Handbook of Eating Disorders

Second Edition

Handbook of Eating Disorders

Second Edition

Edited by

Janet Treasure
Institute of Psychiatry, London, UK

Ulrike Schmidt
Maudsley Hospital, London, UK

Eric van Furth
Robert-Fleury Stichting, Leidschendam, The Netherlands

WILEY

Copyright © 2003   John Wiley & Sons Ltd, The Atrium,
Southern Gate, Chichester,
West Sussex PO19 8SQ, England

Telephone   (+44) 1243 779777

Email (for orders and customer service enquiries): cs-books@wiley.co.uk
Visit our Home Page on www.wileyeurope.com or www.wiley.com

This publication is designed to provide accurate and authoritative information in regard to the
subject matter covered. It is sold on the understanding that the Publisher is not engaged in
rendering professional services. If professional advice or other expert assistance is required, the
services of a competent professional should be sought.

Other Wiley Editorial Offices

John Wiley & Sons Inc., 111 River Street, Hoboken, NJ 07030, USA

Jossey-Bass, 989 Market Street, San Francisco, CA 94103-1741, USA

Wiley-VCH Verlag GmbH, Boschstr. 12, D-69469 Weinheim, Germany

John Wiley & Sons Australia Ltd, 33 Park Road, Milton, Queensland 4064, Australia

John Wiley & Sons (Asia) Pte Ltd, 2 Clementi Loop #02-01, Jin Xing Distripark, Singapore 129809

John Wiley & Sons Canada Ltd, 22 Worcester Road, Etobicoke, Ontario, Canada M9W 1L1

Wiley also publishes its books in a variety of electronic formats. Some content that appears in print may not be
available in electronic books.

Library of Congress Cataloging-in-Publication Data

Handbook of eating disorders / edited by Janet Treasure, Ulrike Schmidt,
Eric van Furth.—2nd ed.
    p. cm.
  Includes index.
  ISBN 0-471-49768-1 (Paper : alk. paper)
  1. Eating disorders.   I. Treasure, Janet.   II. Schmidt, Ulrike.   III. Furth, Eric van.

RC552.E18 H36   2003
616.85′26—dc21   2002015347

British Library Cataloguing in Publication Data

A catalogue record for this book is available from the British Library

ISBN 0-471-49768-1

Typeset in 10/12pt Times by TechBooks, New Delhi, India
Printed and bound in Great Britain by Antony Rowe Ltd, Chippenham, Wiltshire
This book is printed on acid-free paper responsibly manufactured from sustainable forestry
in which at least two trees are planted for each one used for paper production.

To Machteld, and our children,
Annick, Wytze and Bram

E.v.F.

Contents

About the Editors

Janet Treasure, *Department of Psychiatry, 5th Floor, Thomas Guy House, Guys Hospital, London, SEI 9RT, United Kingdom*

Professor Treasure is a psychiatrist who has specialised in the treatment of eating disorders for over 20 years. She trained with Professor Gerald Russell at the Maudsley Hospital and the Institute of Psychiatry. The clinic provides treatment for a population of 2 million in south-east London and is a national referral centre. The unit is active in research and development.

Ulrike Schmidt, *Maudsley Hospital, Denmark Hill, London, SE5 8AZ, United Kingdom*

Dr Ulrike Schmidt is a Consultant Psychiatrist in the Eating Disorders Unit at the Maudsley Hospital and Senior Lecturer at the Institute of Psychiatry. Her research interests include all aspects of eating disorders, but in particular brief psychological and self-help treatments. She has co-authored two self-help books and accompanying clinicians' guides.

Eric van Furth, *Robert-Fleury Stichting, National Centre for Eating Disorders, PO Box 2260, AK Leidschendam, The Netherlands*

Dr Eric van Furth is a psychologist-psychotherapist in the National Centre for Eating Disorders at the Robert-Fleury Stichting (Robert-Fleury Foundation), a general psychiatric hospital in Leidschendam, The Netherlands. He is Honorary Lecturer at the Department of Psychiatry of Leiden University and Honorary Senior Research Fellow at the Department of Psychiatry at St. George's Hospital Medical School, London (UK).

Contributors

Eia Asen, *Marlborough Family Service, London, UK*

Núria Bará-Carril, *Eating Disorders Unit, Institute of Psychiatry, De Crespigny Park, London SE5 8AF, UK*

Beatrice Bauer, *Università Luigi Bocconi, Via Bocconi 8, 20135 Milan, Italy*

Helen Birchall, *University of Leicester, Brandon Mental Health Unit, Leicester General Hospital, Gwendolen Road, Leicester LE5 4PW, UK*

Runi Børresen, *Department of Psychology, University of Tromsø, Åsgårdveien 9, N-9037 Tromsø, Norway*

Tijs Bruna, *National Centre for Eating Disorders, Robert-Fleury Stichting, PO Box 422, 2260 AK Leidschendam, The Netherlands*

Rachel Bryant-Waugh, *Department of Psychological Medicine, Great Ormond Street Hospital, Great Ormond St, London WC1N 3JH, UK*

David Collier, *Eating Disorders Unit, Institute of Psychiatry, De Crespigny Park, London SE5 8AF, UK*

Frances Connan, *Vincent Square Eating Disorders Clinic, Osbert Street, London SW1P 2QU, UK*

Padmal de Silva, *Eating Disorders Unit, Institute of Psychiatry, De Crespigny Park, London SE5 8AF, UK*

Martina de Zwaan, *Department of General Psychiatry, Wahringer Gurtel 18–20, 1090 Wien, Austria*

Ivan Eisler, *Adolescent Eating Disorder Service, Maudsley Hospital and Psychotherapy Section, Institute of Psychiatry, De Crespigny Park, London SE5 8AF, UK*

Manfred Fichter, *Department of Psychiatry, University of Munich and Klinik Roseneck, AM Roseneck 6, D-83209 Prien am Hiemsee, Germany*

Jaap Fogteloo, *Department of General Internal Medicine, Leiden University Medical Centre, PO Box 9600, 2300 RC, Leiden, The Netherlands*

Simon Gowers, *Professor of Adolescent Psychiatry, Pine Lodge Adolescent Unit, 79 Liverpool Road, Chester CH2 1AW, UK*

Stephen Herpertz, *Clinic of Psychosomatic Medicine and Psychotherapy, University of Essen, Virchowstraße 174, D-45147 Essen, Germany*

Wolfgang Herzog, *Ruprecht Karls Universitat, Medizinische Klinkum, Bergheimer Strasse 58, 69115 Heidelberg, Germany*

Hans Wijbrand Hoek, *Department of Psychiatric Residency and Research, Parnassia, The Hague Psychiatric Institute, Albardastraat 100, 2555 VZ The Hague, The Netherlands*

Melanie Katzman, *29 West, 88th Street, New York, NY 10024, USA*

Helen Kennerley, *Oxford Cognitive Therapy Centre, Department of Clinical Psychology, Warneford Hospital, Oxford OX3 7JX, UK*

Heidelinde Krenn, *Department of Psychiatry, University of Munich and Klinik Roseneck, AM Roseneck 6, D-83209 Prien am Hiemsee, Germany*

Daniel le Grange, *Eating Disorders Program, Assistant Professor of Psychiatry, The University of Chicago, 5841 S. Maryland Avenue, MC 3077, Chicago, IL 60637, USA*

Bernd Löwe, *Ruprecht Karls Universitat, Medizinische Klinkum, Bergheimer Strasse 58, 69115 Heidelberg, Germany*

Mervat Nasser, *Department of Psychiatry, 5th Floor, Thomas Guy House, Guys Hospital, London SE1 9RT, UK*

Dasha Nicholls, *Department of Child and Adolescent Mental Health, Great Ormond Street Hospital, Great Ormond St, London WC1N 3JH, UK*

Søren Nielsen, *Psychiatric Youth Centre, Storstrøm County Psychiatric Services, Ringstedgade 61, DK-4700 Næstved, Denmark*

Greta Noordenbos, *Department of Clinical Psychology, Leiden University, Wassenaarseweg 52, 2333 AK Leiden, The Netherlands*

Bob Palmer, *University of Leicester, Brandon Mental Health Unit, Leicester General Hospital, Gwendolen Road, Leicester LE5 4PW, UK*

Lorna Richards, *Eating Disorders Unit, Bethlem Royal Hospital, Monks Orchard Road, Beckenham, Kent, BR3 3BX, UK*

Paul Robinson, *Royal Free Eating Disorders Service, Department of Psychiatry, Royal Free Hospital, Pond Street, London NW3 2QG, UK*

Sheelagh Rodgers, *Adult Psychological Therapies, Pontefract General Infirmary, Friarwood Lane, Pontefract, W. Yorkshire, SF8 1PL, UK*

Jan Rosenvinge, *Department of Psychology, University of Tromsø, Åsgårdveien 9, N-9037 Tromsø, Norway*

Ulrike Schmidt, *Eating Disorders Unit, Institute of Psychiatry, De Crespigny Park, London SE5 8AF, UK*

Jacob Seidell, *Department for Chronic Diseases Epidemiology, National Institute of Public Health and the Environment, PO Box 1, 3720 BA Bilthoven, The Netherlands*

Lucy Serpell, *Eating Disorders Unit, Institute of Psychiatry, De Crespigny Park, London SE5 8AF, UK*

Roz Shafran, *Oxford University, Department of Psychiatry, Warneford Hospital, Oxford, OX3 7JX, UK*

Finn Skårderud, *Regional Centre for Child and Adolescent Psychiatry, University of Oslo and The Norwegian Olympic Training Centre, Oslo, Norway*

Sarah Stanley, *Clinical Lecturer, Department of Metabolic Medicine, Faculty of Medicine, ICSMT, Hammersmith Campus, London W12 0NN, UK*

Rick Stein, *The State University of New York, Department of Paediatrics, Division of Behavioural Medicine, Room G56, Farber Hall, 3435 Main Street, Building #26, Buffalo, NY 14214-3000, USA*

Jorunn Sundgot-Borgen, *The Norwegian University of Sport and Physical Education and The Norwegian Olympic Training Centre, Oslo, Norway*

Claire Tanner, *26 Vancouver Road, Forest Hill, London SE23 2AF, UK*

Janet Treasure, *Department of Psychiatry, 5th Floor, Thomas Guy House, Guys Hospital, London SE1 9RT, UK*

Nicholas Troop, *Department of Psychology, London Metropolitan University, Calcutta House, Old Castle Street, London E1 7NT, UK*

Daphne van Hoeken, *Department of Research, Parnassia, The Hague Psychiatric Institute, Albardastraat 100, 2555 VZ The Hague, The Netherlands*

Glenn Waller, *Department of Psychiatry, St George's Hospital Medical School, University of London SW17 0RE, UK*

Anne Ward, *Psychotherapy Department, Maudsley Hospital, Denmark Hill, London SE5 8AZ, UK*

Peter Webster, *Eating Disorders Unit, Institute of Psychiatry, De Crespigny Park, London SE5 8AF, UK*

Robinson Welch, *Department of Psychiatry, Washington University School of Medicine, Campus Box 8134, 660 South Euclid Avenue, St Louis, MO 63110-1093, USA*

Denise Wilfley, *Washington University School of Medicine, Department of Psychiatry 660 South Euclid, Campus Box 8134, St. Louis, MO 63110, USA*

Elizabeth Winchester, *Eating Disorders Unit, Institute of Psychiatry, De Crespigny Park, London SE5 8AF, UK*

Anthony Winston, *Eating Disorders Unit, Woodleigh Beeches Centre, Warwick Hospital, Lakin Road, Warwick CV34 5BW, UK*

Stephen Zipfel, *Ruprecht Karls Universitat, Medizinische Klinkum, Bergheimer Strasse 58, 69115 Heidelberg, Germany*

Preface

This is the second edition of this very popular book. The drive behind the first edition was to honour the retirement of Professor Gerald Russell and many of the chapters were written by the diaspora of clinicians and scientists emanating from his academic and clinical leadership. Within the decade since that edition was conceived, developed and executed there have been changes in the balance of clinical and academic connections. A European school has started to emerge. In part EEC funding has facilitated this but, in addition, curiosity into the contrasts and similarities between countries and the willingness and ability to communicate has cemented this approach. Thus this second edition now represents a European perspective. There have been marked advances in knowledge and understanding of the eating disorder over this time. Also the spectrum of what is called 'eating disorders' has gradually expanded into obesity as new conditions such as binge eating disorder have been introduced into the diagnostic system. The dialectical process of synthesis between the body of knowledge from the obese and the lean end of the spectrum can enrich our understanding. Many chapters embody this structure. We also used a rather unique method to foster a synthesis and consensus approach. We tried whenever possible to pair authors on the chapters with colleagues in other schools, countries or disciplines.

This has meant that all of the chapters have been rewritten. However, we did not want to lose sight of the original edition, which had provided a coherent, readable and authoritative overview of this rapidly developing field.

There are inherent paradoxes in such a task. How can you satisfy the quality demands of evidence-based science with the need by clinicians, carers and users for clear, concise, coherent models? We hope that we have been able to fulfil this task. Thus, for the clinician, there is a strong practical emphasis with a problem-based approach, which means that this book has a richness of detail and wisdom that will be valued by all of the professional disciplines involved in caring for people with an eating disorder.

J.T.
U.S.
E.v.F.

Preface to the First Edition

This volume marks the occasion of the retirement of Professor Gerald Russell. It is our tribute to his seminal influence on our understanding of the eating disorders. To do this we have organised a scholarly volume charting the achievements in the field over the past three decades, an epoch during which he was such an important leader. We know that a series of personal tributes along the lines of a traditional *festschrift* would be unwelcome to him: indeed they are unnecessary since his research and that of those associated with him speak for themselves.

Our aim has been to provide an up-to-date review of the eating disorders, anorexia nervosa and bulimia nervosa. Space does not permit a detailed account of these disorders. Rather we have asked the contributors to focus on the powerful ideas, hypotheses, or models which have dominated the field. The extent to which these ideas have supporting evidence, what they do and do not explain, and how they might be developed further are highlighted. The evolution of principles governing the treatment of these disorders is similarly treated. We invited contributors to take a broad view of their areas of special interest, to present arguments in favour of the best models, to challenge them with rigour, and to examine their implications for our patients.

The style of this volume, we hope, mirrors the approach exemplified by Gerald Russell. It is that of the clinician scientist—forever alert and faithful to clinical observation, discerning in its apparent mysteries explanations able to be fashioned into hypotheses for scientific testing, and forever maintaining a keen but critical eye on the implications of the results for the care of his or her patients. All of the contributors have been closely associated with him. Nearly all have worked with him in one of his units at various times over the past 30 years. All have imbibed his methods and strived to maintain his high standards. They have participated in a programme of research where findings have been shared by all, so that, for example, the family therapy has been informed by genetics and nutritional physiology, and investigations of follicular growth in the ovary have been sensitive to issues in psychosocial development and cognitive theory. Such interchange between disciplines has deterred any tendency to sectarian thinking or refuge in unchallenged ideas inhibiting further developments. Many of the contributors continue to work in the Eating Disorders Unit at the Institute of Psychiatry and the Maudsley Hospital. The current addresses of many of the others incidate that they went on to establish units of their own in the United Kingdom (Royal Free Hospital, Bristol, Liverpool, Westminster Hospital), Australia (Sydney and Melbourne), and the United States (Johns Hopkins).

The organisation of the book is a little unusual. We have tried to provide a framework which compelled the authors to clarify their ideas as far as possible and to see how far they might be pushed. We probably would all agree that the eating disorders are multifactorial in origin, but by asking contributors to explore discrete models to see how much they might explain, we hoped to arrive at a richer understanding of what 'multifactorial' actually means. In the introductory section the editors prevailed upon Gerald Russell to allow us to include a paper by him examining the history of anorexia nervosa and bulimia which he recently presented at a conference at the Royal College of Psychiatrists. We invited comments on his ideas from two senior figures in the field, Sten Theander and Joseph Silverman. Katherine Halmi examines current concepts and definitions. The separation of causal influences in terms of aetiological versus maintaining factors (which are consequences of the disorders) was also planned as a spur to contributors to ask how our current models, involving different levels of abstraction, really explicate the origins of the eating disorders. Similar principles informed the section dealing with treatment, the editors hoping that the range and limitations of our key interventions would emerge, together with an appreciation of what they might tell us about the nature of the disorders. Then the difficult question of prevention is addressed. Finally, we include an evaluation of Gerald Russell's contribution by Walter Vandereycken, but wish to add that many colleagues offered to contribute personal tributes.

We hope this volume pleases its dedicatee and its readers as much as its preparation has pleased its compilers. In seeing the contributions as a whole, we have become even more keenly aware of Gerald Russell's influence, especially his ability to newly create what he saw, thus opening fresh directions for others to follow.

G.S.
C.D.
J.T.

CHAPTER 1

Concepts of Eating Disorders

Bob Palmer

University of Leicester, Brandon Mental Health Unit,
Leicester General Hospital, UK

The nosology of mental disorders inevitably dithers between the wish to delineate useful categories and the hope of discovering natural kinds. It would be good to achieve both but each aspiration alone is elusive enough. Indeed, some would reckon the second hope to be forlorn and there has been a tendency to emphasise the pragmatic and the descriptive. The current classifications—ICD-10 and DSM-IV—are the offspring of this tendency (WHO, 1992; APA, 1994). Yet there is a nagging feeling that there are 'real' disorders out there to be discovered rather than merely defined.

Within the field of eating disorders, anorexia nervosa crystallised out as a separate and distinct disorder over the course of the last century (Mount Sinai, 1965). It had the advantage of one criterion that was both undisputed and easy to measure, namely low weight. However, it was the description of the characterising beliefs and behaviours that led to the disorder being separated off from other states with weight loss. Furthermore, it was the description of similar beliefs and behaviours in people of unremarkable weight that led to the definition of bulimia nervosa and its relatives. However, it is arguably when the definition of mental disorder relies upon the mental state—as it almost inevitably should—that classification becomes more difficult. Can we really measure people's thoughts and feelings reliably and is it reasonable to expect that they should fit neatly into categories? Even classifying behaviour is problematic enough. However, if we do observe that people come to suffer in similar ways and with similar beliefs then this may give clues not only about sociological generalisations but also, perhaps especially, about innate and probably biological mechanisms which may underpin their disorder.

People may come to be more similar when they are stuck within a morbid process than when they are well because the range of their behaviour and experience is at least in part constrained by potentially definable processes in which such biological mechanisms are playing some limiting part. Tolstoy wrote, 'all happy families resemble one another, but each unhappy family is unhappy in its own way'. This is questionable even with regard to families and unhappiness, but with individuals and disorder it seems likely that the reverse is true. The range of what is morbid is narrower than the range of the non-morbid. Anti-psychiatrists tend to emphasise the prescriptive nature of 'normality' and to portray the person who is 'labelled' mentally disordered as something of a free spirit. However, the

Handbook of Eating Disorders. Edited by J. Treasure, U. Schmidt and E. van Furth.

psychiatric perspective is different. The patient suffering from a mental disorder is seen as constrained and trapped by forces that are outwith his or her control. It is the sufferer who is the tram compared with the normal person who resembles the bus in having much more freedom. Both the bus and the tram are limited by their physical attributes but the tram is additionally constrained by the rails. Study of the patterns of disorder could give clues as to the nature of these 'rails'.

So what is the status of our current attempts at classification? What patterns can we discern in people with eating disorders? How well do our conventional diagnoses map these patterns? And do any of these patterns suggest the presence of plausible mechanisms of aetiological significance? Do our categories promise to be more than convenient pigeonholes? Are there 'real' disorders out there?

What follows is a clinician's view of our present classifications and some speculation about what mechanisms and natural kinds might lurk beneath the surface of their syndromes and diagnostic criteria.

CURRENT CLASSIFICATION

An ideal classification should consist of categories that are mutually exclusive and collectively exhaustive. Its entities should be discreet and together they should cover the ground. The classification of eating disorders measures up to these standards rather poorly. The canon contains only two major categories—anorexia nervosa (AN) and bulimia nervosa (BN). Anorexia nervosa has low weight as an essential criterion. Bulimia nervosa has binge eating as a necessary criterion. The two disorders share the criterion of what in broad terms might be described as an over-concern about body weight and size although some would see a major difference in degree or emphasis in the typical ideas held by sufferers from AN and BN. In DSM-IV, AN takes precedence over BN in the sense that the presence of the former bars the diagnosis of the latter. In contrast in the earlier version, DSM-III-R, it was possible to make the dual diagnosis of both AN and Bulimia Nervosa (APA, 1987). There is in DSM-IV, however, a new subclassification of AN into binge–purging and pure restricting subtypes. The rules in both of these sets of criteria represent different responses to the fact that low weight and bingeing occur together commonly and that, hence, the cardinal features of AN and BN are closely related even in cross-section. When longitudinal course over time is considered then the overlap becomes even more striking. In many series, a substantial minority of BN sufferers have a past history of AN. The reverse transition from BN to AN is less common, but does occur. Thus, AN and BN are far from being entirely discreet disorders and can be made to seem so only by dint of a certain sophistry. However, if the classification of the eating disorders fails to meet fully the ideal of providing discreet entities, it fails even more in respect of the second criterion, that of covering the ground. Many people present with eating disorders that fulfil criteria for neither of the two main disorders. How are these to be classified?

DSM-IV does provide two additional diagnoses, namely binge eating disorder (BED) and eating disorder not otherwise specified (EDNOS). Binge eating disorder is included only as a provisional category 'for further study'. It is strictly a variety of EDNOS within DSM-IV although, in practice, it has come already to be accorded the status of a diagnosis in its own right. However in general, EDNOS is defined essentially by exclusion, that is as being any clinical eating disorder that does not fulfil criteria for AN or BN.

THE PROBLEM OF EDNOS

The classification of the eating disorders achieves the standard of being collectively exhaustive only through having the 'rag bag' or residual category of EDNOS. The EDNOS category has only one positive criterion and one negative criterion. The positive criterion is that the individual being thus diagnosed should be deemed to have an eating disorder of clinical severity—a disorder that matters. The negative criterion is that the disorder should not fulfil criteria for AN or BN.

The EDNOS category thus defined is common. In many clinical series of people presenting to eating disorders services it is the single most common diagnosis and in some forms the majority of cases. Furthermore, as with AN and BN, the longitudinal perspective is illuminating but complicating. Many cases of the two main disorders change their characteristics over time so that those who have suffered from either at one time come later to suffer from neither but continue to have a clinically significant eating disorder (Sullivan et al., 1998; Fairburn et al., 2000). They can then be diagnosed only as being in a state of EDNOS. It is less clear whether people commonly move from a time of sustained EDNOS into one of the classic disorders.

A weakness of the EDNOS category resides in the limitations of its two criteria. The positive criterion is not defined. Where is the line to be drawn that defines a state as an *eating* disorder and of *clinical* significance? This is a matter of judgement. For instance, someone who is eating little and has lost a great deal of weight through severe major depression or because of delusions of poisoning would clearly have a disorder of clinical significance but would still not be diagnosed as EDNOS. The diagnosis is not appropriate because the state is not construed as an eating disorder. There is an implicit further criterion operating here; that is, that EDNOS should be diagnosed only if no non-eating disorder diagnosis is adequate. The positive criterion is further tested when there is uncertainty about whether an individual with eating disorder symptoms, such as maladaptive weight concern or self-induced vomiting, is affected to an extent that constitutes a disorder of clinical significance. Interestingly the judgement may sometimes depend upon the degree not only of the eating disorder symptoms but also of the associated non-specific symptoms. Thus, if the person has important associated anxiety and depressive symptoms or major problems of self-esteem albeit not amounting to diagnosable syndromes in their own right—this may contribute to the decision that a diagnosis of EDNOS is appropriate. However, DSM-IV does not set out how these judgements should be made.

The negative criterion is also questionable when an individual fails narrowly to fulfil just one criterion for one of the major disorders. For instance, amenorrhoea is a difficult symptom to evaluate and yet some criteria demand that it should be present for the diagnosis of AN in females. The use of an oral contraceptive pill can complicate the issue and, furthermore, there is evidence to suggest that the presence or absence of this symptom makes little difference. Should someone who shows an otherwise typical picture of AN really be denied the diagnosis because of continuing menstruation? The ICD-10 system makes the sensible provision for a diagnosis of so-called 'Atypical AN' (or indeed 'Atypical BN') in cases where an individual narrowly misses fully meeting criteria but is clearly in a state very closely akin to one of these main disorders. However, once again these categories are not really defined and the atypical categories merely provide a buffer zone between the full disorders and others. There is still disputed territory at the other margin. In epidemiological work, the term 'partial syndrome' is often used to describe these sorts of states. The decision about whether to count a subject as a 'case' in a survey may require a different kind of judgement to that of the clinician who must decide whether a patient fits a diagnosis. In the former case, the decision may affect aetiological inference; in the latter, the decision may influence the nature of the treatment offered. Sometimes whether or not treatment will be offered at all may be at stake. These things can be important.

Thus the EDNOS category inevitably includes some less severe cases that nevertheless pass the test of being of clinical significance. Many of these will be 'partial syndromes' of a kind that just miss out on fulfilling criteria for one of the main disorders. They will often do so in ways which may be quantitative—the bulimic who does not binge quite often enough—or qualitative, that is, their difference does not seem to threaten the essence of the disorder—e.g. the previously cited case of the female 'anorectic' whose periods persist surprisingly despite important weight loss. However, there will also be people who have disorders which are diagnosed as EDNOS but who seem to be caught up in patterns of difficulty that are qualitatively different in ways which do seem to be significant.

ATYPICAL BEHAVIOURS

Some unusual cases differ in terms of the behaviour that they show. A not uncommon clinical picture is that of the person who is at an unremarkable weight and does not binge. She is thereby barred by definition from being diagnosed as having either AN or BN. She nevertheless induces vomiting after almost every meal. This pattern is one of the examples of EDNOS cited in the DSM-IV manual. A similar behavioural variant would be the person who eats nothing at all because of fear of weight gain but sustains a fair body weight entirely through the consumption of calorific fluids. Another important condition is eating disorder associated with insulin-dependent diabetes mellitus which may sometimes be severe without involving either weight loss or bingeing. Omitting or using insulin erratically in the service of weight control may constitute a clear eating disorder and be life threatening without even approximating to either classic AN or BN (Peveler, 1995). All such states are truly atypical but nevertheless they seem to be sufficiently akin to the typical eating disorders that it does not offend our clinical sensibilities to include them as interesting variants. We seem to feel that in essence they are the same. Is this because we feel that the essence of the eating disorders lies in the beliefs and ideas of the sufferer? But what of people who are atypical in their ideas?

ATYPICAL IDEAS

Controversies about details notwithstanding, both AN and BN include among their necessary criteria the issue of what, for the sake of brevity, might be called 'weight concern'. The different systems use different words but they all clearly refer to ideas which are at least similar. Furthermore, these ideas are held to be the central psychopathology of the disorders. They are deemed to be of the essence and to provide the motivation for the eating restraint which seems to be a key to the pathogenesis of AN and probably of BN too. And yet, there seem to be eating disordered people who do not have them or at least do not talk about them. Every clinician has come across many sufferers who initially deny concern about body weight and shape. Some later reveal that they had had such ideas but that they had been wary and kept quiet about them. Others continue to deny having such weight concerns. Some convince some clinicians that this is truly the case. But is it possible to have, say, anorexia nervosa without weight concern? The diagnostic criteria would say not. However, the clinicians who first described anorexia nervosa in the nineteenth century did not emphasise weight concern. Indeed, the early accounts by Gull and Lasegue do not mention it even though their clinical descriptions are in other respects both vivid and thorough (Mount Sinai, 1965). Likewise, colleagues working in China describe many young women who otherwise seem to have anorexia nervosa but who lack evident weight concern (Lee, Ho & Hsu, 1993). So sure are they that these are cases of 'anorexia nervosa' that they are so designated in the papers which describe them. So much for diagnostic criteria. But then, surely, Lee and his colleagues are following what most would regard as clinical common sense. Perhaps, such common sense rests upon an as yet unmentioned third attribute of a good classification—along with discreet entities and covering the ground—namely that of utility in practice. The Chinese patients without weight concern probably need to be managed in much the same way as their more typical equivalents. But what does such pragmatism do to ideas about the essence of eating disorders?

MOTIVATED EATING RESTRAINT

It is possible to make only a modest change to the diagnostic criteria for the eating disorders and thereby encompass some of the non-weight concerned sufferers. If eating restraint is promoted to be a central or even necessary component of the mechanism of the eating disorders, then weight concern may be seen as one motivation for such restraint among many that are possible (Palmer, 1993). For, instance, restraint may be motivated by religious ideas, ideas of fitness, ideas of asceticism and so on. Many clinicians will recognise some patients for whom such ideas seem to occupy the same position as ideas of weight concern in more typical cases. They reflect the same 'entanglement' between ideas of weight and eating control and wider personal issues such as self-esteem and emotional control. Such atypical ideas may be more common in atypical sufferers such as males.

It is not difficult to think that motivated eating restraint might occupy a central position in the pathogenesis of the eating disorders. Restraint in some sense is clearly involved in AN. Furthermore, it may be plausibly invoked in BN via the kind of rebound effect that has been called 'counterregulation' (Herman & Polivy, 1984; Palmer, 1998). However, such explanations seem to require that the sufferer is fighting her natural urges to eat. She is seen as not having lost her appetite but rather as attempting not to give in to it—'successfully' in the case of the AN sufferer; unsuccessfully in the case of the BN sufferer. Indeed it may be thought an advantage of accounts of eating disorders which give a central place to eating restraint that they are parsimonious in having no need to postulate some primary disorder of appetite or drive to eat. The effects of eating restraint upon individuals with an intact appetite are well documented (Herman & Polivy, 1984; Polivy & Herman, 1995). Restraint leads to distortion. Indeed, a story can be told about these effects that can be spun into a plausible account of the eating disorders. However, although parsimony of explanation may be a virtue, the simplest accounts are not always true. There could be a place for some more primary abnormality of appetite. Surprisingly there is a deal of uncertainty about appetite in eating disorders.

THE VEXED QUESTION OF APPETITE

Hunger or appetite in eating-disordered people have received rather little systematic study. There remains considerable uncertainty. This seems to be for at least three reasons. Firstly, there are inherent difficulties in measuring the subjective strength of hunger or appetite. Secondly, ratings of hunger are likely to be unreliable in people who have complex and distorting ideas about what they should be eating. The sufferer may mislead others, and perhaps even herself, when putting her subjective experiences into words or filling in a rating scale. On the other hand, for obvious reasons, what an eating-disordered individual actually eats cannot be taken as a simple behavioural indicator of the drive to eat. Lastly, clinicians and other experts may assume that they know about hunger and the like in eating-disordered subjects. However, various experts have various views. Especially with respect to AN, some claim that they 'know' that sufferers characteristically experience an enhanced urge to eat which is kept under tight control (see many of the present author's writings). Others say that the drive to eat must be less than normal if the subjects are to 'successfully' stop themselves from eating in the face of gross self-deprivation (Pinel, Assanand & Lehman, 2000). Many are impressed—or perhaps bewildered—by the variety of accounts which their patients give to them.

With regard to the problems of measurement or even description, there are conceptual as well as technical difficulties about what hunger or appetite or drive to eat may be taken to mean as definable terms. These terms do not seem to be used consistently or reliably and may need to be thought of as far from synonymous. For instance, an eating-disordered person may say that she is never hungry but may nevertheless acknowledge a strong urge to eat. It is as if the term hunger had too positive a connotation for it to be used about such a problematic experience.

In principle, hunger or the drive to eat might be abnormal in being reduced or increased. In practice, in many cases in which hunger is *reduced*—i.e. where there is true anorexia—a diagnosis of an eating disorder is not seriously considered. For instance, weight loss associated with physical illness with loss of appetite or depressive illness with true anorexia is not appropriately described as anorexia *nervosa*. The 'nervosa' implies that the relationship between the person's eating and their weight loss is more complex—more entangled with wider personal issues—than that of being simply 'off their food'. Once again, there is some lack of clarity here. Even those who would claim that AN sufferers do have a diminished appetite would want to reserve the diagnosis for those people who seem to be not eating for broadly 'psychological' reasons and who have relevant and related ideas often about weight concern. For instance, a sufferer may couch her immediate aversion to eating in terms of bloating or discomfort, but also have wider ideas of guilt or whatever. At the extreme, it is certainly conceivable that a person could present at low weight who was without both 'weight concern' and motivated eating restraint and who seemed to have some true anorexia. Under what conditions, if any, should she (or he) be considered for a diagnosis of AN? Strictly, such a patient should be diagnosed as EDNOS if no other diagnosis fits. Such people probably do exist although they seem to be scarce (perhaps they present to other kinds of clinician). However, their apparent rarity in practice may suggest that their characteristics should not be considered as threatening refutation of hypotheses about the nature of AN itself. Perhaps they are truly different. At the other end of the dimension of appetite or urge to eat, it seems likely that those who suffer from Binge Eating Disorder (BED) might also have an unusual—this time increased—appetite which is not based upon the distortions of restraint.

A primary *increase* in appetite or drive to eat might possibly be present in AN where it would trigger the restraint as a reaction. However, there seems to be little evidence for this. Such a primary increase is more plausible as a component of the mechanisms of BN and even more so for BED. In BN, the model of restraint acting upon an intact but unremarkable appetite is plausible. Most BN subjects report that the onset of attempted restraint preceded the onset of binge eating. However, this is not the case for a small but interesting minority of BN sufferers and for most of those who suffer with BED. Characteristically BED subjects either do not consistently restrain or the onset of their bingeing precedes that of restraint (Mussell et al., 1995, 1997). The different average outcome of BN and BED in terms of weight change at follow-up provides further support for a possible primary problem of increased appetite in the latter group. Fairburn et al. (2000) have shown that a community group of BED sufferers put on an average of 4.2 kg over the five-year follow-up period and that the rate of obesity rose from 22% to 39%. This weight gain occurred whether or not they continued to have BED. In contrast, BN sufferers gained on average only 3.3 kg from a lower base line and only 15% were obese at follow-up. Thus, many sufferers from BED are or become obese. Perhaps most are grappling with a drive to eat which is truly increased and which destines them for obesity, all other things being equal. Perhaps those who have a more 'straightforward' psychology become straightforwardly obese in the face of this increased drive to eat rather than becoming caught up in BED.

SET POINTS OR SETTLING POINTS?

Restraint-based models of eating disorder tend to go along with models of eating control which emphasise regulation of body weight. This may be seen as involving a regulation of weight around a set point or at least a set range that is variable across individuals but relatively constant for any one individual (Keesey, 1995). Some people regulate around a low weight, some around a high weight and most, by definition, around an average weight. Or so this story goes. The chief drive to eat is thought of as resulting from a biology in which even minor deprivation triggers the urge to eat in order to restore the well-fed state. Such set point models have an intuitive appeal. Furthermore, they can have an ideological utility in simplified form as the basis of a way of talking about eating disorders (Palmer, 1989). However, they have been criticised as not adequately accounting for important phenomena (Pinel, Assanand & Lehman, 2000). Especially, such models seem to overestimate the degree of the inherent stability of people's body weight, especially with regard to the evidently widespread vulnerability to weight gain and obesity. Although there are anecdotes about Sumo wrestlers and evidence from studies that sometimes weight gain is difficult, for many people much of the time weight gain is all too easy (Sims & Horton, 1968). This seems to apply even to weight gain to levels that carry significant disadvantages for health (Pinel, Assanand & Lehman, 2000). The degree to which the bodies of many people 'defend' an upper limit around any set point seems to be less than the models would predict. There seems to be at least an asymmetry between the lower and upper limits. Any dieter knows this. Set point ideas seem to have merit with regard to downward deviations in weight but are rather less good in accounting for weight gain above 'normal' levels. In as much as an eating disorder involves low weight and restraint, set point models may be useful. However, this may not be the case with respect to eating disorders at normal or above normal weight.

Set point ideas are often dressed up with evolutionary stories. It is suggested that regulatory mechanisms would have evolved which tended to keep an individual within a range which was optimal for survival and reproduction. However, a criticism of set point theory suggests that in the ancestral environment, where food would have been scarce, mechanisms would have been favoured that allowed an animal to eat more food when it was available than would be necessary for its immediate needs. Storage of potential energy and substance— putting on weight—would be advantageous in circumstances of erratic food supply in a way that would not be the case for strong satiety mechanisms which cut consumption when immediate needs were met. Furthermore, it is plausible that such permissive mechanisms might be more advantageous for younger females of reproductive age and, indeed, some sexual difference in satiety mechanisms can be observed (Goodwin, Fairburn & Cowen, 1987). But if restraint models are not fully adequate, what other models are available? One is that of so-called positive-incentive theory. This emphasises the rewards of eating, including its hedonic properties. Feeding is intrinsically rewarding and this is especially the case with respect of foods which might well have been valuable but scarce in the ancestral environment such as sweet foods, fatty foods and salty foods. Eating such foods was—and of course still is—especially rewarding. In the past this meant they were especially sought out despite the difficulty in finding them. Now that they are readily available, they are eaten to excess. Positive-incentive theory may hold more promise in explaining aspects of those eating disorders in which restraint seems to play little or no part and which occur at normal or high body weight. There may be complex entanglement between the hedonics of eating and emotion in people with binge eating. And less dramatically the positive incentives may be relevant to obesity.

Pinel, Assanand and Lehman (2000) have proposed a tentative theory of anorexia nervosa in which they suggest that the under-eating characteristic of that disorder may reflect a change of the usually positive incentive of eating towards the negative. However, it is not clear that such an interpretation fits the facts. Thus, as mentioned above, there is controversy about the nature of the subjective urge to eat in AN. Furthermore, it seems highly plausible that deprivation might well be the key drive to eating in those who are at a low weight and hungry and that the positive incentive to eat might well take over when the animal or human is well fed. Sensory specific satiety is a real phenomenon and bread and butter may well suffice when one is deprived, but it takes chocolate pudding to override that full feeling after two or three previous courses. While it may seem more parsimonious to invoke either a set point theory or a positive incentive theory, perhaps both kinds of ideas are required; the first in discussing states of deprivation and weight loss and the second in discussing the regulation of eating in times of plenty and higher weight. It is at least as easy to tell evolutionary stories around such a dual mechanism as it is around a simpler model.

The notion that there is a mechanism that regulates body weight around a set point may be contrasted with the idea that any apparent stability of body weight reflects a settling point which is the net result of two or more mechanisms that may have quite different functions. The implication for intervention may well be different, perhaps especially for the treatment of obesity where the idea of a set point that is defended even when it is problematically high tends to promote therapeutic pessimism (Garner & Wooley, 1991).

CONCLUSIONS

Our cherished diagnoses of AN and BN are here to stay. They clearly describe many patients in the clinic and are useful. Furthermore, the use of definite diagnostic criteria has made an important contribution to research. However, an undue concentration upon individuals who fulfil diagnostic criteria may lead to a somewhat blinkered view. The testing out of new formulations such as that of BED is useful although it would be a pity if such categories invented 'for further study' were routinely and prematurely reified as diagnoses. We need ideas to inform our observations but to be sufficiently open-minded to be able to notice the unexpected.

The view from the clinic can potentially provide suggestions about where it might be profitable to look for more basic physiological and pathological mechanisms.

Returning to the metaphor used above, it may be possible to guess at the location of some of the 'tramlines' that constrain our patients. The following are some summary comments based upon the view through this particular pair of eyes.

1. In looking for mechanisms underlying the eating disorders, ideas which invoke essentially normal regulatory mechanisms which have been pushed out of kilter are to be preferred as more parsimonious if they are adequate.
2. Models based upon eating restraint seem to have merit and may even be adequate for most cases of AN and BN.
3. 'Motivated eating restraint' is a more inclusive and arguably better formulation than 'weight concern' as the criterion for the core psychopathology of most eating disorders.
4. The 'normal mechanisms' invoked may need to include positive-incentive ideas as well as or instead of ideas of restraint if eating disorders at normal or high weight are to be adequately explained.
5. True abnormalities of appetite or drive to eat may play a part in some cases of BN, in BED and in obesity. Likewise, some cases of restricting AN may have some primary change in appetite although this is more speculative. Such variation of appetite may be genetically determined.
6. There should be more research into the difficult topic of the phenomenology of appetite in the eating disorders.
7. Such research should go hand in hand with biological research into the complex mechanisms that are doubtless involved in normal and pathological feeding in animals and human beings.
8. Whenever practical, research should include atypical (EDNOS) cases as well as the typical.
9. A future classification may include a major divide between 'disorders of restraint' and 'disorders of increased appetite'.
10. All true eating disorders—disorders with 'nervosa'—are characterised by an 'entanglement' between the relevant basic weight and eating control mechanisms and the sufferer's interpretation of the meaning of the effects of these within his or her own

individual experience. And, although some generalisations can be made, such interpretations are likely to be varied or even idiosyncratic and to defy neat classification.

REFERENCES

APA (1987) *Diagnostic and Statistical Manual of Mental Disorders* (3rd Edition) Revised. Washington, D.C.: American Psychiatric Association.

APA (1994) *Diagnostic and Statistical Manual of Mental Disorders* (4th Edition). Washington, D.C.: American Psychiatric Association.

Fairburn, C.G., Cooper, Z., Doll, H.A., Norman, P. & O'Connor, M. (2000) The natural course of bulimia nervosa and binge eating disorder in young women. *Archives of General Psychiatry*, **57**, 659–665.

Garner, D.M. & Wooley, S.C. (1991) Confronting the failure of behavioural and dietary treatments of obesity. *Clinical Psychology Review*, **11**, 729–780.

Goodwin, G.M., Fairburn, C.G. & Cowen, P.J. (1987) Dieting changes serotonergic function in women, not men: Implications for the aetiology of anorexia nervosa. *Psychological Medicine*, **17**, 839–842.

Herman, C.P. & Polivy, J. (1984) A boundary model for the regulation of eating. In A.J. Stunkard & E. Stellar (Eds), *Eating and its Disorders*. New York: Raven Press.

Keesey, R.E. (1995) A set-point model of body weight regulation. In K.D. Brownell & C.G. Fairburn (Eds), *Eating Disorders and Obesity: A Comprehensive Handbook*. New York: Guilford Press.

Lee, S., Ho, T.P. & Hsu, L.K.G. (1993) Fat phobic and non-fat phobic anorexia nervosa: A comparative study. *Psychological Medicine*, **23**, 999–1017.

Mount Sinai (1965) Evolution of psychosomatic concepts—anorexia nervosa: A paradigm. *The International Psycho-Analytic Library* No. 65. London: Hogarth Press.

Mussell, M.P., Mitchell, J.E., Weller, C.L., Raymond, N.C., Crow, S.J. & Crosby, R.D. (1995) Onset of binge eating, dieting, obesity, and mood disorders among subjects seeking treatment for binge eating disorder. *International Journal of Eating Disorders*, **17**, 395–410.

Mussell, M.P., Mitchell, J.E., Fenna, C.J., Crosby, R.D., Miller, J.P. & Hoberman, H.M. (1997). A comparison of binge eating and dieting in the development of bulimia nervosa. *International Journal of Eating Disorders*, **21**, 353–360.

Palmer, R.L. (1989) The Spring Story: A way of talking about clinical eating disorder. *British Review of Anorexia Nervosa and Bulimia*, **4**, 33–41.

Palmer, R.L. (1993) Weight concern should not be a necessary criterion for the eating disorders; a polemic. *International Journal of Eating Disorders*, **14**, 459–465.

Palmer, R.L. (1998) The aetiology of bulimia nervosa. In H.W., Hoek, J.L. Treasure & M.A. Katzman (Eds), *Neurobiology in the Treatment of Eating Disorders*. Chichester and New York: John Wiley & Sons.

Peveler, R.C. (1995) Eating disorders and diabetes. In K.D. Brownell & C.G. Fairburn (Eds), *Eating Disorders and Obesity; a Comprehensive Handbook*. New York: Guilford Press.

Pinel, J.P.J., Assanand, S. & Lehman, D.R. (2000) Hunger, eating and ill health. *American Psychologist*, **55**, 1105–1116.

Polivy, J. & Herman, C.P. (1995) Dieting and its relation to eating disorders. In K.D. Brownell & C.G. Fairburn (Eds), *Eating Disorders and Obesity; A Comprehensive Handbook*. New York: Guilford Press.

Sims, E.A.H. & Horton, E.S. (1968) Endocrine and metabolic adaptation to obesity and starvation. *American Journal of Clinical Nutrition*, **21**, 1455–1470.

Sullivan, P.F., Bulik, C.M., Fear, J.L. & Pickering, A. (1998) Outcome of anorexia nervosa: a case-control study. *American Journal of Psychiatry*, **155**, 939–946.

WHO (1992) *The ICD-10 Classification of Mental and Behavioural Disorders: Clinical Descriptions and Diagnostic Guidelines*. Geneva: World Health Organisation.

CHAPTER 2

Epidemiology

Daphne van Hoeken
Parnassia, The Hague Psychiatric Institute, The Netherlands
Jacob Seidell
*Department of Nutrition and Health,
Free University of Amsterdam, The Netherlands*
and
Hans Wijbrand Hoek
*Parnassia, The Hague Psychiatric Institute, The Netherlands and
Department of Epidemiology, Mailman School of Public Health,
Columbia University, New York, USA*

SUMMARY

- The average prevalence rate for young females is 0.3% for anorexia nervosa and 1% for bulimia nervosa. The overall prevalence of obesity may be in the order of 5–10%. The overall incidence is at least 8 per 100 000 person-years for anorexia nervosa and 12 per 100 000 person-years for bulimia nervosa. No reliable incidence data are available for obesity. The standardized mortality rate in the first 10 years after detection is 9.6 for anorexia nervosa, 7.4 for bulimia nervosa. For obesity it is assumed that mortality is elevated by about 50–150% in most adult populations.
- The incidence rate of anorexia nervosa has increased during the past 50 years, particularly in females 10–24 years old. The registered incidence of bulimia nervosa has increased, at least during the first five years after bulimia nervosa was introduced in the DSM-III. The prevalence of obesity is increasing in most of the established market economies. Without societal changes a substantial and steadily rising proportion of adults will succumb to the medical complications of obesity.
- Risk factor research is still sparse, both for eating disorders and for obesity. There is a need for prospective, follow-up designs using initially healthy subjects at high risk for developing an eating disorder or obesity. Depending on the question to be answered, these could be matched on sex, age and socio-economic status with initially healthy intermediate- and low-risk groups.
- Detailed and reliable registration of case definition, demographic and other characteristics of the patient, symptoms and concomitants the disease or disorder remain of the utmost importance to advance evidence-based treatment and prevention.

Handbook of Eating Disorders. Edited by J. Treasure, U. Schmidt and E. van Furth.
© 2003 John Wiley & Sons, Ltd.

INTRODUCTION

As defined by Regier and Burke (2000) 'mental disorder epidemiology is the quantitative study of the distribution and causes of mental disorder in human populations'. Populations are groups sharing a common feature, and the features distinguishing a population with a higher disease rate from another with a lower disease rate serve as clues to aetiology. Incidence and prevalence rates are the basic measures of disease frequency.

In this chapter the incidence and prevalence of eating disorders and obesity are discussed. In eating disordered patients, there is a weight continuum from underweight in anorexia nervosa through normal weight in normal weight bulimics to overweight in the majority of binge-eating disorder patients. It is likely that a number of obese persons have an underlying eating disorder. Traditionally, however, epidemiological research in the fields of obesity and of eating disorders have been two separate lines of study. By addressing the epidemiology of eating disorders and the epidemiology of obesity together in one chapter, a preliminary step is made to share ideas and knowledge.

- *Prevalence*: The prevalence is the total number of cases in the population. The point prevalence is the prevalence at a specific point in time. The one-year period prevalence rate is the point prevalence rate plus the annual incidence rate. The prevalence rate is most useful for planning facilities, as it indicates the demand for care. Prevalent cases reflect the disease itself as well as coexisting factors.
- *Incidence*: The incidence is the number of new cases in the population in a specified period of time (usually one year), and is commonly expressed per 100 000 of the population per year. Incidence rates of eating disorders represent the situation at the moment of detection, which is not necessarily the same as the true start of the disorder.

Studies on the incidence of eating disorders in the general population are lacking, and the incidence rates available have been based on cases presenting to health care. Very few studies have attempted to calculate the incidence rate of obesity. The criterion for obesity is a matter of definition on a gliding scale from low to high weight. It is difficult and probably not meaningful to define at what moment overweight becomes incident obesity.

Incidence rate differences between groups are better clues to aetiology than prevalence rate differences, because they refer to recently started disease (Eaton et al., 1995).

Mortality

Mortality rates are common measures in health statistics. They are often used as indicator for the severity of a disorder. The standard measures are the crude mortality rate (CMR) and the standardized mortality rate (SMR). The CMR is the fraction of deaths within the study population. The SMR is the fraction of the observed mortality rate (CMR) compared to the expected mortality rate in the population of origin, e.g. all young females.

Risk Factors

Population differences in morbidity or mortality rates point out risk factors. A risk factor is a measurable characteristic of a subject that precedes the outcome of interest and which dichotimises the population into a high- and a low-risk group. When it can be changed, and manipulation of the factor changes the outcome, it is a causal risk factor (Kraemer et al., 1997). A risk factor may be an individual characteristic, or a characteristic of the subject's context. The method of choice for assessing the impact of individual characteristics is a prospective follow-up study. Risk factors can be identified by comparing initially healthy subjects who have developed an unfavourable outcome at follow-up with those who have not.

Methodological Aspects

Epidemiological studies have to counter a number of methodological problems (see Szmukler, 1985, and Hoek, 1993, for overviews). Problems specific to the eating disorders are their low prevalence and the tendency of eating disorder subjects to conceal their illness and avoid professional help (Hsu, 1996). These make it necessary to study a very large number of subjects from the general population in order to reach enough differential power for the cases. This is highly time- and cost-intensive. Several strategies have been used to circumvent this problem, in particular case register and other record-based studies, two-stage studies, and studies of special populations.

The limitations of record-based studies are considerable (Hsu, 1996). Register-based frequencies represent cases detected in inpatient, and occasionally outpatient, care. Treated cases represent only a minority of all cases. Findings from case registers/hospital records are of more value to treatment planning than for generating hypotheses on the aetiology of disease, because there is no direct access to the subjects and the additional information that is available is usually limited and of a demographic nature only.

At present a two-stage screening approach is the most widely accepted procedure for case identification. First a large population is screened for the likelihood of an eating disorder by means of a screening questionnaire, identifying an at-risk population (first stage). Then definite cases are established using a personal interview on subjects from this at-risk population as well as on a randomly selected sample of those not at risk (second stage) (Williams et al., 1980). Methodological problems of two-stage studies are poor response rates, sensitivity/specificity of the screening instrument and the often restricted size of the interviewed groups, particularly of those not at risk (Fairburn & Beglin, 1990).

Studies of special populations address a particular segment of the general population, selected a priori for being at increased risk, such as female high school/university students, athletes or a particular age cohort. The major methodological problem associated with this type of study is the specificity of the findings to the selected subset of the general population.

Both two-stage studies and studies of special populations have the potential for providing information relevant to the aetiology, because there is direct access to the subjects and the availability of additional information is not restricted by a predetermined registration system. Register-based prevalence studies and prevalence studies of eating disorders using only questionnaires will not be discussed in this chapter.

There are several types of risk. One is the risk one runs as a member of a particular group. This is usually assessed by comparing prevalence or incidence rates between demographic subgroups (relative risks or risk ratios). Another is the risk one runs because of individual characteristics. A common approach for this has been to use a case-control design. In studies of this type one looks for premorbid differences between prevalent cases and a control group of subjects, usually matched on age, gender and social class. Methodological difficulties centre around the interpretation of the results. The issues are the directionality (cause/consequence) of the findings and the reliability of information gathered retrospectively on premorbid differences. Whether the differences found represent true risk factors that precede—not follow or accompany—the onset of disorder and which developmental mechanisms are operant can only be uncovered in prospective follow-up studies. In such studies, risk factors can be identified by comparing initially healthy subjects who have developed a disorder at follow-up to those who have not. Thus, the preferred method for assessing individual risk is a study with a prospective follow-up design.

EATING DISORDERS

Classification

In the paragraphs on anorexia nervosa and bulimia nervosa only studies using strict definitions of these eating disorders (meeting Russell, DSM or ICD criteria) are discussed. Another category, the Eating Disorders Not Otherwise Specified (EDNOS) is a mixed category. It includes a heterogeneity of patients who do not meet all criteria for anorexia nervosa or bulimia nervosa but who do have symptoms severe enough to qualify them as having a clinically significant eating disorder. This heterogeneity makes it a difficult category for the search on possible aetiologic factors. Hardly any reliable epidemiological information is available. Therefore the EDNOS is not included in this overview. In DSM-IV (APA, 1994) a provision was made for a separate eating disorder category to be researched further, the Binge Eating Disorder (BED). Only limited epidemiological information is available on this category to date.

The epidemiology of eating disorders has been reviewed before, e.g. Hoek (1993), Hsu (1996), van Hoeken et al. (1998). The section on eating disorders is an adaptation and update of the review by van Hoeken and colleagues.

ANOREXIA NERVOSA

Prevalence

The current standard for prevalence studies of eating disorders are studies employing a two-stage selection of cases. Table 2.1 summarizes the two-stage surveys of anorexia nervosa in young females.

All studies have succeeded in obtaining high response rates of 85% or more, except Meadows et al. (1986), who reached a response rate of 70%. Those two-stage surveys that identified cases found a prevalence rate of strictly defined anorexia nervosa of between 0.2 and 0.8% of young females, with an average prevalence of 0.3%. These rates are possibly minimum estimates. Most studies found much higher prevalence rates for partial syndromes of anorexia nervosa.

Two other studies are discussed here because they are not confined to high-risk populations and give prevalence figures for the entire population. A drawback is that these studies did not use a two-stage procedure for case finding. In a general practice study in the

Table 2.1 Two-stage surveys of prevalence of anorexia nervosa in young females

| Study | Subjects | | | Methods | | Prevalence |
	Source	Age	n	Screening[a]	Criteria	%
Button and Whitehouse (1981)	College students	16–22	446	EAT	Feighner	0.2
Szmukler (1983)	Private schools	14–19	1331	EAT	Russell	0.8
	State schools	14–19	1676	EAT	Russell	0.2
King (1989)	General practice	16–35	539	EAT	Russell	0
Meadows et al. (1986)	General practice	18–22	584	EAT	DSM-III	0.2[b]
Johnson-Sabine et al. (1988)	Schoolgirls	14–16	1010	EAT	Russell	0
Råstam et al. (1989)	Schoolgirls	15	2136	Growth chart + questionnaire	DSM-III	0.47
					DSM-III-R	0.23
Whitaker et al. (1990)	Highschool girls	13–18	2544	EAT	DSM-III	0.3
Whitehouse et al. (1992)	General practice	16–35	540	Questionnaire	DSM-II-R	0.2
Rathner and Messner (1993)	Schoolgirls + case register	11–20	517	EAT	DSM-II-R	0.58
Wlodarczyk-Bisaga and Dolan (1996)	Schoolgirls	14–16	747	EAT	DSM-II-R	0
Steinhausen et al. (1997)	Schoolgirls	14–17	276	EDE-S	DSM-II-R	0.7
Nobakht and Dezhkam (2000)	Schoolgirls	15–18	3100	EAT	DSM-IV	0.9

[a]EAT—Eating Attitudes Test; EDE-S—Eating Disorders Examination, Screening Version.
[b]Not found by screening (EAT score below threshold).

Netherlands, Hoek (1991) found a raw point-prevalence rate of 18.4 per 100 000 of the total population (95% CI 12.7–26.8) on 1 January 1985. Lucas et al. (1991) used a very extensive case-finding method. It included all medical records of health care providers, general practitioners and specialists in the community of Rochester, Minnesota. They also screened records mentioning related diagnostic terms for possible non-detected cases. They found an overall sex- and age-adjusted point prevalence of 149.5 per 100 000 (95% CI 119.3–179.7) on 1 January 1985.

A main explanation for this difference can be found in the inclusion of probable and possible cases by Lucas et al. Definite cases constituted only 39% (82 out of 208) of all incident cases identified in the period 1935–1989 (Lucas et al., 1999). Applying this rate to the point prevalence of 149.5 gives an estimated point prevalence of 58.9 per 100 000 for definite cases in Rochester, Minnesota, on 1 January 1985. The remaining difference with the point prevalence reported by Hoek (1991) could be explained by the greater variety of medical sources searched by Lucas et al. (1991).

Incidence

The incidence studies of anorexia nervosa have used psychiatric case registers, medical records of hospitals in a circumscribed area, registrations by general practitioners or medical records of health care providers in a community. Table 2.2 summarizes the results of the

Table 2.2 Incidence of anorexia nervosa per year per 100 000 population

Study	Region	Source	Period	Incidence
Theander (1970)	Southern Sweden	Hospital records	1931–1940	0.10
			1941–1950	0.20
			1951–1960	0.45
			(1931–1960)	(0.24)
Willi et al. (1983, 1990); Martz et al. (2001)	Zurich	Hospital records	1956–1958	0.38
			1963–1965	0.55
			1973–1975	1.12
			1983–1985	1.43
			1993–1995	1.17
Jones et al. (1980)	Monroe County	Case register + hospital records	1960–1969	0.37
			1970–1976	0.64
Kendell et al. (1973)	NE Scotland	Case register	1960–1969	1.60
Szmukler et al. (1986)	NE Scotland	Case register	1978–1982	4.06
Kendell et al. (1973)	Camberwell	Case register	1965–1971	0.66
Hoek and Brook (1985)	Assen	Case register	1974–1982	5.0
Møller-Madsen and Nystrup (1992)	Denmark	Case-register	1970	0.42
			1988	1.36
			1989	1.17
Lucas et al. (1999)	Rochester, MN	Medical records	1935–1949	9.1
			1950–1959	4.3
			1960–1969	7.0
			1970–1979	7.9
			1980–1989	12.0
			(1935–1989)	(8.3)
Hoek et al. (1995)	Netherlands	Gen. practitioners	1985–1989	8.1
Turnbull et al. (1996)	England, Wales	Gen. practitioners	1993	4.2

studies on the incidence of anorexia nervosa that report overall rates for a general population sample.

The overall rates vary considerably, ranging from 0.10 in a hospital-records-based study in Sweden in the 1930s to 12.0 in a medical-records-based study in the USA in the 1980s, both per 100 000 population per year.

Incidence rates derived from general practices on average represent more recently started eating disorders than those based on other medical records. There were two studies of this type (Hoek et al., 1995, and Turnbull et al., 1996). In the study by Hoek and colleagues, general practitioners using DSM-III-R criteria have recorded the rate of eating disorders in a large (1985: $N = 151\,781$), representative sample (1.1%) of the Dutch population. The incidence rate of anorexia nervosa was 8.1 per 100 00 person years (95% CI 6.1–10.2) during the period 1985–1989. During the study period 63% of the incident cases were referred to mental health care, accounting for an incidence rate of anorexia nervosa in mental health care of 5.1 per year per 100 000 population. Turnbull et al. (1996) searched the UK General Practice Research Database (GPRD), covering 550 general practitioners and 4 million patients, for first diagnoses of anorexia in the period 1988–1993. A randomly selected subset of cases was checked with DSM-IV criteria, from which estimates for adjusted incidence rates were made. For anorexia nervosa they found an age- and sex-adjusted incidence rate of 4.2 (95% CI 3.4–5.0) per 100 000 population in 1993.

Lucas et al. (1991, 1999) used the most extensive case-finding method (see the section on prevalence). Over the period of 1935–1989, they report an overall age- and sex-adjusted incidence rate of anorexia nervosa of 8.3 per 100 000 person-years (95% CI 7.1–9.4).

Age and Sex

Incidence rates of anorexia nervosa are highest for females 15–19 years old. These constitute approximately 40% of all identified cases and 60% of female cases. For example, Lucas et al. (1999) report an incidence rate of 73.9 per 100 000 person-years for 15–19-year-old women over the period of 1935–1989, with a continual rise since the 1930s to a top rate of 135.7 for the period 1980–1989.

Although it is clear that anorexia nervosa occurs in men as well as in women, and in younger as well as in older people, few studies report incidence rates for males or for people beyond the age of 35. This makes it difficult to evaluate the size of the problem for them. The majority of male incidence rates reported was below 0.5 per 100 000 population per year (e.g. Turnbull et al., 1996). In those studies where it is reported, the female to male ratio usually is around 11 to 1 (e.g. Hoek et al., 1995). On an overall female rate of 15.0 per 100 000 population per year, Lucas et al. (1999) report a rate of 9.5 for 30–39-year-old women, 5.9 for 40–49-year-old women, 1.8 for 50–59-year-old women, and 0.0 for women aged 60 and over.

Time Trends

There has been considerable debate whether the incidence of eating disorders is, or has been, on the increase. Since the 1970s, the number of incidence studies has increased. Case register studies prior to the 1980s show at most a slight increase over time of incident anorexia nervosa cases (Hoek, 1993). The studies in the 1980s show widely diverging incidence rates. Most likely, there is a methodological explanation for these differences. The main problem lies in the need for long study periods. This results in a sensitivity of these studies to minor changes in absolute incidence numbers and in methods, for example variations in registration policy, demographic differences between the populations, faulty inclusion of readmissions, the particular methods of detection used, or the availability of services (Williams & King, 1987; Fombonne, 1995).

From the studies that have used long study periods, it may now be concluded that there is an upward trend in the incidence of anorexia nervosa since the 1950s. The increase is most substantial in females 15–24 years of age. Lucas et al. (1999) found that the age-adjusted incidence rates of anorexia nervosa in females 15–24 years old showed a highly significant linear increasing trend from 1935 to 1989, with an estimated rate of increase of 1.03 per 100 000 person-years per calendar year. In 10–14-year-old females a rise in incidence was observed for each decade since the 1950s. The rates for men and for women aged 25 and over remained relatively low.

All record-based studies will grossly underestimate the true incidence, because not all cases will be referred to mental health care or become hospitalized. The increase in incidence rates of registered cases implies at least that there is an increased demand for health care facilities for anorexia nervosa.

Mortality

Sullivan (1995) conducted a meta-analysis on crude mortality rates (CMR) for anorexia nervosa in 42 published studies. The CMR found was 5.9% (178 deaths in 3006 patients), translating into 0.56% per year or 5.6% per decade. In the studies specifying cause of death, 54% of the subjects died as a result of eating disorder complications, 27% committed suicide and the remaining 19% died of unknown or other causes.

Nielsen (2001) has conducted an update of a previous meta-analysis on standardized mortality rates (SMR). The overall aggregate SMR of anorexia nervosa in studies with 6–12 years follow-up is 9.6 (95% CI 7.8–11.5) and in studies with 20–40 years follow-up 3.7 (95% CI 2.8–4.7). Thus in the long run subjects with anorexia nervosa have an almost four-fold risk of dying compared to healthy people the same age and sex.

BULIMIA NERVOSA

Prevalence

In 1990 Fairburn and Beglin gave a review of the prevalence studies on bulimia nervosa. This landmark review yielded the generally accepted prevalence rate of 1% of young females with bulimia nervosa according to DSM criteria. Table 2.3 summarizes two-stage surveys of bulimia nervosa in young females that have been published since the review by Fairburn and Beglin.

Despite the different classifications used (DSM-III versus DSM-III-R) and different types of prevalence rates provided (lifetime prevalence, e.g. Bushnell et al., 1990, versus point prevalence, e.g. Rathner & Messner, 1993), the aggregated prevalence rate according to

Table 2.3   Two-stage surveys of prevalence of bulimia nervosa in young females

| Study | Subjects | | | Method | | Prevalence % |
	Source	Age	N	Screening[a]	Criteria	
Whitaker et al. (1990)	Highschool girls	13–18	2544	EAT	DSM-III	4.2
Bushnell et al. (1990)	Household census	18–24		DIS	DSM-III	4.5
		25–44				2.0
		(18–44)	(777)			(2.6)
Szabó and Túry (1991)	Schoolgirls	14–18	416	EAT, BCDS, ANIS	DSM-III	0
					DSM-III-R	0
	College girls	19–36	224	EAT, BCDS, ANIS	DSM-III	4.0
					DSM-III-R	1.3
Whitehouse et al. (1992)	General practice	16–35	540	Questionnaire	DSM-III-R	1.5
Rathner and Messner (1993)	Schoolgirls + case register	11–20	517	EAT	DSM-III-R	0
Wlodarczyk-Bisaga and Dolan (1996)	Schoolgirls	14–16	747	EAT	DSM-III-R	0
Santonastaso et al. (1996)	Schoolgirls	16	359	EAT	DSM-IV	0.5
Steinhausen et al. (1997)	Schoolgirls	14–17	276	EDE-S	DSM-III-R	0.5
Nobakht and Dezhkam (2000)	Schoolgirls	15–18	3100	EAT	DSM-IV	3.2

[a]EAT—Eating Attitudes Test; DIS—Diagnostic Interview Schedule; BCDS—Bulimia Cognitive Distortions Scale; ANIS—Anorexia Nervosa Inventory Scale; EDE-S—Eating Disorder Examination, Screening Version.

DSM criteria remains 1%. The prevalence of subclinical eating disorders is substantially higher than that of full-syndrome bulimia nervosa (e.g. Whitehouse et al., 1992: 1.5% for full-syndrome, and 5.4% for partial syndrome bulimia nervosa).

The results of three studies not using a two-stage procedure for case finding are also reported here, because they address the prevalence for the entire population and not just for the high-risk group of young females. In a study of incident cases reported by general practitioners, Hoek (1991) reports a point-prevalence rate of 20.4 per 100 000 of the total population. Garfinkel et al. (1995) assessed eating disorders in a random, stratified, non-clinical community sample, using a structured interview for the whole sample. They reported a lifetime prevalence for bulimia nervosa of 1.1% in women and of 0.1% in men aged 15–65, using DSM-III-R criteria. In a study by Soundy et al. (1995) no attempt to determine prevalence rates for bulimia nervosa was made because they considered the information about how long symptoms had persisted and the long duration (mean 39.8 months) of symptoms before diagnosis to be too unreliable.

Incidence

There have been only few incidence studies of bulimia nervosa. The most obvious reason is the lack of criteria for bulimia nervosa in the past. Most case registers use the International Classification of Diseases (currently ICD-10; WHO, 1992). The ICD-9 (WHO, 1978) and previous versions did not provide a separate code for bulimia nervosa. Bulimia nervosa has been distinguished as a separate disorder by Russell in 1979 and DSM-III in 1980 (APA, 1980). Before 1980 the term 'bulimia' in medical records designated symptoms of heterogeneous conditions manifested by overeating, but not the syndrome as it is known today. Therefore it is difficult to examine trends in the incidence of bulimia nervosa or a possible shift from anorexia nervosa to bulimia nervosa, which might have influenced the previously described incidence rates of anorexia nervosa.

Three studies are reviewed here: those of Soundy et al. (1995), Hoek et al. (1995) and Turnbull et al. (1996). Soundy and colleagues used methodology similar to that in the long-term anorexia nervosa study by Lucas et al. (1991), screening all medical records of health care providers, general practitioners and specialists in Rochester, Minnesota, over the period of 1980–1990 for a clinical diagnosis of bulimia nervosa as well as for related symptoms. Hoek and colleagues studied the incidence rate of bulimia nervosa using DSM-III-R criteria in a large general practice study representative of the Dutch population, covering the period 1985–1989. Turnbull and colleagues screened the General Practice Research Database (GPRD), covering a large representative sample of the English and Welsh population, for first diagnoses of anorexia nervosa and bulimia nervosa in 1993. Another general population study by Pagsberg and Wang (1994) is not discussed here, because the population under consideration is relatively small (<50 000 inhabitants from the island of Bornholm, Denmark).

The three studies under consideration all report an annual incidence of bulimia nervosa around 12 per 100 000 population: 13.5 for Soundy et al., 11.5 for Hoek et al., and 12.2 for Turnbull et al.

Age and Sex

Soundy et al. (1995) report an incidence of bulimia nervosa of 26.5 for females, and of 0.8 for males per 100 000 population, yielding a female to male ratio of 33:1. Hoek et al. (1995) report similar rates of 21.9 for females and 0.8 for males per 100 000 population, yielding a female to male ratio of 27:1. For the highest risk group of 20–24-year-old females rates close to 82 per 100 000 are found: 82.7 for Soundy et al. and 82.1 for Hoek et al. Hoek and colleagues report a rate of 8.3 per 100 000 for women aged 35–64. Turnbull et al. (1996) report an annual incidence of 1.7 per 100 000 people (men and women) aged 40 and over.

Time Trends

Soundy et al. (1995) found yearly incidence rates to rise sharply from 7.4 per 100 000 females in 1980 to 49.7 in 1983, and then remain relatively constant around 30 per 100 000 females. This would seem to be related to the publication, and following implementation in the field, of DSM-III in 1980, introducing bulimia nervosa as an official diagnostic category. Hoek et al. (1995) report a non-significant trend for the incidence rates of bulimia nervosa to increase by 15% each year in the period 1985–1989. Turnbull et al. (1996) noted a highly significant, three-fold increase in bulimia nervosa incidence rates for women aged 10–39 in the period 1988–1993, increasing from 14.6 in 1988 to 51.7 in 1993.

These incidence rates of bulimia nervosa can only serve as minimum estimates of the true incidence rate. The reasons are the lack of data, the greater taboo around bulimia nervosa and its smaller perceptibility compared to anorexia nervosa.

Mortality

Combination of the results of the meta-analyses of the crude mortality rate (CMR) by Keel and Mitchell (1997) and Nielsen (2001) yields a CMR of bulimia nervosa of 0.4% (11 deaths in 2692 patients). No information is available as to the distribution of causes of death.

Nielsen (2001) has conducted an update of a previous meta-analysis on standardized mortality rates (SMR). The overall aggregate SMR of bulimia nervosa in studies with 5–11 years follow-up is 7.4 (95% CI 2.9–14.9). Longer follow-up periods are not yet available. However, as suggested by Nielsen (personal communication), there may be serious publication bias in this rate. When mortality information of all 42 bulimia nervosa cohorts is used, not just that of the 5 cohorts reporting SMR, the SMR changes to 1.56 (95% C.I. 0.8 –2.7).

Thus, within the first 10 years after detection, subjects with bulimia nervosa run an increased risk of dying compared to healthy people of the same age and sex. But it is still open to debate as to whether this risk is only moderately increased (1.5 times) or, with a seven-fold increase, is close to the risk (more than nine-fold increase) of anorexia nervosa.

BINGE EATING DISORDER

The Binge Eating Disorder (BED) has the status of 'Diagnostic Category in Need of Further Research' in the 1994 version of the *Diagnostic and Statistical Manual of Mental Disorders* (DSM-IV; APA, 1994). A general problem with the comparison of studies of BED—and bulimia nervosa for that matter—lies in the diagnosis of a binge. Studies may differ in the way the boundaries of a binge were set, resulting in subject groups that are not fully comparable.

As for anorexia nervosa and bulimia nervosa, the focus here is on prevalence studies using a two-stage case identification procedure in the general population. Cotrufo et al. (1998) were the only researchers to use a two-stage procedure. They identified two cases of BED in a group of 919 13–19-year-old females, giving a prevalence rate of 0.2%. The low rate may be due to the relatively young age of the investigated population. Also the sample size is rather small for a low-frequency disorder.

Hay (1998) conducted interviews to determine the prevalence of bulimic type eating disorders on all subjects in a large general population sample (3001 interviews). The mean age of the cases was 35.2 years. Using DSM-IV criteria, a (point) prevalence for BED of 1% was found. Using a broader definition by Fairburn and Cooper (1993), the prevalence was estimated at 2.5%. A weakness of the study was that diagnoses were based on a very limited number of questions (two gating questions, and three further probes). No information was given regarding the sensitivity/specificity of the instrument.

No reports on crude or standardized mortality rates have been located for BED.

RISK FACTORS

Context of the Individual

Social Class

Most psychiatric disorders show a higher prevalence in the lower socio-economic classes. It is difficult to determine whether this is the result of the social selection process, or whether it is caused by social factors (Dohrenwend et al., 1992).

For anorexia nervosa, there has been a traditional belief of an upper social class preponderance. In reviewing the evidence, Gard and Freeman (1996) concluded that the relationship between anorexia nervosa and high socio-economic status is unproven, due to data collection biases including sample size, clinical status and referral patterns. A recent study on a large comprehensive clinical database, covering 692 referrals to a UK national specialist centre over a time lapse of 33 years, challenges this conclusion: McClelland and Crisp (2001) found referrals for anorexia nervosa from the two highest social classes to be almost twice as high as expected. They present evidence that their findings are unrelated to differences in clinical features or in access to their service.

For bulimia nervosa, Gard and Freeman (1996) conclude that—similar to most psychiatric disorders—there seems to be a preponderance in the low socio-economic groups.

Level of Industrialization

It is commonly thought that anorexia nervosa is a western illness: there appears to be a developmental gradient across countries, with a predominance in industrialized, developed countries, linking the disorder to an affluent society (Hoek, 1993). This gradient has been hypothesized to be connected with the sociocultural theory, which holds that eating disorders are promoted by a 'western' culture favouring slimness as a beauty ideal for females. By consequence, eating disorders would be less prevalent in underdeveloped, non-western cultures. Unfortunately, up to date few developing countries have the facilities and means needed to arrive at reliable epidemiological data.

Some recent publications cast doubts on the validity of the sociocultural theory, at least for anorexia nervosa. For example, Hoek et al. (1998) found an incidence of anorexia nervosa on the Caribbean island of Curaçao within the range of rates reported in western countries. A methodological problem of this type of study is the definition and assessment of what typifies a culture as 'non-western'. For more discussion on this matter, the reader is referred to Chapter 8 in this book and Nasser et al. (2001).

Level of Urbanization

Hoek et al. (1995) report that the incidence of bulimia nervosa is three to five times higher in urbanized areas and cities than in rural areas, while anorexia nervosa is found with almost equal frequency in areas with different degrees of urbanization. The drift-hypothesis, relating urbanization differences to migration for educational reasons, is rejected because the differences remain after adjusting for age. Other social factors involved might be an increased pressure to be slender and decreased social control in urbanized areas. If these hold true, this would imply that anorexia nervosa is less sensitive to social factors than bulimia nervosa, has a more biological origin, and is more driven by other factors such as a tendency towards asceticism and compulsive behaviour.

Occupation

Some occupations appear to run a greater potential risk of being linked to the development of an eating disorder (Vandereycken & Hoek, 1993). Typical examples of these are professions within the world of fashion and ballet. We do not know whether this is a causal factor or the result of disturbed attitudes around body and shape. In other words, are pre-anorexics attracted by the ballet world, or are the requirements of the profession conducive to the development of anorexia nervosa?

Individual Characteristics

The method of choice for assessing individual risk is a prospective follow-up study. Unfortunately, none of the few prospective studies reported employs a two-stage case identification procedure and they address only a subsample of the general population. Wlodarczyk-Bisaga and Dolan (1996) re-interviewed a high- and a low-risk group of 14–16-year-old schoolgirls, defined by their scores on the EAT, 10 months after initial assessment. No clinical cases were detected at either measurement point. Patton et al. (1999) conducted a cohort study over three years with six-month intervals in students initially aged 14–15 years. All new cases of eating disorder developed during the study had partial/subclinical syndromes of bulimia nervosa. Both dieting and psychiatric morbidity were implicated as risk factors, but from this study it is not clear whether this also holds for full-syndrome eating disorders.

Although case control studies in general are not discussed here because of their methodological drawbacks, an exception is made for the studies by Fairburn and colleagues (1997, 1998, 1999). They compared subjects with bulimia nervosa (1997), binge eating disorder (1998) and anorexia nervosa (1999) with each other, with healthy control subjects without an eating disorder (general risk factors), and with subjects with other psychiatric disorders (specific risk factors), recruited from general practices in Oxfordshire, England. After screening with self-report questionnaires, a retrospective risk-factor interview was carried out that addressed the premorbid period. This interview focused on biological, psychological and social factors thought to place persons at risk for the development of eating disorders. For anorexia nervosa and bulimia nervosa, the great majority of the risk factors found were general risk factors, separating eating disorder cases from healthy controls. For BED only a few general risk factors were identified.

Some specific risk factors, separating eating disorder cases from other psychiatric cases were also found. For anorexia nervosa subjects they were personal vulnerability factors, particularly childhood characteristics of negative self-evaluation and perfectionism. For bulimia nervosa these were dieting vulnerability factors, such as parental obesity, childhood obesity and negative comments from family members about eating, appearance and weight. The results suggest that both bulimia nervosa and binge eating disorder are most likely to develop in dieters who are at risk of obesity and psychiatric disorder in general (Fairburn et al., 1997, 1998). This result is in line with the conclusions of Patton et al. (1999).

OBESITY

Classification

The epidemiology of obesity has for many years been difficult to study because many countries had their own specific criteria for the classification of different degrees of overweight. Gradually during the 1990s, however, the body mass index (BMI = weight/squared height) became a universally accepted measure of the degree of overweight, and now identical cut-points are recommended. In the most recent classification of weight in adults by the World Health Organization (WHO, 1998a), four levels over overweight are defined. The first three each cover 5 units of BMI, from pre-obese starting at a BMI of 25.0, through obese class I at 30.0 and obese class II at 35.0 to the highest level of overweight (obese class III) at a BMI of 40.0 and upwards. The associated health risks are deemed to increase accordingly from increased at pre-obese to very severely increased at obese class III.

The BMI is used because it is highly correlated with body fat percentage and is unrelated to stature. The correlation between BMI and body fat percentage is usually in the range of 0.7 to 0.9 in adults aged 25–65, but lower in subjects at other ages. The level of body fatness for a given BMI varies greatly by age, sex and ethnicity (Deurenberg et al., 1991). This may necessitate sex-, age- and ethnic-specific criteria for the use of the BMI. This issue is currently under intense debate in the obesity research community. Already researchers in Asian countries have criticized the WHO cut-off points. The absolute health risks seem to be higher at any level of the BMI in Chinese and South-Asian people, which is probably also true for Asians living elsewhere. This implies that for Asians the cut-off points to designate overweight or obesity should be lowered by several units of BMI. Because China and India alone each have over a billion inhabitants, small changes in the criteria for overweight or obesity potentially increase the world estimate of the number of obese people by several hundred million (currently estimates are about 250 million world wide).

Much research over the last decade has suggested that for an accurate classification of weight with respect to health risks one needs to factor in the abdominal fat distribution (e.g. Lean et al., 1998). In June 1998 the National Institute of Health (National Heart, Lung and Blood Institute) adopted the BMI classification and combined this with waist cut-off points (NIH, 1998). In this classification the combination of overweight (BMI between 25 and 30 kg/m^2) or moderate obesity (BMI between 30 and 35 kg/m^2) with a large waist circumference (≥ 102 cm in men or ≥ 88 cm in women) is proposed to carry additional health risk.

Prevalence

In many reviews it has been shown that obesity (defined as a body mass index of 30 kg/m^2 or higher) is a prevalent condition in most countries with established market economies (Seidell, 1997), and there is wide variation in prevalence of obesity between and within these countries: e.g. Toulouse in France with a prevalence of obesity of 9% in men and 11% in women and Strasbourg in France with 22% of the men and 23% of the women meeting the obesity criterion. In industrialized countries obesity is usually more frequent among those with relatively low socio-economic status. In cross-sectional surveys the prevalence increases with age until about 60–70 years of age after which the prevalence declines (Seidell & Flegal, 1997). For an explanation of the age effect a combination of selective survival, cohort effect and general weight loss after the age of 60 has been proposed.

There is uncertainty about most national prevalence estimates of obesity due to a lack of solid data, large differences between regions within the same country and secular trends. The numbers corresponding to the midpoint of the estimates add up to about 250 million obese adults, which is about 7% of the total adult world population. It does not seem unreasonable that the true prevalence of obesity is in the order of 5–10%. In most countries the prevalence of overweight (BMI between 25 and 30 kg/m^2) is about two to three times as large as the prevalence of obesity. This means that as many as one billion people may be overweight or obese.

Time Trends

In most of these established market economies it has been shown that the prevalence is increasing over time (Seidell & Flegal, 1997). Figures 2.1 and 2.2 show the changes in the prevalence of obesity (BMI $\geq$ 30) in men and women aged 35–64 years in several centres participating in the WHO MONICA project. In this project cardiovascular risk factors were monitored through independent cross-sectional population surveys over a 10-year period. The surveys included random samples of at least 200 people of each sex for each 10-year age group for the age range 36–64 years (Molarius et al., 2000).

There is a rapid increase in the prevalence of obesity in most centres from countries in the European Union, particularly in men. In centres in countries from central and eastern Europe the prevalence at follow-up of obesity in women remains among the highest in Europe, even though it may have stabilized or even slightly decreased over time.

The study by Molarius et al. (2000) also showed that social class differences in the prevalence of obesity are increasing with time. Obesity increasingly seems to be becoming an almost exclusive lower class problem in Europe.

Regional Differences

The most recent (1988–1994) estimates of obesity prevalence in adults in the USA are about 20% in men and 25% in women (Seidell & Flegal, 1997). In other parts of the world obesity is also frequent. Martorell et al. (2000) recently described the prevalence of obesity in young adult women aged 15–49 years. It was on average 10% in countries from Latin America and 17% in countries in North Africa and the middle east. Obesity is uncommon in Sub-Saharan Africa, China and India, although in all regions the prevalence seems to be increasing, particularly among the affluent parts of the population in the larger cities (Seidell & Rissanen, 1997). In these countries we quite often see the paradoxical combination of increasing under- and overnutrition. This is quite obviously related to growing inequalities in income and access to food in these regions. In addition, as already mentioned, classification criteria based on white populations might not be appropriate for Asian populations.

Incidence

Very few studies have attempted to calculate the incidence rate of obesity. The criterion for obesity is a matter of definition on a gliding scale from low to high weight. This makes it difficult to determine at what moment overweight becomes (incident) obesity and to separate incident from prevalent cases at the moment of registration. In one report a four-year incidence rate of obesity was calculated from data collected in a mixed longitudinal study carried out between 1980 and 1984 in young adults aged 19–31 years in The Netherlands (Rookus et al., 1987). The incidence was determined to be 0.9% per 4 years (95% CI: 0.1–3.4%) in men and 2.5% in 4 years (95% CI: 0.9–5.5%) in women aged 29–31 years of age. It increased with age, particularly in women.

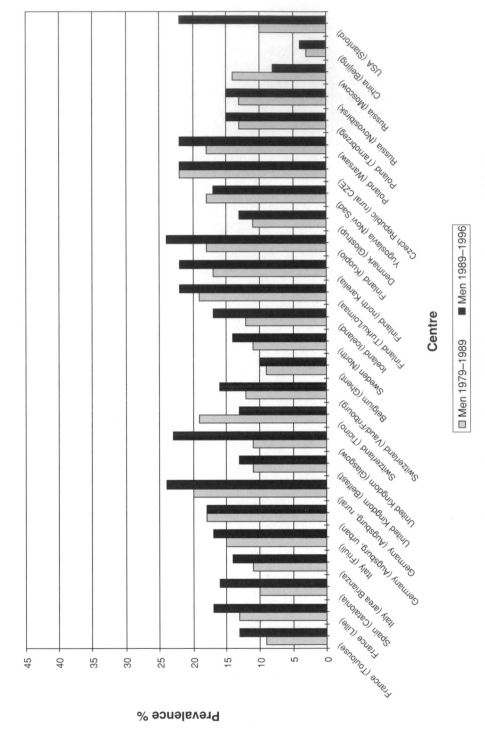

Figure 2.1 The WHO MONICA project: Changes in the prevalence of obesity over 10 years in men aged 35–64 years

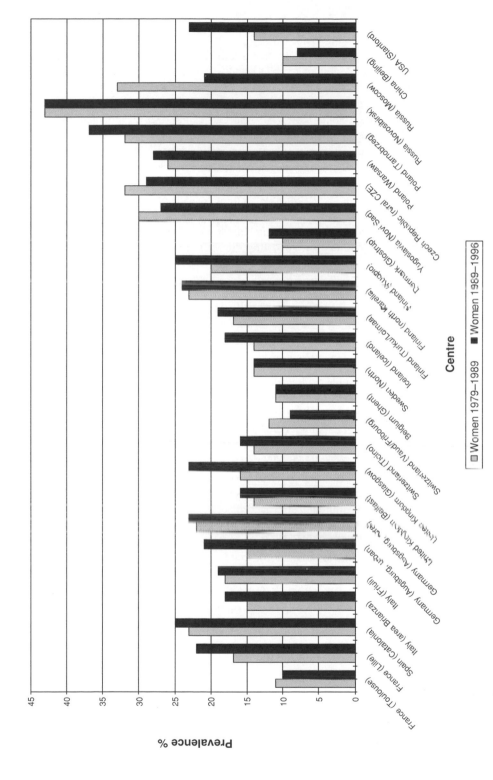

Figure 2.2 The WHO MONICA project: Changes in the prevalence of obesity over 10 years in women aged 35–64 years

Mortality

The relation between high body mass index and mortality has been studied for many decades in many populations. Available evidence shows that obesity is clearly associated with an increased risk of mortality. For instance, recently pooled analyses of six large American prospective studies showed that the number of deaths attributable to obesity is in the order of 300 000 per year in the United States alone (Allison et al., 1999). It is difficult and probably not meaningful to give a single figure for a standardized mortality rate (SMR) in the obese. Research has shown that the SMR for obesity is strongly dependent upon sex, age and ethnicity. In addition, the SMR strongly depends upon the presence of covariates such as smoking habits. It is generally assumed that mortality is elevated by about 50–150% in most adult populations (Seidell et al., 1999). Obesity is a major cause of mortality in most affluent countries. More important, however, is that obesity is associated with a dramatic increase in morbidity and impairment of quality of life. In essence, the true burden of obesity is measured by the increase in number of unhealthy life-years rather than by the reduction in total life-years.

Risk Factors

Context of the Individual

The relation between obesity and social class is highly variable across cultures. In most industrialized countries obesity is more common in people with relatively low socio-economic status. This phenomenon is generally more pronounced in women than in men. The exact reasons for this social class gradient are unknown but generally are assumed to result from both sociocultural perceptions of body shape in combinations with obesity-promoting lifestyles (high consumption of high fat foods and relatively low consumption of fruits and vegetables as well as relatively low physical activity level during leisure time). The reason why this is more pronounced in women than in men probably reflects the stronger emphasis on thinness among women with high education and income. In non-industrialized countries, however, obesity is usually much more common among those with relatively high socio-economic status. In these circumstances obesity is usually being regarded as a sign of material wealth and is thus considered to be a desirable trait. In many countries undergoing an economic transition and industrialization, the relations between social class are subject to change and can vary greatly by region. In rural China, for instance, obesity is still more common among those with relatively high socio-economic status but an inverse association between social class and obesity is observed in large cities such as Beijing (Seidell & Rissanen, 1997).

Individual Characteristics

On an ecological or population level the time trends in the prevalence of obesity are not too difficult to explain although exact quantification of different factors is almost impossible.

On the one hand there is an increase in the average energy supply per capita. The World Health Report (WHO, 1998b) has estimated that the average energy supply per capita in the world has risen from 2300 kcal in 1963 to 2720 kcal in 1992, with an estimated 2900 kcal in 2010. These increases are obviously not evenly distributed across the world's population and, sadly, many remain undernourished. In Asia (particularly China and India) and most of Latin America undernourishment is declining. The number of people with access to at least 2700 kcal has increased from 0.145 billion in 1969–1971 to 1.8 billion in 1990–1992 and is estimated to grow to 2.7 billion in 2010. Even when corrected for the increase in the world's population this implies a more than ten-fold increase in the number of people with access to high calorific diets. The globalization of agricultural production and food processing has not only affected the quantity of energy available per capita but also the energy density.

On the other hand, there is a decrease in the average energy expenditure per capita. Increasing sedentary behaviour has been proposed to be another main reason for the increase in the prevalence of obesity in countries with established market economies. Large and important differences can be seen in the number of hours spent at sedentary jobs and behind television or computer screens during leisure time. Also, the type of transportation is almost certainly a factor. For example, 30% of short trips in the Netherlands are done by bicycle and 18% by walking. In the UK these percentages are 8% by bicycling and 12% walking and, in the USA, 1% by bicycle and 9% by walking (Pucher, 1997).

Given the changes in lifestyles and resulting changes in energy balance over the last decades in many parts of the world it is not surprising that, on average, people gain weight. With small changes in average body weight the prevalence of obesity increases rapidly. For every unit increase in average BMI there is an increase in the prevalence of obesity of 5% (WHO, 1998a).

CONCLUSIONS

For anorexia nervosa an average prevalence rate of 0.3% was found for young females. Although Soundy et al. (1995) caution for the possibility of unreliable information, figures of an average prevalence rate of bulimia nervosa of 1% in women and 0.1% in men seem accurate. A tentative conclusion is that the prevalence of binge eating disorder (BED) is more likely to be 1% than 4% or more. The true prevalence of obesity may be in the order of 5–10%.

Assuming that even the studies with the most complete case finding methods yield an underestimate of the true incidence, as state of the art we conclude that the overall incidence of anorexia nervosa is at least 8 per 100 000 population per year and the incidence of bulimia nervosa is at least 12 per 100 000 population per year. The incidence rate of anorexia nervosa has increased during the past 50 years, particularly in females 10–24 years old. The registered incidence of bulimia nervosa has increased, at least during the first five years after bulimia nervosa was added to the DSM-III. For BED and obesity not enough incidence information is available for an accurate summary.

Risk factor research is still sparse, both for eating disorders and for obesity, and some group and individual characteristics, particularly related to dieting, have been tentatively identified as carrying with them an increased risk.

COMMENTS

The value of epidemiology lies in its particular methodology that gives rise to population-based disease rates and ratios. When properly established, these rates and ratios provide a scientific basis on the community level for treatment planning and aetiologic model building. Epidemiological information is needed to examine and extend on clinical observations.

The basic epidemiological measures are incidence and prevalence rates. For the purpose of treatment planning, there is an ongoing need for prevalence information at the local level. For reasons of time- and cost-efficiency, this is best done by monitoring existing health care consumption registers. Attention must be paid to the interpretation of changing consumption rates in relation to changes in health care recruitment and admission policy. When the adequacy or accuracy of case definition and registration is questioned, efforts are needed to improve registration.

For the purpose of aetiological model building, the mere determination of prevalence and incidence rates is not enough. Although more is becoming known on general and specific risk factors for the onset of an eating disorder, there still is an impressive gap. Furthermore, the developmental mechanisms of these factors are largely unknown. The general conclusion is that dieting behaviour plays a role in the pathogenesis of anorexia nervosa, bulimia nervosa and binge eating disorder. For more information on this matter, see also Chapter 9 in this book. However, not all dieters proceed to develop an eating disorder. A prospective follow-up study of initially healthy dieters sampled from the general population may shed light on the mechanisms that turn dieting into an eating disorder.

To circumvent the power- and cost-problems caused by the relatively low rates of eating disorders in the general population, a few suggestions for the design of economically feasible studies providing generalizable, reliable results on risk factors and mechanisms are given:

- There is a need for prospective, follow-up designs using initially healthy subjects at high risk for developing an eating disorder, such as young females, dieters and participants in weight-restricted sports including ballet dancing. Depending on the question to be answered, these could be matched on sex, age and socio-economic status with initially healthy intermediate- and low-risk groups.
- For lower risk groups, such as males or older persons, a prospective design is too cost-inefficient and a case-control design is more appropriate. Cases should be collected at as low a level of entry into the health care system as possible, preferably primary care. As controls, same-sex siblings and other same-sex persons matched for age and socio-economic status could be of use. To facilitate hypothesis testing and the exchange of knowledge and ideas, the formation of a multi-centre database of these rare cases would mean a great improvement.
- For both prospective follow-up studies and case-control studies of eating disorders, a comprehensive assessment of biological, psychological, familial and social variables is needed. The factors and mechanisms studied should be based on findings from previous research such as that by Fairburn et al. (1997). To decide on the effect of weight- and shape-centred beauty ideals on the frequency of eating disorders, studies are needed that compare the distribution of eating disorders between groups differing in weight- and shape-related attitudes.

Finally, an issue to be solved for epidemiological studies on eating disorders is the reliance on a categorical approach of caseness, particularly for the 'newer' diagnoses of bulimia nervosa, the eating disorders not otherwise specified, and BED. By focusing on incident clinical cases and ignoring atypical or subclinical cases, aetiological reasoning may miss the crucial developmental elements in what have been called 'broad spectrum' disorders.

Obesity is a complex disorder with biological, sociological and psychological dimensions. The fundamental causes of the increase in obesity rates are sedentary lifestyles and high-fat, energy-dense diets. The rising rates reflect the profound changes in society and in the behavioural patterns of the communities, although some individuals may become obese partly because they have a genetic or other biological predisposition to gain more readily when they are exposed to an unfavourable environment. Identifying environmental, behavioural, and biological factors that contribute to an individual's weight gain is particularly difficult.

The World Health Organization has concluded that the global epidemic of obesity is so serious that public health action is urgently required. It is thus essential to develop new preventive public health strategies which affect the entire society. Without societal changes a substantial and steadily rising proportion of adults will succumb to the medical complications of obesity. Indeed, the medical burden of obesity already threatens to overwhelm health services. The spectrum of problems seen in both developing and developed countries is having so negative an impact that the World Health Organization considers obesity to be regarded as today's principal neglected public health problem (WHO, 1998b).

Unless a miracle occurs, it will not be possible to predict an individual's risk at developing an eating disorder or becoming obese, let alone arrive at evidence-based successful preventive measures, for quite a few years.

REFERENCES

Allison, D.B., Fontaine, K.R., Manson, J.E., Stevens, J. & VanItallic, T.B. (1999) Annual deaths attributable to obesity in the United States. *Journal of the American Medical Association*, **282**, 1530–1538.

APA (1980) *Diagnostic and Statistical Manual of Mental Disorders* (3rd Edition). Washington, D.C.: American Psychiatric Association.

APA (1994) *Diagnostic and Statistical Manual of Mental Disorders* (4th Edition). Washington, D.C.: American Psychiatric Association.

Bushnell, J.A., Wells, J.E., Hornblow, A.R., Oakly-Browne, M.A. & Joyce, P. (1990) Prevalence of three bulimia syndromes in the general population. *Psychological Medicine*, **20**, 671–680.

Button, E.J. & Whitehouse, A. (1981) Subclinical anorexia nervosa. *Psychological Medicine*, **11**, 509–516.

Cotrufo, P., Barretta, V., Monteleone, P. & Maj, M. (1998) Full-syndrome, partial-syndrome and subclinical eating disorders: An epidemiological study of female students in Southern Italy. *Acta Psychiatrica Scandinavica*, **98**, 112–115.

Deurenberg, P., Weststrate, J.A. & Seidell, J.C. (1991) Body mass index as a measure of body fatness: Age- and sex-specific prediction formulas. *British Journal of Nutrition*, **65**, 105–114.

Dohrenwend, B.P., Levav, I., Shrout, P.E., Schwartz, S., Naveh, G., Link, B.G., Skodol, A.E. & Stueve, A. (1992) Socioeconomic status and psychiatric disorders: The causation-selection issue. *Science*, **255**, 946–952.

Eaton, W.W., Tien, A.Y. & Poeschla, B.D. (1995) Epidemiology of schizophrenia. In J.A. Den Boer, H.G.M. Westenberg & H.M. Van Praag (Eds), *Advances in the Neurobiology of Schizophrenia* (pp. 27–57). Chichester: John Wiley & Sons.

Fairburn, C.G. & Beglin, S.J. (1990) Studies of the epidemiology of bulimia nervosa. *American Journal of Psychiatry*, **147**, 401–408.

Fairburn, C.G. & Cooper, Z. (1993) The Eating Disorder Examination (12th Edn). In C.G. Fairburn & G.T. Wilson (Eds), *Binge Eating: Nature, Assessment and Treatment* (pp. 317–360). New York: Guilford Press.

Fairburn, C.G., Cooper, Z., Doll, H.A. & Welch, S.L. (1999) Risk factors for anorexia nervosa. Three integrated case-control comparisons. *Archives of General Psychiatry*, **56**, 468–476.

Fairburn, C.G., Doll, H.A., Welch, S.L., Hay, P.J., Davies, B.A. & O'Connor, M.E. (1998) Risk factors for binge eating disorder. A community-based, case-control study. *Archives of General Psychiatry*, **55**, 425–432.

Fairburn, C.G., Welch, S.L., Doll, H.A., Davies, B.A. & O'Connor, M.E. (1997) Risk factors for bulimia nervosa. A community-based case-control study. *Archives of General Psychiatry*, **54**, 509–517.

Fombonne, E. (1995) Anorexia nervosa. No evidence of an increase. *British Journal of Psychiatry*, **166**, 464–471.

Gard, M.C.E. & Freeman, C.P. (1996) The dismantling of a myth: A review of eating disorders and socioeconomic status. *International Journal of Eating Disorders*, **20**, 1–12.

Garfinkel, P.E., Lin, E., Goering, P., Spegg, C., Goldbloom, D.S., Kennedy, S., Kaplan, A.S. & Woodside, D.B. (1995) Bulimia nervosa in a Canadian community sample: Prevalence and comparison of subgroups. *American Journal of Psychiatry*, **152**, 1052–1058.

Hay, P. (1998) The epidemiology of eating disorder behaviors: An Australian community-based survey. *International Journal of Eating Disorders*, **23**, 371–382.

Hoek, H.W. (1991) The incidence and prevalence of anorexia nervosa and bulimia nervosa in primary care. *Psychological Medicine*, **21**, 455–460.

Hoek, H.W. (1993) Review of the epidemiological studies of eating disorders. *International Review of Psychiatry*, **5**, 61–74.

Hoek, H.W., Bartelds, A.I.M., Bosveld, J.J.F., van der Graaf. Y, Limpens, V.E.L., Maiwald, M. & Spaaij, C.J.K. (1995) Impact of urbanization on detection rates of eating disorders. *American Journal of Psychiatry*, **152**, 1272–1278.

Hoek, H.W. & Brook, F.G. (1985) Patterns of care of anorexia nervosa. *Journal of Psychiatric Research*, **19**, 155–160.

Hoek, H.W., van Harten, P.N., van Hoeken, D. & Susser, E. (1998) Lack of relation between culture and anorexia nervosa: Results of an incidence study on Curaçao. *New England Journal of Medicine*, **338**, 1231–1232.

Hsu, L.K.G. (1996) Epidemiology of the eating disorders. *The Psychiatric Clinics of North America*, **19**, 681–700.

Johnson-Sabine, E., Wood, K., Patton, G., Mann, A. & Wakeling, A. (1988) Abnormal eating attitudes in London schoolgirls—a prospective epidemiological study: Factors associated with abnormal response on screening questionnaires. *Psychological Medicine*, **18**, 615–622.

Jones, D.J., Fox, M.M., Babigian, H.M. & Hutton, H.E. (1980) Epidemiology of anorexia nervosa in Monroe County, New York: 1960–1976. *Psychosomatic Medicine*, **42**, 551–558.

Keel, P.K. & Mitchell, J.E. (1997) Outcome in bulimia nervosa. *American Journal of Psychiatry*, **154**, 313–321.

Kendell, R.E., Hall, D.J., Hailey, A. & Babigian H.M. (1973) The epidemiology of anorexia nervosa. *Psychological Medicine*, **3**, 200–203.

King, M.B. (1989) Eating disorders in a general practice population. Prevalence, characteristics and follow-up at 12 to 18 months. *Psychological Medicine*, Suppl. **14**, 1–34.

Kraemer, H.C., Kazdin, A.E., Offord, D.R., Kessler, R.C., Jensen, P.S. & Kupfer, D.J. (1997) Coming to terms with the terms of risk. *Archives of General Psychiatry*, **54**, 337–343.

Lean, M.E.J., Han, T.S. & Seidell, J.C. (1998) Impairment of health and quality of life in men and women with a large waist. *Lancet*, **351**, 853–856.

Lucas, A.R., Beard, C.M., O'Fallon, W.M. & Kurland, L.T. (1991) 50-Year trends in the incidence of anorexia nervosa in Rochester, Minn.: a population-based study. *American Journal of Psychiatry*, **148**, 917–922.

Lucas, A.R., Crowson, C.S., O'Fallon, W.M. & Melton, L.J. (1999) The ups and downs of anorexia nervosa. *International Journal of Eating Disorders*, **26**, 397–405.

Martorell, R., Khan, L.K., Hughes, M.L. & Grummer-Strawn, L.M. (2000) Obesity in women from developing countries. *European Journal of Clinical Nutrition*, **54**, 247–252.

Martz, J. (2001) Entwickling der Inzidenz und andere Aspekte von Anorexia Nervosa im Kanton Zurich, 1956–1995. Doctoral dissertation, Zurich University.

McClelland, L. & Crisp, A. (2001) Anorexia nervosa and social class. *International Journal of Eating Disorders*, **29**, 150–156.

Meadows, G.N., Palmer, R.L., Newball, E.U.M. & Kenrick, J.M.T. (1986) Eating attitudes and disorder in young women: A general practice based survey. *Psychological Medicine*, **16**, 351–357.

Molarius, A., Seidell, J.C., Sans, S., Tuomilehto, J. & Kuulasmaa, K. (2000) Educational level and relative body weight and changes in their associations over ten years—an international perspective from the WHO MONICA project. *American Journal of Public Health*, **90**, 1260–1268.

Møller-Madsen, S. & Nystrup, J. (1992) Incidence of anorexia nervosa in Denmark. *Acta Psychiatrica Scandinavica*, **86**, 197–200.

Nasser, M. (1997) *Culture and Weight Consciousness.* London: Routledge.

Nasser, M., Katzman, M.A. & Gordon, R.A. (Eds) (2001) *Eating Disorders and Cultures in Transition*, London: Brunner Routledge.

NIH (1998) *Clinical Guidelines on the Identification, Evaluation, and Treatment of Overweight and Obesity in Adults. The Evidence Report.* National Institute of Health, NHLBI.

Nielsen, S. (2001) Epidemiology and mortality of eating disorders. *Psychiatric Clinics of North America*, **24**, 201–214.

Nobakht, M. & Dezhkam, M. (2000) An epidemiological study of eating disorders in Iran. *International Journal of Eating Disorders*, **28**, 265–271.

Pagsberg, A.K. & Wang, A.R. (1994) Epidemiology of anorexia nervosa and bulimia nervosa in Bornholm County, Denmark, 1970–1989. *Acta Psychiatrica Scandinavica*, **90**, 259–265.

Patton, G.C., Selzer, R., Coffey, C., Carlin, J.B. & Wolfe, R. (1999) Onset of adolescent eating disorders: Population based cohort study over 3 years. *British Medical Journal*, **318**, 765–768.

Pucher, J. (1997) Bicycling boom in Germany: A revival engineered by public policy. *Transportation Quarterly*, **51**, 31–46.

Råstam, M., Gillberg, C. & Garton, M. (1989) Anorexia nervosa in a Swedish urban region: A population based study. *British Journal of Psychiatry*, **155**, 642–646.

Rathner, G. & Messner, K. (1993) Detection of eating disorders in a small rural town: An epidemiological study. *Psychological Medicine*, **23**, 175–184.

Regier, D.A. & Burke, J.D. (2000) Epidemiology. In B.J. Sadock & V.A. Sadock (Eds), *Comprehensive Textbook of Psychiatry* (pp. 500–522). Philadelphia: Lippincott Williams & Wilkins.

Rookus, M.A., Burema, van 't Hof, M.A., Deurenberg, P. & Hautvast, J.G.A.J. (1987) The development of the body mass index in young adults, II. Interrelationships of level, change and fluctuation, a four-year longitudinal study. *Human Biology*, **59**, 617–630.

Russell, G.F.M. (1979) Bulimia nervos: An ominous variant of anorexia nervosa. *Psychological Medicine*, **9**, 429–448.

Santonastaso, P., Zanetti, T., Sala, A., Favaretto, G., Vidotto, G. & Favaro, A. (1996) Prevalence of eating disorders in Italy: A survey on a sample of 16-year-old female students. *Psychotherapy and Psychosomatics*, **65**, 158–162.

Seidell, J.C. (1997) Time trends in obesity: An epidemiological perspective. *Hormone and Metabolic Research*, **29**, 155–158.

Seidell, J.C. & Flegal, K.M. (1997) Assessing obesity: Classification and epidemiology. *British Medical Bulletin*, **53**, 238–252.

Seidell, J.C. & Rissanen, A. (1997) World-wide prevalence of obesity and time-trends. In G.A. Bray, C. Bouchard & W.P.T. James (Eds), *Handbook of Obesity* (pp. 79-91). New York: M. Dekker Inc.

Seidell, J.C., Visscher, T.L.S. & Hoogeveen, R.T. (1999) Overweight and obesity in the mortality rate data: Current evidence and research issues. *Medical Science Sports Exercises*, **31**, 597–601.

Soundy, T.J., Lucas, A.R., Suman, V.J. & Melton, L.J. (1995) Bulimia nervosa in Rochester, Minnesota, from 1980 to 1990. *Psychological Medicine*, **25**, 1065–1071.

Steinhausen, H.C., Winkler, C. & Meier, M. (1997) Eating disorders in adolescence in a Swiss epidemiological study. *International Journal of Eating Disorders*, **22**, 147–151.

Sullivan, P.F. (1995) Mortality in anorexia nervosa. *American Journal of Psychiatry*, **152**, 1073–1074.

Szabó, P. & Túry, F. (1991) The prevalence of bulimia nervosa in a Hungarian college and secondary school population. *Psychotherapy and Psychosomatics*, **56**, 43–47.

Szmukler, G.I. (1983) Weight and food preoccupation in a population of English schoolgirls. In G.I. Bargman (Ed.), *Understanding Anorexia Nervosa and Bulimia: Report of 4th Ross Conference on Medical Research* (pp. 21–27). Ross, Columbus, Ohio.

Szmukler, G.I. (1985) The epidemiology of anorexia nervosa and bulimia. *Journal of Psychiatric Research*, **19**, 143–153.

Szmukler, G., McCance, C., McCrone, L. & Hunter, D. (1986) Anorexia nervosa: A psychiatric case register study from Aberdeen. *Psychological Medicine*, **16**, 49–58.

Theander, S. (1970) Anorexia nervosa: A psychiatric investigation of 94 female patients. *Acta Psychiatrica Scandinavica*, Suppl. **214**.

Turnbull, S., Ward, A., Treasure, J., Jick, H. & Derby, L. (1996) The demand for eating disorder care. An epidemiological study using the General Practice Research Database. *British Journal of Psychiatry*, **169**, 705–712.

Van Hoeken, D., Lucas, A.R. & Hoek, H.W. (1998) Epidemiology. In H.W. Hoek, J.L. Treasure & M.A. Katzman (Eds), *Neurobiology in the Treatment of Eating Disorders* (pp. 97–126). Chichester: John Wiley & Sons.

Vandereycken, W. & Hoek, H.W. (1993) Are eating disorders culture-bound syndromes? In K.A. Halmi (Ed.), *Psychobiology and Treatment of Anorexia Nervosa and Bulimia Nervosa* (pp. 19–36). Washington DC: American Psychopathological Association.

Whitaker, A., Johnson, J., Shaffer, D., Rapoport, J.L., Kalikow, K., Walsh, B.T., Davies, M., Braiman, S. & Dolinsky, A. (1990) Uncommon troubles in young people: Prevalence estimates of selected psychiatric disorders in a nonreferred adolescent population. *Archives of General Psychiatry*, **47**, 487–496.

Whitehouse, A.M., Cooper, P.J., Vize, C.V., Hill, C. & Vogel, L. (1992) Prevalence of eating disorders in three Cambridge general practices: Hidden and conspicuous morbidity. *British Journal of General Practice*, **42**, 57–60.

WHO (1978) *Mental Disorders: Glossary and Guide to their Classification in Accordance with the Ninth Revision of the International Classification of Diseases*. Geneva: World Health Organization.

WHO (1992) *The ICD-10 Classification of Mental and Behavioural Disorders: Clinical Descriptions and Diagnostic Guidelines*. Geneva: World Health Organization.

WHO (1998a) *Obesity: Preventing and Managing the Global Epidemic*. Geneva: WHO (WHO/NUT/NCD/98.1).

WHO (1998b) *The World Health Report 1998. Life in the 21st Century—A Vision for All*. Geneva: WHO.

Willi, J., Giacometti G. & Limacher, B. (1990) Update on the epidemiology of anorexia nervosa in a defined region of Switzerland. *American Journal of Psychiatry*, **147**, 1514–1517.

Willi, J. & Grossman, S. (1983) Epidemiology of anorexia nervosa in a defined region of Switzerland. *American Journal of Psychiatry*, **140**, 564–657.

Williams, P. & King, M. (1987) The 'epidemic' of anorexia nervosa: another medical myth? *The Lancet*, **i**, 205–207.

Williams, P., Tarnopolsky, A. & Hand, D. (1980) Case definition and case identification in psychiatric epidemiology: Review and reassessment. *Psychological Medicine*, **10**, 101–114.

Wlodarczyk-Bisaga, K. & Dolan, B. (1996) A two-stage epidemiological study of abnormal eating attitudes and their prospective risk factors in Polish schoolgirls. *Psychological Medicine*, **26**, 1021–1032.

CHAPTER 3

Genetic Aetiology of Eating Disorders and Obesity

Elizabeth Winchester and **David Collier**

Eating Disorders Unit, Institute of Psychiatry, London, UK

INTRODUCTION

Eating disorders (anorexia nervosa (AN) and bulimia nervosa (BN)) and obesity have complex aetiologies involving numerous and interacting environmental and genetic risk factors. This chapter will cover the current understanding about the role of genetics in the aetiology of eating disorders and obesity. The influence of the environment on the development of these complex diseases is discussed in several other chapters. This chapter will summarise the following:

- Theory of complex diseases
- Methods used to determine the genetic effects influencing complex disorders
- Evidence for a genetic component to the aetiology of eating disorders and obesity
- Molecular genetic methods of identifying genetic risk factors (susceptibility genes) for complex diseases
- Identification of susceptibility genes for eating disorders and obesity.

THEORY OF COMPLEX DISEASES

Disorders or traits that are not inherited in a Mendelian fashion are known as complex or multifactorial diseases, which result from a complex interplay between multiple environmental and genetic risk factors. The genetic component may be oligogenic, involving a small number of gene variants, or polygenic, involving the simultaneous action of many gene variants each of individually small effect. The genetic variants that contribute to complex diseases are common in the population, whereas Mendelian diseases are caused by relatively rare deleterious variants (mutations) in single genes (monogenic disorder). The genetic variants of genes involved in the predisposition to a complex disease are called *susceptibility alleles* and are neither necessary nor sufficient to cause disease.

Handbook of Eating Disorders. Edited by J. Treasure, U. Schmidt and E. van Furth.

Polygenic traits will be continuously distributed in the population, i.e. they are quantitative traits. However, many complex diseases are qualitative (dichotomous) disorders, where you either have or do not have the disease, but are also polygenic. A liability-threshold model has been proposed for polygenic dichotomous diseases. In this model the underlying polygenic liability is continuously (normally) distributed in the population (i.e. there is a continuum of genetic risk) and there is a threshold of liability (Plomin et al., 2001). A disease will only develop when the number of susceptibility alleles exceeds the liability threshold. Gene–gene interactions (epistasis), in which a gene variant will only confer susceptibility in the presence of another gene variant, and gene–environment interactions, in which susceptibility alleles will have their deleterious effects only in the presence of a particular environmental factor, are likely to be involved in the predisposition to complex diseases. Environmental factors are important and complex diseases will develop in those carrying the greatest genetic and environmental loading.

HERITABILITY OF COMPLEX DISEASES

Family, twin and adoption studies are used to determine the relative contribution of genetic and environmental risk factors in the aetiology of complex diseases, such as eating disorders and obesity (Plomin et al., 2001). In family studies the frequency of a disease in the relatives of an affected individual is compared with the frequency in the general population. A higher disease frequency in relatives compared to the general population provides evidence for a genetic susceptibility to a disease. However, familial aggregation of a disease could also be explained by shared family environment. Twin and adoption studies are powerful methods of disentangling genetic from environmental sources of family resemblance (Plomin et al., 2001).

In twin studies, the similarity of monozygotic (MZ) (genetically identical) twin pairs is compared with the similarity of dyzygotic (DZ) (non-identical) twin pairs for a particular trait. MZ twin pairs share all of their genes and DZ twin pairs share, on average, half of their genes. Therefore, MZ twin pairs will be more similar than DZ twin pairs for a trait that is, to some extent, influenced by genetic factors. However, MZ twin pairs may share a more similar environment than DZ twin pairs. The greater resemblance of MZ twins could therefore be caused by environmental factors that are experienced by MZ twin pairs but not by DZ pairs. To ensure that the greater similarity in MZ twins reflects shared genetic factors, twin studies should demonstrate that both types of twins are equally exposed to aetiological environmental factors (Plomin et al., 2001). This is known as the equal environment assumption (EEA), one of several assumptions in twin methodology. Violation of the EEA would exaggerate estimates of genetic influence.

In adoption studies the resemblance of genetically related individuals who do not share a common family environment, e.g. adopted children and their genetic parents, or the resemblance of family members who are not genetically related but share the same environment, e.g. adopted children and their adoptive parents, are examined. The former situation will estimate the genetic contribution and the latter the postnatal environmental contribution to familial resemblance.

In twin and adoption studies the size of the genetic and environmental effects are calculated by comparing sets of phenotypic correlations between different types of relative pairs. The relative proportion of phenotypic variance that is attributable to additive genetic effects (the cumulative influence of multiple individual genes), shared environmental effects (factors that are common to both members of relative pair), and non-shared environmental effects (influences that are unique to one member of a relative pair), can be estimated from these comparisons. There is insufficient statistical power in twin and adoption analyses to estimate other genetic influences, such as gene–gene interactions (epistasis) and dominance effects. The proportion of the total variation of a trait that is attributable to additive genetic factors is known as the *heritability* of a trait and provides an indication of the importance of genetic factors. A detailed description of twin and adoption methodology is beyond the scope of this chapter but is discussed in detail in Plomin et al. (2001).

HERITABILITY OF EATING DISORDERS

Family Studies of Eating Disorders

The majority of family studies have shown that eating disorders are familial (reviewed by Strober et al., 2000). In the largest case-control family study to date, the risk for AN in female relatives of anorexic probands was 11.4 times higher than the risk in the relatives of control subjects, and the risk for BN in female relatives of bulimic probands was 3.7 times higher (Strober et al., 2000). Some family studies have also reported familial aggregation of milder, broader (subthreshold) phenotypes of AN and BN among female relatives of AN and BN probands respectively (Stein et al., 1998; Strober et al., 2000). Cross-transmission of eating disorders in families is evident from family and twin studies suggesting that AN and BN share or have common familial aetiologic factors (Walters & Kendler, 1995). The prevalence of full and subthreshold BN has been shown to be greater in female relatives of AN probands than in the relatives of control subjects, and the converse for relatives of BN probands (Strober et al., 2000; Walters & Kendler, 1995). Based on the above observations it has been proposed that the full and subthreshold forms of eating disorders form a spectrum of clinical severity in which there is a continuum of familial liability (Strober et al., 2000). The familial aggregation of full and subclinical eating disorders suggests that genetic factors are likely to be involved in causation. The relative contribution of genetic and environmental factors in the aetiology of eating disorders has been determined in twin studies.

Twin Studies of AN and BN

Different estimates of heritability have been obtained from twin studies of AN. The reliability of these estimates are limited due to the ascertainment bias, small sample sizes, or violation of the EEA in several of these studies (Fairburn et al., 1999). In a study of clinically ascertained twins, concordance for AN was substantially greater in MZ twin pairs than in DZ twin pairs, and the heritability was estimated at about 70% (Treasure & Holland, 1989). In contrast, a population-based study of twins found that the concordance rates for AN were higher in DZ twins than in MZ twin pairs (Walters & Kendler, 1995). However, due to the small sample size, the rarity of AN and the possible violation of the EEA in this study inferences regarding the aetiology of AN have not been made from these results (Fairburn et al., 1999). The heritability of AN was estimated to be 76% in another population-based twin sample (Klump et al., 2001) and 58% in a bivariate analysis of AN and major depression (Wade et al., 2000). The magnitude of the genetic contribution to AN remains unresolved. Large-scale twin studies are needed to define the extent and nature of the genetic and environmental contributions to the aetiology of AN.

Three clinically ascertained twin pair studies of BN (Fichter & Noegal, 1990; Hsu et al., 1990; Treasure & Holland, 1989) and two population-based twin studies of BN (Wade et al., 1999; Bulik et al., 1998; Kendler et al., 1991, 1995) have been conducted and have consistently demonstrated significant genetic contributions in the liability to BN. Reanalysis of the data from the twin studies of BN produced estimates of heritabilty ranging from 31% to 83% (Bulik et al., 2000). In general non-shared environmental effects were shown to account for the remaining variance in liability to BN. The magnitude of the contribution of shared environmental effects is unclear but in the majority of the twin studies it appears to be less important than additive genetic effects and non-shared environmental effects (Bulik et al., 2000).

Several of the symptoms, behaviours and attitudes associated with disordered eating have been shown to be heritable in different populations of twins. These continuous traits are assessed using psychometric questionnaires, such as the Eating Disorder Inventory (EDI; Garner et al., 1984) and the Eating Disorders Examination (EDE; Fairburn & Cooper, 1993). The Drive for Thinness subscale of the EDI, was shown to be heritable in one twin population (Holland et al., 1988), and in another twin study several EDI subscales showed heritabilities ranging from 28% to 52% (Rutherford et al., 1993). Heritabilities of 46% and 70% have been reported for binge eating and self-induced vomiting respectively (Sullivan et al., 1998). There is evidence of age-related differences in genetic and environmental influences on these traits. Marked differences in heritabilities for EDI subscales have been reported for a preadolescent (aged 11 years) and an adolescent (aged 17 years) twin sample from the same population (Klump et al., 2000). The contribution of additive genetic effects for the EDI subscales was greater in the adolescent twin sample than in the preadolescent group. Based on this finding it has been proposed that puberty may activate the heritability of eating disorders (Klump et al., 2001). Measures from the EDE such as dietary restraint, and concerns about eating, weight and shape also appear to be heritable (Wade et al., 1998).

Several family and twin studies have investigated the causes of comorbidity between eating disorders and personality traits and other psychiatric disorders. Family studies investigating the relationship between personality traits and eating disorders have shown that some personality traits are significantly elevated in the unaffected relatives of probands with an eating disorder compared to the relatives of the control group (Kaye et al., 1999; Lilenfeld et al., 2000). For example perfectionism, ineffectiveness, and interpersonal distrust has been found to be significantly elevated in the unaffected relatives of BN probands compared to the relatives of the control group (Lilenfeld et al., 2000). There is evidence to suggest that the familial cotransmission of eating pathology and some personality traits results from the sharing of common genetic risk factors. Results from twin studies suggest that the comorbidity between AN and major depression and between BN and major depression is most likely due to genetic factors that influence both disorders (Wade et al., 2000; Walters et al., 1992). It is evident from these studies that there are also unique genetic effects influencing eating disorders that are independent of those contributing to the personality traits and psychiatric disorders.

Model of Inheritance of Eating Disorders

Overall family and twin studies provide evidence for a genetic contribution to the aetiology of eating disorders. However the magnitude of the genetic effect remains uncertain because of problems with case ascertainment and the low statistical power of the studies to date. Non-shared environmental effects appear to play a substantial role in the liability to eating disorders. The development of eating disorders is likely to involve interactions between multiple environmental and genetic risk factors.

HERITABILITY OF HUMAN OBESITY

Family, Twin and Adoption Studies

Family, twin, and adoption studies have indicated that genetic factors play a significant role in the aetiology of obesity and obese phenotypes (Echwald, 1999). Once again in these studies estimates of heritability vary, and thus the relative importance of genetic factors in the causation of obesity remain controversial.

Obesity shows strong familial aggregation but, except for rare monogenic forms of obesity, it does not exhibit a clear pattern of Mendelian inheritance. Many family studies have shown that the risk of obesity (BMI > 30) is higher in the biological relatives of obese individuals compared to the risk in the general population (reviewed in Ravussin & Bouchard, 2000). Overall, family studies have shown that between 20 and 50% of the variation in obesity phenotypes is attributable to genetic factors (reviewed in Echwald, 1999).

Twin studies have reported the highest estimates of heritability for obese phenotypes. In a review of twin studies, concordance rates for BMI were higher in MZ twin pairs than in DZ twin pairs and the heritability estimates ranged from 50% to 90% (Barsh et al., 2000). Adoption studies suggest that shared environment in childhood has much less effect on BMI than genes (Echwald, 1999).

Model of Inheritance for Obesity

The segregation of obesity in families is consistent with a polygenic model of inheritance, with the exception of the rare Mendelian (caused by a single-gene mutation) forms of obesity (Comuzzie & Allison, 1998; Echwald, 1999). The polygenic component of obesity is likely to involve multiple additive gene variants, each of which has a small effect on phenotypic variation, and interacts with other genes and environmental factors. Each gene variant is neither sufficient nor necessary for the development of obesity (Sorensen & Echwald, 2001).

Its is clear from the heritability estimates of obesity that environmental factors are important to the aetiology of obesity. However, the relative genetic and environmental contributions remain unclear. Epidemiological studies indicate that obesity is strongly influenced by environmental factors. For example, differences in prevalence of obesity between populations and between different groups within populations are closely associated with socio-economic and behavioural factors (Sorensen & Echwald, 2001). The rising epidemic of obesity throughout the western world and developing countries cannot be explained by recent changes in genetic inheritance but as a result of rapid environmental changes, such as the availability and composition of food.

A model of the development of obesity has been proposed, in which susceptibility to obesity is mainly determined by genetic factors but a favourable environment is necessary for the expression of the genetic predisposition (Barsh et al., 2000). This putative interaction between genes and environment suggests that the effects of a high level of genetic susceptibility would be amplified in a high-risk environment. Based on this model the rising prevalence of obesity can be explained by environmental changes that have led to the full expression of an underlying pool of obesity susceptibility genes. A good example are the Pima Indians living in the USA who have a much higher prevalence of obesity and type 2 diabetes than the Pima Indians living in Mexico, where food availability is restricted (Ravussin & Bouchard, 2000). There has been much speculation over why the human genome contains genetic variants that predispose to obesity. One explanation is the 'thrifty genotype hypothesis' (Neel, 1962). This hypothesis suggests that evolution through alternating periods of famine with periods of food abundance positively selected for genetic variants that confer survival advantages in famine periods, e.g. 'thrifty genes' (Ravussin & Bouchard, 2000). These 'thrifty genes' are deleterious in modern western societies where calorie-rich foods are abundant.

MOLECULAR GENETIC METHODOLOGY FOR IDENTIFYING SUSCEPTIBILITY GENES FOR COMPLEX DISEASES

Two convergent approaches are used to identify gene variants contributing to the susceptibility of complex diseases: linkage and association studies. Candidate genes for a complex trait are genes that have been implicated in the pathophysiology of a disease based on genetic, physiological or pharmacological evidence. The role of a candidate gene in a complex disorder can be examined in targeted linkage studies and/or association studies.

Linkage Studies

Non-parametric ('model-free') methods of linkage analysis are used for complex traits because this method does not require prior knowledge about the inheritance of a disease. In non-parametric linkage analysis the segregation of variants of anonymous, highly variable deoxyribonucleic acid (DNA) loci (marker alleles) is examined in affected family member pairs, e.g. affected sister pairs. Marker alleles shared by affected relative pairs more often than would be expected by chance provide evidence that there is a linkage between the marker and the disease under investigation, which can either be a dichotomous complex trait or a quantitative trait. The affected sib-pair design is the most widely used approach. Linkage analysis is a statistical approach involving the calculation of LOD scores, which are the logarithms to the base 10 of the likelihood ratios for linkage verses non-linkage. For complex diseases LOD scores >3.3 are considered the most appropriate threshold for evidence of significant linkage (Lander & Kruglyak, 1995). This threshold for significance minimizes the risk of false positive results.

In genome-wide linkage studies DNA markers spaced at regular intervals throughout the genome are examined in affected relative pairs. The DNA markers with significant linkages identify novel candidate chromosomal regions (susceptibility loci) that may encompass unknown or unexpected susceptibility genes. Quantitative trait loci (QTL), which are chromosomal regions that may contain genes that contribute to a quantitative trait, can be identified in genome-wide linkage studies using sib-pairs who both have extreme scores on a measure of a quantitative trait. QTL linkage analysis is a powerful approach for identifying genetic variants with a small to moderate effect on phenotypic variance because quantitative traits are more likely to have a direct relationship with individual genetic variants.

In targeted sib-pair linkage studies the segregation of a genetic variant of a candidate gene or a marker allele close to a candidate gene is examined in affected relative pairs.

Association Studies

Two sample designs are used in association studies: case controls and family trios. Both designs are used to evaluate the role of variants of candidate genes in a complex disorder. In case control association studies the frequency of a genetic variant of a gene (an allele) or marker allele in an affected group is compared with the frequency of the allele in a control group from the same population. An allele, which is either directly involved in the genetic susceptibility of a disease, or closely linked to the causative allele, will occur more often in cases than in controls than would be expected by chance. The differences in allele frequencies between cases and controls are tested for statistical significance using a statistical measure such as the chi squared or odds ratio test. The risk of false positive or false negative findings is a major problem with case-control association studies, particularly in studies based on small sample sizes or in studies using a heterogeneous population where the cases and controls may consist of genetically distinct subsets, e.g. different ethnic groups (Barsh et al., 2000). The problem of poor matching between cases and controls can be overcome by using family trios, which consist of an affected child and both parents. In family based (family trios) association studies the alleles that the parents do not pass onto their child act as internal controls. The risk of false negative results is inherent in the low-frequency and small biological impact of the genetic variants involved in the susceptibility of complex diseases (Sorensen & Echwald, 2001). Hence it is important that candidate genes are not excluded on the basis of negative findings and that positive associations are replicated in different samples to confirm true associations.

For both linkage and association studies of complex traits, large sample sizes are needed to provide sufficient statistical power to detect genetic variants that confer a small effect on phenotypic variance.

CHOOSING THE PHENOTYPE FOR MOLECULAR GENETIC STUDIES

The definition of the phenotype or the diagnostic criteria used to classify individuals as affected or unaffected is an important consideration when designing molecular genetic research strategies for complex diseases. It is important that the diagnostic criteria used in genetic studies are robust and reliable, so that results from different studies are comparable.

Eating Disorders

The eating disorders have been classified into three categories: anorexia nervosa, bulimia nervosa and binge eating disorder (DSM-IV; APA, 1994). Subgroups within the AN and BN groups have been defined on the basis of variations in eating and compensatory behaviours. Individuals with AN are divided into those with restricting AN (RAN) and those with binge-purging AN (AN/BP). Individuals with BN are divided into a purging type in which individuals engage in laxative abuse, self-induced vomiting and/or enemas, and a non-purging type where individuals engage in fasting or extreme exercise. Although this diagnostic classification system is useful for genetic research, it has many pitfalls and appears to be somewhat arbitrary. The difficulties with categorizing the eating disorders are discussed in depth in other chapters in this book. Firstly, AN and BN are not discreet disorders and approximately 50% of women with AN develop BN over the course of their illness (Treasure & Collier, 2001). The boundaries between other eating disorder categories also overlap. For example, it is difficult to distinguish between non-purging BN and BED. Secondly, a substantial proportion of the individuals presenting with an eating disorder do not fulfil the diagnostic criteria for the main categories and are classified as having an eating disorder not otherwise specified (EDNOS). This group includes individuals presenting with 'partial syndromes'. It has been proposed that it might be more appropriate to view all eating disorders as lying on a spectrum with a continuum of eating symptoms from under-eating to over-eating (Treasure & Collier, 2001). It is conceivable that many of the differences between eating disorder categories, such as between BN and obesity, may be quantitative rather than qualitative.

Several of the personality traits and Axis II disorders that are frequently associated with eating disorders have been shown to precede the development of eating disorders and to persist after long-term recovery, suggesting that they could contribute to the pathogenesis of eating disorders (Kaye et al., 2000a). It has been suggested that eating disorders should not only be classified in terms of eating symptoms but also by personality types. Three personality domains have been identified: a high functioning, self-critical, perfectionistic group, which was mainly associated with BN; a constricted, overcontrolled group restricting pleasure, needs, emotions, relationships and self-knowledge, which was associated with RAN; and an impulsive, undercontrolled and emotionally dysregulated group (Goldner et al., 1999).

Defining the phenotype for eating disorder research is far from simple. Many genetic studies to date have used eating disorder subgroups such as RAN, AN/BP, binge-purging BN, or non-purging BN because the genes underlying these types are likely to be more homogeneous than those underlying the main eating disorder categories. The use of narrow diagnostic criteria increases the chance of detecting small genetic effects. However, the number of individuals in each subgroup would be very small because AN and BN are rare and this would reduce the statistical power of the study. Conversely, a broad eating disorder phenotype that includes 'partial symptoms' would increase the sample size but the heterogeneity of the sample would reduce statistical power. Future research may benefit from conceptualizing the eating disorders as a spectrum.

Obesity

Obesity and obesity-related phenotypes are quantitative traits. The use of quantitative traits, where the effects of individual genes may be more pronounced, increases the statistical power of genetic studies (Barsh et al., 2000). There are several different measures of obesity and related phenotypes. The most widely used measure of general obesity is the body mass index (BMI), which is defined as the weight in kilograms (kg) divided by body area. In practice the BMI is usually estimated by dividing the weight (kg) by the height squared (m^2). This measure is reliable, inexpensive and convenient for large sample numbers, however it does not account for the proportion of fat to muscle mass in the body and is influenced by factors unrelated to obesity, e.g. organ mass (Perusse & Chagnon, 1997). The total amount of body fat mass expressed as a percentage of the total body weight (% FAT) is a more accurate measure of obesity and can be assessed from underwater weighing or bioelectrical impedance. The amount of subcutaneous fat distribution can be assessed by the sum of skinfold thickness measured at different sites around the body or various skinfold ratios (Perusse & Chagnon, 1997). Abdominal obesity is measured using the ratio of waist to hip circumference (WHR) and waist circumference, which is the best correlate of visceral fat (Despres et al., 2001). Intermediary phenotypes, which relate more to the underlying physiology of obesity, such as resting metabolic rate (RMR), respiratory quotient (RQ), insulin sensitivity, and leptin levels can also be measured and are often used in molecular genetic studies. The different obesity-related phenotypes are likely to have unique and shared genetic risk factors.

The heritable personality traits often associated with eating disorders and other eating disorder symptoms that appear to have a heritable component, such as drive for thinness, are quantitative traits and can be used in QTL analysis for the eating disorders. Multiple quantitative phenotypes can be analysed to increase the statistical power of linkage and association studies. However, multiple comparisons will be necessary, which raises the threshold required to achieve statistical significance and this will result in a reduction in power.

IDENTIFICATION OF SUSCEPTIBILITY GENES FOR EATING DISORDERS AND OBESITY

Genetic research into eating disorders is in its infancy and to date only one genome-wide linkage study has been completed for eating disorders, the results of which have not yet been published. However, other genome-wide linkage studies in large populations are currently underway. Several candidate gene association studies have been completed, but the majority have reported negative findings.

Two approaches have been adopted in obesity research: one has studied the rare single-gene (monogenic) mutations causing obesity in rodents and in humans, and the other has studied the genetics of common variation in body weight. Identification of some of the genes responsible for Mendelian forms of obesity in rodents and humans has directly resulted in the unravelling of a fundamental pathway involved in body weight regulation (Barsh et al.,2001). In the effort to identify genetic variants contributing to common obesity, QTL have been mapped in human populations and in polygenic animal models of obesity and many candidate genes have been evaluated in linkage and association studies. A forum known as the 'Human Obesity Gene Map' has been established, in which the results from all the published studies on the genetics of obesity are collected with the aim of helping to guide the design of future studies (Perusse et al., 2001).

Remarkable progress has been made over the last decade in understanding the genetic mechanisms underlying human body weight regulation (Barsh et al., 2000). As a result of these discoveries, candidate gene analyses for eating disorders and obesity have focused on the genes involved in both the central and peripheral control of energy intake and expenditure. This section will summarize:

• The monogenic causes of obesity in rodents and humans
• The association and linkage results for the genes involved in body weight regulatory pathways
• Other candidate genes for eating disorders
• Other candidate genes for obesity
• Obesity QTL identified in human populations through genome-wide linkage studies and in polygenic animal models of obesity
• The search for lean genes.

Mongenic Rodent Models of Obesity

The genes responsible for six naturally occurring single-gene (monogenic) mutation mouse models of obesity have been identified and their protein products characterized (Table 3.1). The human homologues of these mouse obesity genes have been isolated and several mutations in the *LEP* and *LEPR* genes have been found as rare causes of human obesity (Perusse et al., 2001). Isolation of the mouse *Lep* gene from the Obesity (*ob*) mutation, the human homologue, *LEP*, and the characterization of the gene product as a circulating satiety protein, now named leptin (from the Greek word for thin, leptos), was a major breakthrough in

Table 3.1 Monogenic mouse models of obesity

Mouse mutation	Mouse gene	Human homologue	Chromosomal location in humans	Protein product of gene	References
Obese (*ob*)	*Lep*	*LEP*	7q31.3	Leptin	Zhang et al. (1994)
Diabetes (*db*)	*Lepr*	*LEPR*	1p31	Leptin receptor	Chen et al. (1996)
Agouti yellow (*A^y*)	*A^y*		20q11.2–q12	Agouti-signalling protein	Wilson et al. (1995)
Fat (*fat*)	*Cpe*	*CPE*	4q32	Carboxy-peptidase	Naggert et al. (1995)
Tubby (*tub*)	*Tub*	*TUB*	11p15.5	Insulin-signalling protein	Kleyn et al. (1996); Kapeller (et al.) 1999
Mahogany (*mg*)	*Atrn*	*ATRN*	20p13	Attractin	Nagle et al. (1999); Gunn et al. (1999)

obesity research (Zhang et al., 1994). Leptin is truncated and inactive in mutant *ob/ob* mice (Zhang et al., 1994) and treatment with recombinant leptin results in weight reduction in these obese mice (Halaas et al., 1995). The characterization of the mouse gene responsible for the Diabetes (*db*) mutation as the leptin receptor (Chen et al., 1996), confirmed the prediction, made from earlier cross-circulation (parabiosis) experiments, that *ob/ob* mice might be deficient in a circulating signal of satiety and *db/db* mice might be deficient in its cognate receptor (Spiegelman & Flier, 2001).

The discovery of leptin and its receptor immediately resulted in the recognition of a fundamental endocrine feedback loop regulating the size of adipose (fat) tissue mass, known as the leptinergic–melanocortinergic system, that is conserved among all mammals (reviewed in chapters in this handbook and in Spiegelman and Flier, 2001). Leptin, which is expressed in adipose tissue and circulates in proportion to adipose tissue mass, serves as the afferent signal of this loop informing the brain about the status of the body's fat stores. It acts through leptin receptors on nerve cells in the arcuate nucleus of the hypothalamus to trigger neuropeptide responses that modulate appetite and energy expenditure.

Through identification of the other rodent obesity genes, knockout and transgenic mice studies and identification of mutant genes in human monogenic obesity, the neuropeptides that coordinate the response to leptin signalling have been defined (Spiegelman & Flier, 2001). Leptin reduces expression of the orexigenic (feeding-inducing) neuropeptides, neuropeptide Y (NPY) and agouti-related protein (AgRP) and induces expression of the anorexigenic (feeding-inhibitors) neuropeptides, cocaine and amphetamine related transcript (CART) and the melanocortin, α-melanocyte-stimulating hormone (α-MSH), via activation of proopiomelanocortin (POMC) neurons. α-MSH is derived from POMC, which is a precursor protein that is cleaved into a number of proteins with diverse physiological roles. α-MSH reduces food intake and increases energy expenditure through activation of melanocortin 3 (Mc3) and melanocortin 4 (Mc4) receptors in the hypothalamus (Spiegelman & Flier, 2001). Knockout studies in mice have demonstrated that *Mc3r* and *Mc4r* have distinct and complementary roles in energy homeostasis (Chen et al., 2000). AgRP is an endogenous antagonist of the *Mc3/4* receptors and thus opposes the action of α-MSH.

The involvement of melanocortins in the leptin-signalling pathway was determined through elucidation of the genetic basis for the dominant agouti yellow (A^y) obesity syndrome. The obesity in the A^y mouse is caused by the abnormal expression of the A^y gene product—the agouti coat-colour protein—in the brain where it mimics AgRP by antagonizing the signalling of α-MSH through the melanocortin 4 receptor (*Mc4r*) (Michaud et al. 1994; Rossi et al., 1998). *Pomc* and *Mc4r* knockout mice and gain-of-function *Agrp* mutations in mice produce an obesity phenotype similar to that displayed by the A^y mice, thereby supporting the central role of the melanocortin system in energy homeostasis (Graham et al., 1997; Huszar et al., 1997; Yaswen et al., 1999).

The functional roles of the Fat (*fat*) and Tubby (*tub*) mutations in causing obesity have not been clearly defined. The gene responsible for the *fat* mutation, *Cpe*, encodes carboxypeptidase E, an enzyme involved in processing many neuropeptides, including POMC (Naggert et al., 1995). The *fat* mutation reduces enzyme activity and it has been proposed that the obesity in the *fat* mouse may be caused, in part, by defective POMC processing (Barsh et al., 2000). The protein product of the *tub* gene is an insulin-signalling protein, which is highly expressed in the hypothalamus and may be involved in the response to leptin (Kleyn et al., 1996; Kapeller et al., 1999). The attractin (*Atrn*) gene is responsible for the Mahogony (*mg*) mutation and is involved in suppressing diet-induced obesity (Nagle et al., 1999; Gunn et al., 1999).

Targeted gene-deletion studies in rodents have identified the components that act downstream of the melanocortin signal, additional components that interact with leptin and other neuropeptide pathways that either stimulate or inhibit feeding. Two examples are the orexigenic neuropeptide melanin-concentrating hormone (MCH) (Ludwig et al., 2001) and the serotonin IIC receptor (*Htr-2c*) (Barsh et al., 2000). A description of these is beyond the scope of this chapter but has been reviewed by Inui (2000) and Spiegelman and Flier (2001). The genes encoding these components provide candidate genes for human obesity and targets for therapeutic intervention.

Monogenic Human Obesity Syndromes

To date, 19 loss of function mutations in six different genes have been found to be the cause of 47 cases of monogenic forms of human obesity (Perusse et al., 2001). Mutations in the *LEP* (Montague et al., 1997; Strobel et al., 1998), *LEPR* (Clement et al., 1998), *MC4R* (Vaisse et al., 1998; Yeo et al., 1998; Hinney et al., 1999), and *POMC* (Krude et al., 1998) genes have been reported in 45 human obesity cases.

The obesity phenotypes in mice and in humans with homologous mutations are very similar, confirming the fundamental nature of the leptinergic–melanocortinergic signalling pathway in the regulation of body weight among mammals. However, important species-specific differences in energy physiology have also been defined; in particular there are differences in the metabolic and endocrinological phenotypes caused by leptin signalling defects in humans and mice (Barsh et al., 2000).

A loss of function mutation in the prohormone convertase 1 (*PC1*) gene has been found as the cause of an obesity syndrome in one three-year-old case (Jackson et al., 1997). This obesity syndrome is very similar to the mouse Fat obesity syndrome caused by mutations in *Cpe*. Although *Cpe* and *PC1* are non-homologous genes they have similar functions and are both involved in processing prohormones, in particular POMC (Barsh et al., 2000). A loss of function mutation in the single-minded (*Drosophila*) homolog 1 (*SIM1*) gene is the most probable cause of obesity in a six-year old case (Holder et al., 2000). In mice the *Sim1* gene is a critical transcription factor for the formation of the paraventricular nuclei in the hypothalamus, which are known to be involved in energy homeostasis (Holder et al., 2000).

MC4R mutations are the most common cause of monogenic human obesity, with 11 mutations responsible for 34 out of the 47 reported cases of obesity with known mutations (Perusse et al., 2001). Several of the mutations appear to influence the function of the gene. Obesity status appears to differ between individuals with *MC4R* mutations and not all individuals with these mutations are obese, which suggests that these mutations show variable penetrance (Vaisse et al., 2000).

Overall the mutations identified in these six genes are very rare, which suggests that they are not responsible for the most common forms of obesity in the population. However, other less harmful variants of these genes may influence common human obesity and the results from linkage and association studies with other variants of these genes are discussed later in this chapter.

There are currently over 26 Mendelian human disorders in which obesity is one of several symptoms (Perusse et al., 2001). The genetic location for 24 of these syndromes have been mapped including Prader–Willi, Alstrom, Bardet-Biedl and Cohen syndromes (Perusse et al., 2001). For some of these syndromes candidate genes have been identified within the genetic location and implicated in causation (Perusse et al., 2001). Although these rare obesity-related Mendelian disorders are distinct from common forms of obesity, identification of the underlying mutant genes may provide candidate genes for extreme human obesity and/or information on the regulation of food intake and energy expenditure. To date many of the known chromosomal regions have not shown significant linkage to common obesity in genome-wide or in targeted linkage studies.

Candidate Gene Analyses for Eating Disorders and Obesity

Genes Involved in Body Weight Regulatory Pathways

Leptin–Melanocortinergic System

Genetic variants of genes encoding components of the leptin–melanocortinergic system have been tested for association with the eating disorders and obesity (see Table 3.2). The finding that disturbances in weight regulation pathways persist after long-term recovery of AN suggest that these disturbances could be involved in the aetiology of AN (Hinney et al., 2000). However, to date no association between genetic variants of these genes and AN or BN has been reported (Hinney et al., 2000). Some of these negative findings may be false negatives due to the use of small sample sizes or the use of an inappropriate control group in some of the studies (Hinney et al., 2000). Alternatively the negative findings could indicate that these variants do not have a significant role in the genetic predisposition to eating disorders.

In contrast variants of the *LEP* (Butler et al., 1998; Hager et al., 1998b; Li et al., 1999; Mammes et al., 1998; Oksanen et al., 1997), *LEPR* (Chagnon et al., 2000b; Mammes et al., 2001; Roth et al., 1998), *MC4R* (Chagnon et al., 1997b), and *POMC* (Hixson et al., 1999) genes have been significantly associated with obesity and obesity-related phenotypes (see Table 3.2). Linkage studies have also reported strong evidence for linkage between variants of these genes and obesity and obesity-related phenotypes (Chagnon et al., 1997b, 1999; Clement et al., 1996; Duggirula et al., 1996; Lapsys et al., 1997; Ohman et al., 1999; Reed et al., 1996; Roth et al., 1997; Rutkowski et al., 1998). Variants of the *NPY* gene have been associated with birth weight (Karvonen et al., 2000), and BMI (Bray et al., 2000). Obesity in Pima Indians was associated with a variant in the NPY receptor Y5 gene (*NPY5R*) (Jenkinson et al., 2000).

Serotonergic and Dopaminergic Neurotransmitter Systems

The serotonergic and dopaminergic neurotransmitter systems are involved in central energy balance pathways (Spiegelman & Flier, 2001). Serotonergic signalling suppresses food intake. The serotonin and leptin pathways can converge since leptin has been shown to increase serotonin turnover.Disturbances in the serotonergic and neurotransmitter systems occur in individuals with AN and BN and appear to persist after recovery (Hinney et al., 2000). Individuals with eating disorders exhibit multiple neuroendocrine and neuropeptide disturbances, the majority of which are secondary to malnutrition and/or weight loss

Table 3.2 Association studies with genes involved in energy homeostasis for anorexia nervosa, bulimia nervosa, and obesity

Regulatory pathway	Gene	Chromosomal location	AN p-value[a]	BN p-value[a]	Phenotype	Obesity p-value[a]
Leptin-melanocortinergic system	*LEP*	7q31.3	NS	NS	Weight loss	$0.006 < p < 0.007$
					Body weight	0.05
					Leptin	0.02
					Leptin	0.04
					BMI	<0.05
					Obesity in women	0.017–0.035
	LEPR	1p31	ND	ND	% fat	0.003
					FFM	0.03–0.05
					BMI	0.041
					BMI, FM	0.005–0.03
					Obesity in children	0.02–0.04
	POMC	2p23.3	NS	NS	Leptin	0.001
	MC4R	18q22	NS	NS	FM, % fat, FFM in females $0.002 < p < 0.004$	
	NPY	7p15.1	ND	ND	Birth weight	0.03
					BMI	0.03–0.04
	NPY5R	4q31–q32	NS	ND	Obesity (BMI 40–47)	<0.05
Serotonergic nuerotransmitter system	*5-HT SERT*		NS NS	ND <0.000		
	5-HTR$_{2a}$	13q14–q21	0.02 0.005 0.0001 0.0001 NS in 3 studies	NS		0.028–0.047
	5-HTR$_{2c}$	Xq24	NS	NS	BMI > 28	0.009–0.02

Dopaminergic neurotransmitter system	DRD2	1q22.2–q22.3	ND	ND	Relative weight	0.002
					Obesity	0.002–0.003
					Iliac and triceps skinfold	0.002–0.039
	DRD3		NS	ND		
	DRD4		NS	ND		
Thermogenesis	UCP-1	4q28–q31			High fat gainers	0.05
					BMI	0.02
					Weight and BMI loss	<0.05
					Weight loss	0.001
	UCP-2	11q13		ND	Significant in 6 studies[b]	0.008–0.04
	UCP-3	11q13		ND	BMI, RQ	0.0037
					BMI	0.02–0.04
					BMI	
	UCP-2/-3		S	ND		
Lipid metabolism	ADRβ2	5q31–q32	ND	ND	Significant in 9 studies[b]	
	ADRβ3	3p12–p11.2	NS	ND	Significant in 20 studies[b]	

S, significant; NS, non-significant; ND, not done.
[a]p-value for the association of the rare allele to the phenotype.
[b]See Perusse et al. (2001) for the Human Obesity Gene Map: The 2000 Update. This details all the association studies.

(Kaye et al., 2000a). Serotonergic neurotransmission appears to remain increased in long-term weight-restored AN and BN patients suggesting that serotonergic dysfunction might be a premorbid trait that contributes to the susceptibility of eating disorders (Kaye et al., 2000a). Serotonin (5-hydroxytryptamine; 5-HT) is involved in a range of physiological and behavioural functions including mood and sex drive. Serotonergic dysfunction could therefore also contribute to other eating disorder symptoms. Increased brain 5-HT activity has been associated with several of the personality traits that appear to occur premorbidly in some eating disorder patients, such as perfectionism, obsessiveness and rigidity (Hinney et al., 2000). The serotonergic system includes serotonin, tryptophan hydroxylase, the 5-HT transporter (SERT) and several 5-HT receptors. A variant of the 5-HT transporter gene was not associated with AN in three studies but showed a positive association with BN in one study (Di Bella et al., 2000; Hinney et al., 1997a; Sundaramurthy et al., 2000)—see Table 3.2. A 5-HT transporter gene variant has also been associated with specific personality traits (Ebstein et al., 2000). Inconsistent findings have been reported for a variant (-1438 G/A) of the $5\text{-}HT_{2a}$ receptor gene and AN. Four studies in different population groups reported an increase in the A-allele of the $5\text{-}HT_{2a}$ variant in AN women compared to controls (Collier et al., 1997; Enoch et al., 1998; Nacmias et al., 1999; Sorbi et al., 1998). However three studies could not replicate this positive association (Campbell et al., 1998; Hinney et al., 1997b; Ziegler et al., 1999)—see Table 3.2. In two of the studies with positive findings the association was only found with the restricting type of AN and not the binge–purging type of AN (Nacmias et al., 1999; Sorbi et al., 1998). Different diagnostic criteria, the use of heterogeneous populations or small sample sizes may, in part, account for the inconsistent results from these studies (Hinney et al., 2000). A meta-analysis of all the results detected no association between AN and the A-allele of this $5\text{-}HT_{2a}$ gene variant (Ziegler et al., 1999). The role of this variant in the aetiology of AN therefore remains to be determined in large-scale association studies. No association has been reported between this $5\text{-}HT_{2a}$ gene variant and BN (Enoch et al., 1998; Nacmias et al., 1999; Ziegler et al., 1999). Tests for association between other variants of the $5\text{-}HT_{2a}$ gene and AN and BN have all been non-significant (Hinney et al., 2000).

A genetic variant of the $5\text{-}HT_{2c}$ receptor gene has been associated with obesity (BMI >28) (Yuan et al., 2000) and an obesity QTL showing suggestive linkage has been identified on chromosome Xq24, which is the chromosomal location of this receptor (Ohman et al., 2000). Dietary energy and carbohydrate and alcohol intake in obese subjects has been associated with a variant in the $5\text{-}HT_{2a}$ receptor gene (Aubert et al., 2000)—see Table 3.2. These positive associations need to be replicated in independent populations. Genetic variants of the dopamine D3 and dopamine D4 receptor genes (DRD3, DRD4) have been tested for association with AN with consistent negative findings (Bruins-Slot et al., 1998; Hinney et al., 2000). Genetic variants of the dopamine D2 receptor gene (DRD2) have been significantly associated with obesity (BMI >30) (Spitz et al., 1999), triceps skinfold (Thomas et al., 2000), and relative weight (Comings et al.,1993).

Thermogenesis

Uncoupling proteins (UCP) are involved in uncoupling mitochondrial respiration (oxidative phosphorylation) from ATP synthesis, resulting in dissipation of energy as heat (Spiegelman & Flier, 2001). Three UCPs have been identified: UCP-1, which is expressed in brown adipose tissue (BAT), *UCP-2*, which is widely expressed in many tissues, and *UCP-3*, expressed in BAT and skeletal muscle. A positive association between AN and a genetic variant near the uncoupling protein-2/uncoupling protein-3 (*UCP-2/UCP-3*) gene cluster has been reported (Campbell et al., 1999)—see Table 3.2. This positive finding needs to be replicated in an independent sample to confirm its importance. Many association studies have reported positive associations between obesity and/or obesity-related phenotypes and variants of the *UCP-1*, *UCP-2* and *UCP-3* genes (Perusse et al., 2001)—see Table 3.2.

Adipose Tissue Metabolism

Beta adrenergic receptors are involved in lipid metabolism by activating lipase, which catalyses lipolysis. A genetic variant of the β_3-adrenergic receptor (*ADRβ3*) was not associated with AN or BN (Hinney et al., 1997c). Numerous association and linkage studies have investigated the role of this genetic variant in common obesity (Perusse et al., 2001). However, the results from these studies are conflicting and the importance of this variant in obesity remains to be determined. Obesity and other related phenotypes have been associated with genetic variants of the β_2-adrenergic receptor (*ADRβ2*) gene in several independent studies (Perusee et al., 2001)—see Table3.2.

Other Candidate Genes for the Eating Disorders

Candidate genes for eating disorders also include those involved in mood, personality and responses to stress. Based on the female predominance of eating disorders and the frequent onset around puberty, it has been suggested that an exaggerated sensitivity of the brain to rising oestrogen levels during puberty, which would have an anorectic effect, may be involved in the development of eating disorders. The gene encoding the oestrogen β-receptor (ERβ) is a candidate gene and the frequency of a variant of this gene was increased in AN cases compared to controls in one association study. This positive association needs to be independently replicated (Rosenkranz et al., 1998).

Animal models of eating disorders could provide other plausible candidate genes. There is one spontaneous mouse model of AN, which is caused by a lethal autosomal recessive mutation on mouse chromosome 2 (Son et al., 1994). This anorexia (*anx*) mutation is associated with marked alterations in many of the known hypothalamic neuropeptides involved in appetite control. The *anx/anx* mouse is a useful model for exploring the role of the hypothalamus in the regulation of food intake and for identifying new therapeutic targets for AN. The *anx* gene and its product(s) have not been identified so far but elucidation of this gene will aid in furthering the understanding of appetite control. The selective breeding for leanness in agricultural farm animals has uncovered recessive mutations causing syndromes related to AN, for example thin sow syndrome. These syndromes could provide valuable models of AN (Treasure & Owen, 1997).

Other Candidate Genes for Obesity

Many other genes have been tested for association with obesity and obesity-related phenotypes including genes encoding the apolipoproteins (APO), which are involved in lipid metabolism, genes involved in adipocyte differentiation such as the peroxisome proliferator-activated receptor (*PPAR*) genes, and the glucocorticoid receptor (*GRL*) gene involved in the hypothalamus–pituitary–adrenal (HPA) axis, which is abnormally regulated in obesity (Rosmond et al., 2001). The list of candidate genes for obesity is vast and the task for researchers is to prioritize the most plausible genes for genetic research.

To date 48 candidate genes have shown significant associations with obesity and obesity-related phenotypes (Perusse et al., 2001). Several of the positive associations have been replicated in independent populations. However it is important to note that the majority of the candidate genes showing positive associations have also shown non-significant associations in different studies. The disparity between different studies may, in part, be due to the methodological limitations of association studies mentioned earlier in this chapter or may reflect differences in genetic background. The formidable task of identifying the true positive associations from the growing list of significant associations remains. In addition, the variants of the candidate genes that have shown positive associations have not been found to affect the function of the gene products and therefore the causative variants to which they are linked need to be identified.

Human Genome-Wide Linkage Studies for Obesity—Identification of QTL

Several genome-wide linkage studies of obesity and obesity-related phenotypes have been conducted in different populations (Perusse et al., 2001). Many QTL have been identified from these genome screens and a full list of the human obesity QTL can be found in *The Human Obesity Gene Map: The 2000 Update* (Perusse et al., 2001). The majority of the QTL identified thus far show suggestive linkages but there are a few showing strong linkages (see Table 3.3). Some of the QTL will be more important than others and some suggestive linkages may reflect true linkages that cannot reach statistical significance because the causative gene(s) underlying the QTL have a small effect. Replication of linkage results in

Table 3.3 Summary of some human QTL showing strong and suggestive evidence of linkage to obesity and obesity-related phenotypes

Chromosomal location of QTL	Obesity phenotype	Lod score[a] or p-value	References
2p21	Leptin, fat mass, BMI	Lod = 4.9/2.8 $0.008 < p < 0.03$	Comuzzie et al. (1997) Rotimi et al. (1999)
20q13	BMI >30, %fat	$3.0 < $ Lod $ < 3.2$	Lee et al. (1999)
20q11.2	24-hour RQ	Lod = 3.0	Norman et al. (1998)
10p12.3	Obesity	Lod = 4.9	Hager et al. (1998a)
10p11.22	Obesity	$1.1 < $ Lod $ < 2.5$	Hinney et al. (2000)
11q24	BMI	Lod = 3.6	Hanson et al. (1998)
11q22	% Fat	Lod = 2.8	Norman et al. (1997)
18q12	Fat free mass	Lod = 3.6	Chagnon et al. (2000a)

[a]For whole genome-wide linkage analyses a lod score >3.3 is considered statistically significant evidence for the presence of linkage.
[For a full list of the human obesity QTL see the latest update of the *Human Obesity Gene Map* (Perusse et al., 2001).

independent populations should eliminate false positive results and confirm the potential importance of a QTL. However, the majority of QTL identified to date have not been replicated. A possible explanation for this is that the genetic variants underlying variation in obesity and related phenotypes differ across populations.

Evidence supporting some QTL is very convincing. The strongest QTL are shown in Table 3.3. A strong QTL on the short arm (p) of chromosome 2 at band 21 (2p21) influencing serum leptin levels has been identified. Evidence for linkage of this locus to serum leptin levels was first reported in a genome-wide linkage study in Mexican-Americans (Comuzzie et al., 1997), and was later replicated in two independent studies, one of French sibling pairs (Hager et al., 1998a) and the other in an African-American population (Rotimi et al., 1999). Replication of this linkage result in different populations provides convincing evidence that 2p21 is an important obesity-related locus. This chromosomal region encompasses several potential candidate genes including the glucokinase regulatory protein (*GCKR*) and *POMC* genes (Comuzzie et al., 1997). Common variants of the *POMC* gene have been associated with normal variation in leptin levels (Hixson et al., 1999).

The chromosomal region, 20q11–q13, has been implicated in human obesity in several linkage studies in humans and in mice (Perusse et al., 2001). In a genome-wide linkage study in an American population BMI (>30) and % fat showed evidence for linkage with 20q13 markers (Lee et al., 1999). In a targeted linkage study BMI, fat mass and the sum of six skinfolds showed evidence of linkage to the *MC3R* gene located at 20q13.2–q13.3 and to the adenosine deaminase (*ADA*) gene located at 20q12–q13 (Lambertas et al., 1997). Suggestive evidence for linkage between the 24-hour respiratory quotient (RQ) and a marker at 20q11.2 was reported in a genome-wide screen in Pima Indians (Norman et al., 1998). A mouse obesity QTL has been identified on mouse chromosome 2, a region syntenic to chromosome 20q (Lembertas et al., 1997; Mehrabian et al., 1998). Thus the evidence supporting a role for chromosome 20q11–q13 in human obesity is convincing. In addition to *ADA* and *MC3R*, this region contains other plausible candidate genes such as the agouti-signalling protein (*ASIP*) gene and the CAAT/enhancer-binding protein beta (*CEBPβ*) gene (Lee et al., 1999). Also the hepatic nuclear factor gene (*4HNF4*), which when mutated causes one form of maturity onset diabetes of the young (MODY1) is located in 20q12 and two susceptibility loci for non-insulin-dependent diabetes (NIDDM) have been localized to 20q (Lee et al., 1999). There is evidence from two genome-wide screens in different populations, for a major susceptibility locus for obesity on chromosome 10p (Hager et al., 1998a; Hinney et al., 2000). However, this region does not contain any obvious candidate genes for obesity.

Identification of QTL in Polygenic Animal Models of Obesity

QTL analysis in polygenic animal models of obesity is relatively easier than in humans and, to date, 115 QTL linked to body weight or body fat have been reported from cross-breeding experiments in various animals (Perusse et al., 2001). Laboratory animals are ideal model systems for QTL analysis because the effects of environmental factors and genetic background can be held constant and specific phenotypes such as adiposity or energy expenditure can be selected for over many generations (Barsh et al., 2000).

A highly dense and reliable mouse gene map for polygenic obesity has been generated (Perusse et al., 2001). On the basis of synteny between the mouse and human genomes, the mouse obesity QTL have been mapped to their putative homologous locations in the human genome (Perusse et al., 2001). The search for the causative gene variants underlying the mouse QTL and candidate genes within the homologous chromosomal regions in humans is currently underway. Some of the mouse QTL have mapped to human genomic regions containing known candidate genes such as the *UCP-1*, *UCP-2* and *UCP-3* genes (Echwald, 1999).

QTL analysis in polygenic animal models of obesity offers the opportunity to investigate specific questions related to human obesity such as the role of genetic factors in determining the response of body fat composition to changes in dietary fat intake (Perusse & Bouchard, 2000). Mouse models of diet-induced obesity provide the most promising approach of identifying the genes responsible for modulating the response to diet. Three QTL determining the response to dietary lipids in a mouse model of diet-induced obesity have been identified and mapped to their syntenic regions in the human genome, chromosomes 1, 3 and 8 (West et al., 1994). Suggestive evidence of linkage has been reported between human chromosome 1 markers and various obesity phenotypes (Chagnon et al., 1997a).

The Search for Lean Genes

An alternative approach to understanding the genetic basis of eating disorders and obesity might be to search for genes involved in the control of body leanness (fat free mass) (Bjorntorp, 2001). Fat free mass (FFM) consists mostly of bone tissues and skeletal muscle and can be calculated from percent body fat. A genome-wide linkage study has been conducted to identify candidate chromosomal regions for FFM. In this study FFM showed significant linkage to a genetic marker within the insulin-like growth factor-1 receptor (*IGF-1R*) gene on chromosome 15q25–q26 and to two markers on chromosome 18q12 (Chagnon et al., 2000a). A moderately significant linkage was observed on chromosome 7p15.3, which contains a plausible candidate gene, the growth hormone-releasing hormone (*GHRH*) receptor gene. These positive linkages need to be replicated in other populations. An association between a variant of the insulin-like growth factor-1 (*IGF-1*) gene and FFM has been reported (Sun et al., 1999). This *IGF-1* gene variant has also been linked to the changes in FFM in response to 20 weeks of endurance exercise (Sun et al., 1999). The roles of variants of the *IGF-1R*, *GHRH*, *IGF-1* genes in eating disorders and obesity need to be assessed in association studies.

Another approach to identify lean genes is to examine genetic variants in people that have managed to keep their bodyweight constant without difficulty. These people are a rare, specific subgroup who might have genetic variants that differ from the general population and that are protecting them from gaining weight. In a study of women who have managed to keep their weight constant from the age of 21 years, a specific variant of the aromatase gene, whose protein product functions more efficiently, has been implicated in their ability to stay lean (Bjorntorp, 2001). The identification of such genes may provide targets for therapeutic intervention in obesity.

CONCLUSION

Thus far, there has been little success in elucidating the polygenic component to the aetiology of either eating disorders or common human obesity.

The majority of candidate gene association studies for eating disorders have reported negative findings. It is impossible to draw conclusions from these results because many of the studies were small and used heterogeneous populations. There have been a few positive associations but these need to be replicated in independent populations to confirm their importance. The *5-HT$_{2a}$* gene is a plausible candidate but its role in the genetic aetiology of AN remains unresolved. It is hoped that the large-scale association and linkage studies that are currently underway will have greater statistical power to detect small genetic effects and lead to the identification of susceptibility genes for eating disorders.

To date, over 250 candidate genes, markers, or chromosomal regions have been linked or associated with common human obesity phenotypes and this number will continue to expand over the coming years (Perusse et al., 2001). These putative obesity loci have been found on all human chromosomes except the Y chromosome. Despite the number of putative obesity loci there are as yet no common obesity susceptibility genes. Identification of the true obesity loci and the causative genetic variants is a formidable task.

Genetic studies in monogenic and polygenic animal models of obesity have provided valuable insight into fundamental pathways regulating appetite and energy expenditure. The number of mouse obesity genes and QTL will continue to increase over the coming years, and this will aid in the identification of new pathways involved in energy homeostasis, additional components of already identified pathways and guide candidate gene analyses in human studies.

A fundamental flaw in current research strategies can in part explain the lack of success in identifying susceptibility genes for these disorders. Current approaches investigate the relationship between a variant in a single gene and a phenotype/disease without controlling for gene–gene interactions and/or environmental factors, neither of which have been clearly defined (Sorensen & Echwald, 2001). Some genetic variants may only show an effect in combination with other gene variants or environmental factors. Polygenic animal models offer the opportunity to explore gene–gene interactions and gene–environment interactions. Another problem is that the sample sizes needed to detect genes of truly small effects are unrealistically large for an individual researcher to collect (Comuzzie & Allison, 1998). More powerful approaches of detecting genes of small effect are being developed, such as whole-genome association studies (Kruglyak, 1999).

The challenge for future research is to determine the combination of genetic variants and epistatic (gene–gene) interactions that contribute to the aetiology of eating disorders and obesity and the environmental circumstances in which the genetic predisposition is fully expressed (Perusse et al., 2001). It is hoped that progress in understanding the genetic basis of these disorders will provide the basis for more rational pharmacological treatment and/or preventative therapeutic strategies for eating disorders and obesity.

REFERENCES

APA, (1994) *Diagnostic and Statistical Manual of Mental Disorders* (4th Edition) Washington, D.C.: American Psychiatric Association.

Aubert, R., Betoulle, D., Herbeth, B., Siest, G. & Fumeron, F. (2000) 5-HT2A receptor gene polymorphism is associated with food and alcohol intake in obese people. *Int. J. Obes. Relat. Metab. Disord.*, **24**, 920–924.

Barsh, G.S., Farooqui, I.S. & O'Rahilly, S. (2000) Genetics of body-weight regulation. *Nature*, **404**, 644–651.

Bjorntorp, P. (2001) Thrifty genes and human obesity: Are we chasing ghosts? *Lancet*, **358**, 1006–1008.

Bray, M.S., Boerwinkle, E. & Hanis, C.L. (2000) Sequence variation within the neuropeptide Y gene and obesity in Mexican Americans. *Obes. Res.*, **8**, 219–226.

Bruins-Slot, L., Gorwood, P., Bouvard, M., Blot, P., Ades, J., Feingold, J., Schwartz, J.C. & Mouren-Simeoni, M.C. (1998) Lack of association between anorexia nervosa and D3 dopamine receptor gene. *Biol. Psychiat.*, **43**, 76–78.

Bulik, C.M., Sullivan, P.F., Wade, T.D. & Kendler, K.S. (2000) Twin sudies of eating disorders: A review. *Int. J. Eat. Disord.*, **27**, 1–20.

Bulik, C.M., Sullivan, P.F. & Kendler, K.S. (1998) Heritability of binge-eating and broadly defined bulimia nervosa. *Biol. Psychiat.*, **44**, 1210–1218.

Butler, M.G., Hedges, L., Hovis, C.L. & Feurer, I.D. (1998) Genetic variants of the human obesity (OB) gene in subjects with and without Prader-Willi Syndrome: comparison with body mass index and weight. *Clin. Genet.*, **54**, 385–393.

Campbell, D.A., Sundaramurthy, D., Gordon, D., Markham, A.F. & Pieri, L.F. (1999) Association between a marker in the UCP-2/UCP-3 gene cluster and genetic susceptibility to anorexia nervosa. *Mol. Psychiat.*, **4**, 68–70.

Campbell, D.A., Sundaramurthy, D., Markham, A.F. & Pieri, L.F. (1998) Lack of association between 5-HT$_{2a}$ gene promoter polymorphism and susceptibility to anorexia nervosa. *Lancet*, **351**, 499.

Chagnon, Y.C., Borecki, I.B., Perusse, L., Roy, S., Lacaille, M., Chagnon, M., Ho-Kim, M.A., Rice, T., Province, M.A., Rao, D.C. & Bouchard, C. (2000a) Genome-wide search for genes related to the fat-free body mass in the Quebec family study. *Metabolism*, **49**, 203–207.

Chagnon, Y.C., Wilmore, J.H., Borecki, I.B., Gagnon, J., Perusse, L., Chagnon, M., Collier, G.R., Leon, A.S., Skinner, J.S., Rao, D.C. & Bouchard, C. (2000b) Associations between the leptin receptor gene and adiposity in middle-aged caucasian males from the HERITAGE family study. *J. Clin. Endoc. Metab.*, **85**, 29–34.

Chagnon, Y.C., Chung, W.K., Perusse, L., Chagnon, M., Leibel, R.L. & Bouchard, C. (1999) Linkages and associations between the leptin receptor (LEPR) gene and human body composition in the Quebec family study. *Int. J. Obes. Relat. Metab. Disord.*, **23**, 278–286.

Chagnon, Y.C., Perusse, L., Lamothe, M., Chagnon, M., Nadeau, A., Dionne, F.T., Gagnon, J., Chung, W.K., Leibel, R.L. & Bouchard, C. (1997a) Suggestive linkages between markers on human 1p32-22 and body fat and insulin levels in the Quebec family study. *Obes Res.*, **5**, 115–121.

Chagnon, Y.C., Chen, W.J., Perusse, L., Chagnon, M., Nadeau, A., Wilkison, W.O. & Bouchard, C. (1997b) Linkage and association studies between the melanocortin receptors 4 and 5 genes and obesity-related phenotypes in the Quebec Family study. *Molec. Med.*, **3**, 663–673.

Chen, H., Charlat, O., Tartaglia, L.A., Woolf, E.A., Weng, X., Ellis, S.J., Lakey, N.D., Culpepper, J., Moore, K.J., Breitbart, R.E., Duyk, G.M., Tepper, R.I. & Morgenstern, J.P. (1996) Evidence that the diabetes gene encodes the lepton receptor: identification of a mutation in the leptin receptor gene in *db/db* mice. *Cell.* **84**, 491–495.

Chen, A., Marsh, D.J., Trumbauer, M.E., Frazier, E.G., Guan, X.M., Yu, H., Rosenblum, C.I., Vongs, A., Feng, Y., Cao, L., Metzger, J.M., Strack, A.M., Camacho, R.E., Mellin, T.N., Nunes, C.N., Min, W., Fisher, J., Gopal-Truter, S., MacIntyre, D.E., Chen, H.Y. & Van der Ploeg, L.H.T. (2000) Inactivation of the mouse melanocortin-3 receptor results in increased fat mass and reduced lean body mass. *Nat. Genet.*, **26**, 97–101.

Clement, K., Vaisse, C., Lahlou, N., Cabrol, S., Pelloux, V., Cassuto, D., Gourmelen, M., Dina, C., Chambaz, J., Lacorte, J.M., Basdevant, A., Bougneres, P., Lebouc, Y., Froguel, P. & Guy-Grand, B. (1998) A mutation in the human leptin receptor gene causes obesity and pituitary dysfunction. *Nature*, **392**, 398–401.

Clement, K., Garner, C., Hager, J., Philippi, A., LeDuc, C., Carey, A., Harris, T.J., Jury, C., Cardon, L.R., Basdevant, A., Demenais, F., Guy-Grand, B., North, M. & Froguel, P. (1996) Indication for linkage of the human OB gene region with extreme obesity. *Diabetes*, **45**, 686–690.

Collier, D.A., Arranz, M.J., Li, T., Mupita, D., Brown, N. & Treasure, J. (1997) Association between 5-HT$_{2a}$ gene promoter polymorphism and anorexia nervosa. *Lancet*, **350**, 412.

Comings, D.E., Flanagan, S.D., Dietz, G., Muhleman, D., Knell, E. & Gysin, R. (1993) The dopamine D2 receptor (DRD2) as a major gene in obesity and height. *Biochem. Med. metab. Biol.*, **50**, 176–185.

Comuzzie, A. & Allison, D. (1998) The search for human obesity genes. *Science*, **280**, 1347–1378.

Comuzzie, A.G., Hixson, J.E., Almasy, L., Mitchell, B.D., Mahaney, M.C., Dyer, T.D., Stern, M.P., MacCluer, J.W. & Blangero, J. (1997) A major quantitative trait locus determining serum leptin levels and fat mass is located on human chromosome 2. *Nat. Genet.*, **15**, 273–275.

Despres, J.P., Lemieux, I. & Prud'homme D. (2001) Treatment of obesity: Need to focus on high risk abdominally obese patients. *BMJ*, **322**, 716–720.

Di Bella, D., Catalano, M., Cavallini, M.C., Riboldi, C. & Bellodi, L. (2000) Serotonin transporter linked polymorphic region in anorexia nervosa and bulimia nervosa. *Molec. Psychiat.*, **5**, 233–234.

Duggirula, R., Stern, M.P., Mitchell, B.D., Reinhart, L.J., Shipman, P.A., Uresandi, O.C., Chung, W.K., Leibel, R.L., Hales, C.N., O'Connell, P. & Blangero, J. (1996) Quantitative variation in obesity-related traits and insulin precursors linked to the OB gene region on human chromosome 7, *Am. J. Hum. Genet.*, **59**, 694–703.

Ebstein, R.P., Benjamin, J. & Belmaker, R.H. (2000) Personality and polymorphisms of genes involved in aminergic neurotansmission. *EJP*, **410**, 205–214.

Echwald, S.M. (1999) Genetics of human obesity: Lessons from mouse models and candidate genes. *J. Int. Med.*, **245**, 653–666.

Enoch, M.A., Kaye, W.H., Rotondo, A., Greenberg, B.D., Murphy, D.L. & Goldman, D. (1998) 5-HT$_{2a}$ promoter polymorphism—1438 G/A, anorexia nervosa, and obsessive-compulsive disorder. *Lancet*, **351**, 1785–1786.

Fairburn, C.G., Cowen, P.J. & Harrison, P.J. (1999) Twin studies and the aetiology of eating disorders. *Int. J. Eat. Disord.*, **26**, 349–358.

Fairburn, C.G., & Cooper, Z. (1993) The eating Disorders Examination. In C. Fairburn & G. Wilson (Eds), *Binge-eating: Nature, Assessment and Treatment* (12th edn; pp. 317–360). New York: Guilford Press.

Fichter, M.M. & Noegal, R. (1990) Concordance for bulimia nervosa in twins. *Int. J. Disord.*, **9**, 255–263.

Garner, D., Olmsted, M. & Polivy, J. (1984) *Eating Disorders Inventory Manual*. New York: Psychological Assessment Resources. .

Goldner, E.M., Srikameswaran, S., Schroeder, M.L., Livesley, W.J. & Birmingham C.L. (1999) Dimensional assessment of personality pathology in patients with eating disorders. *Psychiat. Res.*, **85**, 151–159.

Graham, M., Shutter, J.T., Sarmiento, U., Sarosi, I. & Stark, K.L. (1997) Overexpression of Agrt leads to obesity in transgenic mice. *Nat. Genet.*, **17**, 273–274.

Gunn, T.M., Miller, K.A., He, L., Hyman, R.W., Davis, R.W., Azarani, A., Schlossman, S.F., Duke-Cohan, J.S. & Barsh, G.S. (1999) The mouse mahagany locus encodes a transmembrane form of human attractin. *Nature*, **398**, 152–156.

Hager, J., Dina, C., Francke, S., Dubois, S., Hourari, M., Vatin, V., Vaillant, E., Lorentz, N., Basdevant, A., Clement, K., Guy-Grand, B. & Froguel, P. (1998a) A genome wide scan for human obesity genes reveals a major susceptibility locus on chromosome 10. *Nat. Genet.*, **20**, 304–308.

Hager, J., Clement, K., Francke, S., Dina, C., Raison, J., Lahlou, N., Rich, N., Pelloux, V., Basdevant, A., Guy-Grand, B., North, M. & Froguel, P. (1998b) A polymorphism in the 5′ untranslated region of the human *ob* gene is associated with low leptin levels. *Int. J. Obes. Relat. Metab. Disord.*, **22**, 200–205.

Halaas, J.L., Gajiwala, K.S., Maffei, M., Cohen, S.L., Chait, B.T., Rabinowitz, D., Lallone, R.L., Burley, S.K. & Friedman, J.M. (1995) Weight-reducing effects of the plasma protein encoded by the obese gene. *Science*, **269**, 543–546.

Han, L., Nielsen, D.A., Rosenthal, N.E., Jefferson, K., Kaye, W., Murphy, D., Altemus, M., Humphries, J., Cassano, G., Rotondo, A., Virkkunen, M., Linnoila, M. & Goldman, D. (1999) No coding variant of the tryptophan hydroxylase gene detected in seasonal affective disorder, obsessive-compulsive disorder, anorexia nervosa, and alcoholism. *Biol. Psychiat.*, **45**, 615–619.

Hanson, R.L., Ehm, M.G., Pettitt, D.J., Prochazka, M., Thompson, D.B., Timberlake, D., Foroud, T., Kobes, S., Baier, L., Burns, D.K., Almasy, L., Blangero, J., Garvey, W.T., Bennett, P.H. & Knowler, W.C. (1998) An autosomal genomic scan for loci linked to type II diabetes mellitus and body-mass index in Pima Indians. *Am. J. Hum. Genet.*, **63**, 1130–1138.

Hebebrand, J. & Remschmidt, H. (1995) Anorexia nervosa viewed as an extreme weight condition: genetic implications. *Hum. Genet.*, **95**, 1–11.

Hinney, A., Remschmidt, H. & Hebebrand, J. (2000) Candidate gene polymorphisms in eating disorders. *EJP*, **410**, 147–159.

Hinney, A., Schmidt, A., Nottebom, K., Heibult, O., Becker, I., Ziegler, A., Gerber, G., Sina, M., Gorg, T., Mayer, H., Siegfried, W., Fichter, M., Remschmidt, H. & Hebebrand, J. (1999) Several mutations in the melanocortin-4 receptor gene including a nonsense and a frameshift mutation associated with dominantly inherited obesity in humans. *J. Clin. Endoc. Metab.*, **84**, 1483–1486.

Hinney, A., Barth, N., Zeigler, A., Von Prittwitz, S., Hamann, A., Hennighausen, K., Lentes, K.U., Heils, A., Rosenkranz, K., Roth, H., Coners, H., Mayer, H., Herzog, W., Siegfried, A., Lehmkuhl, G., Poustka, F., Schmidt, M.H., Schafer, H., Grzeschik, K.H., Pirke, K.M., Lesch, K.P. Remschmidt, H. & Hebebrand, J. (1997a) Serotonin transporter gene-linked polymorphic region: Allele distributions in relationship to body weight and in anorexia nervosa. *Life Sci.*, **61**, L295–PL303.

Hinney, A., Zeigler, A., Nothen, M.M. Remschmidt, H. & Hebebrand, J. (1997b) 5-HT$_{2a}$ receptor gene polymorphisms, anorexia nervosa and obesity. *Lancet*, **350**, 1324–1325.

Hinney, A., Lentes, K.U., Rosenkranz, K., Barth, N., Roth, H., Zeigler, A., Hennighausen, K., Coners, H., Wurmser, H., Jacob, K., Romer, G., Winnekes, U., Mayer, H., Herzog, W., Lehmkuhl, G., Poutska, F., Schmidt, M.H., Blum, W.F., Pirke, K.M., Schafer, H., Grzeschik, K.H., Remschmidt, H., Hebebrand, J. (1997c) Beta 3-adrenergic-receptor allele distributions in children, adolescents and young adults with obesity, underweight or anorexia nervosa. *Int. J. Obes. Relat. Metab. Disord.*, **21**, 224–230.

Hixson, J.E., Almasy, L., Cole, S., Birnbaum, S., Mitchell, B.D., Mahaney, M.C., Stern, M.P., MacCluer, J.W., Blangero, J. & Comuzzie, A.G. (1999) Normal variation in leptin levels is associated with polymorphisms in the proopiomelanocortin gene, POMC. *J. Clin. Endoc. Metab.*, **84**, 3187–91.

Holder, J.L., Butte, N.F. & Zinn, A.R. (2000) Profound obesity associated with a balanced translocation that disrupts the SIM1 gene. *Hum. Molec. Genet.*, **9**, 101–108.

Holland, A.J., Sicotte, N. & Treasure, J. (1988) Anorexia nervosa: Evidence for a genetic basis. *J. Psychosom. Res.*, **32**, 561–571.

Hsu, L.K.G., Chesler, B.E. & Santhouse, R. (1990) Bulimia nervosa in eleven sets of twins: A clinical report. *Int. J. Eat. Disord.*, **9**, 275–282.

Huszar, D., Lynch, C.A., Fairchild-Huntress, V., Dunmore, J.H., Fang, Q., Berkemeier, L.R., Gu, W., Kesterson, R.A., Boston, B.A., Cone, R.D., Smith, F.J., Campfield, L.A., Burn, P. & Lee, F. (1997) Targeted disruption of the melanocortin-4 receptor results in obesity in mice. *Cell*, **88**, 131–141.

Inui, A. (2000) Transgenic study of energy homeostasis equation: Implications and confounding influences. *FASEB Jl*, **14**, 2158–2170.

Jackson, R.S., Creemers, J.W., Ohagi, S., Raffin-Sanson, M.L., Sanders, L., Montague, C.T., Hutton, J.C. & O'Rahilly, S. (1997) Obesity and impaired prohormone processing associated with mutations in the prohormone convertase 1 gene. *Nat. Genet.*, **16**, 303–306.

Jenkinson, C.P., Cray, K., Walder, K., Herzog, H., Hanson, R. & Ravussin, E. (2000) Novel polymorphisms in the neuropeptide-Y Y5 receptor associated with obesity in Pima Indians. *Int. J. Obes. Relat. Metab. Disord.*, **24**, 580–584.

Kapeller, R., Moriarty, A., Strauss, A., Stubdal, H., Theriault, K., Siebert, E., Chickering, T., Morgenstern, J.P., Tartaglia, L.A. & Lillie, J. (1999) Tyrosine phosphorylation of tub and its association with Src homology 2 domain-containing proteins implicate tub in intracellular signalling by insulin. *J. Biol. Chem.*, **274**, 24980–24986.

Karvonen, M.K., Koulu, M., Pesonen, U. et al. (2000) Leucine 7 to proline 7 polymorphism in the preproneuropeptide Y is associated with birth weight and serum triglyceride concentration in preschool aged children. *J. Clin. Endoc. Metab.*, **85**, 1455–1460.

Kaye, W.H., Klump, K.L., Frank, G.K.W. & Strober, M. (2000a) Anorexia and bulimia nervosa. *Ann. Rev. Med.*, **51**, 299–313.

Kaye, W.H., Lilenfeld, L.R., Wade, H., Berrettini, Strober, M., Devlin, B., Klump, K.L., Goldman, D., Bulik, C.M., Halmi, K.A., Fichter, M.M., Kaplan, A., Woodside, A.B., Treasure, J., Plotinov, K., Pollice, C., Radhika, R. & McConaha, C.W. (2000b) A search for susceptibility loci for anorexia nervosa: Methods and sample description. *Biol. Psychiat.*, **47**, 794–803.

Kendler, K.S., Walters, E.E., Neale, M.C., Kessler, R.C., Heath, A.C. & Eaves, L.J. (1995) The structure of the genetic and environmental risk factors for six major psychiatric disorders in women:

Phobis, generalised anxiety disorder, panic disorder, bulimia, major depression, and alcoholism. *Arch. Gen. Psychiat.*, **52**, 374–383.

Kendler, K.S., Maclean, C., Neale, M.C., Kessler, R.C., Heath, A.C. & Eaves, L.J. (1991) The genetic epidemiology of bulimia nervosa. *Am. J. Psychiat.*, **148**, 1627–1627.

Kleyn, P.W., Fan, W., Kovats, S.G., Lee, J.J., Pulido, J.C., Wu, Y., Berkemeier, L.R., Misumi, D.J., Holmgren, L., Charlat, O., Woolf, E.A., Tayber, O., Brody, T., Shu, P., Hawkins, F., Kennedy, B., Baldini, L., Ebeling, C., Alperin, G.D., Deeds, J., Lakey, N.D., Culpepper, J., Chen, H., Glucksmann-Kuis, M.A., Moore, K.J., et al. (1996) Identification and characterization of the mouse obesity gene tubby: A member of a novel gene family. *Cell*, **85**, 281–290.

Klump, K.L., Bulik, C.M., Kaye, W.H. & Strober, M. (2001) The genetics of eating disorders. Manuscript in preparation.

Klump, K.L., McGue, M. & Iacono, W.G. (2000) Age differences in genetic and environmental influences on eating attitudes and behaviours in preadolescent and adolescent twins. *J. Abnorm. Psychol.*, **109**, 239–251.

Klump, K.L., Kaye, W.H., Plotinov, K., Pollice, C. & Rao R. (1999) Familial transmission of personality traits in women with anorexia nervosa and their first-degree relatives. Poster presented at the Academy for Eating Disorders Annual Meeting, San Diego, California.

Krude, H., Biebermann, H., Luck, W., Horn, R., Brabant, G. & Gruters, A. (1998) Severe early-onset obesity, adrenal insufficiency, and red hair pigmentation caused by POMC mutations in humans. *Nat. Genet.*, **19**, 155–157.

Kruglyak, L. (1999) Prospects for whole-genome linkage disequilibrium mapping of common disease genes. *Nat. Genet.*, **22**, 139–144.

Lambertas, A.V., Perusse, L., Chagnon, Y.C., Fisler, J.S., Warden, C.H., Purcell-Huynh, D.A., Dionne, F.T., Gagnon, J., Nadeau, A., Lusis, A.J. & Bouchard, C. (1997) Identification of an obesity quantitative trait locus on mouse chromosome 2 and evidence of linkage to body fat and insulin on the human homologous region 20q. *J. Clin. Invest.*, **100**, 1240–1247.

Lander, E. & Kruglyak, L. (1995) Genetic dissection of complex traits: Guidelines for interpreting and reporting linkage results. *Nat. Genet.*, **11**, 241–247.

Lapsys, N.M., Furler, S.M., Moore, K.R., Nguyen, T.V., Herzog, H., Howard, G., Samaras, K., Carey, D.G., Morrison, N.A., Eisman, J.A. & Chisholm, D.J. (1997) Relationship of a novel polymorphic marker near the human obese (OB) gene to fat mass in healthy woman. *Obes Res.*, **5**, 430–433.

Lee, J.H., Reed, D.R., Li, W.D., Xu, W., Joo, E.J., Kilker, R.L., Nanthakumar, E., North, M., Sakul, H., Bell., A. & Price R. (1999) Genome scan for human obesity and linkage to markers in 20q13. *Am. J. Hum. Genet.*, **64**, 196–209.

Li, W.D., Reed, D.R., Lee, J.H., Xu, W., Kilker, R.L., Sodam, B.R. & Price, R.A. (1999) Sequence variants in the 5′ flanking region of the leptin gene are associated with obesity in woman. *Ann. Hum. Genet.*, **63**, 227–234.

Lilenfeld, L.R., Stein, D., Bulik, C.M., Strober, M., Plotinov, K., Pollice, C., Rao, R., Merikangas, K.R., Nagy, L. & Kaye, W.H. (2000) Personality traits among currently eating-disordered, recovered and never ill first-degree female realtives of bulimic and control woman. *Psychol. Med.*, **30**, 1399–1410.

Ludwig, D.S., Tritos, N.A., Mastaitis, J.W., Kulkarni, R., Kokkotou, E., Elmquist, J., Lowell, B., Flier, J.S. & Maratos-Flier, E. (2001) Melanin-concentrating hormone overexpression in transgenic mice leads to obesity and insulin resistance. *J. Clin. Invest.*, **107**, 379–386.

Mammes, O., Aubert, R., Betoulle, D., Pean, F., Herberth, B., Visvikis S., Siest G. & Fumeron F. (2001) *LEPR* gene polymorphisms: Associations with overweight, fat mass and response to diet in women. *Eur. J. Clin. Invest.*, **31**, 398–404.

Mammes, O., Betoulle, D., Aubert, R., Giraud, V., Tuzet, S., Petiet, A., Colas-Linhart, N. & Fumeron, F. (1998) Novel polymorphisms in the 5′ region of the LEP gene: Association with leptin levels and response to low-calorie diet in human obesity. *Diabetes*, **47**, 487–489.

Mehrabian, M., Wen, P.Z., Fisler, J., Davis, R.C. & Lusis, A.J. (1998) Genetic loci controlling body fat, lipoprotein metabolism, and insulin levels in a multifactorial mouse model. *J. Clin. Invest.*, **101**, 2485–2496.

Michaud, E.J., Bultman, S.J., Klebig, M.L., van Vugt, M.J., Stubbs, L.J., Russell, L.B. & Woychik, R.P. (1994) A molecular model for the genetic and phenotypic characteristics of the mouse lethal yellow (A^y) mutation. *Proc. Natl. Acad. Sci. USA*, **91**, 2562–2566.

Montague, C.T., Farooqi, I.S., Whitehead, J.P., Soos, M.A., Rau, H., Wareham, N.J., Sewter, C.P., Digby, J.E., Mohammed, S.N., Hurst, J.A., Cheetham, C.H., Earley, A.R., Barnett, A.H., Prins, J.B. & O'Rahilly, S. (1997) Congenital leptin deficiency is associated with severe early-onset obesity in humans. *Nature*, **387**, 903–908.

Nacmias, B., Ricca, V., Tedde, A., Mezzani, B., Rotella, C.M. & Sorbi, S. (1999) 5-HT$_{2a}$ receptor gene polymorphisms in anorexia nervosa and bulimia nervosa. *Neurosci Lett.*, **277**, 134–136.

Naggert, J.K., Fricker, L.D., Varlamov, O., Nishina, P.M., Rouille, Y., Steiner, D.F., Carroll, R.J., Paigen, B.J. & Leiter, E.H. (1995) Hyperproinsulinaemia in obese fat/fat mice associated with a carboxypeptidase E mutation which reduces enzyme activity. *Nat Genet.*, **10**, 135–142.

Nagle, D.L., McGrail, S.H., Vitale, J., Woolf, E.A., Dussault, B.J., DiRocco, L., Holmgren, L., Montagno, J., Bork, P., Huszar, D., Fairchild-Huntress, V., Ge, P., Keilty, J., Ebeling, C., Baldini, L., Gilchrist, J., Burn, P., Carlson, G.A. & Moore, K.J. (1999) The mahogany protein is a receptor involved in supression of obesity. *Nature*, **398**, 148–152.

Neel, J.V. (1962) Diabetes mellitus: A 'thrifty' genotype rendered detrimental by progress? *Am. J. Hum. Genet.*, **14**, 353–363.

Norman, R.A., Tataranni, P.A., Pratley, R., Thompson, D.B., Hanson, R.L., Prochazka, M., Baier, L., Ehm, M.G., Sakul, H., Foroud, T., Garvey, W.T., Burns, D., Knowler, W.C., Bennett, P.H., Bogardus, C. & Ravussin, E. (1998) Autosomal genomic scan for loci linked to obesity and energy metabolism in Pima Indians. *Am. J. Hum. Genet.*, **62**, 659–668.

Norman, R.A., Thompson, D.B., Foroud, T., Garvey, W.T., Bennett, P.H., Bogardus, C., & Ravussin, E. (1997) Genome-wide search for genes influencing percent body fat in Pima Indians: Suggestive linkage at chromosome 11q21–q22. Pima Diabetes Gene Group. *Am. J. Hum. Genet.*, **60**, 166–173.

Ohman, M., Oksanen, L., Kaprio, J., Koskenvuo, M., Mustajoki, P., Rissanen, A., Salmi, J., Kontula, K., Peltonen, L. (2000) Genome-wide scan of obesity in Finnish sib-pairs reveals linkage to chromosome Xq24. *J. Clin. Endocrinol. Metab.*, **85**, 3183–3190.

Ohman, M., Oksanen, L., Kainulainen, K., Janne, O.A., Kaprio, J., Koskenvuo, M., Mustajoki, P., Kontula, K. & Peltonen, L. (1999) Testing of human homologues of murine obesity genes as candidate regions in Finnish obese sib pairs. *Eur. J. Hum. Genet.*, **7**, 117–124.

Oksanen, L., Ohman, M., Heiman, M., Kainulainen, K., Kaprio, J., Mustajoki, P., Koivisto, V., Koskenvuo, M., Janne, O.A., Peltonen, L. & Kontula, K. (1997) Markers for the gene *ob* and serum leptin levels in human morbid obesity. *Hum. Genet.*, **99**, 559–564.

Rutkowski, M.P., Klanke, C.A., Su, Y.R., Reif, M., Menon, A.G. (1998) Genetic markers at the leptin (OB) locus are not significantly linked to hypertension in African Americans. *Hypertension*, **31**, 1230–1234.

Perusse, L. & Bouchard, C. (2000) Gene-diet interactions in obesity. *Am. J. Clin. Nutr.*, **72** (suppl), 1285S–1290S.

Perusse, L., Chagnon, Y.C., Weisnagel, S.J., Rankinen, T., Snyder, E., Sands, J. & Bouchard, C. (2001) The Human Obesity Gene Map: The 2000 update. *Ob. Res.* **9**, 135–168.

Perusse, L. & Chagnon, Y.C. (1997) Summary of human linkage and association studies. *Behav. Genet.*, **27**, 359–372.

Plomin, R., Defries, J.C., McClearn, G.E. & McGuffin, P. (2001) *Behavioural Genetics* (4th edition). Worth Publishers and W.H. Freeman & Company.

Ravussin, E., & Bouchard, C. (2000) Human genomics and obesity: Finding appropriate drug targets. *EJP*, **410**, 131–145.

Reed, D.R., Ding, Y., Xu, W., Cather, C., Green, E.D. & Price, R.A. (1996) Extreme obesity may be linked to markers flanking the human OB gene. *Diabetes*, **45**, 691–694.

Roth, H., Hinney, A., Ziegler, A., Barth, N., Gerber, G., Stein, K., Bromel, T., Mayer, H., Siegfried, W., Schafer, H., Remschmidt, H., Grzeschik, K.H. & Hebebrand, J. (1997) Further support for linkage of extreme obesity to the obese gene in a study group of obese children and adolescents. *Exp. Clin. Endocrinol. Diabetes*, **105**, 341–344.

Rotimi, C.N., Comuzzie, A.G., Lowe, W.L., Luke, A., Blangero, J. & Cooper, R.S. (1999) The quantitative trait locus on chromosome 2 for serum leptin levels is confirmed in African-Americans. *Diabetes*, **48**, 643–644.

Rosenkranz, K., Hinney, A., Ziegler, A., Hermann, H., Fichter, M., Mayer, H., Siegfried, W., Young, J.K., Remschmidt, H. & Hebebrand, J. (1998) Systematic mutation screening of the oestrogen receptor beta gene in probands of different weight extremes: Identification of several genetic variants. *J. Clin. Endocrinol. Metab.*, **83**, 4524–4527.

Rosmond R., Bouchard C. & Bjorntorp P. (2001) Tsp5091 polymorphism in exon 2 of the glucocorticoid receptor gene in realtion to obesity and cortisol secretion: Cohort study. *BMJ*, **322**, 652–653.

Rossi, M., Kim, M.S., Morgan, D.G., Small, C.J., Edwards, C.M., Sunter, D., Abusnana, S., Goldstone, A.P., Russell, S.H., Stanley, S.A., Smith, D.M., Yagaloff, K., Ghatei, M.A. & Bloom, S.R. (1998) A C-terminal fragment of agouti-related protein increases feeding and antagonises the effect of alpha-melanocyte stimulating hormone in vivo. *Endocrinology*, **139**, 4428–4431.

Roth, H., Korn, T., Rosenkranz, K., Hinney, A., Ziegler, A., Kunz, J., Siegfried, W., Mayer, H., Hebebrand, J. & Grzeschik, K.H. (1998) Transmission disequilibrium and sequence variants at the leptin receptor gene in extremely obese German children and adolescents. *Hum. Genet.*, **103**, 540–546.

Rutherford, J., McGuffin, P., Katz, R. & Murray, R. (1993) Genetic influences on eating attitudes in a normal female twin population. *Psychol. Med.*, **23**, 425–436.

Son, J.H., Baker, H., Park, D.H. & Joh, T.H. (1994) Drastic and selective hyperinnervation of central serotonergic neurons in a lethal neurodevelopmental mouse mutant, Anorexia (anx). *Mol. Brain. Res.*, **25**, 129–134.

Sorbi, S., Nacmias, B., Tedde, A., Ricca, V., Mezzani, B. & Rotella, C.M. (1998) 5-HT$_{2a}$ promoter polymorphism in anorexia nervosa. *Lancet*, **351**, 1785.

Sorensen, T.I.A. & Echwald, S.M. (2001) Obesity genes. *BMJ*, **322**, 639–631.

Spiegelman B.M. & Flier J.S. (2001) Obesity and the regulation of energy balance. *Cell*, **104**, 531–543.

Spitz, M.R., Detry, M.A., Pillow, P. et al. (1999) Variant alleles of the D2 dopamine receptor gene and obesity. *Nutr. Res.*, **20**, 371–380.

Stein, D., Lilenfeld, L.R., Plotnicov, K., Pollice, C., Rao, R., Strober, M. & Kaye, W. (1998) Familial aggregation of eating disorders: Results from a controlled family study of bulimia nervosa. *Int. J. Eat. Disord.*, **26**, 211–215.

Strobel, A., Issad, T., Camoin, L., Ozata, M. & Strosberg, A.D. (1998) A leptin missense mutation associated with hypogonadism and morbid obesity. *Nat. Genet.*, **18**, 213–215.

Strober, M., Freeman, R., Lampert, C., Diamond, J. & Kaye, W. (2000) Controlled family study of anorexia nervosa and bulimia nervosa: Evidence of shared liability and transmision of partial syndromes. *Am. J. Psychiat.*, **157**, 393–401.

Sullivan, P.F., Bulik, C.M., & Kendler, K.S. (1998) The genetic epidemiology of binging and vomiting. *Br. J. Psychiat.*, **173**, 75–79.

Sun, G., Gagnon, J., Chagnon, Y.C., Perusse, L., Despres, J.P., Leon, A.S., Wilmore, J.H., Skinner, J.S., Borecki, I., Rao, D.C. & Bouchard, C. (1999) Association and linkage between an insulin-like growth factor-1 gene polymorphism and fat free mass in the HERITAGE family study. *Int. J. Obes. Relat. Metab. Disord.*, **23**, 929–935.

Sundaramurthy, D., Pieri, L.F., Gape, H., Markham, A.F. & Campbell, D.A. (2000) Analysis of the serotonin transporter gene linked polymorphism (5-HTTLPR) in anorexia nervosa. *Am. J. Med. Genet.*, **96**, 53–55.

Tartaglia, L.A., Dembski, M., Weng, X., Deng, N., Culpepper, J., Devos, R., Richards, G.J., Campfield, L.A., Clark, F.T., Deeds, J. et al. (1995) Identification and expression cloning of a leptin receptor, OB-R. *Cell*, **83**, 1263–1271.

Thomas, G.N., Tomlinson, B. & Critchley, J.A. (2000) Modulation of blood pressure and obesity with the dopamine D2 receptor gene *Taq*1 polymorphism. *Hypertension*, **36**, 177–182.

Treasure, J.L. & Collier, D. (2001) The spectrum of eating disorders in humans. In J.B. Owen, J.L. Treasure & D. Collier (Eds), *Animal Models—Disorders of Eating Behaviour and Body Composition* (pp.19–49). Boston: Kluwer Academic Publishers.

Treasure, J. & Holland, A. (1989) Genetic vulnerability to eating disorders: Evidence from twin and family studies. In H. Remschmidt & M.H. Schmidt (Eds), *Child and Youth Psychiatry: European Perspectives* (pp. 59–68). New York: Hogrefe & Huber.

Treasure, J.L. & Owen, J.B. (1997) Intriguing links between animal behaviour and anorexia nervosa. *Int. J. Eat. Disord.*, **21**, 307–311.

Vaisse, C., Clement, K., Guy-Grand, B. & Froguel, P. (1998) A frameshift mutation in human MC4R is associated with a dominant form of obesity. *Nat. Genet.*, **20**, 113–114.

Vaisse, C., Clement, K., Durand, E., Hercber, S., Guy-Grand, B. & Froguel, P. (2000) Melanocortin-4 receptor mutations are a frequent and heterogeneous cause of morbid obesity. *J. Clin. Invest.*, **106**, 253–262.

Wade, T.D., Bulik, C.M., Neale, M. & Kendler, K.S. (2000) Anorexia nervosa and major depression: Shared genetic and environmental risk factors. *Am. J. Psychiat.*, **157**, 469–471.

Wade, T.D., Neale, M.C., Lake, R.I.E. & Martin, N.G. (1999) A genetic analysis of the eating and attitiudes associated with bulimia nervosa: Dealing with the problem of ascertainment. *Behav. Genet.*, **29**, 1–10.

Wade, T.D., Martin, N. & Tiggerman, M. (1998) Genetic and environmental risk factors for the weight and shape concerns characteristic of bulimia nervosa. *Psychol. Med.*, **28**, 761–771.

Walters, E.E. & Kendler, K.S. (1995) Anorexia nervosa and anorexic-like syndromes in a population-based twin sample. *Am. J. Psychiat.*, **152**, 64–71.

Walters, E.E., Neale, M.C., Eaves, L.J., Heath, A.C., Kessler, R.C. & Kendler, K.S. (1992) Bulimia nervosa and major depression: A study of common genetic and environmental factors. *Psychol. Med.*, **22**, 617–622.

West, D.B., Goudey-Lefevre, J., York, B. & Truett, G.E. (1994) Dietary obesity linked to genetic loci on chromosomes 9 and 15 in a polygenic mouse model. *J. Clin. Invest.*, **94**, 1410–1416.

Wilson, B.D., Ollmann, M.M., Kang. L., Stoffel. M., Bell. G.I. & Barsh, G.S. (1995) Structure and function of ASP, the human homolog of the mouse agouti gene. *Hum. Mol. Genet.*, **4**, 223–230.

Yaswen, L., Diehl, N., Brennan, M.B. & Hochgeschwender, U. (1999) Obesity in the mouse model of proopiomelanocortin deficiency responds to peripheral melanocortin. *Nature Med.*, **5**, 1066–1070.

Yeo, G.S.H., Farooqi, I.S., Aminian, S., Halsall, D.J. & Stanhope, R.G. (1998) A frameshift mutation in MC4R associated with dominantly inherited human obesity. *Nat. Genet.*, **20**, 111–112.

Yuan, X., Yamada, K., Ishiyama-Shigemoto, S., Koyama, W. & Nonaka, K. (2000) Identification of polymorphic loci in the promoter region of the serotonin 5-HT2C receptor gene and their association with obesity and type II diabetes. *Diabetologia*, **43**, 373–376.

Zhang, Y., Proenca, R., Maffei, M., Barone, M., Leopold, L. & Friedman, J.M. (1994) Positional cloning of the mouse obese gene and its human homologue. *Nature*, **372**, 425–432.

Ziegler, A., Hebebrand, J., Gorg, T., Rosenkranz, K., Fichter, M., Herpertz-Dahlmann, B., Remschmidt, H. & Hinney, A. (1999) Further lack of association between the 5-HT$_{2a}$ gene promoter polymorphism and susceptibility to eating disorders and a meta-analysis pertaining to anorexia nervosa. *Mol. Psychiat.*, **4**, 410–412.

CHAPTER 4

Biology of Appetite and Weight Regulation

Frances Connan

Vincent Square Eating Disorders Clinic, London, UK

and

Sarah Stanley

Department of Metabolic Medicine, ICSMT, London, UK

INTRODUCTION

Understanding the basic science underpinning appetite and weight homeostasis is vital if we are to pose useful hypotheses and interpret findings appropriately in the study of eating disorders. Peripheral signals of energy homeostasis, such as leptin and insulin, modulate appetite and energy expenditure via complex orexigenic and anorexigenic neuroendocrine pathways of the hypothalamus. Here, information from higher centres, such as those governing motivation and reward, can be integrated before an appropriate response is elicited.

Anorexia nervosa is characterised by severe energy deficit that may reflect impairment of appetite. Studies implicate impaired hypothalamic function, rather than peripheral energy-signalling deficits. Neuroendocrine stress response and serotonergic systems may be particularly relevant.

Bulimia nervosa is characterised by periods of over-eating coupled with efforts to compensate in order to achieve lower weight. Reduced leptin signalling may enhance activity in orexigenic pathways such that there is a tendency to gain weight. Overweight in the context of low self-esteem and emotional dysregulation may increase the risk of engagement in weight reduction behaviours. Once established, these behaviours appear to maintain the disorder via effects upon mood, satiety and appetite.

Binge eating disorder is characterised by a tendency towards over-eating and excessive weight gain, in the absence of food restriction. Little is known about the biology of appetite in this group as yet. The reward value of food is high and it is likely that there is an imbalance between central orexigenic and anorexigenic pathways of the hypothalamus, favouring positive energy balance.

It is hoped that a better understanding of the abnormalities of appetite and weight regulation contributing to the aetiology of eating disorders will lead to improved treatment.

Handbook of Eating Disorders. Edited by J. Treasure, U. Schmidt and E. van Furth.
© 2003 John Wiley & Sons, Ltd.

THE BIOLOGY OF APPETITE AND WEIGHT HOMEOSTASIS

In most adult mammals, body weight and body fat remain remarkably constant in spite of great variation in the calories consumed from one meal to the next and in the amount of energy expended (Edholm, 1977). When measured over months, energy intake and energy expenditure are finely balanced. Active mechanisms are involved. Reduction in food intake results in weight loss and this is primarily body fat. But when food is freely available once more, intake increases and body weight returns to its previous point (Harris et al., 1986). Similarly, if food intake is massively increased, as is seen in some cultures, body weight and fat mass increase greatly. However, with a return to regular habits, body weight returns to normal (Pasquet & Apfelbaum, 1994). In addition to these changes in food intake, energy expenditure is also reduced or increased until body weight is restored. Thus, there is some evidence to suggest that body weight appears to be tightly regulated in most cases. However, Pinel et al. (2000) have argued that unpredictable food supplies have resulted in an evolutionary pressure to eat without limit when food is readily available. The disparity between the environment where these systems evolved and the modern day environment with unlimited resources may contribute to the over-eating seen in the developed world.

Although the control of appetite is complex, recent studies have identified that both peripheral and central signalling molecules are important in the regulation of body weight. Circulating inhibitory signals, produced in proportion to fat mass, act on the brain to reduce appetite (Kennedy, 1953). As weight is lost, the level of these signals falls and food intake increases until weight is restored. In addition, inhibitory signals are generated in response to an individual meal. These signals are satiety factors.

PERIPHERAL SIGNALS OF ENERGY HOMEOSTASIS

There are several circulating peptides that are putative markers of adiposity, and, of these, the pancreatic hormone, insulin, and the adipose tissue hormone, leptin, are the most extensively studied.

Leptin

The identification of leptin arose from examination of two obese mutant mice, *ob/ob* (Coleman, 1973) and *db/db* (Chua et al., 1996). Although originally described over 30 years ago, the nature of their defect was unclear until 1995 when the *ob* gene product was identified as leptin (Zhang et al., 1994). Leptin is a 16 kDa, 146 amino acid protein that is expressed and secreted from adipose tissue in most mammals, including humans. Circulating leptin concentrations are directly proportional to fat mass in both animals and man (Considine et al., 1996).

The leptin receptor gene encodes a single transmembrane receptor belonging to the class I cytokine receptor family (Tartaglia et al., 1995). Subsequent work revealed multiple variants of OB-R with variable C-terminal portions. The functioning form appears to have both a large extracellular domain and a long intracellular region, in contrast to the shorter intracellular domains of the non-functioning receptors. In the hypothalamus, the long, functioning leptin receptor predominates and is found in areas important in the regulation of body weight: the arcuate, ventromedial, paraventricular and dorsomedial nuclei (Elmquist et al., 1998). In particular, leptin receptors are present on neurons containing the neuro-transmitters neuropeptide Y (NPY)/Agouti-related peptide (AgRP) (Baskin et al., 1999a) and proopiomelanocortin (POMC)/cocaine and amphetamine-regulated transcript (CART) (Cheung et al., 1997). These peptides appear to play a fundamental role in the control of appetite.

The importance of leptin as a signal of fat mass is seen in the *ob/ob* and *db/db* mice. The *ob/ob* mice fail to secrete mature leptin (Zhang et al., 1994) while in the *db/db* mouse the leptin receptor is defective and these mice are resistant to leptin (Ghilardi et al., 1996; Lee et al., 1996). In the absence of leptin or leptin signalling, negative feedback is disrupted and there is no brake on food intake or up-regulation of energy expenditure (Hall et al., 1986). Thus both *ob/ob* and *db/db* mice are hyperphagic, obese and hypothermic. In the *ob/ob* mouse, the receptor is present and functional so exogenous leptin treatment completely reverses the syndrome, reducing food intake, increasing thermogenesis and reducing body weight (Pelleymounter et al., 1995). Leptin-deficient and -resistant humans have also been identified, although they are rare. Leptin-deficient children lack the negative feedback signal of increasing leptin as fat mass increases. They too are hyperphagic, massively obese and hyperinsulinaemia (Montague et al., 1997) and respond to exogenous leptin (Farooqi et al., 1999).

Since circulating leptin levels are correlated with fat mass, leptin falls dramatically in starvation. Many neuroendocrine and other abnormalities are seen in starvation: including suppression of the gonadal axis (Yu et al., 1997), somatotrophic axis (Sinha et al., 1975), thyroid axis and immune function (Lord et al., 1998) and stimulation of the hypothalamo–pituitary–adrenal axis. These changes are due, in part, to leptin deficiency. The genetic absence of leptin, as in the *ob/ob* mouse, is actually a model of low circulating leptin and thus starvation. Many of the abnormalities seen in these animals, and in humans with congenital leptin deficiency, are similar to those seen in starvation. If leptin is replaced in *ob/ob* animals then these abnormalities are reversed. Similarly, in normal animals, if the starvation-induced fall in leptin is prevented by exogenous replacement, these changes are blunted (Lord et al., 1998; Yu et al., 1997). Therefore, the adaptive responses to leptin deficiency appear to be as important as its role in the regulation of weight gain. Although circulating leptin levels are sensitive to changes in fat mass, they also vary with acute changes in caloric balance. Fasting results in a greater fall in leptin than might be expected for the change in fat mass and, conversely, food intake results in a post-prandial rise in circulating leptin (Weigle et al., 1997).

Insulin

Insulin was one of the first hormonal signals known to be secreted in proportion to adipose mass. Insulin receptors are present in the CNS, particularly in hypothalamic regions important in the control of appetite, such as the arcuate nucleus. Both insulin receptor mRNA and specific insulin binding sites are found in the arcuate (Werther et al., 1987).

Insulin appears to provide negative feedback on food intake. Chronic central infusion of insulin dose-dependently reduces daily food intake (Chavez et al., 1995; Foster et al., 1991). This effect is not immediate and is maximal only after 24 hours. Central administration of insulin not only reduces appetite but also activates brown fat thermogenesis and increases energy expenditure (Muller et al., 1997). Animals that are insulin deficient show marked hyperphagia and this effect is reversed by administration of insulin just into the CNS (Sipols et al., 1995). Anti-insulin antibodies given into the CNS result in increased appetite and weight gain in normal animals (Strubbe & Mein, 1977).

Peripheral signals are also involved in increasing food intake. One such signal is the recently identified peptide, ghrelin (Tschop et al., 2000). This 28 amino acid peptide was identified in 1999 having been purified from rat stomach and subsequently cloned in man. Ghrelin is the endogenous agonist of the growth hormone secretagogue receptor (GHS-R). Synthetic growth hormone secretagogues act to stimulate growth hormone, prolactin and ACTH release both at the hypothalamus and pituitary but, in addition, they have marked actions on food intake. Recent work has demonstrated that serum ghrelin concentrations increase with fasting and fall with re-feeding. Subcutaneous, intraperitoneal and intracerebroventricular injection of ghrelin increased food intake and body weight in rats and mice. Thus ghrelin may act as a peripheral signal to regulate energy homeostasis.

Peripheral Satiety Factors

While insulin and leptin may act as long-term regulators of energy balance, they appear to have little role in the initiation of a meal. The biological signals that are responsible for this are still little understood. In rodents, there is a small drop in blood glucose just prior to a meal. If feeding does not occur immediately, blood glucose returns to normal and a meal will occur after the next spontaneous fall in glucose. If such a decrease is produced experimentally, the animal will feed, but if the fall in glucose is prevented, feeding still continues as normal (Campfield & Smith, 1990).

The signals generated to limit a meal size have been much more extensively investigated. In addition to the neural signals from the stomach, duodenum and the liver, a number of peptides are secreted from the gastrointestinal tract. Stomach stretch receptor activation is important in limiting food intake but if the stomach size remains constant due to the presence of a fistula, feeding still ceases. This effect may be mediated by peptides released from the gastrointestinal tract to suppress feeding, and one of these is the duodenal peptide, cholecystokinin (CCK) (Houpt, 1982).

CCK activates CCK-A receptors on small unmyelinated vagal afferents which project to the brain stem (Reidelberger, 1994). Administration of CCK into the peritoneal cavity reduces food intake (Batt, 1983) and this action is abolished by vagotomy (Reidelberger, 1992). Rodents lacking CCK-A receptors are obese and do not respond to exogenous CCK (Takiguchi et al., 1997). Similarly, chronic administration of CCK antagonists also results in obesity (Meereis et al., 1998). CCK acts synergistically with leptin. A single dose of CCK, given into the abdominal cavity, potentiates the reduction in food intake seen after leptin (Barrachina et al., 1997; Emond et al., 1999). Thus CCK may play a role in the long-term regulation of body weight through its interaction with leptin. Conversely, leptin may act to potentiate the effects of CCK and other satiety signals.

A further candidate as a peripheral regulator of appetite in both man and animals is the GI peptide, glucagon-like peptide 1 (GLP-1). GLP-1 is a product of post-translational processing of pre-proglucagon in the intestinal L cells of the distal gut. Circulating GLP-1 increases in response to food (Hotamisligil et al., 1995). Central administration of GLP-1 potently reduces food intake in rodents (Turton et al., 1996) while peripheral administration of GLP-1 reduces food intake and meal duration (Rodriquez et al., 2000) and these effects occurred at plasma levels equivalent to those observed post-prandially.

It seems likely that further molecules derived from adipose tissue will be identified and found to play a role in the peripheral signalling of fat mass.

Hypothalamic Regulation

Peripheral signals of body fat mass, such as leptin and insulin, maintain body weight via activation of central circuits. Many neuropeptides have been shown to modulate appetite and body weight but for these peptides to play a physiological role they also need to be regulated by insulin and leptin. The hypothalamus appears to be the critical site for the action of these peripheral signals and, in particular, the arcuate nucleus, paraventricular nucleus and the lateral hypothalamus. Recent studies have proposed a model of first-order hypothalamic neurons in the arcuate nucleus, directly influenced by leptin and insulin, which then project to, and modulate, second-order neuronal pathways that in turn regulate energy homeostasis (Elias et al., 1998a; Schwartz et al., 2000).

The arcuate nucleus appears to play an essential role in the regulation of energy balance since destruction of the arcuate nucleus (ARC) produces obesity (Olney, 1969). This nucleus contains a high density of neurons that produce orexigenic peptides: neuropeptide Y (NPY) (Elias et al., 1999), the opioids dynorphin (Zamir et al., 1984) and β-endorphin (Merimee & Fineberg, 1976), galanin (Skofitsch & Jacobowitz, 1985), gamma amino butyric acid (Everitt et al., 1986; Melander et al., 1986), the endogenous antagonist of the central melanocortin receptors, agouti gene related peptide, AgRP (Elias et al., 1998a) and also the recently identified ghrelin. However, the anorectic peptides, alpha melanocyte stimulating hormone (α-MSH) (Mezey et al., 1985) and cocaine- and amphetamine-regulated transcript (CART) (Kristensen et al., 1998) are also found in arcuate neurons. Morphological evidence has demonstrated that NPY and AgRP are co-localised in a subpopulation of medial ARC neurons which then project to the PVN (Broberger et al., 1998). In the lateral ARC, α-MSH and CART are co-localised to neurons with a much wider pattern of projection (Elias et al., 1998b).

The ARC lies outside the blood brain barrier and is therefore ideally placed to respond to peripheral signals such as insulin, leptin and ghrelin. Both NPY/AgRP and α-MSH/CART neurons in the ARC express leptin receptors (Baskin et al., 1999b; Cheung et al., 1997). Food intake is reduced with microinjection of leptin into the ARC (Satoh et al., 1997) and if the arcuate nucleus is destroyed, there is no response to leptin (Dawson et al., 1997). Similarly, insulin receptors are present in the ARC (Werther et al., 1987) and insulin also inhibits the expression of NPY mRNA (Weigle et al. 1995). In addition, GHS-R, at which ghrelin acts, are expressed on arcuate NPY neurons.

Increases in circulating leptin due to increased fat mass have dual effects. Leptin stimulates the expression of POMC and CART mRNA (Broberger et al., 1998), peptides that reduce food intake, both directly and by a reduction in inhibitory GABA inputs (Cowley et al., 1999). In addition, leptin inhibits the expression of NPY and AgRP mRNA, potent stimulators of appetite (Schwartz et al., 1997; Vrang et al., 1999).

Conversely, in starvation, when circulating leptin levels are low, NPY/AgRP mRNA expression increases and these neurons are stimulated to increase the release of anabolic peptides that stimulate appetite. In addition, POMC/CART mRNA expression is reduced

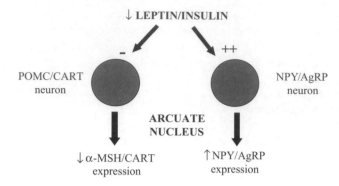

Figure 4.1 Role of the arcuate neurons in adiposity signalling. Decreasing leptin and insulin inhibits the POMC/CART anorexic pathway and stimulates the NPY/AgRP orexigenic pathway

(Vrang et al., 1999) and release of the catabolic peptides, α-MSH and CART, is reduced (see Figure 4.1).

The arcuate neurons project to a number of downstream pathways, second-order neurons, in the paraventricular nucleus (PVN) and lateral hypothalamus (LH) in particular.

The role of the PVN in the control of food intake has been extensively investigated. Destruction of the PVN results in weight gain while electrical stimulation decreases appetite (Weingarten et al., 1985). Almost all known orexigenic and anorectic signals, including leptin, injected into the PVN modulate appetite (Dube et al., 1999; Grandison & Guidotti, 1977; Kelly et al., 1979; Krahn et al., 1988; Kuru et al., 2000; Kyrkouli et al., 1990; Laorden et al., 2000; Li et al., 1994; Satoh et al., 1997; Stanley et al., 1985).

The projections from the ARC to the PVN are extensive and are rich in NPY and AgRP (Broberger et al., 1998). Fasting increases the release of NPY from the PVN (Chua et al., 1991a, 1991b; Kalra et al., 1991). Alpha-MSH and CART immunoreactive neurons also project from the ARC to the PVN (Dall et al., 2000). Electrophysiological studies have demonstrated that the NPY/AgRP and POMC/CART inputs from the arcuate nucleus are integrated in the PVN (Cowley et al., 1999). Interneurons expressing the inhibitory transmitter, GABA, are thought to mediate the actions of arcuate neurotransmitters on second-order effector neurons. These GABAergic neurons have both melanocortin and NPY receptors. When circulating leptin is low and NPY is released in the PVN, NPY receptors on the GABA interneurons are activated. These receptors inhibit adenylate cyclase activity and reduce intracellular cyclic AMP. This results in decreased activity of these inhibitory neurons and a decrease in the release of GABA. The inhibition mediated by GABA is reduced and feeding increases.

In contrast, activation of the melanocortin receptors by α-MSH stimulates adenylate cyclase activity and increases intracellular cAMP. The activity of the inhibitory neurons is thus increased and this activation can be blocked by the melanocortin antagonist, AgRP. However, the identity of the second-order neurons on which GABA acts remains unclear (see Figure 4.2).

A number of peptides present in the PVN are modulated by leptin. Corticotrophin-releasing hormone (CRH) neurons are in close contact with arcuate NPY immunoreactive fibres. In addition, CRH expression is regulated by peripheral leptin and central administration of CRH inhibits feeding (Brunetti et al., 2000). Similarly, thyrotrophin-releasing

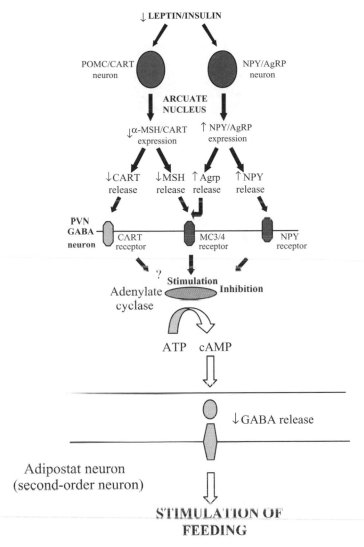

Figure 4.2 Model of neuronal response in the arcuate nucleus and PVN in response to circulating leptin and insulin

hormone (TRH) neurons are innervated by NPY (Legradi & Lechan 1999) and α-MSH immunoreactive fibres and leptin has been shown to increase TRH mRNA (Fekete et al., 2000; Nillni et al., 2000). Central injection of TRH suppresses appetite and reduces food intake (Jackson, 1982). If these are the effectors of the arcuate nucleus neurons, they should be stimulated by α-MSH and CART and inhibited by NPY. This remains to be shown.

The lateral hypothalamus (LH) receives inputs from the arcuate nucleus (Elias et al., 1998a). The LH expresses the orexigenic peptide, melanin-concentrating hormone (MCH). Central injection of MCH increases feeding (Rossi et al., 1997), MCH mRNA is increased by food restriction (Herve & Fellmann, 1997) and loss of MCH in the knockout mouse results in

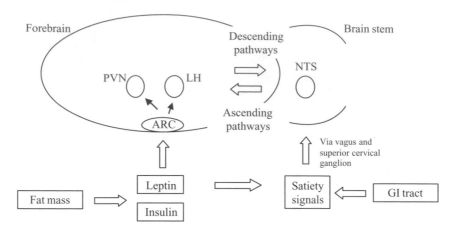

Figure 4.3 Schematic representation of pathways by which adipose and satiety signals interact with central pathways and the interaction between hypothalamic and brain stem pathways

low body weight (Shimada et al., 1998). Also, MCH signals via the SLC-1 receptor (Hervieu et al., 2000) and, similar to the NPY receptor, this reduces adenylate cyclase activity and intracellular cAMP. In addition, the LH neurons contain orexins. Orexin expression changes with fasting and orexin injection increases food intake (Sakurai et al., 1998). If these neurons are further downstream effectors of leptin and insulin signalling on the arcuate, one would expect CART and α-MSH to inhibit orexin and MCH neuronal activity and NPY to stimulate their signalling. This too remains to be demonstrated.

The short-term satiety signals, such as CCK, act via the nucleus of the solitary tract (NTS) in the brain stem rather than the hypothalamus. The NTS receives afferents from and projects to the hypothalamus, particularly the PVN. The NTS expresses POMC mRNA (Bronstein et al., 1992) and leptin receptors (Elias et al., 2000). In addition, the brain stem contains noradrenergic neurons (Simonian & Herbison, 1997) which project to the hypothalamus. Noradrenaline increases food intake (Wellman et al., 1993) and leptin inhibits the release of noradrenaline in the hypothalamus (Brunetti et al., 1999). Serotonin is also synthesised in the brain stem and serotonergic fibres project widely (Steinbusch & Nieuwenhuys, 1981). Compounds that increase 5HT receptor signalling suppress food intake (Leibowitz & Alexander, 1998) and $5HT_{2C}$ receptor knockout mice are hyperphagic and obese (Heisler et al., 1998). Leptin increases serotonin turnover (Calapai et al., 1999). Thus the brain stem might respond both to short-term satiety signals and to circulating signals such as leptin and insulin and in turn influence hypothalamic pathways via ascending fibres (see Figure 4.3).

MOTIVATION AND REWARD

The areas of the brain mediating reward and reinforcement have been mapped by intracranial stimulation and these studies have implicated areas within the limbic system, the septum and prefrontal cortex along with the catecholaminergic projections from the brain stem (Robbins & Everitt, 1996). In particular, work has focused on the ventral striatum and the nucleus accumbens (Pecina & Berridge, 2000).

Both the opioid system and the dopaminergic system have been implicated in mediating reward. Opioids increase food intake partly by increasing the reward aspects of food. Studies in animals have shown systemic or central injection of morphine to amplify the positive aspects of food while opioid antagonists cause sweet tastes to become less positive and bitter tastes to become more aversive (Pecina & Berridge, 2000). In humans, systemic administration of the opioid antagonist, naltrexone, decreases subjective ratings of food palatability (Yeomans & Gray, 1997). One area of the nucleus accumbens shell, the medial caudal subregion, appears to mediate much of the rewarding actions of opioids (Pecina & Berridge, 2000). There is also considerable evidence for a role of the dopaminergic system in the mediation of reward. The reinforcing effects of psychomotor stimulants are mediated by modulating dopamine availability in the ventral striatum (Volkow et al., 1997) and, in addition, natural reinforcers such as food also depend on dopamine release in this area (Robbins & Everitt, 1996). The rewarding effect of cocaine is diminished by systemic and intra-accumbens administration of dopamine antagonists (Romach et al., 1999).

Dopamine and opiates mediate different aspects of the reward circuits. Dopamine increases the appetitive or preparatory phases before eating, for example, the locomotor responses. Dopamine release in the ventral striatum is associated with the increase in lever operation in order to obtain food but falls when the animals start to consume the food (Berridge, 1996). In addition, dopamine release is enhanced by food deprivation and by novel food. In contrast, dopamine depleted rats will exert less behaviour to gain access to food. Opioids appear to increase the consummatory behaviour itself (Berridge, 1996).

Peripheral signals also appear to influence reward. Leptin acts to attenuate the reward produced by self-stimulation in some areas of the brain but to enhance these effects in other areas (Fulton et al., 2000). Thus leptin acts not only on the circuits influencing appetite and energy expenditure but also on the motivation to eat.

The regulation of appetite and energy balance is only now being unravelled. While much work has focused on investigation of obesity, these studies have extended knowledge of the physiological mechanisms regulating body weight. We are now better able than ever to explore and understand the pathophysiology of eating disorders.

DYSREGULATION OF APPETITE AND WEIGHT HOMEOSTASIS IN EATING DISORDERS

Anorexia Nervosa

Anorexia Nervosa and Appetite

Anorexia nervosa (AN) is clearly a disorder of under-eating, but the question of whether appetite is impaired remains controversial and poorly researched. Studies employing subjective assessment have consistently reported reduced hunger and desire to eat and enhanced satiety and sensation of fullness in people with AN (e.g. Halmi & Sunday, 1991; Robinson, 1989). Furthermore, the subjective reward value of food is reduced (Drewnowski et al., 1987; Sunday & Halmi, 1990), and the rate of eating is slow (Halmi & Sunday, 1991). Some authors argue that these findings reflect tight cognitive control of normal appetite

(Palmer, 2000). However, relative to healthy comparison women, those with AN show reduced salivation (LeGoff et al., 1988) and a heightened autonomic response to food (Leonard et al., 1998). Images of food elicit fear and disgust (Ellison et al., 1998). These objective data suggest that appetite may indeed be impaired in AN (Pinel et al., 2000), although some capacity to respond to hunger and satiety cues clearly remains (Cugini et al., 1998; Rolls et al., 1992).

A predisposition to leanness may be a risk factor for AN (Hebebrand & Remschmidt, 1995), supporting the notion that heritable risk for the disorder may be exerted through the biological systems regulating appetite and weight.

Peripheral Signals in AN

In acute AN, basal and fasting insulin and IGF-1 concentrations are reduced (e.g. Alderdice et al., 1985; Argente et al., 1997; de Rosa et al., 1983; Fukuda et al., 1999; Stoving et al., 1999a) while growth hormone (GH) (de Rosa et al., 1983; Stoving et al., 1999b) and cortisol concentrations are elevated (Stoving et al., 1999c for review). These findings are consistent with the need to promote gluconeogenesis in the starving state and resolve with weight gain (Casper et al., 1988; Casper, 1996; Golden et al., 1994), suggesting that they arise as an adaptive response to prolonged negative energy balance. Similarly, altered thyroid function in acute AN does not differ from that associated with malnutrition (de Rosa et al., 1983) and normalises with weight restoration (e.g. Komaki et al., 1992).

The endocrine response to a meal may be abnormal in AN. For example, the insulin response to a meal is delayed and reduced (Alderdice et al., 1985; Blickle et al., 1984). This may be attributable to delayed absorption and, in chronic cases, impaired pancreatic beta cell function (Nozaki et al., 1994). Insulin sensitivity appears to vary greatly between individuals with AN (Kiriike et al., 1990) and there may be a tendency towards increased glucose utilisation rather than storage (Franssila-Kallunki et al., 1991). Blunting of the glucose and insulin response to a meal persists even after full recovery from AN, when there is also evidence of an abnormal cortisol response to the meal (Ward et al., 1998). It remains unclear whether these findings reflect vulnerability factors for the disorder, or a scar of the illness.

Interestingly, the biology of restricting and binge–purge subtypes of AN may differ significantly. For example, relative to the binge–purge subtype, the restricting subtype is associated with higher basal and growth hormone-releasing hormone stimulated GH concentrations, lower basal IGF-1 (Brambilla et al., 2001) and elevated cortisol release (Connan et al., 2003a).

Enhanced satiety resulting from elevated basal and post-prandial CCK release (e.g. Brambilla et al., 1995a; Fujimoto et al., 1997) might contribute to the aetiology of AN. However, this finding has not been consistently replicated (e.g. Pirke et al., 1994) and, when present, resolves with partial weight gain (e.g. Tamai et al., 1993). Furthermore, the satiating effect of CCK may be reduced by the impairment of 5HT function associated with AN (Stallone et al., 1989). Pancreatic polypeptide release is elevated in response to a meal during the acute illness (Alderdice et al., 1985; Fujimoto et al., 1997) although the significance of this finding is unclear.

Although a wealth of studies have examined a possible role for leptin in the aetiology of AN, little evidence of functional abnormality has been unearthed. During the acute illness, leptin concentrations are low (Casanueva et al., 1997; Herpertz et al., 2000; Monteleone et al., 2000a) but proportional to BMI and fat mass (Ferron et al., 1997; Grinspoon et al., 1996; Monteleone et al., 2000a), except at extremely low weight (Casanueva et al., 1997; Pauly et al., 2000). The diurnal rhythm of leptin and its relationship with insulin and IGF-1 release are preserved, but the temporal relationship with cortisol is disrupted until weight is restored (Eckert et al., 1998; Herpertz et al., 1998, 2000).

Interestingly, there is a dissociation between BMI and leptin levels during weight gain (Hebebrand et al., 1997; Mantzoros et al., 1997) which could contribute to difficulty achieving full weight restoration with rapid refeeding. Similarly, leptin levels are elevated above that expected for BMI in those with the purging subtype of AN (Mehler et al., 1999). Elevation of the CSF : plasma leptin ratio in acute AN (Mantzoros et al., 1997) suggests that central levels may be relatively elevated, perhaps contributing to impairment of appetite. However, normalisation following full recovery from AN (Mantzoros et al., 1997) indicates that altered leptin dynamics are a state-related phenomena. In keeping with this hypothesis, leptin levels are predictive of amenorrhoea in eating-disordered patients (Kopp et al., 1997) and restoration of normal levels is necessary, but not sufficient, for restoration of menses (Audi et al., 1998).

Central Regulation of Appetite and Weight in AN

Far less is known about the central mechanisms regulating appetite and weight in AN. Data examining the role of hypothalamic peptides in the eating disorders are limited to estimations of plasma and CSF levels because of the inherent difficulty in measuring regional brain peptide activity in vivo.

In terms of orexigenic networks of the hypothalamus, NPY levels are elevated in the CSF of those with AN (Kaye et al., 1990), consistent with a reduced leptin signal from the periphery and an orexigenic response to starvation. Levels normalise with full recovery (Gendall et al., 1999; Kaye et al., 1990), at which time CSF polypeptide Y (PPY) levels are also reported normal (Gendall et al., 1999). The NPY Y5 receptor mediates the orexigenic effects of NPY (Schaffhauser et al., 1997) and there is no evidence for an association between receptor gene polymorphisms and AN (Rosenkranz et al., 1998). Galanin has been measured only in peripheral plasma, in which levels do not differ from normal (Baranowska et al., 1997). There are no data currently available regarding orexin, AgRP, MCH or ghrelin function in AN, but all are potential candidates for an aetiological role.

Plasma β-endorphin (β-EP) levels are reduced in acute AN (Baranowska et al., 1997). Circadian rhythmicity is lost and there is some evidence of disrupted regulation of POMC-derived peptide secretion (Brambilla et al., 1991). CSF levels appear to be reduced, but only in the most severely underweight patients (Kaye et al., 1987a). Although β-EP stimulates feeding, there is some evidence that infusion of an opioid antagonist improves weight gain during refeeding in AN (Moore et al., 1981). This may reflect blockade of central motivation and reward systems, or more direct effects on the hypothalamic regulation of feeding.

Again, little is known about the functional activity of anorexigenic peptides, such as MSH and CART, in AN. One recent study found elevated plasma CART concentrations in those with the acute disorder, and normal concentrations in women who had fully recovered (Sarah Stanley, personal communication). This finding must be interpreted with caution, because recent data suggests that CART may have orexigenic properties in at least some areas of the hypothalamus (Abbott et al., 2001).

Studies of HPA axis activity in AN suggest that an impairment of feedback inhibition at the level of the hypothalamus gives rise to elevated CRH activity. This is turn overrides feedback inhibition at the level of the pituitary, giving rise to the HPA axis hyperactivity associated with AN (Kaye et al., 1987b; Licinio et al., 1996). Elevated concentrations of CRH in the CSF (Kaye et al. 1987b) and blunting of the ACTH and β-EP responses to exogenous CRH (Brambilla et al., 1996; Hotta et al., 1986) are consistent with this hypothesis. Although HPA axis AVP activity is up-regulated in the context of chronic stress in animals and depression in humans, there is no evidence of elevated AVP activity in acute AN (Connan et al., 2003b, 2003c). This is significant because AVP modulates CRH release and sensitivity of the axis to feedback inhibition via altered glucocorticoid receptor activity (Felt et al., 1984; Plotsky et al., 1984). An abnormal HPA axis response to chronic stress may therefore contribute to persistently elevated CRH activity in AN. In addition to the inhibitory effect on appetite and feeding, elevated CRH activity has widespread behavioural and physiological effects, which include many of the features of AN, such as: increased locomotor activity; cardiovascular changes; reduced social and sexual behaviour; impaired sleep; and increased anxiety behaviours (Dunn & Berridge, 1990).

There is some evidence to suggest that a heightened cortisol response to stress and a blunted cortisol response to a meal may persist even after full recovery (Connan 2003a; Ward et al., 1998). Subtle abnormalities of HPA axis regulation might therefore contribute to susceptibility to AN.

Bulimia Nervosa

Disturbance of Appetite in Bulimia Nervosa

While the majority of those with bulimia nervosa (BN) are of normal weight, caloric restriction and compensatory behaviours are a core part of the phenomenology of the disorder and may be accompanied by milder biological changes of the type seen in AN. However, in contrast to AN, the subjective sense of satiety is reduced in BN (Kissileff et al., 1996), the salivary response to food presentation fails to habituate in BN (Wisniewski et al., 1997), and the prevalence of parental and premorbid obesity are elevated (Fairburn et al., 1997). These data suggest that a tendency to over-eat may be a vulnerability factor for BN.

Peripheral Signals in BN

Several factors may contribute to impaired satiety in BN. CCK release following a meal is reduced in BN (Devlin et al., 1997) and there is some evidence to support the hypothesis that a functional reduction of vagal signal transduction also contributes (Faris et al., 2000). Gastric emptying is delayed (Devlin et al., 1997) although pancreatic glucagon, insulin and glucose responses to a meal do not differ from normal (Johnson et al., 1994). However, binge-eating episodes are associated with relatively elevated insulin and cortisol responses (Kaye et al., 1989; Weltzin et al., 1991). Following purging, glucose and insulin levels fall rapidly (Johnson et al., 1994) and these fluctuations of insulin and glucose are likely to be a significant factor in promoting further binge eating.

The fall in leptin levels associated with fasting is blunted in those with BN (Monteleone et al., 2000b). Additionally, although plasma leptin levels are positively correlated with BMI (Monteleone et al., 2000a), leptin levels are lower than those of healthy comparison women, even after adjusting for low BMI (Brewerton et al., 2000; Jimerson et al., 2000; Monteleone et al., 2000a)—a finding that persists even after recovery (Jimerson et al., 2000). Duration of illness and severity of disorder are related to the reduced leptin levels in BN (Monteleone et al., 2000a). Among obese binge eaters, lower leptin levels are associated with greater dietary restraint (d'Amore et al., 2001) and restraint might similarly contribute to low leptin levels in those vulnerable to BN. These data suggest that while the body fat sensing function of leptin is intact, there is a tendency for a lower leptin secretion per fat mass and thus a higher settling point for weight in BN. A degree of restrained eating may therefore be necessary to maintain a healthy low weight in these individuals. The impaired capacity for the leptin system to respond to acute changes in energy intake could contribute to maintenance of disordered eating in BN.

Central Regulation of Appetite and Weight in BN

Milder variants of the HPA axis hyperactivity associated with AN may occur in BN (Coiro et al., 1992; Kennedy et al., 1989). In contrast to AN, relative to healthy comparison women, those with BN exhibit reduced cortisol and sympathetic nervous system (SNS) responses to mental stress (Laessle et al., 1992), suggesting that BN may be associated with stress hyporesponsivity.

Reduced levels of central β-ED in BN correlate with severity of depressive symptoms (Brewerton et al., 1992), but data regarding peripheral β-ED levels are highly inconsistent (Brambilla et al., 1995b; Fullerton et al., 1986; Waller et al., 1986). Opioid antagonists reduce binge–purge frequency in both BN and the binge–purge subtype of AN, consistent with an 'auto-addiction' model of the disorder (Jonas & Gold, 1986; Marrazzi et al., 1995a). This hypothesis is supported by the finding that in BN the reward value of food is high (Franko et al., 1994; LeGoff et al., 1988) and opioid antagonists reduce both the hedonic value and the amount of food consumed by women with BN, but not simple obesity (Drewnowski et al., 1995). These factors may be important in the aetiology of emotional precipitants to bingeing.

Following short-term abstinence from binge–purge behaviour, CSF levels of PYY and somatostatin are elevated relative to both acute BN and healthy controls (Kaye et al., 1988, 1990). A relative excess activity in the orexigenic pathways of the hypothalamus might therefore be stimulating over-eating in BN. However, levels of both PYY and NPY in CSF are normal after full recovery, suggesting that this is unlikely to be a trait phenomenon (Gendall et al., 1999).

BED AND OBESITY

At the opposite end of the eating and weight spectrum from AN, binge eating disorder (BED) is associated with obesity and over-eating, in the absence of behaviours to compensate. The biology of BED is therefore likely to overlap with that of BN, but in the absence of the biological consequences of food restriction.

The little available data examining biological contributions to dysregulated appetite and weight in obese binge eaters can be summarised as follows. This group do not differ from obese non-binge eaters in terms of resting energy expenditure, body composition, serum lipids, insulin and thyroid hormones (Adami et al., 1995; Wadden et al., 1993).

Cephalic phase plasma insulin, free fatty acid and glucose levels also do not differ with respect to binge eating in obesity (Karhunen et al., 1997). While the salivary response to food exposure is reduced, those with BED experience a greater subjective desire to eat than women with simple obesity when presented with food (Karhunen et al., 1997). As in BN, opioid antagonists ameliorate binge eating in BED (Marrazzi et al., 1995b). Binge eating may therefore be driven more by emotional cues than hunger in BED. Leptin levels are elevated and proportional to BMI in women with BED (Monteleone et al., 2000a), but it remains to be seen whether leptin levels differ between obese binge and non-binge eaters after adjustment for BMI.

Thus, as in BN, the reward value of food is high and there is a tendency to obesity which might be hypothesised to arise from above-average appetite. Emotional regulation also appears to be an important aetiological factor. Studies examining satiating factors and physiological responses to food in BED, relative to both non-purging BN and simple obesity, will be important in furthering understanding of each of these disorders.

CONCLUSIONS

On the whole, peripheral energy balance and satiety signals appear to function normally given the state of under-nutrition in acute AN. However, enhanced CCK satiety signalling and elevated central leptin concentrations might play a role in maintenance of the disorder, while elevated leptin for BMI during rapid refeeding may contribute to difficulty restoring weight. Subtle abnormalities of the insulin and cortisol response to a meal following recovery could reflect residual damage to gastrointestinal function, or a vulnerability factor for the disorder. Imbalance between the orexigenic and anorexigenic pathways of the hypothalamus may therefore be implicated in the appetite disturbance of AN. An aberrant HPA axis response to chronic stress, characterised by persistently elevated CRH activity, may be one factor that contributes to the pathophysiology of AN. However, it is likely that other neuropeptide and neurotransmitter systems also play an important role. Indeed, the serotonin system may be particularly relevant in this regard because of the well-recognised effects on appetite (Blundell, 1986; Dourish et al., 1986) and reciprocal regulatory interactions with the HPA axis (Dinan, 1996; Grignaschi et al., 1996; Lowry et al., 2000). This underpins some of the response to treatment. Preliminary evidence suggests that olanzepine, which acts on the serotonin system at multiple sites, may improve weight gain during refeeding in AN (Hanson, 1999; La Via et al., 2000; Mehler et al., 2000) and that fluoxetine may prevent relapse after weight restoration (Kaye et al., 2001).

In BN, a tendency to overweight may arise from a variety of constitutional factors, including reduced leptin signalling from stored body fat. Overweight in the context of low self-esteem and emotional dysregulation (see Chapter 9, by Serpell & Troop) increases the risk of engaging in weight reduction behaviours. Once initiated, food restriction gives rise to both hunger and dysphoric mood (see Chapter 5 by deZwaan), which are key triggers for binge eating. Reduced satiety signalling from peripheral factors such as CCK, leptin and the vagal nerve may impair the capacity to terminate binges, but there is no evidence currently to suggest that these are primary problems. Similarly, altered insulin and glucose dynamics appear to be secondary to disordered eating, but nevertheless may play an important role in perpetuating binge–purge behaviour. At the central level, overactivity of orexigenic pathways in acute BN is in keeping with low leptin levels relative to body mass. However, other factors may contribute because orexigenic peptide levels in CSF return to normal after recovery, despite persistence of low leptin levels. The high reward value of food for those with BN may also be secondary to chronic food restriction and low leptin levels, and could serve to both establish and reinforce binge eating as a strategy for emotional regulation.

Understanding the biological components of appetite and weight regulation is vital if we are to develop better aetiological and treatment models for eating disorders. Functional neuroimaging, neuroendocrine and candidate gene studies will help to further elucidate the central mechanisms maintaining low appetite and weight in AN, and the drive to overeat in BN and BED. However, emerging differences in the biology of restricting and binge–purge subtypes of AN highlight the need for good phenotypic description of study participants, and a consensus definition of diagnostic subtypes, stage of illness and recovery for future research.

Peptides that provoke potent and long-lasting increases in appetite and ultimately in body weight have already been identified. For example, both neuropeptide Y and AgRP stimulate food intake and promote fat storage—effects that are undiminished after seven days' treatment. Orexigenic peptide analogues and CRH antagonists may prove fruitful therapeutic options for the treatment of AN. Safe and effective anti-obesity drugs that target central orexigenic pathways are likely to proliferate in the future, providing potentially useful treatments for BN and BED.

REFERENCES

Abbott, C.R., Rossi, M., Wren, A.M., Murphy, K.G., Kennedy, A.R., Stanley, S.A., Zollner, A.N., Morgan, I., Ghatel, M.A., Small, C.J. & Bloom, S.R. (2001) Evidence of an orexigenic role for cocaine- and amphetamine-regulated transcript (CART) following administration into discrete hypothalamic nuclei.

Adami, G.F., Gandolfo, P., Campostano, A., Cocchi, F., Bauer, B. & Scopinaro, N. (1995) Obese binge eaters: Metabolic characteristics, energy expenditure and dieting. *Psychol. Med.*, **25** (1), 195–198.

Alderdice, J.T., Dinsmore, W.W., Buchanan, K.D. & Adams, C. (1985) Gastrointestinal hormones in anorexia nervosa. *J. Psychiat. Res.*, **19** (2–3), 207–213.

Argente, J., Caballo, N., Barrios, V., Munoz, M.T., Pozo, J., Chowen, J.A., Morande, G. & Hernandez, M. (1997) Multiple endocrine abnormalities of the growth hormone and insulin like growth factor axis in patients with anorexia nervosa: Effect of short- and long-term weight recuperation. *J. Clin. Endocrinol. Metab.*, **82** (7), 2084–2092.

Audi, L., Mantzoros, C.S., Vidal-Puig, A., Vargas, D., Gussinye, M. & Carrascosa, A. (1998) Leptin in relation to resumption of menses in women with anorexia nervosa [see comments]. *Mol. Psychiat.*, **3** (6), 544–547.

Baranowska, B., Wasilewska-Dziubinska, E., Radzikowska, M., Plonowski, A. & Roguski, K. (1997) Neuropeptide Y, galanin, and leptin release in obese women and in women with anorexia nervosa. *Metabolism*, **46** (12), 1384–1389.

Barrachina, M.D., Martinez, V., Wang, L., Wei, J.Y. & Tache, Y. (1997) Synergistic interaction between leptin and cholecystokinin to reduce short-term food intake in lean mice. *Proc. Natl. Acad. Sci. USA*, **94** (19), 10455–10460.

Baskin, D.G., Breininger, J.F. & Schwartz, M.W. (1999a) Leptin receptor mRNA identifies a subpopulation of neuropeptide Y neurons activated by fasting in rat hypothalamus. *Diabetes*, **48** (4), 828–833.

Baskin, D.G., Hahn, T.M. & Schwartz, M.W. (1999b) Leptin sensitive neurons in the hypothalamus. *Horm. Metab. Res.*, **31** (5), 345–350.

Batt, R.A. (1983) Decreased food intake in response to cholecystokinin (pancreozymin) in wild-type and obese mice (genotype ob/ob). *Int. J. Obes.*, **7** (1), 25–29.

Berridge, K.C. (1996) Food reward: Brain substrates of wanting and liking. *Neurosci. Biobehav. Rev.*, **20** (1), 1–25.

Blickle, J.F., Reville, P., Stephan, F., Meyer, P., Demangeat, C. & Sapin, R. (1984) The role of insulin, glucagon and growth hormone in the regulation of plasma glucose and free fatty acid levels in anorexia nervosa. *Horm. Metab. Res.*, **16** (7), 336–340.

Blundell, J.E. (1986) Serotonin manipulations and the structure of feeding behaviour. *Appetite*, **7** (Suppl), 39–56.

Brambilla, F., Bellodi, L., Arancio, C., Ronchi, P. & Limonta, D. (2001) Central dopaminergic function in anorexia and bulimia nervosa: A psychoneuroendocrine approach. *Psychoneuroendocrinology*, **26** (4), 393–409.

Brambilla, F., Ferrari, E., Brunetta, M., Peirone, A., Draisci, A., Sacerdote, P. & Panerai, A. (1996) Immunoendocrine aspects of anorexia nervosa. *Psychiat. Res.*, **62** (1), 97–104.

Brambilla, F., Brunetta, M., Peirone, A., Perna, G., Sacerdote, P., Manfredi, B. & Panerai, A.E. (1995a) T-lymphocyte cholecystokinin-8 and beta-endorphin concentrations in eating disorders: I. Anorexia nervosa. *Psychiat. Res.*, **59** (1–2), 43–50.

Brambilla, F., Brunetta, M., Draisci, A., Peirone, A., Perna, G., Sacerdote, P., Manfredi, B. & Panerai, A.E. (1995b) T-lymphocyte concentrations of cholecystokinin-8 and beta-endorphin in eating disorders: II. Bulimia nervosa. *Psychiat. Res.*, **59** (1–2), 51–56.

Brambilla, F., Ferrari, E., Petraglia, F., Facchinetti, F., Catalano, M. & Genazzani, A.R. (1991) Peripheral opioid secretory pattern in anorexia nervosa. *Psychiat. Res.*, **39** (2), 115–127.

Brewerton, T.D., Lesem, M.D., Kennedy, A. & Garvey, W.T. (2000) Reduced plasma leptin concentrations in bulimia nervosa. *Psychoneuroendocrinology*, **25** (7), 649–658.

Brewerton, T.D., Lydiard, R.B., Laraia, M.T., Shook, J.E. & Ballenger, J.C. (1992) CSF beta-endorphin and dynorphin in bulimia nervosa. *Am. J. Psychiat.*, **149** (8), 1086–1090.

Broberger, C., Johansen, J., Johansson, C., Schalling, M. & Hokfelt, T. (1998) The neuropeptide Y/agouti gene-related protein (AGRP) brain circuitry in normal, anorectic, and monosodium glutamate-treated mice. *Proc. Natl. Acad. Sci. USA*, **95** (25), 15043–15048.

Bronstein, D.M., Schafer, M.K., Watson, S.J. & Akil, H. (1992) Evidence that beta-endorphin is synthesized in cells in the nucleus tractus solitarius: Detection of POMC mRNA. *Brain Res.*, **587** (2), 269–275.

Brunetti, L., Orlando, G., Michelotto, B., Recinella, L. & Vacca, M. (2000) Cocaine- and Amphetamine-regulated transcript (CART) peptide (55-102) inhibits hypothalamic dopamine release. *82nd Annual Meeting of American Endocrine Society*.

Brunetti, L., Michelotto, B., Orlando, G. & Vacca, M. (1999) Leptin inhibits norepinephrine and dopamine release from rat hypothalamic neuronal endings. *Eur. J. Pharmacol.*, **372** (3), 237–240.

Calapai, G., Corica, F., Corsonello, A., Sautebin, L., Di Rosa, M., Campo, G.M., Buemi, M., Mauro, V.N. & Caputi, A.P. (1999) Leptin increases serotonin turnover by inhibition of brain nitric oxide synthesis. *J. Clin. Invest.*, **104** (7), 975–982.

Campfield, L.A. & Smith, F.J. (1990) Transient declines in blood glucose signal meal initiation. *Int. J. Obes.*, **14** (Suppl. 3), 15–31.

Casanueva, F.F., Dieguez, C., Popovic, V., Peino, R., Considine, R.V. & Caro, J.F. (1997) Serum immunoreactive leptin concentrations in patients with anorexia nervosa before and after partial weight recovery. *Biochem. Mol. Med.*, **60** (2), 116–120.

Casper, R.C. (1996) Carbohydrate metabolism and its regulatory hormones in anorexia nervosa. *Psychiat. Res.*, **62** (1), 85–96.

Casper, R.C., Pandey, G., Jaspan, J.B. & Rubenstein, A.H. (1988) Eating attitudes and glucose tolerance in anorexia nervosa patients at 8-year followup compared to control subjects. *Psychiat. Res.*, **25** (3), 283–299.

Chavez, M., Kaiyala, K., Madden, L.J., Schwartz, M.W. & Woods, S.C. (1995) Intraventricular insulin and the level of maintained body weight in rats. *Behav. Neurosci*, **109** (3), 528–531.

Cheung, C.C., Clifton, D.K. & Steiner, R.A. (1997) Proopiomelanocortin neurons are direct targets for leptin in the hypothalamus. *Endocrinology*, **138** (10), 4489–4492.

Chua-SC, J., Chung, W.K., Wu, P., X, Zhang, Y., Liu, S.M., Tartaglia, L. & Leibel, R.L. (1996) Phenotypes of mouse diabetes and rat fatty due to mutations in the OB (leptin) receptor [see comments]. *Science*, **271** (5251), 994–996.

Chua-SC, J., Brown, A.W., Kim, J., Hennessey, K.L., Leibel, R.L. & Hirsch, J. (1991a) Food deprivation and hypothalamic neuropeptide gene expression: effects of strain background and the diabetes mutation. *Brain Res. Mol. Brain Res.*, **11** (3–4), 291–299.

Chua-SC, J., Leibel, R.L. & Hirsch, J. (1991b) Food deprivation and age modulate neuropeptide gene expression in the murine hypothalamus and adrenal gland. *Brain Res. Mol. Brain Res.*, **9** (1–2), 95–101.

Coiro, V., Volpi, R., Marchesi, C., Capretti, L., Speroni, G., Rossi, G., Caffarri, G., De Ferri, A., Marcato, A. & Chiodera, P. (1992) Abnormal growth hormone and cortisol, but not thyroid-stimulating hormone, responses to an intravenous glucose tolerance test in normal- weight, bulimic women. *Psychoneuroendocrinology*, **17** (6), 639–645.

Coleman, D.L. (1973) Effects of parabiosis of obese with diabetes and normal mice. *Diabetologia*, **9** (4), 294–298.

Connan, F., Campbell, I.C., Lightman, S.L., Landau, S., Wheeler, M. & Treasure, J. (2003a) Hyper-cortisolaemia in anorexia nervosa. Submitted.

Connan, F., Campbell, I.C., Lightman, S.L., Landau, S., Wheeler, M. & Treasure, J. (2003b) The combined dexamethasone/corticotrophin releasing hormone challenge test in anorexia nervosa. Submitted.

Connan, F., Campbell, I.C., Lightman, S.L., Landau, S., Wheeler, M. & Treasure, J. (2003c) An arginine vasopressin challenge test in anorexia nervosa. Submitted.

Considine, R.V., Sinha, M.K., Heiman, M.L., Kriauciunas, A., Stephens, T.W., Nyce, M.R., Ohannesian, J.P., Marco, C.C., McKee, L.J., Bauer, T.L. et al. (1996) Serum immunoreactive-leptin concentrations in normal-weight and obese humans [see comments]. *N. Engl. J. Med.*, **334** (5), 292–295.

Cowley, M.A., Pronchuk, N., Fan, W., Dinulescu, D.M., Colmers, W.F. & Cone, R.D. (1999) Integration of NPY, AGRP, and melanocortin signals in the hypothalamic paraventricular nucleus: Evidence of a cellular basis for the adipostat. *Neuron*, **24** (1), 155–163.

Cugini, P., Ventura, M., Ceccotti, P., Cilli, M., Marciano, F., Salandri, A., Di Marzo, A., Fontana, S., Pellegrino, A.M., Vacca, K. & Di Siena, G. (1998) Hunger sensation: a chronobiometric approach to its within-day and intra-day recursivity in anorexia nervosa restricting type. *Eat. Weight. Disord.*, **3** (3), 115–123.

d'Amore, A., Massignan, C., Montera, P., Moles, A., De Lorenzo, A. & Scucchi, S. (2001) Relationship between dietary restraint, binge eating, and leptin in obese women. *Int. J. Obes. Relat. Metab. Disord.*, **25** (3), 373–377.

Dall, V.S., Lambert, P.D., Couceyro, P.C., Kuhar, M.J. & Smith, Y. (2000) CART peptide immunoreactivity in the hypothalamus and pituitary in monkeys: Analysis of ultrastructural features and synaptic connections in the paraventricular nucleus. *J. Comp. Neurol.*, **416** (3), 291–308.

Dawson, R., Pelleymounter, M.A., Millard, W.J., Liu, S. & Eppler, B. (1997) Attenuation of leptin-mediated effects by monosodium glutamate-induced arcuate nucleus damage. *Am. J. Physiol.*, **273** (1), E202–E206.

de Rosa, G., Corsello, S.M., de Rosa, E., Della, C.S., Ruffilli, M.P., Grasso, P. & Pasargiklian, E. (1983) Endocrine study of anorexia nervosa. *Exp. Clin. Endocrinol.*, **82** (2), 160–172.

Devlin, M.J., Walsh, B.T., Guss, J.L., Kissileff, H.R., Liddle, R.A. & Petkova, E. (1997) Postprandial cholecystokinin release and gastric emptying in patients with bulimia nervosa. *Am. J. Clin. Nutr.*, **65** (1), 114–120.

Dinan, T.G. (1996) Serotonin and the regulation of hypothalamic-pituitary-adrenal axis function *Life Sci.*, **58** (20), 1683–1694.

Dourish, C.T., Hutson, P.H., Kennett, G.A. & Curzon, G. (1986) 8-OH-DPAT-induced hyperphagia: Its neural basis and possible therapeutic relevance. *Appetite*, **7** (suppl.), 127–140.

Drewnowski, A., Krahn, D.D., Demitrack, M.A., Nairn, K. & Gosnell, B.A. (1995) Naloxone, an opiate blocker, reduces the consumption of sweet high-fat foods in obese and lean female binge eaters. *Am. J. Clin. Nutr.*, **61** (6), 1206–1212.

Drewnowski, A., Halmi, K.A., Pierce, B., Gibbs, J. & Smith, G.P. (1987) Taste and eating disorders. *Am. J. Clin. Nutr.*, **46** (3), 442–450.

Dube, M.G., Kalra, S.P. & Kalra, P.S. (1999) Food intake elicited by central administration of orexins/hypocretins: identification of hypothalamic sites of action. *Brain Res.*, **842** (2), 473–477.

Dunn, A.J. & Berridge, C. W. (1990) Physiological and behavioral responses to corticotropin-releasing factor administration: Is CRF a mediator of anxiety or stress responses? *Brain Res. Rev.*, **15** (2), 71–100.

Eckert, E.D., Pomeroy, C., Raymond, N., Kohler, P.F., Thuras, P. & Bowers, C.Y. (1998) Leptin in anorexia nervosa [see comments]. *J. Clin. Endocrinol. Metab.*, **83** (3), 791–795.

Edholm, O.G. (1977) Energy balance in man studies carried out by the Division of Human Physiology, National Institute for Medical Research. *J. Hum. Nutr.*, **31** (6), 413–431.

Elias, C.F., Kelly, J.F., Lee, C.E., Ahima, R.S., Drucker, D.J., Saper, C.B. & Elmquist, J.K. (2000) Chemical characterization of leptin-activated neurons in the rat brain. *J. Comp. Neurol.*, **423** (2), 261–281.

Elias, C.F., Aschkenasi, C., Lee, C., Kelly, J., Ahima, R.S., Bjorbaek, C., Flier, J.S., Saper, C.B. & Elmquist, J.K. (1999) Leptin differentially regulates NPY and POMC neurons projecting to the lateral hypothalamic area. *Neuron*, **23** (4), 775–786.

Elias, C.F., Saper, C.B., Maratos, F.E., Tritos, N.A., Lee, C., Kelly, J., Tatro, J.B., Hoffman, G.E., Ollmann, M.M., Barsh, G.S., Sakurai, T., Yanagisawa, M. & Elmquist, J.K. (1998a) Chemically defined projections linking the mediobasal hypothalamus and the lateral hypothalamic area. *J. Comp. Neurol.*, **402**, (4), 442–459.

Elias, C.F., Lee, C., Kelly, J., Aschkenasi, C., Ahima, R.S., Couceyro, P.R., Kuhar, M.J., Saper, C.B. & Elmquist, J.K. (1998b) Leptin activates hypothalamic CART neurons projecting to the spinal cord. *Neuron*, **21** (6), 1375–1385.

Ellison, Z., Foong, J., Howard, R., Bullmore, E., Williams, S. & Treasure, J. (1998) Functional anatomy of calorie fear in anorexia nervosa [letter]. *Lancet*, **352** (9135), 1192.

Elmquist, J.K., Bjorbaek, C., Ahima, R.S., Flier, J.S. & Saper, C.B. (1998) Distributions of leptin receptor mRNA isoforms in the rat brain. *J. Comp. Neurol.*, **395** (4), 535–547.

Emond, M., Schwartz, G.J., Ladenheim, E.E. & Moran, T.H. (1999) Central leptin modulates behavioral and neural responsivity to CCK. *Am. J. Physiol.*, **276** (5), R1545–R1549.

Everitt, B.J., Meister, B., Hokfelt, T., Melander, T., Terenius, L., Rokaeus, A., Theodorsson, N.E., Dockray, G., Edwardson, J., Cuello, C., et al. (1986) The hypothalamic arcuate nucleus-median eminence complex: Immunohistochemistry of transmitters, peptides and DARPP-32 with special reference to coexistence in dopamine neurons. *Brain Res.*, **396** (2), 97–155.

Fairburn, C.G., Welch, S.L., Doll, H.A., Davies, B.A. & O'Connor, M.E. (1997) Risk factors for bulimia nervosa. A community-based case-control study. *Arch. Gen. Psychiatry*, **54** (6), 509–517.

Faris, P.L., Kim, S.W., Meller, W.H., Goodale, R.L., Oakman, S.A., Hofbauer, R.D., Marshall, A.M., Daughters, R.S., Banerjee-Stevens, D., Eckert, E.D. & Hartman, B.K. (2000) Effect of decreasing afferent vagal activity with ondansetron on symptoms of bulimia nervosa: A randomised, double-blind trial. *Lancet*, **355** (9206), 792–797.

Farooqi, I.S., Jebb, S.A., Langmack, G., Lawrence, E., Cheetham, C.H., Prentice, A.M., Hughes, I.A., McCamish, M.A. & O'Rahilly, S. (1999) Effects of recombinant leptin therapy in a child with congenital leptin deficiency [see comments]. *N. Engl. J. Med.*, **341** (12), 879–884.

Fekete, C., Legradi, G., Mihaly, E., Huang, Q.H., Tatro, J.B., Rand, W.M., Emerson, C.H. & Lechan, R.M. (2000) Alpha-melanocyte-stimulating hormone is contained in nerve terminals innervating thyrotropin-releasing hormone-synthesizing neurons in the hypothalamic paraventricular nucleus and prevents fasting-induced suppression of prothyrotropin-releasing hormone gene expression. *J. Neurosci*, **20** (4), 1550–1558.

Felt, B.T., Sapolsky, R.M. & McEwen, B.S. (1984) Regulation of hippocampal corticosterone receptors by a vasopressin analogue. *Peptides*, **5** (6), 1225–1227.

Ferron, F., Considine, R.V., Peino, R., Lado, I.G., Dieguez, C. & Casanueva, F.F. (1997) Serum leptin concentrations in patients with anorexia nervosa, bulimia nervosa and non-specific eating disorders correlate with the body mass index but are independent of the respective disease. *Clin. Endocrinol. (Oxf)*, **46** (3), 289–293.

Foster, L.A., Ames, N.K. & Emery, R.S. (1991) Food intake and serum insulin responses to intraventricular infusions of insulin and IGF-I. *Physiol. Behav.*, **50** (4), 745–749.

Franko, D.L., Wolfe, B.E. & Jimerson, D.C. (1994) Elevated sweet taste pleasantness ratings in bulimia nervosa. *Physiol. Behav.*, **56** (5), 969–973.

Franssila-Kallunki, A., Rissanen, A., Ekstrand, A., Eriksson, J., Saloranta, C., Widen, E., Schalin-Jantti, C. & Groop, L. (1991) Fuel metabolism in anorexia nervosa and simple obesity. *Metabolism*, **40** (7), 689–694.

Fujimoto, S., Inui, A., Kiyota, N., Seki, W., Koide, K., Takamiya, S., Uemoto, M., Nakajima, Y., Baba, S. & Kasuga, M. (1997) Increased cholecystokinin and pancreatic polypeptide responses to a fat-rich meal in patients with restrictive but not bulimic anorexia nervosa. *Biol. Psychiat.*, **41** (10), 1068–1070.

Fukuda, I., Hotta, M., Hizuka, N., Takano, K., Ishikawa, Y., Asakawa-Yasumoto, K., Tagami, E. & Demura, H. (1999) Decreased serum levels of acid-labile subunit in patients with anorexia nervosa. *J. Clin. Endocrinol. Metab.*, **84** (6), 2034–2036.

Fullerton, D.T., Swift, W.J., Getto, C.J. & Carlson, I.H. (1986) Plasma immunoreactive beta-endorphin in bulimics. *Psychol. Med.*, **16** (1), 59–63.

Fulton, S., Woodside, B. & Shizgal, P. (2000) Modulation of brain reward circuitry by leptin. *Science*, **287** (5450), 125–128.

Gendall, K.A., Kaye, W.H., Altemus, M., McConaha, C.W. & La Via, M.C. (1999) Leptin, neuropeptide Y, and peptide Y Y in long-term recovered eating disorder patients. *Biol. Psychiat.*, **46** (2), 292–299.

Ghilardi, N., Ziegler, S., Wiestner, A., Stoffel, R., Heim, M.H. & Skoda, R.C. (1996) Defective STAT signaling by the leptin receptor in diabetic mice. *Proc. Natl. Acad. Sci. USA*, **93** (13), 6231–6235.

Golden, N.H., Kreitzer, P., Jacobson, M.S., Chasalow, F.I., Schebendach, J., Freedman, S.M. & Shenker, I.R. (1994) Disturbances in growth hormone secretion and action in adolescents with anorexia nervosa. *J. Pediatr.*, **125** (4), 655–660.

Grandison, L. & Guidotti, A. (1977) Stimulation of food intake by muscimol and beta endorphin. *Neuropharmacology*, **16** (7–8), 533–536.

Grignaschi, G., Sironi, F. & Samanin, R. (1996) Stimulation of 5-HT2A receptors in the paraventricular hypothalamus attenuates neuropeptide Y-induced hyperphagia through activation of corticotropin releasing factor. *Brain Res.*, **708**, (1–2), 173–176.

Grinspoon, S., Gulick, T., Askari, H., Landt, M., Lee, K., Anderson, E., Ma, Z., Vignati, L., Bowsher, R., Herzog, D. & Klibanski, A. (1996) Serum leptin levels in women with anorexia nervosa. *J. Clin. Endocrinol. Metab.*, **81** (11), 3861–3863.

Hall, A., Leibrich, J., Walkey, F.H. & Welch, G. (1986) Investigation of 'weight pathology' of 58 mothers of anorexia nervosa patients and 204 mothers of schoolgirls. *Psychol. Med.*, **16** (1), 71–76.

Halmi, K.A. & Sunday, S. R. (1991) Temporal patterns of hunger and fullness ratings and related cognitions in anorexia and bulimia. *Appetite*, **16** (3), 219–237.

Hanson, L. (1999) Olanzepine in the treatment of anorexia nervosa (letter). *Br. J. Psychiat.*, **175** (592).

Harris, R.B., Kasser, T.R. & Martin, R.J. (1986) Dynamics of recovery of body composition after overfeeding, food restriction or starvation of mature female rats. *J. Nutr.*, **116** (12), 2536–2546.

Hebebrand, J., Blum, W.F., Barth, N., Coners, H., Englaro, P., Juul, A., Ziegler, A., Warnke, A., Rascher, W. & Remschmidt, H. (1997) Leptin levels in patients with anorexia nervosa are reduced in the acute stage and elevated upon short-term weight restoration [see comments]. *Mol. Psychiat.*, **2** (4), 330–334.

Hebebrand, J. & Remschmidt, H. (1995) Anorexia nervosa viewed as an extreme weight condition: genetic implications. *Hum. Genet.*, **95** (1), 1–11.

Heisler, L.K., Chu, H.M. & Tecott, L.H. (1998) Epilepsy and obesity in serotonin 5-HT2C receptor mutant mice", *Ann. NY Acad. Sci.*, **861**, 74–78.

Herpertz, S., Albers, N., Wagner, R., Pelz, B., Kopp, W., Mann, K., Blum, W.F., Senf, W. & Hebebrand, J. (2000) Longitudinal changes of circadian leptin, insulin and cortisol plasma levels and their correlation during refeeding in patients with anorexia nervosa. *Eur. J. Endocrinol.*, **142** (4), 373–379.

Herpertz, S., Wagner, R., Albers, N., Blum, W.F., Pelz, B., Langkafel, M., Kopp, W., Henning, A., Oberste-Berghaus, C., Mann, K., Senf, W. & Hebebrand, J. (1998) Circadian plasma leptin levels in patients with anorexia nervosa: Relation to insulin and cortisol. *Horm. Res.*, **50** (4), 197–204.

Herve, C. & Fellmann, D. (1997) Changes in rat melanin-concentrating hormone and dynorphin messenger ribonucleic acids induced by food deprivation. *Neuropeptides*, **31** (3), 237–242.

Hervieu, G.J., Cluderay, J.E., Harrison, D., Meakin, J., Maycox, P., Nasir, S. & Leslie, R.A. (2000) The distribution of the mRNA and protein products of the melanin-concentrating hormone (MCH) receptor gene, slc-1, in the central nervous system of the rat. *Eur. J. Neurosci.*, **12** (4), 1194–1216.

Hotamisligil, G.S., Arner, P., Caro, J.F., Atkinson, R.L. & Spiegelman, B. M. (1995) Increased adipose tissue expression of tumor necrosis factor-alpha in human obesity and insulin resistance. *J. Clin. Invest.*, **95** (5), 2409–2415.

Hotta, M., Shibasaki, T., Masuda, A., Imaki, T., Demura, H., Ling, N. & Shizume, K. (1986) The responses of plasma adrenocorticotropin and cortisol to corticotropin-releasing hormone (CRH) and cerebrospinal fluid immunoreactive CRH in anorexia nervosa patients. *J. Clin. Endocrinol. Metab.*, **62** (2), 319–324.

Houpt, K.A. (1982) Gastrointestinal factors in hunger and satiety. *Neurosci Biobehav. Rev.*, **6** (2), 145–164.

Jackson, I.M. (1982) Thyrotropin-releasing hormone. *N. Engl. J. Med.*, **306** (3), 145–155.

Jimerson, D.C., Mantzoros, C., Wolfe, B.E. & Metzger, E.D. (2000) Decreased serum leptin in bulimia nervosa. *J. Clin. Endocrinol. Metab.*, **85** (12), 4511–4514.

Johnson, W.G., Jarrell, M.P., Chupurdia, K.M. & Williamson, D.A. (1994) Repeated binge/purge cycles in bulimia nervosa: role of glucose and insulin. *Int. J. Eat. Disord.*, **15** (4), 331–341.

Jonas, J.M. & Gold, M. S. (1986) Treatment of antidepressant-resistant bulimia with naltrexone. *Int. J. Psychiat. Med.*, **16** (4), 305–309.

Kalra, S.P., Dube, M.G., Sahu, A., Phelps, C.P. & Kalra, P.S. (1991) Neuropeptide Y secretion increases in the paraventricular nucleus in association with increased appetite for food. *Proc. Natl. Acad. Sci. USA*, **88** (23), 10931–10935.

Karhunen, L.J., Lappalainen, R.I., Tammela, L., Turpeinen, A. K. & Uusitupa, M. I. (1997) Subjective and physiological cephalic phase responses to food in obese binge-eating women. *Int. J. Eat. Disord.*, **21** (4), 321–328.

Kaye, W.H., Nagata, T., Weltzin, T.E., Hsu, L.K., Sokol, M.S., McConaha, C., Plotnicov, K.H., Weise, J. & Deep, D. (2001) Double-blind placebo-controlled administration of fluoxetine in restricting-type anorexia nervosa. *Biol. Psychiat.*, **49** (7), 644–652.

Kaye, W.H., Berrettini, W., Gwirtsman, H. & George, D.T. (1990) Altered cerebrospinal fluid neuropeptide Y and peptide YY immunoreactivity in anorexia and bulimia nervosa. *Arch. Gen. Psychiat.*, **47** (6), 548–556.

Kaye, W.H., Gwirtsman, H.E. & George, D.T. (1989) The effect of bingeing and vomiting on hormonal secretion. *Biol. Psychiat.*, **25** (6), 768–780.

Kaye, W.H., Rubinow, D., Gwirtsman, H.E., George, D.T., Jimerson, D.C. & Gold, P. W. (1988) CSF somatostatin in anorexia nervosa and bulimia: Relationship to the hypothalamic pituitary-adrenal cortical axis. *Psychoneuroendocrinology*, **13**, (3), 265–272.

Kaye, W.H., Berrettini, W.H., Gwirtsman, H.E., Chretien, M., Gold, P.W., George, D.T., Jimerson, D.C. & Ebert, M.H. (1987a) Reduced cerebrospinal fluid levels of immunoreactive pro-opiomelanocortin related peptides (including beta-endorphin) in anorexia nervosa. *Life Sci.*, **41** (18), 2147–2155.

Kaye, W.H., Gwirtsman, H.E., George, D.T., Ebert, M., Jimerson, D.C., Tomai, T.P., Chrousos, G.P. & Gold, P.W. (1987b) Elevated cerebrospinal fluid levels of immunoreactive corticotrophin-releasing hormone in anorexia nervosa: Relation to state of nutrition, adrenal function and intensity of depression. *J. Clin. Endocrin. and Metab.*, **64**, 203–208.

Kelly, J., Rothstein, J. & Grossman, S.P. (1979) GABA and hypothalamic feeding systems. I. Topographic analysis of the effects of microinjections of muscimol. *Physiol. Behav.*, **23** (6), 1123–1134.

Kennedy, G.C. (1953) The role of depot fat in the hypothalamic control of food intake in the rat. *Proc. R. Soc. London*, **140**, 578–592.

Kennedy, S.H., Garfinkel, P.E., Parienti, V., Costa, D. & Brown, G.M. (1989) Changes in melatonin levels but not cortisol levels are associated with depression in patients with eating disorders. *Arch. Gen. Psychiat.*, **46** (1), 73–78.

Kiriike, N., Nishiwaki, S., Nagata, T., Okuno, Y., Yamada, J., Tanaka, S., Fujii., A. & Kawakita, Y. (1990) Insulin sensitivity in patients with anorexia nervosa and bulimia. *Acta. Psychiatr. Scand.*, **81** (3), 236–239.

Kissileff, H.R., Wentzlaff, T.H., Guss, J.L., Walsh, B.T., Devlin, M.J. & Thornton, J.C. (1996) A direct measure of satiety disturbance in patients with bulimia nervosa. *Physiol. Behav.*, **60** (4), 1077–1085.

Komaki, G., Tamai, H., Mukuta, T., Kobayashi, N., Mori, K., Nakagawa, T. & Kumagai, L.F. (1992) Alterations in endothelium-associated proteins and serum thyroid hormone concentrations in anorexia nervosa. *Br. J. Nutr.*, **68** (1), 67–75.

Kopp, W., Blum, W.F., von Prittwitz, S., Ziegler, A., Lubbert, H., Emons, G., Herzog, W., Herpertz, S., Deter, H.C., Remschmidt, H. & Hebebrand, J. (1997) Low leptin levels predict amenorrhea in underweight and eating disordered females [see comments]. *Mol. Psychiat.*, **2** (4), 335–340.

Krahn, D.D., Gosnell, B.A., Levine, A.S. & Morley, J.E. (1988) Behavioral effects of corticotropin-releasing factor: Localization and characterization of central effects. *Brain Res.*, **443** (1–2), 63–69.

Kristensen, P., Judge, M.E., Thim, L., Ribel, U., Christjansen, K.N., Wulff, B.S., Clausen, J.T., Jensen, P.B., Madsen, O.D., Vrang, N., Larsen, P.J. & Hastrup, S. (1998) Hypothalamic CART is a new anorectic peptide regulated by leptin. *Nature*, **393** (6680), 72–76.

Kuru, M.M., Ueta, Y., Serino, R., Nakazato, M., Yamamoto, Y., Shibuya, I. & Yamashita, H. (2000) Centrally administered orexin/hypocretin activates HPA axis in rats. *Neuroreport*, **11** (9), 1977–1980.

Kyrkouli, S., Stanley, B., Seirafi, R. & Leibowitz, S. (1990) Stimulation of feeding by galanin: Anatomical localization and behavioral specificity of this peptide's effects in the brain. *Peptides*, **11**, 995–1001.

La Via, M.C., Gray, N. & Kaye, W.H. (2000) Case reports of olanzapine treatment of anorexia nervosa. *Int. J. Eat. Disord.*, **27** (3), 363–366.

Laessle, R.G., Fischer, M., Fichter, M.M., Pirke, K.M. & Krieg, J.C. (1992) Cortisol levels and vigilance in eating disorder patients. *Psychoneuroendocrinology*, **17** (5), 475–484.

Laorden, M.L., Castells, M.T., Martinez, M.D., Martinez, P.J. & Milanes, M.V. (2000) Activation of c-fos expression in hypothalamic nuclei by mu- and kappa-receptor agonists: Correlation with catecholaminergic activity in the hypothalamic paraventricular nucleus. *Endocrinology*, **141** (4), 1366–1376.

Lee, G.H., Proenca, R., Montez, J.M., Carroll, K.M., Darvishzadeh, J.G., Lee, J.I. & Friedman, J.M. (1996) Abnormal splicing of the leptin receptor in diabetic mice. *Nature*, **379** (6566), 632–635.

LeGoff, D.B., Leichner, P. & Spigelman, M.N. (1988) Salivary response to olfactory food stimuli in anorexics and bulimics. *Appetite*, **11** (1), 15–25.

Legradi, G. & Lechan, R.M. (1999) Agouti-related protein containing nerve terminals innervate thyrotropin-releasing hormone neurons in the hypothalamic paraventricular nucleus. *Endocrinology*, **140** (8), 3643–3652.

Leibowitz, S.F. & Alexander, J.T. (1998) Hypothalamic serotonin in control of eating behavior, meal size, and body weight. *Biol. Psychiat.*, **44** (9), 851–864.

Leonard, T., Perpina, C., Bond, A. & Treasure, J. (1998) Assessment of test meal induced autonomic arousal in anorexic, bulimic and control females. *Eur. Eat. Disord. Rev.*, **6**, 188–200.

Li, B.H., Xu, B., Rowland, N.E. & Kalra, S.P. (1994) c-fos expression in the rat brain following central administration of neuropeptide Y and effects of food consumption. *Brain. Res.*, **665** (2), 277–284.

Licinio, J., Wong, M.-L. & Gold, P.W. (1996) The hypothalamic-pituitary-adrenal axis in anorexia nervosa. *Psychiat. Res.*, **62**, 75–83.

Lord, G.M., Matarese, G., Howard, J.K., Baker, R.J., Bloom, S.R. & Lechler, R.I. (1998) Leptin modulates the T-cell immune response and reverses starvation-induced immunosuppression. *Nature*, **394** (6696), 897–901.

Lowry, C.A., Rodda, J.E., Lightman, S.L. & Ingram, C.D. (2000) Corticotropin-releasing factor (CRF) increases in vitro firing rates of serotonergic neurons in the rat dorsal raphe nucleus: Evidence for activation of a topographically organised mesolimbocortical serotonergic system. *J. Neurosci.*, **20** (7), 7728–7736.

Mantzoros, C., Flier, J.S., Lesem, M.D., Brewerton, T.D. & Jimerson, D.C. (1997) Cerebrospinal fluid leptin in anorexia nervosa: Correlation with nutritional status and potential role in resistance to weight gain. *J. Clin. Endocrinol. Metab.*, **82** (6), 1845–1851.

Marrazzi, M.A., Bacon, J.P., Kinzie, J. & Luby, E.D. (1995a) Naltrexone use in the treatment of anorexia nervosa and bulimia nervosa. *Int. Clin. Psychopharmacol.*, **10** (3), 163–172.

Marrazzi, M.A., Markham, K.M., Kinzie, J. & Luby, E.D. (1995b) Binge eating disorder: response to naltrexone. *Int. J. Obes. Relat. Metab. Disord.*, **19** (2), 143–145.

Meereis, S.K., Klonowski, S.H., Herberg, L. & Niederau, C. (1998) Long-term effects of CCK-agonist and -antagonist on food intake and body weight in Zucker lean and obese rats. *Peptides*, **19** (2), 291–299.

Mehler, C., Wewetzer, C., Schulze, U., Theisen, F., Dittman, W. & Warnke, A. (2000) Olanzepine in children and adolescents wit chronic anorexia nervosa. A study of five cases. *Eur. J. Child Adolesc. Psychiat.*, **10**, 151–157.

Mehler, P.S., Eckel, R.H. & Donahoo, W.T. (1999) Leptin levels in restricting and purging anorectics. *Int. J. Eat. Disord.*, **26** (2), 189–194.

Melander, T., Hokfelt, T., Rokaeus, A., Cuello, A.C., Oertel, W.H., Verhofstad, A. & Goldstein, M. (1986) Coexistence of galanin-like immunoreactivity with catecholamines, 5-hydroxytryptamine, GABA and neuropeptides in the rat CNS. *J. Neurosci.*, **6** (12), 3640–3654.

Merimee, T.J. & Fineberg, E.S. (1976) Starvation-induced alterations of circulating thyroid hormone concentrations in man. *Metabolism*, **25** (1), 79–83.

Mezey, E., Kiss, J.Z., Mueller, G.P., Eskay, R., O'Donohue, T.L. & Palkovits, M. (1985) Distribution of the pro-opiomelanocortin derived peptides, adrenocorticotrope hormone, alpha-melanocyte-stimulating hormone and beta-endorphin (ACTH, alpha-MSH, beta-END) in the rat hypothalamus. *Brain Res.*, **328** (2), 341–347.

Montague, C.T., Farooqi, I.S., Whitehead, J.P., Soos, M.A., Rau, H., Wareham, N.J., Sewter, C.P., Digby, J.E., Mohammed, S.N., Hurst, J.A., Cheetham, C.H., Earley, A.R., Barnett, A.H., Prins, J.B. & O'Rahilly, S. (1997) Congenital leptin deficiency is associated with severe early-onset obesity in humans. *Nature*, **387** (6636), 903–908.

Monteleone, P., Di Lieto, A., Tortorella, A., Longobardi, N. & Maj, M. (2000a) Circulating leptin in patients with anorexia nervosa, bulimia nervosa or binge-eating disorder: Relationship to body weight, eating patterns, psychopathology and endocrine changes [In Process Citation]. *Psychiat. Res.*, **94** (2), 121–129.

Monteleone, P., Bortolotti, F., Fabrazzo, M., La Rocca, A., Fuschino, A. & Maj, M. (2000b) Plamsa leptin response to acute fasting and refeeding in untreated women with bulimia nervosa *J. Clin. Endocrinol. Metab.*, **85** (7), 2499–2503.

Moore, R., Mills, I.H. & Forster, A. (1981) Naloxone in the treatment of anorexia nervosa: Effect on weight gain and lipolysis. *J. R. Soc. Med.*, **74** (2), 129–131.

Muller, C., Voirol, M.J., Stefanoni, N., Surmely, J.F., Jequier, E., Gaillard, R.C. & Tappy, L. (1997) Effect of chronic intracerebroventricular infusion of insulin on brown adipose tissue activity in fed and fasted rats. *Int. J. Obes. Relat. Metab. Disord.*, **21** (7), 562–566.

Nillni, E.A., Vaslet, C., Harris, M., Hollenberg, A.N., Bjorbaek, C. & Flier, J.S. (2000) Leptin regulates prothyropin releasing hormone (proTRH) biosynthesis: Evidence for direct and indirect pathways. *J. Biol. Chem.*, **275**, 36124–36133.

Nozaki, T., Tamai, H., Matsubayashi, S., Komaki, G., Kobayashi, N. & Nakagawa, T. (1994) Insulin response to intravenous glucose in patients with anorexia nervosa showing low insulin response to oral glucose. *J. Clin. Endocrinol., Metab.*, **79** (1), 217–222.

Olney, J.W. (1969) Brain lesions, obesity, and other disturbances in mice treated with monosodium glutamate. *Science*, **164** (880), 719–721.

Palmer, R.L. (2000) *Managment of Eating Disorders.* Chichester: John Wiley & Sons.

Pasquet, P. & Apfelbaum, M. (1994) Recovery of initial body weight and composition after long-term massive overfeeding in men. *Am. J. Clin. Nutr.*, **60** (6), 861–863.

Pauly, R.P., Lear, S.A., Hastings, F.C. & Birmingham, C.L. (2000) Resting energy expenditure and plasma leptin levels in anorexia nervosa during acute refeeding [In Process Citation]. *Int. J. Eat. Disord.*, **28** (2), 231–234.

Pecina, S. & Berridge, K.C. (2000) Opioid site in nucleus accumbens shell mediates eating and hedonic 'liking' for food: Map based on microinjection Fos plumes. *Brain Res.*, **863** (1–2), 71–86.

Pelleymounter, M.A., Cullen, M.J., Baker, M.B., Hecht, R., Winters, D., Boone, T. & Collins, F. (1995) Effects of the obese gene product on body weight regulation in ob/ob mice [see comments]. *Science*, **269** (5223), 540–543.

Pinel, J.P.J., Assanand, S. & Lehman, D.R. (2000) Hunger, eating, and ill health. *Am. Psychol.*, **55** (10), 1105–1116.

Pirke, K.M., Kellner, M.B., Friess, E., Krieg, J.C. & Fichter, M.M. (1994) Satiety and cholecystokinin. *Int. J. Eat. Disord.*, **15** (1), 63–69.

Plotsky, P.M., Bruhn, T.O. & Vale, W. (1984) Central modulation of immunoreactive corticotrophin-releasing factor secretion by arginine vasopressin. *Endocrinology*. **115**, 1639–1641.

Reidelberger, R.D. (1994) Cholecystokinin and control of food intake. *J. Nutr.*, **124** (8), 1327S–1333S.

Reidelberger, R.D. (1992) Abdominal vagal mediation of the satiety effects of exogenous and endogenous cholecystokinin in rats. *Am. J. Physiol.*, **263** (6), R1354–R1358.

Robbins, T.W. & Everitt, B.J. (1996) Neurobehavioural mechanisms of reward and motivation. *Curr. Opin. Neurobiol.*, **6** (2), 228–236.

Robinson, P.H. (1989) Perceptivity and paraceptivity during measurement of gastric emptying in anorexia and bulimia nervosa. *Br. J. Psychiat.*, **154**, 400–405.

Rodriquez, d.F., Navarro, M., Alvarez, E., Roncero, I., Chowen, J.A., Maestre, O., Gomez, R., Munoz, R.M., Eng, J. & Blazquez, E. (2000) Peripheral versus central effects of glucagon-like peptide-1 receptor agonists on satiety and body weight loss in Zucker obese rats. *Metabolism*, **49** (6), 709–717.

Rolls, B.J., Andersen, A.E., Moran, T.H., McNelis, A.L., Baier, H.C. & Fedoroff, I.C. (1992) Food intake, hunger, and satiety after preloads in women with eating disorders. *Am. J. Clin. Nutr.*, **55** (6), 1093–1103.

Romach, M.K., Glue, P., Kampman, K., Kaplan, H.L., Somer, G.R., Poole, S., Clarke, L., Coffin, V., Cornish, J., O'Brien, C.P. & Sellers, E.M. (1999) Attenuation of the euphoric effects of cocaine by the dopamine D1/D5 antagonist ecopipam (SCH 39166) [see comments]. *Arch. Gen. Psychiatry*, **56** (12), 1101–1106.

Rosenkranz, K., Hinney, A., Ziegler, A., von Prittwitz, S., Barth, N., Roth, H., Mayer, H., Siegfried, W., Lehmkuhl, G., Poustka, F., Schmidt, M., Schafer, H., Remschmidt, H. & Hebebrand, J. (1998) Screening for mutations in the neuropeptide Y Y5 receptor gene in cohorts belonging to different weight extremes. *Int. J. Obes. Relat. Metab. Disord.*, **22** (2), 157–163.

Rossi, M., Choi, S.J., O'Shea, D., Miyoshi, T., Ghatei, M.A. & Bloom, S.R. (1997) Melanin-concentrating hormone acutely stimulates feeding, but chronic administration has no effect on body weight. *Endocrinology*, **138** (1) 351–355.

Sakurai, T., Amemiya, A., Ishii, M., Matsuzaki, I., Chemelli, R.M., Tanaka, H., Williams, S.C., Richardson, J.A., Kozlowski, G.P., Wilson, S., Arch, J.R., Buckingham, R.E., Haynes, A.C., Carr, S.A., Annan, R.S., McNulty, D.E., Liu, W.S., Terrett, J.A., Elshourbagy, N.A., Bergsma, D.J. & Yanagisawa, M. (1998) Orexins and orexin receptors: A family of hypothalamic neuropeptides and G protein-coupled receptors that regulate feeding behavior [comment]. *Cell*, **92**, (5), p. 1.

Satoh, N., Ogawa, Y., Katsuura, G., Hayase, M., Tsuji, T., Imagawa, K., Yoshimasa, Y., Nishi, S., Hosoda, K. & Nakao, K. (1997) The arcuate nucleus as a primary site of satiety effect of leptin in rats. *Neurosci. Lett.*, **224** (3), 149–152.

Schaffhauser, A.O., Stricker-Krongrad, A., Brunner, L., Cumin, F., Gerald, C., Whitebread, S., Criscione, L. & Hofbauer, K.G. (1997) Inhibition of food intake by neuropeptide Y Y5 receptor antisense oligodeoxynucleotides. *Diabetes*, **46** (11), 1792–1798.

Schwartz, M.W., Woods, S.C., Porte, D., Seeley, R.J. & Baskin, D.G. (2000) Central nervous system control of food intake. *Nature*, **404** (6778), 661–671.

Schwartz, M.W., Seeley, R.J., Woods, S.C., Weigle, D.S., Campfield, L.A., Burn, P. & Baskin, D.G. (1997) Leptin increases hypothalamic pro-opiomelanocortin mRNA expression in the rostral arcuate nucleus. *Diabetes*, **46** (12), 2119–2123.

Shimada, M., Tritos, N.A., Lowell, B.B., Flier, J.S. & Maratos, F.E. (1998) Mice lacking melanin-concentrating hormone are hypophagic and lean. *Nature*, **396** (6712), 670–674.

Simonian, S.X. & Herbison, A.E. (1997) Differential expression of estrogen receptor and neuropeptide Y by brainstem A1 and A2 noradrenaline neurons. *Neuroscience*, **76** (2), 517–529.

Sinha, Y.N., Salocks, C.B. & Vanderlaan, W.P. (1975) Prolactin and growth hormone secretion in chemically induced and genetically obese mice. *Endocrinology*, **97** (6), 1386–1393.

Sipols, A.J., Baskin, D.G. & Schwartz, M.W. (1995) Effect of intracerebroventricular insulin infusion on diabetic hyperphagia and hypothalamic neuropeptide gene expression. *Diabetes*, **44** (2), 147–151.

Skofitsch, G. & Jacobowitz, D.M. (1985) Immunohistochemical mapping of galanin-like neurons in the rat central nervous system. *Peptides*, **6** (3), 509–546.

Sorbi, S., Nacmias, B., Tedde, A., Ricca, V., Mezzani, B. & Rotella, C. M. (1998) 5-HT2A promoter polymorphism in anorexia nervosa [letter]. *Lancet*, **351** (9118), 1785.

Stallone, D., Nicolaidis, S. & Gibbs, J. (1989) Cholecystokinin-induced anorexia depends on serotoninergic function. *Am. J. Physiol.*, **256** (5), R1138–R1141.

Stanley, B.G., Chin, A.S. & Leibowitz, S.F. (1985) Feeding and drinking elicited by central injection of neuropeptide Y: evidence for a hypothalamic site(s) of action. *Brain Res. Bull.*, **14** (6), 521–524.

Steinbusch, H.W. & Nieuwenhuys, R. (1981) Localization of serotonin-like immunoreactivity in the central nervous system and pituitary of the rat, with special references to the innervation of the hypothalamus. *Adv. Exp. Med. Biol.*, **133**, 7–35.

Stoving, R.K., Flyvbjerg, A., Frystyk, J., Fisker, S., Hangaard, J., Hansen-Nord, M. & Hagen, C. (1999a) Low serum levels of free and total insulin-like growth factor I (IGF-I) in patients with anorexia nervosa are not associated with increased IGF-binding protein-3 proteolysis. *J. Clin. Endocrinol. Metab.*, **84** (4), 1346–1350.

Stoving, R.K., Veldhuis, J.D., Flyvbjerg, A., Vinten, J., Hangaard, J., Koldkjaer, O.G., Kristiansen, J. & Hagen, C. (1999b) Jointly amplified basal and pulsatile growth hormone (GH) secretion and increased process irregularity in women with anorexia nervosa: Indirect evidence for disruption of feedback regulation within the GH-insulin- like growth factor I axis. *J. Clin. Endocrinol. Metab.*, **84** (6), 2056–2063.

Stoving, R.K., Hangaard, J., Hansen-Nord, M. & Hagen, C. (1999c) A review of endocrine changes in anorexia nervosa. *J. Psychiatr. Res.*, **33** (2), 139–152.

Strubbe, J.H. & Mein, C. G. (1977) Increased feeding in response to bilateral injection of insulin antibodies in the VMH. *Physiol. Behav.*, **19** (2), 309–313.

Sunday, S.R. & Halmi, K.A. (1990) Taste perceptions and hedonics in eating disorders. *Physiol. Behav.*, **48** (5), 587–594.

Takiguchi, S., Takata, Y., Funakoshi, A., Miyasaka, K., Kataoka, K., Fujimura, Y., Goto, T. & Kono, A. (1997) Disrupted cholecystokinin type-A receptor (CCKAR) gene in OLETF rats. *Gene.*, **197** (1–2), 169–175.

Tamai, H., Takemura, J., Kobayashi, N., Matsubayashi, S., Matsukura, S. & Nakagawa, T. (1993) Changes in plasma cholecystokinin concentrations after oral glucose tolerance test in anorexia nervosa before and after therapy. *Metabolism*, **42** (5), 581–584.

Tartaglia, L.A., Dembski, M., Weng, X., Deng, N., Culpepper, J., Devos, R., Richards, G.J., Campfield, L.A., Clark, F.T., Deeds, J. et al. (1995) Identification and expression cloning of a leptin receptor, OB-R. *Cell*, **83** (7), 1263–1271.

Tschop, M., Smiley, D. L. & Heiman, M.L. (2000) Ghrelin induces adiposity in rodents. *Nature*, **407**, 908–913.

Turton, M.D., O'Shea, D., Gunn, I., Beak, S.A., Edwards, C.M., Meeran, K., Choi, S.J., Taylor, G.M., Heath, M.M., Lambert, P.D., Wilding, J. P., Smith, D.M., Ghatei, M.A., Herbert, J. & Bloom, S.R. (1996) A role for glucagon-like peptide-1 in the central regulation of feeding [see comments]. *Nature*, **379** (6560), 69–72.

Volkow, N.D., Wang, G.J., Fischman, M.W., Foltin, R.W., Fowler, J.S., Abumrad, N.N., Vitkun, S., Logan, J., Gatley, S.J., Pappas, N., Hitzemann, R. & Shea, C.E. (1997) Relationship between subjective effects of cocaine and dopamine transporter occupancy. *Nature*, **386** (6627), 827–830.

Vrang, N., Tang, C. M., Larsen, P.J. & Kristensen, P. (1999) Recombinant CART peptide induces c-Fos expression in central areas involved in control of feeding behaviour. *Brain Res.*, **818** (2), 499–509.

Wadden, T.A., Foster, G.D., Letizia, K.A. & Wilk, J.E. (1993) Metabolic, anthropometric, and psychological characteristics of obese binge eaters. *Int. J. Eat. Disord.*, **14** (1), 17–25.

Waller, D.A., Kiser, R.S., Hardy, B.W., Fuchs, I., Feigenbaum, L.P. & Uauy, R. 1986, Eating behavior and plasma beta-endorphin in bulimia. *Am. J. Clin. Nutr.*, **44** (1), 20–23.

Ward, A., Brown, N., Lightman, S., Campbell, I.C. & Treasure, J. (1998) Neuroendocrine, appetitive and behavioural responses to d-fenfluramine in women recovered from anorexia nervosa. *Br. J. Psychiat.*, **172**, 351–358.

Weigle, D.S., Duell, P.B., Connor, W.E., Steiner, R.A., Soules, M.R. & Kuijper, J.L. (1997) Effect of fasting, refeeding, and dietary fat restriction on plasma leptin levels. *J. Clin. Endocrinol. Metab.*, **82** (2), 561–565.

Weigle, D.S., Bukowski, T.R., Foster, D.C., Holderman, S., Kramer, J.M., Lasser, G., Lofton-Day, C.E., Prunkard, D.E., Raymond, C. & Kuijper, J.L. (1995) Recombinant ob protein reduces feeding and body weight in the ob/ob mouse. *J. Clin. Invest.*, **96** (4), 2065–2070.

Weingarten, H.P., Chang, P.K. & McDonald, T.J. (1985) Comparison of the metabolic and behavioral disturbances following paraventricular- and ventromedial-hypothalamic lesions. *Brain Res. Bull.*, **14** (6), 551–559.

Wellman, P.J., Davies, B.T., Morien, A. & McMahon, L. (1993) Modulation of feeding by hypothalamic paraventricular nucleus alpha 1- and alpha 2-adrenergic receptors. *Life Sci.*, **53** (9), 669–679.

Weltzin, T.E., McConaha, C., McKee, M., Hsu, L.K., Perel, J. & Kaye, W.H. (1991) Circadian patterns of cortisol, prolactin, and growth hormonal secretion during bingeing and vomiting in normal weight bulimic patients. *Biol. Psychiat.*, **30** (1), 37–48.

Werther, G.A., Hogg, A., Oldfield, B.J., McKinley, M.J., Figdor, R., Allen, A. M. & Mendelsohn, F.A. (1987) Localization and characterization of insulin receptors in rat brain and pituitary gland using in vitro autoradiography and computerized densitometry. *Endocrinology*, **121** (4), 1562–1570.

Wisniewski, L., Epstein, L.H., Marcus, M.D. & Kaye, W. (1997) Differences in salivary habituation to palatable foods in bulimia nervosa patients and controls. *Psychosom. Med.*, **59** (4), 427–433.

Yeomans, M.R. & Gray, R.W. (1997) Effects of naltrexone on food intake and changes in subjective appetite during eating: Evidence for opioid involvement in the appetizer effect. *Physiol. Behav.*, **62** (1), 15–21.

Yu, W.H., Kimura, M., Walczewska, A., Karanth, S. & McCann, S.M. (1997) Role of leptin in hypothalamic-pituitary function [published erratum appears in *Proc. Natl. Acad. Sci. U.S.A.* 1997, Sep. 30; **94** (20), 11108]. *Proc. Natl. Acad. Sci. U.S.A.*, **94** (3), 1023–1028.

Zamir, N., Palkovits, M. & Brownstein, M. J. (1984) Distribution of immunoreactive dynorphin A1–8 in discrete nuclei of the rat brain: Comparison with dynorphin A. *Brain Res.*, **307** (1–2), 61–68.

Zhang, Y., Proenca, R., Maffei, M., Barone, M., Leopold, L. & Friedman, J.M. (1994) Positional cloning of the mouse obese gene and its human homologue [published erratum appears in *Nature*, 1995, Mar 30; **374** (6521), 479] [see comments]. *Nature*, **372** (6505), 425–432.

CHAPTER 5

Basic Neuroscience and Scanning

Martina de Zwaan

Department of General Psychiatry, Währinger Gürtel, Wien, Austria

SUMMARY

Structural neuroimaging techniques:

- There is sufficient evidence of a relationship between eating disorders and altered brain structures.
- Morphological brain alterations are most likely a consequence of endocrine and metabolic reactions to starvation, regardless of whether starvation leads to an underweight state ('pseudoatrophy').
- However, there are individual cases in whom the brain alterations continue to exist.
- Improvement in MRI technique will shed more light on the regional distribution of structural brain abnormalities.

Functional neuroimaging techniques:

- The functional abnormalities may be partly secondary to weight loss but may also reflect underlying primary brain dysfunction.
- Cognitive activation and symptom provocation paradigms might elucidate typical brain activation patterns in eating disorder patients.
- Re-assessment should be performed upon recovery to determine if the structural and functional abnormalities are strictly secondary to the abnormal eating behavior or related to underlying traits.
- The enormously rapid development of new technology in structural and functional neuroimaging techniques will allow more precise observation of the brain.

Serotonin activity:

- Disturbances of brain serotonin activity have been described in patients with anorexia nervosa and bulimia nervosa.
- Whether abnormalities are a consequence or a potential antecedent of pathological eating behavior remains a major question.

Handbook of Eating Disorders. Edited by J. Treasure, U. Schmidt and E. van Furth.

- There are distinct differences in serotonin activity between recovered and ill patients with anorexia or bulimia nervosa (challenge tests, CSF 5-HIAA).
- It cannot be ruled out that subjects at risk of an eating disorder might have trait abnormalities in the regulation of brain serotonin function that might make them vulnerable to abnormal eating behavior (as a way to 'treat' abnormal serotonin activity) or to dieting-induced decreases in plasma tryptophan.
- In addition, a disturbance of serotonin activity may also explain associated psychopathological features (e.g. obsessionality, depression) that are common to both anorexia and bulimia nervosa.

Other neurochemicals:

- Altered regulation in several neurotransmitter systems (e.g. dopamine) may contribute to the disorder.

NEUROIMAGING

The correlations between eating disorders and brain abnormalities are best assessed using neuroimaging techniques, both structural and functional. Structural techniques assess brain anatomy and include computerised tomography (CT) and magnetic resonance imaging (MRI). Functional techniques assess brain physiology and chemistry and include positron emission tomography (PET), single photon emission tomography (SPECT), magnetic resonance spectroscopy (MRS) and functional magnetic resonance imaging (fMRI).

Structural Imaging

CT and MRI

Krieg et al. (1986, 1987) reported that 82% of patients with anorexia and 46% of patients with bulimia show one or more morphological brain alteration. The most consistent finding in the brains of patients with anorexia nervosa has been an enlargement of the external CSF spaces (sulcal widening) and, less frequently, internal CSF spaces (ventricular enlargement); both have been shown to be largely reversible after weight gain ('pseudoatrophy') (e.g. Golden et al., 1996; Swayze et al., 1996). See Table 5.1. The findings for patients with bulimia nervosa are less consistent, with some studies showing no morphological changes (Lakenau et al., 1985) while others show sulcal widening and ventricular enlargement (Krieg et al., 1987). Other findings using MRI have included a mild atrophy of the thalamus and midbrain area in patients with anorexia nervosa (Husain et al., 1992) and a decrease in pituitary size in patients with both anorexia nervosa and bulimia nervosa (Doraiswamy et al., 1990). Katzman et al. (1996) reported an MRI study showing that adolescent patients with anorexia nervosa had significant reductions in both total gray matter and total white matter volumes when compared to healthy controls. The authors observed that these abnormalities were present in adolescents with relatively short duration of illness.

Table 5.1   Results of CT and MRI studies in patients with eating disorders

- Enlargement of external CSF spaces (enlargement of cortical sulci, narrowing of the gyri)
- Enlargement of internal CSF spaces (ventricular enlargement)
- Decreased total gray matter volume
- Decreased total white matter volume
- Mild atrophy of the thalamus and midbrain area
- Reduced pituitary size

Since a considerable number of normal-weight bulimic patients display the same kind of sulcal widening as anorexic patients, malnutrition cannot be the only explanation for these structural brain abnormalities. However, bulimic patients show low T_3 and elevated β-HBA values as a consequence of intermittent starvation. Hypercortisolemia may contribute directly to the brain abnormalities. Hypercortisolism is a common finding in eating disorders and similar structural brain changes can be found in patients with Cushing syndrome and those taking corticosteroids (Table 5.2).

As mentioned previously, the abnormalities are usually reversible with weight restoration; however, there are individual cases in whom the brain alterations continue to exist unaltered over a period of one year after the body weight has returned to normal. Change that persists might be due to residual damage of the brain ('scar') or persistent abnormal metabolism. The results of neuropathologic examinations of patients who died of anorexia nervosa revealed ventricular enlargement, but also neuronal loss and gliosis in the cerebral cortex. However, persistence of changes might also be a consequence of comorbid disorders such as alcoholism. Even though there is no good evidence for a primary structural deficit, this possibility for explaining a persistent brain alteration can not be completely excluded. Technological advances in MRI should shed more light on the regional distribution of tissue shrinkage.

From a clinical standpoint, CT and MRI are useful for identifying structural lesions involving the hypothalamus which have been reported in emaciated patients ('diencephalic

Table 5.2   Significant clinical correlates with CT and MRI findings

Positive correlations between
- serum/urinary cortisol and total/cortical CSF volumes
- lowest BMI and total gray matter volumes
- serum creatinine and total/cortical gray matter volumes
- total protein and central gray matter volume

Negative correlations between
- urinary free cortisol and central gray matter volumes
- body weight and external CSF volumes
- lowest BMI and total/external CSF volumes
- T_3 (as a sign of starvation) and CSF volumes

No correlations
- estradiol, LH, FSH, prolactin
- duration of illness
- age

wasting'), but such cases are extremely rare. Both CT and MRI should be used clinically in patients who have atypical symptoms of eating disorders such as food aversions without body image disturbances (Swayze, 1997).

Functional Imaging

These techniques allow the identification of possible brain dysfunction even where there are no structural changes. Currently, SPECT, PET, MRS and fMRI have only research applications for patients with eating disorders. PET and SPECT require the introduction of manufactured radioactive compounds. The major advantage of SPECT over PET is the longer half-lives of SPECT's isotopes, which do not require an on-site cyclotron. A major disadvantage is that SPECT has poorer image resolution than PET.

Positron Emission Tomography

Most PET studies of eating disorders have evaluated glucose metabolism (metabolic rate, blood flow) with the use of 18-fluorodeoxyglucose (FDG). At rest with eyes closed, patients with anorexia nervosa usually present an absolute global and regional hypometabolism of glucose. However, this can also be found in low-weight patients with depression and is most likely a consequence of starvation since it disappears after weight gain. Most recently regional cerebral blood flow (rCBF) was investigated using PET in 9 women in long-term recovery from BN (Frank et al., 2000). There were no differences between bulimics and controls, suggesting that alterations in rCBF during the ill state of bulimia nervosa may be a state-related phenomenon. Both, anorexic and normal-weight bulimic patients have been shown to have relative parietal hypometabolism which persisted after weight gain in some anorexic patients (Delvenne et al., 1995, 1997a, 1997b, 1999). The authors hypothesise that this might be a characteristic of eating disorders, a primary cerebral dysfunction, which may be related to distortions of body image. However, it might also be a particular sensitivity of this cortical region to nutritional factors. In their most recent study Delvenne et al. (1999) found that patients with anorexia nervosa showed an increased relative glucose metabolism in the inferior frontal cortex and in the basal ganglia compared to controls, confirming the finding by Herholz et al. (1987). This might be due to a more pronounced reduction in cortical than in basal ganglia glucose metabolism and may be related to increased vigilance or anxiety in patients compared to controls.

Two studies of glucose metabolism in bulimia applied PET scans together with cognitive activation tasks which stimulate particular regions of brain activity (Wu et al., 1990; Andreason et al., 1992). Bulimics showed an abnormal hemispheric lateralization (left greater than right hemispheric asymmetry as opposed to healthy controls in whom right is greater than left) in the parietotemporal region and parts of the frontal lobes, which appeared to be independent of the mood state (similar findings were reported for depression and OCD). It is an open question whether the loss of normal right activation in some areas has a role in the aetiology of this disorder.

Another option is symptom provocation studies, which have already been performed in patients with anxiety disorders. In healthy subjects the confrontation with desirable food stimuli was associated with decreases in left temporo-insular cortical blood flow (Gordon et al., 2000). Further studies are needed to elucidate brain activity patterns in patients with eating disorders using the same provocation paradigms.

Specific ligands for serotonin and dopamine sites can be utilised to clarify the involvement of these neurotransmitter systems in eating disorders. Data of PET with altanserin, a serotonergic ligand that binds to 5-HT$_{2a}$ receptors, in 9 women who had recovered from bulimia nervosa versus 12 normal controls, have shown reduced 5-HT$_{2a}$ binding in the medial orbital frontal cortex, an area involved in regulating emotional and impulse control (Kaye et al., 2001). A study in 16 women recovered from anorexia nervosa versus 23 controls demonstrated significantly reduced altanserin binding in mesial temporal and cingulate cortical regions (Frank et al., 2002). These studies suggest that altered 5-HT neuronal system activity may persist after recovery from BN or AN.

Single Photon Emission Tomography

SPECT is a functional imaging technique that is mainly used for studies of regional cerebral blood flow (rCBF). SPECT studies in adults with eating disorders have been inconclusive. Krieg et al. (1989) reported no change in regional blood flow in patients with anorexia nervosa before and after eating or when compared with a control group. Nozoe et al. (1993) reported an increase in rCBF in response to food intake in the left inferior frontal cortex in patients with anorexia nervosa. Gordon et al. (1997) showed unilateral temporal lobe hypoperfusion in 13 out of 15 children and adolescent patients with anorexia nervosa. The authors speculate as to whether this is a primary finding since temporal lobe hypoperfusion persisted in three patients who had regained normal weight. Furthermore, changes in the brain secondary to starvation would be expected to produce global and symmetrical changes.

SPECT can also be used to study neurotransmitter systems. In addition to those compounds used for measuring blood flow, iodine labeled ligands for the muscarinic, dopaminergic, and serotonergic receptors can be used. [123]Beta-CIT SPECT studies are used to investigate the availability of brain serotonin transporters (SERT) and dopamine transporters (DAT). Tauscher et al. (2000) performed scans in 10 medication-free, bulimic patients and 10 age-matched controls. They found a 17% reduced SERT availability in hypothalamus and thalamus and a similar reduction in striatal DAT availability. In addition, there was a negative correlation between illness duration and SERT availability. As with other alterations it remains unclear whether reduced SERT availability might be an etiologic defect, adaptive mechanism or an unrelated epiphenomenon of another etiologic lesion.

Functional Magnetic Resonance Imaging

fMRI studies offer an important opportunity to look at cognitive processing. Ellison et al. (1998) studied cerebral blood oxygenation changes with fMRI in six adult patients with anorexia nervosa and six healthy controls. Images were obtained while the participants viewed a 5-minute videotape that showed pictures of labelled high and low calorie drinks.

The group with anorexia nervosa showed more extreme and powerful signal changes in response to the contrasting stimuli, especially in the left insula, anterior cingulate gyrus and left amygdala–hippocampal region. Anxiety was also rated and found to be much higher in the anorexic group when viewing the high calorie drinks. The authors suggest that the left amygdala–hippocampal region may mediate conditioned fear of high calorie foods and that the insula and anterior cingulate may be involved in autonomic arousal and attentional processes.

Magnetic Resonance Spectroscopy

With MRS a wide range of metabolic processes can be studied. Roser et al. (1999) found that patients with anorexia nervosa showed a decrease in myo-inositol (by 15%) and lipid compounds (by 50%) within the frontal white matter. Interestingly, myo-inositol is a metabolite which is found in reduced levels also in patients treated with corticosteroids. The concentration was further reduced with decreasing BMI. Again, the metabolic changes seem to be a consequence of nutritional deficiency and hormonal changes typical in patients with anorexia nervosa. The authors could not find evidence for neuronal degeneration or damage.

NEUROTRANSMITTER SYSTEMS

Central Nervous System Serotonin Activity

Brain serotonin (5-HT) systems (Table 5.3) play a role in the modulation of appetite, depression, anxiety, impulse control, obsessionality, and neuroendocrine function. Central serotonin pathways, particularly involving the paraventricular nucleus of the hypothalamus,

Table 5.3 Research methods of assessing serotonin function

Pharmacological challenge strategy
Administration of an agent (e.g. mCPP, fenfluramine, L-tryptophan) with serotonin-specific properties and the subsequent assessment of changes in behavior or hormonal release (e.g. prolactin). Measure of hypothalamic–pituitary neuroendocrine responsiveness

Acute tryptophan depletion
Methodology that induces a rapid and substantial lowering of plasma tryptophan levels and markedly reduces brain 5-HT synthesis in humans followed by the examination of behavioral responses (mood, urge to eat, food consumption)

Platelet measures of serotonin function
Peripheral measures of 5-HT activity as an indirect means of assessing central 5-HT function: ^{3}H-imipramine binding, platelet uptake of serotonin, serotonin-amplified platelet aggregation, serotonin-induced platelet calcium mobilization, ^{3}H-LSD binding, platelet MAO activity

Precursor and metabolite studies
Tryptophan levels and plasma TRP/LNAA ratio, CSF concentrations of 5-HIAA, the major metabolite of serotonin

Treatment trials with serotonergic agents
Serotonin antagonists (cyproheptadine), serotonin agonists (SSRIs)

---

seems to play a major role in the development of postprandial satiety and the determination of the amount of food eaten (Blundell, 1991). Treatments which increase intrasynaptic serotonin or directly activate serotonin receptors tend to reduce food consumption. Thus, a brain serotonergic dysfunction may contribute to the etiology and/or pathophysiology of eating disorders.

There are studies in symptomatic patients with eating disorders and in women who have long recovered from anorexia and bulimia nervosa. Studies in individuals who have achieved stable remission from anorexia or bulimia nervosa provide better opportunity to identify trait-related characteristics that may have constituted a risk factor in the original development of the disorder. Nevertheless, it is not entirely possible to differentiate if alterations of serotonergic activity are the cause of an eating disorder, a reversible consequence of the eating disorder (which might contribute to the perpetuation of the disorder), or a 'scar' caused by the abnormal eating behavior which persists after recovery.

In addition to affecting eating behavior directly, alterations in CNS serotonin function could contribute to other psychological symptoms associated with eating disorders. The diminished CNS serotonin could play a role in the high prevalence of depressive disorders in patients with bulimia nervosa. An impulsive-aggressive behavioral style which is frequently seen in bulimic patients may also be associated with diminished CNS serotonin function. Consequently, altered central serotonin function may reflect a shared neurobiological diathesis across several psychiatric disorders.

Anorexia Nervosa

Underweight patients with anorexia nervosa have a significant reduction of basal CSF 5-HIAA compared to healthy controls, which normalises after short-term weight restoration. In long-term weight-recovered patients even increased concentrations have been observed (Kaye et al., 1984, 1988a, 1991) indicating increased 5-HT activity. This could reflect a disturbance of serotonin neuronal activity that is a premorbid trait contributing to the pathogenesis of eating disorders. In addition, long-term weight-recovered patients show persistent psychopathological traits such as behavioral constraint, perfectionism, anxiety and obsessionality. These psychological characteristics have shown to be independently associated with elevated CSF 5-HIAA. However, one cannot rule out the possibility that elevated CSF 5-HIAA levels after recovery are a physiological consequence of prior chronic malnutrition.

In most studies anorexic patients have a significant blunting of plasma prolactin response to drugs with serotonin activity (Brewerton & Jimerson, 1996; Hadigan et al., 1995; Monteleone et al., 1998b). There is some evidence that reduced brain serotonin activity persists after short-term weight recovery (Frank et al., 2001). However, in long-term weight-recovered patients with a history of anorexia nervosa this blunted response could no longer be found (O'Dwyer et al., 1996; Ward et al., 1998). In the study of Ward et al. (1998) the recovered group showed diminished responses to the appetite-suppressant effects of d-fenfluramine relative to the control subjects. Consequently, it cannot be ruled out that the appetitive and neuroendocrine responses are mediated by different serotonin systems. It must be kept in mind that there are multiple brain 5-HT pathways and several subtypes of 5-HT receptors.

Human platelets are a model for studying serotonergic systems because of similarities to those in the central nervous system. Anorexic patients have been found to have reduced

[3]H-imipramine binding, but normal serotonin uptake in platelets (Weizman et al., 1986; Zemishlany et al., 1987).

Together these findings suggest that CNS serotonergic responsiveness is substantially reduced in low-weight patients with anorexia nervosa and increases toward normal with weight restoration.

There is evidence that the serotonin/histamine antagonist cyproheptadine has a therapeutic benefit in hospitalised patients with anorexia nervosa. Halmi et al. (1986) found that cyproheptadine hydrochloride, at a dose of 32 mg/day, had a small but significant effect in accelerating weight gain in restricting anorexic patients, but not in bulimic anorexic patients, when compared to treatment with amitriptyline. Antidepressants are modestly if at all effective in severely weight reduced AN patients (Attia et al., 1998). However, in a controlled study Kaye et al. (2001) reported that fluoxetine may be effective in weight restored AN patients in preventing relapse.

Bulimia Nervosa

As opposed to anorexia nervosa, normal weight patients with bulimia nervosa had normal CSF 5-HIAA levels compared to healthy controls (Jimerson et al., 1992; Kaye et al., 1990). However, patients with a history of bingeing twice a day had 5-HIAA levels lower than less symptomatic patients. As in anorexia nervosa, long-term recovered bulimic patients showed elevated levels of 5-HIAA (Kaye et al., 1998).

Also, the results of pharmacological challenge studies resemble those in anorexia nervosa: blunted prolactin response to serotonin agonists in acutely ill bulimic patients (Goldbloom et al., 1990; Brewerton et al., 1992; Levitan et al., 1997; Jimerson et al., 1997; McBride et al., 1991; Monteleone et al., 1998a; Monteleone et al., 2000) and no difference in prolactin response between remitted patients and controls (Wolfe et al., 2000; Kaye et al., 1998). Studies have shown an inverse relationship between symptom severity and prolactin response to a serotonergic challenge (Monteleone et al., 2000) and there is evidence for an association between self-destructiveness, a history of sexual abuse, and impulsivity and reduced serotonin function (Steiger et al., 2001a, 2001b, 2001c).

When depleted of tryptophan, bulimic patients showed increased caloric intake (Weltzin et al., 1994, 1995) and an increased desire to binge (Kaye et al., 2000). Consequently, lowering serotonin function can increase the clinical severity of bulimia nervosa in actively ill subjects. In abstinent patients one study found no effect of tryptophan depletion on food intake (Oldman et al., 1995), although in another study subjects with a history of bulimia nervosa had significant increases in ratings of body image concern and subjective loss of control of eating (Smith et al., 1999). The authors conclude that subjects at risk of bulimia nervosa might have trait abnormalities in the regulation of brain serotonin function that might make them vulnerable to dieting-induced decreases in plasma tryptophan. Dieting is a common precursor to bulimia nervosa. Dieting significantly lowers plasma tryptophan which results in a decreased plasma ratio of tryptophan to large neutral amino acids (TRP/LNAA). This reduces the availability of tryptophan to the brain and reduced brain serotonin synthesis. Even though a study of baseline measures found no difference in the TRP/LNAA ratio between patients with bulimia nervosa and normal control subjects (Lydiard et al., 1988), patients who fail to exhibit an increase in the TRP/LNAA ratio during bingeing may experience prolongation of the binge–purge cycle (Kaye et al., 1988b) suggesting a self-medicating model of restoration of 5-HT activity.

With regard to platelet measures, high platelet 5-HT uptake, which may reflect increased 5-HT uptake at central nervous system synapses (Goldbloom et al., 1990) and decreased platelet ^{3}H-imipramine binding have been reported (Marazziti et al. 1988). Others found evidence of an increased sensitivity of 5-HT$_{2a}$ receptor activity (platelet aggregation, calcium mobilization) in patients with bulimia but not with anorexia (McBride et al., 1991; Okamoto et al., 1995). However, this might be related more to difficulty with impulse control in general rather than with bulimic attitudes specifically (Okamoto et al., 1999). In addition, platelet MAO activity was significantly lower in bulimic patients and was inversely correlated with scores on impulsivity (Carrasco et al., 2000).

Further support for the serotonergic hypothesis of BN comes from evidence of a satisfactory response to treatment with SSRIs in these patients. Most double-blind, placebo-controlled studies of medications that have actions on serotonin are efficacious in reducing symptoms in bulimia nervosa (FBNC Study Group, 1992; Goldstein et al., 1995; Wood, 1993).

The available data do not indicate whether disturbances of serotonergic function as described above predate the onset of bulimic symptoms or result from dietary abnormalities or other changes characteristic of the disorder. Disordered eating behavior could produce alterations in serotonin function. Alternatively, patients with bulimia nervosa could engage in abnormal eating behavior to 'treat' an intrinsic defect in serotonergic activity. Studies of unaffected first-degree relatives of eating disorder patients and other high-risk individuals prior to the development of an eating disorder may be clarifying.

Central Nervous System Activity of Other Neurochemicals

However strong the link between eating disorders and serotonin seems to be, it is unlikely that a specific dysfunction of one neurotransmitter system can fully explain the pathogenesis of anorexia nervosa and bulimia nervosa. Preclinical studies indicate that other neurochemicals are involved in the initiation, continuation, and termination of a meal. CNS norepinephrine and neuropeptide Y contribute to enhanced food intake, possibly by increasing hunger. Dopamine and endogenous opiates are likely to play a role in food reward. Cholecystokinin, like serotonin, appears to contribute to post-ingestive satiety. Leptin is thought to serve as a metabolic signal for decreased food intake and increased energy metabolism. Finally, ghrelin, a recently discovered gastric peptide, has been demonstrated to increase appetite and food intake in humans. Fasting plasma levels of ghrelin have been found to be elevated in patients diagnosed with anorexia nervosa (Otto et al., 2001).

Homovanillic acid (HVA), the major metabolite of dopamine, was decreased in CSF of underweight anorexic subjects (Kaye et al., 1984) and in bulimic patients who had a high binge frequency (Kaye et al., 1990; Jimerson et al., 1992). Kaye et al. (1999) studied women who had recovered from anorexia and bulimia nervosa and compared them to healthy controls. CSF HVA was significantly lower in former restricting-type anorexic women compared to bulimia nervosa, bulimic-type anorexic women and control women. CSF MHPG, a norepinephrine metabolite, showed similar values in all groups. Consequently, a trait-related disturbance of dopamine metabolism may contribute to a vulnerability to develop restricting-type anorexia nervosa.

REFERENCES

Andreason, P.J., Altemus, M., Zametkin, A.J., King, A.C., Lucinio, J. & Cohen, R.M. (1992) Regional cerebral glucose metabolism in bulimia nervosa. *American Journal of Psychiatry*, **149**, 1506–1513.

Attia, E., Haiman, C., Walsh, B.T. & Flater, S.R. (1998) Does fluoxetine augment the inpatient treatment of anorexia nervosa? *American Journal of Psychiatry*, **155**, 548–551.

Blundell, J.E. (1991) Pharmacological approaches to appetite suppression. *Trends in Pharmacological Science*, **12**, 147–157.

Brewerton, T.D. & Jimerson, D.C. (1996) Studies of serotonin function in anorexia nervosa. *Psychiatry Research*, **62**, 31–42.

Brewerton, T.D., Mueller, E.A., Lesem, M.D., Brandt, H.A., Quearry, B., George, D.T., Murphy, D.L. & Jimerson, D.C. (1992) Neuroendocrine responses to m-Chlorophenylpiperazine and l-Tryptophan in bulimia. *Archives of General Psychiatry*, **49**, 852–861.

Carrasco, J.L., Diaz-Marsa, M., Hollander, E., Cesar, J. & Saiz-Ruiz, J. (2000) Decreased platelet monoamine oxidase activity in female bulimia nervosa. *European Neuropsychopharmacology*, **10**, 113–117.

Delvenne, V., Goldman, S., Biver, F., De Maertalaer, V., Wikler, D., Damhaut, P. & Lotstra, F. (1997a) Brain hypometabolism of glucose in low-weight depressed patients and in anorectic patients: a consequence of starvation? *Journal of Affective Disorders*, **44**, 69–77.

Delvenne, V., Goldman, S., Simon, Y., De Maertalaer, V. & Lotstra, F. (1997b) Brain hypometabolism of glucose in bulimia nervosa. *International Journal of Eating Disorders*, **21**, 313–320.

Delvenne, V., Goldman, S., Simon, Y., De Maertalaer, V. & Lotstra, F. (1999) Brain glucose metabolism in eating disorders as assessed by positron emission tomography. *International Journal of Eating Disorders*, **25**, 29–37.

Delvenne, V., Lotstra, F., Goldman, S., Biver, F., De Maertalaer, V., Appelboom-Fondu, J., Schoutens, A., Bidaut, L.M., Luxen, A. & Mendlewicz, J. (1995) Brain hypometabolism of glucose in anorexia nervosa: a PET scan study. *Biological Psychiatry*, **37**, 161–169.

Doraiswamy, P.M., Krishan, K.R., Figiel, G.S., Husain, M.M., Boyko, O.B., Rockwell, W.J.K. & Ellinwood, E.H. (1990) A brain magnetic resonance imaging study of pituitary gland morphology in anorexia nervosa and bulimia. *Biological Psychiatry*, **28**, 110–116.

Ellison, Z., Foong, J., Howard, R., Bullmore, E., Williams, S. & Treasure, J. (1998) Functional anatomy of calorie fear in anorexia nervosa. *Lancet*, **352**, 1192 (Research letter).

Fluoxetin Bulimia Nervosa Collaborative Study Group (1992) Fluoxetine in the treatment of bulimia nervosa: A multicenter placebo-controlled double-blind trial. *Archives of General Psychiatry*, **49**, 139–147.

Frank, G.K., Kaye, W.H., Greer, P., Meltzer, C.C. & Price, J.C. (2000) Regional cerebral blood flow after recovery from bulimia nervosa. *Psychiatry Research*, **20**, 31–39.

Frank, G.K., Kaye, W.H., Meltzer, C.C., Price, J.C., Greer, P., McConaha, C. & Skovira, K. (2002) Reduced 5-HT2A receptor binding after recovery from anorexia nervosa. *Biological Psychiatry*, **52**, 896–906.

Frank, G.K., Kaye, W.H., Weltzin, T.E., Perel, J., Moss, H., McConaha, C. & Pollice, C. (2001) Altered response to meta-chlorophenylpiperazine in anorexia nervosa: Support for a persistent alteration of serotonin activity after short-term weight restoration. *International Journal of Eating Disorders*, **30**, 57–68.

Goldbloom, D.S., Hicks, L. & Garfinkel, P.E. (1990) Platelet serotonin uptake in bulimia nervosa. *Biological Psychiatry*, **28**, 644–647.

Goldbloom, D.S., Garfinkel, P.E., Katz, R. & Brown, G. (1990) The hormonal response to intravenous 5-hydroxytryptophan in bulimia nervosa. *Psychosomatic Medicine*, **52**, 225–226.

Golden, N.H., Ashtari, M., Kohn, M.R., Patel, M., Jacobson, M.S., Fletcher, A. & Shenker, I.R. (1996) Reversibility of cerebral ventricular enlargment in anorexia nervosa, demonstrated by quantitative magnetic resonance imaging. *Journal of Pediatrics*, **128**, 296–301.

Goldstein, D.J., Wilson, M.G., Thompson, V.L., Potvin, J.H., Rampey, A.H. & The Fluoxetine Bulimia Nervosa Research Group (1995) Long-term fluoxetine treatment of bulimia nervosa. *British Journal of Psychiatry*, **166**, 660–666.

Gordon, C.M., Dougherty, D.D., Rauch, S.L., Emans, S.J., Grace, E., Lamm, R., Alpert, N.M., Majzoub, J.A. & Fischman, A.J. (2000) Neuroanatomy of human appetitive function: a positron emission tomography investigation. *International Journal of Eating Disorders*, 27, 163–171.

Gordon, I., Lask, B., Bryant-Waugh, R., Christie, D. & Timimi, S. (1997) Childhood-onset anorexia nervosa: towards identifying a biological substrate. *International Journal of Eating Disorders*, 22, 159–165.

Hadigan, C.M., Walsh, B.T., Buttinger, C. & Hollander, E. (1995) Behavioural and neuroendocrine responses to mcta-CPP in anorexia nervosa. *Biological Psychiatry*, 37, 504–511.

Halmi, K.A., Eckert, E., LaDu, T.J. & Cohen, J. (1986) Anorexia nervosa: treatment efficacy of cyproheptadine and amitriptyline. *Archives of General Psychiatry*, 43, 177–181.

Herholz, K., Krieg, J.C., Emrich, H.M., Pawlik, G., Bell, C., Pirke, K.M., Pahl, J.J., Wagner, R., Wienhard, K., Ploog, D. & Heiss, W.D. (1987) Regional cerebral glucose metabolism in anorexia nervosa measured by positron emission tomography. *Biological Psychiatry*, 22, 43–51.

Husain, M.M., Black, K.J., Doraiswamy, P.M., Shah, S.A., Rockwell, W.J.K., Ellinwood, E.H. & Krishan, K.R. (1992) Subcortical brain anatomy in anorexia and bulimia. *Biological Psychiatry*, 31, 735 738.

Jimerson, D.C., Lesem, M.D., Kaye, W.H. & Brewerton, T.D. (1992) Low serotonin and dopamine metabolite concentration in cerebrospinal fluid from bulimic patients with frequent binge episodes. *Archives of General Psychiatry*, 49, 132–138.

Jimerson, D.C., Wolfe, B.E., Metzger, E.D., Finkelstein, D.M., Cooper, T.B. & Levine, J.M. (1997) Decreased serotonin function in bulimia nervosa. *Archives of General Psychiatry*, 54, 529 534.

Katzman, D.K., Lambe, E.K., Mikulis, D.J., Ridgley, J.N., Goldbloom, D.S. & Zipursky, R.B. (1996) Cerebral gray matter and white matter volume deficits in adolescent girls with anorexia nervosa. *Journal of Pediatrics*, 129, 794–803.

Kaye, W.H., Ballenger, J.C., Lydiard, R.B., Stuart, G.W., Laraia, M.T., O'Neil, P., Fossey, M.D., Stevens, V., Lesser, S.C. & Hsu, G. (1990) CSF monoamine levels in normal weight bulimia: evidence for abnormal noradrenergic activity. *American Journal of Psychiatry*, 147, 225–229.

Kaye, W.H., Ebert, M.H., Raleigh, M. & Lake, R. (1984) Abnormalities in CNS monoamine metabolism in anorexia nervosa. *Archives of General Psychiatry*, 41, 350–355.

Kaye, W.H., Frank, G.K.W. & McConaha, C. (1999) Altered dopamine activity after recovery from restricting-type anorexia nervosa. *Neuropsychopharmacology*, 21, 503–506.

Kaye, W.H., Frank, G.K., Meltzer, C.C., Price, J.C., McConaha, C.W., Crossan, P.J., Klump, K.L. & Rhodes, L. (2001) Altered serotonin 2A receptor activity in women who have recovered from bulimia nervosa. *American Journal of Psychiatry*, 158, 1152–1155.

Kaye, W.H., Gendall, K.A., Fernstrom, M.H., Fernstrom, J.D., McConaha, C.W. & Weltzin, T.E. (2000) Effects of acute tryptophan depletion on mood in bulimia nervosa. *Biological Psychiatry*, 47, 151–157.

Kaye, W.H., Greeno, C.G., Moss, H., Fernstrom, J., Fernstrom, M., Lilenfeld, L.R., Weltzin, T.E. & Mann, J.J. (1998) Alterations in serotonin activity and psychiatric symptoms after recovery from bulimia nervosa. *Archives of General Psychiatry*, 55, 927 935.

Kaye, W.H., Gwirtsman, H.E., Brewerton, T.D., George, D.T. & Wurtman, R.J. (1988b) Bingeing behavior and plasma amino acids: a possible involvement of brain serotonin in bulimia nervosa. *Psychiatry Research*, 23, 31–43.

Kaye, W.H., Gwirtsman, H.E., George, D.T., Jimerson, D.C. & Ebert, M.H. (1988a) CSF 5-HIAA concentrations in anorexia nervosa: reduced values in underweight subjects normalise after weight restoration. *Biological Psychiatry*, 23, 102–105.

Kaye, W.H., Gwirtsman, H.E., George, D.T. & Ebert, M.H. (1991) Altered serotonin activity in anorexia nervosa after long-term weight restoration: does elevated cerebrospinal 5-hydroxyindoleacetic acid level correlate with rigid and obsessive behavior? *Archives of General Psychiatry*, 48, 556–562.

Kaye, W.H., Nagata, T., Weltzin, T.E., Hsu, L.K., Sokol, M.S., McConaha, C., Plotnikov, K.H., Weise, J. & Deep, D. (2001) Double-blind placebo-controlled administration of fluoxetine in restricting- and purging-type anorexia nervosa. *Biological Psychiatry*, 49, 644–652.

Krieg, J.C., Backmund, H. & Pirke, K.M. (1986) Endocrine, metabolic and brain morphological abnormalities in patients with eating disorders. *International Journal of Eating Disorders*, 5, 999–1005.

Krieg, J.C., Backmund, H. & Pirke, K.M. (1987) Cranial computed tomography findings in bulimia. *Acta Psychiatrica Scandinavica*, **75**, 144–149.

Krieg, J.C., Lauer, C., Leisinger, G., Pahl, J., Wolfgang, S., Pirke, K.M. & Moser, E.A. (1989) Brain morphology and regional cerebral blood flow in anorexia nervosa. *Biological Psychiatry*, **25**, 1041–1048.

Lakenau, H., Swigar, M.E., Bhimani, S., Luchins, D. & Quilan, D.M. (1985). Cranial CT scans in eating disorder patients and controls. *Comprehensive Psychiatry*, **26**, 136–147.

Levitan, R.D., Kaplan, A.S., Joffe, R.T., Levitt, A.J. & Brown, G.M. (1997) Hormonal and subjective responses to intravenous meta-Chlorphenylpiperazine in bulimia nervosa. *Archives of General Psychiatry*, **54**, 521–527.

Lydiard, R.B., Brandy, K.T., O'Neil, P.M., Schlesier-Carter, B., Hamilton, S., Rogers, Q. & Ballenger, J.C. (1988) Precursor amino acid concentrations in normal weight bulimics and normal controls. *Progress in Neuropsychopharmacology and Biological Psychiatry*, **12**, 893–898.

Marazziti, D., Macchi, E., Rotondo, A., Placidi, G.F. & Cassano, G.B. (1988) Involvement of the serotonin system in bulimia. *Life Sciences*, **43**, 2123–2126.

McBride, P.A., Anderson, G.M., Khait, V.D., Sunday, S.R. & Halmi, K.A. (1991) Serotonergic responsivity in eating disorders. *Psychopharmacology Bulletin*, **27**, 365–372.

Monteleone, P., Brambilla, F., Bortolotti, F., Ferraro, C. & Maj, M. (1998a) Plasma prolactin response to D-fenfluramine is blunted in bulimic patients with frequent binge episodes. *Psychological Medicine*, **28**, 975–983.

Monteleone, P., Brambilla, F., Bortolotti, F. & Maj, M. (2000) Serotonergic dysfunction across the eating disorders: relationship to eating behaviour, nutritional status and general psychopathology. *Psychological Medicine*, **30**, 1099–1110.

Monteleone, P., Brambilla, F., Bortolotti, F., La Rocca, A. & Maj, M. (1998b) Prolactin response to D-fenfluramine is blunted in people with anorexia nervosa. *British Journal of Psychiatry*, **172**, 438–442.

Nozoe, S., Naruo, T., Nakabeppu, Y., Soejima, Y., Nakajo, M. & Tanaka, H. (1993) Changes in cerebral blood flow in patients with anorexia nervosa detected through single photon emission tomography imaging. *Biological Psychiatry*, **34**, 578–580.

O'Dwyer, A.M., Lucey, J.V. & Russell, G.M.F. (1996) Serotonin activity in anorexia nervosa after long-term weight restoration: response to D-fenfluramine challenge. *Psychological Medicine*, **26**, 353–359.

Okamoto, Y., Okamoto, Y., Kagaya, A., Horiguchi, J. & Yamawaki, S. (1999) The relationship of the platelet 5-HT-induced calcium response to clinical symptoms in eating disorders. *Psychopharmacology*, **142**, 289–294.

Okamoto, Y., Okamoto, Y., Kagaya, A., Tamiya, S., Fujita, Y., Tohoda, Y., Motohashi, N. & Yamawaki, S. (1995) Serotonin-induced platelet calcium mobilization is enhanced in bulimia nervosa but not in anorexia nervosa. *Biological Psychiatry*, **38**, 274–276.

Oldman, A., Walsh, A., Salkovskis, P., Fairburn, C.G. & Cowen, P.J. (1995) Biochemical and behavioural effects of acute tryptophan depletion in abstinent bulimic subjects: a pilot study. *Psychological Medicine*, **25**, 995–1001.

Otto, B., Kuntz, U., Fruehauf, E., Wawarta, R., Folwaczny, C., Riepl, R.L., Heiman, M.L., Lehnert, P., Fichter, M. & Tschop, M. (2001) Weight gain decreases elevated plasma ghrelin concentrations of patients with anorexia nervosa. *European Journal of Endocrinology*, **145**, 5–9.

Roser, W., Bubl, R., Buergin, D., Seelig, J., Radue, E.W. & Rost, B. (1999) Metabolic changes in the brain of patients with anorexia and bulimia nervosa as detected by proton magnetic resonance spectroscopy. *International Journal of Eating Disorders*, **26**, 119–139.

Smith, K.A., Fairburn, C.G. & Cowen, P.J. (1999) Symptomatic relapse in bulimia nervosa following acute tryptophan depletion. *Archives of General Psychiatry*, **56**, 171–176.

Steiger, H., Gauvin, L., Israel, M., Koerner, N., Ng Ying Kin N.M.K., Paris, J. & Young, S.N. (2001b) Association of serotonin and cortisol indices with childhood abuse in bulimia nervosa. *Archives of General Psychiatry*, **58**, 837–843.

Steiger, H., Koerner, N., Engelberg, M.J., Israel, M., Ng Ying Kin N.M.K. & Young, S.N. (2001a) Self-destructiveness and serotonin function in bulimia nervosa. *Psychiatry Research*, **103**, 15–26.

Steiger, H., Young, S.N., Ng Ying Kin N.M.K., Koerner, N., Israel, M., Lageix, P. & Paris, J. (2001c) Implications of impulsive and affective symptoms for serotonin function in bulimia nervosa. *Psychological Medicine*, **31**, 85–95.

Swayze, V.W. (1997) Brain imaging and eating disorders. *Eating Disorders Review*, **8**, 1–4.

Swayze, V.W., Nadersen, A., Arndt, S., Rajarethinam, R., Fleming, F., Sato, Y. & Andreasen, N.C. (1996) Reversibility of brain tissue loss in anorexia nervosa assessed with a computerised Talairach 3-D proportional grid. *Psychological Medicine*, **26**, 381–390.

Tauscher, J., Pirker, W., Willeit, M., de Zwaan, M., Bailer, U., Neumeister, A., Asenbaum, S., Lennkh, C., Praschak-Rieder, N., Brücke, T. & Kasper, S. (2001) [^{123}]Beta-CIT and single photon emission computed tomography reveal reduced brain serotonin transporter availability in bulimia nervosa. *Biological Psychiatry*, **49**, 326–332.

Ward, A., Brown, N., Lightman, S., Campbell, I.C. & Treasure, J. (1998) Neuroendocrine, appetitive and behavioural responses to d-fenfluramine in women recovered from anorexia nervosa. *British Journal of Psychiatry*, **172**, 351–358.

Weizman, R., Carmi, M., Tyano, S., Apter, A. & Rehavi, M. (1986) High affinity ^{3}H-imipramine binding and serotonin uptake to platelets of adolescent females suffering from anorexia nervosa. *Life Sciences*, **38**, 1235–1242.

Weltzin, T.E., Fernstrom, J.D., McConaha, C.& Kaye, W.H. (1994) Acute tryptophan depletion in bulima: effects on large neutral amino acids. *Biological Psychiatry*, **35**, 388–397.

Weltzin, T.E., Fernstrom, M.H., Fernstrom, J.D., Neuberger, S.K. & Kaye, W.H. (1995) Acute tryptophan depletion and increased food intake and irritability in bulimia nervosa. *American Journal of Psychiatry*, **152**, 1668–1671.

Wolfe, B.E., Metzger, E.D., Levine, J.M., Finkelstein, D.M., Cooper, T.B. & Jimerson, D.C. (2000) Serotonin function following remission from bulimia nervosa. *Neuropsychopharmacology*, **22**, 257–263.

Wood, A. (1993) Pharmacotherapy of bulimia nervosa—experience with fluoxetine. *International Clinical Psychopharmacology*, **8**, 295–299.

Wu, J.C., Hagman, J., Buchsbaum, M.S., Blinder, B., Derfler, M., Tai, W.Y., Hazlett, E. & Sicotte, N. (1990) Greater left cerebral hemispheric metabolism in bulimia assessed by positron emission tomography. *American Journal of Psychiatry*, **147**, 309–312.

Zemishlany, Z., Modai, A., Apter, A., Jerushalmy, Z., Samuel, E. & Tyano, S. (1987) Serotonin (5-HT) uptake by blood platelets in anorexia nervosa. *Acta Psychiatrica Scandinavica*, **75**, 127–130.

CHAPTER 6

Attachment and Childhood Development

Anne Ward

Psychotherapy Department, Maudsley Hospital, London, UK

and

Simon Gowers

Pine Lodge Adolescent Unit, Chester, UK

INTRODUCTION

Although the aetiology of eating disorders is generally regarded as multidimensional, encompassing a range of biological and psychosocial variables, distinction should be drawn between those factors which act as proximal *precipitants* of dieting behaviour or the associated psychological concerns and those earlier influences that *predispose* to eating disorders. The longitudinal study of Marchi and Cohen (1990) which followed up 800 children at three time points, demonstrated that weight and shape concerns are rare in young children, thus they appear to develop through childhood, becoming common by later adolescence. Very recently, reports have appeared of children as young as 5 expressing fears of becoming fat and with concerns about their body image (Feldman et al., 1988). Shapiro et al. (1997) meanwhile showed that dieting and exercise were used to control weight in as many as 29% of boys and 41% of girls aged 8–10 years. Clearly the seeds for the development of the typical concerns of eating disorders are sown early. In this chapter we explore some of the early biological and family factors which shape personality and future human relationships and which may subsequently confer a vulnerability to their development.

It is widely accepted that parent–child relationships play a central role in children's psychological development and so we will focus largely on these. The quality and form of these relationships are thought to predict later interpersonal relationships and have a profound influence on personality development and related psychological functioning, such as in the areas of self-esteem and social confidence. Surprisingly, there has been until relatively recently, only a small body of good empirical evidence to support the importance of these relationships in development. It is largely within the area of attachment that a lucid and comprehensive theory of early relationships has evolved. The grounds for attachment theory

Handbook of Eating Disorders. Edited by J. Treasure, U. Schmidt and E. van Furth.

were laid by Bowlby from the late 1950s (Bowlby, 1958, 1969, 1973, 1980). However, it only formally emerged as a scientific discipline in the 1980s with the development of appropriate research instruments. A means of assessing individual differences in attachment behaviour was later developed through the work of Mary Ainsworth (Ainsworth et al., 1978). This has been enormously helpful in enabling intensive, ongoing attempts to assess the psychological effects of early relationships on development.

We will begin then by reviewing the major influences on child development starting with attachment theory and then examine the research evidence for their role in the development and maintenance of eating disorders.

ATTACHMENT

Origins of Attachment Theory

Bowlby's early theories were influenced by ethology, attachment behaviour being seen as a 'safety regulating system' to protect against predators. In this formulation attachment is seen as protective, in as much as children need protection from disease, injury and at times human predation and thus their distress at separation is viewed as adaptive. Attachment is seen as a feature of a relationship and not a characteristic of the infant alone; it develops as a function of a caregiver's general sensitivity to an infant's signals. Thus Bowlby suggested, the child learns about the caregivers emotional and physical availability and responds accordingly. Bringing together elements from cognitive psychology and object relations theory, Bowlby proposed that children internalise their experience with attachment figures to form *internal working models* of the relationships between themselves and others.

Responsive parenting and sensitivity to infant and child signals is thought within this theory to have an important impact on one's sense of self-efficacy, that is the child's belief that they have control over life events. Children who have experienced caring and responsive caregiving, generally see others as caring and reliable and themselves as lovable and worthy of care. If they have been ignored or rejected they may grow to see others as uncaring and unreliable and themselves as unworthy or unlovable.

Many of the first attempts to study the impact of early care and relationships on development focused on the consequences of poor or inconsistent care. Children raised in orphanages, without consistent caregivers were found to suffer developmental delays and also displayed unusual social and emotional behaviour. They seemed unable to form close relationships and were sometimes indiscriminately friendly to strangers. Initially these deficits were ascribed to '*maternal deprivation*' but subsequent research has drawn attention to the role of fathers, siblings and family life as well as the opportunities for healthy attachment and subsequent social development offered by substitute care-givers provided they are consistent and offer quality one-to-one relationships.

A scheme for measuring attachment was developed by Ainsworth who classified the responses of infants to separation from mothers, followed by reunion in a laboratory setting (the so-called Strange Situation). Thus attachments could be rated secure, avoidant or resistant, and ambivalent denoted by the letters B, A and C. Furthermore, this classification was found to be a marker for behaviour in the home. More recently a fourth category of disorganised/disorientated attachment has been added to the scheme.

Influences on Attachment

Early relationships play such a crucial part in a child's early years that it is difficult to separate influences on attachment from other influences on development. Similarly, while attachment relationships depend on the interaction between parent and child, factors in the child, in the parent and issues outside the relationship will have a bearing on their quality.

Factors in the Child

Temperament

Most parents who have brought up more than one child will say that they noticed differences between them right from the beginning. These early infant characteristics include such factors as activity level, predominant mood, readiness to approach new experiences and sleep pattern, often referred to as temperamental factors. On the one hand temperament theory provides a challenge to attachment theory as an explanation for the quality of parent–child relationships, but on the other can be seen as an influence on it. Thomas et al. (1968) were responsible for initiating much temperament research and in an attempt to reduce the blame on parents for children's behavioural disorders, suggested that some children were much harder to parent than others.

Developmental Maturity

The ability of a child to develop social relationships including attachment relationships will depend on its developmental maturity. Usually social maturity equates broadly to general maturity but in certain disorders such as autism, social maturity may be specifically retarded.

Health

Certain physical disorders may adversely affect the child's ability to respond to signals put out by caregivers; this will particularly be the case for deficits in hearing or vision. Disfiguring conditions meanwhile, particularly those affecting the child's face, such as cleft palate or port-wine stain may also affect parental bonding. Life-threatening conditions in infancy may influence attachment because of their influence on the parents' ability to maintain physical closeness, if the child is for example nursed in an incubator or subject to multiple surgical procedures. Alternatively, the fear of the potential loss of the child may inhibit the parents' willingness to allow themselves to engage in an intimate relationship. On occasions the child's ill-health may promote a 'high concern' or overprotective style of parenting, which may continue after the health problem has been resolved.

Factors in Parents

Attitudes towards the child develop from the point of conception, through fantasies about the sex, appearance and personality of the child. At the point of birth, the feelings towards the child, particularly from the mother, will generally be positive, but ambivalent or negative feelings may predominate, particularly if the pregnancy was unwanted or if the relationship with the father is poor.

Parental high concern or an overprotective style of parenting may result from parental anxiety or a perceived physical or psychological weakness in the child irrespective of objective evidence of the child's vulnerability (Shoebridge & Gowers, 2000).

Parental Health and Personality

Parental anxiety may be a constitutional trait or arise from a specific child-related antecedent such as a problematic past obstetric history. The index child may be born after a period of infertility or the loss of an earlier child.

Parental ill-health can have an effect on the quality of attachment through a number of routes. The parent may be unavailable either physically or emotionally and the relationship may suffer frequent disruptions. Where disruptions occur without warning, for example as a result of emergency hospitalisation, they are likely to be particularly bewildering, while children's ability to understand the implications of ill-health will be governed by their developmental maturity. Serious ill-health in one parent may be compensated for by a good quality relationship with the other, or a substitute caregiver, but healthy parents are likely in turn to be adversely affected in terms of their physical availability and their own psychological adjustment to their spouse's illness.

Mental ill-health in a parent poses particular challenges for the relationship with the child and his or her psychological development. A parent who is anxious or fearful of the world may transmit such attitudes, while depressive mood will have an impact on emotional responsiveness and availability and may present a gloomy outlook on life. Psychotic disorders may confront a child with both disturbances of behaviour and belief. For an older child a negative effect on peer relationships may ensue, with the child being reluctant to bring friends home, he or she may suffer bullying.

Eating disorders provide a good example of the effects of the interplay between parental attitudes and behaviours (in themselves and directed to the child). Mothers who diet or have weight concerns themselves are more likely to bottle feed (Crisp, 1969). The mother's attitude to feeding is likely to be a more important influence than the direct effect of bottle feeding on infant growth.

Children's perceptions of their parents' health in turn impact on their feelings of security and their view of their own health and resilience. The development of an external locus of control or a feeling of personal ineffectiveness may be particularly potent as risk factors for eating disorders.

Parental Attachment Status

There are good grounds for supposing that parents' own experiences of being parented and their attachment relationships in their families of origin will predict the quality of their own children's attachments. Until recently there were few ways of linking intergenerational attachment representations.

The Adult Attachment Interview (AAI; George et al., 1984) is a semi-structured interview-based measure for adults which enables evaluation of the quality of past attachments in childhood. It is designed to assess the adults 'state of mind' with respect to attachment, by enquiring about relationships in childhood and evaluating the coherence of their accounts.

It is concerned not so much with what happened as what the subject feels about what happened and whether what the subject says is backed up by evidence. The general quality of child–caregiver relationships is probed, together with experiences of early separation, illnesses, losses, rejection, and maltreatment; the interviewer probes for specific memories to illustrate general statements. There are three main categories in this classification system: Free-autonomous (F), Dismissive (D), and Preoccupied (E). Secure adults categorised (F) are said to value intimate relationships, and acknowledge their effects. In addition, some interviews are characterised by an apparent failure to resolve mourning over loss or abuse, and are separately classified as Unresolved (U). Subjects who simultaneously possess E and D qualities are described as Cannot Classify (CC). All interviews are rated on a number of scales concerning 'Probable Experience' (of attachment figures) and current 'State of Mind' of the interviewee; these scales contribute to the overall classification (D/E/F/U).

The AAI has been shown to have predictive validity for the quality of infant attachment in the next generation (van IJzendoorn, 1995), in as much as two-thirds of infant attachments on the ABCD classification match their parents attachment category on the AAI.

Other Influences on Attachment

Genetics

There is a growing body of evidence from twin studies to suggest a significant genetic contribution to attachment patterns. It may be that genetic contributions to the temperamental component of distress proneness is greater than that for security/insecurity (Goldberg, 2000).

Siblings

Brothers and sisters can facilitate or impair attachment formation in a number of ways. They may display jealousy towards the new child or else their behaviour or temperament may influence parental expectations of subsequent infants.

Living Conditions

Good quality attachment is likely to occur when the family is not pressed by financial hardship or overcrowding. Good quality family relationships can, however, overcome severe material deprivation.

Effects of Attachment beyond Infancy

Bowlby considered attachment to be a feature of significant relationships throughout the lifespan, as early experiences are coded as internal working models, which are then carried forward to influence later personality and behaviour. These internal models contain both affective and cognitive information. Emotional expressions become more complex and subtle as children get older and they learn implicit rules about displaying affect, including the masking of negative emotions (Lewis & Michalson, 1983). Attachment theory has been concerned with two aspects of emotional development: the way in which attachment figures respond to affect and the ways in which attachment relationships vary with individual differences in emotional expression and regulation. Attachment relationships are also thought to influence information processing through their effects on selective attention and memory. By the age of about 6, children develop a *'theory of mind'*, i.e. a notion that they and others have thoughts about the world, which may not be the same and which are independent of external objects. Internal working models of attachment come prominently to include attributions of key relationships, e.g. 'Mummy likes to bake cakes for me'.

Parental (and to a lesser extent, sibling) attitudes to their own body shape may affect children in two ways (Stein, 1995). Firstly, children model themselves on their same sex parent and elder siblings. Secondly, parents with eating disorders may influence their children through their attitudes to their children's weight, shape and eating habits and the importance they attach to these. Agras et al.'s (1999) controlled, prospective study of 41 mothers with eating disorders and 153 without a history of eating disorder, demonstrated that food tended to be used for reward or behavioural control more in the former. Also the mothers with eating disorders were more concerned about their daughter's weight from the age of 2 onwards. At 5 years, the children of mothers with eating disorders had greater negative affect than controls. Although most studies have shown that children of eating-disordered mothers tend to be thinner than controls (Stein et al., 1996), a group of mothers in this study overfed their children through a belief that infant weight was an important index of health and successful parenting.

Attachment and Health

The notion that internal working models play a key role in linking early attachment experiences to later social and psychological consequences is appealing, but not widely tested. A simple hypothesis might be that insecure attachment increases vulnerability to behavioural problems or psychological disorder. The second part of this chapter will address the evidence for associations between attachment style and the development of eating disorders, followed by a review of non-attachment developmental influences.

ATTACHMENT AND EATING DISORDERS

Historical Perspective

Hilde Bruch, writing in the 1970s, linked emergent attachment ideas to her clinical observations. In her seminal work, *Eating Disorders: Anorexia Nervosa, Obesity and the Person Within* (1974), she offers an unusual insight into Mary Ainsworth's thinking, as the precursor of the Strange Situation appears associated with early mother–infant feeding interactions:

> When rated at 12 months, the infants in whom the feeding interaction had been most appropriate to their needs, permitting them active participation, showed the strongest attachment to their mothers, with a clear-cut tendency to seek her proximity, and to express distress at her absence. They made active efforts to gain and maintain contact with her. In contrast babies with inappropriate feeding experiences, showed little or no tendency to seek proximity, interaction, or contact with the mother and little or no tendency to cling when picked up or to resist being released. They tended either to

ignore the mother on her return, or to turn away or go away from her. There was a third group which included the one of pseudo-demand with overfeeding (i.e. mother impatient with the baby and staves them off with food), in which children were distressed by separation, but showed less ability to use the mother as a secure base from which they could enjoy exploring the strange environment. They generally displayed more maladaptive behaviour in relation to new and strange situations.

(Ainsworth & Bell, 1969; quoted in Bruch, 1974)

Developing these ideas to describe her own patient population, Bruch's formulation was of a mother–child interaction in which mother does not respond appropriately to her infant's needs, instead superimposing her own needs such that the infant does not learn to discriminate self. The infant adapts, such that the situation may pass unnoticed throughout a 'well-behaved' childhood, only becoming evident as the adolescent striving for autonomy/identity can no longer be ignored. Although this is clearly an oversimplification of Bruch's rich theory, it serves to highlight the interweaving of attachment ideas with some of the earlier clinical literature, providing a basis from which to explore subsequent developments.

Background Research

The application of attachment research instruments to the field of eating disorders was initially slow, but has recently mushroomed. Thus, in the space of four years between two comprehensive reviews, the number of published studies in the field approximately doubled (O'Kearney, 1996; Ward et al., 2000). In the earlier review, strong evidence of attachment disturbance in eating-disordered populations was found, and connected to key elements of eating disorder psychopathology (O'Kearney, 1996). However, this reviewer also pointed to limitations in the methodology of published work, such that few conclusions could be drawn about direction of causality, or about the role of attachment disturbance in the maintenance of eating disorders. In addition, of the ten studies surveyed, six were based on the Parental Bonding Instrument (Parker et al., 1979), which, although it taps into childhood experience, only indirectly relates to Bowlby's attachment constructs.

Since 1996 there has been increased attention to the topic and the use of instruments has tended to become more refined. In particular, the Adult Attachment Interview (AAI), currently regarded as the 'gold standard' in attachment research, has been applied to eating-disordered populations. Thus one might anticipate that greater clarity would emerge from a later review. Questions have also been asked about the association between attachment style and eating disorder diagnosis. Following Bowlby, insecure attachment is usually classified as anxious/resistant/avoidant/dismissive, or angry/preoccupied/enmeshed. Although no association between attachment status and eating disorder subtype emerged from O'Kearney's (1996) work, there was a belief that such an association might emerge in a larger review with more refined instruments. Clinically, anorexic women appear avoidant, not only of food but of life in the raw, whereas bulimic women are more often angry and chaotic. Williams (1997) has described bulimic patients as 'porous', unable to protect themselves from mother's toxic projections as an infant, whereas anorexic patients have developed a 'no-entry' system of defences against this style of mothering. Whereas this has echoes of the avoidant/entangled attachment classification, it is a psychoanalytic rather than an empirical description. A more up-to-date review might expect to bridge these different stances.

Review of the Literature

A search of the relevant databases reveal nothing new since the publication of the last review (Ward et al., 2000). However, the findings of two recent studies from the South London and Maudsley Eating Disorders Unit are included here, one paper in press (Ward et al., in press) and one study submitted for publication (Ward et al., submitted). Otherwise a summary of the review is presented as the state of the art. To facilitate ease of presentation, studies are grouped according to the attachment measure used. Studies involving non-clinical groups will not be discussed further, as these are typically milder cases of eating disorders, picked up by screening questionnaires. The clinical populations constitute a purer diagnostic group and are thus of more relevance in a search for specific associations between diagnosis and attachment status. Any such associations could be tested in the broader groups at a later date. Similarly, studies using the Parental Bonding Instrument are excluded, as they are of more peripheral concern. However, for interested readers, further details of all these publications are presented in the more recent review.

Separation Anxiety Test

Hansburg's Separation Anxiety Test is a semi-projective measure of separation anxiety, derived from Bowlby's attachment theory. Armstrong and Roth (1989) compared eating disordered inpatients to controls chosen to reflect other developmental stages likely to trigger separation anxiety. The patient group showed significantly more severe separation and attachment difficulties than controls. Ninety-six percent of the eating-disordered subjects showed anxious attachment, 85% severely. Moreover, the patient group did not appear to distinguish cognitively between brief, common separations, and more permanent leaving. The authors suggest that restrictive eating provides a form of distant, safe, but unacknowledged attachment, and that bingeing may fill a need for nurturance in a non-threatening way.

Parental Attachment Questionnaire

The Parental Attachment Questionnaire which is based on Ainsworth's concepts of attachment was administered to eating-disordered inpatients and to controls (Kenny & Hart, 1992). The results suggested that weight preoccupation, bulimic behaviour, and feelings of ineffectiveness were associated with the lack of affectively positive and emotionally supportive parental relationships, together with poor parental fostering of autonomy. The authors felt that their results challenged traditional conceptualisations of eating disorders that focused on separation difficulties but gave little attention to parental attachment.

Relationship Questionnaire

Based on the ideas of cognitive constructivists, the authors hypothesised that eating-disordered individuals would have an enmeshed or preoccupied attachment style (Friedberg & Lyddon, 1996). The Relationship Questionnaire assesses respondents' relative commitments to four descriptive paragraphs consistent with four attachment styles (Secure,

Preoccupied, Dismissing and Fearful). Participants were inpatients and outpatients with an eating disorder, and controls. The contention was supported, in that Secure and Preoccupied attachment styles on the RQ significantly predicted membership in either the non-clinical or eating-disordered groups respectively. The patients were a mixed diagnostic group, but no attempt was made to link attachment style with eating disorder diagnosis.

Attachment History Questionnaire

The Attachment History Questionnaire, which is a structured interview designed to elicit information about experiences with primary and later attachment figures, was administered to inpatients with eating disorders and to controls (Chassler, 1997). Eating-disordered patients experienced early attachment figures as significantly less responsive, available and trustworthy than did controls. Patients felt more unwanted, alone and helpless, and experienced more shame and guilt than did controls. Finally, eating-disordered patients felt significantly more responsible for their parents' happiness than did controls. While acknowledging the limitations of the study, the author points out that it highlights likely transference difficulties in therapy with this group of patients.

Adolescent Attachment Interview

Salzman (1997) reports links between a particular attachment pattern and two clinically significant correlates, affective instability and eating disorders (anorexia, or anorexia with bulimia). Although not a patient study in the sense above, all reported cases of eating disorder had been diagnosed by family physicians, and so the findings are included here for discussion. The interview sample was preselected by a screening questionnaire to yield a group of women, who appeared to meet the criteria for secure ($n = 10$), ambivalent ($n = 11$), or avoidant ($n = 7$) attachment to their mothers. All partook in the Adolescent Attachment Interview (developed separately from, but overlapping with the AAI), which was classified into the three categories of secure, avoidant, and ambivalent. The most striking observations were among the ambivalently attached subgroup, where 7 of 11 had experienced clinically significant anorexia nervosa, and 9 of the 11 reported states of distressingly intense feeling. In contrast, none of the secure or avoidant subjects suffered from diagnosed anorexia in adolescence. Daughters reported that their mothers described a similar mixture of anger, longing, and dependence in their own attachments to the subjects' grandmothers. Salzman links the adolescents' descriptions of attachment to their mothers to the particular type of disturbed feeding pattern 'pseudo-demand with impatient mothers' quoted earlier in this chapter (Ainsworth & Bell, 1969; quoted in Bruch, 1974).

Reciprocal Attachment Questionnaire

Ward et al. (2000) surmised that attachment insecurity in eating-disordered patients would extend from the family of origin to other adult attachment relationships. The Reciprocal Attachment Questionnaire (RAQ) operationalises the key components of reciprocal attachment and is in close theoretical agreement with the Adult Attachment Interview. Subjects were inpatients and outpatients with eating disorders, and controls. Patients scored significantly higher than controls on most of the RAQ scales, most notably on the subscales *Compulsive Care-Seeking* and *Compulsive Self-Reliance*. No associations were found between disorder diagnoses and particular attachment profiles. The results illuminate a basic 'pull–push' dilemma in the reciprocal adult attachment relationships of eating-disordered subjects. The authors argue that this dilemma bedevils attempts at therapy and may illuminate the strong feelings elicited by these patients in their therapists.

Adult Attachment Interview

The Adult Attachment Interview (AAI) was used in a study of the relationship between attachment style and psychiatric status in non-psychotic inpatients in a therapeutic community (Fonagy et al., 1996). Case-matched controls were selected from a hospital outpatient department. The AAI was administered to both groups, and an additional scale, Reflective Self-Functioning (RSF), which assesses the clarity of an individual's representation of the mental states of others as well as of his or her own mental state, was applied to the transcripts.

Seventeen percent ($n = 14$) of the inpatients had an eating disorder, although the type was not specified. Using a three-way classification (D/E/F), one patient with an eating disorder was Free/Autonomous (F), 9 were Preoccupied (E), and 4 were Dismissive (D). Of the 14 patients, 13 were Unresolved (U) with respect to loss or abuse. The CC classification was not available at the time of rating. Findings specifically relating to a diagnosis of eating disorder (compared to other Axis I diagnoses) were a positive association with idealisation of attachment figures on the State of Mind score, and low Reflective Self-Functioning. The authors comment that idealisation of parents echoes the clinical observation that patients with eating disorders are perfectionists whose eating disorder may stem from exaggerated standards that are also applied to parents. Results from this study also suggest that individuals rated as D on the AAI are more likely to show improvement in psychotherapy than are preoccupied or secure patients, at least by the time of discharge. As idealisation is the hallmark of the D individual, and idealisation was associated with an eating disorder diagnosis, this result is of interest to therapists working with this group of patients.

Candelori and Ciocca (1998) administered their adolescent version of the AAI to inpatients on an Eating Disorders Unit. Twelve patients had restricting anorexia nervosa (AN-R), 12 had bulimia nervosa (BN), and 12 were anorexic, binge–purging subtype (AN-BP) (DSM-IV). Classifying attachment in the group as a whole: 9 (25%) patients were Dismissing (D), 6 (16.7%) Secure (F), 15 (41.7%) Preoccupied (E), 1 (2.8%) Unresolved/Dismissing (U/D), and 5 (13.9%) were rated Cannot Classify (CC). Fisher's Exact Test showed a significant association between classification and diagnosis (our analysis, $p = 0.023$). Specifically AN-R is over-represented in the Dismissing and BN in the Preoccupied subgroups. Likewise, AN-BP is most commonly found in the Preoccupied or more difficult to classify subgroups. The authors argue against the DSM classification of eating disorders, pointing to the mounting evidence that the restricting type of anorexia is quite different from the bingeing–purging subtype, which in turn is more akin to bulimia nervosa. They interpret Dismissive Idealisation as a reflection of the mind's capacity to organise itself independently of experience and reality. This dissociative ability, they believe, is only momentary in bulimia, but lasting and enduring in anorexia.

Clinical studies have addressed mother–daughter interactions in eating-disordered populations, but there has been little empirical research into the mother's own attachment patterns, and whether there might be intergenerational transmission of these patterns. In a recent study, the AAI was administered to inpatients with anorexia nervosa ($n = 20$) and, where possible, to their mothers ($n = 12$) (Ward et al., 2001). Nineteen (95%) daughters and 10 (83%) mothers were rated insecure on the AAI. Of these, 15 (79%) daughters and 7 (70%) mothers were rated Dismissive in type. No association was found between mothers' and daughters' attachment styles. The incidence of Unresolved loss was high among the mothers (67%), as was the broader category of Unresolved trauma among the daughters (50%). Compared to published norms for controls and for general psychiatric patients (Fonagy et al., 1996), Idealisation scores were high, and Reflective Self-Functioning scores low in both mother and daughter groups. The authors concluded that women with anorexia nervosa and their mothers commonly have a Dismissive attachment style. (Women with a primary diagnosis of bulimia nervosa were not included in this study and so the association with Preoccupied attachment style could not be tested.) Low Reflective Self-Functioning and high Idealisation are also common, and may be learned (or transmitted) from mother to daughter. A difficulty in emotional processing, highlighted by difficulties in processing trauma, may be transmitted to daughters, and act as a risk factor for the development of anorexia nervosa.

OTHER INFLUENCES ON DEVELOPMENT

The following is a brief review of some of the childhood factors thought to predispose to the development of eating disorders. A fuller account is provided by Gowers and Shore (in press).

Physical Influences

Growth and Puberty

Childhood is, of course, a time of immense physical growth. Linear growth occurs up to the age of 15 in girls and 17 in boys, while increase in weight continues into adulthood. Growth is maximal in infancy with a further growth spurt typically spanning two years during puberty. Puberty leads to changes in shape as well as size and results in the development of secondary sexual characteristics. The timing of puberty is very variable between individuals and has a differential impact on self-esteem between sexes, early puberty generally having an adverse impact on bodily self-esteem in girls and a more positive effect in boys (Alsaker, 1992). The impact of puberty on weight is striking for both genders. Boys' mean weight rises from 40.5 kg at thirteenth birthday to 56 kg at 15, a growth of 38% in two years. Girls, meanwhile grow on average from 34 kg at eleventh birthday to 47.5 kg by 13, a rise of 40% during their (earlier) two years of maximum growth (Tanner & Whitehouse, 1975). The mean proportion of body fat in females also changes from 8% in middle childhood to 22% after puberty (Tanner, 1989). The hormonal changes of puberty are also thought to have an impact on provoked aggressive behaviour in the case of testosterone in boys (Olweus, 1986) and on the vulnerability to depressive symptomatology in girls (Brooks-Gunn & Warren, 1989).

Chronic Physical Illness

The rate of psychological disorder in those with chronic illness is reported as approximately double that in healthy children (Gortmaker et al., 1990). Physical illness may impact on children and increase their vulnerability in a number of ways, particularly in adolescence when identity and self-image are developing. Having a chronic illness can get in the way of normal childhood activities such as playing sports, while those disorders requiring adherence to a special diet, such as diabetes mellitus and cystic fibrosis, might be expected to influence attitudes to 'healthy' or 'forbidden' foods.

Adversity and Negative Life Events

Adversities are usually classified as acute and chronic. The former usually have a rapid onset and are of short duration, while the latter, such as chronic parental ill-health, exert their influence over time. While acute life events may result in depressive reactions or in extreme cases post-traumatic stress disorder, chronic stressors are thought to have a more lasting effect on psychological health (Compas, 1989). The impact of negative events varies between individuals depending on the resources at their disposal, generally referred to as resilience factors. These include 'personal' factors such as intelligence, high self-esteem, internal locus of control and having problem-focused coping skills. 'Environmental' factors such as having a close, supportive family and good friendships have an additive effect in conferring resilience. Clearly, both personal and environmental factors are unlikely to be independent of attachment relationships.

Severe adverse life events are not especially common as immediate precipitants of anorexia nervosa compared to other adolescent psychiatric disorders and where they have occurred, they confer a relatively good prognosis (North et al., 1997).

Intellectual Impairment

Behavioural problems, autistic type disorders, hyperactivity and psychoses have generally been found to be three to four times more common in mentally retarded children than in control children of similar age. Eating disorders, however, are rare in this group of children, probably because of the complexity of the necessary, underlying cognitive processes.

School

The school environment encompasses a wide range of factors such as class size and teacher expectations having an effect on a child's development. Disaffection with school may lead to poor performance and subsequently to truancy and school exclusion. Those who drop out of school are more likely to suffer low self-esteem, depression and commit delinquent acts, though the cause and effect pathway is not clearly established. At the other end of the spectrum, schools may encourage the development of perfectionist traits by strongly reinforcing educational attainment. For those with the ability to succeed, but with poor self-esteem and a sense of ineffectiveness in other spheres of life, control over school achievement may result in a general sense of being in control in a threatening world. This may extend to control of food and weight, highly valued in current society.

Peers

Children who enjoy intimate confiding friendships have been found to be less hostile, less anxious and more sociable than others (Parker & Asher, 1987). Peer groups can, however, take on a powerful and sometimes unhelpful role, particularly in adolescence, where they may encourage risk-taking behaviours. Being rejected or bullied by peers has a negative effect on self-esteem and has been associated with the development of a range of behavioural and emotional disorders. In some young people adverse peer experience may promote a change in behaviour or appearance in an attempt to gain acceptance. Many adolescents who develop eating disorders recount negative comments about fatness as a precipitant to their dieting. These are often single experiences however and, as Hill and Palin (1995) point out, they are often made by boys. Whether those who develop eating disorders have suffered more such comments than their healthy peers or are more vulnerable to their effects is unclear.

DISCUSSION

There is clearly a multifactorial pathway to the development of eating disorders, with the main childhood influences outlined above. The specific contribution of each influence may be debated, although there would be little dispute about its general relevance. However, as the main focus of this chapter has been the influence of attachment status on the development of eating disorders, our discussion will centre on this area. Moreover, as research findings in the area proliferate and often seem confusing, a critical synthesis of the findings is important.

Attachment Research: Main Findings

The overwhelming message from the research literature is of abnormal attachment patterns in eating-disordered populations. The preponderance of insecure attachment is also consistent with the older clinical literature on the subject. In particular, both the ideas of Hilde Bruch and the writings of the early family therapists remain alive in these studies.

Two main themes emerge, the first concerning attachment status and diagnosis, the second revolving around loss. Firstly, using the 'gold standard' Adult Attachment Interview in groups of inpatients with eating disorders, the predicted association between attachment style and eating disorder diagnosis is found by Candelori and Ciocca (1998) and, to a lesser extent, by Ward et al. (2000). Specifically, restricting anorexic patients tended to be Dismissive, whereas those with bulimic behaviours, whether anorexic or bulimic, tended to be Preoccupied. Using the Adolescent Attachment Interview, Salzman (1997) found a strong association between Ambivalent attachment and a history of anorexia nervosa. Similarly, Friedberg and Lyddon (1996) found that a Preoccupied (Ambivalent) stance differentiated eating-disordered patients from controls. However, this latter finding may reflect the fact that there were more bulimic than anorexic patients in their group. In addition, it is not clear how many of the anorexic group had bulimic features. Salzman's findings are interesting, as the anorexia is presented as historical. It is probable that the patients underwent some kind of therapy, as all were diagnosed by family physicians, and that their attachment stance may have shifted as a result. A shift from Dismissive to Preoccupied would be consistent with Candelori and Ciocca's argument that Dismissive strategies are more pathological than those of the Preoccupied group. Again, however, it is not clear how many of the anorexic patients also had bulimic features. It would be reasonable to summarise the evidence to date as suggestive of a bulimic/preoccupied, anorexic/dismissive association, although it would be premature to draw firm conclusions on the basis of these findings.

The second theme emerging is that of unresolved trauma. Ward et al. (2001), using the AAI, found a high incidence of Unresolved loss among the mothers of anorexic woman, and a somewhat lower but still noteworthy level of unresolved trauma among their daughters. Fonagy et al. (1996), also using the AAI, found that the majority of their eating-disordered patients (13/14) were Unresolved (U) with respect to abuse or loss. Many of these patients, however, had Axis II diagnoses in addition to the eating disorder, and so the finding is less specific. The relatively low incidence of U in Candelori's study (1/36) is surprising, given that approximately 16–30% of eating-disordered patients have suffered childhood sexual abuse, and approximately 10–30% direct or indirect violence within the childhood home (Schmidt et al., 1993). It may be that these patients have become absorbed in the Cannot Classify group, as U status typically renders an AAI script harder to rate. To continue the theme of trauma, and more specifically that of loss, an excess of severe obstetric loss prior to the daughter's birth has been shown in families with an adolescent anorexic daughter (Shoebridge & Gowers, 2000). In addition, Wentz-Nilsson et al. (1998) found significantly more deaths among the first-degree relatives of teenagers with anorexia nervosa than among controls. Linking these findings with the AAI studies, the relevant variable may be how those losses/traumas are processed within the family. Shoebridge and Gowers record high levels of parental concern in the parents of later anorexic adolescents, and suggest that this may derive, in part, from abnormal grief reactions. Interestingly, Armstrong and Roth (1989), using the SAT, showed that eating-disordered patients did not appear to distinguish cognitively between brief and more permanent leavings. A theme of unresolved loss would be consistent with the older clinical literature, which emphasises early separation difficulties in the aetiology of anorexia nervosa. In a situation in which there are difficulties with emotional processing, the risk of various kinds of abuse would be increased.

Recurring Difficulties in the Literature

Focusing on clinical groups has allowed the emergence of a number of themes: the high incidence of insecure attachment in eating-disordered groups, the possible link between attachment stance and eating disorder symptomatology, and the potential importance of unresolved loss/trauma in these families. However, if we look at the larger literature (Ward et al., 2000) a less coherent picture emerges. It is still the case that insecurity is rife in subjects with eating difficulties, but any more precise associations are lost. We have argued that the study of non-patient groups has blurred the picture. However, there are several other problems with the literature, which are worth airing.

Terminology

Different terms have been used to describe the various attachment categories, several of which overlap to a greater or lesser extent. Alternatively, the same term (e.g. 'anxious' attachment) is used in different sense in different studies. Similarly, there are important differences in the various authors' use of the anorexia/bulimia category, for some it means anorexia with bulimic symptoms, for others, bulimia with a history of anorexia.

Methodologies

As mentioned earlier, there are relevant differences in the various populations studied, and in the methods used to establish a diagnosis of eating disorder in each study. Apparent contradictions raise the question of what the various instruments are actually measuring, and at what level of consciousness. A desire to please, which is a feature of eating-disordered women, together with idealisation of parents (Fonagy et al., 1996) may lead to a falsely positive picture of attachments on a relatively straightforward questionnaire. Age, chronicity and cultural differences are other potential confounders that are not often addressed in these studies.

The use of appropriate control groups is important when considering the specificity of a study's findings. Their selection is not straightforward, however. For example, there is an argument for using general psychiatric patients as controls to tease out the specific contribution of the eating disorder. However, a general psychiatric population may well contain patients with eating disorders, and patients with eating disorders often have comorbidity. To screen out the comorbidity, as some studies have attempted to do, may be to distort the clinical picture, as the most severely affected eating disordered patients in a naturalistic setting may well have a comorbid depression or personality disorder. Most studies have adopted the solution of enrolling 'normal' controls, which brings us back to the problem of specificity of the findings for eating disorders.

Attachment and Eating Disorders: Where Next?

Attachment theorists have been criticised for assuming a 'single pathway' model, as if they believe that an account of attachment disruption alone would provide a sufficient explanation of particular psychopathologies (O'Kearney, 1996). Thus Halmi has proposed a biopsychosocial model for bulimia nervosa, at the same time acknowledging that the ideal prospective risk factor study is probably prohibited by cost (Halmi, 1997). While not wishing to diminish these complexities, we now have suggestive empirical evidence linking Bruch's and Ainsworth's ideas on abnormal mother–child interactions and eating disorders with attachment insecurity in later life. The question is how realistically to continue investigating these findings.

It may be unhelpful to pursue the search for tighter associations between attachment style and diagnosis as, both clinically and experimentally, detailed study reveals the Avoidant subject to be closer to her Ambivalent neighbour than is consciously apparent. The Ambivalent subject oscillates between over-involvement and flight, akin to the claustroagarophobic, whereas her Avoidant counterpart associates closeness with overwhelming pain. Each thus carries aspects of the other and instruments that address the conscious aspects of attachment only are likely to miss this overlap. The trend is for more complex studies to examine specific aspects of attachment rather than global attachment style, and this may prove more fruitful in testing clinical ideas. Further work needs to be done on how insecure attachment styles, including difficulties with loss/abuse, are transmitted across the generations. Although transgenerationally transmitted (Fonagy et al., 1991), attachment style may also be modified by therapy (Fonagy et al., 1996; Byng-Hall, 1995). Links with family theorists may help to marry the two historically influential aetiological schools of individual and family therapists. To recognise that attachment is but one aspect of development is not to diminish its importance, but to acknowledge the complexity of human development.

REFERENCES

Ainsworth, M.D.S., Blehar, M.C., Waters, E. & Wall, S. (1978) *Patterns of Attachment: A Psychological Study of the Strange Situation*. Hillsdale, NJ: Erlbaum Associates.

Agras, S., Hammer, L. & McNicholas, F. (1999) A prospective study of the influence of eating-disordered mothers on their children. *International Journal of Eating Disorders*, **25**, 253–262.

Alsaker, F.D. (1992) Pubertal timing, overweight and psychological adjustment. *Journal of Early Adolescence*, **12**, 396–419.

Armstrong, J.G. & Roth, D.M. (1989) Attachment and separation difficulties in eating disorders: A preliminary investigation. *International Journal of Eating Disorders*, **8**, 141–155.

Bowlby, J. (1958) The nature of the child's tie to his mother. *International Journal of Psychoanalysis*, **3**, 1–23.

Bowlby, J. (1969) *Attachment and Loss*, vol. 1, *Attachment*. New York: Basic Books, and London: Hogarth (2nd revised edn, 1982).

Bowlby, J. (1973) *Attachment and Loss*, vol. 2, *Separation: Anxiety and Anger*. New York: Basic Books, and London: Hogarth.

Bowlby, J. (1980) *Attachment and Loss*, vol. 3, *Loss: Sadness and Depression*. New York: Basic Books, and London: Hogarth.

Brooks-Gunn, J. & Warren, M.P. (1989) Biological and social contributions to negative affect in young adolescent girls. *Child Development*, **62**, 40–55.

Bruch, H. (1974) *Eating Disorders: Obesity, Anorexia Nervosa and the Person Within* (pp. 59–60). London: Routledge & Kegan Paul.

Byng-Hall, J. (1995) *Rewriting Family Scripts: Improvisation and Systems Change*. New York: The Guilford Press.

Candelori, C. & Ciocca A. (1998) Attachment and eating disorders. In *Psychotherapeutic Issues in Eating Disorders: Models, Methods, and Results*. Roma: Società Editrice Universo.

Chassler, L. (1997) Understanding anorexia nervosa and bulimia nervosa from an attachment perspective. *Clinical Social Work Journal*, **25**, 407–423.

Compas, B.E. (1989) Risk factors for emotional and behavioural problems in young adolescents. *Journal of Consulting and Clinical Psychology*, **57**, 732–740.

Crisp, A.H. (1969) Psychological aspects of breast feeding with particular reference to Anorexia Nervosa. *British Journal of Medical Psychology*, **42**, 119–132.

Feldman, W., Feldman, E. & Goodman, J.T. (1988) Culture vs. biology: Children's attitude toward thinness and fatness. *Pediatrics*, **81**, 190–194.

Fonagy, P., Leigh, T., Steele, M., Steele, H., Kennedy, R., Mattoon, G., Target, M. & Gerber, A. (1996) The relation of attachment status, psychiatric classification, and response to psychotherapy. *Journal of Consulting and Clinical Psychology*, **64**, 22–31.

Fonagy, P., Steele, M. & Steele, H. (1991) Maternal representations of attachment during pregnancy predict the organisation of mother–infant attachment at one year of age. *Child Development*, **62**, 880–893.

Friedberg, N.L. & Lyddon, W.J. (1996) Self-other working models and eating disorders. *Journal of Cognitive Psychotherapy: An International Quarterly*, **10**, 193–203.

George, C., Kaplan, N. & Main, M. (1984) *The Adult Attachment Interview* (revised in 1985 and 1996). Unpublished scoring manual. Dept of Psychology, University of California: Berkeley.

Goldberg, S. (2000) *Attachment and Development*. London: Arnold.

Gortmaker, S.L., Walker, D., Weitzman, M. & Sobol, A.M. (1990) Chronic conditions socio-economic risks and behavioural problems in children and adolescents. *Pediatrics*, **85**, 267–276.

Gowers, S.G. & Shore, A. (in press) Development of weight and shape concerns in the aetiology of eating disorders. *British Journal of Psychiatry*.

Halmi, K.A. (1997) Models to conceptualize risk factors for bulimia nervosa. *Archives of General Psychiatry*, **54**, 507–508.

Hill, A.J. & Palin, V. (1995) Low self-esteem and weight control: Related issues in 8-year old girls but not boys. *International Journal of Obesity*, **19** (Suppl. 2), 128.

Kenny, M.E. & Hart, K. (1992) Relationship between parental attachment and eating disorders in an inpatient and a college sample. *Journal of Counseling Psychology*, **39**, 521–526.

Lewis, M. & Michalson, L. (1983) *Children's Emotions and Moods*. New York: Plenum Press

Marchi, M. & Cohen, P. (1990) Early childhood eating behaviours and adolescent eating disorders. *Journal of the American Academy of Child and Adolescent Psychiatry*, **29** (1), 112–117.

North, C.D., Gowers, S.G. & Byram, V. (1997) Family functioning and life events in the outcome of adolescent anorexia nervosa. *British Journal of Psychiatry*, **171**, 545–549.

O'Kearney, R. (1996) Attachment disruption in anorexia nervosa and bulimia nervosa: A review of theory and empirical research. *International Journal of Eating Disorders*, **20**, 115–127.

Olweus, D. (1986) Aggression and hormones: Behavioural relationships with testosterone and adrenaline. In D. Olweus, J. Block & M. Radke-Yarrow (Eds), *Development of Antisocial and Prosocial Behaviour: Research Theories and Issues* (pp. 51–72) Orlando, FL: Academic Press.

Parker, J.G. & Asher, S.R. (1987) Peer relations and later adjustment: are low-accepted children 'at risk'. *Psychology Bulletin*, **102**, 357–389.

Parker, G., Tupling, H. & Brown, L.B. (1979) A parental bonding instrument. *British Journal of Medical Psychology*, **52**, 1–10.

Salzman, J.P. (1997) Ambivalent attachment in female adolescents: Association with affective instability and eating disorders. *International Journal of Eating Disorders*, **21**, 251–259.

Schmidt, U.H., Tiller, J.M. & Treasure, J. (1993) Setting the scene for eating disorders: Childhood care, classification and course of illness. *Psychological Medicine*, **23**, 663–672.

Shapiro, S., Newcomb, M. & Loeb, T.B. (1997) Fear of fat, disregulated-restrained eating, and body-esteem: Prevalence and gender differences among eight to ten year old children. *Journal of Clinical Child Psychology*, **26** (4), 358–365.

Shoebridge, P. & Gowers, S. (2000) Parental high concern and adolescent onset anorexia nervosa. *British Journal of Psychiatry*, **176**, 132–137.

Stein, A. (1995) Eating disorders and childrearing. In K.D. Brownell & C.G. Fairburn (Eds), *Eating Disorders and Obesity: A Comprehensive Handbook* (pp. 188–190). New York: Guilford Press.

Stein, A., Murray, L., Cooper, P. & Fairburn, C. (1996) Infant growth in the context of maternal eating disorders and maternal depression: A comparative study. *Psychological Medicine*, **26** (3), 569–574.

Tanner, J.M. (1989) *Foetus into Man: Physical Growth from Conception to Maturity* (2nd edn). Ware, Herts: Castlemead publications.

Tanner, J.M. & Whitehouse, R.H. (1975) *Growth and Development Records for Boys and Girls*. Ware, Herts: Castlemead Publications.

Thomas, A., Chess, S. & Birch, H.G. (1968) *Temperament and Behaviour Disorders in Children*. New York: New York University Press.

van IJzendoorn, M.H. (1995) Adult attachment presentations, parental responsiveness and infant attachment. A meta-analysis on the predictive validity of the AAI. *Psychological Bulletin*, **117**, 387–403.

Ward, A., Ramsay, R. & Treasure, J. (2000) Attachment research in eating disorders. *British Journal of Medical Psychology*, **73**, 35–51.

Ward, A., Ramsay, R., Turnbull, S., Benedettini, M. & Treasure, J. (2000) Attachment patterns in eating disorders: Past in the present. *International Journal of Eating Disorders*, **27**, 279–287.

Ward, A., Ramsay, R., Turnbull, S., Steele, M., Steele, H. & Treasure, J. (2001) Attachment in anorexia nervosa: A transgenerational perspective. *British Journal of Medical Psychology*, **74**, 497–505.

Wentz-Nilsson, E., Gillberg, C. & Rastam, M. (1998) Familial factors in anorexia nervosa. *Comprehensive Psychiatry*, **39**, 392–399.

Williams, G. (1997) *Internal Landscapes and Foreign Bodies: Eating Disorders and Other Pathologies*. London: Duckworth.

CHAPTER 7

Cognitive-Behavioural Models

Roz Shafran
Department of Psychiatry, Warneford Hospital, Oxford, UK
and
Padmal de Silva
Eating Disorders Unit, Institute of Psychiatry, London, UK

INTRODUCTION

In keeping with the rest of this handbook, this chapter not only focuses on the two most widely research eating disorders—anorexia nervosa and bulimia nervosa—but it also includes obesity. The relationship between these eating disorders and obesity is described in other chapters and it is notable that a personal or family history of obesity is a specific risk factor for the development of bulimia nervosa (Fairburn, Cooper, Doll & Welch, 1999). The strong relationship between anorexia nervosa and bulimia nervosa is well documented with over one-quarter of patients with bulimia nervosa having experienced an episode of anorexia nervosa (Braun, Sunday & Halmi, 1994; Bulik et al., 1995). It is therefore no surprise to see some overlap in the cognitive-behavioural accounts of anorexia nervosa, bulimia nervosa and obesity. Despite the similarities, there are also important differences that must be taken into account by cognitive-behavioural models of these disorders.

This chapter begins by describing the purpose of cognitive-behavioural models and introducing general principles that guide cognitive-behavioural models of disorders. An important distinction is drawn between models of the aetiology of these disorders and their maintenance. It is argued that the cognitive-behavioural models of the maintenance of these disorders are more likely to lead to developments in the effective treatments than models of aetiology. A critical review of cognitive-behavioural models of each of these disorders is provided. Experimental and treatment outcome data are used to evaluate the models. The chapter ends by calling for further research to directly evaluate the models and their derived cognitive-behavioural treatments.

THE PURPOSE OF COGNITIVE-BEHAVIOURAL MODELS

In this context, the term 'models' is used to describe theoretical schemes for ordering information in a broad and comprehensive way (Gelder, 1997). Cognitive-behavioural models

Handbook of Eating Disorders. Edited by J. Treasure, U. Schmidt and E. van Furth.

can have many functions, depending on whether they are accounts of the development of the disorder or the maintenance of the disorder. They have two main purposes. First, they provide a means of understanding the development or maintenance of the most important cognitive and behavioural aspects of the phenomenology of the disorder. In anorexia nervosa, the cognitive aspects that need to be explained include (but are not limited to) the determination to actively maintain a low weight, negative self-evaluation, body image disturbance, preoccupation with eating, shape and weight, and the egosyntonicity of the disorder. The primary behaviour in need of explanation is dietary restriction. Other behaviours that may require explanation are episodes of binge eating, excessive exercise and self-induced vomiting or taking of laxatives (American Psychiatric Association, 1994).

In bulimia nervosa, the cognitive aspects are similar to those of in anorexia nervosa but the additional behaviours that require explanation include the objective episodes of binge eating and the resultant compensatory behaviour (APA, 1994). In obesity, the cognitive aspect that needs to be explained is debatable but may relate to beliefs about the positive effects of eating and the negative consequences of not eating. In addition, people with obesity who are trying to control their weight have to impose control over their energy intake/expenditure (Wilson, 1993). The behaviour that needs to be explained is over-eating and, for a minority of patients, binge eating.

The second purpose of cognitive-behavioural models is to improve the treatment of the disorder. Put succinctly, 'some of the most effective psychological treatments for emotional disorders have been developed by constructing a model of the development and maintenance of the disorder and then devising a set of treatment procedures that focus on the core pathology and reverse the maintaining factors' (Clark, 1997, p. 121). There is often overlap between factors leading to the development of a disorder and their maintenance (e.g. dieting). Nevertheless, it is important to draw the neglected distinction between development and maintenance (see Cooper, 1997) since it is the maintenance mechanisms that need to be reversed if the therapeutic intervention is to be effective. Understanding the development of a disorder may give some *clues* as to the processes that might reverse the development of the disorder, and may give a good indication of how to prevent relapse. However, better information regarding intervention is obtained by understanding the mechanisms that maintain the disorder since reversing these maintaining mechanisms will result in an effective treatment intervention. This has been shown to be the case for the anxiety disorders (e.g. panic disorder; Clark, 1997) and bulimia nervosa (Fairburn, 1997).

The two purposes of the cognitive-behavioural model are connected. Understanding the phenomenology of the disorder allows for treatment interventions, and treatment interventions based on the model can help inform our understanding of the disorder. This is the case in a general way but the same principle applies within therapy. Presenting a patient with a model that makes sense of the development or maintenance of their disorder is important in engaging the patients (particularly those with anorexia nervosa) and in providing a cognitive-behavioural formulation of the problem to guide a specific treatment intervention (see Persons, 1989).

GENERAL PRINCIPLES OF COGNITIVE-BEHAVIOURAL MODELS

As their name suggests, cognitive-behavioural models combine two approaches. First, models incorporating behavioural theories and therapies which were proposed by Watson early in the twentieth century (Watson, 1925). Behavioural theories and therapies were based on the principles of learning and were effective in the treatment of anxiety disorders (Wolpe, 1958). The majority of existing therapies for obesity are behavioural (e.g. Wing, 1998; Wadden et al., 1998). Dissatisfaction due to the lack of advancement in theorising about behaviour therapy and the lack of success in dealing with depression led to the development of cognitive theories and therapy in the 1970s (see Rachman, 1997).

Second, models incorporate cognitive theories, such as those of Beck (Beck, 1976, 1985), that propose that one's emotions are influenced by one's thoughts, and that emotional disorders result from particular interpretation of events. For example, if clothes feel tight and this is interpreted as 'I'm fat' then such an interpretation is likely to result in low mood and body dissatisfaction; if the person interprets the tightness of the clothes as 'these have been shrunk by the drycleaners', then the resulting emotion may be anger. Cognitive therapy uses the cognitive model to identify and correct cognitive distortions and deficiencies by encouraging the patient to use rules of evidence and logic, and to consider alternative explanations (Beck, 1976). For example, a patient with an eating disorder who thinks 'I'm fat' can be encouraged to distinguish between the thought 'I think I am fat', the feeling 'I feel fat' and the real situation 'I am significantly overweight' (Fairburn, Marcus & Wilson, 1993).

Pure behavioural or pure cognitive models are rarely postulated nowadays as providing explanatory accounts of complex behaviours. What are commonly found instead are cognitive-behavioural models, where cognitive and behavioural concepts are integrated and used as major elements. There have been detailed theoretical discussion of these issues (e.g. Brewin, 1988; Williams et al., 1988; Wolpe, 1993). Similarly in treatment, cognitive and behavioural techniques are interwoven, most notably in the form of behavioural experiments that the patient uses to gather evidence to examine the validity of the patient's thoughts or assumptions (Beck, 1995). For example, the negative automatic thought, 'If I eat an extra biscuit a day for the next week, I will gain at least three kilograms' can be tested behaviourally by determining the amount of weight gain (if any) that results from eating the extra biscuit for a week.

SPECIFIC VS GENERAL COGNITIVE-BEHAVIOURAL MODELS

Beck's cognitive model of emotional disorders (Beck, 1979) was originally postulated to account for depression. It also provides a general framework for understanding the development and maintenance of emotional disorders. Beck proposes that different types of thinking (termed 'negative automatic thoughts', 'dysfunctional assumptions' and 'core beliefs') are characterised by cognitive distortions such as 'all-or-nothing thinking' (e.g. 'I'm either fat or I'm thin') or 'discounting positive information' (e.g. 'She's only saying I look nice because she feels sorry for me') (see Beck, 1995).

Some of the cognitive-behavioural models described below (e.g. Garner & Bemis, 1982, 1985; Wolff & Serpell, 1998) stick closely to Beck's framework and make particular use of Beck's general cognitive-behavioural techniques. Other models take the principle that cognitive-behavioural processes maintain the disorder but are specific to the disorder. For example, the leading model of bulimia nervosa (Fairburn, 1997) proposes that the central cognitive maintaining process is the judging of self-worth largely, or even exclusively, in terms of shape or weight. In this type of approach, the particular cognitive-behavioural model of maintenance indicates a specific cognitive-behavioural intervention. Given that the most successful psychological treatment interventions have derived from specific models of the maintenance of the disorder (e.g. panic disorder, Clark, 1986; bulimia nervosa, Fairburn, 1985), it is our view that specific models of maintenance are likely to generate more treatment advances than the generic models.

ANOREXIA NERVOSA

Models of Development

For the reasons stated above, it is important to separate models of the development and maintenance of disorders, although the two overlap. Cognitive-behavioural (and other) models of the development of anorexia nervosa are usually multifactorial in nature (see Garner & Garfinkel, 1997). The origins of the disorder are likely to be related to numerous predisposing and precipitating factors including individual variables such as perfectionism (Dally & Gomez, 1979; Fairburn et al., 1999; Lilenfeld, 1998), environmental factors, and genetic factors (see Lilenfeld & Kaye, 1998). Issues such as adolescent conflict, family problems, a negative comment about shape and weight, the sense of failure and loss of control can all serve as precipitating factors (Beumont, George & Smart, 1976; Garfinkel & Garner, 1983; Gilbert, 1986).

Models of Maintenance

Behavioural Models

The earliest behavioural theories suggested that the 'impairment of food intake in anorexia nervosa can be viewed as a specific learned behavior, perpetuated by environmental re-inforcements' (Blinder, Freeman & Stunkard, 1970, p. 1093). The individual engages in excessive dieting. The resultant weight loss may be positively reinforced (at least initially) by the reactions of peer groups and negatively reinforced by the absence of being overweight (which can be met with disapproval and even peer rejection). This over-simplistic model leaves many questions unanswered. Some suggest that general societal pressure are too remote to act as an immediate reinforcer for dietary restriction; other positive reinforcers that have been suggested are attention (Allyon, Haughton & Osmond, 1964), stimuli in the environment (Bachrach, Erwin & Mohr, 1965), an empty stomach (Gilbert, 1986) or an endogenously produced substance (Szmukler & Tantam, 1984). Avoiding anxiety associated with eating and weight gain has also been suggested to negatively reinforce dietary restriction (Leitenberg, Agras & Thomson, 1968).

Slade's Functional Analysis

In one of the most fully developed accounts of the origins and maintenance of anorexia nervosa, Slade (1982) proposes that general dissatisfaction with life and oneself arises from a combination of interpersonal problems and conflicts of adolescence. Such dissatisfaction is proposed to interact with perfectionism to give rise to a need to control and achieve success in some aspect of life. If dieting is triggered, for example by the critical comments of a peer, this need for control and achievement becomes focused on the dieting behaviour. The dieting is reinforced positively by feelings of success and satisfaction, and is negatively reinforced through the fear of weight gain and avoidance of stressors, which preceded the onset of the disorder. These reinforcers intensify the dieting behaviour and weight spirals downwards. Together with the endocrine disturbance, which may be a direct effect of stress or indirect effect caused through weight loss, this eventually leads to anorexia nervosa.

Vitousek's Approach[1]

Hilde Bruch (1973, 1982) was critical of the purely behavioural approach and, despite being a psychoanalyst in orientation, she stressed the importance of these patients' thinking style (Bruch, 1973) and the person's idiosyncratic interpretation of the meaning of events. Bruch's ideas were subsequently refined and extended by Garner and Bemis in two key articles (Garner & Bemis, 1982, 1985) in which they applied to anorexia nervosa the principles of Beck's cognitive theory and therapy of depression (Beck, 1979). Their cognitive-behavioural view has since been elaborated by Vitousek and colleagues in a series of articles that have focused on the role of self-esteem (Garner & Bemis, 1985), information processing (Vitousek & Hollon, 1990), self-representation (Vitousek & Ewald, 1993), personality variables (Vitousek & Manke, 1994) and motivation respectively (Vitousek, Watson & Wilson, 1999). This is the leading cognitive-behavioural account and it 'holds that anorexic and bulimic symptoms are maintained by a characteristic set of beliefs about weight and shape' (Vitousek & Orimoto, 1993, p. 193). They propose that the core cognitive disturbance can be understood in terms of 'schema' (organised cognitive structures) that unite the views of the self and the culturally derived beliefs about the virtue of thinness for female appearance (Vitousek, 1996; Vitousek & Hollon, 1990; Vitousek & Manke, 1994). Such schema give rise to the belief that the solution to a view of the self as unworthy, imperfect and overwhelmed is thinness and weight loss, which are therefore pursued relentlessly.

According to this account, anorexic beliefs and behaviour are reinforced in four main ways. First, they are positively reinforced by feelings of success, achievement, moral superiority and control that result from successful dietary restriction. Second, they are negatively reinforced by the avoidance of being fat. Over time, the margin of safety needed to avoid 'fatness' increases, which is proposed to explain the need for an ever-decreasing target weight. Third, self-worth is defined in terms of shape and weight which gives rise to a series of cognitive processing biases that maintain the anorexic beliefs and behaviour. Finally, the effects of starvation contribute in various ways to the maintenance of the disorder, for example, by increasing concrete thinking. Additional reinforcements include social reinforcement for being slim, concern and attention from family members as weight loss increases and the development of an anorexic identity in which the individual becomes increasingly isolated so that her dysfunctional thinking and behaviour comprise the essence of her personality.

Other Cognitive-Behavioural Models emphasising Weight and Shape

Other cognitive-behavioural perspectives have emerged (see Cooper, 1997, for a review) including that of Kleifield and colleagues (Kleifield, 1996), Williamson et al. (1990) and the Maudsley unit (Wolff & Serpell, 1998). These models differ slightly but have the same focus on the central anorexic premise of the importance of weight and shape. For example, typical

---

[1] Also known as Bemis's approach.

anorexic assumptions are described as 'If I'm thin, I'm special, if I'm fat, I'm worthless' (Wolff & Serpell, 1998, p. 406). Other examples of cognitive distortions are:

- Selective abstraction (selecting out small parts of a situation while ignoring other evidence, and coming to conclusions on that basis), e.g. 'Other people will like me more if I am thin.'
- Dichotomous reasoning (thinking in terms of extremes and absolutes), e.g. 'If I am not thin, then I am fat.'
- Overgeneralisation (deriving a rule from one event and applying it to other situations or events), e.g. 'I was unhappy when I was at normal weight. So I know that putting on weight is going to make me unhappy.'
- Magnification (exaggerating the significance of events), e.g. 'Gaining two pounds has made me unattractive.'
- Superstitious thinking (assuming causal relationships between unrelated things), e.g. 'If I eat this, it will be converted into fat on my stomach immediately.'

The account by the Maudsley group incorporates advances in the role of cognitive theory. The result is a model that includes metacognitions ('thoughts about thoughts'), safety behaviours (behaviours designed to protect the individual from 'threat' but that actually serve to magnify the perception of threat (Salkovskis, 1996)) and the Interacting Cognitive Subsystems model (Teasdale, 1993) in which weight/shape are linked with self-esteem (Wolff & Serpell, 1998). In this account, particular emphasis is placed on the patients' 'pro-anorexia' (p. 411) beliefs about the disorder as a factor in its maintenance, e.g. 'if I didn't have anorexia, my whole world would fall apart, I wouldn't be able to cope' (p. 412).

Guidano and Liotti (1983)

The cognitive-behavioural model of Guidano and Liotti (1983) proposed that the central feature of anorexia nervosa was a deficit in cognitive structures relating to personal identity rather than weight and shape. They suggested that the personal identity in anorexia nervosa comprises beliefs of ineffectiveness, failure, and the futility of disclosing personal views or emotions. The difficulties with personal identity are suggested to arise from a failure to develop autonomy in childhood and lack of individuality during development. Such patients are suggested to use dieting and weight loss as inappropriate means of coping with the difficulties in personal identity.

Fairburn, Shafran & Cooper (1999)

The model of Fairburn, Shafran & Cooper (1999) proposes that the core psychopathology of anorexia nervosa is a need for self-control that becomes focused on controlling eating, shape and weight. This model suggests that dietary restriction is maintained in three ways. First, dietary restriction is maintained by positive reinforcement from a temporary increase in feelings of self-control and self-worth. Dietary restriction is suggested to become an index of self-control and self-worth. Second, the physiological sequalae of starvation are suggested to be interpreted as a threat to perceived control over eating, or a failure of control over eating. For example, feeling full after eating only a small amount (heightened satiety) is hypothesised to lead to the interpretation 'I've eaten too much' i.e., a perceived failure of control over-eating. As a consequence, dietary restriction may result. These two mechanisms are culturally independent.

The third mechanism suggested to maintain dietary restriction in patients with restricting anorexia nervosa proposes that controlling one's shape and weight is used as an index of self-control in general in western cultures. This third mechanism concerns the over-importance of shape and weight, and addresses behaviours such as frequent weighing and checking of one's body shape. It is hypothesised that frequent weighing or checking of one's body shape results in a perceived failure of control over eating, shape and weight as any perceived imperfections are likely to be magnified by such frequent body checking or weighing. Active avoidance of body checking or weighing is suggested to maintain the perception of a failure of control over eating, shape and weight as the person has no means by which to disconfirm her view that she is 'too large'. This model is currently being evaluated but has been somewhat superseded by a 'transdiagnostic' cognitive-behavioural model which attempts to account for eating disorder psychopathology across all the eating disorders, i.e. anorexia nervosa, bulimia nervosa and atypical eating disorders (Fairburn, Cooper & Shafran, in press).

Evaluation of Models

Some of the above models generate testable hypotheses and predictions that are open to empirical investigation (see Vitousek & Hollon, 1990), while others are less amenable to such evaluation. Empirical data evaluating the models has been considered in terms of self-report questionnaire data, experimental data and data on treatment outcome.

Self-Report and Interview Data

While self-report may be particularly vulnerable to bias and distortion in this population (Vitousek, Daly & Heiser, 1991), an abundance of studies have shown that patients with anorexia nervosa have a distinct set of cognitions regarding eating, shape and weight (e.g. Clark, Feldman & Channon, 1989; Cooper, Todd & Cohen-Tovee, 1996; Cooper & Turner, 2000; Mizes, 1992). Such studies provide support for the prediction deriving from the cognitive-behavioural models that patients with anorexia nervosa have 'negative automatic thoughts', 'underlying assumptions' and 'core beliefs' related to eating, shape and weight (see Vitousek, 1996, and Cooper, 1997, for reviews). However, since such cognitions are consistent with all the cognitive-behavioural models, the studies cannot provide particular support for any one model.

Experimental Data

Information-processing tasks have been used to test predictions deriving mainly from Vitousek's cognitive-behavioural account (e.g. Vitousek & Hollon, 1990). Cognitive-behavioural theories predict that attention will be biased towards stimuli related to body fatness and to fattening food since these stimuli are threatening to people with eating disorders (Williamson et al., 1999). Studies of attention have been conducted using the Stroop colour-naming task (Stroop, 1935) and patients with anorexia nervosa are slower to colour-name words relevant to their concerns than normal controls (e.g. Ben-Tovim et al.,

1989; Channon, Hemsley & de Silva, 1988; Cooper & Fairburn, 1992a; Green, McKenna & de Silva, 1994; Long, Hinton & Gillespie, 1994). (For reviews, see Vitousek, 1996, and Williamson, Mathews & McLeod, 1996.) Data from these Stroop experiments are difficult to interpret; they may be assessing state-like salient concerns instead of stable attentional biases and they do not provide definitive evidence of biases in attention (Vitousek, 1996). Nevertheless, they are at least consistent with the cognitive-behavioural theories described above. There have been no studies with patients with anorexia nervosa using the dichotic listening task or lexical decision tasks although such studies have been done in people with bulimia nervosa (Schotte, McNally & Turner, 1990; see later) and women with body dysphoria (Fuller, Williamson & Anderon, 1995).

Cognitive-behavioural theories suggest that personally salient information concerning shape and weight will be more readily encoded and recalled than neutral stimuli. People with 'body dysphoria' have been shown to recall more body-related words and difficulty recalling thinness words than those low in 'body dysphoria' (Baker, Williamson & Sylve, 1995; Watkins et al., 1995). A memory bias for words concerning 'fatness' was found in a mixed group of patients with eating disorders (Sebastian, Williamson & Blouin, 1996) and an explicit memory bias for anorexia-nervosa related words was recently demonstrated in a small sample of patients with anorexia nervosa compared to non-dieting controls (Herman et al., 1998). This finding could not be attributed to the valence of the words.

In summary, such experimental data have provided support for the leading cognitive-behavioural model of anorexia nervosa (Garner & Bemis, 1985; Vitousek & Hollon, 1990). However, as with the case of the questionnaire studies, the experimental data do not provide particular support for any one specific model as opposed to another.

Treatment Outcome Data

It is worth noting that an effective cognitive-behavioural treatment that is derived from a cognitive-behavioural model does not 'prove' that the model is correct since the treatment could be effective for a number of other, non-specific reasons. Such data can only be taken as being consistent with the cognitive-behavioural model and providing indirect support for it. It is, however, possible to conclude that the maintenance model is incorrect if the therapy reverses the proposed maintaining mechanisms yet the disorder persists.

Based on the early behavioural accounts, operant paradigms were implemented consisting of (a) isolating patients from reinforcers and (b) providing the reinforcers in response to specified criteria such as weight gain or calorie intake. At least 60 publications describing operant techniques for anorexia nervosa were published in the 1960s and 1970s and the literature has been thoroughly reviewed elsewhere (Halmi, 1985). Reviews indicate the effectiveness of operant conditioning in the short-term but the technique has questionable utility for long-term improvement (see Bemis, 1982). More recently, behaviour therapy plus education has been shown to be successful in a recent controlled study (Treasure et al., 1995), indicating the promise of this type of therapy.

Cognitive-behavioural therapy, however, is considered to be indicated for AN in adults by 90% of clinicians (Herzog et al., 1992). As with the cognitive-behavioural models, the leading account of the cognitive-behavioural treatment of anorexia nervosa is that proposed by Garner and Bemis (1982, 1985). To date, the descriptions of this treatment have tended to be schematic rather than detailed, although two recent publications have provided rather more information (Pike, Loeb & Vitousek, 1996; Garner, Vitousek & Pike, 1997).

There have been three controlled studies of a cognitive behavioural treatment (Channon et al., 1989; Halmi et al., 2000; Pike, 2000) for anorexia nervosa but all have methodological limitations. In the first study (Channon et al., 1989), no group could be considered clinically recovered by the end of the study period and it is unclear whether the treatment did derive directly from the cognitive-behavioural theory of Garner and Bemis (1982). In the second study (Halmi et al., 2000), the drop-out rate from all conditions was extremely high, which makes the results difficult to interpret. In the third study, the best to date, CBT was compared to nutritional counselling and found to be more effective (Pike, 2000). However, this sample of patients were weight-restored patients with 'anorexia nervosa'. The effectiveness of this intervention in a sample of underweight patients with anorexia nervosa is unknown.

In summary, the treatment outcome data neither support nor refute any of the proposed cognitive-behavioural models. At present, there is no generally accepted treatment and anorexia nervosa 'is one of the most frustrating and recalcitrant forms of psychopathology' (Vitousek, Watson & Wilson, 1998).

BULIMIA NERVOSA

Behavioural Models

As was the case in anorexia nervosa, purely behavioural models were developed first to account for the maintenance of the disorder. One of the earliest behavioural accounts proposed that purging was positively reinforced because it reduces anxiety associated with binge eating (Rosen & Leitenberg, 1982). This purely behavioural model can, at best, account for only part of the maintenance of bulimia nervosa and does not address psychosocial and cognitive factors. Furthermore, the theoretical model on which it is based (the two-stage fear-reduction model of Mowrer, 1960) has been shown to be an inadequate explanation for a range of disorders (see Rachman, 1984, for a critique of this model).

Fairburn's Cognitive-Behavioural Model

At the same time as the behavioural model was proposed, Fairburn (1981) described a cognitive-behavioural model of bulimia nervosa. This cognitive-behavioural model attempts to explain the core cognitive and behavioural components of the disorder, in particular low self-esteem, overconcern with shape and weight, rigid dietary restriction, binge eating and purging. Although the importance of affect in binge eating has been noted since the earliest accounts (e.g. Fairburn, Cooper & Cooper, 1986), more recently the model has been extended to specify the importance of the role of affect in binge eating and the influence of perfectionism and dichotomous (all-or-nothing) thinking (Fairburn, 1997). The cognitive-behavioural model is shown in Figure 7.1.

In essence, this model proposes that the core cognitive disturbance in bulimia is the tendency to judge the self largely, or even exclusively, in terms of shape and weight. These extreme concerns about shape and weight lead to characteristic extreme and rigid dieting. Such dieting is characterised by rigid rules (e.g. 'I must eat less than 1000 calories'; 'I must not eat any chocolate') which render the dietary restriction brittle and vulnerable to being disrupted. The disruption occurs when dietary rules are violated, for example the person may eat a piece of chocolate. Such rigid dietary rules are particularly vulnerable to violation in

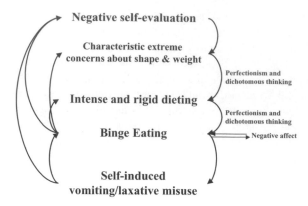

Figure 7.1 Cognitive-Behavioural Model of the Maintenance of Bulimia Nervosa (Fairburn, 1997). Reprinted by permission of Oxford University Press.

the context of an adverse mood state. Since patients have perfectionistic standards (Fairburn et al., 1999) and dichotomous thinking, the violation of the rule is suggested to be interpreted by patients in an all-or-nothing manner so the person may well think 'I've blown it now—if I have had one piece of chocolate I've failed so I may as well eat all of it'.

In this model, such dichotomous thinking, along with the physiological and psychological effects of dietary restraint, is suggested to lead to episodes of objective over-eating accompanied by a sense of loss of control (i.e. an episode of binge eating). Such binge eating tends to moderate negative affect in the short term but also activates and reinforces concerns about shape and weight, and the person attempts to ameliorate the impact of episode of binge eating by purging, commonly by inducing vomiting. Vomiting, in turn, is suggested to reinforce binge eating and, in particular, the size of the binge. This is for two reasons: first, people learn that it is easier to vomit if they have eaten a large amount; second, people discount calories consumed in a binge if they believe that they are 'getting rid' of them by purging.

Wilson (1989) has proposed a similar account and this account includes fear and social factors. A broader model which includes other psychopathological mood states (e.g. depression), distorted body image and cognitive biases has been proposed by Williamson and colleagues (1985, 1990, 1999). A model in which binge eating is suggested to function as an 'escape from awareness' has been proposed (Heatherton & Baumeister, 1991; Waller et al., 1995). This model has been developed further by Waller and colleagues who propose a 'multilevel model of processing where abandonment issues play an early role in the activation of food schemata . . . and hence inducing bulimic behavior as a means of reducing awareness of such cognitions' (Meyer & Waller, 2000, p. 333). Yet another model suggests that there are two pathways to bulimia nervosa, the first concerning dietary restraint and the second relating to affect regulation (Stice, Nemeroff & Shaw, 1996; Stice, Shaw & Nemeroff, 1998; Stice et al., 1996).

Evaluation

Self-Report Questionnaires, Interview and Experimental Data

As with anorexia nervosa, it has been demonstrated that patients with bulimia nervosa have a distinct set of cognitions regarding eating, shape and weight (e.g. Cooper & Fairburn,

1992b; Mizes, 1992; Phelan, 1987) and interview studies also support the importance of the core cognitive disturbance in bulimia nervosa as the over-importance of shape and weight in the judgement of self-worth (Goldfein, Walsh & Midlarsky, 2000). Information-processing studies using a dichotic listening task (Schotte, McNally & Turner, 1990), location of attention (Newman et al., 1993) and, most commonly, the Stroop colour-naming task support the model (see Vitousek, 1996, for a review) although it has correctly been stated that the theoretical implications of the Stroop task are difficult to determine. Other information-processing studies, most notably those conducted by Glenn Waller and colleagues (e.g. McManus, Waller & Chadwick, 1996; Meyer & Waller, 1999; Waller, Quinton & Watson, 1995), provide support for other cognitive-behavioural models that place central emphasis on the role of emotional factors in binge eating rather than shape and weight concerns.

Studies on counter-regulation have also been used to investigate the cognitive-behavioural model and the hypothesis that over-eating is likely to occur in the context of restraint and negative affect. Although such studies are usually conducted on 'restrained eaters' rather than patients with bulimia nervosa, they provide general support for the cognitive-behavioural model (see Polivy & Herman, 2002). A recent review on such laboratory studies supports their use as a means of testing theories of eating disorders (Mitchell et al., 1998). The dual-pathway model has also received empirical support from both cross sectional and longitudinal studies (e.g., Stice, 2001; Stice & Agras, 1999, Shepherd & Ricciardelli, 1998). Cross-sectional and longitudinal studies have also been used to evaluate Fairburn's (1997) model of bulimia nervosa. In the cross-sectional study using structural equation modelling, many of the main predictions of the theory were supported although the findings regarding binge eating and purging are hard to interpret owing to the methods of assessment (Byrne & McLean, 2002). A well-controlled five year longitudinal prospective study of the natural course of bulimia also supports the model since it was found that the baseline level of over-evaluation of shape and weight predicted persistence of binge eating over 15 months, and this relationship was partially mediated by dietary restraint (Fairburn et al., in press).

Treatment Outcome Data

The strongest evidence in support of the cognitive account comes from studies of the cognitive-behavioural treatment of the disorder. Indirect support for the account is provided by over 25 randomised-controlled trials (Wilson & Fairburn, 2002). Overall, such trials have demonstrated that cognitive-behavioural therapy for bulimia nervosa based on the above account is a lasting and effective treatment for approximately 40% of cases, and it is superior to comparison treatments that control for non-specific effects (see Wilson & Fairburn, 2002). More direct support is provided from treatment studies that have 'dismantled' the cognitive-behavioural treatment (e.g. by comparing it to behavioural treatment) which have demonstrated that the absence of cognitive procedures greatly influences long-term outcome (Fairburn et al., 1995). Most directly, among patients who have responded to treatment, the residual level of attitudinal disturbance has been shown to predict subsequent outcome (Fairburn et al., 1993). Additional support comes from a study of mediators of response to CBT which found that the treatment's effect on binge eating was mediated by a decrease in dietary restraint (Wilson et al., 2002). It is worth noting that interpersonal psychotherapy has been found in two large studies to be as effective as cognitive-behavioural therapy but takes longer to produce change (Fairburn et al., 1995; Agras et al., 2000).

OBESITY

Behavioural Models

Behavioural treatments of obesity have dominated the field since the 1960s (Ferster, Nurnberger & Levitt, 1962; Stuart, 1967). In essence, behavioural models propose that obesity results from (1) maladaptive eating habits that lead to over-eating that is reinforced, and (2) the absence of exercise which is also reinforced according to the principles of learning theory (Wilson, 1993; Bray, Bouchard & James, 1998). As would be expected, the behavioural treatment deriving from the behavioural models is a set of principles and techniques to help overweight individuals modify inappropriate eating and activity habits (Wadden & Foster, 2000).

Cognitive-Behavioural Models

The limitations of behavioural models have been noted elsewhere (Wooley, Wooley & Dyrenforth, 1979). Criticisms include the assumption of distinctive eating patterns in people with obesity and the failure to incorporate information about the biology of weight regulation. The poor long-term outcome of patients with obesity has also been noted (see Brownell & Fairburn, 2002; Stunkard & Penick, 1979).

With the advent of cognitive theory, an alternative model was proposed in the form of a 'food dependency model' (Goodrick & Foreyt, 1991), which focused on cognitions and emotions related to obesity and to social support (see Wilson, 1993). The need for a combined cognitive-behavioural approach to the understanding and treatment of obesity was highlighted by Wilson (1996) who argued for recognition of combining behavioural treatment with cognitive change, particularly the value of accepting whatever shape and weight changes result from the treatment. However, until recently, cognitive-behavioural treatments of obesity primarily comprised adding cognitive components such as negative thinking or help in decision making to behavioural treatments (Sbrocco et al., 1999). A recent review (Foreyt & Poston, 1998) indicated that most forms of CBT for obesity included five strategies. These were (1) self-monitoring and goal setting, (2) stimulus control for the modification of eating style and activity, (3) cognitive restructuring techniques that focus modifying dysfunctional thinking, (4) stress management, and (5) social support.

Recently, however, a new approach has been taken to cognitive-behavioural accounts of obesity. Recognising that the problem is not one of initial weight loss but rather of the poor long-term outcome of behavioural treatment for obesity (Kramer et al., 1989; Safer, 1991; Wadden et al., 1989), a new approach focuses on factors that account for weight regain after successfully losing weight (Cooper & Fairburn, 2001; in press). According to this new cognitive-behavioural approach, patients with obesity who lose weight fail to maintain their gains for two reasons. First, they do not achieve their weight loss goals, nor the anticipated benefits of achieving them. For example, the patient may anticipate feeling 'more confident' after losing 10 kg but either loses only 5 kg or does not feel any differently about his or her confidence. As a consequence, efforts to lose weight are abandoned (Cooper & Fairburn, 2001). A second, interrelated reason, for failing to maintain weight loss is that when the patient does not achieve his or her goal or its anticipated benefits, the patient neglects the need to acquire skills to maintain the new, lower weight but instead resumes previous eating and exercise habits, and therefore regains the lost weight (Cooper & Fairburn, 2001).

The new cognitive-behavioural therapy based on this theory is delivered on an individual basis and addresses weight loss, the maintenance of weight *lost*, body image, weight goals and, originally, 'primary goals' (Cooper & Fairburn, in press). These 'primary goals' are defined as the objectives which patients hope to achieve as a result of weight loss and include improving self-confidence, increasing one's social life, etc. Equally distinct and original is the emphasis given to the long-term maintenance of weight rather than continuing and indefinite weight loss (Cooper & Fairburn, in press).

Evaluation

Treatment Outcome Studies

The majority of evidence that addresses the cognitive-behavioural models of obesity relate to treatment outcome data which, as previously stated, can only provide indirect support for a theory. Behavioural treatment—with or without the cognitive component—typically incorporates a 1200 kcal/day diet and results in a weight loss of approximately 10% of initial body weight (Wing, 1998; Wadden & Foster, 2000). Therapy is usually conducted in groups in the format of 'lessons' that address self-monitoring of eating, setting of behavioural goals regarding eating and exercise, education about nutrition, problem solving, challenging of cognitions and relapse prevention. Unfortunately, the weight is regained by the majority of patients within the subsequent three years (e.g. Kramer et al., 1989; Safer, 1991; Wadden et al., 1989).

It was these data which led to the development of Cooper & Fairburn, (2001, in press) new cognitive-behavioural treatment of obesity. This treatment is currently being evaluated in a randomised-controlled treatment trial and the format of treatment is deliberately different from existing group interventions for obesity.

In summary, the treatment outcome data are consistent with cognitive-behavioural models of obesity but the long-term outcome of cognitive-behavioural therapy of obesity is poor. It is hoped that a new form of cognitive-behavioural therapy focusing on weight regain will improve treatment outcome as well as testing a new cognitive-behavioural conceptualisation of weight gain following treatment for obesity.

SUMMARY AND CONCLUSIONS

At the beginning of this chapter it was argued that cognitive-behavioural models had two purposes. First, to provide a means of understanding the development or maintenance of the most important cognitive and behavioural aspects of the phenomenology of the disorder and, second, to improve treatments of the disorder. The cognitive-behavioural models of anorexia nervosa have provided a way of understanding the phenomenology of this problem, although they have not yet been demonstrated to lead to any major breakthroughs in the treatment of this disorder and there is little evidence to favour one model over another. On the other hand, the leading cognitive-behavioural model of bulimia nervosa (Fairburn, 1997) has led to the development of a relatively effective treatment for the disorder. It is argued that further theoretical developments are now needed to improve therapies for those patients who do not improve with the existing treatment. Such a development has recently been proposed in the form of a 'transdiagnostic' cognitive behavioural theory and treatment for all forms of clinical eating disorder (Fairburn et al., in press). Finally, the cognitive-behavioural mechanisms in the maintenance of obesity are ill-understood and, at present, the long-term outcome of cognitive-behavioural therapy for this disorder is poor. It is hoped that the new theoretical developments, particularly the focus on mechanisms contributing to weight regain after successful weight loss (Cooper & Fairburn, in press-a), will improve our understanding of these mechanisms and, consequently, the treatment of obesity.

ACKNOWLEDGEMENTS

RS is supported by a Wellcome Trust Research Career Development Fellowship (063209).

REFERENCES

Agras, W.S., Walsh, T., Fairburn, C.G., Wilson, G.T. & Kraemer, H.C. (2000) A multicenter comparison of cognitive-behavioral therapy and interpersonal psychotherapy for bulimia nervosa. *Archives of General Psychiatry*, **57**, 459–466.

Allyon, T., Haughton, E. & Osmond, H.P. (1964) Chronic anorexia: A behaviour problem. *Canadian Psychiatric Association Journal*, **9**, 147–157.

APA (1994) *Diagnostic and Statistical Manual of Mental Disorders* (4th edition). Washington, D.C.: American Psychiatric Association.

Bachrach, A.J., Erwin, W.J. & Mohr, J.P. (1965) The control of eating behavior in an anorexic by operant conditioning techniques. In L.P. Ullman & L. Krasner (Eds), *Case Studies in Behavior Modification*. New York: Holt, Rinehart & Winston.

Baker, J.D., Williamson, D.A. & Sylve, C. (1995) Body image disturbance, memory bias and body-dysphoria: Effects of negative mood induction. *Behavior Therapy*, **26**, 747–759.

Beck, A.T. (1976) *Cognitive Therapy and the Emotional Disorders*. New York: International Universities Press.

Beck, J.S. (1995). *Cognitive Therapy: Basics and Beyond*. New York: Guilford Press.

Ben-Tovim, D.I., Walker, M.K., Fok, D. & Yap, E. (1989) An adaptation of the Stroop test for measuring shape and food concerns in eating disorders. A quantitative measure of psychopathology? *International Journal of Eating Disorders*, **6**, 681–687.

Beumont, P.J.V., George, G.C.W. & Smart, D.E. (1976) 'Dieters' and 'vomiters and purgers' in anorexia nervosa. *Psychological Medicine*, **6**, 617–622.

Blinder, B.J., Freeman, D.M. & Stunkard, A.J. (1970) Behavior therapy of anorexia nervosa: Effectiveness of activity as a reinforcer of weight gain. *American Journal of Psychiatry*, **126**, 1093–1098.

Braun, D.L., Sunday, S.R. & Halmi, K.A. (1994) Psychiatric comorbidity in patients with eating disorders. *Psychological Medicine*, **24**, 859–867.

Bray, G.A., Bouchard, C. & James, W.P.T. (1998) *Handbook of Obesity*. New York: Marcel Dekker.

Brewin, C. (1988) *Cognitive Foundations of Clinical Psychology*. Hove, UK: Lawrence Erlbaum.

Bruch, H. (1973) *Eating Disorders*. New York: Basic Books.

Bruch, H. (1982) Anorexia nervosa: Therapy and theory. *American Journal of Psychiatry*, **139**, 1531–1538.

Bulik, C.M., Sullivan, P.F., Joyce, P.R. & Carter, F.A. (1995) Tempereament, character and personality disorder in bulimia nervosa. *Journal of Nervous and Mental Diseases*, **183**, 593–598.

Byrne, S.M. & McLean, N.J. (2002) The cognitive-behavioural model of bulimia nervosa: a direct evaluation. *International Journal of Eating Disorders*, **31**, 17–31.

Channon, S., de Silva, P., Hemsley, D. & Perkins, R. (1989) A controlled trial of cognitive-behavioural and behaviour treatment of anorexia nervosa. *Behaviour Research and Therapy*, **27**, 529–535.

Channon, S., Hemsley, D. & de Silva, P. (1988) Selective processing of food words in anorexia nervosa. *British Journal of Clinical Psychology*, **27**, 259–260.

Clark, D.A., Feldman, J. & Channon, S. (1989) Dysfunctional thinking in anorexia and bulimia nervosa. *Cognitive Therapy and Research*, **13**, 377–387

Clark, D.M. (1986) A cognitive approach to panic. *Behaviour Research and Therapy*, **24**, 461–470.

Clark, D.M. (1997) Panic disorder and social phobia. In D.M. Clark & C.G. Fairburn (Eds), *Science and Practice of Cognitive Behaviour Therapy*. Oxford Medical Publications. Oxford: Oxford University Press.

Cooper, M.J. (1997) Cognitive theory in anorexia nervosa and bulimia nervosa: A review. *Behavioural and Cognitive Psychotherapy*, **25**, 113–145.

Cooper, M., Cohen-Tovee, E., Todd, G., Wells, A. & Tovee, M. (1997) The eating disorder belief questionnaire: Preliminary development. *Behaviour Research and Therapy*, **35**, 381–388.

Cooper, M. & Fairburn, C.G. (1992a) Selective processing of eating, weight and shape related words in patients with eating disorders and dieters. *British Journal of Clinical Psychology*, **31**, 363–365.

Cooper, M. & Fairburn, C.G. (1992b) Thoughts about eating, weight and shape in anorexia nervosa and bulimia nervosa. *Behaviour Research and Therapy*, **30**, 501–511.

Cooper, M. & Turner, H. (2000) Underlying assumptions and core beliefs in anorexia nervosa and dieting. *British Journal of Clinical Psychology*, **39**, 215–218

Cooper, Z., & Fairburn, C.G. (2001) A new cognitive behavioural approach to the treatment of obesity. *Behaviour Research and Therapy*, **39**, 499–511

Cooper, Z. & Fairburn, C.G. (in press) Cognitive behaviour therapy for obesity. In T.A. Wadden & A.J. Stunkard (Eds), *Obesity: Theory and Therapy*. New York: Guilford Press.

Dally, P. & Gomez, J. (1979) *Anorexia Nervosa*. London: Heinemann.

Fairburn, C.G. (1981) A cognitive-behavioural approach to the management of bulimia. *Psychological Medicine*, **11**, 697–706.

Fairburn, C.G. (1985) A cognitive-behavioural treatment of bulimia. In D.M. Garner & P.E. Garfinkel (Eds), *Handbook of Psychotherapy for Anorexia Nervosa and Bulimia*. New York: Guilford Press.

Fairburn, C.G. (1995) Short-Term psychological treatments for bulimia nervosa. In K. Brownell & C.G. Fairburn (Eds), *Eating Disorders and Obesity: A Comprehensive Handbook* (pp. 289–378). New York: Guilford Press.

Fairburn, C.G. (1997) Eating disorders. In D.M. Clark & C.G. Fairburn (Eds), *Science and Practice of Cognitive Behaviour Therapy*. Oxford Medical Publications. Oxford: Oxford University Press

Fairburn, C.G. & Brownell, K.D. (Eds) (2002) *Eating Disorders and Obesity: A Comprehensive Handbook* (2nd edn). New York: Guilford Press.

Fairburn, C.G., Cooper, Z., Doll, H.A. & Welch, S.L. (1999) Risk factors for anorexia nervosa: Three integrated case control comparisons. *Archives of General Psychiatry*, **56**, 468–476.

Fairburn, C.G., Cooper, Z. & Shafran, R. (in press) Cognitive-behaviour therapy for eating disorders: a 'transdiagnostic' theory and treatment. *Behaviour Research and Therapy*.

Fairburn, C.G., Marcus, M.D. & Wilson, G.T. (1993) Cognitive-behavioral therapy for binge eating and bulimia nervosa: A comprehensive treatment manual. In C.G. Fairburn, G. Christopher & G.T. Wilson (Eds), *Binge Eating: Nature, Assessment, and Treatment*. New York: Guilford Press.

Fairburn, C.G., Norman, P.A., Welch, S.L., O'Connor, M.E., Doll, H.A. & Peveler, R.C. (1995) A prospective study of outcome in bulimia nervosa and the long-term effects of three psychological treatments. *Archives of General Psychiatry*, **52**, 304–312.

Fairburn, C.G., Peveler, R.C., Jones, R., Hope, R. A. & Doll, H.A. (1993) Predictors of 23-month outcome in bulimia nervosa and the influence of attitudes to shape and weight. *Journal of Consulting and Clinical Psychology*, **61**, 696–698.

Fairburn, C.G., Shafran, R. & Cooper, Z. (1999) A cognitive-behavioural theory of anorexia nervosa. *Behaviour Research and Therapy*, **37**, 1–13.

Fairburn, C.G., Stice, E., Cooper, Z., Doll, H.A., Norman, P.A. & O'Connor, M.E. (in press) Understanding persistence in bulimia nervosa: a five-year naturalistic study. *Journal of Consulting and Clinical Psychology*.

Ferster, C.B., Nurenberger, I. & Levitt, E.B. (1962) The control of eating. *Journal of Mathetics*, **1**, 87–109.

Fuller, R.D., Williamson, D.A. & Anderson, T.W. (1995) Selective information processing of body size and food related stimuli in women who are preoccupied with body size. *Advances in Health Care Research*, **14**, 61–66.

Garfinkel, P.E. & Garner, D.M. (1983) *Anorexia Nervosa: A Multi-dimensional Perspective*. New York: Brunner/Mazel.

Garner, D.M. & Garfinkel, P.E. (Eds), *Handbook of Treatment for Eating Disorders* (2nd edn). New York: Guilford Press.

Garner, D.M. & Bemis, K.M. (1982) A cognitive-behavioral approach to anorexia nervosa. *Cognitive Therapy and Research*, **6**, 123–150.

Garner, D.M. & Bemis, K.M. (1985) Cognitive therapy for anorexia nervosa. In D.M. Garner & P.E. Garfinkel (Eds), *Handbook of Psychotherapy for Anorexia Nervosa and Bulimia*. New York: Guilford Press.

Garner, D.M., Vitousek, K.M. & Pike, K.M. (1997) Cognitive-behavioral therapy for anorexia nervosa. In D.M. Garner & P.E. Garfinkel (Eds), *Handbook of Treatment for Eating Disorders* (2nd edn). New York: Guilford Press.

Gelder, M. (1997) The scientific foundations of cognitive behaviour therapy. In D.M. Clark & C.G. Fairburn (Eds), *Science and Practice of Cognitive Behaviour Therapy*. Oxford Medical Publications. Oxford: Oxford University Press.

Gilbert, S. (1986) *Pathology of Eating*. London: Routledge & Kegan Paul.

Goldfein, J.A., Walsh, B.T. & Midlarsky, E. (2000) Influence of shape and weight on self-evaluation in bulimia nervosa. *International Journal of Eating Disorders*, **27**, 435–445.

Goodrick, G.K. & Foreyt, J.P. (1991) Why treatments for obesity don't last. *Journal of American Dietetic Association*, **91**, 1243–1247.

Green, M.W., McKenna, F.P. & deSilva, M.S.L. (1994) Habituation patterns to colour-naming of eating-related stimuli in anorexics and non-clinical controls. *British Journal of Clinical Psychology*, **33**, 499–508.

Guidano, V.F. & Liotti, G. (1983) *Cognitive Processes and Emotional Disorders*. New York: Guilford Press.

Halmi, K.A. (1983) The state of research in anorexia nervosa and bulimia. *Psychiatric Development*, **1**, 247–262.

Halmi, K.A., Agras, S., Crow, S. & Mitchell, J. (2000) *Anorexia Nervosa: Multicentre Treatment Study*. Ninth International Conference on Eating Disorders, Academy for Eating Disorders, 4–7 May 2000, New York.

Heatherton, T.F. & Baumeister, R.F. (1991) Binge eating as escape from self-awareness. *Psychological Bulletin*, **110**, 86–108.

Hermans, D., Pieters, G. & Eelen, P. (1998) Implicit and explicit memory for shape, body weight, and food-related words in patients with anorexia nervosa and nondieting controls. *Journal of Abnormal Psychology*, **107**, 193–202.

Herzog, D.B., Keller, M.B., Strober, M., Yeh, C.J. et al. (1992) The current status of treatment for anorexia nervosa and bulimia nervosa. *International Journal of Eating Disorders*, **12**, 215–220.

Kleifield, E.I., Wagner, S. & Halmi, K.A. (1996) Cognitive-behavioral treatment of anorexia nervosa. *Psychiatric Clinics of North America*, **19**, 715–737.

Kramer, F.M., Jeffery, R.W., Forster, J.L. & Snell, M.K. (1989) Long-term follow-up of behavioral treatment for obesity: Patterns of weight regain among men and women. *International Journal of Obesity*, **13**, 123–136.

Leitenberg, H., Agras, W.S. & Thompson, L.G. (1968) A sequential analysis of the effect of positive reinforcement in modifying anorexia nervosa. *Behaviour Research and Therapy*, **6**, 211–218.

Lilenfeld, L. & Kaye, W.H. (1998) Genetic studies of anorexia and bulimia. In H.W. Hoek, J.L. Treasure & M.A. Katzman (Eds), *Neurobiology in the Treatment of Eating Disorders*. Wiley series on Clinical and Neurobiological Advances in Psychiatry. Chichester: John Wiley & Sons.

Lilenfeld L.R., Kaye, W.H., Greeno, C.G., Merikangas K.R., Plotnicov, K., Pollice, C., Rao, R., Strober, M., Bulik, C.M. & Nagy, L. (1998) A controlled family study of anorexia nervosa and bulimia nervosa: Psychiatric disorders in first degree relatives and effects of proband comorbidity. *Archives of General Psychiatry*, **55**, 603–610.

McManus, F., Waller, G. & Chadwick, P. (1996) Biases in the processing of different forms of threat in bulimic and comparison women. *Journal of Nervous and Mental Disease*, **184**, 547–554.

Meyer, C. & Waller, G. (1999) The impact of emotion upon eating behavior: The role of subliminal visual processing of threat cues. *International Journal of Eating Disorders*, **25**, 319–326.

Mitchell, J.E., Crow, S., Peterson, C.B., Wonderlich, S. & Crosby, R. D. (1998) Feeding laboratory studies in patients with eating disorders: A review. *International Journal of Eating Disorders*, **24**, 115–124.

Mizes, J.D. (1992). Validity of the Mizes Anorectic Cognitions scale: A comparison between anorectics, bulimics, and psychiatric controls. *Addictive Behaviors*, **17**, 283–289.

Mowrer, O.H. (1960) *Learning Theory and Behavior.* New York: John Wiley & Sons.

Newman, J.P., Wallace, J.F., Strauman, T.J., Skolaski, R.L., Oreland, K.M., Mattek, P.W., Elder, K.A. & McNeely, J. (1993) Effects of motivationally significant stimuli on the regulation of dominant responses. *Journal of Personality and Social Psychology*, **65**, 165–175.

Persons, J.B. (1989) *Cognitive Therapy in Practice: A Case Formulation Approach.* New York: W.W. Norton & Co. Inc.

Phelan, P.W. (1987) Cognitive correlates of bulimia: The bulimia Thoughts Questionnaire. *International Journal of Eating Disorders*, **6**, 593–607.

Pike, K.M. (2000) How do we keep patients well? Issues of relapse prevention. *Plenary Session II: New Clinical Trials.* Ninth International Conference on Eating Disorders, Academy for Eating Disorders, 4–7 May 2000, New York.

Pike, K.M., Loeb, K. & Vitousek, K. (1996) Cognitive behavioral therapy for anorexia nervosa and bulimia nervosa. In J. K. Thompson (Ed.), *Body Image, Eating Disorders and Obesity: An Integrated Guide for Assessment and Treatment.* Washington, DC: American Psychological Association.

Polivy, J. & Herman, C.P. (2002) Experimental studies of dieting. In C.G. Fairburn & K.D. Brownell (Eds), *Eating Disorders and Obesity: A Comprehensive Handbook.* (2nd edn) (pp. 84–87). Guilford Press: New York.

Rachman, S. (1984) Anxiety disorders: Some emerging theories. *Journal of Behavioral Assessment*, **6**, 281–299.

Rachman, S. (1997) The evolution of cognitive behaviour therapy. In D.M. Clark & C.G. Fairburn (Eds), *Science and Practice of Cognitive Behaviour Therapy.* Oxford Medical Publications. Oxford: Oxford University Press.

Rosen, J.V. & Leitenberg, E. (1982) Bulimia nervosa: Treatment with exposure and response prevention. *Behaviour Research and Therapy*, **14**, 125–131.

Salkovskis, P.M. (1996) The cognitive approach to anxiety: threat beliefs, safety-seeking behavior, and the special case of health anxiety and obsessions. In P.M. Salkovskis (1996). *Frontiers of Cognitive Therapy.* New York: Guilford Press.

Schotte, D.E., McNally, R.J. & Turner, M.L. (1990) A dichotic listening analysis of body weight concern in bulimia nervosa. *International Journal of Eating Disorders*, **9**, 109–113.

Sebastian, S.B., Williamson, D.A. & Blouin, D.C. (1996) Memory bias for fatness stimuli in the eating disorders. *Cognitive Therapy and Research*, **20**, 275–286.

Shepherd, H. & Ricciardelli, L.A. (1998) Test of Stice's dual pathway model: dietary restraint and negative affect as mediators of bulimic behavior. *Behaviour Research and Therapy*, **36**, 345–352.

Slade, P. (1982) Towards a functional analysis of anorexia nervosa and bulimia nervosa. *British Journal of Clinical Psychology*, **21**, 167–179.

Stice, E. (2001) A prospective test of the dual-pathway model of bulimic pathology: mediating effects of dieting and negative affect. *Journal of Abnormal Psychology*, **110**, 124–135.

Stice, E. & Agras, W.S. (1999) Subtyping bulimic women along dietary restraint and negative affect dimensions. *Journal of Consulting and Clinical Psychology*, **67**, 460–469.

Stice, E., Nemeroff, C. & Shaw, H.E. (1996) Test of the dual pathway model of bulimia nervosa: Evidence for dietary restraint and affect regulation mechanisms. *Journal of Social and Clinical Psychology*, **15**, 340–363.

Stice, E., Shaw, H. & Nemeroff, C. (1998) Dual pathway model of bulimia nervosa: Longitudinal support for dietary restraint and affect-regulation mechanisms. *Journal of Social and Clinical Psychology*, **17**, 129–149.

Stice, E., Ziemba, C., Margolis, J. & Flick, P. (1996) The dual pathway model differentiates bulimics, subclinical bulimics, and controls: Testing the continuity hypothesis. *Behavior Therapy*, **27**, 531–549.

Stroop, J.R. (1935) Studies of interference in serial verbal reactions. *Journal of Experimental Psychology*, **18**, 643–662.

Stuart, R.B. (1967) Behavioural control of overeating. *Behaviour Research and Therapy*, **5**, 357–365.

Stunkard, A.J. & Penick, S.B. (1979) Behavior modification in the treatment of obesity—the problem of maintaining weight loss. *Archives of General Psychiatry*, **36**, 801–806.

Szmukler, G.I. & Tantam, J. (1984) Anorexia nervosa: Starvation dependence. *British Journal of Medical Psychology*, **57**, 303–310.

Treasure, J., Todd, G., Brolly, M., Tiller, J., Nehmed, A. & Denman, F. (1995) A pilot study of a randomised trial of cognitive analytical therapy vs educational behavioral therapy for adult anorexia nervosa. *Behaviour Research and Therapy*, **3**, 363–367.

Vitousek, K.B. & Hollon, S.D. (1990) The investigation of schematic content and processing in eating disorders. *Cognitive Therapy and Research*, **14**, 191–214.

Vitousek, K.B., & Ewald, L.S. (1993) Self-representation in eating disorders: A cognitive perspective. In Z.V. Segal & S.J. Blatt (Eds), *The Self in Emotional Distress: Cognitive and Psychodynamic Perspectives*. New York: Guilford Press.

Vitousek, K.B. Daly, J. & Heiser, C. (1991) Reconstructing the internal world of the eating-disordered individual: Overcoming denial and distortion in self-report. *International Journal of Eating Disorders*, **10**, 647–666.

Vitousek, K.M. (1996) The current status of cognitive-behavioral models of anorexia nervosa and bulimia nervosa. In P.M. Salkovskis (Ed.), *Frontiers of Cognitive Therapy*. New York: Guilford Press.

Vitousek, K. & Manke, F. (1994) Personality variables and disorders in anorexia nervosa and bulimia nervosa. *Journal of Abnormal Psychology*, **103**, 103–147.

Vitousek, K., Watson, S. & Wilson, G.T. (1998) Enhancing motivation for change in treatment-resistant eating disorders. *Clinical Psychology Review*, **18**, 391–420.

Wadden, T.A., Sternberg, J.A., Letizia, K.A., Stunkard, A.J. & Foster, G.D. (1989) Treatment of obesity by very low calorie diet, behavior therapy, and their combination: A five-year perspective. *Journal of Consulting and Clinical Psychology*, **66**, 429–433.

Wadden, T.A., Vogt, R.A., Foster, G.D. & Anderson, D.A. (1998) Exercise and the maintenance of weight loss: 1-year follow-up of a controlled clinical trial *Journal of Consulting and Clinical Psychology*, **66**, 429–433.

Watson, J.B. (1925) *Behaviorism*. New York: North Holland.

Williams, J.M.G., Watts, F.N., MacLeod, C. & Mathews, A. (1988) *Cognitive Psychology and Emotional Disorders*. Chichester: John Wiley & Sons.

Williamson, D.A., Muller, S.L., Reas, D.L. & Thaw, J.M. (1999) Cognitive bias in eating disorders: Implications for theory and treatment. *Behaviour Modification*, **23**, 556–577.

Williamson, D., Kelley, M.L., Davis, C.J., Ruggiero, L. & Vietia, M.C. (1985) The psychophysiology of bulimia. *Advances in Behaviour Research and Therapy*, **7**, 163–172.

Williamson, D.A., Davis, C.J., Duchmann, G.G., McKenzie, S.J. & Watkins, P.C. (1990) *Assessment of Eating Disorders: Obesity, Anorexia and Bulimia Nervosa*. New York: Pergamon.

Wilson, G.T. (1989) The treatment of bulimia nervosa: A cognitive-social learning analysis. In A.J. Stunkard & A. Baum (Eds), *Perspectives in Behavioral Medicine: Eating, Sleeping and Sex*. Hillsdale, NJ: Lawrence Earlbaum.

Wilson, G.T. (1993) Behavioral treatment of obesity: Thirty years and counting. *Advances in Behaviour Research and Therapy*, **16**, 31–75.

Wilson, G.T. (1996) Acceptance and change in the treatment of eating disorders and obesity. *Behaviour Therapy*, **27**, 417–439.

Wilson, G.T. & Fairburn, C.G. (2002) Treatments for eating disorders. In P.E. Nathan & J.M. Gorman, *A guide to treatments that work* (2nd edn) (pp. 559–592). New York: Oxford University Press.

Wilson, G.T., Fairburn, C.G., Agras, W.S., Walsh, B.T. & Kraemer, H. (2002) Cognitive-behavior therapy for bulimia nervosa: time course and mechanisms of change. *Journal of Consulting and Clinical Psychology*, **70**, 267–274.

Wing, R.R. (1998) Behavioral approaches to the treatment of obesity. In G.A. Bray, C. Bouchard & W.P.T. James (Eds), *Handbook of Obesity*. New York: Marcel Dekker.

Wolff, G. & Serpell, L. (1998) A cognitive model and treatment strategies for anorexia nervosa. In H.W. Hoek, J.L. Treasure & M.A. Katzman (Eds), *Neurobiology in the Treatment of Eating Disorders*. Wiley series on Clinical and Neurobiological Advances in Psychiatry. Chichester John Wiley & Sons.

Wolpe, J. (1958) *Psychotherapy by Reciprocal Inhibition*. Stanford: Stanford University Press.

Wolpe, J. (1993) The cognitivist oversell and comments on symposium contributions. *Journal of Behavior Therapy Experimental Psychiatry*, **24**, 141–147.

Wooley, S.C., Wooley, O.W. & Dyrenforth, S.R. (1979) Theoretical, practical and social issues in behavioral treatment of obesity. *Journal of Applied Behavior Analysis*, **12**, 3–25.

CHAPTER 8

Sociocultural Theories of Eating Disorders: An Evolution in Thought

Mervat Nasser

Department of Psychiatry, Thomas Guy House, London, UK

and

Melanie Katzman

29 West, 88th Street, New York, USA

In this chapter we trace the evolution of cultural explanations for disordered eating. Beginning with the individual's interface with the environment and traditional psychodynamic forces, we work through gender-focused and western-oriented explanations until we conclude with global changes, the role of technology and even some theorising about prevention. Table 8.1 at the end of this chapter provides a visual map of this journey.

EATING PATHOLOGY: THE INTERFACE BETWEEN THE INDIVIDUAL AND THE ENVIRONMENT

Self-starvation: The Psychological Predicament

The embodiment of the psyche in human form and the dialectic of this body with its environment has been central to all causal theories of eating disorders long before the study of sociocultural influences became the vogue. In fact early psychodynamic descriptions of the anorexic syndrome did not ignore the importance of placing the phenomenon within the context of the individual's environment. Initially psychodynamic attention was understandably focused on the contribution of the dysfunctional family as a microcosmic environment. As early as the 1800s authors remarked upon the importance of 'placing in parallel the morbid condition of the patient and the preoccupation of those who surround her. The moral medium amid which the patient lives, exercises and influences would be regrettable to overlook or misunderstand' (Laségue, 1873).

Handbook of Eating Disorders. Edited by J. Treasure, U. Schmidt and E. van Furth.

Table 8.1 Eating disorders: The sociocultural model

1873–1971	
Non-specific neurosis	Environmentally responsive
1970s	
Specific neurosis	Ego/family dynamics
1980s	
Culture-specific neurosis	Western culture dynamics
	Symbolic morbidity: Reflects notions of thinness promoted by culture
	Continuum morbidity: Subclinical forms merging with normality
	Cultural epidemiological evidence/(? increase over 50 years)
	Cross-cultural evidence/(? absent/rare in non-western cultures)
1990s	
Gender specific	Gender dynamics: Metaphorical manipulation of the body
The New Millennium	
Worldwide neurosis	Worldwide culture dynamics
	'Cultures in transition'/confused identities in the flesh

From a psychoanalytic perspective, the anorexic disorder was considered an unusual variation on the neurotic theme and its historical relationship to hysteria is well established in the literature (see Silverstein & Perlick, 1995). Anorexia nervosa remained fairly inconspicuous and only gained prominence in the past 30 years when it moved from being a 'mere' manifestation of neurosis to a specific neurotic syndrome in its own right (Russell, 1970).

Self-starvation: Specific Neurosis Reactive to the Cult of Thinness

The specific diagnostic status acquired by anorexia nervosa has been attributed to a raise in incidence, an increase that is debatably one of perception, detection, or real presentation change. However, several publications have documented an increase over the past 50 years in western nations (Lucas et al., 1991; Hoek, 1993).

This apparent rise was curiously noted to take place against a background of declining hysteria. This was interpreted as an indication of a change in social preoccupations which consequently changed our perception and definition of what we regard as 'morbid'. Both hysteria and anorexia nervosa were seen as representing 'adaptive processes' in the face of particular environmental factors. Hysteria was commonly thought to be the product of a sexually repressive environment while the anorexic thinness began to be viewed as responding to new environmental demands that promoted the desirability of thinness (Swartz, 1985).

The cultural shift towards a 'thin ideal' was noted in art, fashion and media advertisements and seemed to have been easily endorsed by women, the common sufferers of the disorder. The pursuit of thinness had metaphorical connotations, which meant a lot more than thinness, such as a pursuit of beauty, attractiveness, health and achievement (Garner & Garfinkel, 1980; Scwarz et al., 1983; Anderson & Di Domenico, 1992).

Self-starvation and Eating Disorders: The Continuum Hypothesis

The growing obsession with thinness was then considered responsible for the pervasive dieting behaviour, which in turn was linked closely to the full anorexic syndrome. This experience, said Crisp (1981), 'is wide spread amongst the female adolescent population and although it becomes very intense in the anorectic to be, it would not appear to be qualitatively different at this stage from the more universal experience'.

The observation that the morbid phenomenon of extreme thinness does in fact blur and merge with what is considered to be normal or culturally acceptable, such as the practice of dieting, formed the basis of the continuum hypothesis. In other words, dieting falls at one end of the spectrum and the extreme forms of disordered eating at the other end with a number of weight-reducing behaviours of variable intensities in between.

The 'continuum' theory of severity was confirmed in a number of community studies which showed the presence of subclinical forms in normal student populations (Button & Whitehouse, 1981; Clarke & Palmer, 1983, Szmukler, 1983; Mann et al., 1983; Johnson-Sabine et al., 1988; Katzman et al., 1984). In fact the subclinical forms were generally estimated to be five times more common than the full-blown syndromes (Dancyger & Garfinkel, 1995).

The epidemiological impression that bulimia and bulimic behaviours appear to be far more prevalent in the community than the anorexic syndrome raised the possibility that the nature of both conditions, despite psychopathological similarities, are different. In the case of anorexia, the cardinal feature is restraint, which requires a strong internal drive; however, the bulimic disorder may be more responsive to external environmental reinforces (Palmer, 1999). It was even suggested that bulimia could be the result from a set of 'socially contagious' behaviours (Chiodo & Latimer, 1983).

Hoek et al. (1995) in their cross-cultural work in Curaçao have suggested that anorexia may be more epidemiologically stable while bulimia may increase with growing urbanization. (For more discussion on epidemiological issues please refer to the chapter by Hoeken, Seidell and Hoek in this volume.)

Whether one looked at anorexia or bulimia over time, one thing was consistent: more women than men were demonstrating clinical and subclinical concerns with weight and diet. Why should this be an issue specific to women and why at this point in history?

Eating Disorders: Gender Specific?

The 'why woman' question in the early 1980s was framed as a feminist issue although, as writers later in the twentieth century revealed, the question of gender is one that impacts all professionals working in the field of eating disorders (Katzman & Waller, 1998).

Women's susceptibility to eating problems and the pursuit of a thin ideal has been viewed as a rebellion against the adult female form and all that is implied with being a woman in today's society—an effort to obtain an androgynous physique at a time when men are still viewed as more powerful, as a means of demonstrating mastery and control, and of course a realistic adaptation to the availability of fashionable clothes and a susceptibility to the 'culture of health' in which leanness is associated with longevity.

Katzman (1998) suggested that it was the female access to power that was critical in the debate and not the chromosomal make-up of eating-disordered sufferers. She suggested that it was power not gender that mattered, and it just so happened that more women had obstacles to independence and achievement. Littlewood (1995) noted that, looking cross-culturally, it was in fact the ability for self-determination that differentiated male and female eating problems. (The gender dimension in eating disorders in males is further explored by Fichter and Krenn in Chapter 23 of this volume; also such psychological factors as the role of power, control, self-esteem and self-regulation are dealt with by Serpell and Troop in Chapter 9.)

Eating Disorders: Culture Specific

The expansion of the gender debate to include a study of social and political impacts on behaviour enabled the field to consider the importance not only of western cultures but of all cultures. While the early 1980s and 1990s enjoyed a fascination with the western women's predicament, and the eastern women's 'protection' from eating distress (by virtue of clearly defined social roles and acceptance of plumpness as a sign of success), further sophistication of these models revealed not only gender myopia but also a cultural visual restriction. No one was immune to eating problems. Perhaps our diagnostic criteria and theoretical lenses had been somewhat selective. Although eating disorders in the 1980s and early 1990s were considered culture bound (Prince, 1983; Swartz, 1985), by the end of the 1990s, with increasing data from the east, the limitations of seeing the problem as exclusive to 'one culture' and 'one sex', namely western culture and western women, were apparent.

Eating Disorders: A Worldwide Concern—from Specific to Global

Nasser (1997) conducted an extensive review of the published studies of eating disorders in the east and west and found few national or societal boundaries that contained the growing detection of eating problems, albeit sometimes with a twist. For example, in the east, the work of Sing Lee and colleagues consistently demonstrated anorexia in the absence of a fear of fat. These findings, along with discoveries of eating issues in unexpected places like the Middle East, challenge us not to ask 'if' problems exist but 'how'? For example: How do they present themselves? How do we understand and treat these problems? How can we be inspired in our aetiological models by data that may challenge our traditional notions of why people choose to alter their bodies or diets in times of distress?

The emergence of eating pathology in the majority of societies was initially linked to an exposure to and identification with western cultural norms in relation to weight and shape preferences—especially for women. The media was considered the main culprit in disseminating these values and in homogenising public perceptions. The pressure to 'remake the body' to match a newly unified global aesthetic ideals was seen to operate through international advertising and worldwide satellite networks. While certainly plausible, the questions remain of why women would be so susceptible to media programming, and what does the globalisation in the marketplace reflect in terms of women's roles that might impact on the development of eating disorders?

In an analysis of 'feminism across cultures', Nasser (1997) pointed to the fact that feminist movements similar to those in the west also arose in other non-western societies, which resulted in questioning and debating traditional gender roles. The majority of non-western women have significantly changed their position, with increasing numbers of them being highly educated and working outside the family. This meant that all women of different cultures and societies increasingly share the pressures that are hypothesised to increase western women's propensity to eating disorders.

So yet again the opening of a theoretical frontier brings with it as many questions as it does inspirations. For example, does 'westernisation' only mean 'image-identification' or is there more to it? How would the issue of westernisation relate to other issues such as urbanisation, modernisation and economic globalisation? And even if we tried to break down the concept into constituent elements, would that be sufficient to explain a universal preoccupation with weight? Or does 'weight' mean perhaps much more than mere body regulation? Is it a quest for refashioning the body? Is the quest for refashioning the self (i.e. remaking of a new identity) able to translate and negotiate the impact of a volatile and constantly changing culture?

THE EVOLUTION OF EATING PSYCHOPATHOLOGY AS A METAPHOR FOR CONTROL

Body Regulation and Identity

In some of the early descriptions of the anorexic syndrome, one can find fashion-driven explanations for the role of environment in the development of eating psychopathology.

Bruch (1982) indicates that the environment of the family with its pathological interactions could indeed create an 'identity deficit'. Within this remit, the anorexic symptomatology serves as a defence against feelings of 'powerlessness', and the act of food refusal becomes symbolic of a strive towards autonomy and mastery over one's self as well as others. The failure of individuality or incomplete identity described in Bruch's analysis was later applied beyond the boundaries of the domestic circle, to include an individual struggle for autonomy against social pressures in a much wider context. The feminist text clearly put the notion of identity at centre stage within the anorexic struggle. Self-starvation is seen as allowing women a sense of power to develop an identity as a person in the absence of real control or power in other areas of their life (Orbach, 1986; Lawrence, 1984).

The current status of our understanding of the conceptual aspects of eating disorders is central to an ongoing debate and a specific chapter in this volume is allocated to a discussion of this topic. The author(s) of this chapter question the validity of our current categories, raising the contention of whether eating disorders are 'real disorders' or mere categories that do not take into account the 'meaning' of these behaviours and serve only as convenient pigeon-holes.

The Cultural Transition and the Social Predicament

Historically the displacement of the locus of power to the body was noted to occur during periods of cultural transition, particularly at times when 'identity definition or redefinition' is called for. Under these conditions, morbid forms of bodily control are seen as symptomatic of the 'transition in culture' and not the 'culture' per se (Di Nicola, 1990; Nasser, 1997; Gordon, 1998).

The notion of the social predicament was therefore advanced as a possible explanatory model for eating disorders. Predicaments, said Taylor (1985), 'are painful social situations or circumstances, complex, unstable, morally charged and varying in their import in time and place'. Di Nicola (1990) suggested that by applying the social predicament model to bulimia and anorexia we could better understand the diversity of cultural experiences and hopefully uncode the metaphors contained within the symptoms.

However, even the sociocultural models of the late twentieth century remained overly focused on weight and media control in an effort to capture how existing social structures could exercise a quantitative and qualitative influence on individual psyches. As a result there are a number of questions that clearly illustrate the limitations of our current approach to understanding the nature of these disorders *vis-à-vis* culture.

- Given that Western Europe and northern America constitute what is commonly known as the 'west', why should the rates of eating morbidity be higher in the American society than in central Europe (Neumarker et al., 1992)?
- Even within Europe itself, why there should there be any differences between east and west Europe, given their shared European heritage (except for a very brief historical period of 50 years or so)? And how true is the claim that eating disorders began to appear in Eastern Europe only after the decline of communism (Rathner et al., 1995)?
- What possibly could be the reasons behind the reported 800% increase of eating morbidity in the Kibbutz in the past 25 years (Kaffman & Sadeh, 1989)?
- Why should there be any differences at all in the rates of eating disorders between the 'north' and the 'south' of Italy—or any culture within a culture for that matter (Ruggiero et al., 2000)?
- What is the explanation for differences in the rates of anorexia nervosa between urban and rural Japan, or indeed the reasons behind their reported 100% increase in only a 5-year period (Ohzeki et al., 1990; Suematsu et al., 1995)?
- What significance could be attached to the apparent rise of eating disorders among black South African girls after the fall of the Apartheid regime (le Grange et al., 1998)?
- Why is anorexic self-starvation in Hong Kong not associated with a fear of fatness, while in the west such fear is considered pathognomonic (Lee, 1995)?

Well the sceptic might just say that these idiosyncrasies prove the unreliability of cultural research (for example, the use of unreliable self-report measures in the absence of clinical interview and the failure to involve random and community samples over time). Would it not also be too simplistic to dismiss them as mere artefacts?

In order to begin to understand the reasons that may lie behind such variabilities, one needs to have a deeper understanding of the type of culture we live in, which appears to be multiple fragments within a globally 'homogeneous/homogenised entity'. There are therefore several 'contradictory' elements within this apparent modern uniformity and the tension at the moment is therefore likely to be between the 'one' and the 'multiple'.

SHAPING APPETITES: GASTRONOMIC DIVERSITY AND STANDARD McDONALDISM—THE PREDICTED RISE OF OBESITY

One notable aspect of modern western societies is their attempt to embrace different cultural/ethnic elements within a unified whole, to enable culture to be one and multiple at the same time. This is achieved through what is now commonly referred to as 'supermarket multiculturalism', i.e. the exposure of the west to other cultures through their cuisine, or other exotic pastiches. Foreign ingredients and ready-made meals have found their way to supermarket shelves and there is a clear proliferation of different foreign restaurants in any big city, from Chinese and Italian to Indian and Thai, etc.

Yet, while this is taking place in the west, many countries in the non-western world are undergoing major changes in their dietary habits, through the introduction of western fast food chains selling beefburgers and fried chicken. The impact of the McDonald's restaurants on the quality and choice of food available was initially studied in highly urbanised western society (Robertson, 1992) and was offered as one of the possible reasons behind the different rates of eating disorders between Europe and the USA. Several studies from non-western societies have extended this hypothesis and now point to a possible link between the changes in traditional diet and the inevitable impact on population weight and shape secondary to the increased fat content of one's diet. These dietary changes could lead to a rise in the rates of obesity worldwide and may in fact prompt greater weight consciousness and possible eating pathology (Nogami et al., 1984; Lee et al., 1989; Nasser, 1997).

Another factor contributing to rates of obesity, apart from the ongoing changes in the nature of food consumption, is the shifting of meal times such that the main meal is now consumed in the evening and often not in the presence of others. Later hours at work or school and the demand for longer uninterrupted hours are some of the consequences of increased urbanisation and modernisation. The need for faster, pre-packaged food to keep pace with changing work demands has impacted family roles and national habits.

Given the dietary changes, confusion in the living patterns and reduced physical activity, it is not surprising that a governmental summit held in London, April 2000, concluded that the average norm for population weight in the UK had significantly increased in the past two decades—particularly for women. As a reflection of this, the popular Marks & Spencer stores began using a size 16 model to promote their clothes lines! Obesity is also a recognised problem in the USA, where there are reports that nearly 30% of the population are classified as obese.

The relationship between obesity and the eating patterns of anorexia and bulimia are well documented (Garner et al., 1980). It is also well known that people tend to over-eat at times of emotional tension; as Bruch (1966) recounted, 'obesity has an important positive function, and it is a compensatory mechanism in a frustrating and stressful life'.

FOOD ABUNDANCE AND FOOD SHORTAGE: ECONOMIC FORCES

With an increase in economic freedom in various countries has come a departure from State-supported privileges. While potentially providing freer opportunity for all there has in fact been greater differentials of wealth and poverty between countries and within the same country. A market economy is based on the principle of cost-effectiveness, which heightens competition as well as standardisation as increases in productivity are sought. A deregulated economy is built on the primacy of individual choice which can produce increased social inequalities as well as social isolation, and is probably associated with increased commercialisation and material aspirations (Nasser, 1997).

Several clinicians and researchers from eastern Europe have suggested that the increase in commercialism and changing gender roles, coupled with the depletion of state-offered benefits (such as education, employment, and health care), may result in the comodificaiton of the human body and modifications to its form to fit with global standardisations of beauty, marketability and adaptability (Nasser et al., 2001). This in turn may make women more susceptible to eating problems as they may be forced not only to adapt their bodies to a new form but to form their identities to a new role. Hence their bodies may become placards for social distress and transition.

CABLE AND ONLINE CULTURES

Just in case the deregulation of markets, family life and meal structure did not impress you as potential risk factors for personal pathology, one final area to consider is the role of online cultures and the power and alienation of the individual. Is it possible that the deregulated media deregulates the relationship between the individual and society? Several authors (e.g. Morley & Robins, 1997) have attempted to explore this concept and have found that changes in computer culture have meant a change in how we relate to our own nation as a geographic entity. As people type and tap into a shared global environment they may in fact be travelling beyond their familiar nexus to ideas and fashions never considered by their homes or home country.

There is no doubt that there are inherent advantages in the potentially unlimited choices, but to negotiate these choices the individual needs to learn how to reformulate an identity amidst an influx of visual information and images. Identities in the new media order will need to be similar and different at the same time! Individual personalised cultures will inevitably arise within the context of the uniform and the universal. This means that the act of transmitting image/information will change from broadcasting to narrow casting with special programming aimed at specific target and differentiated audiences. How does one fit in, and where? How does one connect to others, and how? These are the psychic and social challenges. Their impact on the body and its form will be the quest for the next level of cultural research and potential treatment planning.

CULTURE TRANSITION AND DISCONNECTION

Predictably, the rising rate of eating disorders will pose a public health challenge to most modernizing countries in Asia, Eastern Europe, Latin America and Africa. In nearly all of these countries, specialized treatment facilities and support groups are barely available. Patients frequently have to detour around various practitioners before they receive some sort of psychological treatment. Many more are not being treated. The outcome of these patients remains a mystery, and the prevention of their distress an intriguing social challenge.

In earlier works Katzman (1998), and Katzman and Lee (1997) have argued that eating disorders may be precipitated by problems with transition, dislocation and oppression that produce solutions in manipulations of weight, diet and food. As one examines the movement of eating disorders from individual neurosis to cultural monitor of distress, it becomes increasingly important to identify ways of operationalising treatment and prevention strategies. By organising our research and clinical questions around ways of assisting women in self-determination, control and connection rather than simply documenting media and weight insults we may be able to progress beyond the limitations of our current strategies and provide alternatives for women struggling with eating disorders as an 'answer' to complex personal social and personal problems.

GLOBAL CONCERNS, GLOBAL CONSIDERATIONS FOR PREVENTION—NOW WHAT?

Nasser and Katzman (1999) have suggested that the prevention of eating problems will be enhanced by the provision of new social supports and the careful work of providing new ways of belonging at the work and school level. Katzman and Leung (1996) demonstrated that teenagers undergoing cultural transition are likely to use food and weight discussions as a common point of connection; alternative means of finding one's place will be key. Piran (1996), in her participatory research, has underscored the need to explore, label, challenge and change small group norms as a means of undoing unhealthy social forces.

Nasser and Katzman (1999), and others (Levine et al., 1999), have also suggested a shift in emphasis towards competencies rather than pathology in prevention and treatment strategies. While the notion of working with people's strength is central to motivational approaches to treatment (Troop et al., 1993), how to deploy potential resources creatively and make healthy links between people has probably not been fully exploited. For example, perhaps advances in information technology can be used to forge dialogues between people in the similar predicaments worldwide.

Several authors in the field of prevention have written about the importance of mentoring and role modelling by women who have managed to 'navigate their way' in this challenging and changing world (Levine, 1994). Nasser and Katzman (1999) suggested that electronic connections may provide a new way of achieving female connectedness, one in which women may be able to help other women with whom they would not have been able to communicate in the past. Linked by computer technology women may be able to overcome their social and political isolation and gain new insights into formulas for success and survival.

As the position of individuals, particularly women, is changed and challenged internationally it may become increasingly important to work towards social change, not merely symptom change, and to look not only at individual cosmetic concerns but at responsible cultural consciousness. This may require a broad examination of social morbidity, and a further examination of the effects that subordinate positions may have on individual psyches. If we can view eating disorders as a marker of cultures in transition then our challenge will be to empower and support individuals as they evolve in new roles.

REFERENCES

Anderson, A. & Di Domenico, L. (1992) Diet vs. shape content of popular male and female magazines: A dose response relationship to the incidence of eating disorders? *Int. J. Eat. Disord.*, **11**, 283–287.

Bruch, H. (1966) Anorexia nervosa and its differential diagnosis, *J. Nrv. Ment. Dis.* **141** (5), 555–566.

Bruch, H. (1982) Anorexia nervosa: Therapy and theory. *American Journal of Psychiatry*, **139**, 12.

Button, E.J. & Whitehouse, A. (1981) Subclinical anorexia nervosa. *Psychol. Med.*, **11**, 509–516.

Chiodo, J. & Latimer, P. (1983) Vomiting as a learned weight control technique in bulimia. *J. Behav. Ther. Exp. Psychiat.*, **14** (2), 131–135.

Clarke, M. & Palmer, R.L. (1983) Eating attitudes and neurotic symptoms in university students. *Br. J. Psychiat.*, **142**, 299–304.

Crisp, A.H. (1981) Anorexia nervosa at normal body weight! The abnormal normal weight control syndrome. *Int. J. Psychiat. Med.*, **11** (3), 203–233.

Dancyger, I. & Garfinkel, P.E. (1995) The relationship of partial syndrome of eating disorders to anorexia nervosa and bulimia nervosa. *Psychol. Med.*, **25**, 1018–1025.

Di Nicola, V.F. (1990) Anorexia: Multiform self-starvation in historical and cultural context. Part II: Anorexia nervosa as a culture reactive syndrome. *Transcultural Psychiat. Res. Rev.*, **27**, 245–285.

Garner, D.M., Garfinkel, P.E., Schwartz, D. & Thompson, M. (1980) Cultural expectations of thinness in women. *Psychiat. Rep.*, **47**, 483–491.

Garner, D.M. & Garfinkel, P.E. (1980) Sociocultural factors in the development of anorexia nervosa, *Psychol. Med.*, **10**, 483–491.

Gordon, R. (1998) Concepts of eating disorders: A historical reflection. In H. Hoek, J. Treasure, & M.A. Katzman. *Neurobiology in the Treatment of Eating Disorders*. London: Wiley.

Hoek, H., Aaad, I., Bartelds, M., Jacquoline, J., Bosveld, M., Yolanda van der Graaf, M., Veronique, E., Limpens, M., Maiwald, M., Carolyine, J., Spaaij, M. (1995) Impact of urbanisation on detection rates of eating disorders. *Am. J. Psychiat.*, **152** (9), 1272–1285.

Hoek, H. (1993) Review of epidemiological studies of eating disorders. *Int. Rev. Psychiat.*, **5**, 61–74

Johnson-Sabine, E., Wood, K., Patton, G., Mann, A. & Wakeling, A. (1988) Abnormal eating attitudes in London school girls: Aprospective epidemiological study: factors associated with abnormal response on screening questionnaires. *Psychol. Med.*, **18**, 615–622.

Kaffman, M. & Sadeh, T. (1989) Anorexia nervosa in the Kibbutz: Factors influencing the development of monoideistic fixation. *Int. J. Eat. Disord.*, **8** (1), 33–53.

Katzman, M.A. & Waller, G. (1998) Implications of therapist gender in the treatment of eating disorders: Daring to ask the questions . In W. Vandereycken (Ed.), *The Burden of the Therapist*. London: The Athlone Press.

Katzman, M.A. (1997) Getting the difference right. It is power not gender that matters. *Euro. Eat. Dis. Rev.*, **5** (20), 71–74.

Katzman, M.A., Wolchik, S.A. & Braver, S.L. (1984) The prevalence of frequent binge eating and bulimia in a non clinical college sample. *Int. J. Eat. Disord.*, **3**, 53–61.

Katzman, M. & Leung, F. (1996, April) *When East meets West: Does disordered eating follow?* Paper presented at the Seventh International Conference on Eating Disorders, New York.

Katzman, M.A. (1998) Feminist approaches to eating disorders: Placing the issues in context. In S. De Risio, P. Bria, & A. Ciocca (Eds), *Psychotherapeutic Issues on Eating Disorders: Models, Methods and Results*. Rome: Societa Editrice Universo.

Laségue, C. (1873) *De l'anorexie hystorique*. Reprinted in R.M. Kaufman & M. Heinman (Eds), *Evolution of Psychosomatic Concepts: Anorexia Nervosa, a Paradigm* (1964). New York: International University Press.

Lawrence, M. (1984) *The Anorexic Experience*. London: The Women's Press.

Le Grange, D., Telch, C.F. & Tibbs, J. (1998) Eating attitudes and behaviours in 1,435 South African Caucasian and non-Caucasian college students. *Am. J. Psychiat.*, **155** (2), 250–254.

Lee, S. (1995) Self-starvation in context: Towards a culturally sensitive understanding of anorexia nervosa. *Soc. Sci. Med.*, **41**, 25–36.

Lee, S., Chiu, H.F.K. & Chen, C. (1989) Anorexia nervosa in Hong Kong. Why not more in China? *Br. J. Psychiat.*, **154**, 683–685.

Levine, M.P. (1994) Beauty myth and the beast: What men can do and be to help prevent eating. *Eat. Disord: J. Treat. Preven.*, **2**, 101–113.

Levine, M.P., Piran, N., Steiner-Adair, C. (1999) *Preventing Eating Disorders: A handbook of interventions and special challenges.* London and Philadelphia: Brunner/Mazel, Taylor & Francis Group.

Littlewood, R. (1995) Psychopathology and personal agency: Modernity, culture change and eating disorders in South Asian societies. *Br. J. Med. Psychol.*, **68**, 45–63.

Lucas, A., Beard, C., O'Fallon, W. & Kurland, L. (1991) 50-year trends in the incidence of anorexia nervosa in Rochester, Minnesota: A population based study. *Am. J. Psychiat.*, **148**, 917–922.

Mann, A.H., Wakeling, A., Wood, K., Monck, E., Dobbs, R. & Szmukler, G. (1983) Screening for abnormal eating attitudes and psychiatric morbidity in an unselected population of 15 year old school girls. *Psychol. Med.*, **13**, 573–580.

Morley, D. & Robins, K. (1997) *Spaces of Identity, Global Media, Electronic Landscapes and Cultural Boundaries.* London: Routledge.

Nasser, M. (1997) *Culture and Weight Consciousness.* London: Routledge.

Nasser, M. & Katzman, M.A. (1999) Transcultural perspectives inform prevention. In *Preventing Eating Disorders: A Handbook of Interventions and Special.*

Nasser, M., Katzman, M. & Gordon, R. (2001) *Eating Disorders and Cultures in Transition.* London and New York: Bruner-Routledge.

Neumarker, U., Dudeck, U., Voltrath, M., Neumarker, K. & Steinhausen, H. (1992) Eating attitudes among adolescent anorexia nervosa patients and normal subjects in former West and East Berlin: A transcultural comparison. *Int. J. Eat. Disord.*, **12** (3), 281–289.

Nogami, Y., Yanaguchi, T. & Ishiwata, H. (1984) *The prevalence of binge eating in the Japanese university and high school population.* Presented at the International Conference of Eating Disorders,. Swansea, UK (unpublished).

Ohzeki, T., Haanaki, K., Motozumi, H., Ishitani, N., Maatsuda-Ohatahra, H., Sunaguchi, M. & Shiraki, K. (1990) Prevalence of obesity, leaness and anorexia nervosa in Japanese boys and girls aged 12–14 years. *Ann. Nutrit. Metab.*, **34**, 208–212.

Orbach, S. (1986) *Hunger Strike: the Anorexic Struggle as a Metaphor for our Age.* New York: Norton.

Palmer, R. (1999) *Eating disorders in the New Millennium.* Presented at the Eating Disorders Congress, Stockholm, Sweden.

Piran, N. (1996) The reduction of preoccupation with body weight and shape in schools: A feminist approach. *Eat. Disord.: J. Treat. Prevent.*, **4**, 323–333.

Piran, N., Levine, M. & Steiner-Adair, C. (2000) *Preventing Eating Disorders. A Handbook of Interventions and Special Challenges.* London and Philadelphia: Brunner/Mazel.

Prince, R. (1983) Is anorexia nervosa a culture-bound syndrome? *Transcult. Psychiat. Res. Rev.*, **20**, 299.

Rathner, G., Tury, F., Szabo, P., Geyer, M., Rumpold, G., Forgaces, A., Sollner, W. & Plottner, G. (1995) Prevalence of eating disorders and minor psychiatric morbidity in central Europe before the political changes of 1989: A cross-cultural study. *Psychol. Med.*, **25**, 1027–1035.

Robertson, M. (1992) *Starving In Silence*: *An Exploration of Anorexia Nervosa.* Sydney: Allen & Unwin.

Rugggiero, G.M., Hannower, W., Mantero, M. & Papa, R. (2000) Body acceptance and culture: A study in northern and southern Italy. *European Eating Disorders Review*, **8**, 40–50.

Russell, G.F.M. (1970) Anorexia nervosa: Its identity as an illness and its treatment. In • . Harding-Price (Ed.), *Modern Psychological Medicine* (Vol. II; pp. 131–164). London: Butterworths.

Scwarz, M., Thompson, M. & Johnson, C. (1983) *Eating Disorders and the Culture, Anorexia Nervosa. Recent Developments in Research* (pp. 83–84) New York: Alan R. Liss.

Silverstein, B. & Perlick, D. (1995) The *cost of competence: Why Inequality Causes Depression, Eating Disorders and Illness in Women.* Oxford: Oxford University Press.

Suematsu, H., Ishikawa, H., Kuboki, T. & Ito, T. (1985) Statistical studies of anorexia nervosa in Japan: Detailed clinical data on 1011 patients. *Psychother. Psychosomat.*, **43**, 96–103.

Swartz, L. (1985) Anorexia nervosa as a culture-bound syndrome. *J. Soc. Sci. Med.*, **20** (7), 725–730.

Szmukler, G. (1983) Weight and food pre-occupation in a population of English school girls. In B.G. Bergman (Ed.), *Understanding Anorexia Nervosa and Bulimia* (pp. 21–27). 4th Ross Conference on Medical Research. Ohio: Ross Laboratories.

Taylor, D. (1985) The sick child predicament. *Aust. N.Z.J. Psychiat.*, **19**, 130–137.

Troop, N., Treasure, J. & Schmidt, U. (1993) From specialist care to self directed treatment. *Br. Med. J.*, **307** (6904), 577–578.

CHAPTER 9

Psychological Factors

Lucy Serpell

Eating Disorders Unit, Institute of Psychiatry, London

and

Nicholas Troop

Department of Psychology, London Metropolitan University, London, UK

INTRODUCTION: WHY STUDY PSYCHOLOGICAL FACTORS?

The aetiologies of AN and BN are incompletely understood but are generally agreed to be multifactorial. A comprehensive model of aetiology is likely to include some combination of genetic and familial (Bulik et al., 2000; Treasure & Holland, 1995), personality and psychological (Vitousek & Manke, 1994), environmental and neurobiological elements. Finally, of course, psychological therapies are generally more successful than drug treatments in eating disorders (EDs). In addition to psychological factors that may be important in the development of eating disorders *per se,* there may be other non-specific psychological factors that may affect crucial but more general aspects of the therapeutic process such as motivation, engagement, drop-out and therapeutic alliance. However, coverage of all of these factors is beyond the scope of this chapter. Although there are many psychological factors that we could potentially include, we focus, in particular, on stress, personality, self-esteem and emotion. In particular we do not discuss dieting as a risk factor for eating disorders in detail as this is dealt with by Børresen and Rosenvinge (Chapter 27 in this volume) although much of what we discuss is related directly to dieting and dietary restraint.

STRESS AND COPING

Although earlier conceptualisations have considered stress to be a feature of the external environment or a feature of the individual (e.g. an internal physiological response), the cognitive transactional theory of stress (Lazarus & Folkman, 1984) places stress as the relationship between an individual and her environment. In this model stress is experienced when the demands of some person–environment encounter exceed an individual's resources for coping with that situation. Although stress can be studied at many levels (e.g. environmental, biological), the cognitive transactional theory of stress is essentially psychological. It requires not only the presence of some (potential) stressor but also the absence

Handbook of Eating Disorders. Edited by J. Treasure, U. Schmidt and E. van Furth.

of adequate coping resources and, hence, suboptimal coping. This section explores the presence of stressors and coping difficulties prior to the onset of eating disorders. For convenience these are divided into factors that are temporally distant from onset (i.e. occurring in childhood) and those occurring immediately prior to onset.

Stressors: Childhood Adversity

A number of studies have shown that patients with eating disorders report trauma in their childhoods more frequently than do women without eating disorders. This includes traumatic events such as childhood sexual abuse (e.g. Welch & Fairburn, 1994; Waller, 1991) but also other features of childhood environment such as parental antipathy, indifference and over-control (Schmidt et al., 1993a) (although such features of parental care often overlap with other aspects of abuse, Bifulco & Moran, 1997). Generally, studies suggest that it is bulimic disorders (including normal weight bulimia nervosa and anorexia nervosa of the binge/purge subtype) that show the highest levels of childhood adversity (Schmidt et al., 1997a).

Stressors: Onset

Several case-note studies report descriptions of events, difficulties and other life changes prior to onset of eating disorders (e.g. Casper & Davis, 1977; Pyle et al., 1981; Kay & Leigh, 1954). These early reports suffer from a number of problems including the lack of a comparison group of non-eating-disordered women, no criteria to determine severity of events and no formal operationalisation either of what constitutes a stressor or even a definition of onset of the eating disorder.

Gowers et al. (1996) assessed life events in the year before onset in 35 adolescent patients with anorexia nervosa and compared rates with those in a control group from a GP list. Groups differed only marginally ($p = 0.06$) and only for those events rated as extremely negative. Welch et al. (1997), however, found that 76% of bulimic women in the community reported negative events in the year before onset compared with just 40% in non-psychiatric controls. Both these studies used checklists of life events and neither assessed chronic difficulties. Unlike Gowers et al. (1996), Welch et al. (1997) did not assess severity of life events although they did provide an operational definition of the onset of the disorder under study (onset of bulimia defined as the date of first episode of binge eating or vomiting).

Schmidt et al. (1997b) interviewed 101 patients with recent onset (less than 5 years) anorexia nervosa and bulimia nervosa using the Life Events and Difficulties Schedule (Brown & Harris, 1978) which describes criteria to determine severe versus non-severe events as well as major, marked and non-marked difficulties. Onset of bulimia nervosa was defined in the same way as in Welch et al. (1997) and onset of anorexia nervosa was defined as the date at which weight loss to a body mass index of 17.5 kg/m^2 was achieved or when amenorrhoea occurred (whichever was the earlier). Schmidt et al. (1997b) found no significant difference in the experience of severe events in the ED and non-psychiatric control groups; however, when both severe events and marked difficulties were included more of those developing anorexia nervosa and bulimia nervosa reported at least one severe event or marked difficulty in the year before onset compared to the comparison group.

In a reanalysis of their data, Schmidt et al. (1999) found that there were differences between subtypes of anorexia nervosa. Those developing anorexia nervosa of the restricting subtype reported rates of severe events and difficulties that were similar to that of women with bulimia nervosa and depression. Women with anorexia of the binge/purge subtype, on the other hand, reported rates of severe events and difficulties that were no higher than would be expected in a general population of women with no psychiatric disorder. However, Strober (1984) reported different results. Using an event checklist, those who developed anorexia nervosa of the binge/purge subtype reported consistently high levels of stress over the 18 months prior to onset whereas those developing anorexia nervosa of the restricting subtype reported levels of stress that rose over the 18 months prior to onset. In other words, onset of the restricting subtype seems to be associated with an increase in stress levels whereas onset of the binge/purge subtype is associated with chronically high levels of stress. It may be possible to reconcile these differences. Schmidt's work suggests that sufferers with anorexia nervosa of the restricting subtype report relatively little childhood adversity (Schmidt et al., 1993a) but they do report severe events and difficulties prior to onset (Schmidt et al., 1998). Women with anorexia nervosa of the binge/purge subtype report high levels of childhood adversity (Schmidt et al., 1993a) but low rates of events and difficulties prior to onset (Schmidt et al., 1998). Thus, R/AN may be associated with acute problems whereas AN/BN may be associated with more chronic problems, which is essentially what Strober (1984) reports. What is puzzling, however, is that such ongoing background difficulties would also have been picked up by the semi-structured interview used by Schmidt et al. (1997b). This matter is clearly not yet resolved.

The studies described above have relied on retrospective reporting. While potential reporting biases due to current mood or psychiatric status can be reduced by semi-structured interviews where events and difficulties are rated objectively according to potentially observable behaviour (rather than purely subjective ratings) longitudinal studies are often held to be the ideal. Those that have been conducted on stress and eating disorders, however, have tended to use self-report measures of life events and eating pathology in a cross-lagged panel design. While Rosen and colleagues found that stress is predictive of an increase in eating disorder symptoms but not dieting (Rosen et al., 1990, 1993). Patton et al. (1990) found that increases in social stress were predictive of the onset of dieting but not the onset of bulimia nervosa at a case level. The problem with such panel designs is that it is impossible to relate the timing of changes in stress to the timing of changes in pathology.

Stone and Brownell (1994) assessed married couples using a diary methodology, measuring the occurrence of stressful events and whether they ate the same, more or less than usual on any particular day. These authors found that level of stress was not related to the likelihood of eating more but was related to the likelihood of eating less. There was also an interesting gender difference in that women appeared to have a lower threshold for the degree of stress likely to cause them to eat less than men did.

While this study found that eating less was related to stress but eating more was not, one problem with the methodology is that no established measure of eating pathology was used. Crowther et al. (2001) however selected 17 binge eaters and 17 non-binge eaters on the basis of scores on measures of eating pathology and participants completed measures of daily hassles, binge episodes and number of calories consumed (using a food diary). Binge eaters and non-binge eaters did not differ in the *frequency* of hassles but binge eaters rated these as more stressful than did non-binge eaters. In addition, on days rated as high in hassles, binge eaters consumed significantly more calories than on days rated as low in hassles. Non-binge eaters did not differ in the calories consumed between high- and low-hassle days.

However, these studies do not generally include severe crises (severe events and/or difficulties), nor do they examine those with clinically diagnosed EDs. In the case of depression, both severe crises and daily hassles are related to changes in symptoms but only severe crises have been shown to be related to onset at a case level (Coyne & Downey, 1991). It is possible that the same may be true for eating disorders. Nevertheless, diary studies are useful in understanding fluctuation in symptoms which has potential clinical importance. For example, hassles may be involved in fluctuations in symptoms in those who have already developed an eating disorder while severe events and difficulties are required to provoke onset in the first place.

Meaning of Events and Difficulties

Events that most often provoke onset of eating disorders are relationship problems (Schmidt et al., 1997b). However, the precise *meaning* (as opposed to *type*) of event is much less often explored. For example, depression is generally provoked by problems involving loss (such as the ending of an important relationship: Finlay-Jones & Brown, 1981), in particular those involving entrapment or humiliation (Brown et al., 1995), while anxiety is generally provoked by problems involving threat (such as news of eviction: Finlay-Jones & Brown, 1981). Those events that involve loss have also been reported as the most common prior to onset of eating disorders (Troop, 1996). However, in attempting to identify events with a specific meaning that provoke onset of eating disorders, Schmidt et al. (1997b) found that pudicity events (crises of a sexual nature that were perceived as shameful, embarrassing or disgusting) were significantly more common in patients developing anorexia nervosa than in those developing bulimia nervosa and in non-psychiatric controls (24%, 3% and 8% respectively). Nevertheless, these still occurred in only a minority of onsets and more research needs to be carried out to explore this issue further.

Coping and Social Support

The coping response is important in determining the impact of life events and difficulties (i.e. whether the life event or difficulty results in high levels of stress). The consensus is essentially that women with AN and BN show high levels of avoidance-coping relative to non-eating-disordered women and that women with BN (but not AN) seek less support and confide less (Soukup et al., 1991; Neckowitz & Morrison, 1990; Yager et al., 1995). This seems to be true regardless of whether questionnaire or interview methods are used (see, for example, Troop et al., 1994, 1998).

To our knowledge, only two studies have attempted to assess coping retrospectively as factors involved in vulnerability to and onset of eating disorders. Troop and Treasure (1997a) explored coping in response to the events and difficulties that directly provoked onset of eating disorders, using a retrospective semi-structured interview in which ratings of coping were based on potentially observable behaviour rather than subjective reports. While cognitive avoidance was associated with the onset of anorexia nervosa, cognitive rumination was associated with the onset of bulimia nervosa (relative to non-eating-disordered women). In addition, onset of an eating disorder was related to higher rates of helplessness in response to the provoking event/difficulty.

In terms of vulnerability, Troop and Treasure (1997b), again using a semi-structured interview, also found higher rates of helplessness in childhood in women who later developed an eating disorder. Overall, women with AN of the restricting subtype reported lower levels of helplessness than the other eating-disordered subgroups (BN and AN of the binge/purge subtype). However, this may be due in part to the lower levels of severe adversity in childhood since in women with AN of the restricting subtype. When only those women with two or more adverse childhood experiences were included (e.g. sexual abuse, parental antipathy, parental indifference, etc.) the rates of helplessness were rather more similar between eating-disordered subgroups, all of which were higher than that found in non-eating-disordered women.

Interestingly, in terms of social support, Tiller et al. (1997) found differences in structural and functional aspects between eating-disordered subtypes. Women with AN, for example, reported fewer support figures than non-eating-disordered women but were equally satisfied with the support they received. BN women, however, reported a similar sized network of potential support figures as non-eating-disordered women but were considerably more dissatisfied. However, this study was cross-sectional and although no significant differences in crisis support were found in response to events/difficulties directly prior to onset (Troop & Treasure, 1997a), AN and BN patients do report fewer friends and more loneliness in their childhoods than do non-ED women (Fairburn et al., 1997, 1999; Karwautz et al., 2001, Troop & Bifulco, 2002).

PERSONALITY

Another widely researched topic in eating disorders is that of personality, in particular perfectionism. Obsessional features such as rigidity, neatness, conscientiousness and pre-occupation with rules and ethics are also common. If such traits are held to an extreme degree such that they result in marked impairment of social or occupational functioning over a considerable period of time, a diagnosis of obsessive-compulsive personality disorder (OCPD) may be warranted (Serpell et al., 2002). In reviewing studies on personality and personality disorders in anorexia nervosa, Sohlberg and Strober (1994) conclude that obsessional symptoms appear to be related to the state of starvation while obsessional traits are stable personality features which are maintained after weight gain.

Perfectionism

Slade (1982) suggested that perfectionism is one of the 'setting conditions' for the development of AN and that it leads to a need for total control over some area of the individual's life. 'Dissatisfied' (or 'neurotic') perfectionism (in which there is an inability to derive pleasure from one's successes because the performance is never good enough) is considered to be particularly important (e.g. Kiemle et al., 1987; Slade et al., 1990, 1991).

There is a high level of perfectionism in both AN and BN (see full review in Goldner et al., 2002) and most studies have found that different eating-disordered subtypes do not differ in levels of perfectionism (e.g. Garner et al., 1983). Two recent studies have suggested that perfectionistic traits remain high after recovery from AN (Pia & Toro, 1999; Srinivasagam et al., 1995), adding to evidence that such traits are stable features rather than simply due to the effects of the illness (e.g. starvation). There is also evidence from retrospective reports of high levels of perfectionism prior to onset. Halmi and colleagues (1977) found 61% of a group of anorexic patients were described by their parents as having perfectionistic personalities prior to onset. In a large case-control study Fairburn et al. (1999) found childhood perfectionism was one of only two factors (among around 100 measured) which was substantially more common in AN than in healthy controls (see also Rastam, 1992, and Srinivasagam et al., 1995).

There is recent evidence that the related trait of rigidity is also of interest (Goldner et al., 1999). This may be manifest in various neuropsychological domains such as perception in AN (Tchanturia et al., 2002). This perceptual rigidity also appears to be a stable trait, even after recovery from AN (Tchanturia et al., in press). It also is somewhat specific to AN since women with BN typically show a fluctuation rather than rigidity in their perceptual processes (Tchanturia et al., 2002).

Obsessive-Compulsive Personality Disorder

A wealth of clinical literature describes the cluster of rigidity, perfectionism and inflexible thinking that is characteristic of obsessive-compulsive personality disorder (OCPD) in anorexia nervosa (Strober, 1980; Casper et al., 1992; Vitousek & Hollon, 1990). Estimates of comorbidity of OCPD and eating disorders vary enormously from 3% (Piran et al., 1988) to 60% (Wonderlich et al., 1990), with the largest study suggesting a concurrent diagnosis of OCPD of 10% in restricting AN and 4% in binge/purge AN (Herzog et al., 1992). Matsunaga et al. (2000) examined individuals who had recovered from AN for at least one year and found that 15% met strict diagnostic criteria for OCPD. Childhood OCPD personality traits also showed a high predictive value for the development of eating disorders (an odds ratio of nearly 7 was found for every additional trait present) (Brecelj et al., in press).

Preliminary data from family studies indicate increased risk of OCPD in relatives of AN probands compared to controls (Lilenfield et al., 1998). These findings suggest the possible existence of a broad, genetically influenced phenotype with core features of rigid perfectionism and propensity for extreme behavioural constraint.

Other Personality Traits/Disorders

Other common personality disorders in AN are those within cluster C. For example, there is a preponderance of avoidant personality disorders in this group (Gillberg et al., 1995).

Patients with a history of BN, in contrast, are more likely to receive diagnoses of cluster B personality disorders, in particular borderline personality disorder (Carroll et al., 1996; Wonderlich & Mitchell, 1997; Matsunaga et al., 2000) although there are wide variations in rates between studies. Reasons for the wide variability in diagnoses are likely to include the difficulty of diagnosing personality disorders in general (Arntz, 1999) and the widely differing measures used to establish the presence of personality disorders. Impulsive traits are also commonly reported in BN (Fahy & Eisler, 1993).

The presence of borderline and impulsive personality traits in BN may be associated with behaviours such as self-harm, shoplifting and other impulsive behaviours (Welch & Fairburn, 1996; Wiederman & Pryor, 1996). In fact, some authors have suggested that a diagnosis of 'multi-impulsive bulimia' may, in some cases, be appropriate for that subset of bulimic individuals who show several impulsive behaviours as well as BN (Lacey & Read,

1993; Lacey, 1993). It should be noted, however, that the distinction between AN and BN on the basis of personality traits is by no means perfect and shows a great deal of overlap. For example, Carroll et al. (1996) showed similar rates of avoidant personality disorder and borderline PD in BN (around 10% of each) and some studies have found no differences in the pattern of PD diagnoses between those with AN and BN (Inceoglu et al., 2000). Also, there is some evidence that those with the binge/purge subtype of AN show higher rates of personality disorders than either AN-restricting subtype or BN sufferers (Piran et al., 1988; Herzog et al., 1992).

Finally, it should be noted that where diagnosable personality disorders occur, they appear to be associated with greater chronicity and poorer functioning (Skodol et al., 1993; Inceoglu et al., 2000; Johnson et al., 1990).

SELF-ESTEEM

Self-esteem refers to a cognitive evaluation of one's competencies. Longitudinal studies have suggested a relationship between low self-esteem and the later development of eating disorder symptoms (e.g. Button et al., 1996; Wood et al., 1994). Retrospective reporting of childhood negative self-evaluation also suggests that this may be higher in women with anorexia nervosa or bulimia nervosa than in either a non-psychiatric comparison group or even in women with other psychiatric disorders (Fairburn et al., 1997, 1999). However, in follow-up studies of patients treated for BN, self-esteem appears to improve with recovery but remains low in those whose eating disorder symptoms persist (e.g Troop et al., 2000).

Although low self-esteem is not unique to eating disorders, the suggestion that weight and shape are particularly over-identified with self-esteem in individuals with eating disorders has received some attention in the literature (Vitousek & Hollon, 1990) and, in this regard, may represent something rather more specific to eating disorders than to other disorders. In particular, Geller and colleagues report on the development of the Shape and Weight Based Self-Esteem (SAWBS) Inventory which is a measure of the elements that make up a person's self-esteem (Geller et al., 1998, 2000). People with eating disorders base more of their self-esteem on their (perceived unsatisfactory) shape and weight than either a non-clinical control group or a mixed psychiatric control group (Serpell et al., submitted). This provides evidence for the contention of Vitousek and Hollon (1990) that it is the strength of the link between self-esteem and weight and shape that differentiates individuals with eating disorders from non-eating-disordered young women (and those with other psychiatric disorders). What is not clear, however, is when this link between self-esteem and weight and shape occurs in relation to the onset of eating disorders. It is assumed to arise out of a background negative evaluation of self, but the link could develop prior to the onset of the eating disorder (hence explaining the process by which low self-esteem becomes a vulnerability for eating disorders), perhaps at the point of the onset of dieting. Alternatively it may develop at or after onset, becoming a symptomatic manifestation of the low self-esteem.

EMOTION

It is well known that sufferers with eating disorders, particularly in those samples recruited from clinics, report high levels of comorbid emotional disorders such as depressive and anxiety disorders (e.g. Fornari et al., 1992). However, here we will restrict our discussion to emotional states rather than disorders of emotion.

Negative Affect

Both dietary restraint and negative affect mediate (at least partially) the relationship between body dissatisfaction and binge eating (Shepherd & Ricciardelli, 1998). Indeed, and consistent with Stice's (1994) dual pathway model, a longitudinal study showed that the main effects of dieting and negative affect both independently predicted the subsequent onset of binge eating (Stice et al., 2000) although this was true only in females.

In contrast to the independent effects of dietary restraint and negative affect described above, experimental studies suggest an interactive effect, in that the relationship between negative affect and over-eating is stronger in restrained eaters than in unrestrained eaters, the so-called disinhibition of dietary restraint (for a review see Ruderman, 1986). The induction of negative emotions generally reduces the amount eaten by unrestrained individuals but significantly increases the amount eaten by restrained individuals. However, the size of this effect may depend on whether the affect is related to the self. For example, sadness induced by a film clip did not lead to over-eating in restrained eaters (Sheppard-Sawyer et al., 2000) but sadness induced by perceived failure at a task did (Heatherton et al., 1991). On the other hand, fear induced by a film clip (which was not ego-related) did lead to over-eating in restrained eaters (Cools et al., 1992) suggesting that ego-relevance may not be the only factor of importance. Interestingly, this same study also showed that positive mood (induced by a comedy film clip) led to over-eating in restrained individuals, although the effect was smaller than for the horror film used to induce fear.

Polivy and Herman (1999) summarise a number of theoretical models to account for the disinhibiting effects of emotion on dietary restraint including:

* the psychosomatic comfort hypothesis which suggests that eating makes people feel better;
* the learned helplessness hypothesis in which the experience of stress/distress generalises to all areas in life including the ability to maintain a diet;
* the distraction hypothesis in which restrained eaters over-eat in order to distract themselves from feeling distressed;
* the masking hypothesis in which the dieter, by over-eating, misattributes her distress to the problem of over-eating rather than to her real problems.

These authors carried out a study to test all these hypotheses simultaneously and found no support for the comfort hypothesis, strong support for the masking hypothesis and partial support for the learned helplessness and distraction hypotheses.

Disgust

Disgust is a particularly interesting emotion to study in the context of eating disorders and yet, surprisingly, has only recently begun to be explored empirically. Disgust is, at its most basic level, related to the avoidance of foodstuffs which may be harmful (Rozin & Fallon,

1987) and the action tendency associated with this emotion is to have the disgusting stimulus removed or otherwise avoided. Rozin and Fallon (1987) also propose that disgust extends beyond the domain of food and becomes one mechanism by which social and cultural values are transmitted.

There is a growing consensus in clinical samples that disgust and disgust sensitivity are higher in eating-disordered women than non-eating-disordered women (Davey et al., 1998; Troop et al., 2002) in particular for categories of food- and body-related stimuli. Troop et al. (2002) showed that women in remission from an eating disorder continued to report high levels of disgust to foodstuffs of animal origin but lower levels of disgust towards the human body and its products than currently ill women (although these were still not at normative levels). This specificity of disgust domains is interesting and differs from people with animal phobias in which there is general disgust rather than disgust related specifically to the target of the disorder (namely animals).

Fear is ascribed a central role in eating disorders, particularly AN (e.g. fear of weight gain, weight phobia, etc.). However, we have recently found that fear and disgust are equally salient emotions in a non-clinical sample with abnormal eating attitudes in response to high calorie foods and overweight body shapes (Harvey et al., 2002). In addition, preliminary evidence from clinical samples seems to replicate this result in patients.

Murray et al. (submitted) have also looked at sensitivity to recognition of emotion in facial expressions. This fascinating study asked eating-disordered patients and non-eating-disordered controls to manipulate the intensity of facial expressions of emotion on a computer screen and to indicate the point at which they recognised the emotion. Eating-disordered patients were significantly more sensitive to the recognition of disgust expressions relative to controls. What is so fascinating about this result is that it begins to take the role of disgust in eating disorders out of *basic* emotions into *complex* emotions, namely shame. Miller (1997) argues that disgust in the face of an observer is associated with the experience of shame in the subject.

Shame

Shame is a complex emotion in which the self is judged to have fallen short of some internalised set of standards. Even if experienced in private it is *as if* the self is being judged by some external other. Thus, shame is considered by some to be the experience that the self is defective (e.g. Tangney, 1993) while others conceptualise shame as a psychological consequence of being judged to be low in social rank (e.g. Gilbert, 1997). Implicit in both these conceptualisations is the notion of social comparison (Lazarus, 1999).

In non-clinical samples shame-proneness is related to eating pathology (Santfner et al., 1995) while Murray et al. (2000) found that shame mediates the relationship between paternal care in childhood and later eating pathology. In a diary study, Sanftner and Crowther (1998) showed that shame was generally higher in those women who reported binge eating but fluctuations in shame were not related to the occurrence of binge episodes. Interestingly, Waller et al. (2000) found that a core belief of Defectiveness/Shame was related to the frequency of vomiting. At a group level, Defectiveness/Shame was one of three core beliefs that differentiated bulimic subgroups (bulimia nervosa, anorexia nervosa of the binge/purge subtype and binge eating disorder) from a non-eating-disordered comparison group (the other two were Insufficient Self-Control and Failure to Achieve).

There is some debate, however, as to whether shame in general is important in eating disorders or whether it is restricted to shame related specifically to the body. For example, Andrews (1997) found that bodily shame was a better predictor of bulimia than body dissatisfaction and that bodily shame mediated the relationship betwen childhood (physical or sexual) abuse and later bulimia. However, to date only one study has examined both general and bodily shame simultaneously. Burney and Irwin (2000) found that only shame related to eating and the body were uniquely predictive of eating pathology. However, this study used a non-clinical female sample and the result requires replication in a clincal group.

Other Emotions

Like shame, jealousy is also a complex emotion involving social comparison (Lazarus, 1999). Two studies have used a sibling-comparison design to assess non-shared childhood environment in relation to the development of anorexia nervosa (Murphy et al., 2000; Karwautz et al., 2001). Both studies found that affected sisters reported having been more jealous of their unaffected sisters in childhood than the unaffected sisters were of them. Women with bulimia nervosa, on the other hand, report their mothers to have been jealous and competitive in their childhoods (Rorty et al., 2000a, 2000b). Thus, while felt jealousy may be a risk factor for anorexia nervosa and the jealousy of others may be a risk factor in bulimia nervosa, these results suggest that the development of both disorders probably involves competition.

Anger and hostility have attracted rather less attention than other emotions in eating disorders but these emotions are higher in patients with eating disorders than non-eating-disordered comparison women (e.g. Tiller et al., 1995). Milligan and Waller (2000) found that state, but not trait, anger was related to bulimic pathology, as was anger suppression. Anger suppression was uniquely related to the presence of binge eating whereas state anger was uniquely related to the presence of vomiting. These authors suggest that their findings support the functional role of bulimia in blocking unpleasant affective states and, in particular, that different symptoms of bulimia may serve different functions.

Alexithymia

Despite the literature described above showing the importance of emotion in eating disorders, it would be remiss not to mention the phenomenon of alexithymia. Alexithymia is a construct in which an individual is unable to recognise an emotion, is unable to differentiate between emotional and physical signals, is unable to communicate emotions, and experiences concrete thinking and a paucity of fantasy. People with eating disorders typically report higher levels of alexithymia than comparison groups (Bourke et al., 1992; Schmidt et al., 1993b; Cochrane et al., 1993) and these do not appear to reduce with improvement in symptoms (Schmidt et al., 1993b). It is possible that women with eating disorders are genuinely uncertain about what emotions they are experiencing or even whether they are experiencing emotions at all, or simply other bodily signals like, say, hunger. However, even if eating-disordered patients are less able to put their emotions into words, most of the studies described above either induce affect experimentally or measure the experience of emotion indirectly (including items relating to behaviours and attitudes) so this should not be a major problem for the above literature.

CONCLUSION

The precise nature of the aetiological role for many of these factors can only be speculated upon. Clearly a number of psychological factors do play a role in the aetiology of eating disorders. However, studies have generally explored each of these factors in isolation and have not fully integrated all the findings. For example, do perfectionism and stress play independent roles in the development of eating disorders or is it only in those with high levels of perfectionism that stress is a risk for eating disorders (i.e. an interactional model)? The negative emotions experienced as a result of stress may be the key to understanding the link between stress and eating disorders, i.e. that negative affect, however it arises, is the important factor and stressful life events are simply one way that negative emotions can arise. However, the relationship between emotion and symptoms and between stress and symptoms is often examined separately. Future research will need to integrate the various factors more fully.

In spite of the lack of a full integration of the relationships between these factors we present, in Figure 9.1, possible models of aetiology for each of anorexia nervosa of the restricting and binge/purge subtypes and for normal weight bulimia nervosa. In this figure Box 1 represents childhood stress (high levels of adversity in combination with high levels of helplessness or inadequate coping). This feature is a risk particularly for bulimic disorders. Perfectionism/rigidity, on the other hand, is a particular risk for the restrictive disorders while negative evaluation of self (low self-esteem) is a risk factor for all eating disorders. What we

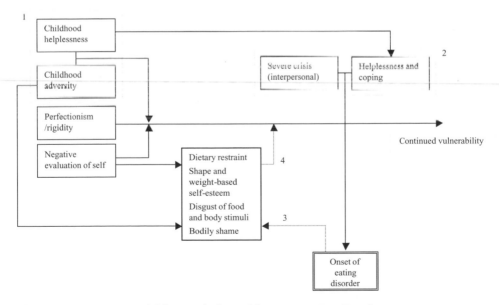

Figure 9.1 Putative model for psychological factors in eating disorders

propose is that these background factors (or some combination of them, depending on the eating disorder subtype) represent an increased risk of eating disorders. However, unless relatively acute stress is experienced at a later date in adolescence or early adulthood individuals will continue to be vulnerable but will not actually develop an eating disorder. (Box 2 shows that stress is the experience of severe interpersonal life events or difficulties in combination with helplessness or inadequate coping.) Those who do experience such an acute stressor, in the presence of the above named risk factors, will be more likely to develop an eating disorder.

Note that negative evaluation of self and childhood adversity are linked to variables concerning dietary restraint, shape and weight-based self-esteem, bodily shame and disgust of food and body stimuli. While some of these diet- and body-related variables have been shown to be premorbid (e.g. dietary restraint), others have not. It is possible (and we therefore speculate) that they all develop as processes involved in dieting behaviour (discussed elsewhere in this book) and so we propose the link between these variables and the main line of vulnerability (line 4). However, it is also possible that some of these variables (e.g. bodily shame) only arise as a consequence of the eating disorder itself and so we have represented this via line 3). It is possible, of course, that both lines 3 and 4 exist, that childhood adversity and negative evaluation of self lead to such dietary and body concerns which increase the risk of an eating disorder, the emergence of which increases these dietary and body concerns still further.

Note also that the role of helplessness in childhood is not limited to its association with adversity in childhood. Harris et al. (1990) have shown that helplessness in childhood is related to helplessness in adulthood. The fact that helplessness in adulthood (at the time of the crisis that provokes onset of the eating disorder directly) may also be implicated, childhood helplessness thus acts towards increasing the risk of an eating disorder via two pathways.

One final point is worth making. We do not hold the view that psychological factors are more important than, or even in competition with, other factors such as genetic and biological factors. For example, there are genetic influences on the development of personality and emotional experience which, by definition, acknowledges the role of biological processes, as well as psychological processes and behavioural responses. Thus, there may be many phenomena that can be explained or explored at a number of different levels (biological, behavioural, psychological). Some researchers may simply prefer to (or be more competent to) study these processes at one level rather than another. However, to the extent that psychological therapies have proved to be more effective than biological therapies in treating eating disorders (especially in the longer term), we would argue that examining psychological factors is essential in understanding the development and treatment of these disorders.

REFERENCES

Andrews, B. (1997) Bodily shame in relation to abuse in childhood and bulimia: A preliminary investigation. *British Journal of Clinical Psychology*, **36**, 41–49.

Arntz, A. (1999) Do personality disorders exist? On the validity of the concept and its cognitive-behavioural formulation and treatment. *Behaviour Research and Therapy*, **37**, S97–S134.

Bastiani, A.M., Rao, R., Weltzin, T. & Kaye, W. (1995) Perfectionism in anorexia nervosa. *International Journal of Eating Disorders*, **17** (2), 147–152.

Bifulco, A. & Moran, P. (1997) *Wednesday's Child*. London: Routledge.

Blouin, A., Bushnik, T., Braaten, J. & Blouin, J. (1989) Bulimia and diabetes: Distinct psychosocial profiles. *International Journal of Eating Disorders*, **8**, 93–100.

Bourke, M.P., Taylor, G.J., Parker, J.D. & Bagby, J.M. (1992) Alexithymia in women with anorexia nervosa: A preliminary investigation. *British Journal of Psychiatry*, **161**, 240–243.

Brecelj, M., Tchanturia, K., Rabe-Hesketh, S. & Treasure, J.L. (in press) Rigidity traits in the childhoods of eating disorder patients. *American Journal of Psychiatry*.

Brown, G.W. & Harris, T.O. (1978) *Social Origins of Depression*. London: Tavistock.

Brown, G.W. & Harris, T.O. (1986) Stressor, vulnerability and depression: A question of replication. *Psychological Medicine*, **16**, 739–744.

Brown, G.W., Harris, T.O. & Hepworth, C. (1995) Loss, humiliation and entrapment among women developing depression: A patient and non-patient comparison. *Psychological Medicine*, **25**, 7–21.

Bulik, C.M., Sullivan, P.F., Wade, T.D. & Kendler, K.S. (2000) Twin studies of eating disorders: A review. *International Journal of Eating Disorders*, **27**, 2–20.

Burney, J. & Irwin, H.J. (2000) Shame and guilt in women with eating disorder symptomatology. *Journal of Clinical Psychology*, **56**, 51–61.

Button, E.J., Sonuga-Barke, E.J.S., Davies, J. & Thompson, M. (1996) A prospective study of self-esteem in the prediction of eating problems in adolescent schoolgirls: Questionnaire Findings. *British Journal of Clinical Psychology*, **35**, 193–203.

Carroll, J.M., Touyz, S.W. & Beumont, P.J.V. (1996) Specific comorbidity between bulimia nervosa and personality disorders. *International Journal of Eating Disorders*, **19** (2), 159–170.

Casper, R.C., Hedeker, D. & McClough, J.F. (1992) Personality dimensions in eating disorders and their subtyping. *Journal of the American Academy of Child and Adolescent Psychiatry*, **31** (5), 830–840.

Casper, R.C. & Davis, J.M. (1977) On the course of anorexia nervosa. *American Journal of Psychiatry*, **134**, 974–978.

Cochrane, C.E., Brewerton, T.D., Wilson, D.B. & Hodges, E.L. (1993) Alexithymia in the eating disorders. *International Journal of Eating Disorders*, **14**, 219–222.

Cools, J., Schotte, D.E. & McNally, R.J. (1992) Emotional arousal and overeating in restrained eaters. *Journal of Abnormal Psychology*, **101**, 348–351.

Coyne, J.C. & Downey, G. (1991) Social factors and psychopathology: Stress, social support and coping processes. *Annual Review of Psychology*, **42**, 401–425.

Crowther, J.H., Sanftner, J., Bonifazi, D.Z. & Shepherd, K.L. (2001) The role of daily hassles in binge eating. *International Journal of Eating Disorders*, **29**, 449–454.

Davey, G.C.L., Buckland, G., Tantow, B. & Dallos, R. (1998) Disgust and eating disorders. *European Eating Disorders Review*, **6**, 201–211.

Fahy, T. & Eisler, I. (1993) Impulsivity and eating disorders. *British Journal of Psychiatry*, **162**, 193–197.

Fairburn, C.G., Welch, S.L., Doll, H.A., Davies, B.A. & O'Connor, M.E. (1997) Risk factors for bulimia nervosa. A community-based case-control study. *Archives of General Psychiatry*, **54**, 509–517.

Fairburn, C.G., Cooper, Z., Doll, H.A. & Welch, S.L. (1999) Risk factors for anorexia nervosa: Three integrated case-control comparison. *Archives of General Psychiatry*, **56**, 468–476.

Finlay-Jones, R.A. & Brown, G.W. (1981) Types of stressful life event and the onset of anxiety and depressive disorders. *Psychological Medicine*, **11**, 803–815.

Fornari, V., Kaplan, M., Sandberg, D.E., Matthews, M., Skolnick, N. & Katz, J.L. (1992) Depressive and anxiety disorders in anorexia nervosa and bulimia nervosa. *International Journal of Eating Disorders*, **12**, 21–29.

Garner, D.M., Olmstead, M.P., & Polivy, J. (1983) Development and validation of a multidimensional eating disorder inventory for anorexia nervosa and bulimia. *International Journal of Eating Disorders*, **2** (2), 15–34.

Geller, J., Johnstone, C., Madsen, K., Goldner, E., Remick, R. & Birmingham, L. (1998) Shape- and weight-based self-esteem and the eating disorders. *International Journal of Eating Disorders*, **24**, 285–298.

Geller, J., Srikameswaran, S., Cockell, S. & Zaitsoff, S.L. (2000) Assessment of shape- and weight-based self-esteem in adolescents. *International Journal of Eating Disorders*, **28**, 339–345.

Gillberg, I., Rastam, M. & Gillberg, C. (1995) Anorexia nervosa 6 years after onset: Part 1. Personality disorders. *Comprehensive Psychiatry*, **36** (1), 61–69.

Gilbert, P. (1997) The evolution of social attractiveness and its role in shame, humiliation, guilt and therapy. *British Journal of Medical Psychology*, **70**, 113–147.

Goldner, E.M., Srikameswaran, S., Schroeder, M.L., Livesley, W.J. & Birmingham, C.L. (1999) Dimensional assessment of personality pathology in patients with eating disorders. *Psychiatry Research*, **85**, 151–159.

Goldner, E.M., Cockell, S.J. & Srikameswaran, S. (2002) Perfectionism and eating disorders. In P.L. Hewitt & G.L. Flett (Eds), *Perfectionism: Theory, Research and Interventions*. APA Books: Washington DC.

Gowers, S.G., North, C.D., Byram, V. & Weaver, A.B. (1996) Life event precipitants of adolescent anorexia nervosa. *Journal of Child Psychology and Psychiatry*, **37**, 469–477.

Halmi, K., Goldberg, S., Eckert, E., Casper, R. & Davis, J. (1977) Pretreatment evaluation in anorexia nervosa. In R.A. Vigersky (Ed.), *Anorexia Nervosa*. New York: Raven Press.

Harvey, T., Troop, N.A., Treasure, J.L. & Murphy, T. (2002) Fear, disgust and eating concerns. *International Journal of Eating Disorders*, **32**, 213–218.

Heatherton, T.F., Herman, C.P. & Polivy, J. (1991) Effects of physical threat and ego threat on eating behavior. *Journal of Personality and Social Psychology*, **60**, 138–143.

Herzog, D., Keller, M., Sacks, N., Yeh, C. & Lavori, P. (1992) Psychiatric comorbidity in treatment-seeking anorexics and bulimics. *Journal of the American Academy of Child and Adolescent Psychiatry*, **31**, 810–818.

Inceoglu, I., Franzen, U., Backmund, H. & Gerlinghoff, M. (2000) Personality disorders in patients in a day-treatment programme for eating disorders. *European Eating Disorders Review*, **8**, 67–72.

Johnson, C., Tobin, D. & Dennis, A. (1990) Difference in treatment outcome between borderline and non-borderline bulimics at one year follow-up. *International Journal of Eating Disorders*, **9**, 616–627.

Karwautz, A., Rabe-Hesketh, S., Hu, X., Zhao, J., Sham, P., Collier, D.A. & Treasure, J.L. (2001) Individual-specific risk factors for anorexia nervosa: A pilot study using a discordant sister-pair design. *Psychological Medicine*, **31**, 317–329.

Kay, D.W.K. & Leigh, D. (1954). The natural history, treatment and prognosis of anorexia nervosa, based on a study of 38 patients. *Journal of Mental Science*, **100**, 411–430.

Kiemle, G., Slade, P.D. & Dewey, M.E. (1987) Factors associated with abnormal eating attitudes and behaviors: Screening individuals at risk of developing an eating disorder. *International Journal of Eating Disorders*, **6**, 713–724.

Lacey, J.H. & Read, T. (1993) Multi-impulsive bulimia: description of an inpatient eclectic treatment programme and a pilot follow-up study of its efficacy. *European Eating Disorders Review*, **1**, 22–31.

Lacey, J.H. (1993) Self-damaging and addictive behaviour in bulimia nervosa. *British Journal of Psychiatry*, **163**, 190–194.

Lazarus, R.S. (1999) *Stress and Emotion: A New Synthesis*. London: Free Association Books.

Lazarus, R.S. & Folkman, S. (1984) *Stress, Appraisal and Coping*. New York: Springer.

Lilenfield, L.R., Kaye, W.H., Greeno, C.G., Merikangas, K.R., Plotnicov, K., Pollice, C., Rao, R., Strober, M., Bulik, C.M. & Nagy, L. (1998) A controlled family study of anorexia nervosa and bulimia nervosa: Psychiatric disorders in first degree relatives and effects of proband comorbidity. *Archives of General Psychiatry*, **55**, 603–610.

Matsunaga, H., Kaye, W. & McConaha, S. (2000) Personality disorders among subjects recovered from eating disorders. *International Journal of Eating Disorders*, **27**, 353–357.

Miller, W. (1997) *Anatomy of Disgust*. Cambridge: Harvard University Press.

Milligan, R.-J. & Waller, G. (2000) Anger and bulimic psychopathology among nonclinical women. *International Journal of Eating Disorders*, **28**, 446–450.

Murphy, F., Troop, N.A. & Treasure, J.L. (2000) Differential environmental factors in anorexia nervosa: A sibling-pair study. *British Journal of Clinical Psychology*, **39**, 193–203.

Murray, L., Murphy, F., Perrett, D. & Treasure, J.L. (submitted) Sensitivity to recognition of facial expressions of emotion in eating disorder patients.

Murray, C., Waller, G. & Legg, C. (2000) Family dysfunction and bulimic psychopathology: The mediating role of shame. *International Journal of Eating Disorders*, **28**, 84–89.

Neckowitz, P. & Morrison, T.L. (1991) Interactional coping strategies of normal-weight bulimic women in intimate and nonintimate stressful situations. *Psychological Reports*, **69**, 1167–1175.

Patton, G.C., Johnson-Sabine, E., Wood, K., Mann, A.H. & Wakeling, A. (1990) Abnormal eating attitudes in London schoolgirls—a prospective epidemiological study: Outcome at twelve month follow-up. *Psychological Medicine*, **20**, 383–394.

Pia, C. & Toro, J. (1999) Anorexia nervosa in a Spanish adolescent sample: An 8-year longitudinal study. *Acta Psychiatrica Scandinavica*, **100**, 441–446.

Piran, N., Lerner, P., Garfinkel, P., Kennedy, S. & Brouillette, C. (1988) Personality disorders in anorexic patients. *International Journal of Eating Disorders*, **7**, 589–599.

Polivy, J. & Herman, P. (1999) Distress and overeating: Why do dieters overeat? *International Journal of Eating Disorders*, **26**, 153–164.

Pyle, R.L., Mitchell, J.E. & Eckert, E.D. (1981) Bulimia: A report of 34 cases. *Journal of Clinical Psychiatry*, **42**, 60–64.

Rastam, M. (1992) Anorexia nervosa in 51 Swedish adolescents: Premorbid problems and comorbidity. *Journal of the American Academy of Child and Adolescent Psychiatry*, **31**, 819–829.

Rorty, M., Yager, J., Buckwalter, J.G., Rossotto, E. & Guthrie, D. (2000a) Development and validation of the Parental Intrusiveness Rating Scale among bulimic and comparison women. *International Journal of Eating Disorders*, **28**, 188–201.

Rorty, M., Yager, J., Rossotto, E. & Buckwalter, G. (2000b) Parental intrusiveness in adolescence recalled by women with a history of bulimia nervosa and comparison women. *International Journal of Eating Disorders*, **28**, 202–208.

Rosen, J.C., Compas, B.E. & Tacy, B. (1993) The relation among stress, psychological symptoms and eating disorder symptoms: A prospective analysis. *International Journal of Eating Disorders*, **14**, 153–162.

Rosen, J.C., Tacy, B. & Howell, D. (1990) Life stress, psychological symptoms and weight reducing behavior in adolescent girls: A prospective analysis. *International Journal of Eating Disorders*, **9**, 17–26.

Rozin, P. & Fallon, A.E. (1987) A perspective on disgust. *Psychological Review*, **94**, 23–41.

Ruderman, A.J. (1986) Dietary restraint: A theoretical and empirical review. *Psychological Bulletin*, **99**, 247–262.

Sanftner, J.L. & Crowther, J.H. (1998) Variability in self-esteem, moods, shame and guilt in women who binge. *International Journal of Eating Disorders*, **23**, 391–397.

Sanftner, J.L., Barlow, D.H., Marschall, D.E. & Tangney, J.P. (1995) The relation of shame and guilt to eating disorder symptomatology. *Journal of Social and Clinical Psychology*, **14**, 315–324.

Schmidt, U.H., Humfress, H. & Treasure, J.L. (1997a) The role of general family environment and sexual and physical abuse in the origins of eating disorders. *European Eating Disorders Review*, **5**, 184–207.

Schmidt, U.H., Jiwany, A. & Treasure, J.L. (1993b) A controlled study of alexithymia in eating disorders. *Comprehensive Psychiatry*, **34**, 54–58.

Schmidt, U.H., Tiller, J.M. & Treasure, J.L. (1993a) Setting the scene for eating disorders: Childhood care, classification and course of illness. *Psychological Medicine*, **23**, 663–672.

Schmidt, U.H., Tiller, J.M., Andrews, B., Blanchard, M. & Treasure, J.L. (1997b) Is there a specific trauma precipitating onset of anorexia nervosa? *Psychological Medicine*, **27**, 523–530.

Schmidt, U.H., Troop, N.A. & Treasure, J.L. (1999) Stress and the onset of eating disorders: Correcting an "age-old" myth. *International Journal of Eating Disorders*, **25**, 83–88.

Serpell, L., Livingstone, A., Lask, B. & Neiderman, M. (2002) Anorexia nervosa: Obsessive compulsive disorder, obsessive compulsive personality or neither. *Clinical Psychology Review*, **22**, 647–669.

Serpell, L., Neiderman, M., Bird, E., Rashid. Z., Roberts, V. & Lask, B. (submitted) The shape and weight-based self-esteem inventory (SAWBS) in *Adolescent Girls with Eating Disorders and Adolescent Controls*.

Shepherd, H. & Ricciardelli, L.A. (1998) Test of Stice's dual pathway model: Dietary restraint and negative affect as mediators of bulimic behaviour. *Behaviour, Research and Therapy*, **36**, 345–352.

Sheppard-Sawyer, C.L., McNally, R.J. & Fischer, J.H. (2000) Film-induced sadness as a trigger for disinhibited eating. *International Journal of Eating Disorders*, **28**, 215–220.

Skodol, A., Oldham, J., Hyler, S., Kellman, H.D., Doidge, N. & Davies, M. (1993) Comorbidity of DSM-III-R eating disorders and personality disorders. *International Journal of Eating Disorders*, **14**, 403–416.

Slade, P.D. (1982) Towards a functional analysis of anorexia nervosa and bulimia nervosa. *British Journal of Clinical Psychology*, **21**, 167–179.

Slade, P.D., Dewey, M.E., Kiemle, G. & Newton, T. (1990) Update on SCANS: A screening instrument for identifying individuals at risk of developing an eating disorder. *International Journal of Eating Disorders*, **9**, 583–584.

Slade, P.D., Newton, T., Butler, N.M. & Murphy, P. (1991) An experimental analysis of perfectionism and dissatisfaction. *British Journal of Clinical Psychology*, **30**, 169–176.

Sohlberg, S. & Strober, M. (1994) Personality in anorexia nervosa: An update and a theoretical integration. *Acta Psychiatrica Scandinavica*, **89** (suppl. 378), 1–15.

Soukup, V.M., Beiler, M.E. & Terrell, F. (1990) Stress, coping style and problem-solving ability among eating disordered inpatients. *Journal of Clinical Psychology*, **46**, 592–599.

Srinivasagam, N.M., Kaye, W.H., Plotnikov, K.H., Greeno, C., Weltzin, T.E. & Rao, R. (1995) Persistent perfectionism, symmetry and exactness after long term recovery from anorexia nervosa. *American Journal of Psychiatry*, **152**, 1630–1634.

Stice, E. (1994) Review of the evidence for a socio-cultural model of bulimia nervosa and an exploration of the mechanisms of action. *Clinical Psychology Review*, **14**, 633–661.

Stice, E., Akutagawa, D., Gaggar, A. & Agras, S. (2000) Negative affect moderates the relation between dieting and binge eating. *International Journal of Eating Disorders*, **27**, 218–229.

Stone, A.A. & Brownell, K.D. (1994) The stress-eating paradox: Multiple daily measurements in adult males and females. *Psychology and Health*, **9**, 425–436.

Strober, M. (1980) Personality and symptomatological features in young non-chronic anorexia nervosa patients. *Journal of Psychosomatic Research*, **24**, 353–359.

Strober, M. (1984) Stressful life events associated with bulimia in anorexia nervosa: Empirical findings and theoretical speculations. *International Journal of Eating Disorders*, **3**, 3–16.

Tangney, J.P. (1993) Shame and guilt. In C.G. Costello (Ed.), *Symptoms of Depression* (pp. 161–180). New York: John Wiley & Sons.

Taylor, G.J., Ryan, D. & Bagby, M.R. (1985) Toward the development of a new self-report alexithymia scale. *Psychotherapy and Psychosomatics*, **44**, 191–199.

Tchanturia, K., Morris, R.G., Surguladze, S. & Treasure, J.L. (in press) An examination of perceptual and cognitive set shifting tasks in acute anorexia and following recovery. *Eating and Weight Disorders*.

Tchanturia, K., Serpell, L., Troop, N., & Treasure, J. (2002) Perceptual illusions in eating disorders: Rigid and fluctuating styles. *Behaviour Therapy and Experimental Psychiatry*, **32**, 107–115.

Tiller, J.M., Schmidt, U.H., Ali, S. & Treasure, J.L. (1995) Patterns of punitiveness in women with eating disorders. *International Journal of Eating Disorders*, **17**, 365–371.

Tiller, J.M., Sloane, G., Schmidt, U.H., Troop, N.A., Power, M. & Treasure, J.L. (1997) Social support in patients with anorexia nervosa and bulimia nervosa. *International Journal of Eating Disorders*, **21**, 31–38.

Treasure, J.L. & Holland, A. (1995) Genetic factors in eating disorders. In G. Szmukler, C. Dare & J. Treasure (Eds), *Handbook of Eating Disorders: Theory, Treatment and Research*. Chichester: John Wiley & Sons.

Troop, N.A. & Bifulco, A. (2002) Childhood social arena and cognitive sets in eating disorders. *British Journal of Clinical Psychology*, **41**, 205–211.

Troop, N.A. & Treasure, J.L. (1997a) Psychosocial factors in the onset of eating disorders: Responses to life events and difficulties. *British Journal of Medical Psychology*, **70**, 373–385.

Troop, N.A. & Treasure, J.L. (1997b) Setting the scene for eating disorders II: Childhood helplessness and mastery. *Psychological Medicine*, **27**, 531–538.

Troop, N.A. (1996) *Coping and crisis support in eating disorders*. Unpublished PhD Thesis, University of London.

Troop, N.A., Holbrey, A. & Treasure, J.L. (1998) Stress, coping and crisis support in eating disorders. *International Journal of Eating Disorders*, **24**, 157–166.

Troop, N.A., Holbrey, A., Trowler, R. & Treasure, J.L. (1994) Ways of coping in women with eating disorders. *Journal of Nervous and Mental Disease*, **182**, 535–540.

Troop, N.A., Treasure, J.L. & Serpell, L. (2002) A further exploration of disgust in eating disorders. *European Eating Disorders Review*, **10**, 218–226.

Troop, N.A., Schmidt, U.H., Turnbull, S. & Treasure, J.L. (2000) Self-esteem and responsibility for change in women with bulimia nervosa. *European Eating Disorders Review*, **8**, 384–393.

Vitousek, K.B. & Hollon, S.D. (1990) The investigation of schematic content and processing in eating disorders. *Cognitive Therapy and Research*, **14** (2), 191–214.

Vitousek, K. & Manke, F. (1994) Personality variables and disorders in anorexia nervosa and bulimia nervosa. *Journal of Abnormal Psychology*, **103**, 137–147.

Waller, G. (1991) Sexual abuse as a factor in eating disorders. *British Journal of Psychiatry*, **159**, 664–671.

Waller, G. & Matoba, M. (1999) Emotional eating and eating psychopathology in nonclinical groups: A cross-cultural comparison of women in Japan and the United Kingdom. *International Journal of Eating Disorders*, **26**, 333–340.

Waller, G., Ohanian, V., Meyer, C. & Osman, S. (2000) Cognitive content among bulimic women: The role of core beliefs. *International Journal of Eating Disorders*, **28**, 235–241.

Welch, S.L., Doll, H.A & Fairburn, C.G. (1997) Life events and the onset of bulimia nervosa: A controlled study. *Psychological Medicine*, **27**, 515–522.

Welch, S.L. & Fairburn, C.G. (1994) Sexual abuse and bulimia nervosa: Three integrated case control comparisons. *American Journal of Psychiatry*, **151**, 402–407.

Welch, S.L. & Fairburn, C.G. (1996) Impulsivity or comorbidity in bulimia nervosa. A controlled study of deliberate self harm and alcohol and drug misuse in a community sample. *British Journal of Psychiatry*, **169** (4), 451–458.

Wiederman, M. W. & Pryor, T. (1996) Multi-impulsivity in bulimia nervosa. *International Journal of Eating Disorders*, **20** (4), 359–365.

Wonderlich, S.A., Swift, W. J., Slotnick, H.B. & Goodman, S. (1990) DSM-III-R personality disorders in eating disorders subtypes. *International Journal of Eating Disorders*, **9**, 607–616.

Wonderlich, S. & Mitchell, J. (1997) Eating disorders and comorbidity: Empirical, conceptual and clinical implications. *Psychopharmacology Bulletin*, **33**, 381–390.

Wood, A., Waller, G. & Gowers, S. (1994) Predictors of eating psychopathology in adolescent girls. *European Eating Disorders Review*, **2**, 6–13.

Yager, J., Rorty, M. & Rossotto, E. (1995) Coping styles differ between recovered and nonrecovered women with bulimia nervosa but not between recovered women and non-eating disordered control subjects. *Journal of Nervous and Mental Disease*, **183**, 86–94.

CHAPTER 10

Medical Complications

Stephen Zipfel, Bernd Löwe and **Wolfgang Herzog**
Ruprecht Karls Universitat, Medizinische Klinkum, Heidelberg, Germany

SUMMARY

Medical complications play an important role in patients with eating disorders, and this chapter diseases some of the treatments/concerns that should be considered:

- Severe biochemical disturbances should be managed in consultation with a physician.
- Oral intervention is generally preferable to rapid, intravenous treatment.
- A cardiovascular examination and an ECG should be carried out in all patients with anorexia nervosa (AN) and those with bulimia nervosa (BN) who have evidence of electrolyte abnormalities.
- In AN patients, drugs which prolong the QT interval should be avoided, whenever possible.
- AN patients with a chronic course are at high risk for the development of osteoporosis.
- To date the best treatment for osteoporosis is a balanced refeeding diet and the resumption of normal menstruation. AN patients with a very low weight (<70% ABW) may benefit from hormone replacement therapy. Although promising new anti-resorptive drug therapies are currently being developed, most are still in the phase of clinical trails.
- Structural brain changes in AN may have both reversible and irreversible components.
- The most common haematological abnormalities in AN are leucopenia and most likely normocytic anaemia.
- Eating disorder patients with an additional medical comorbidity (e.g. diabetes mellitus) have an increased risk for medical complications and should be managed in consultation with a physician or specialist.
- Markedly obese patients face a variety of severe medical complications, which could best be treated with an interdisciplinary team.

INTRODUCTION

Although it is well accepted that the aetiology of eating disorders is best understood from a biopsychosocial model, the complex nature of these disorders makes it sometimes difficult

Handbook of Eating Disorders. Edited by J. Treasure, U. Schmidt and E. van Furth.
© 2003 John Wiley & Sons, Ltd.

to determine which might be the leading aspect in a particular eating-disordered patient—the psyche or the soma. The serious neuropsychological impairments and medical complications which are often associated with eating disorders (Becker et al., 1999; Zipfel et al., 1998) have important implications for clinical practice, particularly for very emaciated anorexic patients.

The first part of this chapter will address the most important acute and chronic medical complications in patients suffering from an eating disorder. In anorexic patients, the consequences of severe malnutrition can be extremely problematic, warranting special consideration during treatment. The clinical picture of bulimia nervosa is influenced by the consequences of purging behaviour, such as self-induced vomiting and the abuse of laxatives and diuretics.

The second part of the chapter will focus on medical complications in individuals with obesity. With nearly every second individual being overweight (BMI > 25 kg/m^2) and one in three being obese (BMI > 30 kg/m^2), the rate of obesity has increased by 50% over the past 20 years, reaching epidemic proportions in industrialised countries (Yanovski & Yanovski, 1999). Although psychological aspects do play an important role in most individuals during the course of marked obesity, it should be noted that only a minority of obese people are suffering primarily from a psychiatric disorder, such as an eating or affective disorder. Therefore, we will address the medical risks and complications of this rapidly growing group of individuals.

ACUTE COMPLICATIONS IN ANOREXIA AND BULIMIA NERVOSA

Since patients with eating disorders, particularly those with anorexia nervosa, tend to deny their disorder and the resulting physical damage, acute somatic complications are often the reason they receive medical treatment for the first time. Even though the diagnosis may be obvious to the examiner based on diagnostic criteria set forth by the DSM-IV or ICD-10, an exact recording of physical findings is strongly recommended. A detailed physical assessment of a patient with a history of weight loss or weight cycling is important for making a differential diagnosis between an eating disorder and other somatic diseases, such as malabsorption syndromes, chronic inflammatory intestinal diseases, tumours, tuberculosis, vasculitis, and diabetes mellitus. Since the majority of eating disorder cases are young females, older females and male cases can be easily overlooked by clinicians. Male patients in particular may not present until marked somatic changes have developed (Siegel et al., 1995). Finally, a detailed medical assessment yields important information regarding the altered nutritional status of a patient, as well as any existing complications from bingeing and purging behaviours (see Table 10.1). This information can help to guide decision making with respect to inpatient, day-patient or outpatient treatment.

CARDIOVASCULAR COMPLICATIONS

Cardiovascular complications are common in patients with eating disorders, particularly with anorexia nervosa. Some of these complications are relatively benign (most forms

Table 10.1 Examinations recommended on admission or in the course of refeeding

Obligatory	Optional
• Full medical and psychiatric history	• Body composition measurement (skinfold, BIA, DEXA)
• *Physical assessment* Body mass index Heart rate blood pressure Temperature	• *In severe anaemia*: Reticulocytes, iron, ferritin, transferrin, vitamin B_{12}
	• *In case of elevated creatinine*: Creatinine clearance
• Full blood count, blood sedimentation rate	• *In case of oedema*: Albumin, total protein, protein electrophoresis
• *Biochemical profile* Serum electrolytes: Sodium Potassium Calcium Magnesium Phosphate Creatinine Urea Liver enzyme profile Blood glucose	• *To rule out hyperthyroidism*: Thyroid function test
	• *In case of cardiovascular abnormalities*: Holder ECG, echocardiography
	• *Differential diagnosis*: Chest X-ray, abdominal ultrasound
	• *To rule out an ulcer*: Gastroscopy
	• *In patients with a long-term course:* Osteodensitometry (DEXA scan) and markers of bone turnover
• Electrocardiogram (ECG)	• *In case of seizures or differential diagnosis*: EEG and neuroimaging (CT, MRI)

of hypotension and bradycardia) and do not usually require treatment unless a patient is symptomatic (Kreipe et al., 1994). However, cardiovascular complications can cause immediate or premature death in these patients (Beumont et al., 1993). The reasons for these complications are mixed, and may include dehydration and electrolyte disturbances secondary to purging behaviour, or occur as a direct effect of malnutrition. In general, cardiac complications occur mostly in patients with purging behaviour (Sharp & Freeman, 1993), but are not always associated with manifest hypokalemia.

ECG Alterations/Arrhythmias

ECG alterations occur in more than 80% of eating-disordered patients (Alvin et al., 1993). In addition to sinus bradycardia, which is frequently seen, ST-depressions and abnormal U-waves may be found on the ECG. They are often associated with electrolyte imbalances and are considered to be warning signals for arrhythmias. These are responsible for a considerable number of deaths in eating disorders (Schocken et al., 1989). In this context, special emphasis is placed on the extension of the QT interval, which is seen in 15% (Cooke & Chambers, 1995) to 40% (Durakovic et al., 1994) of cases. This QT extension is considered to be a significant predictor of ventricular tachyarrhythmias or of sudden cardiac death.

Kreipe et al. (1994) investigated a possible dysfunction of the autonomic nervous system using the heart rate power spectrum analysis. His results indicate that there is a decrease in sympathetic control of the heart rate. Other recent investigations (for review see Winston &

Stafford, 2000) have examined the extent to which additional tests of heart rate variability can provide further diagnostic information when assessing the risk of fatal arrhythmia. Changes in repolarisation, such as an extension of the corrected QT interval in AN patients, showed a significant tendency to revert to normal after refeeding. Only a few studies have focused on cardiovascular disorders in BN. The increased incidence of arrhythmia reported in some studies was usually directly associated with hypokalemia due to frequent vomiting. Consequently, in eating-disordered patients drugs should be avoided which may prolong the QT interval (e.g. tricyclic antidepressants and neuroleptics).

Morphological Changes

Weight loss in AN is associated with a loss in heart muscle mass. Echocardiographic studies of AN patients reported a decreased left ventricular mass and an increased incidence of mitral valve prolapse (MVP) (de Simone et al., 1994). In 62% of the patients, abnormalities of mitral valve motion were found to occur as a result of an imbalance between valve size and ventricle volume, possibly leading to a mitral valve prolapse. The occurrence of MVP in these patients is related to two different factors. First, it is known that MVP is associated with a higher risk of arrhythmia. Second, there is some evidence for an association between MVP and anxiety disorders.

Cardiac failure can also occur as a complication during refeeding (Kahn et al., 1991), especially in cases of simultaneous hypophosphataemia (Schocken et al., 1989). Malnutrition, electrolyte imbalance, and ipecac abuse (Mitchell et al. 1987) can result in a possibly irreversible secondary cardiomyopathy. Male AN patients with an increased heart rate are particularly susceptible to the possibility of congestive heart failure (Siegel et al., 1995). Studies of patients suffering from malnutrition have shown a decrease in heart size and a rotation of the heart's axis into a vertical position during the course of weight loss. These changes were mostly reversible in the refeeding period.

Refeeding Oedema

Peripheral oedema occurs in a substantial proportion of patients undergoing refeeding (Winston, 2000). This may be due to a rapid weight gain of several kilograms and is often alarming for patients and doctors. Why 'rebound oedema' typically develops during the initial weeks of refeeding is unclear, but its effect on body weight should be considered (Bihun et al., 1993). It is very unlikely that this phenomenon is caused by hypoproteinaemia, because this sort of oedema is associated with normal serum albumin levels. It has been suggested that salt and water depletion lead to the development of secondary hyperaldosteronism, which might predispose to the development of oedema when water and salt intake is increased during refeeding. From a clinical point of view this kind of oedema has to be differentiated from cardiac oedema, caused by heart failure, as well as renal and hepatic failure.

GASTROINTESTINAL SYSTEM

Many changes occur in the gastrointestinal physiology in patients suffering from an eating disorder (Robinson, 2000). Some of these changes are particularly important to consider, because they may indicate a chronic course of these disorders.

Hyperamylasemia/Enlargement of the Parotid Gland/Pancreatitis

An increase in serum amylase levels is found in about 50% of patients treated in the hospital. In most cases it is due to vomiting and is not a result of pancreatitis (Mitchell et al., 1983). Correspondingly, this increase is caused by the isoamylase of the parotid gland (Humphries et al., 1987). A distinct enlargement of the parotid gland is often observed, especially in BN. Acute pancreatitis can be assumed if the increase in the serum amylase level is more than three-fold above normal and is associated with abdominal pain. If in doubt, it may be helpful to measure lipase levels. Pancreatitis as a complication of eating disorders is rare; it can, however, develop as a result of refeeding or binge eating.

Impaired Gastric Emptying/Obstipation/Ileus

An impairment of oesophageal motility and gastric emptying is a typical consequence of malnutrition but has also been found variably in patients with bulimia nervosa. After an increase of food intake and stabilisation of weight, this disturbance seems to be fully reversible (Szmukler et al., 1990). It manifests itself as a sensation of fulness after food ingestion, which can make refeeding difficult. Megaduodenum and duodenal immobility are also secondary complications but are reversible (Buchman et al., 1994). Constipation is frequent and is in most cases a result of poor nutrition and hypokalemia due to purging behaviour such as laxative abuse. Abrupt cessation of laxatives could lead to severe water and sodium retention and oedema mainly due to secondary hyperaldosteronism. The possibility of constipation due to antidepressant medication, particularly tricyclic antidepressants, should be considered. Drug treatment with cisapride is not helpful due to cardiovascular side-effects and in many countries, including the UK, this medication has been banned.

Gastric Dilation/Perforation

Gastric dilation typically occurs after binge eating and becomes manifest in spontaneous vomiting and upper abdominal pain. Conservative treatment is usually sufficient; in rare cases, however, circulation disorders of the gastric wall occur, leading to necrosis and gastric perforation (Abdu et al., 1987). In these cases, immediate surgery is required. Five of the 60 cases with spontaneous gastric rupture described since 1960 have been AN patients (Schou et al., 1994). Diagnosis may be difficult since more than 50% of the patients suffer from vomiting, upper abdominal pain, and gastrointestinal disorders.

Gastroduodenal Ulcers/Upper Gastrointestinal Bleeding

Ulcers develop in about one-sixth of the patients (Hall et al., 1989). They can cause bleeding, which may lead to anaemia and circulatory decompensation. However, bleeding can also occur as a result of tears of the oesophagus (Mallory-Weiss Syndrome) due to vomiting.

Hepatitis

Elevated liver function tests are found in about one-third of patients treated in the hospital ('nutritional hepatitis'). Transaminase levels are usually raised and bilirubin can be elevated. If there is no infectious or autoimmune cause, additional treatment is not necessary

(Colombo et al., 1995). If the indirect bilirubin levels are elevated, one should consider the manifestation of Gilbert's syndrom (5% of the total population is affected) in the starving period. Hypercholesterolemia is a result of a reduced bile acid requirement.

HAEMATOLOGICAL AND IMMUNE SYSTEM

Bone Marrow Hypoplasia

A frequent consequence of malnutrition is a reversible, reactive bone marrow hypoplasia (Lambert & Boland, 2000). It leads to anaemia in about 25% of patients, to leukopenia in about 30%, and to thrombopenia in about 10% of cases. Only two of 67 AN patients showed pancytopenia (Devuyst et al., 1993). The bleeding risk is increased if thrombocyte values fall below 30/nl. Anaemia may be accompanied by iron deficiency, rarely by vitamin B12 or folic acid deficiency. In severe anaemia, gastrointestinal bleeding should also be considered. Recently, a significant association between peripheral blood parameters and nutritional parameters has been demonstrated, especially between leucocyte levels and BMI. Blood changes have also prove to be reversible with weight gain. Haematological abnormalities are much less common in patients with BN.

(Bacterial) Infections

Although leukocyte counts and immunoglobulin and other factor levels are often reduced, the immunologic competence is intact in most cases, and serious or opportunistic infections are quite rare. Devuyst et al. (1993), however, reports a 9% rate of serious infections in AN patients, especially occurring in those individuals with neutropenia or very low weight on admission. In any case, infection as a complication of AN has to be taken seriously, since as a result of hypothermia and leukopenia it can take a course without fever or leukocytosis (Tenholder & Pike, 1991). Therefore, weekly controls of the blood sedimentation rate or C-reactive protein are recommended when treating serious cases of anorexia. Zipfel et al. (2000a) demonstrated in a long-term follow-up study, that causes of death in one-third of their patients was directly related to infections (bronchial pneumonia and sepsis).

BIOCHEMICAL ABNORMALITIES

Hypokalemia

($K < 3.5$ mmol/l)   Hypokalemia is found in about one-third of all patients with eating disorders treated in the hospital. The majority of cases are the result of chronic purging, but can also result from an acute case of purgative behaviour. Some of the patients adapt to very low values (<2.0), and symptoms in these patients may be missing (Bonne et al., 1993). Hypokalemia may have fatal consequences, including tachyarrhythmias, paralytic ileus, muscle weakness, cramps, tetany, polyuria or nephropathy. Supplementation should be done slowly and primarily orally. I.V. supplementation with strict heart rate monitoring is rarely necessary.

Hyponatremia

(Na < 135 mmol/l)   In the event of hyponatremia, hydration status as well as urinary sodium and osmolality has to be investigated. It is often due to hypotonic dehydration caused by chronic purging (Challier & Cabrol, 1995). The symptoms are disorientation, myasthenia, and circulatory disorders. In the majority of cases, only oral salt and water replacement is sufficient. In rare cases of fluid overload, a restriction of fluid intake is indicated.

Hypophosphataemia

(Phos < 0.8; severe: <0.3 mmol/l)   A quick decrease in the phosphate levels typically occurs during the refeeding period ('nutritional recovery syndrome', especially in cases of parenteral refeeding) (Fisher et al., 2000; Beumont & Large, 1991), but also as a result of diuretic abuse, renal failure and rapid correction of hypokalaemia. Severe hypophosphatemia can be fatal (Beumont & Large, 1991). It can result in cardiopulmonary decompensation (Cariem et al., 1994), arrhythmia, metabolic acidosis, polyneuropathia, delirium, as well as disorders of the erythrocyte and leukocyte function. As a preventative or supplementary measure, milk powder should be given.

Hypomagnesaemia

(Mg < 0.7 mmol/l)   Severe magnesium deficiency can be caused by diarrhoea, diuretic and alcohol misuse as well as severe malnutrition. It can lead to muscle cramps, intestinal spasms, hypokalaemia, and arrhythmias (Hall et al., 1989).

Hypocalcaemia

(Ca < 2.15 mmol/l)   Hypocalcaemia can be a symptom of calcium deficiency due to chronic malnutrition, but also of alkalosis. It may be associated with ECG changes (Beumont et al., 1993). In the differential diagnosis, possible hypocalcaemic tetany should be distinguished from hyperventilation syndrome.

Glucose Metabolism

In most cases of AN, glucose levels are low and glucose tolerance is reduced (Fukushima et al., 1993). Insulin stimulates glucose oxidation rather than glucose storage. Hypoglycemic coma may develop (Ratcliffe & Bevan, 1985). If the patient is conscious, sugar/glucose drinks should be given. If the patient is unconscious, a 20–50 ml 40% glucose intravenous infusion is recommended.

Metabolic Alkalosis

Generally, metabolic alkalosis occurs in association with the loss of gastric acid due to self-induced vomiting. However, it can also be caused by hypokalaemia, which leads to the loss of renal acid. About one-fourth of BN patients are affected by this disorder (Mitchell et al., 1983). The Pseudo-Bartter Syndrome, which consists of metabolic alkalosis, hypokalaemia, hypochloraemia, polyuria, and dehydration, is a typical result of severe purging behaviour. The Pseudo-Bartter Syndrome should be differentially diagnosed from the syndrome of inadequate ADH secretion (Schwartz–Bartter Syndrome) (Challier & Cabrol, 1995).

Metabolic Acidosis

Metabolic acidosis affects about 8% of BN patients and is a result of enteral bicarbonate loss in cases of laxative abuse (Mitchell et al., 1987). Possible additional causes are a markedly increased endogenous acid formation in AN as well as reduced acid excretion in connection with renal insufficiency.

Water Balance

Dehydration occurs as a result of reduced fluid supply or of chronic purging behaviour and is often associated with circulatory disorders and electrolyte imbalances (hypokalaemia, hypotonic dehydration, see above), which have to be considered in rehydration. Some patients are water loading, sometimes due to weight manipulation or due to additional psychiatric disorders. As a consequence, these patients show a pseudo-anaemia, and a hyponatriemia.

CENTRAL NERVOUS SYSTEM

Imaging methods such as computerised tomography (CT) or magnetic resonance imaging (MRI) play a secondary role in the basic diagnostics of patients with eating disorders. Therefore, the routine use of these methods is not recommended by the guidelines for eating disorders of the American Psychiatric Association (APA, 1994). In individual cases, however, the use of these methods may be indicated. For example, CT or MRI may be useful in excluding the presence of a possible brain tumour, or if a compressive intracerebral process is suspected.

Seizures

About 5% of eating disorder patients are affected by seizures (Patchell et al., 1994). Disturbances in calcium, sodium and glucose metabolism as well as uraemia due to renal failure can be responsible for myoclonic and generalised tonoclonic seizures. Nevertheless, these patients should be examined by an EEG and, if necessary, head CT for differential diagnosis of possible morphological causes.

Morphological and Functional Cerebral Changes

Systematic studies on brain changes in AN patients show dilated and/or enlarged cortical sulci (Golden et al., 1996; Kornreich et al., 1991). Kingston et al. (1996) tested neuropsychological and structural brain changes in AN before and after refeeding. The AN group performed significantly worse than the controls on tasks measuring attention, visuospatial ability, and memory. This group also demonstrated enlarged lateral ventricle sulci on both cortical and cerebellar surfaces. In this study, the correlation between morphological brain changes and cognitive impairment were weak. Lower weight was associated with greater ventricular size on MRI, but not with the duration of illness. However, there are contradictory results as to whether the cognitive deficits occurring in the acute phase were directly connected to the morphological changes (Laessle et al., 1989). In a series of further studies (Schlegel & Kretzschmar, 1997) it was shown that during weight normalisation there was an increase of brain tisssue size of up to 25 vol.% compared to the time of minimum weight.

Interestingly, ventricular enlargements have also been found in patients with BN. Thus, they are not exclusively associated with malnutrition (Krieg, 1991).

Additional Findings

Unspecific EEG changes (i.e. abnormal background activity) are often found in AN as a result of the effect of starvation on cerebral metabolism (Hughes, 1996). Although these atypical EEG findings were seen in a number of studies measuring EEG and sleep-EEG, it has been shown that, compared to other disease groups, these changes were not specific to eating disorders (Rothenberger et al., 1991). Moreover, there were no significant correlations to the body mass index (Delvenne et al., 1996).

Neuromuscular Abnormalities

Nearly 50% of eating-disordered patients are affected by neuromuscular abnormalities. Main symptoms include general muscular weakness, peripheral neuropathy, and headaches (Patchell et al., 1994). Pulmonary function can be severely disturbed due to an impairment of diaphragmatic contractility. A condition which is reversible after malnutrition is treated.

CHRONIC COMPLICATIONS IN ANOREXIA AND BULIMIA NERVOSA

Endocrine System and Reproductive Function

Amenorrhoea

The impairment of the hormonal axes is a main symptom of AN and was included as a diagnostic guideline in the ICD-10 as well as in the DSM-IV. Involvement of the hypothalamo-pituitary-gonadal axis is associated with primary or secondary amenorrhoea, depending on the age of the patient at first manifestation. Although endocrine disorders are not a part of the diagnostic criteria of BN, 20 to 50% of BN patients are found to be amenorrhoic. Menstruation disorders are reported by 40% of BN patients (Fairburn & Cooper, 1984). Studies by Pirke et al. (1989) have shown, however, that self-reports often underestimate the rate of menstrual cycle disorders, especially in BN. For example, he showed by repeatedly measuring plasma oestradiol levels, that the rate of patients with levels of <120 pg/ml was high, making follicle maturation unlikely. Moreover, in 50% of the patients, the progesterone levels measured in the subsequent luteal phase were very low due to an insufficient pulsatile gonadotropin release. In AN, it has also been shown that persistent hypothalamic amenorrhoea does not require permanent inhibition of the GnTH pulse generator (Allouche et al., 1991). At least for some patients in this study, a transient inhibition of pulsatility and qualitative abnormalities of the gonadotropins might be involved in the pathomechanism of amenorrhea. A comparably short fasting period has led to a prepubertal pattern of gonadotropin levels, especially LH levels (Schweiger et al., 1987). Recent studies on the role of leptin in the female cycle (Hebebrand et al., 1997) demonstrated the importance of this protein as a signalling trigger to puberty and link between nutritional status and female cycle (Köpp et al., 1997; Zipfel et al., 1998). In conclusion, the available evidence suggests that disorders of the menstrual cycle are a secondary phenomenon of malnutrition, possibly explaining why amenorrhea often precedes a massive weight loss and may continue even if there is an increase in weight again. Nevertheless, it is still not known whether factors other than malnutrition and weight loss are involved in the development of hormonal disorders.

Eating Disorders and Pregnancy

Hormonal changes also affect fertility. Thus, a reduced fertility and increased spontaneous abortion rate was found due to disturbances of the follicular and luteal phase (Bates et al., 1982). There is evidence that even in successful pregnancy, the infants are clearly underweight. Brinch et al. (1988) carried out a follow-up study on 140 patients with AN after 10–12 years. This study showed that 50 former patients had had children in the interim, 10% had problems with infertility and 20% became pregnant while they continued to be anorectic. In this sample, the rate of premature births was twice as high as in an age-matched population and perinatal mortality was increased by a factor of 6. Willis and Rand (1988) reported a miscarriage rate increased by a factor of 2. There is also evidence that patients with BN have an increased rate of malformations due to laxative and diuretic abuse, as well as due to the increased incidence of alcohol and drug abuse found among these patients (for review see Key et al., 2000).

Non-reproductive Endocrine Abnormalities

In most cases, hormonal changes associated with the eating disorders are directly associated with insufficient energy intake. Beumont (1998) reported an increased basal growth hormone (GH) level in about 50% of patients with AN. The elevated GH level is probably an adaptation to the low energy intake and it is necessary to combat the accompanying hypoglycaemia by mobilising fat tissue. A low T3 syndrome is usually found which helps to conserve energy in the presence of undernutrition. The circulating levels of cortisol are often elevated. Fichter and Pirke (1990) showed that patients with AN have an abnormal

24 hour cortisol secretion, an impaired suppression by dexamethasone, reduced catabolism, and greater hypothalamic effect on cortisol production. In the Munich fasting experiment, five healthy female subjects participated in a starvation experiment. In total they lost about 8 kg in a 3-week phase of complete food abstinence. During this fasting period 24 hours plasma cortisol levels showed a significant increase with blunted dexamethasone suppression tests in half of the subjects. During fasting, basal thyroid-stimulating hormone (TSH) values were lowered and the TSH response to thyrotropin-releasing hormone (TRH) was blunted. The plasma level of growth hormone (GH) over 24 hours was elevated during fasting (Fichter et al., 1986).

OSTEOPOROSIS IN EATING DISORDERS

One of the most serious medical complications in patients suffering from *anorexia nervosa*, is profound osteopenia and osteoporosis of the trabecular and cortical bone compartments (Herzog et al., 1993; Zipfel et al., 2000b). A recent study (Klibanski et al., 1995) demonstrated significantly low bone mineral density (BMD < 2SD) in up to 45% of an anorexic patient sample. In a sample of patients with an average duration of AN of 5.8 years, Rigotti et al. (1991) found a seven-fold increased annual fracture rate in the second and third decade of life compared to an age-matched control. In a long-term follow-up study of anorexic patients, osteoporotic-related fractures were found in 44% of the poor outcome group (Herzog et al., 1993). Such fractures may lead to early invalidism and contribute to the suffering of these patients. Further, a considerable portion of the hospitalisation rate of chronic anorexic patients was due to the consequences of osteoporosis and related fractures. In an intermediate term follow-up study (3.6 years after initial inpatient treatment), Zipfel et al. (in press) showed that non-recovered AN with binge-eating/purging type showed a significantly reduced bone mineral density compared to patients with a restricting type.

Several studies investigating the risk of osteoporosis in patients with bulimia nervosa (BN) have been published over the last 10 years. Unfortunately, these studies have yielded inconsistent findings, making it difficult to reach a consensus regarding the relationship between bone mineral density and bulimia nervosa. One study found no significant differences in bone mineral density levels between BN patients and normal controls (Newman & Halmi, 1989), whereas another demonstrated significantly lower BMD in bulimic patients at the radius and femoral neck than a control group (Joyce et al., 1990). Other findings have further complicated the issue by demonstrating considerable variability in BMD between subgroups of BN patients. A significantly lower BMD of the lumbar spine was found in a subgroup of BN patients with long-lasting secondary amenorrhea (Newton et al., 1993). Additionally, a recent study found differences in BMD between patients classified as sedentary and patients who exercised regularly (Sundgot-Borgen et al., 1998). Specifically, sedentary patients had a lower BMD at the total body, spine, and hip. The authors concluded that weight-bearing exercise prevented or attenuated bone loss in normal weight BN patients. In another recent study, Goebel et al. (1999) demonstrated that a subsample of bulimic patients with a history of low weight had a reduced BMD at the lumbar spine compared to a BN sample without such a low weight history. Zipfel et al. (in press) showed that BN patients without a history of AN had BMD values and markers of bone turnover mostly within the normal range.

Aetiology of Osteoporosis in AN and BN Patients

The precise aetiology of bone demineralisation in patients with AN and BN remains unclear. The development of osteopenia and osteoporosis can be characterised by two major mechanisms that supplement and reinforce each other. Due to the early onset of the eating disorder, often during puberty, the patients fail to reach their peak bone mass, a process which is normally finished at the end of puberty or early adulthood. Second, there is premature and increased bone destruction in patients suffering from these disorders (Ruegsegger et al., 1991). The greatest risk factor for the development of osteoporosis is an oestrogen deficiency, which is reflected by the secondary (sometimes primary) amenorrhea. However, case reports have demonstrated that male anorexic patients can also suffer from osteoporosis, most likely due to testosterone deficiency. In addition, glucocorticoid excess, malnutrition, reduced body mass, and hyperactivity further influence bone turnover in both sexes. Previous studies on recovery from osteoporosis have yielded conflicting results. Some studies conclude that in many cases recovery is possible (Herzog et al., 1993), while others suggest that only partial improvement of BMD can be achieved (Ward et al., 1997).

Essential and Optional Investigations at Assessment and Follow-up

Relatively few clinical risk factors have been identified which can be used to predict or determine affected individuals. Factors associated with an increased risk of osteoporosis include a family history of osteoporosis, low body weight, low calcium intake, immobilisation, and lifestyle factors such as smoking, alcoholism, lack of exercise or excessive exercise. Additionally, it was demonstrated that the duration of the eating disorder is associated with cortical bone mass, whereas the duration of amenorrhea is associated with reduced BMD at the lumbar spine (Herzog et al., 1997a). During assessment, medical problems associated with an increased risk of osteoporosis should be carefully examined. Such medical conditions include: prolonged glucocorticoid therapy, chronic liver and renal disease, proven malabsorptive disorders, and problems associated with thyroxine excess. In addition to a patient history and physical examination, a routine blood test should be conducted to rule out the presence of other medical illnesses which cause bone loss.

Biochemical markers of bone turnover are non-invasive, comparatively inexpensive, and helpful when assessing this process (Seibel et al., 1993). For clinical purposes, markers of bone turnover are classified as either formation markers (e.g. osteocalcin, OC) or bone resorption markers (e.g. desoxypyridinoline, DPD). To ensure the correct interpretation of these markers, it is important to consider other influential factors, such as circadian rhythms, seasonal changes in growth, ageing, diseases, and drugs. The clinical use of biochemical markers in osteoporosis may be especially interesting for the selection of a specific antiresorptive therapy as well as for evaluating treatment outcome. Table 10.1 summarises the routine and additional parameters for the assessment of osteoporotic risk.

Treatment and Prevention Options

The primary goal of preventing or treating osteoporosis in eating-disordered patients should focus on achieving a normal body weight through a calcium-enriched, balanced diet.

Although immense efforts are made by eating disorder researchers to find the optimal treatment for osteoporosis, it is too early to present general guidelines. A selection of bone-specific treatment options are listed below, along with the corresponding research findings.

Serpell and Treasure (1997) are currently involved in a double blind trial to assess the efficacy of calcium and vitamin D supplements in increasing bone density in both current anorexics and those who have recovered from anorexia nervosa. Klibanski et al. (1995) conducted a randomised trial using oestrogen and progesterone replacement therapy (HRT) in anorexic patients. After a mean duration of 1.5 years, the HRT-treated group had no significant change in BMD compared with the control group. However, there was a 4.0% increase in mean BMD in patients with an initial body weight of less than 70% of normal weight who were treated with HRT. Grinspoon et al. (1997) investigated the effect of short-term recombinant human insulin-like growth factor 1 (IGF-1) administration on bone turnover in osteoporotic women with anorexia nervosa. During short-term administration of IGF-1 at a dose of 30 μg/kg, there was a significant increase in markers of bone formation as well as an insignificant increase of bone resorption. At this stage, there are no data on chronic IGF-1 administration. Gordon et al. (1999) studied changes in bone turnover markers and menstrual function after short-term oral dehydroepiandrosterone (DHEA) therapy. Despite the small number of patients ($n = 15$), markers of bone resorption had decreased significantly at 3 months. Resumption of menses in over half of the subjects suggested that DHEA therapy may also lead to oestradiol levels sufficient to stimulate the endometrium. Bisphosphonates have been shown to increase bone mineral density in patients with established osteoporosis as well as those with osteopenia. This group of drugs are safe and effective and are the only agents shown in prospective trails to reduce the risk of hip fractures and other non-vertebral fractures. However to date, they are approved by the US FDA for prevention of bone loss in recently menopausal women, for treatment of postmenopausal osteoporosis, and for management of glucocorticoid-induced bone loss (for review see Watts, 2001). To our knowledge, to date there are no published trials in patients with anorexia nervosa.

Common Problems with Recommended Action

A number of limitations exist in the treatment of osteoporosis in eating disordered patients, especially those suffering from anorexia nervosa. It is generally accepted that the best treatment option is a balanced refeeding diet with the goal of weight gain, so that the patients resume their normal menstrual cycles. However, the 'weight phobia' characteristic of these disorders often prevents the successful implementation of this physiological, cost-effective and 'side-effect free' treatment option. Although aerobic exercise has been found to prevent bone loss in healthy subjects, anorexic patients should be enrolled in supervised programmes, which could carefully monitor exercise levels, due to the tendency of these patients to over-exercise. Chronic patients who are very low weight (<70% of actual body weight) may benefit from HRT. Due to the resumption of menses, however, a considerable portion of these patients are reluctant to take HRT over a longer period of time. Although promising and new antiresorptive drug therapies are currently being developed, most are still in the phase of clinical trials. Future studies with a broader scope and longer follow-up periods will hopefully improve both treatment recommendations and our understanding of osteoporosis in eating-disordered patients.

Dental defects in patients with eating disorders have increasingly been the focus of attention in the past years. Oral changes are often the first indication that an eating disorder is present. The effect of acid regurgitation on the teeth is well appreciated (Robb et al., 1995), and a history of vomiting may have far-reaching consequences for the condition of the teeth. Apart from deterioration, vomiting increases the need for dental work and increased loss of teeth. A common sign of frequent and long-term vomiting is erosion of the dental enamel (Simmons et al., 1986). Enamel is lost from the lingual and palatal surfaces of the anterior teeth. Touyz et al. (1993) showed that patients with both AN and BN had changes indicative of gingivitis and gingival recession but not of periodontitis.

RENAL SYSTEM

A long-term follow-up study by Herzog et al. (1997b) showed that serum creatinine levels at first admission showed a robust main effect on the likelihood of first recovery which was not confounded by other variables. High serum creatinine (>120 mmol/l) and urea (>6.5 mmol/l) levels were indicators of reduced renal function and may be due to fluid loss. Serum creatinine levels correlated significantly with the frequency of vomiting. In addition, increased creatinine levels were seen in those patients who demonstrated purging behaviour but concealed this information. Finally, an increase in creatinine levels may be a sign of permanent kidney damage after a chronic course of disease and in individual AN patients may even cause death (Deter & Herzog, 1994). Good hydration maximises renal function. However in very dehydrated subjects, a slow rehydration is necessary to avoid fluid overload and electrolyte disturbances. In some patients with a very chronic impaired of renal function, referral to a renal physician becomes necessary, sometime with the need for haemodialysis.

MORTALITY

Neumärker (2000) found a crude mortality rate in eating disorders which ranged from 0 to 20%. A more precise method to analyse and document the mortality rate is the standardised mortality ratio (SMR), which is defined as the relationship between observed and expected deaths, using the subject years method. In his review, MR varied between 1.4 and 17.8. In our own long-term follow-up study (Löwe et al., 2001; Zipfel et al., 2000a), we found a SMR of 9.8, very similar to the SMR (9.6) published by Herzog et al. (2000). This relatively broad range of estimates is mainly due to methodological limitations, such as study design and reporting of missing data. The main causes of death in AN patients are suicide and ventricular tachyarrhythmia. Other important causes of death, however, include disorders of the electrolyte balance (including hypophosphataemia), infections (pneumonia, sepsis), terminal renal failure, shock, ileus and gastric perforation. The mortality in AN patients of the binge-eating/purging type is about twice as high as that of the restricting type (Moller et al., 1996; Norring & Sohlberg, 1993). Mortality rates in BN patients are lower than AN and are mainly due to suicide. This reduced mortality is due to the lack of starvation-related causes, but may also in part be due to the shorter follow-up periods of outcome studies.

OBESITY

More than half of all US adults are classified as overweight (BMI > 25 kg/m^2) and one in three is considered to be obese (BMI > 30 kg/m^2). The rate of obesity has increased by 50% over the past 20 years in the USA (Yanovski & Yanovski, 1999), but a similar increase has been shown world wide. For example, the MONICA study and more recent studies in England (see Seidell & Rissannen, 1998) have demonstrated that the percentage of obesity in Europe has also undergone a sharp increase, making obesity the most common nutritional disease in industrialised countries. Binge eating disorder (BED), which is classified as an 'eating disorder not otherwise specified' in the DSM-IV (APA, 1994), has been described as the most relevant eating disorder for overweight individuals. It has been estimated, that approximately 20–30% of overweight persons seeking help at weight loss programmes are classified as binge eaters (Spitzer et al., 1993). This is one of the reasons why mental health professionals need to know about the highly prevalent condition of obesity (Devlin et al., 2000).

Excess weight increases the risk of other severe illnesses, including hypertension, diabetes, coronary heart disease (CHD) and some forms of cancer. Any treatment approach must recognise that obesity is a chronic, stigmatised, and costly disease. Recently, major advances have been made in identifying the components of the homeostatic system which regulate the control of food intake and body weight (Schwartz et al., 2000). The identification of obesity-related genes and hormones as well as the development of new drugs raises hope for the treatment of this serious epidemic.

HEALTH RISKS ASSOCIATED WITH OBESITY

In clinical practice, body fat is most commonly estimated by using the body mass index (BMI = kg/m^2). A graded classification of overweight and obesity using BMI values provides valuable information about increasing body fatness. A World Health Organisation (WHO) expert committee has proposed a classification for overweight and obesity based on the BMI with the following cut-off points (Table 10.2). There are a number of recent studies which demonstrated a close relationship between BMI and the incidence of type 2 diabetes, hypertension, coronary heart disease and cholelithiasis (Willett et al., 1999). This

Table 10.2 Cut-off points proposed by the WHO expert committee for the classification of body weight

Body mass index (kg/m^2)	WHO classification	Popular description
<18.5	Underweight	Thin
18.5–24.9	—	Healthy, normal, acceptable
25.0–29.9	Grade 1 overweight	Overweight
30.0–39.9	Grade 2 overweight	Obesity
≥40.0	Grade 3 overweight	Morbid obesity

The data presented in this table reflect knowledge acquired largely from epidemiological studies in developed countries (adapted from Kopelman, 2000).

relationship is approximately linear for a range of BMI less than 29 kg/m^2, but the risks are greatly increased for both genders above this cut-off. In addition, waist circumferences and waist-to-hip ratio provide measures for assessing upper body fat deposition. The waist circumference in particular is associated with the risk of CHD, hypertension, and blood lipid levels. Lean et al. (1995) demonstrated cut-offs for gender-specific waist circumferences associated with increased risk for metabolic complications. An expert panel on overweight has recently suggested that increased risks of metabolic complications exist if waist circumference is greater than 102 cm in men and 89 cm in women (for review, see Willett et al., 1999). Han et al. (1995) found that, in men, a waist circumference of 94 to 102 cm was associated with a relative risk of 2.2 of having one or more cardiovascular risk factors, and in women a circumference of 80 to 88 cm was associated with a relative risk of 1.6.

Metabolic Complications

Obesity is characterised by elevated fasting plasma insulin and exaggerated insulin response to an oral glucose load. Particularly upper body obesity is associated with measures of insulin resistance. The different fat depots vary in their response to hormones that regulate lipolysis, such as noradrenaline and cortisol. As a consequence, the elevated abdominal adipose tissue contributes to an exaggerated release of free fatty acids (FFA). This elevation of FFA leads to an inappropriate maintenance of glucose production and impaired hepatic glucose utilisation responsible for an impaired glucose tolerance. Prospective studies confirm a close relationship between increasing body fat and type 2 diabetes. In women, the risk for diabetes after adjustment for age for those with a BMI of 35 or greater was increased 93-fold, compared with women with a BMI of less than 21 (Colditz et al., 1995). Similar results had been demonstrated for obese men.

Cardivascular Complications

Kopelman (2000) summarises the changes and impairment of cardiovascular function in obesity. Progressive weight gain is accompanied with an increase in blood volume. As a consequence, there is an increase in the heart's pumping capacity and cardiac output. A combination of elevated circulatory preload and after load led to left ventricular (LF) dilatation and hypertrophy. In the long run, the combination of systolic and diastolic dysfunction can lead to clinically significant heart failure. In the Framingham Heart Study, Kim et al. (2000) demonstrated, that body weight was directly related to an increase in the prevalence of coronary heart disease, particularly in men. In addition, the often marked systemic vascular resistance seen in obese individuals results in a marked rise in blood pressure (hypertension) and concentric LV hypertrophy. As a consequence, these factors are responsible for an increased risk of morbidity and mortality from CHD or sudden death, due to ventricular arrhythmia. This may also be due to an increase in sympathetic and decrease in parasympathetic nervous tone (Rosenbaum et al., 1997). Other mediators, such as altered rates of blood flow, altered thrombocyte function, as well as hyperinsulinaemia or sleep apnoea may be important cofactors. Calle et al. (1999) demonstrated the risk of death from cardiovascular diseases throughout the range of moderate to severe obesity for both men and women in all age groups. The risk associated with a high BMI is greater for whites than for blacks. A weight gain of 5–8 kg is associated with an increase for CHD of 25% (Willet et al., 1995)

Additional Complications

In addition to metabolic or cardiovascular impairments, individuals with a significant excess weight show obesity-related changes in respiratory function, particularly during sleep. Besides daytime somnolence, this sleep apnoea syndrome can cause pulmonary hypertension and is associated with an increased risk of myocardial and cerebral infarction.

Studies have shown a positive association between obesity and osteoarthritis of the hand, hip and knee. The Framingham study demonstrated that a decrease in BMI of 2 units or more over 10 years decreased the odds for developing knee osteoarthritis by over 50% (Felson et al., 1992).

There is evidence that obesity is associated with an increased risk for a gall bladder carcinoma in both sexes. In addition, a higher rate of breast carcinomas and endometrium carcinomas was found in female obese individuals.

HEALTH RISKS ASSOCIATED WITH WEIGHT CYCLING

Weight loss in overweight and obese individuals improves the physical, metabolic, endocrinological and psychological complications. Intentional weight loss may also reduce obesity-related mortality. However, recent clinical guidelines, e.g. *Obesity in Scotland* (Scottish Intercollegiate Guidelines Network, 1996) have recommended that there should be a shift away from major weight loss to weight management and risk factor reduction. A modest weight reduction of 5–10 kg is associated with many beneficial health effects, including a fall of 10 mmHg systolic and 20 mmHg diastolic blood pressure, a decrease in fasting glucose levels of up to 50%, and a significant reduction in total cholesterol and LDL cholesterol. Modest weight reductions improve back and joint pain, lung function and reduce the frequency of sleep apnoea. Unbalanced 'crash' diets should be avoided, because of the high risk of weight cycling and protein depletion. Several prospective studies have outlined some disadvantages of weight loss including (a) an increased risk for women who lose 4–10 kg to develop a clinically relevant gallstone disease and (b) a loss of bone mass. These findings provide further support for the shift towards risk factor reduction and weight maintenance, rather than major weight loss.

SUMMARY AND CONCLUSIONS

Medical complications play an important role in patients with eating disorders. In particular the following patient groups are at high risk for medical complications: malnourished anorexic patients, bulimic patients with a severe symptomatology of bingeing and purging, patients with a somatic comorbidity (e.g. diabetes mellitus) as well as those individuals with a marked overweight or weight fluctuations. Therefore it is important to take a full medical history, including current medication. In view of the multiple physical problems which may occur, and their potentially serious consequences, it is advisable that all patients have a thorough physical examination, with a special focus on the cardiovascular system. In addition there is general agreement, that particularly anorexic patients should have a range of screening investigations (e.g. full blood count, biochemical profile). An electrocardiogram (ECG) is mandatory in all patients with anorexia nervosa and for those eating-disordered patients with severe electrolyte disturbances. In anorexic patients with a chronic course or additional risk factors for osteoporosis, it might be advisable to perform an assessment of bone density by dual energy X-ray absorptiometry (DEXA). It is strongly advisable that all cases of medical complications in eating disorders should be managed in consultation with a physician or a specialist (e.g. endocrinologist, cardiologist).

ACKNOWLEDGEMENT

The authors would like to thank Deborah Reas for her assistance with the translation of this chapter.

REFERENCES

Abdu, R.A., Garritano, D. & Culver, O. (1987) Acute gastric necrosis in anorexia nervosa and bulimia. Two case reports. *Arch. Surg.*, **122**, 830–832.

Allouche, J., Bennet, A., Barbe, P., Plantavid, M., Caron, P. & Louvet, J.P. (1991) LH pulsatility and in vitro bioactivity in women with anorexia nervosa-related hypothalamic amenorrhea. *Acta Endocrinol. Copenh.*, **125**, 614–620.

Alvin, P., Zogheib, J., Rey, C. & Losay, J. (1993) Severe complications and mortality in mental eating disorders in adolescence. On 99 hospitalised patients. *Arch. Fr. Pediat.*, **50**, 755–762.

APA (1994) *Diagnostic and Statistical Manual of Mental Disorders* (DSM-IV), Fourth edition. Washington, DC.: American Psychiatric Association.

Bates, G.W., Bates, S.R. & Whitworth, N.S. (1982) Reproductive failure in women who practice weight control. *Fertil. Steril.*, **37**, 373–378.

Becker, A.E., Grinspoon, S.K., Klibanski, A. & Herzog, D.B. (1999) Eating disorders. *N. Engl. J. Med.*, **340**, 1092–1098.

Beumont, P.J. & Large, M. (1991) Hypophosphataemia, delirium and cardiac arrhythmia in anorexia nervosa. *Med. J. Aust.*, **155**, 519–522.

Beumont, P.J.V., Russell, J.D. & Touyz, S.W. (1993) Treatment of anorexia nervosa. *Lancet*, **341**, 1635–1640.

Beumont, P.J.V. (1998) The neurobiology of eating behaviour and weight control. In H.W., Hoeck, J.L., Treasure & M.A., Katzman (Eds), *Neurobiology in the Treatment of Eating Disorders* (pp. 237–253). Chichester: John Wiley & Sons.

Bihun, J.A., McSherry, J. & Marciano, D. (1993) Idiopathic edema and eating disorders: Evidence for an association. *Int. J. Eat. Disord.*, **14**, 197–201.

Bonne, O.B., Bloch, M. & Berry, E.M. (1993) Adaptation to severe chronic hypokalemia in anorexia nervosa: A plea for conservative management. *Int. J. Eat. Disord.*, **13**, 125–128.

Brinch, M., Isager, T. & Tolstrup, K. (1988) Anorexia nervosa and motherhood: Reproduction pattern and mothering behavior of 50 women. *Acta Psychiat. Scand.*, **77**, 611–617.

Buchman, A.L., Ament, M.E., Weiner, M., Kodner, A. & Mayer, E.A. (1994) Reversal of megaduodenum and duodenal dysmotility associated with improvement in nutritional status in primary anorexia nervosa. *Dig. Dis. Sci.*, **39**, 433–440.

Calle, E.E., Thun, M.J., Petrelli, J.M., Rodriguez, C. & Heath-CW, J. (1999) Body-mass index and mortality in a prospective cohort of U.S. adults. *N. Engl. J. Med.*, **341**, 1097–1105.

Cariem, A.K., Lemmer, E.R., Adams, M.G., Winter, T.A. & O'Keefe, S.J. (1994) Severe hypophosphataemia in anorexia nervosa. *Postgrad. Med. J.*, **70**, 825–827.

Challier, P. & Cabrol, S. (1995) Severe hyponatremia associated with anorexia nervosa: role of inappropriate antidiuretic hormone secretion?. *Arch. Pediat.*, **2**, 977–979.

Colditz, G.A., Willett, W.C., Rotnitzky, A. & Manson, J.E. (1995) Weight gain as a risk factor for clincial diabetes mellitus in women. *Ann. Int. Med.*, **122**, 481–486.

Colombo, L., Altomare, S., Castelli, M., Bestetti, A., Stanzani, M., Colombo, N., Picollo, S., Pietrasanta, E.R., Gnocchi, P. & Giavardi, L. (1995) Kinetics of hepatic enzymes in anorexia nervosa. *Recent Prog. Med.*, **86**, 204–207.

Cooke, R.A. and Chambers, J.B. (1995) Anorexia nervosa and the heart. *Br. J. Hosp. Med.*, **54**, 313–317.

De Simone, G., Scalfi, L., Galderisi, M., Celentano, A., Di Biase, G., Tammaro, P., Garofalo, M., Mureddu, G.F., de Divitiis, O. & Contaldo, F. (1994) Cardiac abnormalities in young women with anorexia nervosa. *Br. Heart J.*, **71**, 287–292.

Delvenne, V., Goldman, S., De, M., V, Simon, Y., Luxen, A. & Lotstra, F. (1996) Brain hypometabolism of glucose in anorexia nervosa: normalization after weight gain. *Biol. Psychiat.*, **40**, 761–768.

Deter, H.C. & Herzog, W. (1994) Anorexia nervosa in a long-term perspective: results of the Heidelberg–Mannheim Study. *Psychosom. Med.*, **56**, 20–27.

Devlin, M.J., Yanovski, S.Z., Wilson, G.T. (2000) Obesity: what mental health professionals need to know. *Am. J. Psychiat.*, **157**, 854–866.

Devuyst, O., Lambert, M., Rodhain, J., Lefebvre, C. & Coche, E. (1993) Haematological changes and infectious complications in anorexia nervosa: a case-control study. *Qtly J. Med.*, **86**, 791–799.

Durakovic, Z., Durakovic, A. & Korsic, M. (1994) Changes of the corrected Q T interval in the electrocardiogram of patients with anorexia nervosa. *Int. J. Cardiol.*, **45**, 115–120.

Fairburn, C G & Cooper, P.J. (1984) The clinical features of bulimia nervosa. *Br. J. Psychiat.*, **144**, 238–246.

Felson, D.T., Zhang, Y., Anthony, J.M., Naimark, A. & Anderson, J.J. (1992) Weight loss reduces the risk for symptomatic knee osteoarthritis in women. The Framingham Study. *Ann. Int. Med.*, **116**, 535–539.

Fichter, M.M., Pirke, K.M. & Holsboer, F. (1986) Weight loss causes neuroendocrine disturbances: Experimental study in healthy starving subjects. *Psychiat. Res.*, **17**, 61–72.

Fichter, M.M. & Pirke, K.M. (1990) Endocrine dystunctions in bulimia nervosa. In M.M., Fichter (Ed.), *Bulimia Nervosa*, Chichester: John Wiley & Sons.

Fisher, M., Simpser, E. & Schneider, M. (2000) Hypophosphatemia secondary to oral refeeding in anorexia nervosa. *Int. J. Eat. Disord.*, **28**, 181–187.

Fukushima, M., Nakai, Y., Taniguchi, A., Imura, H., Nagata, I. & Tokuyama, K. (1993) Insulin sensitivity, insulin secretion, and glucose effectiveness in anorexia nervosa: A minimal model analysis. *Metabolism*, **42**, 1164–1168.

Goebel, G., Schweiger, U., Kruger, R. & Fichter, M.M. (1999) Predictors of bone mineral density in patients with eating disorders. *Int. J. Eat. Disord.*, **25**, 143–150.

Golden, N.H., Ashtari, M., Kohn, M.R., Patel, M., Jacobson, M.S., Fletcher, A. & Shenker, I R (1996) Reversibility of cerebral ventricular enlargement in anorexia nervosa, demonstrated by quantitative magnetic resonance imaging. *J. Pediat.*, **128**, 296–301.

Gordon, C., Grace, E, Emans, S, Goodman, E,. Crawford, M. & Leboff, M. (1999) Changes in bone turnover markers and menstrual function after short-term oral DHEA in young women with anorexia nervosa. *J. Bone Miner. Res.*, **14**, 136–145.

Grinspoon, S., Herzog, D. & Klibanski, A. (1997) Mechanisms and treatment options for bone loss in anorexia nervosa. *Psychopharmacol. Bull.*, **33**, 399–404.

Hall, R.C., Beresford, T.P. & Hall, A.K. (1989) Hypomagnesemia in eating disorder patients: clinical signs and symptoms. *Psychiat. Med.*, **7**, 193–203.

Hall, R.C. & Beresford, T.P. (1989) Medical complications of anorexia and bulimia. *Psychiat. Med.*, **7**, 165–192.

Han, T.S., van Leer, E.E., Seidell, J.C., Lean, M.E. (1995) Waist circumference action levels in the identification of cardiovascular risk factors: prevalence study in a random sample. *Br. Med. J.*, **311**, 1401–1405.

Hebebrand, J., Blum, W.F., Barth, N., Coners, H., Englaro, P., Juul, A., Ziegler, A., Warnke, A., Rascher, W. & Remschmidt, H. (1997) Leptin levels in patients with anorexia nervosa are reduced in the acute stage and elevated upon short-term weight restoration. *Mol. Psychiat.*, **2**, 330–334.

Herzog, D.B., Greenwood, D.N., Dorer, D.J., Flores, A.T., Ekeblad, E. R., Richards, A., Blais, M.A. & Keller, M.B. (2000) Mortality in eating disorders: a descriptive study. *Int. J. Eat. Disord.*, **28**, 20–26.

Herzog, W., Minne, H., Deter, C., Leidig, G., Schellberg, D., Wuster, C., Gronwald, R., Sarembe, E., Kroger, F., Bergmann, G. et al. (1993) Outcome of bone mineral density in anorexia nervosa patients 11.7 years after first admission. *J. Bone Miner. Res.*, **8**, 597–605.

Herzog, W., Deter, H.C., Fiehn, W. & Petzold, E. (1997a) Medical findings and predictors of long-term physical outcome in anorexia nervosa: a prospective, 12-year follow-up study. *Psychol. Med.*, **27**, 269–279.

Herzog, W., Schellberg, D. & Deter, H.C. (1997b) First recovery in anorexia nervosa patients in the long-term course: a discrete-time survival analysis. *J. Consult. Clin. Psychol.*, **65**, 169–177.

Hughes, J.R. (1996) A review of the usefulness of the standard EEG in psychiatry. *Clin. Electroenceph.*, **27**, 35–39.

Humphries, L.L., Adams, L.J., Eckfeldt, J.H., Levitt, M.D. & McClain, C.J. (1987) Hyperamylasemia in patients with eating disorders. *Ann. Int. Med.*, **106**, 50–52.

Joyce, J.M., Warren, D.L., Humphries, L.L., Smith, A.J. & Coon, J.S. (1990) Osteoporosis in women with eating disorders: comparison of physical parameters, exercise, and menstrual status with SPA and DPA evaluation. *J. Nucl. Med.*, **31**, 325–331.

Kahn, D., Halls, J., Bianco, J.A. & Perlman, S.B. (1991) Radionuclide ventriculography in severely underweight anorexia nervosa patients before and during refeeding therapy. *J. Adolesc. Health.*, **12**, 301–306.

Key, A., Mason, H., Bolton, J. (2000) Reproduction and eating disorders: a fruitless union. *Eur. Eat. Disord. Rev.*, **8**, 98–107.

Kingston, K., Szmukler, G., Andrewes, D., Tress, B. & Desmond, P. (1996) Neuropsychological and structural brain changes in anorexia nervosa before and after refeeding. *Psychol. Med.*, **26**, 15–28.

Kim, K.S., Owen, W.L., Williams, D. & Adams-Campbell, L.L. (2000) A comparison between BMI and conicity index on predicting coronary heart disease: the Framingham Heart Study. *Ann. Epidemiol.*, **10**, 424–431.

Klibanski, A., Biller, B.M., Schoenfeld, D.A., Herzog, D.B. & Saxe, V.C. (1995) The effect of estrogen administration on trabecular bone loss in young women with anorexia nervosa. *J. Clin. Endocrinol. Metab.*, 898–904.

Kopelman, P.G. (2000) Obesity as a medical problem. *Nature*, **404**, 635–643.

Köpp, W., Blum, W.F., Ziegler, A., Lubbert, H., Emons, G., Herzog, W., Herpertz, S., Deter, H.C., Remschmidt, H. & Hebebrand, J. (1997) Low leptin levels predict amenorrhea in underweight and eating disordered females. *Mol. Psychiat.*, **2**, 335–340.

Kornreich, L., Shapira, A., Horev, G., Danziger, Y., Tyano, S. & Mimouni, M. (1991) CT and MR evaluation of the brain in patients with anorexia nervosa. *Am. J. Neuroradiol.*, **12**, 1213–1216.

Kreipe, R.E., Goldstein, B., DeKing, D.E., Tipton, R. & Kempski, M.H. (1994) Heart rate power spectrum analysis of autonomic dysfunction in adolescents with anorexia nervosa. *Int. J. Eat. Disord.*, **16**, 159–165.

Krieg, J.C. (1991) Eating disorders as assessed by cranial computerised tomography (CCT, dSPECT, PET). *Adv. Exp. Med. Biol.*, **291**, 223–229.

Laessle, R.G., Krieg, J.C., Fichter, M.M. & Pirke, K.M. (1989) Cerebral atrophy and vigilance performance in patients with anorexia nervosa and bulimia nervosa. *Neuropsychobiology*, **21**, 187–191.

Lambert, M. and Boland, B. (2000) Haematological complications. *Eur. Eat. Disord. Rev.*, **8**, 158–163.

Lean, M.E., Han, T.S. & Morrison, T.E. (1995) Waist circumference as a measure for indicating need for weight management. *Br. Med. J.*, **331**, 158–161.

Löwe, B., Zipfel, S., Buchholz, C., Dupont, Y., Reas, D.L. & Herzog, W. (2001) Long-term outcome of anorexia nervosa in a prospective 21-year follow-up study. *Psychol. Med.*, **31**, 881–890.

Mitchell, J.E., Pyle, R.L., Eckert, E.D., Hatsukami, D. & Lentz, R. (1983) Electrolyte and other physiological abnormalities in patients with bulimia. *Psychol. Med.*, **13**, 273–278.

Mitchell, J.E., Seim, H.C., Colon, E. & Pomeroy, C. (1987) Medical complications and medical management of bulimia. *Ann. Int. Med.*, **107**, 71–77.

Moller, M.S., Nystrup, J., and Nielsen, S. (1996) Mortality in anorexia nervosa in Denmark during the period 1970–1987. *Acta Psychiat. Scand.*, **94**, 454–459.

Neumärker, K.J. (2000) Mortality rates and causes of death. *Eur. Eat. Disord. Rev.*, **8**, 181–187.

Newman, M.M. & Halmi, K.A. (1989) Relationship of bone density to estradiol and cortisol in anorexia nervosa and bulimia. *Psychiat. Res.*, **29**, 105–112.

Newton, J.R., Freeman, C.P., Hannan, W.J. & Cowen, S. (1993) Osteoporosis and normal weight bulimia nervosa—which patients are at risk? *J. Psychosom. Res.*, **37**, 239–247.

Norring, C.E. and Sohlberg, S.S. (1993) Outcome, recovery, relapse and mortality across six years in patients with clinical eating disorders. *Acta Psychiat. Scand.*, **87**, 437–444.

Patchell, R.A., Fellows, H.A. & Humphries, L.L. (1994) Neurological complications of anorexia nervosa. *Acta Neurol. Scand.*, **89**, 111–116.

Pirke, K.M., Schweiger, U., Strowitzki, T., Tuschl, R.J., Laessle, R.G., Broocks, A., Huber, B. & Middendorf, R. (1989) Dieting causes menstrual irregularities in normal weight young women through impairment of episodic luteinizing hormone secretion. *Fertil. Steril.*, **51**, 263–268.

Ratcliffe, P.J. & Bevan, J.S. (1985) Severe hypoglycaemia and sudden death in anorexia nervosa. *Psychol. Med.*, **15**, 679–681.

Rigotti, N.A., Neer, R.M., Skates, S.J., Herzog, D.B. & Nussbaum, S.R. (1991) The clinical course of osteoporosis in anorexia nervosa. A longitudinal study of cortical bone mass *JAMA*, **265**, 1133–1138.

Robb, N.B., Smith, B.G. & Geidrys, L.E. (1995) The distribution of erosion on the dentitions of patients with eating disorders. *Br. Dent. J.*, **178**, 171–174.

Robinson, P.H. (2000) The gastrointestinal tract in eating disorders. *Eur. Eat. Disord. Rev.*, **8**, 88–97.

Rosenbaum, M., Leibel, R.L. & Hirsch, J. (1997) Obesity. *N. Engl. J. Med.*, **337**, 396–407.

Rothenberger, A., Blanz, B. & Lehmkuhl, G. (1991) What happens to electrical brain activity when anorectic adolescents gain weight? *Eur. Arch. Psychiat. Clin. Neurosci.*, **240**, 144–147.

Ruegsegger, P., Durand, E.P. & Dambacher, M.A. (1991) Differential effects of ageing and disease on trabecular and compact bone density of the radius. *Bone*, **12**, 99–105.

Schlegel, S. & Kretzschmar, K. (1997) Value of computerised tomography and magnetic resonance tomography in psychiatric diagnosis. *Nervenarzt*, **68**, 1–10.

Schocken, D.D., Holloway, J.D. & Powers, P.S. (1989) Weight loss and the heart. Effects of anorexia nervosa and starvation. *Arch Int. Med.*, **149**, 877–881.

Schou, J.A., Lund, L. & Sandermann, J. (1994) Spontaneous ventricular rupture in adults. *Ugeskr. Laeger*, **156**, 3299–3305.

Schwartz, M.W., Woods, S.C., Porte, D., Seeley, R.J. & Baskin, D.G. (2000) Central nervous system control of food intake. *Nature*, **404**, 661–671.

Schweiger, U., Laessle, R.G., Pfister, H. et al. (1987) Diet induced menstrual irregularities: Effect of age and weight loss. *Fertil. Steril.*, **48**, 746–751.

Scottish Intercollegiate Guidelines Network (1996) *Obesity in Scotland. Integrating Prevention with Weight Management.* http://www.show.scot.nhs.uk/sign/sign8inf.html.

Seibel, M.J., Cosman, F., Shen, V., Gordon, S., Dempster, D.W., Ratcliffe, A. & Lindsay, R. (1993) Urinary hydroxypyridinium crosslinks of collagen as markers of bone resorption and estrogen efficacy in postmenopausal osteoporosis. *J. Bone Miner. Res.*, **8**, 881–889.

Seidell, J.C. & Rissannen, A.M. (1998) Time trends in the world-wide prevalence of obesity. In G.A., Bray, C., Bouchard & W.P.T., James (Eds), *Hanbook of Obesity*, (pp. 79–91). New York: Dekker.

Serpell, L. & Treasure, J. (1997) Osteoporosis: A serious health risk in chronic anorexia nervosa. *Eur. Eat. Disord. Rev.*, **5**, 149–157.

Sharp, C.W. and Freeman, C.P. (1993) The medical complications of anorexia nervosa. *Br. J. Psychiat.*, **162**, 452–462.

Siegel, J.H., Hardoff, D., Golden, N.H. & Shenker, I.R. (1995) Medical complications in male adolescents with anorexia nervosa. *J. Adolesc. Health.*, **16**, 448–453.

Simmons, M.S., Grayden, S.K. & Mitchell, J.E. (1986) The need for psychiatric-dental liaison in the treatment of bulimia. *Am. J. Psychiat.*, **143**, 783–784.

Spitzer, R.L., Yanovski, S., Wadden, T., Wing, R., Markus, M.D. Stunkard, A. (1993) Binge eating disorder: its further validation in a multisite study. *Int. J. Eat. Disord.*, **13**, 137–153.

Sungot-Borgen, J., Bahr, R., Falch, J.A. & Sundgot-Schneider, L. (1998) Normal bone mass in bulimic women. *J. Clin. Endocrinol. Metab.*, 3144–3149.

Szmukler, G.I., Young, G.P., Lichtenstein, M. & Andrews, J.T. (1990) A serial study of gastric emptying in anorexia nervosa and bulimia. *Aust. N.Z. J. Med.*, **20**, 220–225.

Tenholder, M.F. & Pike, J.D. (1991) Effect of anorexia nervosa on pulmonary immunocompetence. *South. Med. J.*, **84**, 1188–1191.

Touyz, S.W., Liew, V.P., Tseng, P. & et al. (1993) Oral and dental complications in dieting disorders. *Int. J. Eat. Disord.*, **14**, 341–347.

Watts, N.B. (2001) Treatment of osteoporosis with bisphosphonates. *Rheum. Dis. Clin. North. Am.*, **27**, 197–214.

Ward, A., Brown, N. & Treasure, J. (1997) Persistent osteopenia after recovery from anorexia nervosa. *Int. J. Eat. Disord.*, **22**, 71–75.

Willett, W.C., Manson, J.E., Stampfer, M.J., Colditz, G.A., Rosner, B. & Speiser, F.E. (1995) Weight, weight change, and coronary heart disease in women. Risk within the normal weight range. *JAMA*, **273**, 461–465.

Willett, W.C., Dietz, W.H. & Colditz, G.A. (1999) Guidelines for healthy weight. *N. Engl. J. Med.*, **341**, 427–434.

Willis, J. & Rand, P. (1988) Pregnancy in bulimic women. *Obstet. Gynecol.*, **71**, 708.

Winston, A.P. & Stafford, P.J. (2000) Cardiovascular effects of anorexia nervosa. *Eur. Eat. Disord. Rev.*, **8**, 117–125.

Yanovski, J.A. & Yanovski, S.Z. (1999) Recent advances in basic obesity research. *JAMA*, **282**, 1504–1506.

Zipfel, S., Specht, T. & Herzog, W. (1998) Medical complications in eating disorders. In H., Hoeck, J., Treasure & M., Katzman (Eds), *The Integration of Neurobiology in the Treatment of Eating Disorders* (pp. 457–484). New York, Toronto: John Wiley & Sons.

Zipfel, S., Specht, T., Blum, W., Englaro, P., Hebebrand, J., Hartmann, M., Wüster, C., Ziegler, R. & Herzog, W. (1998) Leptin—a parameter for body fat measurment in patients with eating disorders. *Eur. Eat. Disord. Rev.*, **6**, 38–47.

Zipfel, S., Lowe, B., Reas, D.L., Deter, H.C. & Herzog, W. (2000a) Long-term prognosis in anorexia nervosa: Lessons from a 21-year follow-up study. *Lancet*, **355**, 721–722.

Zipfel, S., Herzog, W., Beumont, P.J. & Russell, J.D. (2000b) Osteoporosis. *Eur. Eat. Disord. Rev.*, **8**, 108–116.

Zipfel, S., Seibel, M,J., Löwe, B., Beumont, P.J., Kasperk, C., Herzog, W. (in press). Osteoporosis in eating disorders: a follow-up study of patients with anorexia and bulimia nervosa. *J. Clin. Endocrinol. Metab.*

CHAPTER 11

Family, Burden of Care and Social Consequences

Søren Nielsen

*Psychiatric Youth Centre, Storstrøm County Psychiatric Services,
Næstved, Denmark*

and

Núria Bará-Carril

Eating Disorders Unit, Institute of Psychiatry, London, UK

SUMMARY

What do we know?

- High levels of distress—personal and intra-familial
- Burden of care high—familial, psychiatric and somatic
- Loss of productive years—through periods of illness and through premature death
- 'Stunting'—emotional, psychosexual, physical and vocational
- Outcome depends on both patient and treatment factors—'experts' do make a difference

What we need to know more about

- Which patients and families benefit most from which type and dose of treatment
- Outcome if treatment is refused, incomplete or prematurely terminated
- Characteristics of cases untraced or refusing follow-up
- Sibling's roles in the disease process and in the treatment process
- Consumer satisfaction—of patients as well as carers
- Quality of life—with and without eating disorder

INTRODUCTION

The concept 'burden of care' has attracted only limited attention in the field of eating disorders (Treasure et al., 2001). It is clear from outcome studies that there is a lot of suffering in and around persons with eating disorders (Tolstrup et al., 1987; Ratnasuria

Handbook of Eating Disorders. Edited by J. Treasure, U. Schmidt and E. van Furth.
© 2003 John Wiley & Sons, Ltd.

et al., 1991; Crisp et al., 1992; Theander, 1970, 1992, 1996; Keller et al., 1992; Wentz, 2000). Personal reports clearly attest to this (MacDonald, 2000). Our aim is to look at the 'burden' from three perspectives: personal, familial and societal. We will attempt to outline what is known, and what deficits there are in our present knowledge.

PERSONAL BURDEN

Misery

In the acute phase of the illness patients do seem to get some satisfaction from the anorectic way of life. However, later the costs become apparent in terms of loneliness, despair and intense mood swings. The rigid control of all aspects of life tends to kill life as other people know it, and indeed as the patient herself has known it. Despite all efforts, no success seems to be really satisfactory, further goals continue to loom on the horizon. No solutions are in sight, only problems. From an outsider's—e.g. most therapists—perspective the condition is enigmatic. Many autobiographical accounts exist, a few of which can be found in authoritative texts, e.g. Haggiag (2000). Some emphasise the suffering brought about by treatment, rather than the suffering originating from the illness *per se*. This point of view is understandable, given the clinical accounts of some of the more drastic treatment approaches (e.g. Theander, 1970, esp. pp. 115–118; Morgan & Crisp, 2000).

Stunting

Social

The 'hibernation' following from years of existence as a person with an eating disorder, with chronic malnutrition, a limited range of interests and few free choices, can lead to sequelae in many areas of life. The potential for development is seldom fulfilled. Anorexia nervosa can lead to developmental delay, emotionally as well as socially. Ratnasuriya et al. (1991) noted that many in their cohort did not obtain full independence, but stayed with relatives in a dependent relationship, with a limited range of interests, neither completing an education nor holding a job. Tolstrup et al. (1987) found a downward slide in social class in the probands from the initial evaluation to the first follow-up in 1981–1982. The long-term significance of this finding will be fully appreciated only after further follow-up interviews. We have reanalysed some of the published raw data from the interesting follow-up study from Sweden, in particular 'the living situation' given in Wentz (2000) using the program package *StatXact4* (Cytel, 2000). The data set consists of singly ordered R × C tables, and consequently the Kruskall-Wallis test (Siegel & Castellan, 1988) is the relevant analytical tool.

A smaller proportion of the AN group (study group) shared a flat, and more live alone than in the COMP group (comparison group). Similar numbers in both groups live with parents, and similar numbers are married/cohabiting in each group. At variance with Tolstrup et al. (1987) and Ratnasuriya et al. (1991), Wentz (2000) found no between-group differences in 'occupation' when the cohort was 24 years old, i.e. after 10 years of follow-up.

Table 11.1 Personal contacts and activities at follow-up[a]

	Distribution across categories. Absolute numbers AN group (N = 51)	Distribution across categories. Absolute numbers. COMP. group (N = 51)	Kruskall–Wallis test. Observed test statistic and 'exact' p-value
Personal contacts at 6 years of follow-up	26 8 11 6	41 5 5 0	11.12; exact p-value 0.0008
Personal contacts at 10 years of follow-up	20 7 20 4	44 1 6 0	23.02; exact p-value 0.0000
Social activities at 6 years of follow-up	27 15 6 3	45 5 1 0	15.81; exact p value 0.0001
Social activities at 10 years of follow-up	23 14 12 2	42 5 4 0	15.05; exact p-value 0.0001

[a] Reanalysis of published raw data from Wentz (2000), Paper III, Table 4, using the program package StatXact4 (Cytel, 2000).

On the other hand, a pronounced difference between the AN group and the COMP group is noted in the quantity and quality of the 'personal contacts'. At the 6-year follow-up the AN group has significantly fewer and more superficial friendships than the COMP group, and the situation seems to be even worse at the 10-year follow-up (see Table 11.1). The findings for the dimension 'social activities' are very similar: significantly fewer in the AN group mix well outside the family and more feel solitary or do not take part in activities outside the family. The findings were similar at the 6-year follow-up and at the 10-year follow-up (see Table 11.1 for details).

Sexual

Many former eating-disordered patients have problems with sexuality in general and consequently with procreation (Key et al., 2000). Brinch et al. (1988a) found fertility reduced to one-third of the expected numbers, twice the rate of prematurity in the offspring, and a six-fold increase in perinatal mortality in a cohort of 140 former female anorexia nervosa patients. It is of note that none of the 11 males cases had offspring. A two-fold increase in miscarriage rate was reported for a bulimic population in a controlled study by Willis and Rand (1988). Increased miscarriage rate is also reported by Abraham (1998). In some cases females are helped by gynaecologists who stimulate ovulation with clomiphene. There is controversy about this as it could be argued that unless someone is ready to accept a biologically healthy body weight for themselves they may not be able to meet the demands of intimacy and motherhood. There are several reports of highly problematic interactions between an eating-disordered mother and her baby (i.e. irritability and inability to cope with the child's demands while bingeing) (Smith & Hanson, 1972; Fahy & Treasure, 1989; Stein & Fairburn, 1989; van Wezel-Meijer & Wit, 1989; O'Donoghue et al., 1991; Stein et al., 1999, 2001; Jacobi et al., 2001). In addition, Evans and le Grange (1995) found that at least half the children of the 10 eating-disordered mothers they studied were suffering from emotional difficulties.

A rather unexpected finding from the Gothenburg cohort (see Paper III in Wentz, 2000) is that 10 out of 51 AN probands had become mothers at age 24 (the latest follow-up), against only 4 of 51 in the COMP group (a statistically non-significant difference; $p = 0.15$). The mothers in both groups had on average 1.5 children—a figure almost identical to that reported by Brinch et al. (1988a). Mothering behaviour has not yet been reported in studies from the Gothenburg cohort.

The findings by Wentz (2000) on sexual attitudes and sexual behaviour were that 82% of the AN group and 96% of the COMP group had a positive attitude towards sexual matters (this difference is approaching statistical significance—Fisher statistic 3.883; exact p-value 0.09). Furthermore, pleasurable sexual relationships were reported in 67% of the AN group, and in 84% of the COMP group (this figure is also approaching statistical signi-ficance—Fisher statistic 4.241; exact p-value 0.06). However, the AN individuals tended to have fewer and less satisfactory love affairs. The findings on marital status reflect the Scandinavian way of life: in both groups about 10% are married, about 40% are cohabitating (with and without children) and about 50% live alone. There is a statistically significant between-group difference, mainly brought about by 9 in the AN group, as opposed to only 2 in the COMP group, cohabitating with children (Fisher statistic 7.92; exact p-value 0.04).

Intellectual and Vocational Functioning

Several long-term follow-up studies (Tolstrup et al., 1987; Ratnasuria et al., 1991; Crisp et al., 1992; Theander, 1970, 1992, 1996) indicate that a significant number of former eating-disordered patients do not fulfil reasonable expectations, given many probands' apparent resources and family background. More recent studies with a shorter follow-up period cannot be expected to contribute definitive evidence on this issue. A recent Swedish multicentre follow-up study (see Paper I in Wallin, 2000) encompassing five child and adolescent psychiatric treatment centres showed that 3.2 years after the end of treatment 70.3% of 111 female with DSM-III-R anorexia nervosa had a 'good outcome'—they were considered recovered, with a body mass index within the normal range, regular menstruation and normalised eating. Two-thirds of the probands had a global assessment of functioning scale (GAF; APA, 1987) score of 80 or above, indicating good psychological, social and occupational function. No deaths were recorded, but one should keep in mind that the average age at follow-up was 17.3 years. Wentz et al. (2001) report significantly lower mean GAF scores in the AN group ($M = 65$) as opposed to a mean GAF score of 84 in the COMP group. In the AN group there was a significant difference in GAF score between those who had received psychiatric treatment during the period of observation (median GAF score 60) and those who had not (median GAF score 75).

Quality of Life

It follows from the above that a reduced quality can be expectable in many areas of life. Very little eating disorder-specific research has been carried out (e.g. Keilen et al., 1994; Padierna et al., 2000). The latter authors evaluated 196 consecutive patients from an eating disorder outpatient clinic. Compared to 18- to 34-year-old women from the general population, eating-disordered patients were more dysfunctional in all areas measured by the SF-36 (Ware et al., 1993). There were no differences between the diagnostic subgroups. Higher levels of psychopathology (measured by eating attitudes test) were associated with greater impairment on all SF-36 subscales.

Consumer Satisfaction

This is one perspective relevant to quality of life, but it is seldom elucidated. Brinch et al. (1988b) evaluated the child psychiatric probands ($n = 64$) of the Copenhagen Anorexia Nervosa Follow-up Study (Tolstrup et al., 1987) on this dimension. Over 80% were interviewed on average 12.5 years after presentation. One question was: 'When you recall your contact with the department do you think of it as something positive, or negative?' Eleven replies were 'clearly plus somewhat positive', 20 were 'neutral' and 22 'negative'. Outcome status was unrelated to consumer satisfaction, and no difference in consumer satisfaction was detected between inpatients and outpatients. Rosenvinge and Klusmeier (2000) received 321 useful self-report questionnaires out of 600 (54%) that were sent to members of the Norwegian organisations for former and present eating-disordered patients. Combining the response categories 'of some help' and 'extremely helpful' the authors concluded that 57% found treatment helpful. They found no difference in response related to 'expertise', i.e. the satisfaction was similar whether the GP or an 'expert' had provided the treatment. Almost one-third found that family therapy 'made the situation worse'. A remarkable finding is that 57 of 115 persons treated in hospital had been detained against their will, and of these only 34% were satisfied with this legal action in retrospect. The probands suggested the following recommendations for improving eating disorder services: 'improving clinical competence and knowledge of EDs among GPs (17%) and schoolteachers (14%)', 'to provide help to relatives ... ' (12.5%), 'more specialists in eating disorders' (11%), and 'suitable inpatient treatment programmes' (9%). This Norwegian study was a replication of a larger British study (Newton et al., 1993) and the findings are largely similar.

FAMILIAL BURDEN

History: The Family as Cause

Ideas about the role of the family have changed over time, as almost all aspects of our understanding of the eating disorders. A good introduction to this field is found in Part I of the first edition of this handbook (Szmukler et al., 1995), and in Chapter 17 of this book. The seminal works of Selvini-Palazzoli (1974) and Minuchin et al. (1978) stimulated a lot of interest in the role of the family in the aetiology of these disorders. Unfortunately this led to families suffering and experiencing guilt and blame. Some of the concepts of Minuchin et al. (1978) proved elusive (Kog et al., 1987; Dare et al., 1994), whereas other researchers (le Grange et al., 1992b; Papers 2–4 in Wallin, 2000) found some terms (e.g. 'enmeshment', 'adaptability' and 'cohesion') useful.

Present: The Consequences for the Family

As research matured and became less impressionistic the focus shifted towards an understanding of the suffering of all it involved. More reliable tools for family observation were employed, on "normal" as well as "clinical" families, and researchers became aware of the fact that very few normal family functions remain after living with an eating-disordered person for a year or more. The concept of 'expressed emotion' (Leff & Vaughn, 1985) has found its way into eating disorder research (van Furth, 1991; le Grange et al., 1992a). Expressed emotion is a measure of family interaction originally developed in the schizophrenia field. It assesses the attitudes and behaviours that family members express towards their ill relative. The interaction in families of eating-disordered patients is characterised by low levels of expressed emotion, and particularly of criticism, as compared to those found in families of schizophrenic patients (Dare et al., 1994; Goldstein, 1981; le Grange et al., 1992a; Hodes et al., 1999; Szmukler et al., 1985; van Furth et al., 1996). However criticism is higher in families of bulimic patients than in those of anorexic patients; it has been argued that this could be a result of the greater disruption and lesser acceptability of the bulimic symptomatology (Hodes & le Grange, 1993). Higher levels of emotional expression have also been associated to other variables such as older age, laxative use, and presence of comorbidity (van Furth et al., 1996).

The measure of expressed emotion (EE) in relatives is associated with a poor outcome for patients with eating disorders (see Butzlaff & Hooley, 1998). The effect size of the relationship between living with a relative with high EE (critical, hostile or emotionally overinvolved) and poor outcome is 0.51. This is higher than the effect size found for schizophrenia or for mood disorders although this finding must be interpreted with caution as it is based on only one study in anorexia nervosa. One study had some weak evidence which suggested that expressed emotion may be used as a predictor to distinguish differential treatment effectiveness, in that families with high expressed emotion did better with separated rather than conjoint family therapy (Eisler et al., 2000).

Collaborating with the Family

There is an increasing awareness of the necessity of a more positive cooperation with the families. This was brought about in part by the de-institutionalisation movement, and partly by the increased influence of family therapy and family therapy research (Russell et al., 1987; Stierlin & Weber, 1989; Dare et al., 1990; Crisp et al., 1991).

Many treatment centres employ parents' groups as an integral part of the treatment programme (Rose & Garfinkel, 1980; Jeammet & Gorge, 1980; Lewis & MacGuire, 1985). At Rigshospitalet in Copenhagen we noticed a sharp decline in unplanned terminations of treatment after the introduction of group work (a parents' group once a month, and weekly patients' groups—one 'talking group' and one art group) at the department of child psychiatry in 1986 (Tolstrup, 1990).

The principles of psychoeducation for groups of patients (Garner, 1997) and for patients and families (Surgenor et al., 2000) are beginning to be used. Another new development is the introduction of the multi-family group (McFarlane, 1983, 1991) in the treatment of eating disorders (Dare & Eisler, 2000; Scholz & Asen, 2001). See Part IV Treatments of this volume.

Care

Thus, despite the lack of agreement about the role that the family plays in the aetiology and/or maintenance of eating disorders, it is now widely accepted that the family plays an important role both in the formal and in the informal care of the eating-disordered patient. Caring for a relative with a psychiatric disorder can be a rewarding experience. However, it can also have an adverse effect in a number of areas of family functioning. The household roles and routines may change, and the family relationships, social life, leisure activities, career and finances may also be affected; in addition to these, the subjective distress of the carers can also be considerable, and both their physical and emotional health can suffer (Perring et al., 1990). This is what has often been conceptualised as burden of care (Schene, 1990) or, from a more constructive perspective, caregiving distress (Szmukler, 1996).

The diagnosis of an eating disorder may give rise to a wide variety of feelings and emotions in the family, including surprise, disbelief, relief and, most commonly, shame and guilt. The carers' guilt is often reflected in their immediate desire to find out what they did wrong. They may even believe that they should have noticed the patient's difficulties earlier and should have provided help sooner, or maybe that they had delayed seeking professional help for too long (Perednia & Vandereycken, 1989). In addition, among younger patients the parents' loss of control over their son's or daughter's eating may result in their feeling that they have failed to fulfil a basic parenting task (Walford & McCune, 1991; Wood et al., 1998).

Family daily routines are usually disrupted, with mealtimes becoming a battle that causes distress for the entire family. The family eating pattern is often altered in an attempt to help the patient eat. Carers may end up preparing different foods at different times for different family members and meals are no longer a social event, but a struggle that adds to the carer's distress.

The patient's behavioural changes may disrupt the family life (Morandé, 1999). Thus, in addition to the isolation and secretiveness that often surround eating disorders, bulimic patients may engage in antisocial behaviours such as lying, stealing, or substance misuse. Carers may be confused by the ambivalent message they seem to be getting: while on the one hand patients seem to be struggling to achieve independence, on the other they fail to fulfil their own basic needs and are indeed perceived as special and in need of extraordinary care.

Patients may thus become the focus of attention in the family. Slowly, there is less time devoted to friends and social activities, and more to the ill family member. Families may become isolated and believe that what they are going through is a unique and shameful experience. As Perednia and Vandereycken (1989) pointed out, these feelings may in turn be reinforced by relatives and friends who, in an attempt to help, give advice to the carer on what they should and should not do, which can be seen to imply that there is something the carer is not doing right.

In a recent pilot study, which appears to be the first to specifically examine the experience of caregiving in eating disorders, the General Health Questionnaire (GHQ; Goldberg & Hillier, 1979) and the Experience of Care Giving Inventory (ECI; Szmukler et al., 1996) were used to compare the experiences of carers of anorexic in patients with those of carers of people with a psychotic illness (Treasure et al., 2001). Although no differences were found with regard to the positive aspects of caregiving, carers of the anorexic patients reported more difficulties and higher levels of psychological distress. In addition, carers of the anorexic patients were also asked to write about their particular experience of caring. Among other issues, feelings of guilt, shame and loss were mentioned, as well as difficulties in family functioning and in dealing with the patient's difficult behaviours. Treasure and colleagues (2001) concluded that carers experience many difficulties and high levels of psychological distress, and highlighted the need of further research into carers' distress in the area of eating disorders.

Siblings

Although it is very likely that siblings of eating-disordered patients may also feel the strain of the eating disorder, little is known about the extent of the effect that the eating disorder may have on them. Roberto (1988) and Colahan and Senior (1995) in Chapter 13 of the first edition of this handbook, mention that the non-sick sibling(s) get some apparent freedom through a process of de-identification from the sick person. This 'freedom' entails a considerable loss of an appropriate sibling relationship and of parental attention. The existing large body of literature regarding the effects that chronic illnesses may have on the family has shown that, although the incidence of psychiatric disorders is not higher than in the general population, healthy siblings may experience high levels of distress and a wide range of adjustment problems (Sahler et al., 1994). There is a great need of research in order to shed some light into the needs and experiences of siblings, who probably constitute one of the most neglected groups of carers in the eating disorder literature (Moulds et al., 2000).

Parenting

The actual treatment of the eating-disordered patient can also have a deep impact on the family functioning. If the patient's condition is severe enough to require inpatient treatment, this may result in an immediate feeling of relief in the carer; however, the family separation may also add to any existing feelings of guilt, failure, isolation and family fragmentation (Vandereycken, et al., 1989). The recovery from the eating disorder will involve the acquisition of new roles not only for the patient, but also for the remaining family members.

SOCIETAL BURDEN

Burden on Health Care Delivery Systems

The impact of these disorders on the health care delivery systems has been the subject of a few register studies (McKenzie & Joyce, 1992; Nielsen et al., 1996), a single case study (Howlett et al., 1995), and one review (Agras, 2001). Deter and Herzog (1994) found after almost 12 years of follow-up a four-fold increase in the use of both psychiatric and somatic beds. Theander (1970) showed (Table 36, p. 93) that the number of hospital days used by seven cases with 'severe anorexia nervosa at review' ranged from 41 to 1006 (mean 364.4 days; median 295 days). The register study of McKenzie and Joyce (1992) showed a similar variation in length of total inpatient care across all admissions ($n = 190$) for the 112 patients first admitted in 1980 and 1981. Furthermore the admission data showed clear indication of non-Gaussian distribution (range: 1–1380 days; mean 139 days; SD 175 days). First admissions had a mean length of 64 days (SD 46 days; range 1–112 days). Only patients with organic disorders and schizophrenia had a higher cumulative length of inpatient stay over the five years of follow-up. The editorial by Howlett et al. (1995) gives details of a case with a cumulated length of stay of 1161 days over a four-year period—a figure that approaches, but does not exceed, the upper range given in McKenzie and Joyce (1992). The study by Nielsen et al. (1996) investigates data from the Danish nationwide register of psychiatric admissions in the period 1970–1993.

Selected findings from that study are summarised in Figures 11.1, 11.2 and 11.3 below.

In Figure 11.1 please note a highly significant change point (Jones and Dey, 1995) in 1980. See the statistical details in Table 11.2.

In both general psychiatry and adolescent psychiatry the proportion of bed days used by anorexia nervosa patients increased five-fold from 1970 to 1993. The number of available beds in general psychiatry was almost halved in that period. In child psychiatry two highly significant change points (Jones and Dey, 1995) were found in 1981 and 1988. See Figure 11.2 and Table 11.3 below.

We also analysed the proportion of bed days used by anorexia nervosa patients relative to the total number of psychiatric bed days for females under 18 years of age (all psychiatric specialties combined). We found a linear increase from 2% around 1970 to 20% in 1993, a ten-fold increase (see Figure 11.3).

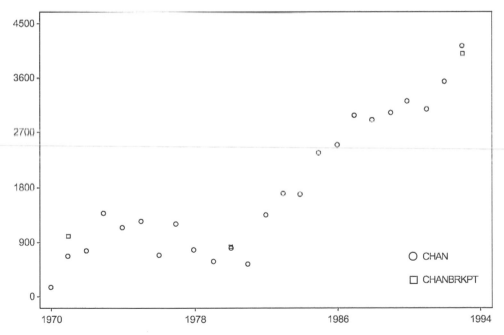

Figure 11.1 Yearly number of child psychiatric bed-days used by AN patients in Denmark 1970–1993. No trend in the period 1971–1980. Note the existence of one significant change point in 1980 where the trend changes into a significant positive value (see text). (*Source*: Nielsen et al., 1996)

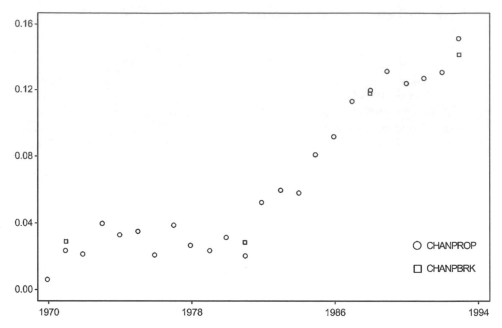

Figure 11.2 Proportion of the the total number of child psychiatric bed-days utilised by AN patients in Denmark 1970–1993. Stable values from 1971 to 1981. Positive trend is evident from 1981 to 1988 where the trend changes into a less positive value. Both change points statistically significant, see Table 11.2. (*Source*: Nielsen et al., 1996)

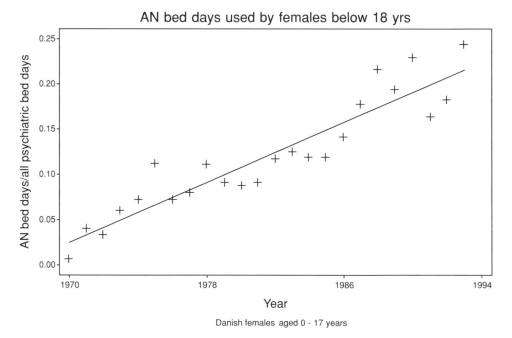

Figure 11.3 Proportion of the total number of psychiatric bed-days utilised by females under 18 years of age, used by AN patients, Denmark 1970–1993. Strong linear trend throughout the period. (*Source*: Nielsen et al., 1996)

Table 11.2 Results of fitting an increasing number of change points to the data in Figure 11.1

| No. of change points | Residual SS | Stepwise F-test | Degrees of freedom | | AIC_C |
			Num.	Den.	
0	5.6545×10^6				315.75
1[a]	1.6125×10^6	23.81	2	19	293.16
2	1.1894×10^6	15.95	4	17	294.10
3	1.0656×10^6	10.77	6	15	301.95

[a] Best model: AIC_C attains minimum

The positive trend in Figure 11.3 is highly significant (t (df 21) = 10.69; p < 0.00001).

Financial Burden

The cost of the bed days used by Danish anorexia nervosa patients in 1993 was estimated (Nielsen et al., 1996) at ~4.6 million euros. Including all eating disorders, this figure rises to ~6.4 million euros. Current prices for non-residents is set to about 240 euros per day for adult psychiatric inpatients, 295 euros for adolescent psychiatric inpatients and from 740 to 1000 euros for child psychiatric inpatients.

Loss of Productive Years

This dimension of societal burden stem from two sources—the time spent too ill to work or study, whether the person is in actual care or not, and from the increased risk of premature death. The first part has been discussed in depth above, and the second part will be discussed below.

PREMATURE DEATH

Mortality in relation to eating disorders has been reviewed recently (Sullivan, 1995; Nielsen et al., 1998; Nielsen, 2001). Below we shall briefly outline what is presently known about mortality for each eating disorder diagnosis.

Table 11.3 Results of fitting an increasing number of change points to the data in Figure 11.2

| No. of change points | Residual SS | Stepwise F-test | Degrees of freedom | | AIC_C |
			Num.	Den.	
0	0.00728377				−155.06
1	0.00188477	27.21	2	19	−179.89
2[a]	0.00102890	25.84	4	17	−185.87
3	0.00098525	15.98	6	15	−176.49

[a] Best model: AIC_C attains minimum

Anorexia Nervosa

Excess mortality is well established (Sullivan, 1995; Møller-Madsen et al., 1996; Nielsen et al., 1998), both in a 10-year perspective and in a longer perspective (Nielsen, 2001). Crude mortality rate is given as 5.9% (178 dead of 3006 AN probands) in Sullivan (1995). Standardised Mortality Ratio (SMR) was 9.6 (95% CI: 7.8 to 11.5) after about 10 years of follow-up and 3.7 (95% CI: 2.8 to 4.7) in four studies with a mean length of follow-up ranging from 20 to 36 years (Nielsen, 2001). Comorbid type 1-diabetes and anorexia nervosa seem to have higher mortality than either disorder alone (Nielsen et al., 2002).

Bulimia Nervosa

A suggested increase in SMR (Nielsen et al., 1998; Nielsen, 2001) seem to be based on a small and highly selected set of studies (Nielsen, submitted). Overviews by Keel and Mitchell (1997) and Nielsen (2001) yielded an overall crude mortality of 0.5% (14 dead of 2692 BN probands). The majority of studies reported no deaths, so selection bias might distort the findings on SMR in BN. Unpublished simulation data by Nielsen (personal communication) indicate that by using information from all 42 available studies instead of just data from the selected studies a highly significant overall aggregate SMR of 7.4 (95% CI: 2.9 to 14.9) changed to a non-significant SMR of 1.56 (95% CI: 0.8 to 2.7). At present the evidence on mortality in bulimia nervosa is inconclusive.

Anorexia Nervosa *and* Bulimia Nervosa

Jørgensen (1992; cited in Nielsen, 2001) report a crude mortality of 20% (5 of 25 probands) after a mean of 12.5 years of follow-up. SMR is 9.9 (95% CI: 3.2 to 23). These findings are almost identical to the overall findings for AN.

Eating Disorder not Otherwise Specified: EDNOS

Jørgensen (1992) found that 4 out of 28 probands (14.3%) had died after 11 years of follow-up. SMR was 2.8 (95% CI: 0.8 to 7.3), a non-significant increase ($p = 0.11$).

CONCLUSION

There seem to be significant differences in mortality from AN to BN (Fisher's exact test $p < 0.0001$). OR for premature death in AN vs BN is 12 (95% CI: 7 to 22.5). More data on BN, EDNOS, BED and atypical and 'subclinical' eating disorders are needed before any firm conclusions can be drawn for these specific eating disorders.

REFERENCES

Abraham, S. (1998) Sexuality and reproduction in bulimia nervosa patients over 10 years. *J. Psychosom. Res.*, **44**, 491–502.

Agras, W.S. (2001) The consequences and costs of the eating disorders. *Psych. Clin. North Am.*, **24**, 371–379.

APA (1987) *Diagnostic and Statistical Manual of Mental Disorders* (3rd edition revised). Wasington, D.C.: American Psychiatric Association.

Brinch, M., Isager, T. & Tolstrup, K. (1988a) Anorexia nervosa and motherhood: reproductional pattern and mothering behavior of 50 women. *Acta Psychiat. Scand.*, **77**, 98–104.

Brinch, M., Isager, T. & Tolstrup, K. (1988b) Patients' evaluation of their former treatment for anorexia nervosa (AN). *Nord. Psykiatr. Tidsskr.*, **42**, 445–448.

Butzlaff, R.L. & Hooley, J.M. (1998) Expressed emotion and psychiatric relapse: a meta-analysis. *Arch. Gen. Psychiat.*, **55**, 547–552.

Colahan, M. & Senior, R. (1995) Family patterns in eating disorders: going round in circles, getting nowhere fasting. In G. Szmukler, C. Dare, & J. Treasure (Eds.), *Handbook of Eating Disorders— Theory, Treatment and Research* (pp. 243–257). Chichester/New York: John Wiley & Sons.

Crisp, A.H., Callendar, J.S., Halek, C. & Hsu, L.K.G. (1992) Long-term mortality in anorexia nervosa. *Br. J. Psychiat.*, **161**, 104–107.

Crisp, A.H., Norton, K. & Gowers, S. (1991) A controlled trial of the effect of therapies aimed at adolescent and family psychopathology in anorexia nervosa. *Br. J. Psychiat.*, **159**, 325–333.

Cytel (2000) *StatXact4.0.1 for Windows. A Statistical Software Program for Exact Nonparametric Inference*. Cambridge MA: CYTEL Software Corporation.

Dare, C., Eisler, I., Russell, G.F.M. & Szmukler, G. (1990) Family therapy for anorexia nervosa: implications from the results of a controlled trial of family and individual therapy. *J. Marital Fam. Ther.*, **16**, 39–57.

Dare, C. & Eisler, I. (2000) A multi-family group day treatment programme for adolescent eating disord. *Eur. Eat. Disord. Rev.*, **8**, 4–18.

Dare, C., le Grange, D., Eisler, I. & Rutherford, J. (1994) Redefining the psychosomatic family: Family process of 26 eating disordered families. *Int. J. Eat. Disord.*, **16**, 211–226.

Deter, H.-C. & Herzog, W. (1994) Anorexia nervosa in a long-term perspective: Results of the Heidelberg-Mannheim study. *Psychosom. Med.*, **56**, 20–27.

Eisler, I., Dare, C., Hodes, M., Russell, G.F.M., Dodge, E. & le Grange, D. (2000) Family therapy for adolescent anorexia nervosa: The results of a controlled comparison of two family interventions. *J. Child Psychol. Psychiat.*, **41**, 727–736.

Evans, J. & le Grange, D. (1995) Body size and parenting in eating disorders: A comparative study of the attitudes of mothers towards their children. *Int. J. Eat. Disord.*, **18**, 39–48.

Fahy, T. & Treasure, J. (1989) Children of mothers with with bulimia nervosa. *Br. Med. J.*, **299**, 1031.

Fernández Aranda, F. & Túron Gil, V. (1998) *Trastornos de la Alimentación. Guia Básica de Tratamiento en Anorexia y Bulimia*. Barcelona: Masson.

Garner, D.M. (1997) Psychoeducational principles in treatment. In Eds *Handbook of Treatment for Eating Disorders* (2nd edition). Garner D.M. & Garfinkel P.E. (Eds), New York: Guilford Press.

Goldberg, D.F. & Hillier, V.F. (1979) A scaled version of the General Health Questionnaire. *Psychol. Med.*, **15**, 139–145.

Goldstein, M.J. (1981) Family factors associated with schizophrenia and anorexia nervosa. *J. Youth Adolesc.*, **10**, 385–405.

Haggiag, T. (2000) The broken jigsaw: A child's perspective. In B. Lask & R. Bryant-Waugh (Eds), *Anorexia Nervosa and Related Eating Disorders in Childhood and adolescence* (2nd edition; pp. 3–10). Hove: Psychology Press.

Hodes, M., Dare, C., Dodge, E. & Eisler, I. (1999) The assessment of expressed emotion in a standardised family interview. *J. Child Psychol. Psychiat.*, **40**, 617–625.

Hodes, M. & le Grange, D. (1993) Expressed emotion in the investigation of eating disorders: a review. *Int. J. Eat. Disord.*, **13**, 279–288.

Howlett, M., McClelland, L. & Crisp, A.H. (1995) The cost of the illness that defies (editorial). *Postgrad. Med. J.*, **71**, 705–706.

Jacobi, C., Agras, W.S. & Hammer, L. (2001) Predicting children's reported eating disturbances at 8 years of age. *J. Am. Acad. Child. Adolesc. Psychiat.*, **40**, 364–372.

Jeammet, P. & Gorge, A. (1980) Une forme de thérapie familiale: Le groupe de parents. *Psychiat. Enfant.*, **23**, 587–636.

Jones, R.H. & Dey, I. (1995) Determining one or more change points. *Chem. Phys. Lipids.*, **76**, 1–6.

Keel, P.K. & Mitchell, J.E. (1997) Outcome in bulimia nervosa. *Am. J. Psychiat.*, **154**, 313–321.

Keilen, M., Treasure, T., Schmidt, U. & Treasure, J. (1994) Quality of life measurements in eating disorders, angina, and transplant candidates: are they comparable?. *J. R. Soc. Med.*, **87**, 441–444.

Keller, M.B., Herzog, D.B., Lavori, P.W. & Bradburn, I.S. (1992) The naturalistic history of bulimia nervosa: Extraordinarily high rates of chronicity, relapse, recurrence, and psychosocial morbidity. *Int. J. Eat. Disord.*, **12**, 1–9.

Key, A., Mason, H. & Bolton, J. (2000) Reproduction and eating disorders: A fruitless union. *Eur. Eat. Disord. Rev.*, **8**, 98–107.

Kog, E., Vertommen, H. & Vandereycken, W. (1987) Minuchin's psychosomatic family model revisited: a concept validation study using a multitrait-multimethod approach. *Fam. Proc.*, **26**, 235–253.

Leff, J. & Vaughn, C.E. (1985) *Expressed Emotion in Families: Its Significance for Mental Illness.* New York: Guilford.

Le Grange, D., Eisler, I., Dare, C. & Hodes, M. (1992a) Family criticism and self starvation: a study of expressed emotion. *J. Fam. Ther.*, **14**, 177–192.

Le Grange, D., Eisler, I., Dare, C. & Russell, G.F.M. (1992b) Evaluation of family treatments in adolescent anorexia nervosa: a pilot study. *Int. J. Eat. Disord.*, **12**, 347–357.

Lewis, H.L. & MacGuire, M.P. (1985) Review of a group for parents of anorexics. *J. Psychiat. Res.*, **19**, 453–458.

MacDonald, M. (2000) Bewildered, blamed and broken-hearted: Parent's views of anorexia nervosa. In B. Lask and R. Bryant-Waugh (Eds), *Anorexia Nervosa and Related Eating Disorders in Childhood and Adolescence* (2nd edition; pp. 11–24). Hove: Psychology Press.

McFarlane, W.R. (1983) Multiple family therapy in schizofrenia. In W.R. McFarlane (Ed.), *Family Therapy in Schizofrenia* (pp. 141–172). New York: Guilford Press.

McFarlane, W.R. (1991) Family psychoeducational treatment. In A.S. Gurman & D.P. Kniskern (Eds), *Handbook of Family Therapy* (Vol. II; pp. 363–395). New York: Brunner/Mazel.

McKenzie, J. & Joyce, P. (1992) Hospitalisation for anorexia nervosa. *Int. J. Eat. Disord.*, **11**, 235–241.

Minuchin, S., Rosman, B.L. & Baker, L. (1978) *Psychosomatic Families: Anorexia Nervosa in Context.* Cambridge, MA: Harvard University Press.

Morandé, G. (1999) *La Anorexia. Cómo Combatir y Prevenir el Miedo a Engordar de las Adolescentes.* Madrid: Colección Vivir Mejor, Ediciones Temas de Hoy.

Morgan, J.F. & Crisp, A.H. (2000) Use of leucotomy for intractable anorexia nervosa: A long-term follow-up study. *Int. J. Eat. Disord.*, **27**, 249–258.

Moulds, M.I., Touyz, S.W., Schotte, D., Beumont, P.J.V., Griffiths, R., Russell, J. & Charles, M. (2000) Perceived expressed emotion in the siblings and parents of hospitalized patients with anorexia nervosa. *Int. J. Eat. Disord.*, **27**, 288–296.

Møller-Madsen, S., Nystrup, J. & Nielsen, S. (1996) Mortality in anorexia nervosa in Denmark during the period 1970–1987. *Acta Psychiatr. Scand.*, **94**, 454–459.

Newton, T., Robinson, P. & Hartley, P. (1993) Treatment for eating disorders in the United Kingdom. Part II. Experiences of treatment: A survey of members of Eating Disorders Association. *Eat. Disord. Rev.*, **1**, 10–21.

Nielsen, S. (2001) Epidemiology and mortality of eating disorders. *Psych. Clin. North Am.*, **24**, 201–214.

Nielsen, S., Emborg, C. & Mølbak, A.G. (2002) Mortality in concurrent type 1 diabetes and anorexia nervosa. *Diabetes Care*, **25**, 309–312.

Nielsen, S., Møller-Madsen, S., Nystrup, J. & Emborg, C. (1996) Utilisation of psychiatric beds in the treatment of ICD-8 eating disorders in Denmark 1970–1993. A register study. Paper read at the AEP Conference in London, July 1996.

Nielsen, S., Møller-Madsen, S., Isager, T., Jørgensen, J., Pagsberg, K. & Theander, S. (1998) Standardized mortality in eating disorders—a quantitative summary of previously published and new evidence. *J. Psychosom. Res.*, **44**, 413–434.

O'Donoghue, G., Treasure, J.L. & Russell, G.F.M. (1991) Eating disorders and motherhood. *Signpost* (newsletter for the Eating Disorders Association), **April**, 1–5.

Padierna, A., Quintana, J.M., Arostegui, I., Gonzalez, N. & Horcajo, M.J. (2000) The health-related quality of life in eating disorders. *Quality of Life Research*, **9**, 667–674.

Perednia, C. & Vandereycken, W. (1989) An explorative study on parenting in eating disorder families. In W. Vandereycken, E. Kog & J. Vanderlinden (Eds), *The Family Approach to Eating Disorders* (pp. 119–146). New York: PMA Publishing Corp.

Perring, C., Twigg, J. & Atkin, K. (1990) *Families Caring for People Diagnosed as Mentally Ill: The Literature Re-examined*. London: HMSO Publications.

Ratnasuriya, R.H., Eisler, I., Szmukler, G.I. & Russell, G.F.M. (1991) Anorexia nervosa: Outcome and prognostic factors after 20 years. *Br. J. Psychiat.*, **158**, 495–502.

Roberto, G. (1988) The vortex: siblings in the eating disordered family. In K.G. Lewis & M.D. Kahn (Eds), *Siblings in Therapy*. New York: W.W. Norton.

Rose, J. & Garfinkel, P.E. (1980) A parent's group in the management of anorexia nervosa. *Can. J. Psychiat.*, **25**, 228–232.

Rosenvinge, J.R. & Klusmeier, A.K. (2000) Treatment of eating disorders from a patient satisfaction perspective: A Norwegian replication of a British study. *Eur. Eat. Disord. Rev.*, **8**, 293–300.

Russell, G.F.M., Szmukler, G., Dare, C. & Eisler, I. (1987) An evaluation of family therapy in anorexia nervosa and bulimia nervosa. *Arch. Gen. Psychiat.*, **44**, 1047–1056.

Sahler, O.J.Z., Roghmann, K.J., Carpenter, P.J., Mulhern, R.K., Dolgin, M.J., Sargent, J.R., Barbarin, O.A., Copeland, D.R. & Zelter, L.K. (1994) Sibling adaptation to childhood cancer collaborative study. Prevalence of sibling distress and definition of adaptation levels. *Develop. Behav. Pediat.*, **15**, 353–366.

Schene, A.H. (1990) Objective and subjective dimensions of family burden. Towards an integrative framework for research. *Soc. Psychiat. Psychiat. Epidemiol.*, **25**, 289–297.

Scholz, M. & Asen, E. (2001) Multiple family therapy with eating disordered adolescents: Concepts and preliminary results. *Eur. Eat. Disord. Rev.*, **9**, 33–42.

Smith, S.M. & Hanson, R. (1972) Failure to thrive and anorexia nervosa. *Postgrad. Med. J.*, **48**, 382–384.

Selvini-Palazzoli, M. (1974) *Self-starvation: From the Intrapsychic to the Transpersonal Approach*. London: Chaucer.

Siegel, S. & Castellan, N.J. (1988) *Nonparametric Statistics for the Behavioral Sciences* (2nd edition). New York: McGraw-Hill.

Stein, A. & Fairburn C.G. (1989) Children of mothers with bulimia nervosa. *Br. Med. J.*, **299**, 777–778.

Stein, A., Woolley, H. & McPherson, K. (1999) Conflict between mothers with eating disorders and their infants during mealtimes. *Br. J. Psychiat.*, **175**, 455–461.

Stein, A., Woolley, H., Murray, L., Cooper, P., Noble, F., Affonso, N. & Fairburn, C.G. (2001) Influence of psychiatric disorder on the controlling behaviour of mothers with 1-year-old infants. A study of women with maternal eating disorders, postnatal depression and a healthy comparison group. *Br. J. Psychiat.*, **179**, 157–162.

Stierlin, H. & Weber, G. (1989) Anorexia nervosa: Lessons from a follow-up study. *Fam. Syst. Med.*, **7**, 120–157.

Sullivan, P.F. (1995) Mortality in anorexia nervosa. *Am. J. Psychiat.*, **152**, 1073–1074.

Surgenor, L.J., Rau, J., Snell, D.L. & Fear, J.L. (2000) Educational needs of eating disorders patients and families. *Eur. Eat. Disord. Rev.*, **8**, 59–66.

Szmukler, G. (1996) From family 'burden' to caregiving. *Psychiat. Bull.*, **20**, 449–451.

Szmukler, G., Burgess, P., Herrman, H., Benson, A., Colusa, S. & Bloch, S. (1996) Caring for relatives with serious mental illness: The development of the Experience of Caregiving Inventory. *Soc. Psychiat. Psychiat. Epidemiol.*, **31**, 137–148.

Szmukler, G., Dare, C. & Treasure, J. (Eds) (1995) *Handbook of Eating Disorders—Theory, Treatment and Research*. Chichester/New York: John Wiley & Sons.

Szmukler, G.I., Eisler, I., Russell, G.F.M. & Dare, C. (1985) Anorexia nervosa, parental 'expressed emotion' and dropping out of treatment. *Br. J. Psychiat.*, **147**, 265–271.

Theander, S. (1970) Anorexia nervosa: a psychiatric investigation of 94 female patients (MD-thesis). *Acta Psychiat., Scand.*, **214** (suppl.), 1–194.

Theander, S. (1992) Chronicity in anorexia nervosa: Results from the Swedish long-term follow-up study. In W. Herzog, H.-C. Deter & W. Vandereycken (Eds), *The Course of Eating Disorders. Long-term Follow-up Studies of Anorexia Nervosa and Bulimia Nervosa* (pp. 214–227). Berlin: Springer.

Theander, S. (1996) Anorexia nervosa with an early onset: Selection, gender, outcome and results of a long-term follow-up study. *J. Youth Adolesc.*, **25**, 419–429.

Tolstrup, K. (1990) Treatment of anorexia nervosa: Current status. In J.G. Simeon & H. Bruce Ferguson (Eds), *Treatment Strategies in Child and Adolescent Psychiatry* (pp. 115–131). New York: Plenum.

Tolstrup, K., Brinch, M., Isager, T., Nielsen, S., Nystrup, J., Severin, B. & Olesen, N.S. (1987) Long-term outcome of 151 cases of anorexia nervosa. The Copenhagen Anorexia Nervosa Follow-up Study. *Acta Psychiat. Scand.*, **71**, 380–387.

Treasure, J., Murphy, T., Todd, G., Gavan, K., Schmidt, U., James, J. & Szmukler, G. (2001) The experience of care giving for severe mental illness: A comparison between anorexia nervosa and psychosis. *Soc. Psychiat. Psychiat. Epidemiol.*, **36**, 343–347.

Vandereycken, W., Vanderlinden, J. & Van Vreckem, E. (1989) The family, the hospitalized patient and the therapeutic team. In W. Vandereycken, E. Kog & J. Vanderlinden (Eds), *The Family Approach to Eating Disorders* (pp. 239–247). New York: PMA Publishing Corp.

Van Furth, E.F. (1991) *Parental expressed emotion and eating disorders*. PhD thesis, University of Utrecht.

Van Furth, E.F., Van Strien, D.C., Martina, L.M.L., Van Son, M.J.M., Hendrickx, J.J.P. & Van Engeland, H. (1996) Expressed emotion and the prediction of outcome in adolescent eating disorders. *Int. J. Eat. Disord.*, **20**, 19–31.

Van Wezel-Meijer, G. & Wit, J.M. (1989) The offspring of mothers with anorexia nervosa: A high-risk group for under nutrition and stunting? *Eur. J. Pediat.*, **149**, 130–135.

Walford, G. & McCune, N. (1991) Long-term outcome in early-onset anorexia nervosa. *Br. J. Psychiat.*, **159**, 383–389.

Wallin, U. (2000) *Anorexia nervosa in adolescence. Course, treatment and family function* (MD thesis). Lund: KFS AB.

Ware, J.E., Snow, K.K., Kosinski, M. & Gandek, B. (1993) *SF-36 Health Survey: Manual and Interpretation Guide*. Boston, MA: The Health Institute, New England Medical Center.

Wentz, E. (2000) *Ten-year outcome of anorexia nervosa with teenage onset* (MD thesis). Göteborg: Kompendiet.

Wentz, E., Gillberg, C., Gillberg, I.C. & Råstam, M. (2001) Ten-year follow-up of adolescent-onset anorexia nervosa: Psychiatric disorders and overall functioning scales. *J. Child Psychol. Psychiat.*, **42**, 613–622.

WHO (1965) *International Classification of Diseases* (8th edition). Geneva: World Health Organization.

Willis, J. & Rand, P. (1988) Pregnancy in bulimic women. *Obstet. Gynecol.*, **71**, 708.

Wood, D., Flower, P. & Black, D. (1998) Should parents take charge of their child's eating disorder? Some preliminary findings and suggestions for future research. *Int. J. Psych. Clin. Pract.*, **2**, 295–301.

CHAPTER 12

Treatment Overview

Janet Treasure

Department of Psychiatry, Thomas Guy House, London, UK

and

Ulrike Schmidt

Eating Disorders Unit, Institute of Psychiatry, London, UK

When we planned the outline of the treatment section for this book we decided to commission a number of chapters which would describe the major therapeutic approaches which have been evaluated in the management of eating disorders, such as cognitive-behavioural therapy (see Chapter 7), family therapy (see Chapter 18) and interpersonal therapy (see Chapter 15). We also wanted to include some of the newer psychological approaches for which there currently is less evidence available, such as cognitive analytical therapy (see Chapter 17) and dialectical behaviour therapy (see Chapter 16) as these have recently generated considerable interest as potentially helpful in the treatment of more complex cases. Likewise, we included separate chapters on different service models, ranging from prevention and early identification models (see Chapters 27 and 28) to day care and inpatient treatment (see Chapters 21 and 22). The advantage of this somewhat artificial separation of topics is to allow in-depth descriptions of different models of therapy, service or intervention, explaining the rationale, theoretical underpinning and the evidence supporting them.

The disadvantage is that for clinical decision making or service planning we need to know much more. We need to know how different treatments or service models compare in terms of their efficacy, acceptability and cost. This involves making a judgement on the quality of the available evidence and taking into account potential harms arising from an intervention or model. We also need to know how treatment efficacy translates into effectiveness in clinical settings outside research studies. Moreover, we need to know how best to sequence interventions and/or whether or how to combine them to maximise efficacy. And perhaps the most difficult question of all is what treatment or intervention or service is the most helpful for a given patient (with a given level of severity, chronicity and comorbidity, motivation and coping skills) at a certain point in time (taking into account previous treatment history and current life circumstances). In order to answer these questions we need to integrate the best research evidence with clinical expertise and patient values (Sackett, 2000).

Handbook of Eating Disorders. Edited by J. Treasure, U. Schmidt and E. van Furth.
© 2003 John Wiley & Sons, Ltd.

Table 12.1 Quality of evidence rating system (adapted from National Health and Medical Research Council, 1995)

Level I	Evidence obtained from a review of all relevant randomised-controlled trials
Level II	Evidence obtained from at least one randomised-controlled trial
Level III	Evidence obtained from controlled trials with randomisation
Level IV	Evidence obtained from multiple time series with or without intervention
Level V	Other evidence (such as opinions or policies of respected authorities based on clinical experience, descriptive studies, or reports of expert committees; summary by writers using a variety of written material; expert testimony; reference to the philosophy of a particular practitioner; reference to personal experience).

HOW GOOD IS THE AVAILABLE EVIDENCE?

Anorexia Nervosa

In anorexia nervosa, while there is a detailed, coherent body of research which documents prognostic features, there is very little in the way of good evidence (Level I or II evidence—for details regarding the system of grading see Table 12.1) about the efficacy of treatment. One systematic review of all randomised-controlled trials which have considered the treatment for anorexia nervosa has been conducted (Schmidt & Treasure, 2001). The protocol for a further, similarly comprehensive systematic review has been registered with the Cochrane library (Hay, personal communication). Additionally, there are two systematic reviews (in German) on psychodynamically informed treatments and on psychological treatments of anorexia nervosa (both conducted by the same group (Herzog & Hartmann, 1997). Moreover, there are other systematic reviews (completed or in progress) that have focused on specific aspects of service provision. One of these has specifically attempted to address the question of how inpatient treatment compares with outpatient or day care treatment (Meads, Gold & Burls, 2001). Another, one protocol registered with the Cochrane library, will be reviewing the evidence for treatments in specialist centres compared to non-specialist settings. Lastly, a systematic review has addressed the question of whether early intervention is important in AN (Schoemaker, 1997). Below we outline the conclusions from our own systematic review which gives the most comprehensive assessment of the available evidence (Schmidt & Treasure, 2001):

- One small randomised-controlled trial (RCT) found limited evidence that various psychotherapies (individual focal therapy, cognitive analytical therapy and family therapy) were more effective than treatment as usual. Three small RCTs found no clear differences between various psychotherapies and dietary advice or treatment as usual. Seven small RCTs found no significant differences between different psychotherapies. However, all the RCTs were small and were unlikely to have been powered to detect a difference between treatments.
- Four RCTs found no evidence that the addition of an antidepressant to treatment improved outcomes.
- Three RCTS found no evidence that cyproheptidine increased weight gain compared with placebo.

- Limited evidence from one small RCT found outpatient treatment to be as effective as inpatient treatment in those individuals not so severely ill as to warrant emergency intervention.
- One small RCT found that zinc was of no benefit in the treatment of anorexia nervosa.
- One small trial found no benefit from cisapride in the treatment of anorexia nervosa.
- We found no good evidence of the effect of hormonal treatment on fracture rates. One small RCT found no effect of oestrogen on bone mineral density.
- We found no RCTs to support the use of neuroleptic medication in anorexia nervosa.

The review also identified wide variability in the quality and reporting of studies, in terms of the CONSORT standards (Moher, Jones & Lepage, 2001; Moher, Schulz & Altman, 2001). Many of the RCTs were small and were unlikely to have been powered to detect a difference between treatments.

Bulimia Nervosa

In contrast to anorexia nervosa, the body of treatment research in bulimia nervosa is much larger and of overall better quality. This has been summarised in several systematic reviews which have either focused on psychological treatments (Hay & Bacaltchuk, 2000), drug treatments (Bacaltchuk, Hay & Mari, 2000) or both (Hay & Bacaltchuk, 2002; Whittal, Agras & Gould, 1999) The main conclusions from these reviews can be summarised as follows: cognitive-behavioural treatment (CBT) is the form of psychological treatment that has been best researched to date. There is evidence that this treatment is at least as effective if not more so than other psychological treatments. CBT delivered in a self-help or guided self-help format seems to be nearly as efficacious as full CBT. There is also evidence supporting the use of interpersonal treatment although this is less strong. Medication is less effective compared to psychological treatments, and the combination of medication and psychological treatment seems to be more effective than either treatment on its own, but with greater drop-out rates. Moreover, there is one systematic review addressing the question of the importance of early intervention (Reas et al., 2001), however, with inconclusive results.

INTEGRATING THE BEST AVAILABLE EVIDENCE ON TREATMENT WITH CLINICAL EXPERTISE AND PATIENT VALUES

Anorexia Nervosa

Connecting information about the best evidence to a specific patient's problem is no easy matter. The patient's problems have to be clearly defined and placed within the context of a clinical risk assessment. This needs to include an assessment both of the acute risk and the longer term prognosis, taking into account physical, psychological, psychosocial, developmental and family variables. Elsewhere we discuss the best approach to foster the exchange of necessary information between the person with the eating disorder and the professional.

Assessment of Short-Term Risk

Decisions on short-term risk involve a combined assessment of the medical risk and the person's psychological capacity to consent to treatment, taking into account the possible resources of motivation and psychosocial support.

Medical risk is critically important in guiding the acute management of anorexia nervosa. In Table 12.1 we illustrate a simple guide given to medical practitioners and other members of the multidisciplinary team as a decision aid when evaluating this acute risk in our Unit. A more detailed account of medical risk is given in Chapters 21 and 22 (day patient/inpatient treatment). Body mass index is a better marker than weight alone as a proxy measure of medical risk but a rigid cut-off point is less good for the extremes of height as the relationship is non-linear. Children have smaller fat stores than mature women and so medical complications occur with less weight loss. Bulimic features or refusal to drink also increase the risk. In turn, these medical markers interact with a variety of clinical and psychosocial factors.

High medical risk is often associated with an impairment of capacity for the consent to treatment. The criteria used to assess capacity are detailed below. Individuals are thought to have capacity if they:

- are able to take in and retain the information material to the decision and understand the likely consequences of having and not having the treatment (thus an acute confusional state may seriously impair the person's ability to process the information)
- believe the information (a compulsive disorder, delusion or phobia may stifle the belief in the information)
- weigh up the information as part of a process of arriving at decisions.

A proportion of patients with anorexia nervosa do not have the capacity to make decisions about their own health and safety and in many countries there is a form of Mental Health Law to allow admission to hospital and treatment in case of this contingency. (See Chapter 22 on inpatient treatment for further details.)

The patients' levels of motivation and their psychosocial resources can act as a buffer against some of these risks. Measuring the early response to treatment, such as a change in weight or the ability to show active involvement in treatment, is a good proxy measure of motivation.

Assessment of Longer Term Risk

In addition to its relevance for the acute risk, body mass index is important in terms of the long-term prognosis whether this is defined as mortality or stages of recovery (Nielsen et al., 1998; Steinhausen, 1995; Steinhausen et al., 2000). Another important risk factor is age, which is a proxy measure of duration of illness. Both age and weight correlate with the standardised mortality rate (Nielsen et al., 1998). Many of the randomised-controlled trials on the treatment of anorexia nervosa see (Schmidt & Treasure, 2001) are, in effect, stratified by age and hence duration of illness. Approximately two-thirds of adolescent patients (typically with illness durations of less than 3 years) have remitted from their illness by two years after outpatient treatment, whereas only one-third of adult patients recover with specialised outpatient treatment.

Choosing Treatments

Let us now consider how one might use the available evidence to choose treatment for an individual patient with anorexia nervosa who may present with a high acute medical risk or a poor long-term prognosis and or a combination of the two.

Anorexia Nervosa with High Acute Medical Risk

Cases with a high medical risk and lack of capacity require intensive care such as that offered by a specialised inpatient unit, although it could be argued that day patient care can also give the requisite level of intensity of care (see Chapter 22). However, given the high mortality associated with this subgroup it would be ethically difficult to conduct a randomised-controlled trial in which either of these treatments was compared to no treatment or even outpatient treatment.

The one systematic review which compared inpatient versus outpatient or day patient treatment of the underweight patient (Meads, Gold & Burls, 2001) only identified one published RCT (Crisp et al., 1991; Gowers et al., 1994) and a second unpublished RCT (Freeman, 1992). The review concludes that for the group of people with anorexia nervosa that is ill enough for inpatient care, *but not severe enough for this to be essential*, outpatient treatment is at least as effective (if not more effective) than inpatient treatment. The italics are our own but are essential. The outcome of *severe malnutrition* is known and there is no doubt that the appropriate treatment is food.

There is some Level III evidence from a large prospective, naturalistic outcome study conducted in Germany where inpatient care is the standard treatment for all forms of eating disorder. The study showed that people with severe anorexia nervosa (i.e. long duration and severe weight loss) benefit from longer admission (Kächele (for the study group MZ-ESS.), 1999; Kaechele et al., 2001)

There is Level IV evidence to suggest that decisions on when to admit and for how long are largely dependent on the model of health service provision used in a particular country. For example, current guidelines of the American Psychiatric Association (2000) suggest that intensive 24-hour care should be used when the BMI drops below 16 kg/m^{2}or when weight falls by 20%. Admissions in the USA tend to be short. In contrast, in the UK some specialist centres have very high thresholds for intensive care (e.g. BMI < 13 kg/m^2). For example, in Leicester only 20% of adult cases require inpatient care (Palmer et al., 2000). The duration of inpatient admissions in specialist units catering for adults in the UK is typically around 3–4 months, whereas admissions to adolescent units are usually longer.

The type of service, skills mix and treatments, which are included in this form of high-intensity care, are discussed in more detail in the chapters on inpatient care (Chapter 22) and day care (Chapter 21).

Medication as an adjunct to inpatient care does not seem to have any clinical benefit in terms of weight gain (Attia et al., 1998). However, there may be a place for the SSRIs to prevent relapse as one small RCT found a better outcome in the group randomised to fluoexetine (Kaye et al., 2001). There is also some Level III evidence from the naturalistic German study that the group on medication after discharge had a lower risk of relapse (Kächele, 1999) The wider role of pharmacotherapy in the outpatient management of anorexia nervosa is an area worthy of further development.

Anorexia Nervosa with a Good Long-Term Prognosis

As mentioned above, this group mainly consists of adolescents with a short duration of illness. There are several RCTs, which suggest that this group of patients can be managed with outpatient treatment. However, even in this good long-term prognostic (adolescent) group approximately 20% will pose an acute medical risk and may need a higher intensity of care such as inpatient treatment (Eisler et al., 2000; Robin et al., 1994). Involvement of the family is beneficial for younger, early onset cases (Eisler et al., 1997; Russell et al., 1987). However, traditional family therapy is not necessary. Indeed parental counselling may be more effective especially if there is high expressed emotion (Eisler et al., 2000). Recent interest is focused on multiple family meetings in a day care setting (Colahan & Robinson, 2001; Dare & Eisler, 2000; Scholtz & Asen, 2001). (Approaches for this group of patients are discussed in more detail in Chapter 18.)

Anorexia Nervosa with a Poor Long-Term Prognosis

In the poorer long-term prognosis (adult) group there is less certainty about the treatments that work. More care (either in terms of intensity or duration) may be most appropriate. However, even in cases with high long-term risk, a case can be made for giving a trial of outpatient therapy, as this is often the most acceptable form of treatment for these patients. One of the advantages of working with anorexia nervosa is that the outcomes can be determined objectively. Thus treatment can be considered to be having an effect if weight loss can be brought to a halt and there is a reduction in some of the other anorexic behaviours.

In adults, one randomised-controlled trial (RCT) found limited evidence that specialised psychotherapies—family therapy (see Chapter 18), focal psychotherapy (see Dare & Crowther, 1995) and cognitive analytical therapy (see Chapter 17)—were more effective than treatment as usual (Dare et al., 2001). However, there is no evidence to suggest that any particular type of specialised psychotherapy produces better outcomes (Treasure et al., 1995; Hall & Crisp 1987). While one small study found no difference in outcome between psychotherapy and dietary management (Hall & Crisp, 1987) another found that standard dietetic management was not accepted by patients as a first-line treatment, with all patients dropping out from this arm of the study (Serfaty, 1999).

Bulimia Nervosa

Bulimia nervosa is an entirely different problem. For the majority of patients the risk to life or limb (for self or others) is not high, the need for admission or even day care is relatively rare and the vast majority of patients can be managed safely as outpatients. There are, however, some particular circumstances in which risk issues need to be identified at assessment and taken into account in planning the patient's care, both in the short and longer term. These concern patients with self-harm and suicidality and other high-risk behaviours; those who are pregnant or have small children; and those with medical comorbidity such as diabetes mellitus. The specific issues involved in planning care for these high-risk groups are discussed later. However, in the absence of major risk issues the main question for clinicians and patients alike is: Is there any evidence that can help us to decide the type of treatment to choose for a particular patient?

Choosing Treatments for the Majority of Patients with Bulimia Nervosa

Although a number of pretreatment prognostic indicators have been identified (Keel & Mitchell, 1997; Vaz, 1998), few of them have been replicated across studies and across different treatments. For example, severity and duration of bulimic symptoms have had an inconsistent link to outcome. There seems to be somewhat more agreement that personality disorder features such as borderline or impulsive features predict a poorer outcome. However, the main conclusion to be drawn with confidence about the literature on pretreatment outcome predictor variables is that none of the ones identified has any major utility in helping us to choose the treatment that is most helpful for a particular patient.

Given the general dearth of information on how to match treatments to patients, it can be argued that the use of a stepped care approach, starting with the least intensive, least costly and least invasive interventions, might generally be best. The obvious candidate for the first step in the treatment of BN is CBT self-help either with or without some therapeutic guidance. However, although there are now a sizeable number of studies on the use of CBT self help, very little work has been done on the additional treatment needs of these patients thereafter or on the potential harms of such an approach as the first step in treatment (e.g. in terms of drop-out or demoralisation of more severely ill patients who may not do well with this approach). There is also some evidence suggesting that those who are more severely symptomatic may do less well with such an approach. On the face of it, medication might also be a good starting point as a Step I intervention. However, the evidence suggests that drug treatments are less acceptable to patients (high drop-out rates, reduced take up, side-effects) and the longer term effects have not been studied in detail.

The Dose of Treatment

Currently most evidence-based packages for the treatment of BN are brief (less than 20 sessions). A meta-analysis of psychotherapy studies of bulimia nervosa up to 1990 found that 36% of the variance in outcome was explained by the number of treatment sessions in combination with relationship orientation (Hartmann, Herzog & Drinkmann, 1992). If a longer duration of treatment yields potentially better outcomes it would be important to know what dose of treatment is needed to treat what proportion of patients presenting and whether there is a point beyond which offering 'more of the same' is unlikely to improve outcome. The work of Ken Howard and others on the dose–effectiveness relationship in psychotherapy addresses precisely these issues (Lutz et al., 2001). In general, the vast majority of people receiving psychotherapy improve quickly within the first few sessions. Those who have failed to improve at an early stage have much less of a chance of getting well and need vastly more input to get well than those who improve early. And there is a point beyond which very few patients get better, if the same sort of treatment is continued. However, the exact shape of this curve of the pattern of improvement varies according to diagnosis, type of symptoms, the presence of interpersonal problems and comorbidity (Lueger, Lutz & Howard, 2000). Unfortunately, at present we don't really know what the shape of this curve looks like for different treatments of bulimia nervosa. What we do know from Level II evidence is that, in CBT treatment, early response within 4 to 6 weeks is an excellent predictor of longer term outcome (Agras et al., 2000) In other words, if someone has failed to show any symptomatic improvement with CBT at an early stage, one seriously needs to consider the reasons for this and think about altering the plan of treatment. However, findings from the German multi-centre TREAT study showed that the response to early intensive treatment (mostly inpatient care) in bulimia nervosa did not predict outcome at 2.5 years and that, in some settings, giving prolonged treatment leads to increasing benefits (Kordy, personal communication).

Intensity of Treatment

Many outpatient treatments for bulimia nervosa offer sessions on a once-weekly basis, but there is evidence that a more intensive outpatient approach is more effective in inducing remission in patients with bulimia nervosa compared with a weekly psychotherapy that uses the same manual-based CBT approach (Mitchell et al., 1993).

SPECIAL CONSIDERATIONS FOR HIGH-RISK GROUPS

Self-harm, Suicidality and Other High-Risk Behaviours

The most commonly identified issues of risk in bulimia nervosa are around repeated self-harm and suicidality. It is rare for bulimic patients to present as acutely suicidal, and indeed the risk of death through suicide in bulimia nervosa patients is low (Keel & Mitchell, 1997; Keel et al., 2000). In those who do present as acutely depressed and suicidal a standard suicide risk assessment should be conducted. Having said that, repeated self-harm through cutting, burning and overdosing is common and occurs in approximately 15–25% of clinic samples (Favaro & Santonastaso, 1997). This is often associated with other high-risk behaviours such as alcohol or substance abuse, unprotected casual sex or repeated shop-lifting. These impulsive features have been found to predict poorer outcome for review (see Vaz, 1998). Therapeutic approaches for the management of these complex cases have been developed (DBT, CAT—see Chapters 16 and 17), and Level II evidence suggests that DBT is promising in those with repeated self-harm (for review see Hawton et al., 2001).

Pregnancy and Motherhood

Sometimes there is also a risk involving the safety of others, especially in cases where the person with bulimia presents during pregnancy or has small children. In the majority of cases bulimic symptoms will improve during pregnancy and for a period of time after the birth, as the woman is aware of needing to eat healthily for the good of the baby (Blais et al., 2000). Nonetheless women with bulimia nervosa are at risk of having small babies, and have higher rates of Caesarian sections and perinatal problems. The risk of postnatal depression is also raised. (Abraham, 1998; Franko et al., 2001). The management of the patient with unremitting bulimic symptoms during pregnancy is difficult. Health professionals can become frustrated, angry and anxious. In this context it is important to remember the principles of motivational interviewing (see Chapter 17) and to try to understand the nature of the woman's inability to ensure the safety of her unborn baby.

Bulimic mothers have been shown to affect the well-being of their young children subtlely through a negative emotional atmosphere and being more intrusive and controlling of their children both at meal and at play times (Stein & Fairburn, 1989; Stein et al., 2001). Thus the risk to the health and safety of the child needs to be thought about, especially if the mother is severely bulimic and/or has severe impulsive features and/or is currently in an abusive relationship.

Comorbid diabetes mellitus

Type I diabetes is associated with an increased risk of developing bulimia nervosa. Typically the development of the diabetes precedes the onset of the bulimia nervosa, which in turn usually arises in the context of other psychiatric disturbance (see Chapter 25 in this book). The risk of severe diabetic complications is raised in diabetics with eating disorders. Standard CBT for bulimia nervosa is not unproblematic for these patients as many of the psycho-educational recommendations of CBT for bulimia nervosa aim to relax control over eating and may conflict with the nutritional advice given to diabetics (Peveler et al., 1993). However, so far no evidence base for treatments for this difficult subgroup exists.

CONCLUSION

Common sense (rather than documented evidence) dictates that patients who present with major risk issues as outlined above are likely to need more intensive and perhaps longer treatments than those without, and of course ongoing risk monitoring and management.

REFERENCES

Abraham, S. (1998) Sexuality and reproduction in bulimia nervosa patients over 10 years. *J. Psychosom. Res.*, **44**, 491–502.

Agras, W.S., Crow, S.J., Halmi, K.A. et al. (2000) Outcome predictors for the cognitive behavior treatment of bulimia nervosa: Data from a multisite study. *Am. J. Psychiat.*, **157**, 1302–1308.

American Psychiatric Association (2000) Practice guideline for the treatment of patients with eating disorders (revision). American Psychiatric Association Work Group on Eating Disorders. *Am. J. Psychiat.*, **157**, 1–39.

Attia, E., Haiman, C., Walsh, B.T. et al. (1998) Does fluoxetine augment the inpatient treatment of anorexia nervosa? *Am. J. Psychiat.*, **155**, 548–551.

Bacaltchuk, J., Hay, P. & Mari, J.J. (2000) Antidepressants versus placebo for the treatment of bulimia nervosa: A systematic review. *Aust. N. Z. J. Psychiat.*, **34**, 310–317.

Blais, M.A., Becker, A.E., Burwell, R.A. et al. (2000) Pregnancy: Outcome and impact on symptomatology in a cohort of eating- disordered women. *Int. J. Eat. Disord.*, **27**, 140–149.

Colahan, M. & Robinson, P. (2001) Multifamily groups in the treatment of young eating disorder adults. *J. Fam. Ther.*

Crisp, A.H., Norton, K., Gowers, S. et al. (1991) A controlled study of the effect of therapies aimed at adolescent and family psychopathology in anorexia nervosa. *Br. J. Psychiat.*, **159**, 325–333.

Dare, C. & Crowther, C. (1995) Psychodynamic models of eating disorders. In G. Szmukler, C. Dare & J. Treasure (Eds), *Handbook of Eating Disorders: Theory, Treatment and Research* (pp. 125–141). Chichester: John Wiley & Sons.

Dare, C. & Eisler, I. (2000) A multi-family group day treatment for adolescent eating disorder. *Eur. Eat. Disord. Rev.*, **8**, 4–18.

Dare, C., Eisler, I., Russell, G. et al. (2001) Psychological therapies for adults with anorexia nervosa: randomised controlled trial of out-patient treatments. *Br. J. Psychiat.*, **178**, 216–221.

Eisler, I., Dare, C., Hodes, M. et al. (2000) Family therapy for adolescent anorexia nervosa: the results of a controlled comparison of two family interventions [In Process Citation]. *J. Child Psychol. Psychiat.*, **41**, 727–736.

Eisler, I., Dare, C., Russell, G.F. et al. (1997) Family and individual therapy in anorexia nervosa. A 5-year follow-up. *Arch. Gen. Psychiat.*, **54**, 1025–1030.

Favaro, A. and Santonastaso, P. (1997) Suicidality in eating disorders: Clinical and psychological correlates. *Acta Psychiat. Scand.*, **95**, 508–514.

Franko, D.L., Blais, M.A., Becker, A.E. et al. (2001) Pregnancy complications and neonatal outcomes in women with eating disorders. *Am. J. Psychiat.*, **158**, 1461–1466.

Freeman, C. (1992) Day patient treatment for anorexia nervosa 6,1:3–8. *Br. Rev. Bulimia Anorexia Nervosa*, **6**, 3–8.

Gowers, S., Norton, K., Halek, C. et al. (1994) Outcome of outpatient psychotherapy in a random allocation treatment study of anorexia nervosa. *Int. J. Eat. Disord.*, **15**, 165–177.

Hall, A. & Crisp, A.H. (1987) Brief psychotherapy in the treatment of anorexia nervosa. Outcome at one year. *Br. J. Psychiat.*, **151**, 185–191.

Hartmann, A., Herzog, T. & Drinkmann, A. (1992) Psychotherapy of bulimia nervosa: What is effective? A meta-analysis. *J. Psychosom. Res.*, **36**, 159–167.

Hawton, K., Townsend, E., Arensma, E., Gunnell, D., Hazell, P., House, A. & van Heeringen, K. (2001) Psychosocial and pharmacological treatments for deliberate selfharm. *Cochrane Rev.*

Hay, P. & Bacaltchuk, J. (2000) Psychotherapy for bulimia nervosa and binging (Cochrane Review). *Cochrane. Database. Syst. Rev.*, **4**, CD000562.

Hay, P. & Bacaltchuk, J. (2002) Bulimia nervosa. *Clinical Evidence*, 642–651.

Herzog, T. & Hartmann, A. (1997) Psychoanalytically oriented treatment of anorexia nervosa. Methodology-related critical review of the literature using meta-analysis methods. *Psychother. Psychosom. Med. Psychol.*, **47**, 299–315.

Kaechele, H., Kordy, H., Richard, M. et al. (2001) Therapy amount and outcome of inpatient psychodynamic treatment of eating disorders in Germany. Data from a multicentre study. *Psychother. Res.*, **11**, 239.

Kaye, W.H., Nagata, T., Weltzin, T.E. et al. (2001) Double-blind placebo-controlled administration of fluoxetine in restricting- and restricting-purging-type anorexia nervosa. *Biol. Psychiat.*, **49**, 644–652.

Kächele, H. (for the study group MZ-ESS) (1999) Eine multizentrische Studie zu Aufwand und Erfolg bei psychodynamischer Therapie von Eßstörungen. *Psychother. med. Psychol.*, **49**, 100–108.

Keel, P.K. & Mitchell, J.E. (1997) Outcome in bulimia nervosa. *Am. J. Psychiat.*, **154**, 313–321.

Keel, P.K., Mitchell, J.E., Miller, K.B. et al. (2000) Social adjustment over 10 years following diagnosis with bulimia nervosa. *Int. J. Eat. Disord.*, **27**, 21–28.

Lueger, R.J., Lutz, W. & Howard, K.I. (2000) The predicted and observed course of psychotherapy for anxiety and mood disorders. *J. Nerv. Ment. Dis.*, **188**, 127–134.

Lutz, W., Lowry, J., Kopta, S.M. et al. (2001) Prediction of dose-response relations based on patient characteristics. *J. Clin. Psychol.*, **57**, 889–900.

Meads, C., Gold, L. & Burls, A. (2001) How effective is outpatient care compared to inpatient care for the treatment of anorexia nervosa? A Systematic review. *Eur. Eat. Disord. Rev.*, **9**, 229–241.

Mitchell, J.E., Pyle, R.L., Pomeroy, C. et al. (1993) Cognitive-behavioral group psychotherapy of bulimia nervosa: Importance of logistical variables. *Int. J. Eat. Disord.*, **14**, 277–287.

Moher, D., Jones, A. & Lepage, L. (2001) Use of the CONSORT statement and quality of reports of randomized trials: A comparative before-and-after evaluation. *JAMA*, **285**, 1992–1995.

Moher, D., Schulz, K.F. & Altman, D.G. (2001) The CONSORT statement: Revised recommendations for improving the quality of reports of parallel group randomized trials. *Med. Res. Methodol.*, **1**, 2.

Nielsen, S., Moller-Madsen, S., Isager, T. (1998) Standardized mortality in eating disorders—a quantitative summary of previously published and new evidence. *J. Psychosom. Res.*, **44**, 413–434.

Palmer, R.L., Gatwood, N., Black, S. & Park S. (2000) Anorexia nervosa: Service consumption and outcome of local patients. *Psychiat. Bull.* **24**, 298–300.

Peveler, R.C., Davies, B.A., Mayou, R.A. et al. (1993) Self-care behaviour and blood glucose control in young adults with type 1 diabetes mellitus. *Diabet. Med.*, **10**, 74–80.

Reas, D.L., Schoemaker, C., Zipfel, S. et al. (2001) Prognostic value of duration of illness and early intervention in bulimia nervosa: A systematic review of the outcome literature. *Int. J. Eat. Disord.*, **30**, 1–10.

Robin, A.L., Siegel, P.T., Koepke, T. et al. (1994) Family therapy versus individual therapy for adolescent females with anorexia nervosa. *J. Dev. Behav. Pediatr.*, **15**, 111–116.

Russell, G.F., Szmukler, G.I., Dare, C. et al. (1987) An evaluation of family therapy in anorexia nervosa and bulimia nervosa. *Arch. Gen. Psychiat.*, **44**, 1047–1056.

Sackett, D.L. (2000) The fall of 'clinical research' and the rise of 'clinical-practice research'. *Clin. Invest. Med.*, **23**, 331–333.

Schmidt, U.H. & Treasure, J.L. (2001) A systematic review of treatments for anorexia nervosa. pp 0–5.

Schoemaker, C. (1997) Does early intervention improve the prognosis in anorexia nervosa? A systematic review of the treatment outcome literature. *Int. J. eat. Disord.*, **21**, 1–15.

Scholtz, M. & Asen, E. (2001) Multiple family therapy with eating disordered adolescents. *Eur. Eat. Disord. Rev.*, **9**, 33–42.

Serfaty, M.A. (1999) Cognitive therapy versus dietary counselling in the outpatient treatment of anorexia nervosa: Effects of the treatment phase. *Eur. Eat. Disord. Rev.*, **7**, 334–350.

Stein, A. & Fairburn, C.G. (1989) Children of mothers with bulimia nervosa [see comments]. *Br. Med. J.*, **299**, 777–778.

Stein, A., Woolley, H., Murray, L. et al. (2001) Influence of psychiatric disorder on the controlling behaviour of mothers with 1-year-old infants. A study of women with maternal eating disorder, postnatal depression and a healthy comparison group. *Br. J. Psychiat.*, **179**, 157–162.

Steinhausen, H.-C. (1995) The course and outcome of anorexia nervosa. In K. Brownell & C.G. Fairburn (Eds), *Eating Disorders and obesity: A Comprehensive Handbook.* (pp. 234–237). New York: Guilford Press.

Steinhausen, H.C., Boyadjieva, S., Grigoroiu-Serbanescu, M. et al. (2000) A transcultural outcome study of adolescent eating disorders. *Acta Psychiat. Scand.*, **101**, 60–66.

Treasure, J., Todd, G., Brolly, M. et al. (1995) A pilot study of a randomised trial of cognitive analytical therapy vs educational behavioral therapy for adult anorexia nervosa. *Behav. Res. Ther.*, **33**, 363–367.

Turnbull, S.J., Schmidt, U., Troop, N.A. et al. (1997) Predictors of outcome for two treatments for bulimia nervosa: Short and long-term. *Int. J. Eat. Disord.*, **21**, 17–22.

Vaz, F.J. (1998) Outcome of bulimia nervosa: Prognostic indicators. *J. Psychosom. Res.*, **45**, 391–400.

Whittal, M.L., Agras, W.S. & Gould, R.A. (1999) Bulimia nervosa: A meta analysis of psychosocial and pharmacological treatments. *Behav. Ther.*, **30**, 117–135.

CHAPTER 13

Assessment and Motivation

Janet Treasure

Department of Psychiatry, Thomas Guy House, London, UK

and

Beatrice Bauer

Università Luigi Bocconi, Milan, Italy

SUMMARY

This chapter discusses the treatment of anorexia nervosa and bulimia nervosa under the following headings:

- Why do we need to consider readiness to change?
- Models of behaviour change
- Tailoring treatment
- How to measure readiness, importance and confidence
- Benefits of motivational strategies
- Limitations of motivational strategies
- The use of information to enhance motivation
- Implementing motivational strategies for patients with eating disorders

WHY DO WE NEED TO CONSIDER READINESS TO CHANGE?

Several assumptions underlie the agenda of the assessment interview. The first is that the client has decided that he or she wants something, a diagnosis or treatment. The health provider works on the usual premise that he or she needs to give information or practical help. To a degree these assumptions are true but there may be disparities between the perceived goals of the two partners. For example, when a women with anorexia nervosa walks into the room she may not want a diagnosis and/or treatment; instead she may be coming to stop her parents or her school nagging her to attend. A woman with bulimia nervosa may want help to stop her bingeing but she may not be prepared to do anything that may jeopardise the solutions for weight control that she has hit upon. An obese person may

Handbook of Eating Disorders. Edited by J. Treasure, U. Schmidt and E. van Furth.
© 2003 John Wiley & Sons, Ltd.

show a very high motivation to lose weight in order to avoid orthopaedic surgery or social stigmatisation. The health provider needs to find the balance between what may be wanted and what his expertise indicates may be needed and realistic. The concept of readiness to change can be a helpful structure to frame this intervention.

MODELS OF BEHAVIOUR CHANGE

The transtheoretical model of change of Prochaska and DiClemente (1984; Velicer, et al., 1996; Prochaska & Velicer, 1997a), is one model that recognises that people do not make a simple black or white decision to change their behaviour. Rather it assumes that there is a gradual process, divided into phases. The transtheoretical model (TTM) posits that health behaviour change involves progress through six stages of change: precontemplation, contemplation, preparation, action, maintenance and termination. In addition this transtheoretical model conceptualises psychotherapeutic change in three dimensions: firstly, the 'stages of change', or the *when* of change, and readiness to work towards a goal; secondly, the 'processes' of change, the *how* of change, and activities brought into play to modify thinking, behaviour or affect in relation to a problem; thirdly, the 'level' of change, the *what* of change, or domain in which change will occur. The other elements of the model comprise decisional balance (the balance of pros and cons (Prochaska & Norcross, 1994; O'Connell & Velicer, 1988), self-efficacy (Temoshok et al., 1985) and temptations. There is some evidence that these factors predict movement through the stages (Prochaska & Velicer, 1997b; Schwab et al., 2000). An analysis of the probability of movement among the stages revealed three findings in support of TTM: the probability of forward movement was greater than that of backward movement; the probability of moving to adjacent stages was greater than the probability of two-stage progression (Martin Velicer & Fava, 1996); and movement through the stages is not always linear . However, the concept of circularity or perhaps a spiral may be a better analogy to describe the movement; that is, people can progress from one stage to another or drop back to an earlier stage before stable change occurs. In the case of smoking, on average people enter the change cycle three times. Basic research has generated a rule of thumb for at-risk populations: 40% in precontemplation, 40% in contemplation, and 20% in preparation (Prochaska & Velicer, 1997a).

This model, however, has had its critics (Davidson, 1998): some argue for a continuum rather a series of stages; others question the processes that have been defined.

TAILORING TREATMENTS

The transtheoretical model has been used to tailor interventions. A computer program—an expert system (Velicer et al., 1993—measures the key elements of the TTM using validated questionnaires (Prochaska et al., 1988; Prochaska & Norcross, 1994; Velicer et al., 1990). From the results of this, an individual's stage, process use, decisional balance, self-efficacy and temptation scores are integrated to predict movement to the next stage (Velicer & Plummer, 1998). This is then given as feedback to the individual along with information about possible strategies, which may facilitate change. Such a system was found to be more effective in smoking cessation in adults than a stage-based manual alone (Velicer et al., 1999). This system has also been tested in adolescents where the results are less conclusive (Pallonen et al., 1998).

The transtheoretical model has been successfully applied to a variety of health behaviours (Prochaska et al., 1994; Nigg et al., 1999), including smoking cessation (Prochaska et al., 1993), weight control (Rossi et al., 1995; Jeffery et al., 1999), fat intake (Greene et al., 1999; Hargreaves et al., 1999), quitting cocaine (Prochaska et al., 1994), exercise acquisition (Marcus et al., 1992; Biddle & Fox, 1998) and the take-up of screening for mammography (Prochaska et al., 1994; Rakowski & Clark, 1998). An adaptation of TTM was proposed to predict engagement in outpatient psychotherapy (Derisley & Reynolds, 2000).

The distribution of individuals across the stages of change can provide a valuable tool for designing health intervention (Laforge et al., 1999; Jeffery et al., 1999; Abrams et al., 2000). Five independent studies from the USA and Australia examined the pattern of distribution across the stages of change for five behavioural risk factors (smoking, low fat diet, regular exercise, reducing stress, and losing weight). These studies showed that the single-item survey measures of the stage of change are readily applicable to population studies and appear to provide important information about the population characteristics linked to readiness to modify behavioural risk factors (Laforge et al., 1999).

We have examined whether the transtheoretical model can be applied to patients with eating disorders (Ward et al., 1996; Blake et al., 1997) as some preliminary work suggested that it could be applied to women with bulimia nervosa (Stanton et al., 1986). We adapted the measurement instruments devised by Prochaska's Rhode Island group to measure stage of change, processes of change and decisional balance (Rossi et al., 1995). We gave these instruments to patients with anorexia nervosa before their first assessment at our eating disorder clinic. Their primary care physicians referred most of the cases although many had had treatment before. We found that less than 50% of patients with anorexia nervosa were in action; 20% were in precontemplationi; and 30% in contemplation (Blake et al., 1997). We also found that the majority of patients with anorexia nervosa in our inpatient unit were in precontemplation or contemplation (Ward et al., 1996). We also examined the processes of change that our patients were currently using. As would be predicted from the model, those in precontemplation used very few processes of change. On the decisional balance questionnaire the precontemplation group endorsed few positive reasons for change and had a greater number of negative expectations from change. In contrast the group who were in action were using strategies such as self-liberation, self re-evaluation and dramatic relief significantly more. The group in action had a greater number of positive reasons for change and a small decrease in the reasons not to change. Patients undergoing treatment on our inpatient unit showed a similar profile (Ward et al., 1996).

We concluded from this research that the transtheoretical approach did seem to be applicable to patients with eating disorders, and studies from other authors support our findings (e.g. Vitousek et al., 1998).

We have also used this model in examining the treatment of obese patients. Fifty-six obese treatment-seekers (41 female and 15 male, age 44 ± 6.7 yr, BMI kg/m^2 37 ± 6.2, $M \pm SD$) were randomly assigned to two treatment groups after clinical assessment. The first group was assigned to an individualised six-month weight loss treatment integrated by the use of a manual. The second group started with a self-help manual for motivation enhancement (four weeks), according to the key construct of the TTM, before beginning the weight loss treatment offered to Group 1.

The reasons for seeking weight loss treatment were similar in the two groups: high pressure from family physicians to improve health (65%), family pressure (22%), difficulties in becoming pregnant (4%) and recent onset of diabetes mellitus and/or hypertension (9%).

All the participants had experienced repeated weight loss treatments during the last 10 years (very low calorie diet, drugs, etc.), while failing to maintain results.

At assessment, no statistically significant differences between the two groups were found in the distribution of individuals among the six stages of change: 17% in precontemplation, 60% in contemplation, 21% in determination and 2% in action. After the end of the first month we observed a large difference between the two groups in the distribution of patients among the six stages of change: in Group 1, at the end of one month of treatment, 15% of patients were in precontemplation, 64% in contemplation, and 21% in action; in Group 2, at the end of the motivation enhancement self-help manual, no patient was in precontemplation, 40% were in contemplation, 52% in determination and 8% in action. At the end of the second month, the difference in drop-out rate was statistically significant between Group 1 (17%) and Group 2 (0%) and these results were confirmed at the end of the treatment programme (Group 1, 27%; Group 2, 3%). Our preliminary findings (not yet published) at follow-up after three and six months have shown a statistically significant ($p < 0.001$) difference in weight loss achieved, between Group 1 (M ± SD respectively 3.7 ± 1.2% and 4.8 ± 3.1% of initial weight) and Group 2 (M ± SD respectively 6.3 ± 1.7% and 8.3.1 ± 3.6%).

The transtheoretical approach seems to offer promising results in the assessment and treatment of obesity, but our data also show that motivation needs to be monitored and enhanced repeatedly; to be successful the process needs time, so to increase motivation means to procrastinate action, even in severe cases of obesity, in favour of more realistic expectations and goals and better compliance with treatment at a later stage. In contrast, pushing patients towards action splits the patient groups into patients who still resist and those more prone to change, and seems to favour a much greater drop-out rate.

Several other models include stages in behaviour change. For example, Weinstein (1988) distinguished five stages in the precaution adoption process; De Vreis and Backbier (1994) describe change in attitudes, social influence and self-efficacy through motivational stages in their Attitude, Social Influence, and Efficacy (ASE) model. Most models of health behaviour change include the idea that there are two components to readiness to change. These are importance/conviction and confidence/self efficacy (Keller & Kemp White 1997; Rollnick 1998; Rollnick et al., 1999) encapsulated in the adage 'ready, willing and able'. *Importance* relates to why change is needed, and this concept includes the personal values and expectations that will accrue from change; confidence relates to a person's belief that he or she has the ability to master behaviour change.

For example, someone with anorexia nervosa may see no reason why she should change. She may not want to eat. However, she may be confident that if she decided to change she could do it. She is sceptical about change. This contrasts with an obese person, who may be very ready to change but may have no confidence that she can instigate or maintain the steps that are necessary, which causes frustration.

READINESS, IMPORTANCE AND CONFIDENCE

Several methods have been used to measure readiness to change.

In 1990 Brownell developed the Diet Readiness Test (DRT) widely used in the obese population as a means of measuring a person's readiness to begin a weight loss programme (Brownell, 1990). This test has had his critics (Carlson et al., 1994; Pendleton et al., 1998; Fontaine & Wiersema, 1999), who found no relationship between the DRT total score and weight loss, suggesting that DRT has no factorial or predictive validity in a clinical population.

There is a 32-item self-report measure called the URICA (University of Rhode Island Change Assessment) which can be used as a continuous change assessment scale (McConnaughty et al., 1989). We used this instrument in our pilot work with eating-disordered patients (Treasure & Ward, 1997). This measure is not designed to allocate individuals to different stages; algorithms have been designed to do this job, and in our preliminary work we adapted algorithms used for other behaviours (Blake et al., 1997). We have developed this approach further and have evaluated a variety of different algorithms for use in anorexia nervosa (Jordan et al., 2002). The most useful algorithm was one which assessed the readiness to stop restricting/bingeing and purging. However, Davidson (1998) has criticised the methodology used for stage allocation. In particular he notes that the chronological cut-offs are arbitrary.

Several groups have also developed different measures specifically for people with eating disorders. Rieger and colleagues have developed a self-report measure (Rieger et al., 2000), and Geller (2002) has introduced an interview measure based on the eating disorder examination (see also Geller et al., 2001).

We would caution against the use of sophisticated measures of motivation to change symptomatic behaviours that clinicians have used for diagnostic purposes as these may bear no relevance for the client herself. Readiness to change is a dynamic concept that can vary within and between sessions, therefore it is not reasonable to spend a great deal of effort measuring readiness accurately at one point in time. One reason driving this interest in measurement was the idea that it might be useful to match treatment to the readiness to change. It can be argued that every clinician should be able to rapidly evaluate these concepts within the session whatever the agenda of the moment. Linear visual analogue scales, which measure readiness and the dimensions of importance and confidence on a continuum, are useful tools (Keller & Kemp White, 1997; Rollnick et al., 1999). The issues of importance and confidence can then be addressed in more detail.

We have also found that it is useful to have an additional scale that measures how eager others (i.e. those who are close to the respondent) are to see change. This highlights the social context and its impact upon change. For example, if there is a great disparity between the readiness of family members for change and the individual's readiness to change, this can cause conflict. In the case of anorexia nervosa the family may be insistent upon change and this may lead to an 'anti-motivational' environment in which there is confrontation and high negative expressed emotion. In obesity family members may be *more* or *less* motivated

Table 13.1 Questions to explore 'Importance'

What would have to happen for it to become more important for you to change?
You have given yourself x on the scale. What would need to happen before your score to move from x to 10?
What stops you moving from x to 10?
What are the things that you take into account which make you give yourself as high a score as you do?
What are the good things about x behaviour? What are some of the less good things about x behaviour?
What concerns do you have about x behaviour?
If you were to change, what would it be like?

Table 13.2   Questions to explore 'Confidence'

What would make you more confident about making these changes?
Why have you given yourself as high a score as you have on 'confidence'?
How could you go up higher so that your score goes from x to y?
How can I or anybody else help you to succeed?
Is there anything that you found helpful in any previous attempts to change?
What have you learned from the way things went wrong last time you tried?
If you decided to change, what might your options be? Do you know of any ways that have
   worked for other people?
What are the practical things you would need to do to achieve this goal? Are they achievable?
Is there anything you can think of that would make you feel more confident?

for change than the individual concerned. In a group of 111 obese patients seeking weight loss treatment, 54% admitted to registering for treatment because of strong family pressure, but considered themselves unable to carry out the programme (Caputo et al., 1993). We can also find obese patients who get highly involved in changing their lifestyle but with their family members *resenting* the time they spend away from home in the gym doing exercise and *opposed* to sharing healthier but less palatable food during meals. A husband may suspect that his wife may become more attractive to other men and be tempted to infidelity. This emphasises the need for a broad exploration of the psychosocial environment.

BENEFITS OF MOTIVATIONAL STRATEGIES TO FACILITATE CHANGE

As we discussed above, the transtheoretical model can be used to tailor self-help interventions (DiClemente & Prochaska 1998; Butler et al., 1999). It may also help to guide the therapist as to how to make the content of sessions congruent with the client's readiness to change. Motivational interviewing is a useful technique which can help to move an individual closer to the position where he or she is ready to change (Miller & Rollnick, 1991) and was used in conjunction with the TTM to examine the concept of psychotherapy matching. The results were somewhat disappointing (Project MATCH Research Group, 1997) in that the motivational enhancement therapy only improved the 15-month outcome in the less-motivated group whereas cognitive-behavioural therapy did relatively better in the short term. There was a large difference in the dose effect where motivational treatment was given in 4 sessions contrasting with 12 sessions of CBT. In a study of bulimia nervosa, comparing 4 sessions of MET with 4 sessions of CBT, there was no difference in the short-term outcome (Treasure et al., 1999).

Thus there is little evidence to support the simple model that patients in the precontemplation and contemplation stages should be given motivational treatment and that those in the action stage should have a skill-based intervention. On the other hand, there is increasing evidence that motivational interviewing is a cost-effective technique to facilitate change. Miller and his group at Albuquerque found that the style of the therapist's interaction was a critical component in facilitating change (for a review of this literature, see Miller, 1995, 1998) as the therapist's expectancies for patient change can influence the patient's compliance and outcomes. Therapists also differ markedly in their retention rates. When patients are randomly assigned to therapists, their outcomes differ substantially depending upon the therapist to whom they are assigned. By changing their therapeutic style between confrontation and client centred, therapists can drive client resistance rates up and down. This non-confrontational style contrasts with the model suggesting that people with alcohol abuse and dependence are resistant because of personality factors that must be broken down. Miller developed a short intervention ('the drinker's check-up') which operationalised some of the factors found to be useful to increase motivation. This check-up with motivational feedback was compared with standard confrontation. The outcome, in terms of drinking one year later, was worse in the group of patients who were given feedback from the drinker's check-up in a confrontational manner (Miller et al., 1993). In a further study it was found that if the motivational feedback of the drinker's check-up was given as an initial intervention prior to entry into an inpatient clinic, patients were found to have a better outcome. The therapists for this group reported that their patients had participated more fully in treatment and appeared to be more motivated (Brown & Miller, 1993; Bien et al., 1993).

Motivational interviewing has been found to be effective in several forms of behaviour change. The effectiveness has been demonstrated in randomised-controlled trials for alcohol abuse (Project Match Research Group, 1997; Heather, 1996; Gentilello et al., 1999; Handmaker et al., 1999; Senft, 1997), smoking (Butler et al., 1999; Colby, 1998), exercise acquisition (Harland et al., 1999), weight loss (Smith et al., 1997), and fat intake (Mhurchu et al., 1998).

Motivational interviewing is a directive, client-centred counselling style that aims to help patients to explore and resolve their ambivalence about behaviour change. It combines elements of style (warmth and empathy) with technique (e.g. key questions and focused reflective listening). One of the principles of this approach is that head to head conflict is unhelpful. What is more helpful is a collaborative, shoulder to shoulder relationship in which therapist and patient tackle the problem together. The patient's motivation to change is enhanced if there is a gentle process of negotiation in which the patient, not the practitioner, articulates the benefits and costs involved.

Rollnick and Miller (1995) were able to define specific and trainable therapist behaviours that they felt led to a better therapeutic alliance and better outcome (Rollnick & Miller, 1995) A good motivational therapist was able to:

(1) understand the other person's frame of reference
(2) express acceptance and affirmation
(3) filter the patient's thoughts so that motivational statements are amplified and non-motivational statements are dampened
(4) elicit self-motivational statements from the client: expressions of problem recognition, concern, desire, intention to change and ability to change
(5) match processes to the stage of change, and ensure that they do not jump ahead of the client
(6) affirm the client's freedom of choice and self-direction.

(1), (3), (4) and (5) cover issues relating to the transtheoretical model of change. They explore the reasons that sustain the behaviour and aim to help the client to shift the decisional balance of pros and cons into the direction of change. Items (2) and (6) cover the interpersonal aspects of the relationship. The therapist needs to provide a warm, optimistic setting and take a subordinate, non-powerful position by emphasising the client's autonomy and right to choose.

The fable about the sun and the wind is a rather nice metaphor about the spirit of motivational interviewing.

> The Sun and the Wind were having a dispute as to who was the most powerful. They saw a man walking along and they challenged each other about which of them would be most successful at getting the man to remove his coat. The Wind started first and blew up a huge gale, the coat flapped but the man only closed all his buttons and tightened up his belt. The Sun tried next and shone brightly making the man sweat. He proceeded to take off his coat.

Therapists need to model themselves on the Sun! Motivational interviewing seems to work by reducing negativity. A low level of resistance predicted change (Miller et al., 1993) and appeared to have a more powerful effect than increasing the number of positive statements about change. Resistance often occurs in the presence of confrontation. Confrontation occurs with low frequency in 5–15% of therapy sessions and unless this behaviour is reduced there is little change in client outcome. In some settings, such as probation/legal services, it is difficult to train workers to reduce the amount of confrontation.

LIMITATIONS OF MOTIVATIONAL STRATEGIES

There are some problems in using the standard techniques of motivational interviewing for patients with eating disorders. The style involves an equal balance of power between client and therapist. Patients with anorexia nervosa are often young adolescents and they may find this approach novel and somewhat alien and threatening. They tend to be wary and suspicious and are sensitised to being misunderstood. In this context the therapist may need to give more structure to the session and not use too many open questions, especially at the beginning. The therapist will be judged during the information exchange process as to whether he or she understands the problem.

One of the tenets of motivational interviewing is that the client is able to choose whether he or she will decide to change. In the case of anorexia nervosa there has to be a limit to this freedom because it is physiologically impossible to make the choice not to eat for longer than 2–3 months, and in most countries there is mental heath legislation limiting the individuals freedom to make such a choice. One way to use this within a motivational framework is for the therapist to bring in the concept of a higher power or authority, which constrains the action of both therapist and patients. This means that the therapist does not have to use confrontation or coercion directly but indirectly through society's rules. For example:

> The rules of good medical practice for the management of anorexia nervosa are to weigh the patient at every session. You can see [from this chart] that your weight is now in the range in which we have to recommend inpatient treatment.

The other problem is that families are intimately involved in the management of anorexia nervosa and they may be much more ready to see change than is your patient. It can be difficult to balance these different agendas. Families are well into action and the danger is that this can merely lead to high levels of confrontation at home which counteracts the non-confrontational approach of the clinic. We have therefore developed an intervention which involves teaching the family the basic principles of motivational interviewing. This approach overlaps with the techniques used to reduce expressed emotion in families. In addition to developing communication skills the family are also taught how to reinforce non eating disorder behaviour and to remove attention from eating disorder behaviour. These techniques are based upon Community Reinforcement Approach—CRAFT (Meyers & Smith, 1995; Meyers et al., 1998).

THE USE OF INFORMATION TO ENHANCE MOTIVATION

Most patients consider themselves well informed about how to solve eating and weight problems. They mainly gather their information from the media (American talk . . . , 1997), but such information can be either wrong, exaggerated or tendentious (Johnson, 1998). Correct information can make a difference in motivation, but this mostly depends on how data and knowledge are offered to patients. The information may lead to new ways of thinking, feeling or acting but may also deaden or destroy whatever curiosity or motivation already exists.

To increase motivation and at the same time reduce treatment costs, most institutions use written material, tapes or lectures for patients, organised in sessions of psychoeducation. These sessions, usually in a group format or in the form of written material or manuals, are mostly standardised, making it easy for less skilled therapists to inform patients about health, eating and weight problems, etc. The importance of delivering this information in the change process has been largely overvalued, and the belief in its intrinsic power to change behaviour has fostered a massive use of it. Often the term psychoeducation is misleading in terms of its pedagogical content.

Lecturing patients gives a sense of control and efficient time management, but inevitably means that the patients' participation will be low—they will be mostly passive. The strength of a lecture is in presenting an example and first of all in generating a stimulus, not in shaping a response. It solicits further work, but does not in itself demand it (Wilkinson, 1984). The therapist in most cases must try to awaken a curiosity that is dormant as a consequence of long periods of strenuously defending one's position in precontemplation and contemplation from excessive stigmatisation. The insights that come from a lecture or an unsupervised reading, however intense, are often random experiences; they cannot duplicate the careful sequence and sustained growth of ideas fostered by a dialogue. In a motivation enhancement session the patient is not only required to absorb notions but is also asked to develop critical thinking skills while answering questions, discussing different positions or searching for solutions. Such probing often reveals fundamental gaps in knowledge and information or misconceptions that must be pointed out before they can be corrected. Once acquired, the new information and conceptual categories need to be related to an untidy reality. The patient must create a link between a well-organised number of facts and a less-structured personal experience. Only by encouraging critical thinking and experimenting can a patient be helped to fully grasp the complexity of a notion and to understand what that notion means when adapted to his or her specific problem (Ventura & Bauer, 1999). This is in contrast to the temptation to reduce the complexity of any human condition and change process to simplistic categories of good and bad, black and white (so typical of mass media information about eating and weight) that may encourage a false confidence and hinder real change.

The discussion during a group treatment, and the white space in a manual where patients are asked to register observations, allow therapists to follow the growth in this direction and monitor the change process through the different stages. The therapist can then orient the treatment according to the information that seems to be needed.

When asking an eating-disordered patient to consider entering a treatment programme, it may be of great importance to explain the why and how of treatment and offer information about the way we want her or him to eat. If we ask the patient to simply increase the amount of daily calories and to trust the therapist that a certain amount of calories are needed for recovery, or if we force the patient to eat whatever food is presented with the explanation that he or she is for the moment unable to decide autonomously, we may be reducing the complexity of this difficult task too much. Furthermore, such a therapeutic attitude may also be inconsistent with the empowerment principle of motivational interviewing. Asking an obese patient to reconsider losing weight after many failures by simply presenting another diet may not increase the confidence level. Introducing new information, like the satiating effect of food, or the psychobiological background of our eating behaviour and the way to control it, may be more inspiring and stimulate enough interest to try a new solution (Ventura & Bauer, 1999).

We should always consider whether the explanation we offer for the causes of past failures or future success stimulates passive compliance or an increase in patient autonomy. The General Causality Orientation Scale was used to test the autonomy orientation in 128 patients in a six-month long (very low calorie) weight-loss program with a 23-month follow-up. Analyses confirmed that participants whose motivation for weight loss was more autonomous would attend the programme more regularly, lose more weight during the programme, and maintain their lower weight after, as measured at follow-up (William et al., 1996). In a smoking cessation programme the movement through the different stages of motivation was influenced favourably by an experientially oriented process, and less favourably when the process was more oriented toward environmental events, such as dramatic relief and social liberation (Prochaska et al., 1985).

The level of involvement offered by a therapist and accepted by a patient may also vary because of cultural factors (Bauer et al., 1999). Even if treatment programmes of different countries share the same treatment principles, some aspects of therapy such as as power differentials, distance and participation are strongly culture-specific and need to be considered when defining the level of involvement and collaboration we initially expect from a patient. In treatment, it may, therefore, be easier to ask Scandinavian participants to express their point of view or their ambivalence in front of the group than in a Mediterranean or Latin American culture, and it may take more time in some cultures to ask patients to do homework than in others. These difficulties, however, should not be an excuse to think that patients don't need to be involved in a decision process.

REFERENCES

Abrams, D.B., Herzog, T.A., Emmons, K.M. & Linnan, L. (2000) Stages of change versus addiction: a replication and extension. *Nicotine Tob. Res.*, **2** (3), 223–229.

American talk about science and medical news: The National Health Report. (1997) New York: Roper Starch Worldwide.

Bauer, B., Katzman, M. & Ventura, M. (1999) Recognizing and working with cultural differences in patient support program. *Int. J. Obes.*, **23** (Suppl. 5), S58.

Biddle, S.J. & Fox, K.R. (1998) Motivation for physical activity and weight management. *Int. J. Obes. Relat. Metab. Disord.*, **22** (Suppl. 2), S39–S47.

Bien, T.H., Miller, W.R. & Tonigan, J.S. (1993) Brief interventions for alcohol problems: A review. *Addiction*, **88**, 315–335.

Blake, W., Turnbull, S. & Treasure, J. (1997) Stages and processes of change in eating disorders. Implications for therapy. *Clin. Psychol. Psychother.*, **4**, 186–191.

Brown, K.L. & Miller, W. (1993) Impact of motivational interviewing on participation and outcome in residential alcoholism treatment. *Psychology of Addictive Behaviours*, **7**, 238–245.

Brownell, K. (1990) Dieting readiness. *Weight Control Digest*, **1**, 5–10.

Butler, C.C., Rollnick, S., Cohen, D., Russell, I., Bachmann, M. & Stott, N. (1999) Motivational counselling versus brief advice for smokers in general practice: A randomised trial. *Br. J. Gen. Prac.*, **49**, 611–616.

Caputo, G., Arovini, C., Cuzzolaro, M. (1993) Restriction and disinhibition in obesity: Biological, behavioural or psychiatric symptoms? In M. Cuzzolaro, G. Caputo, V. Guidetti, G. Ripa di Meana (Eds), *Proceedings of the 2nd International Rome Symposium on Eating Disorders*, pp. 316–322.

Carlson, S., Sonnenberg, L.M. & Cummings, S. (1994) Dieting readiness test predicts completion in a short-term weight loss program. *J. Am. Diet. Assoc.*, **94**, 552–554.

Colby, S.M., Monti, P.M., Barnett, N.P., Rohsenow, D.J., Weissman, K., Spirito, A., Woolard, R.H. & Lewander, W.J. (1998) Brief motivational interviewing in a hospital setting for adolescent smoking: A preliminary study. *J. Consult. Clin. Psychol.*, **66**, 574–578.

Davidson, R. (1998) The transtheoretical model. A critical overview. In W. Miller & N. Heather (Eds), *Treating Addictive Behaviours* (2nd edn; pp. 25–38). New York: Plenum Press.

Derisley, J. & Reynolds, S. (2000) The transtheoretical stages of change as a predictor of premature termination, attendance and alliance in psychotherapy. *Br. J. Clin. Psychol.*, **39** (Pt 4), 371–382.

De Vries, H. & Backbier, E. (1994) Self-efficacy as an important determinant of quitting among pregnant women who smoke the Ø pattern. *Preventive Medicine*, **23**, 167–174.

DiClemente, C. & Prochaska, J.O. (1998) Towards a comprehensive, transtheoretical model of change. In W. Miller & N. Heather (Eds), *Treating Addictive Behaviours* (pp. 3–24) New York: Plenum Press.

Fontaine, K.R. & Wiersema, L. (1999) Dieting readiness test fails to predict enrollment in a weight loss program. *J. Am. Diet. Assoc.*, **99**, 664.

Geller, J. (2002) Estimating readiness for change in anorexia nervosa: Comparing clients, clinicians, and research assessors. *Int. J. Eat. Disord.*, **31**, 251–260.

Geller, J., Cockell, S.J. & Drab, D.L. (2001) Assessing readiness for change in the eating disorders: The psychometric properties of the readiness and motivation interview. *Psychol. Assess.*, **13**, 189–198.

Gentilello, L.M., Rivara, F.P., Donovan, D.M., Jurkovich, G.J., Daranciang, E., Dunn, C.W., Villaveces, A., Copass, M. & Ries, R.R. (1999) Alcohol interventions in a trauma center as a means of reducing the risk of injury recurrence. *Ann. & Surg.*, **230**, 473–480.

Greene, G.W., Rossi, S.R., Rossi, J.S., Velicer, W.F., Fava, J.L. & Prochaska, J.O. (1999) Dietary applications of the stages of change model. *J. Am. Diet. Assoc.*, **99**, 673–678.

Handmaker, N.S., Miller, W.R. & Manicke, M. (1999) Findings of a pilot study of motivational interviewing with pregnant drinkers. *J. Stud. Alcohol.*, **60**, 285–287.

Hargreaves, M.K., Schlundt, D.G., Buchowski, M.S., Hardy, R.E., Rossi, S.R. & Rossi, J.S. (1999) Stages of change and the intake of dietary fat in African-American women: Improving stage assignment using the Eating Styles Questionnaire. *J. Am. Diet. Assoc.*, **99**, 1392–1399.

Harland, J., White, M., Drinkwater, C., Chinn, D., Farr, L. & Howel, D. (1999) The Newcastle exercise project: A randomised controlled trial of methods to promote physical activity in primary care. *Br. Med. J.*, **319**, 828–832.

Heather, N. (1996) The public health and brief interventions for excessive alcohol consumption: The British experience. *Addict. Behav.*, **21**, 857–868.

Jeffery, R.W. & French, S.A. (1999) Preventing weight gain in adults: The pound of prevention study. *Am. J. Public Health*, **89**, 747–751.

Johnson, T. (1998) Shattuck lecture — medicine and the media *N. Engl. J. Med.*, **339**, 87–92.

Jordan, T. (in press) Measurement. *Int. J. Eat. Disord.*

Keller, V.F. & Kemp-White, M. (1997) Choices and changes: A new model for influencing patient health behavior. *J. Clin. Outcome Management*, **4**, 33–36.

Laforge, R.G., Rossi, J.S., Prochaska, J.O., Velicer, W.F., Levesque, D.A. & McHorney, C.A. (1999) Stage of regular exercise and health-related quality of life. *Prev. Med.*, **28**, 349–360.

Marcus, B.H., Banspach, S.W., Lefebvre, R.C., Rossi, J.S., Carleton, R.A. & Abrams, D.B. (1992) Using the stages of change model to increase the adoption of physical activity among community participants. *Am. J. Health Promot.*, **6**, 424–429.

Martin, R.A., Velicer, W.F. & Fava, J.L. (1996) Latent transition analysis to the stages of change for smoking cessation. *Addict. Behav.*, **21**, 67–80.

McConnaughy, E., DiClemente, C.C., Prochaska, J.O. & Velicer, W.F. (1989) Stages of change in psychotherapy. *Psychotherapy*, **26**, 494–503.

Meyers, R.J. & Smith, J.E. (1995) *Clinical Guide to Alcohol Treatment: The Community Reinforcement Approach*. New York: Guilford Press.

Meyers, R.J., Smith, J.E. & Miller, E.J. (1998) Working through the concerned significant other. In W.R. Miller & N. Heather (Eds), *Treating Addictive Behaviours* (2nd edn; pp. 149–161). New York: Plenum Press.

Mhurchu, C.N., Margetts, B.M. & Speller, V. (1998) Randomized clinical trial comparing the effectiveness of two dietary interventions for patients with hyperlipidaemia. *Clin. Sci. (Lond.)*, **95**, 479–487.

Miller, W.R., Benefield, R.G. & Tonigan, J.S. (1993) Enhancing motivation for change in problem drinking: A controlled comparison of two therapist styles. *J. Consult. Clin. Psychol.*, **61**, 455–461.

Miller, W. (1995) Increasing Motivation for change. In M. Hetherington & W. Miller (Eds), *Handbook of Alcoholism Treatment Approaches* (2nd edn). Needham Heights. MA: Allyn & Bacon.

Miller, W.R. (1998) Enhancing motivation to change. In W.R. Miller & N. Heather (Eds), *Treating Addictive Behaviours: Processes of change* (2nd edn; pp. 121–132). New York: Plenum Press.

Miller, W. & Rollnick, S. (1991) *Motivational Interviewing: Preparing People to Change Addictive Behaviour*. New York: Guilford.

Nigg, C.R., Burbank, P.M., Padula, C., Dufresne, R., Rossi, J.S., Velicer, W.F., Laforge, R.G. & Prochaska, J.O. (1999) Stages of change across ten health risk behaviors for older adults. *Gerontologist*, **39**, 473–482.

O'Connell, D. & Velicer, W.F. (1988) A decisional balance measure and the stages of change model for weight loss. *Int. J. Addict.*, **23**, 729–750.

Pallonen, U.E., Prochaska, J.O., Velicer, W.F., Prokhorov, A.V. & Smith, N.F. (1998) Stages of acquisition and cessation for adolescent smoking: an empirical integration. *Addict. Behav.*, **23**, 303–324.

Pendleton, V.R., Poston, W.S., Goodrick, G.K., Willems, E.P., Swank, P.R., Kimball, K.T. & Foreyt, J.P. (1998) The predictive validity of the Diet Readiness Test in a clinical population. *Int. J. Eat. Disord.*, **24**, 363–369.

Prochaska, J.O. & Norcross, J. (1994) *Systems of Psychotherapy: A Transtheoretical Analysis* (3rd edn). Pacific Grove California: Brooks /Cole Publishing Company.

Prochaska, J.O., DiClemente, C.C., Velicer, W.F., Ginpil, S. & Norcross, J.C. (1985) Predicting change in smoking status for self-changers. *Addict. Behav.*, **10**, 395–406.

Prochaska, J.O., Diclemente, C.C., Velicer, W.F. & Rossi, J.S. (1993). Standardized, individualized, interactive, and personalized self-help programs for smoking cessation. *Health Psychol.*, **12**, 399–405.

Prochaska, J.O. & Velicer, W.F. (1997a) Misinterpretations and misapplications of the transtheoretical model. *Am. J. Health Promot.*, **12**, 11–12.

Prochaska, J.O. & Velicer, W.F. (1997b) The transtheoretical model of health behavior change. *Am. J. Health Promot.*, **12**, 38–48.

Prochaska, J.O., Velicer, W.F., DiClemente, C.C. & Fava, J. (1988) Measuring processes of change: applications to the cessation of smoking. *J. Consult. Clin. Psychol.*, **56**, 520–528.

Prochaska, J. & DiClemente, C. (1984) *The Transtheoretical Approach: Crossing the Traditional Boundaries of Therapy*. Homewood, IL: Dow Jones Irwen.

Project MATCH Research Group (1997) Matching alcoholism treatments to client heterogeneity: Project MATCH posttreatment drinking outcomes. *J. Stud. Alcohol.*, **58**, 7–29.

Rakowski, W. & Clark, M.A. (1998) Do groups of women aged 50 to 75 match the national average mammography rate? *Am. J. Prev. Med.*, **15**, 187–197.

Rieger, E., Touyz, S., Schotte, D., Beumont, P., Russell, J., Clarke, S., Kohn, M. & Griffiths, R. (2000) Development of an instrument to assess readiness to recover in anorexia nervosa [In Process Citation]. *Int. J. Eat. Disord.*, **28**, 387–396.

Rollnick, S. (1998) Readiness, importance and confidence: Critical conditions of change in treatment. In W.R. Miller & N. Heather (Eds), *Treating Addictive Behaviours* (2nd edn; pp. 49–60). New York: Plenum Press.

Rollnick, S., Mason, P. & Butler, C. (1999) *Health Behaviour Change*. Edinburgh: Churchill Livingstone.

Rollnick, S. & Miller, W.R. (1995) What is motivational interviewing? *Behav. Cognit. Psychother.*, **23**, 325–335.

Rossi, J., Rossi, S., Velicer, W. & Prochaska, J. (1995) Motivational readiness to control weight. In D. Allison (Ed.), *Handbook of Assessment Methods for Eating Behaviours and Weight Related Problems* (pp. 387–430). London: Sage Publications.

Schwab, M., Schmidt, K., Witte, H. & Abrams, M. (2000) Investigation of nonlinear ECG changes during spontaneous sleep state changes and cortical arousal in fetal sheep. *Cereb. Cortex*, **10**, 142–148.

Senft, R.A., Polen, M.R., Freeborn, D.K. & Hollis, J.F. (1997) Brief intervention in a primary care setting for hazardous drinkers. *Am. J. Prev. Med.*, **13**, 464–470.

Smith, K.A., Fairburn, C.G. & Cowen, P.J. (1997) Relapse of depression after rapid depletion of tryptophan [see comments]. *Lancet*, **349**, 915–919.

Stanton, A.L., Rebert, W.M. & Zinn, L.M. (1986) Self change in bulimia: A preliminary study. *Int. J. Eat. Disord.*, **5**, 917–924.

Temoshok, L., Heller, B.W., Sagebiel, R.W., Blois, M.S., Sweet, D.M., DiClemente, R.J. & Gold, M.L. (1985) The relationship of psychosocial factors to prognostic indicators in cutaneous malignant melanoma. *J. Psychosom. Res.*, **29**, 139–153.

Treasure, J.L. & Ward, A. (1997) A practical guide to the use of motivational interviewing in anorexia nervosa. *Eur. Eat. Disord. Rev.*, **5**, 102–114.

Treasure, J.L., Katzman, M., Schmidt, U., Troop, N., Todd, G. & de Silva, P. (1999) Engagement and outcome in the treatment of bulimia nervosa: First phase of a sequential design comparing motivation enhancement therapy and cognitive behavioural therapy. *Behav. Res. Ther.*, **37**, 405–418.

Velicer, W.F., DiClemente, C.C., Rossi, J.S. & Prochaska, J.O. (1990) Relapse situations and self-efficacy: An integrative model. *Addict. Behav.*, **15**, 271–283.

Velicer, W.F. & Plummer, B.A. (1998) Time series analysis in historiometry: A comment on Simonton. *J. Pers.*, **66**, 477–486.

Velicer, W.F., Prochaska, J.O., Bellis, J.M., DiClemente, C.C., Rossi, J.S., Fava, J.L. & Steiger, J.H. (1993) An expert system intervention for smoking cessation. *Addict. Behav.*, **18**, 269–290.

Velicer, W.F., Prochaska, J.O., Fava, J.L., Laforge, R.G. & Rossi, J.S. (1999) Interactive versus noninteractive interventions and dose-response relationships for stage-matched smoking cessation programs in a managed care setting. *Health Psychol.*, **18**, 21–28.

Velicer, W.F., Rossi, J.S., DiClemente, C.C. & Prochaska, J.O. (1996) A criterion measurement model for health behavior change. *Addict. Behav.*, **21**, 555–584.

Ventura, M. & Bauer, B. (1999) Empowerment of women with purging-type bulimia nervosa through nutritional rehabilitation. *Eat. Weight Disord.*, **4**, 55–62.

Vitousek, K., Watson, S. & Wilson, G.T. (1998) Enhancing motivation for change in treatment-resistant eating disorders. *Clin. Psychol. Rev.*, **18**, 391–420.

Ward, A., Ward, A., Troop, N., Todd, G. & Treasure, J. (1996) To change or not to change—'how' is the question? *Br. J. Med. Psychol.*, **69** (Pt 2), 139–146.

Weinstein, N.D., Rothman, A.J. & Sutton, S.R. (1998) Stage theories of health behavior: Conceptual and methodological issues. *Health Psychol.*, **17**, 290–299.

Wilkinson, J. (1984) *The Art and Craft of Teaching*. Cambridge, MA: Harvard Press.

Williams, G.C., Grow, V.M., Freedman, Z.R., Ryan, R.M. & Deci, E.L. (1996) Motivational predictors of weight loss and weight-loss maintenance. *J. Pers. Soc. Psychol.*, **70**, 115–126.

CHAPTER 14

Cognitive-Behavioural Treatments

Glenn Waller

*Department of Psychiatry, St. George's Hospital Medical School,
University of London, London, UK
and*

Helen Kennerley

Department of Clinical Psychology, Warneford Hospital, Oxford, UK

Cognitive-behaviour therapy (CBT) has been the most exhaustively researched form of treatment for the eating disorders. The focus in this literature has largely been on work with bulimia nervosa and binge eating disorder, and there is substantially less evidence regarding its long-term efficacy with anorexia nervosa or obesity. In polls of specialist clinicians' preferred mode of practice (e.g. Mussell et al., 2000), many report that their therapeutic work with the eating disorders involves some elements of CBT. However, it is clear that many clinicians who describe their work as CBT are not actually practising within a recognisable CBT framework—either using protocol-driven therapies in the appropriate manner or using cognitive-behavioural theory to drive individualised assessment, formulation and treatment. Therefore, we think that it is important that we should start by defining our central terms.

WHAT IS COGNITIVE-BEHAVIOURAL THERAPY?

Any cognitive therapy recognises the reciprocal role of cognitions (mental representations in the form of thoughts or images), affect and behaviour. The way we think affects the way we feel and behave, which then affect the way we think. Simply put, if our cognitions or interpretations are valid, we feel and react appropriately: if our interpretations are skewed or distorted, we feel and behave in ways that do not reflect reality and can cause difficulties.

Cognitive-behavioural therapy was developed by A.T. Beck throughout the 1960s and 1970s, and is one of several cognitive therapies that emerged at this time. Beck's cognitive therapy emphasises the understanding of the cognitive element of a problem, and stresses

Handbook of Eating Disorders. Edited by J. Treasure, U. Schmidt and E. van Furth.
© 2003 John Wiley & Sons, Ltd.

the powerful role of behaviour in maintaining and changing the way that we think and feel. In his original description of emotional problems, Beck recognised that biology and external environment impact on our well-being. He noted that readily accessible cognitions and observable behaviours were underpinned by fundamental belief systems (or schemata). However, 'classic' CBT was evolved to exploit the fact that much radical change (impacting on deeper structures) can be effected through active work at the level of current cognitions and behaviours.

The aim of CBT is first to help the client to identify the cognitions that underpin problem behaviours and/or emotional states, and then to help that person to reappraise these cognitions. Insights that are evolved in this way are then 'tested', in that the client is encouraged to check out the veracity of the new belief. Insights are developed using guided discovery (or 'Socratic questioning'), often combined with self-monitoring in the form of 'daily thought records'. Clients are taught the technique of appraising automatic thoughts and images, identifying cognitive distortions and substituting statements (or images) that carry greater validity and which do not promote the problem affect/behaviour. Clients are also encouraged to use structured data collection and behavioural tests to evaluate all new perspectives.

Although clearly structured, CBT has always been more than a protocol-driven therapy that can be applied to particular psychological problems. Beck et al. (1979) emphasise the importance of developing and using the therapeutic relationship (p. 27) and stress the need to tailor the therapy to meet the needs of the individual (p. 45). Beck also warns the therapist against being overly didactic or interpretative, encouraging genuine 'collaborative empiricism' instead (p. 6).

The model underpinning this form of psychological therapy provides such a general heuristic for understanding human learning, behaviour, emotion and information processing that it is almost impossible to encounter a client who does not 'fit' the model. However, this does not mean that every patient can benefit from CBT. Safran and Segal (1990) have identified certain client characteristics as being necessary if CBT is to match the style and needs of the client. Those characteristics include: an ability to access relevant cognitions; an awareness of and ability to differentiate emotional states; acceptance of the cognitive rationale for treatment; acceptance of personal responsibility for change; and the ability to form a real 'working alliance' with the therapist. This means that there will be clients who are better suited to other forms of psychotherapy (such as analytical, systemic, social and pharmacological approaches), and it is the task of the assessing therapist to consider the most appropriate intervention.

How is CBT Relevant to the Eating Disorders?

Anyone who works with clients with eating disorders will appreciate the interacting role of cognitions, feelings and behaviours in the maintenance of the problem, whatever the presentation. Figure 14.1 shows examples of some of the ways in which cognition and affect are related to the behavioural manifestations of the eating disorders. In principle, given this interaction of cognition, emotion and behaviour, CBT should be an appropriate intervention for a range of eating disorders, enabling the client to identify prominent maintaining cycles in their problem and, ultimately, to break these cycles through cognitive and behavioural

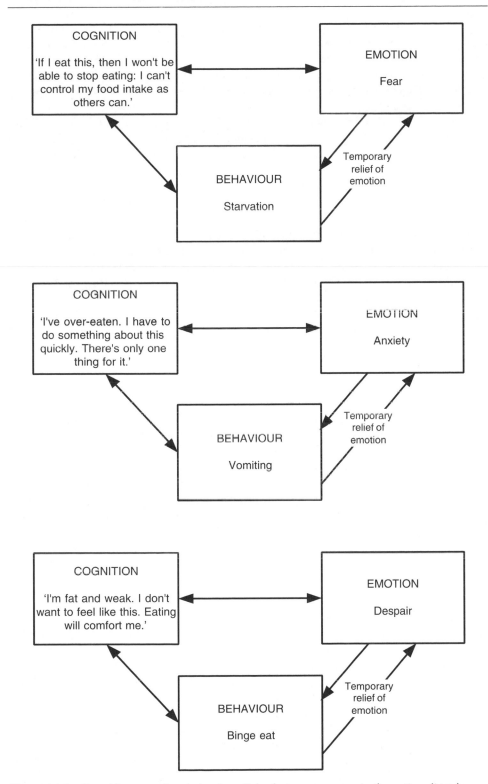

Figure 14.1   Cognition–emotion–behaviour links that are common in the eating disorders

methods. As outlined above, the practical utility of CBT is such cases will be limited if the client is not able to identify with the model and collaborate with the methods. Given the nature of some aspects of eating pathology (outlined below), it will be important to consider ways of helping some clients to overcome their difficulties with CBT (e.g. recognition of emotion, or coping with abandonment fears and control issues for long enough to develop a working relationship).

Cognitive-behavioural theory has been used as the basis for treatment programmes for eating disorders since the early 1980s. Garner and Bemis (1982) suggested a CBT approach to the management of anorexia nervosa, while Fairburn (1981; Fairburn & Cooper, 1989) developed a similar programme for bulimia nervosa. More recently, various clinicians and researchers have extended this work to address binge eating disorder, and others (e.g. Agras et al., 1997) have discussed the application of CBT methods as part of the broad-based approach that is most likely to be effective in working with obesity. However, CBT is still relatively underdeveloped in work with children and adolescents with eating disorders. In addition, CBT in this field has been limited by a focus on diagnosable cases, with inevitable difficulties of generalisability to the many atypical cases. Nevertheless, understanding the principles of CBT should enable us to develop a focus for understanding, and perhaps managing, problem eating behaviours.

THE DEVELOPMENT AND NATURE OF EXISTING FORMS OF CBT IN THE EATING DISORDERS

CBT for eating disorders has been developed over the past two decades, and is the most extensively researched and validated psychological therapy used with the eating disorders. Its scientific base means that such research has employed strong designs and allows for clear conclusions. However, that same scientific approach means that we need to be critical of our models and the treatments that have been developed from them. Therefore, the review that follows will consider the strengths and weaknesses of CBT as it stands. In order to understand the added value of introducing the cognitive element, we will begin by considering the earlier literature regarding the impact of treatments based solely on behavioural principles.

Behavioural Treatments

There is a long tradition of using behavioural methods in working with *anorexia nervosa*, particularly to reinforce weight gain or address weight 'phobias'. In the short term, such methods are relatively effective in ensuring weight gain, and have a clear role in stabilising physiological and physical health status. However, the long-term benefit of these methods is dubious, since there is often marked weight loss after treatment. Clinical experience would suggest that this is often due to the behavioural programmes addressing the wrong behaviour. For example, the clinician may intend to reinforce 'positive' behaviour (eating), while the patient may see eating as a means to a completely different contingency (e.g. getting out of hospital, and being able to re-establish personal control). While the initial effect on the overt behaviour will be identical (eating more), the impact on eating attitudes and ultimate weight gain might be minimal. In short, the perceived success of behavioural methods in this group (as with all others) depends on an emphasis on behavioural analysis, rather than an understanding of the contingencies involved.

In *bulimia nervosa*, behaviour therapy has been examined both in isolation and as an adjunct to cognitive work. In isolation, it has produced disappointing results, yielding much lower remission rates than either CBT or interpersonal psychotherapy (IPT; Fairburn et al., 1995). By analogy with the addiction literature, it has been argued that a key behavioural technique in working with bulimia will be exposure with response prevention. For example, a person might be dissuaded from purging after a binge. In theory, this would promote extinction or habituation of the anxiety that follows a binge. However, a number of researchers (e.g. Bulik et al., 1998) have concluded that exposure and response prevention adds nothing to the therapeutic benefits of CBT, thus calling into doubt the usefulness of a behavioural approach and of the addiction link.

Until relatively recently, psychological treatment for *obesity* and *binge eating disorder* (BED) has been based largely upon a mixture of behavioural and dietary methods. Results in the published literature (i.e. a research base that is likely to be biased in favour of positive findings) indicate that weight loss and its maintenance are generally poor (e.g. Wooley & Garner, 1991). The best impact is on the frequency of binge eating, rather than weight loss. Although normalisation of eating patterns is a major achievement, weight loss is not achieved reliably in the obese. Several authors (e.g. Levine, Marcus & Moulton, 1996) have demonstrated that introducing an exercise component to a treatment programme for obese women with BED can have positive benefits in terms of abstinence from bingeing but, again, there is no comparable impact on weight loss. Overall, we have a very limited understanding of individual prognosis and suitability for a behavioural treatment of obesity and BED. While there is generally a modest amount of weight reduction during treatment (e.g. Wooley & Garner, 1991), this gain is usually poorly maintained at follow-up. While some individuals are able to sustain and improve upon the therapeutic gain, we lack a clear picture of what is different about the psychology of those successful individuals. Our understanding is further confused because researchers tend not to differentiate obese patients from obese binge eaters. In addition, treatment programmes for these complex disorders lack diversity. Wilson (1996) suggests that part of the failure of behaviour therapy to produce change in weight levels among obese patients is that this approach fails to address the concept of self-acceptance, in the way that CBT does. In other words, if the clinician's target is for the patient to achieve a modest but stable level of weight loss over an extended time period, that may conflict with the patient's own goal (often substantial and rapid weight loss). If behaviour therapy fails to address the utility of their goals, then it is not surprising that patients will come to see the therapy as unhelpful.

Summary

The failure of behaviour therapy in the eating disorders has indicated a need to develop cognitive-behavioural approaches to the eating disorders, with a greater stress on modifying the belief structures of these patients. As will be seen in the next section, these formulations and the resulting treatments have yielded a very mixed pattern of utility, ranging from poor to relatively successful.

The Conceptual Base of Existing Cognitive-Behavioural Treatments

To date, CBT with the eating disorders has been based on models where the central pathology involves cognitions and behaviours that are highly focused on food, weight and body shape (e.g. Fairburn, 1981; Garner & Bemis, 1982). The aims of treatment within these models have been clearly described elsewhere (e.g. Fairburn & Cooper, 1989), but centre on the modification of behaviours and cognitions that maintain the existing behaviour. In CBT terms, the main foci are the modification of negative automatic thoughts and dysfunctional assumptions relating to food, weight and shape, and the breaking of behavioural and physiological chains that maintain the unhealthy eating behaviours and cognitions. This model has been used to develop clearly operationalised treatments, although it would be a mistake to conclude that these manualised protocol-driven treatments lack an individualised component (see above). Nor are these models static, as evidenced by the recent modifications to Fairburn's model of bulimia nervosa (Fairburn, 1997). From a clinical and scientific perspective, the benefit of the clear operationalisation of these (or any other) treatments is that one can be more conclusive about their effectiveness and limitations.

The Effectiveness of Existing CBT with Different Eating Disorders

There is only a relatively limited evidence base for the efficacy of CBT with *anorexia nervosa*, possibly due to the inadequacy of most cognitive and behavioural models of restrictive behaviours. It is also important to note that some studies are based on work with restrictive anorexics only, while others involve mixed groups of restrictive and bulimic anorexics. The little evidence that has been generated by controlled trials tends to suggest that individual CBT is moderately effective for anorexia nervosa, but no more effective than less focused psychotherapies (Channon et al., 1989). At the symptomatic level, however, there is some strong evidence that CBT can be effective in producing change in specific aspects of anorexia nervosa. For example, body image disturbance has been shown to respond to exposure and cognitive challenge (e.g. Norris, 1984). Although group work has been advocated for anorexia nervosa, the evidence regarding group CBT with anorexics shows that has very poor therapeutic efficacy (Leung, Waller & Thomas, 1999a), and it cannot be recommended at present.

In contrast, the evidence base for conventional CBT with *bulimia nervosa* is very strong, particularly given its basis in well-controlled studies with long follow-up times (e.g. Fairburn et al., 1995). At the syndromal level, individual CBT induces remission in approximately 40–50% of cases, and an overall level of symptom reduction of approximately 60–70% (e.g. Vitousek, 1996; Wilson, 1999). This level of symptom reduction is only marginally lower when CBT is presented in a group format (Leung, Waller & Thomas, 2000). Indeed, there is evidence that a proportion of bulimics can benefit substantially from the use of self-help manuals (e.g. Cooper, Coker & Fleming, 1996). In controlled trials, existing CBT methods have been established to be superior to most other therapies in terms of either the magnitude or the immediacy of effect. They also have a clear superiority over the impact of antidepressant medication (e.g. Johnson, Tsoh & Varnado, 1996). While the most widely validated forms of CBT for bulimia tend to require between 16 and 20 sessions, Bulik et al. (1998) have reported equivalent results from an eight-session programme (although there are no long-term follow-up data on this variant).

The picture is somewhat less well developed in the case of *binge eating disorder* and *obesity*, partly due to the tendency to confound the two disorders. However, the conclusion is relatively similar to that with behaviour therapy—CBT is effective in reducing binge frequency, but not in reducing weight substantially in the long term. Long-term weight reduction (albeit modest) is more dependent on achieving abstinence from binge eating during the CBT (Agras et al., 1997). In the case of the non-binge-eating obese, a multifactorial approach to therapy (e.g. CBT plus exercise plus diet) appears to promote the most sustained weight loss (e.g. Leermakers et al., 1999), although the amount of weight lost is still only moderate in most cases. In the case of failure to benefit from the standard course of CBT, it is worth extending the treatment for binge eating disorder patients, since this helps a substantial number of individuals to achieve abstinence from binge eating (Eldredge et al., 1997).

Summary: Strengths and Limitations of Existing CBT for the Eating Disorders

Existing forms of CBT have been researched well enough that we can conclude that they have a number of strengths and limitations (Wilson, 1999). First, they are effective in reducing the presence of bulimic behaviours, cognitions and syndromes (Vitousek, 1996), and show clear advantages in the magnitude of change, the rapidity of change, or both. There is clearly a need to understand why CBT does not induce remission or symptom reduction in a large number of bulimics, and this may require consideration of the sufficiency of existing cognitive-behaviour models that have been applied to bulimia (Hollon & Beck, 1994). Second, CBT is no more effective than other approaches in some domains, particularly in the treatment of restrictive disorders and in the long-term reduction of obesity. Third, as is the case with other therapies, there is some evidence that CBT is less effective in working with complex cases, such as those bulimics with a history of trauma, high levels of dissociation or comorbid personality disorders (e.g. Sansone & Fine, 1992; Waller, 1997). Finally, since the basis of these forms of CBT was laid down (in the early 1980s), there have been substantial developments in the cognitive psychology of the eating disorders (see Shafran & de Silva, this volume) and in the conceptual base of CBT itself.

CBT remains demonstrably as or more effective than other forms of therapy for the eating disorders. However, given these strengths and limitations, it is clear that we should treat existing forms of CBT as necessary but not sufficient in this field. Therefore, it is timely to consider how to integrate the literature on the cognitive psychology of the eating disorders with the existing forms of CBT, in order to develop therapies that might be more effective. It will also be valuable to consider whether this elaboration of the cognitive structure of the eating disorders might explain the benefits found with some other (non-CBT) therapies. Rather than leaping in with suggestions about more advanced forms of CBT that might be considered when working with the eating disorders, it is important to consider the advances in our understanding of the eating disorders over recent years. Such an approach should have the benefit of allowing us to suggest more appropriate, theory-based formulations of eating psychopathology, which in turn should inform the development of CBT.

RECENT DEVELOPMENTS IN COGNITIVE-BEHAVIOURAL FORMULATIONS OF THE EATING DISORDERS

Whether in the eating disorders or elsewhere, the progressive development of models of psychopathology should be seen as an inherent part of clinical and research work. Such development needs to be both 'top–down' (driven by theories of psychological function) and 'bottom–up' (driven by the data that emerge from clinical practice and research). There is bound to be some lag time, as existing models are properly tested. However, it is clear that progress in the field of the eating disorders has been relatively slow, with a failure to absorb the lessons that have been present for some time both in our conceptualisation of CBT (Hollon & Beck, 1994) and in the evidence base (e.g. Meyer, Waller & Waters, 1998). Clearly, the most pressing issue is the failure of CBT (and other therapies) to have any substantial impact in two areas—the level of restriction in anorexia, and weight loss in conditions that include obesity. However, it is also necessary to consider how we can build on the strong start that has been made in the field of reducing bulimic behaviours. While pioneering work in this field (e.g. Bulik et al., 1998; Fairburn et al., 1995) shows that CBT for bulimia nervosa has impressive results (Vitousek, 1996), there are still many with bulimia who do not benefit from it (e.g. Wilson, 1996, 1999).

The Role of Individual Formulations

At the heart of any form of CBT, there must lie two things. The first is a broad assessment, driven both by the existing evidence base and by the material that the patient brings to the session. The second is an individualised formulation, which takes into account both the aetiology and the maintenance of the relevant cognitions, behaviours and emotions (e.g. Persons, 1989). Such a formulation needs to be based both on the broad psychology and physiology of eating problems and on the individual's circumstances. This formulation will act as the key in illustrating the cognitive and behavioural factors that need to be addressed in therapy.

There are two errors commonly made in constructing such formulations. The first is ignoring the individual's idiosyncratic situation and experience, instead falling back on generalised formulations of the disorder (e.g. Fairburn & Cooper, 1989; Lacey, 1986; Slade, 1982). This ignores the fact that these broad formulations are better used as templates, using existing theory and evidence to assist in deciding what elements are relevant to the individual case. The second error is forgetting that an individual formulation is a working hypothesis rather than a proven fact—an error that often leads us to assume that we understand the individual, thereby blinding us to evidence that we are wrong. A formulation is never anything more than the best model that we can achieve at the time, and we should always be ready to find that we have to reformulate to accommodate the unexpected (e.g. when treatment is failing, or when the patient tells us that we are wrong). Within CBT, both assessment and formulation have a strong evidence base to draw upon, meaning that our templates of the general case are likely to have some relevance to the individual patient. However, there is still plenty of room for improvement in our models (and always will be, however well developed they might become).

Emerging Themes in the Formulation of the Eating Disorders

As outlined above, CBT models of the eating disorders have been very much driven by a focus on cognitions and behaviours regarding food, shape and weight (Fairburn, 1981; Fairburn & Cooper, 1989; Garner & Bemis, 1982). While the evidence to date shows that understanding these negative automatic thoughts and dysfunctional assumptions is necessary to understand the eating disorders (e.g. Channon, Hemsley & de Silva, 1989; Cooper, 1997), these cognitions are clearly not sufficient explanatory constructs. Both research and clinical reports have suggested that comprehensive cognitive-behavioural models of eating disorders will need to include the following (often overlapping) factors.

Social and Interpersonal Issues

The impact of interpersonal psychotherapy on bulimic psychopathology (Fairburn et al., 1995) gives us the strongest clue that there are important interpersonal and social issues that contribute to eating pathology. Those issues include abandonment fears (e.g. Patton, 1992; Meyer & Waller, 1999), fear of negative social evaluation (e.g. Steiger et al., 1999), and the socially-marked experience of shame (e.g. Murray, Waller & Legg, 2000; Striegel-Moore, Silberstein & Rodin, 1993). However, this research is in its early stages, and needs considerable extension to determine the role of social factors across the eating disorders.

Control Issues

It has often been noted that control is a particularly powerful factor in the aetiology and maintenance of restrictive disorders. Slade (1982) incorporated a need for control into his early formulation of anorexia nervosa. However, the construct was largely overlooked within the more predominant early models (e.g. Fairburn, 1981; Garner & Bemis, 1982). It is only recently that Fairburn, Shafran and Cooper (1999) have revisited the issue of control, elaborating on Slade's work in order to develop a more refined cognitive-behavioural model of restrictive pathology. Where there has been research into the construct (e.g. King, 1989), it has largely focused on the role of perceived control over life and events. However, Slade's model really addresses the discrepancy between *perceived* and *desired* control. While control has generally been considered in relation to the restrictive aspects of anorexia, it is also possible to see a critical role for control in bulimia. In particular, bulimic symptoms often serve an emotion regulation function (Lacey, 1986; Root & Fallon, 1989). There is a clear, long-standing gap in our understanding of the impact of control discrepancies, and this gap needs to be closed in order to refine our understanding of this factor in CBT. Such research would benefit from distinguishing between discrepancies in control over life and discrepancies in control over affective states, to determine whether these patterns distinguish different forms of eating psychopathology.

Motivation

Given the ego-syntonic nature of some eating pathology (e.g. Serpell et al., 1999), it has been suggested that there is a need to enhance motivation in eating-disordered patients before treatment can have its maximal effect. This principle would apply as much to CBT as to any other disorder (if not more, given the importance of the working alliance in CBT). However, it seems to be too early to be optimistic. While it is clear that women with eating disorders often have very low levels of motivation to change (e.g. Serpell et al., 1999), it is far from evident that adding a motivational element to CBT for the eating disorders actually produces any improvement in therapeutic outcome (Treasure et al., 1999). It appears either that we lack a good motivational enhancement method in such cases at present, or that the motivational enhancement model used is inappropriate to the eating disorders.

Cognitive Content and Process

Perhaps the most critical issue in existing CBT for the eating disorders is that it is based on cognitive-behavioural formulations that fail to reflect contemporary knowledge about the cognitive psychology of the eating disorders. This point has been identified in restrictive anorexia by Fairburn, Shafran and Cooper (1999), although their control-based model is still in the early days of testing. Recent conceptualisations of psychopathology (e.g. Wells & Matthews, 1994; Williams et al., 1997) have stressed the importance of understanding both cognitive content (beliefs and emotions) and cognitive process (attentional processes, cognitive avoidance, dissociation, etc.). Both of these aspects have begun to be addressed in contemporary research into the eating disorders.

As has been mentioned above, cognitive-behavioural formulations have stressed the role of two levels of *cognitive representation*—negative automatic thoughts (which are largely immediate, conscious cognitions) and underlying assumptions (conditional rules, such as: 'Gaining one pound will mean that I put on a hundred pounds'). These can be characterised as 'superficial' levels of cognition, and each primarily involves beliefs that are focused on weight, shape and eating. However, it has been suggested that this superficial level of analysis is responsible for the failure of much contemporary CBT for the eating disorders (Hollon & Beck, 1994). Recent research has supported Kennerley's (1997) and Cooper's (1997) arguments that we need to understand the role of 'deeper' schema-level representations in the eating disorders. Eating psychopathology (at the diagnostic and the behavioural levels) appears to be directly related to unconditional core beliefs that are unrelated to eating, weight and shape, such as defectiveness/shame and emotional inhibition beliefs (e.g. Leung, Waller & Thomas, 1999b; Waller et al., 2000). In addition, the presence of unhelpful core beliefs has a negative impact on the outcome of 'conventional' CBT for bulimia nervosa (Leung, Waller & Thomas, 2000), thus suggesting that the failure of some CBT cases is a product of pathological schema-level representations.

Reflecting this core belief literature, there is now substantial evidence that bulimics process *threat cognitions* preferentially, being influenced by threats that are not directly relevant to food, shape and weight. For example, bulimic psychopathology is associated with a strong attentional bias towards self-esteem threats, with a lower level of bias towards physical threats (Heatherton & Baumeister, 1991; Heatherton, Herman & Polivy, 1991; McManus, Waller & Chadwick, 1996; Schotte, 1992). In addition, bulimic women have been shown to avoid processing self-esteem threats, where the task involves strategic processing (Meyer et al., under consideration). Finally, a number of studies have used subliminal visual presentation of cues to show that non-clinical women with disturbed eating attitudes are influenced by preconscious processing of information that they are not even aware of. Such women eat more after being exposed to subliminal abandonment threat cues, but not by subliminal appetitive cues (Meyer & Waller, 1999). Overall, these findings show that eating psychopathology is strongly associated with threat cognitions that are unrelated to the overt pathology of the disorders.

Affect

Finally, there is now substantial evidence for the role of emotionally driven eating behaviours (e.g. Agras & Telch, 1998; Meyer, Waller & Waters, 1998; Waters, Hill & Waller, 2001). This element has now been added to (although not incorporated into) Fairburn's model of bulimia nervosa (Fairburn, 1997), but has not been widely investigated. Any clinically useful formulation of the eating disorders needs to take full account of phenomena such as emotional eating in bulimic and restrictive pathologies (e.g. Arnow, Kenardy & Agras, 1992, 1995; Herman & Polivy, 1980).

Summary

We have briefly reviewed the current state of the cognitive-behavioural models that underpin CBT for the eating disorders, and have identified a number of psychological and interpersonal domains that existing cognitive-behavioural formulations and treatments fail to take into account adequately. In keeping with the spirit of scientific enquiry that drives CBT, these deficits should be seen as giving directions to the future content and format of CBT for the eating disorders. At one level, one could suggest adding these to the targets of existing forms of CBT (e.g. adding treatment components that address social and emotional issues). However, this would be a radical revision, given the limited focus of existing CBT and the models that have underpinned it (Fairburn, 1981; Garner & Bemis, 1982).

Before adopting a 'bottom–up' approach (changing CBT in line with data alone), we should revisit broader cognitive-behavioural models, to see whether there is a case for 'top–down', conceptually driven change in our understanding and treatment of the eating disorders. Cognitive-behavioural models and treatments in other areas of psychopathology have moved on in the 20 years since the bases of our current cognitive-behavioural models of the eating disorders were first formulated (e.g. Garner & Bemis, 1982). Therefore, in the next section, we will consider recent developments in cognitive-behavioural and related therapies, in order to determine whether those developments have therapeutic potential, given the developments in cognitive-behavioural formulations outlined in this section. We will then outline some of the key principles of the cognitive-behavioural model and therapy that we argue best compensates for the shortfall in our therapeutic efficacy and effectiveness—schema-focused CBT.

NEW DEVELOPMENTS IN CBT: POTENTIAL APPLICATION TO THE EATING DISORDERS

We have suggested that there is a need to return to the principles of cognitive-behavioural theory in order to understand the eating disorders better. Using these principles, models can be developed that incorporate the wide range of empirical and clinical findings that have been generated since our existing CBT models of the eating disorders were first proposed. There have been a number of developments in cognitive-behavioural models and therapies in recent years, and we will briefly consider some of the more important of them. Each will be considered in terms of its capacity to address the elements of the cognition–emotion–behaviour matrix that have been shown to be most relevant to eating psychopathology (see above). This explanatory power also needs to take account of cognition, emotion and behaviour in their social/interpersonal context.

A number of clinicians (e.g. Wiser & Telch, 1999) have considered the clinical utility of *dialectical behaviour therapy* (DBT; Linehan, 1993) with the eating disorders. Telch (1997) has published a case suggesting that DBT is potentially useful with binge eating disorder. However, it should be stressed that this case study appears to show some substantial deviations from the protocol that Linehan suggests (using individual skills training only; re-ordering skills modules). Nor is it clear whether DBT per se was necessary, or whether individual skills were the effective elements of successful treatment. Finally, there is no clear rationale for using DBT with restrictive behaviours, and there is no evidence that it will be effective in treating purging behaviours.

It has been suggested that *cognitive analytic therapy* (CAT; Ryle, 1997) is appropriate for complex cases where eating disturbance is present (Bell, 1996). However, while there is now some preliminary evidence of effectiveness with borderline personality disorder (e.g. Wildgoose, Clarke & Waller, 2001), CAT has been developed largely with personality pathology features in mind, and it is not clear how appropriate it is for understanding and treating the specific features of eating pathology. Given its foci, it might be expected to share some of the beneficial characteristics of *interpersonal psychotherapy* (Fairburn et al., 1995), but there is no empirical base to support this as yet.

SCHEMA-FOCUSED COGNITIVE-BEHAVIOUR THERAPY

We argue that schema-focused cognitive-behaviour therapy (SFCBT) is likely to be beneficial in complex eating cases, both on the basis of our clinical experience (Kennerley, 1997; Ohanian & Waller, 1999) and on theoretical grounds. The schema-focused approach is the development of CBT that most comprehensively addresses all of the elements of eating psychopathology that we have described as important (above). The conceptual basis for SFCBT accommodates the possibility of working with cognitions (at a range of levels), emotions, behaviours and interpersonal function. There is also a growing empirical base that stresses the need to consider schemata in our understanding of eating psychopathology (see below). However, we would also acknowledge that the empirical base for therapeutic outcome is small and is, to date, dependent on case studies (e.g. Kennerley, 1997; Ohanian & Waller, 1999). In order to explain the potential utility of SFCBT in the eating disorders, it is first necessary to expand on its general principles and practice.

The obvious first question is: What is a schema? Generally, this is defined as a mental structure that: 'consists of a stored domain of knowledge which interacts with the processing of new information' (Williams et al., 1997). It is a mental 'filter', shaped by our previous experiences and which colours subsequent interpretations. Recently, several theoretical models have been advanced to refine this definition of the schema (e.g. Beck, 1996; Layden et al., 1993; Power, 1997; Teasdale, 1996), and these definitions have several common features. First, schemata are seen as multi-modal structures—a schema is rich in meaning,

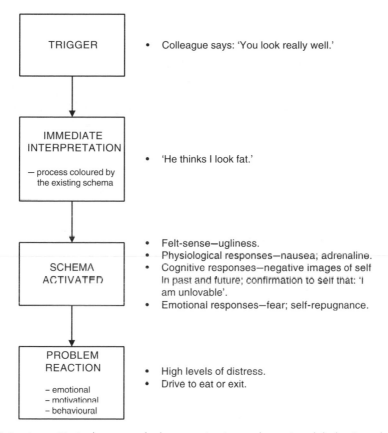

Figure 14.2   Anna: Typical pattern of schema activation and emotional–behavioural responses

and represents much more than a single belief. They comprise 'meaning' held in physical, emotional, verbal, visual, acoustic, kinetic, olfactory, tactile and kinaesthetic form. These aspects of meaning interact to convey the powerful 'sense' that is carried by the schema. The following example (see Figure 14.2) illustrates the complexity of schemata, explaining their resilience to 'classic' challenging:

> Anna had a schema that was best represented by the simple label: 'I am unlovable'. It was this that made sense of her low self-esteem, her difficulty maintaining her relationships, and her comfort-eating. When a colleague said: 'You look well', her interpretation (coloured by her belief system) was: 'He thinks that I look fat.' This activated her schemata, which triggered a powerful 'felt sense' of ugliness, fatness and self-revulsion, resulting in a physiological reaction of nausea and a flood of adrenaline. She also had an uneasy sense of *déjà vu* and a negative projection into the future, accompanied by a fleeting image of being rejected—which was actually a restimulation of a past experience. This promoted a drive to protect herself through escape (e.g. eating to dissociate, exiting the situation). For Anna, in an instant, she had experienced something powerfully awful that she could not easily put into words but which was best represented by the component core belief: 'I am unlovable.' Sometimes this phrase echoed in her mind.

Schema-focused cognitive-behavioural therapy addresses the schemata directly. It is an extension or elaboration of CBT, rather than being distinct from CBT. 'Classic' CBT, though effective with a range of psychological problems, has de-emphasised the role of schemata and often fails to generate sufficient understanding of complex, chronic and characterological problems. Fortunately, by the late 1980s, the aetiological factors in the development of persistent dysfunctional beliefs and schemata were made more explicit by cognitive therapists, and the role of those factors in the maintenance of problems was refined (Beck et al., 1990; Young, 1994). This development has helped us to understand the persistence and complexity of certain psychological problems.

Schema Identification

In order to develop a schema-based conceptualisation, key schemata need to be identified. This is often achieved using guided discovery, as in 'classic' CBT, although the use of phrases like 'How does that feel?' and 'What's happening in your body?' might commonly supplement 'What images or thoughts run through your mind?'. The process of 'unpacking' meaning can be lengthy and should take into account a client's difficulty in accessing and/or acknowledging painful core belief systems. Assessment might be supplemented by questionnaires devised to aid schema identification (e.g. Cooper et al., 1997; Young, 1994), although care should be taken not to lose idiosyncratic meanings, which might not be reflected in such measures.

Strategies to Effect Change

Clearly, schemata may shift as a direct result of a 'classic' CBT intervention creating sustainable changes that impact on these fundamental structures. However, some schemata are resilient and require interventions that address them directly. SFCBT has evolved to meet this need.

Beck and colleagues (1990), Padesky (1994) and Young (1994) all provide useful descriptions of schema change strategies. Schema-focused strategies in cognitive therapy often require relatively simple modification of standard techniques. Commonly used schema change approaches include scaling, positive data logs, historical review and visual restructuring. *Scaling/continuum techniques* are an elaboration of the exploration and balancing of a dichotomous thinking style that is commonly used in CBT. *Positive data logs* (Padesky, 1994) require focused, systematic collection of evidence supporting the development of an adaptive core belief. As such, the technique has its roots in the data collection exercises typical of traditional CBT. *Historical reviews* (Young, 1994) represent an elaboration of the familiar 'daily thought records', but the identification and challenging of key cognitions becomes a retrospective exercise to re-evaluate schema-relevant experiences and beliefs. Also, much *visual restructuring* (Layden et al., 1993), which aims to transform the meanings held by memories and images, has built on the imagery exercises that have been a component of CBT since the 1970s. *Imagery rescripting* has also been developed to allow individuals to modify schemata that are not encoded verbally (Ohanian, 2002; Smucker et al., 1995). More recently, there have been clinical developments in helping clients to combat unhelpful 'felt-sense' (Kennerley, 1996; Mills & Williams, 1997; Rosen, 1997), using *guided discovery and challenging*. Thus, schema-change strategies can target meanings that are held in verbally, visually and somatically accessible modalities, each of which interacts with affect and motivation. Finally, Safran and Segal (1990) have established a further branch of

SFCBT that targets *interpersonal schemata*, using the interpersonal domain as a medium for change.

Can SFCBT Contribute to our Work with the Eating Disorders?

We are developing a much better understanding of the 'inner world' of people with eating disorders, well beyond their concerns about weight, shape and food. For example, Waller et al. (2000) have used Young's Schema Questionnaire (1994) to show that the prominent belief systems of women suffering from bulimic disorders include core beliefs regarding defectiveness and shame, poor self-control, emotional inhibition, and vulnerability to harm. Similarly, Serpell et al. (1999) have shown that a fundamental sense of worthlessness, badness and powerlessness are central to eating pathology in anorexia nervosa, and Cooper and Hunt (1998) have demonstrated the prominence of such beliefs in bulimia nervosa. Although some of these fundamental beliefs can shift as a direct result of challenging the underlying assumptions concerning weight, shape and food, some will require a more direct approach, such as is offered by SFCBT.

In addition, it is pertinent that SFCBT was developed for use with clients with characterological difficulties, as most of us will have met eating-disordered clients with complex social and interpersonal problems, who relapse frequently and who seem ambivalent about therapy. In fact, Baker and Sansone (1997) suggest that the majority of non-responders to eating disorder programmes may be individuals with axis II pathology. Thus, SFCBT might well contribute to our work with this client group.

Finally, schema theory and SFCBT recognise the relevance of somatic or kinetic meaning, which can contribute to the persistence of eating disorders—how often does the therapist hear: '... but I just *feel* fat'? We all have mental representations of our body size, state and position (i.e. 'body schemata'; Berlucchi & Aglioti, 1997). These internal representations of body state can be distorted, even to the extent that a person can experience 'phantom' limbs (Ramachandran, 1998). It has long been recognised that abnormality of body image frequently plays a part in the maintenance of eating disorders, and this remains one of the diagnostic criteria for both anorexia nervosa and bulimia nervosa (APA, 1994). In fact, Rosen (1997) concludes that: 'Of all psychological factors that are believed to cause eating disorders, body image dissatisfaction is the most relevant and immediate antecedent.' Again, within the field of schema-focused work, there is scope for helping clients to recognise and restructure distorted body image (or 'felt-sense'), as well as tackling the complex belief systems and the interpersonal difficulties that can contribute to the chronicity and complexity of some disorders.

Who will Benefit?

Just as we cannot assume that a person will benefit from CBT because she or he can identify key cognitions, we cannot assume that someone will benefit from SFCBT simply because the problem is schema-driven. Although SFCBT particularly targets the client who presents with diffuse problems, interpersonal difficulties, rigid and inflexible traits, and avoidance of cognition and affect (McGinn & Young, 1996), this form of therapy (like 'classic' CBT) requires that the client is able to establish a collaborative alliance and has an ability to relate to psychological models. Some clients will not be at the stage of engagement that would allow them to use SFCBT, and might possibly benefit from preliminary motivational counselling. Such work would aim particularly to reduce the perceived positive benefits of the eating problem, which appear to be the best predictors of the severity of eating pathology (Serpell et al., 1999). Others might experience such pronounced interpersonal difficulties that an analytic intervention would best meet their needs. Finally, some patients will have ongoing environmental stresses that need to be addressed (through social or systemic intervention) before they can engage in any cognitive therapy. Again, we are reminded of the importance of a rigorous assessment of our clients.

WHERE TO NEXT? THE NEED FOR FURTHER INQUIRY

Cognitive-behavioural models and therapy have made the greatest contribution to date to our understanding and treatment of bulimic disorders. However, they do not appear to explain all cases of bulimia, and have very poor therapeutic power in explaining and treating restrictive pathology and obesity. There is a clear need to address these deficits, drawing on developments in the broader fields of cognitive-behavioural theory, principles and therapy. Current developments (e.g. Cooper, 1997; Fairburn, Shafran & Cooper, 1999; Kennerley, 1997) suggest that there is now a movement towards returning to the combination of flexibility, innovation and empiricism that characterises CBT. This gives us some hope that it will be possible to add to the existing therapeutic benefits of CBT, applying it to a much broader range of those cases that have so far defeated this form of therapy.

REFERENCES

Agras, W.S., Telch, C.F., Arnow, B., Eldredge, K. & Marnell, M. (1997) One-year follow-up of cognitive-behavioral therapy for obese individuals with binge eating disorder. *Journal of Consulting and Clinical Psychology*, **65**, 343–347.

Agras, W.S. & Telch, C.F. (1998) The effects of caloric deprivation and negative affect on binge eating in obese binge eating disordered women. *Behaviour Therapy*, **29**, 491–503.

APA (1994) *Diagnostic and Statistical Manual of Mental Disorders* (4th edition). Washington, D.C.: American Psychiatric Association.

Arnow, B., Kenardy J. & Agras, W.S. (1992) Binge eating among the obese: a descriptive study. *Journal of Behavioral Medicine*, **15**, 155–170.

Arnow, B., Kenardy, J. & Agras, W.S. (1995) The Emotional Eating Scale: The development of a measure to assess coping with negative affect by eating. *International Journal of Eating Disorders*, **18** 79–90.

Baker, D.A. & Sansone, R.A. (1997) Treatment of patients with personality disorders. In D. Garner & P.E. Garfinkel (Eds), *Handbook of Treatments for Eating Disorders*. New York: Guilford Press.

Beck, A.T. (1996) Beyond belief: A theory of modes, personality and psychopathology. In P.M. Salkovskis (Ed.), *Frontiers of Cognitive Therapy*. New York: Guilford Press.

Beck, A.T., Rush, A.J., Shaw, B.F. & Emery, G. (1979) *Cognitive Therapy of Depression*. New York: Guilford Press.

Beck, A.T. and *co-workers* (1990) *Cognitive Therapy of Personality Disorders*. New York: Guilford Press.

Bell, L. (1996) Cognitive analytic therapy: Its value in the treatment of people with eating disorders. *Clinical Psychology Forum*, **92**, 5–10.

Berlucchi, G. & Aglioti, S. (1997) The body in the brain: neural bases of corporeal awareness. *Trends in Neuroscience*, **20**, 560–564.

Bulik, C.M., Sullivan, P.F., Carter, F.A., McIntosh, V.V. & Joyce, P.R. (1998) The role of exposure with response prevention in the cognitive-behavioural therapy for bulimia nervosa. *Psychological Medicine*, **28**, 611–623.

Channon, S., de Silva, P., Hemsley, D. & Perkins, R. (1989) A controlled trial of cognitive-behavioural and behavioural treatment of anorexia nervosa. *Behaviour Research and Therapy*, **27**, 529–35.

Cooper, P.J., Coker, S. & Fleming, C. (1996) An evaluation of the efficacy of supervised cognitive behavioral self-help bulimia nervosa. *Journal of Psychosomatic Research*, **40**, 281–287.

Cooper, M. (1997) Cognitive theory in anorexia nervosa and bulimia nervosa: A review. *Behavioural and Cognitive Psychotherapy*, **25**, 113–145.

Cooper, M., Cohen-Tovée, E., Todd, G., Wells, A. & Tovée, M. (1997) The Eating Disorder Belief Questionnaire: Preliminary development. *Behaviour Research and Therapy*, **35**, 381–388.

Cooper, M. & Hunt, J. (1998) Core beliefs and underlying assumptions in bulimia nervosa and depression. *Behaviour Research and Therapy*, **36**, 895–898.

Eldredge, K.L., Agras, W.S., Arnow, B., Telch, C.F., Bell, S. & Castonguay, L. (1997) The effects of extending cognitive-behavioral therapy for binge eating disorder among initial treatment nonresponders. *International Journal of Eating Disorders*, **21**, 347–352.

Fairburn, C.G. (1981) A cognitive behavioural approach to the treatment of bulimia. *Psychological Medicine*, **11**, 707–711.

Fairburn, C.G. (1997) Eating disorders. In D.M. Clark & C.G. Fairburn (Eds), *Science and Practice of Cognitive Behaviour Therapy*. Oxford: Oxford University Press.

Fairburn, C.G. & Cooper, P. (1989) Eating disorders. In K. Hawton, P.M. Salkovskis, J. Kirk, & D.M. Clark (Eds), *Cognitive Behaviour Therapy for Psychiatric Problems*. New York: Oxford University Press.

Fairburn, C.G., Norman, P.A., Welch, S.L., O'Connor, M.E., Doll, H.A. & Peveler, R.C. (1995) A prospective study of outcome in bulimia nervosa and the long-term effects of three psychological treatments. *Archives of General Psychiatry*, **52**, 304–312.

Fairburn, C.G., Shafran, R. & Cooper, Z. (1999) A cognitive-behavioural theory of anorexia nervosa. *Behaviour Research and Therapy*, **37**, 1–13.

Garner, D. & Bemis, K.M. (1982) A cognitive-behavioural approach to anorexia nervosa. *Cognitive Therapy and Research*, **6**, 123–150.

Heatherton, T.F., Herman, C.P. & Polivy, J. (1991) Effects of physical threat and ego threat on eating behaviour. *Journal of Personality and Social Psychology*, **60**, 138–143.

Heatherton, T.F. & Baumeister, R.F. (1991) Binge-eating as an escape from self-awareness. *Psychological Bulletin*, **110**, 86–108.

Herman, C.P. & Polivy, J. (1980) Restrained eating. In A.J. Stunkard (Ed.), *Obesity* (pp. 208–225) Philadelphia: Saunders.

Hollon, S.D. & Beck, A.T. (1994) Cognitive and cognitive-behavioural therapies. In A.E. Bergin & S.L. Garfield (Eds), *Handbook of Psychotherapy and Behavioural Change* (pp. 428–466) Chichester: John Wiley & Sons.

Johnson, W.G., Tsoh, J.Y. & Varnado, P.J. (1996) Eating disorders: Efficacy of pharmacological and psychological interventions. *Clinical Psychology Review*, **16**, 457–478.

Kennerley, H. (1996) Cognitive therapy of dissociative symptoms associated with trauma. *British Journal of Clinical Psychology*, **35**, 325–340.

Kennerley, H. (1997, July) Managing complex eating disorders using schema-based cognitive therapy. Paper presented at the British Association of Behavioural and Cognitive Psychotherapy conference, Canterbury, UK.

King, M. (1989) Locus of control in women with eating pathology. *Psychological Medicine*, **19**, 183–187.

Lacey, J.H. (1986) Pathogenesis. In L.J. Downey & J.C. Malkin (Eds), *Current Approaches: Bulimia Nervosa*. Southampton: Duphar.

Layden, M.A., Newman, C.F., Freeman, A. & Morse, S.B. (1993) *Cognitive Therapy of Borderline Personality Disorder*. Boston: Allyn & Bacon.

Leermakers, E.A., Perri, M.G., Shigaki, C.L. & Fuller, P.R. (1999) Effects of exercise-focused versus weight-focused maintenance programs on the management of obesity. *Addictive Behaviors*, **24**, 219–227.

Leung, N., Waller, G. & Thomas, G.V. (1999a) Group cognitive-behavioural therapy for anorexia nervosa: A case for treatment? *European Eating Disorders Review*, **7**, 351–361.

Leung, N., Waller, G. & Thomas, G.V. (1999b) Core beliefs in anorexic and bulimic women. *Journal of Nervous and Mental Disease*, **187**, 736–741.

Leung N., Waller G. & Thomas G.V. (2000) Outcome of group cognitive-behavior therapy for bulimia nervosa: The role of core beliefs. *Behaviour Research and Therapy*, **38**, 145–156.

Leung, N., Thomas, G.V. & Waller, G. (2000) The relationship between parental bonding and core beliefs in anorexic and bulimic women. *British Journal of Clinical Psychology*, **39**, 203–213.

Levine, M.D., Marcus, M.D. & Moulton, P. (1996) Exercise in the treatment of binge eating disorder. *International Journal of Eating Disorders*, **19**, 171–177.

Linehan, M.M. (1993) *Cognitive-Behavioural Treatment for Borderline Personality Disorder: The Dialectics of Effective Treatment*. New York: Guildford Press.

McGinn, L.K. & Young, J. (1996) Schema-focused Therapy. In P.M. Salkovskis (Ed.), *Frontiers of Cognitive Therapy*. New York: Guilford Press.

McManus, F., Waller, G. & Chadwick, P. (1996) Biases in the processing of different forms of threat in bulimic and comparison women. *Journal of Nervous and Mental Disease*, **184**, 547–554.

Meyer, C., Serpell, L., Waller, G., Murphy, F., Treasure, J. & Leung, N. (under consideration) Schema avoidance in the strategic processing of ego threats: Evidence from eating—disordered patients. *British Journal of Clinical Psychology*.

Meyer, C., Waller, G. & Waters, A. (1998) Emotional states and bulimic psychopathology. In H. Hoek, M. Katzman & J. Treasure (Eds), *The Neurobiological Basis of Eating Disorders*. Chichester: John Wiley & Sons.

Meyer, C. & Waller, G. (1999) The impact of emotion upon eating behaviour: The role of subliminal visual processing of threat cues. *International Journal of Eating Disorders*, **25**, 319–26.

Mills, N. & Williams, R. (1997) Cognitions are never enough: The use of 'body metaphor' in therapy with reference to Barnard and Teesdale's ICS model. *Clinical Psychology Forum*, **110**, 9–13.

Murray, C., Waller, G. & Legg, C. (2000) Family dysfunction and bulimic psychopathology: The mediating role of shame. *International Journal of Eating Disorders*, **28**, 84–89.

Mussell, M.P., Crosby, R.D., Crow, S.J., Knopke, A.J., Peterson, C.B., Wonderlich, S.A. & Mitchell, J.E. (2000) Utilization of empirically supported psychotherapy treatments for individuals with eating disorders: A survey of psychologists. *International Journal of Eating Disorders*, **27**, 230–237.

Norris, D.L. (1984) The effects of mirror confrontation on self-estimation of body dimensions in anorexia nervosa, bulimia and two control groups. *Psychological Medicine*, **14**, 835–842.

Ohanian, V. (2002) Imagery rescripting within cognitive behaviour therapy for bulimia nervosa: An illustrative case report. *International Journal of Eating Disorders*, **31**, 352–357.

Ohanian, V. & Waller, G. (1999, April) Cognitive behavioural treatment of complex cases of bulimia: Use of schema-focused therapy and imagery rescripting. Conference paper presented at *Eating Disorders'99*, London.

Padesky, C. (1994) Schema change processes in cognitive therapy. *Clinical Psychology and Psychotherapy*, **1**, 267–278.

Patton, C.J. (1992) Fear of abandonment and binge eating: A subliminal psychodynamic activation investigation. *Journal of Nervous and Mental Disease*, **180**, 484–490.

Persons, J. (1989) *Cognitive Therapy in Practice: A Case Formulation Approach*. New York: Norton.

Power, M. (1997) Conscious and unconscious representations of meaning. In M. Power & C. Brewin (Eds), *The Transformation of Meaning in Psychological Therapies*. Chichester: John Wiley & Sons.

Ramachandran, V.S. (1998) Consciousness and body image: lessons from phantom limbs, Capgrass syndrome and pain asymbolia. *Philosophical Transactions of the Royal Society of London: Brain and Biological Sciences*, **353**, 1851–1859.

Root, M.P.P. & Fallon, P. (1989) Treating the victimized bulimic. *Journal of Interpersonal Violence*, **4**, 90–100.

Rosen, J. (1997) Cognitive behavioural body image therapy. In D. Garner & P. Garfinkel (Eds), *Handbook of Treatments for Eating Disorders*. New York: Guilford Press.

Ryle, A. (1997) The structure and development of borderline personality disorder: A proposed model. *British Journal of Psychiatry*, **170**, 82–87.

Safran, J.D. & Segal, Z.V. (1990) Interpersonal process. In *Cognitive Therapy*. New York: Basic Books.

Sansone, R.A. & Fine, M.A. (1992) Borderline personality disorder as a predictor of outcome in women with eating disorders. *Journal of Personality Disorders*, **6**, 176–186.

Schotte, D.E. (1992) On the special status of 'ego threats'. *Journal of Personality and Social Psychology*, **62**, 798–800.

Serpell, L., Treasure, J., Teasdale, J. & Sullivan V. (1999) Anorexia nervosa: Friend or foe? *International Journal of Eating Disorders*, **25**, 177–186.

Slade, P. (1982) Towards a functional analysis of anorexia nervosa and bulimia nervosa. *British Journal of Clinical Psychology*, **21**, 167–179.

Smucker, M.R., Dancu, C., Foa, E.B. & Niederee, J.L. (1995) Imagery rescripting: A new treatment for survivors of childhood sexual abuse suffering from posttraumatic stress. *Journal of Cognitive Psychotherapy: An International Quarterly*, **9**, 3–17.

Steiger, H., Gauvin, L., Jabalpurwala, S., Seguin, J.R. & Stotland, S. (1999) Hypersensitivity to social interactions in bulimic syndromes: Relationship to binge eating. *Journal of Consulting and Clinical Psychology*, **67**, 765–775.

Striegel-Moore, R.H., Silberstein, L.R. & Rodin, J. (1993) The social self in bulimia nervosa: Public self-consciousness, social anxiety, and perceived fraudulence. *Journal of Abnormal Psychology*, **102**, 297–303.

Teasdale, J.D. (1996) Clinically relevant theory: Integrating clinical insight with cognitive science. In P.M. Salkovskis (Ed.), *Frontiers of Cognitive Therapy*. New York: Guilford Press.

Telch, C.F. (1997) Skills training treatment for adaptive affect regulation in a woman with binge-eating disorder. *International Journal of Eating Disorders*, **22**, 77–81.

Treasure, J.L., Katzman, M., Schmidt, U., Troop, N., Todd, G. & de Silva, P. (1999) Engagement and outcome in the treatment of bulimia nervosa: First phase of a sequential design comparing motivation enhancement therapy and cognitive behavioural therapy. *Behaviour Research and Therapy*, **37**, 405–418.

Vitousek, K.B. (1996) The current status of cognitive behavioural models of anorexia nervosa and bulimia nervosa. In P.M. Salkovskis (Ed.), *Frontiers of Cognitive Therapy* (pp. 383–418) New York: Guilford Press.

Waller, G. (1997) Drop-out and failure to engage in individual outpatient cognitive-behaviour therapy for bulimic disorders. *International Journal of Eating Disorders*, **22**, 35–41.

Waller, G., Ohanian, V., Meyer, C. & Osman, S. (2000) Cognitive content among bulimic women: The role of core beliefs. *International Journal of Eating Disorders*, **28**, 235–241.

Waters, A., Hill, A. & Waller, G. (2001) Bulimics' responses to food cravings: Is binge-eating a product of hunger or emotional state? *Behaviour Research and Therapy*, **39**, 877–886.

Wells, A. & Matthews, G. (1994) *Attention and Emotion. A Clinical Perspective*. Hillsdale, NJ: Lawrence Erlbaum Associates.

Wildgoose, A., Clarke, S. & Waller, G. (2001) Treating personality fragmentation and dissociation in borderline personality disorder: A pilot study of the impact of cognitive analytic therapy. *British Journal of Medical Psychology*, **74**, 47–55.

Williams, J.M.G., Watts, F.N., MacLeod, C. & Mathews, A. (1997) *Cognitive Psychology and Emotional Disorders* (2nd edition). New York: John Wiley & Sons.

Wilson, G.T. (1996) Treatment of bulimia nervosa: When CBT fails. *Behaviour Research and Therapy*, **34**, 197–212.

Wilson, G.T. (1999) Cognitive behavior therapy for eating disorders: Progress and problems. *Behaviour Research and Therapy*, **37**, S79–S95.

Wiser, S. & Telch, C.F. (1999) Dialectical behavior therapy for binge-eating disorder. *Journal of Clinical Psychology*, **55**, 755–768.

Wooley, S.C. & Garner, D.M. (1991) Obesity treatment: The high cost of false hope. *Journal of the American Dietetic Association*, **91**, 1248–1251.

Young, J.E. (1994) *Cognitive Therapy for Personality Disorders: A Schema-Focused Approach* (2nd edition). Sarasota, FL: Professional Resource Exchange.

CHAPTER 15

Interpersonal Psychotherapy

Denise Wilfley

Department of Psychiatry, Washington University in St. Louis School of Medicine, USA

Rick Stein

The State University of New York, Department of Paediatrics, USA

and

Robinson Welch

Department of Psychiatry, Washington University in St. Louis School of Medicine, USA

SUMMARY

- IPT is a focused, goal-driven treatment which targets interpersonal problem(s) associated with the onset and/or maintenance of the eating disorder.
- IPT is supported by substantial empirical evidence documenting the role of interpersonal factors in the onset and maintenance of eating disorders.
- IPT is a viable alternative to CBT for the treatment of BN and BED and is under investigation for the treatment of AN.
- Future research directions include the identification of mechanisms and predictors of IPT, the dissemination of IPT in applied settings, and the examination of IPT with specific subgroups of eating-disordered patients.

INTRODUCTION

Interpersonal psychotherapy (IPT), initially developed as a short-term, outpatient psychological treatment for major depression (Klerman et al., 1984), has been successfully adapted to treat other types of mood and several non-mood disorders including bulimia nervosa (BN) and binge eating disorder (BED) (for a review see Weissman et al., 2000). Although cognitive-behavioral therapy (CBT) for BN produces more rapid changes in the short-term, IPT for BN has consistently demonstrated equal efficacy in the long-term (Agras et al., 2000; Fairburn et al., 1991, 1993, 1995). In treating BED, IPT has demonstrated similar efficacy to CBT in both the short and long term (Wilfley et al., 1993, 2002). At this time,

Handbook of Eating Disorders. Edited by J. Treasure, U. Schmidt and E. van Furth.
© 2003 John Wiley & Sons, Ltd.

there are no empirical data on the use of IPT for AN, but a psychotherapy trial is currently underway to evaluate its effectiveness (McIntosh et al., 2000).

IPT is derived from theories in which interpersonal function is recognized to be a critical component of psychological adjustment and well-being. It is also based on empirical research which has linked change in the social environment to the onset and maintenance of depression. As applied to eating disorders, IPT assumes that the development of eating disorders occurs in a social and interpersonal context. Both the maintenance of the disorder and response to treatment are presumed to be influenced by the interpersonal relationships between the eating-disordered patient and significant others. Consequently, IPT for eating disorders focuses on identifying and altering the interpersonal context in which the eating problem has been developed and maintained. This chapter provides the empirical basis of IPT for eating disorders and describes its application to eating disorders. Emphasis is placed on the use of IPT with BN and BED, given that the status of IPT as an effective treatment for AN still remains unknown. Case examples are provided to illustrate IPT methods, strategies and techniques. Areas in need of further investigation are also delineated.

EMPIRICAL BASIS FOR AN INTERPERSONAL APPROACH TO EATING DISORDERS

There is compelling evidence that interpersonal factors play a significant role in the etiology and maintenance of eating disorders. As basic examples, many AN and BN patients report having experienced serious stressors related to relationships with family or friends prior to the onset of the disorder (Schmidt et al., 1997). With BN and BED, a history of exposure to negative interpersonal factors (e.g. critical comments from family about shape, weight, or eating; low parental contact) are among the specific retrospective correlates (Fairburn et al., 1997, 1998). Identification of such interpersonal factors fills a gap in other etiological theories. For example, restraint theory, a widely embraced theory emphasizing the role of dieting in the etiology of binge-eating problems does not seem satisfactory to account for the development of BED, particularly since only about half of BED patients dieted before the onset of their eating disorder (Spurrell et al., 1997). According to interpersonal vulnerability models of eating disorders (e.g. Wilfley et al., 1997), some of the missing factors in the restraint model include interpersonal functioning, mood, and self-esteem, all of which are empirically supported as related to the onset/maintenance of eating disorder symptoms.

First, there is a great deal of evidence that interpersonal problems and deficits play a significant role in all three eating disorders. Individuals with eating disorders are more lonely (O'Mahony & Hollwey, 1995) and perceive lower social support than do non-eating-disordered individuals. They have fewer support figures, less emotional and practical support, and are less likely to seek out support as a way to cope with problems (Ghaderi & Scott, 1999; Rorty et al., 1999; Tiller et al., 1997; Troop et al., 1994). Eating disorders are associated with difficulty in various areas of social adjustment including work, social/leisure, extended family, and global functioning (Herzog et al., 1987). Eating disordered women also report and demonstrate lower competence, relative to subclinical and normal control women, in coping with social stress and social problem situations, including independence from family, family conflict, female peer conflict, and male rejection (Grissett & Norvell, 1992; McFall et al., 1999). This lack of competence is especially relevant because serious life stresses that involve the patients relationships with family or friends tend to precede

AN and BN (Schmidt et al., 1997). Interpersonal stress may create more disinhibited eating among restrained eaters (Tanofsky-Kraff et al., 2000) and bulimics (Tuschen-Caffier & Vögele, 1999) than do other types of stressors. In addition, obese women with BED experience significantly higher levels of interpersonal problems than those without BED (Telch & Agras, 1994). This set of findings indicates that some eating-disordered individuals may lack the social skills necessary to establish and/or sustain supportive relationships and to cope with problem social situations, and these problems may be directly linked with the onset and maintenance of eating disorder symptomatology.

Some research has focused on difficulties that eating-disordered women may have in their relationships with men. For example, level of bulimic symptomatology among female college students is significantly correlated with dissatisfaction in relationships with men, as well as reported level of difficulty forming and maintaining friendships and romantic relationships with men (Thelen et al., 1990, 1993). Other data indicate that eating disorder symptomatology is correlated with lower ratings of closeness in romantic relationships (O'Mahony & Hollwey, 1995), and that eating-disordered women may even avoid sexual activity within their romantic relationships (see, e.g., McIntosh et al., 2000; Segrin, in press, for reviews; see also Woodside et al., 1993). Indeed, married women seeking treatment for an eating disorder had levels of marital distress comparable to couples seeking marital therapy (Van Buren & Williamson, 1988). This set of findings suggests that eating-disordered women may have difficulty negotiating their roles within their platonic and romantic relationships with men.

A considerable amount of research has focused on the family-of-origin history prior to the onset of the disorder. Eating disorders are associated with low perceived family cohesion (see Segrin, in press). Eating-disordered individuals are more likely to receive critical comments from their families about shape, weight, or eating, and experience low parental contact (Fairburn et al., 1997, 1998). They may also experience parental pressure that is inappropriate for their age, gender, or abilities (Horesh et al., 1996). In addition, several aspects of family dynamics—warmth, communication, affective expression, and control— have been identified as problematic for some eating-disordered patients (see Segrin, in press, for a review). These kinds of problems in family relationships and family environment have been prospective predictors of the later development of eating disorders (e.g. Calam & Waller, 1998). Finally, women with BN and BED report more sexual and physical abuse experiences than non-eating-disordered women, but similar levels as individuals with other psychiatric disorders (e.g. Striegel-Moore et al., 2001; Welch & Fairburn, 1994).

In addition, many studies have supported the notion that interpersonal problems may be linked to eating disorder symptomatology through lowered self-esteem and negative affect. Low self-esteem often predates AN and may be a core aspect of problematic thinking patterns in AN (Garner et al., 1997). Similarly, retrospective risk factor research indicates that negative self-evaluation predates the eating disorder and distinguishes BN patients from both normal and general psychiatric controls (Fairburn et al., 1997); it may also be associated with a desire to binge in the face of stress (Cattanach et al., 1988). Eating-disordered women may experience self-esteem problems specifically in the social domain, for example, they have elevated concern with how others view them, and have a high need for social approval, relative to non-eating-disordered individuals (see Wilfley et al., 1997).

In terms of mood, evidence supports that affective restraint is a common distinguishing personality trait of premorbid AN patients (Wonderlich, 1995), and that negative affect strengthened the relation between dietary restraint and binge eating among a community sample of adolescents (Stice et al., 2000). For eating-disordered individuals, data indicates that negative affect often precipitates a binge-eating episode (e.g. Greeno et al., 2000; Kenardy et al., 2001; Steiger et al., 1999; Telch & Agras, 1996). Purging among bulimics may partly serve to manage negative affect (e.g. Powell & Thelen, 1996; Schupak-Neuberg & Nemeroff, 1993). Even more specifically relevant for IPT, a recent experience-sampling study among bulimics found that negative social interactions are associated with increased self-criticism and lowered mood (Steiger et al., 1999). In this study, negative social interactions, self-criticism, and lowered mood all tended to precede binge episodes. After bingeing, participants experienced further deteriorations in self-esteem and mood, as well as more negative perceptions of social experiences. These findings underscore the theoretical link among eating disorder symptomatology and these three factors—interpersonal functioning, self-esteem, and mood, all of which are targeted by IPT (see also reviews by Heatherton & Baumeister, 1991; McManus & Waller, 1995; Wilfley et al., 1997).

Overall, it appears that eating-disordered individuals have a history of more frequent difficult social experiences, including problematic family histories and specific interpersonal stressors, than non-eating-disordered individuals. They also experience a wide range of social problems such as loneliness, lack of perceived social support, low social adjustment, and poor social problem-solving skills, possibly leaving them with inadequate resources and social competence to cope with interpersonal stressors. Finally, interpersonal difficulties, low self-esteem, and negative affect may all be interconnected and related to eating disorder problems. These factors may thus create a vicious cycle of exacerbating each other and combine to precipitate and/or maintain symptoms among eating-disordered individuals. IPT aims to improve interpersonal functioning, self-esteem, and negative affect, as they relate to each other and to eating disorder symptoms. The specific areas of interpersonal functioning that are identified and targeted by IPT are consistent with the pattern of problems described above.

IMPLEMENTATION OF THE TREATMENT

Timeline for Therapy

The typical course of IPT for eating disorders lasts 15–20 sessions over a four-to five-month time period (Fairburn et al., 1998; Wilfley et al., 1998). Treatment progresses through three distinct phases: the initial phase of identifying the problem area in significant relationships, the middle phase of working on the target problem area(s), and the late phase of consolidating work and preparing patients for future work on their own.

Interpersonal Problem Areas

IPT focuses on the resolution of problems within four social domains that are associated with the onset and/or maintenance of the disorder namely: grief, interpersonal deficits, interpersonal role disputes, and role transitions. Grief is identified as the problem area when the onset of the patients symptoms are associated with the loss of a person or a relationship, either recent or past. Interpersonal deficits apply to those patients who are socially isolated or who are in chronically unfulfilling relationships. Interpersonal role disputes are conflicts with a significant other (e.g. a partner, other family member, coworker, or close friend) which emerge from differences in expectations about the relationship. Role transition includes any difficulties resulting from a change in life status (e.g. leaving a job or one's home, going away to school, divorce, other economic, health, or family changes). See Table 15.1 for a fuller description of the interpersonal problem areas, as well as treatment goals and therapeutic strategies.

Generally, one of the four IPT problem areas can be readily applied to eating-disordered patients. For example, in Table 15.2, the distribution of primary problem areas are presented across the three disorders. The percentages of problem areas were obtained from psychotherapy studies for BN and BED (Fairburn et al., 1993; Wilfley et al., 2002), and from an interview-based study for AN (McIntosh et al., 2000). For all three disorders, grief was uncommon whereas role disputes were fairly common. The notable differences among the disorders were that interpersonal deficits were more likely to be found among BED and AN patients, and role transitions were more common among BN patients.

TREATMENT PHASES, GOALS AND STRATEGIES

The *initial phase*, ordinarily four to five sessions, includes diagnostic assessment and psychiatric history and establishes the context for the treatment. After a standardized diagnostic symptom review is conducted, the patient is diagnosed as having an eating disorder and assigned a sick role. The sick role identifies patients as in need of help, exempts them from additional social pressures and elicits their cooperation in the process of recovery. Because many eating-disordered individuals camouflage their own social difficulties by meeting others' needs rather than their own, the sick role is assigned to relieve them of excessive caretaking tendencies. It is explained to them that only by confronting their need to please others and redirecting some of this energy toward themselves, will they be able to recover from their eating problems. The therapist and patient then discuss the diagnosis and what the patient might expect from treatment. Symptom relief starts with helping the patient to understand that the eating disorder symptoms (e.g. recurrent pattern of binge eating, extreme dietary restriction, and dysfunctional attitudes about shape and weight) are part of a known syndrome, which responds to several treatments and has a good prognosis. Patients are informed that IPT focuses on altering current interpersonal patterns and life situations in order to eliminate their eating disorder.

The therapist conducts an interpersonal inventory which includes a review of the patient's past/current social functioning and close relationships. For each person who is important in the patient's life the following information is assessed: frequency of contact, activities shared, satisfactory and unsatisfactory aspects of the relationship, and ways that the patient would like to change the relationship. The interpersonal inventory provides a structure for elucidating the social and interpersonal context of the onset and maintenance of eating disorder symptoms and delineates the focus of treatment. Of particular importance are changes in relationships proximal to the onset of symptoms (e.g. the death of a significant other, changing to a new job, increasing marital discord, or disconnection from a friend). The therapist obtains a chronological history of significant life events, fluctuations in mood and self-esteem, interpersonal relationships, and eating disorder symptoms. From this review, the therapist can make a connection between certain life experiences and eating disorder symptoms. As this interrelationship is delineated, patients understand more clearly the rationale of IPT.

Table 15.1 Interpersonal problem areas: description, goals, and strategies (Klerman et al., 1984; Weissman et al., 2000)

Interpersonal problem area	Description	Goals	Strategies
Grief	Complicated bereavement following the death of a loved one	• Facilitate the mourning process • Help patient re-establish interest in new activities and relationships to substitute for what has been lost	• Reconstruct the patient's relationship with the deceased • Explore associated feelings (negative and positive) • Consider ways of becoming re-involved with others
Interpersonal deficits	A history of social impoverishment, inadequate, or unsustaining interpersonal relationships	• Reduce patient's social isolation • Enhance quality of any existing relationships • Encourage the formation of new relationships	• Review past significant relationships including negative and positive aspects • Explore repetitive patterns in relationships • Note problematic interpersonal patterns in the session and relate them to similar patterns in the patient's life
Interpersonal role disputes	Conflicts with a significant other: a partner, other family member, coworker, or close friend	• Identify the nature of the dispute • Explore options to resolve the dispute • Modify expectations and faulty communication to bring about a satisfactory resolution • If modification is unworkable, encourage patient to reassess the expectations for the relationship and to generate options to either resolve it or to dissolve it and mourn its loss	• Determine the stage of the dispute: renegotiation (calm down participants to facilitate resolution); impasse (increase disharmony in order to reopen negotiation); dissolution (assist mourning and adaptation) • Understand how non-reciprocal role expectations relate to the dispute • Identify available resources to bring about change in the relationship
Role transitions	Economic or family change: the beginning or end of a relationship or career, a move, promotion, retirement, graduation, diagnosis of a medical illness	• Mourn and accept the loss of the old role • Recognize the positive and negative aspects of the new role, and assets and liabilities of the old role • Restore self-esteem by developing a sense of mastery regarding the demands of the new role	• Review positive and negative aspects of old and new roles • Explore feelings about what is lost • Encourage development of social support system and new skills called for in new role

Table 15.2   Distribution of problem areas

Problem areas	Anorexia nervosa[a]	Bulimia nervosa[b]	Binge eating disorder[c]
Grief	6%	12%	6%
Interpersonal disputes	33%	16%	60%
Role disputes	33%	64%	30%
Role transitions	17%	36%	4%
Other	11%	N/A	N/A

[a] It is important to note that the percentages of problem areas for AN were taken as patient report during a 10-year follow-up by Sullivan et al. Patients were asked in an open-ended fashion what they believed contributed to their eating disorder. Their answers were then coded into one of the four problem areas. Patient answers that could not be coded into one of the four problem areas were placed in other. (*Source*: McIntosh et al., 2000.)
[b] The percentages total over 100% because some patients were identified as having more than a single problem area. (*Source*: Fairburn, 1997.)
[c] The percentages total 100% as they reflect each patient's primary problem area. (*Source*: Wilfley et al., 2000a.)

The therapist then links the eating disorder syndrome to one of the four interpersonal problem areas: grief, interpersonal deficits, interpersonal role disputes, or role transitions. Although the therapist explicitly assigns a problem area (i.e. the interpersonal formulation), the patient needs to concur with the salience of the problem area proposed and agree to work on it in treatment. Because the four problem areas are relatively inclusive, it is typically quite easy for the therapist to provide an individualized formulation. While patients may fit into several problem areas, the time-limited nature of treatment dictates limiting the choice to one, or at most two, problem areas, in order to clearly define a treatment focus. Once the problem area(s) is agreed upon, a treatment plan with specified goals to work on is formulated. These goals guide day-to-day work and are referenced at each meeting in order to maintain the focus of treatment. If more than one problem area is identified, the patient may elect to work on both simultaneously or to address first the problem that seems to be most responsive to treatment.

During the *intermediate phase* of treatment, typically eight to ten sessions, the therapist implements treatment strategies that are specific to the identified problem area as specified by Klerman and colleagues (1984). For grief, the goals include facilitating mourning and helping the patient find new activities and relationships to substitute for the loss. For role transition, the therapist helps the patient to manage the change by recognizing positive and negative aspects of the new role he or she is assuming, as well as the pros and cons of the old role this replaces. For interpersonal role disputes, the therapist assists the patient in identifying the nature of the dispute and generates options to resolve it. If the patient and therapist conclude that resolution is impossible, the therapist assists the patient in dissolving the relationship and in mourning its loss. For interpersonal deficits, the goal is to improve the patient's social skills and to reduce the patient's social isolation by helping to enhance the quality of existing relationships and encourage the formation of new relationships.

In the *termination phase* of treatment, usually four to five sessions, patients are encouraged to describe specific changes in their eating behaviors, especially as they relate to improvements in the identified problem area(s). The therapist assists the patient in evaluating and consolidating gains, acknowledging the feelings associated with termination, detailing plans for maintaining improvements in the identified interpersonal problem area(s), and outlining remaining work for the patient to continue on his or her own. Patients are also encouraged to identify early warning signs of symptom recurrence (e.g. dietary restriction) and to identify plans of action.

Throughout the three phases, focus stays on the interpersonal context of a patient's life. Thus, in the case of a patient with eating disorder symptoms, the therapist will focus on relationship difficulties that exacerbate the symptoms rather than review cognitions or inner conflict associated with the eating disorder. Once the treatment goals have been established, the therapist refers to them in each session. Descriptive phrases such as moving forward on your goals, and making important changes are used to encourage patients to be responsible for their treatment while reminding them that altering interpersonal patterns requires attention and persistence. Indeed, research on IPT maintenance treatment for recurrent depression has demonstrated that the therapist's ability to maintain focus on interpersonal themes is associated with better outcomes (Frank et al., 1991). In session, unfocused discussions are redirected to the key interpersonal issues, and abstract or general discussions are minimized in order to preserve focus. Therapists refrain from making inquiries that evoke vague or passive responses, such as general questions about the patient's week. Rather, sessions begin with questions such as what would you like to work on today? Or how have you worked on your goals since we last met? These questions provide more direction for the patient and focus them on the present. The therapist assists the patient in drawing connections between interpersonal events and eating problems. Patients are asked to pay careful attention to what triggers binge eating, as these episodes are often precipitated by interpersonal stressors and negative mood. Consequently, patients begin to recognize that problematic eating is often an important indicator of interpersonal problems that might otherwise go unnoticed (Fairburn, 1997).[1]

THERAPEUTIC STANCE AND TECHNIQUES

Similar to many other therapies, in IPT, the focus is on establishing a positive therapeutic alliance. Specifically, the IPT therapeutic stance is one of warmth, support, and empathy. The therapist is active and serves as patient advocate. The therapist helps the patient feel comfortable by phrasing comments positively in order to foster a safe and supportive working environment. In addition, the therapist conveys a hopeful stance and optimistic attitude about the patient's ability to recover. Confrontations and clarifications are offered in a gentle and timely manner and the therapist is careful to encourage the patient's positive expectations of the therapeutic relationship.

Techniques include exploratory questions, encouragement of affect, clarification, communication analysis, use of therapeutic relationship, behavior change techniques, and adjunctive techniques (for a description of these techniques, see Klerman et al., 1984). IPT's focus on affect evocation and exploration is especially relevant for eating-disordered patients, given that problematic eating often functions as a way to regulate negative affect. Specifically, the IPT therapist helps patients: (1) acknowledge and accept painful affects, (2) use affective experiences to bring about desired interpersonal changes, and (3) experience suppressed affects.

---

[1] To minimize procedural overlap with CBT, research applications of IPT have not included a symptom focus during the second and third phases of treatment.

CASE EXAMPLES

The first case example illustrates the therapist's presentation to the patient of the interpersonal formulation that links the onset of the eating disorder to one of the four interpersonal problem areas. The therapist's ability to rapidly discern patterns in interpersonal relationships, connect events with the onset and maintenance of the disorder, and formulate goals are crucial to the time-limited nature of IPT. In addition, the case vignettes illustrate the strategies and techniques used with each of the four problem areas (i.e., role transitions, role disputes, interpersonal deficits, and grief, respectively).

The Interpersonal Formulation/Role Transitions: The Case of W

W is a 51-year-old woman who presented for treatment of BED. She is college educated, has her own business, and is a divorced mother of one adult son in his early twenties. Prior to treatment, W had a BMI of 42 and had been binge eating approximately 10–15 days per month for the last eight years. Along with her current diagnosis of BED, W struggled with recurrent major depression.

During the *Initial Phase*, W and her therapist began to review her history and the interpersonal events that were associated with her binge eating. W shared that she began over-eating and gaining weight at age 14. When she was age 18 she moved to a foreign country with her parents. Soon after the move, W's father left her and her mother to return to the United States. W was enraged at her father for leaving them, and still gets very tearful and angry when discussing the separation. W and her mother decided to stay abroad since W had started university and W's mother was working. Both had developed strong social ties and felt comfortable in their new home. During this time, W continued to gain weight, and started dieting. Shortly after graduating from university, W met and married a foreign national and at age 28 delivered their only son. Two years later, W and her husband went through a very bitter divorce. Although we described this as a terrible time in her life, she maintained close ties with her friends and her mother. During this time, she began to diet and reached her lowest adult weight. At age 35 when W's mother died of a heart condition, she had her first episode of major depression, which was treated and resolved with antidepressants and a brief course of psychotherapy. Although W had previous cycles of weight loss and weight regain, she did not evidence any sign of eating disturbance at this point. W continued to maintain close social ties and enjoyed her close relationship with her son. When W was in her early forties, an economic downturn in her adopted country forced her to return to the USA. Having lost all of her savings, W struggled financially while she looked for work. During this time, W started binge eating and gaining weight. Within a year of this move, W's son decided to return to live with his father (who was very wealthy). W felt angry and betrayed. Yet, when her son would visit, she would assume a subservient role with him, as she was afraid of losing his affection. He, in turn, became quite demanding and critical of her. Prior to seeking treatment, her heightened feelings of isolation and loneliness were leading to increased binge eating, depression and weight gain.

By session 3 of the Initial Phase, W's therapist began to consider which problem area would be the focus of the remainder of treatment. W had a history of important relationship losses and subsequent grief: the loss of her father, her husband, her mother, and most recently, her son when he went back to live with his father. However, none of these losses were associated with the development of binge-eating problems (although her dieting was clearly linked to her feelings of anger after the divorce from her husband, and her depression was intimately linked with her mother's death). W's anger at her son for returning to live with the enemy was clearly a role dispute, yet her binge eating had begun two years prior to his departure (although it clearly worsened after he left). Since neither of these problem areas were directly linked to the onset of the eating disorder, W's therapist decided that the focus of treatment would be to assist W in managing her role transition. W's move back to the USA, with the subsequent loss of her support and friendship networks, were clearly associated with the onset and continued maintenance of her binge eating. During the fourth session of the Initial Phase, W's therapist shared her formulation of the problem area with her:

> From what you have described, your binge eating really began after you returned to the USA. After that transition, you were more isolated and alone than you have ever been. It seems that binge eating was a way for you to manage that transition and the subsequent feelings of isolation and loneliness. Your transition has also had a negative impact on your relationship with your son. Even though you are a very social person and enjoy the company of others, you have yet to develop the kind of support that you had before you moved. Although you have struggled with some very significant issues over the course of your life your father leaving, the pain of the divorce, and the death of your mother your friends and support systems sustained you. If we work together to help you find and develop more intimate and supportive relationships here, I believe you will be much less likely to turn to food and binge eating as a source of support or comfort.

W agreed with the formulation and worked with her therapist to establish some treatment goals to help her resolve the problem area. First, W was encouraged to become more aware of her feelings (especially isolation and loneliness) when she was binge eating, and how binge eating seemed to be the way she managed those feelings. A second goal was for W to take steps to increase her social contacts and develop more friendships. The third goal, which was identified as a secondary problem area, centered on helping W resolve the role dispute with her son. Specifically, the therapist developed a goal with W to help her establish a clearer parental role with her son.

During the *Intermediate Phase*, the therapist helped W grieve the loss of her previous role and the extensive support that she once had. W and her therapist worked to identify several sources of support and friendships of which she had not been aware. Soon after, W reported significant progress in initiating and establishing relationships with others. This change appeared to help give her confidence in her new roles. In fact, she had begun to receive a few social invitations. She was more attuned to the ways that she would rely on food especially when she felt lonely or felt that she was not receiving enough time from others. The connection between the lack of supportive contacts and binge eating was becoming very clear to her in these intermediate sessions. During this phase, the therapist also assisted W in setting appropriate limits in her relationship with her adult son, and recognizing his adult-like responses in return.

By the *Termination Phase*, W reported that she no longer felt so lonely and isolated and that her binge eating had all but disappeared. She remarked how the quality of her relationship with her son had changed dramatically. He was more supportive and respectful, visited more frequently, and stayed with her for longer periods of time. In the final sessions, she talked about her need to let go of the past and move on to her life as it is now, assuming her new roles more fully. She worked closely with her therapist to develop a plan to maintain the gains that she had made in treatment and used the final session to review the important work that she had accomplished.

Interpersonal Role Disputes: The Case of S

S is a 35-year-old woman who presented for treatment of her BN. S is married to a lawyer and has one child. When she came in for treatment, she was bingeing and vomiting an average of five times per week. Her pattern was to binge and purge when she was alone on the weekend and during the week when husband was at work and her son at school. Although S did not work, she was actively involved in her community church, and attended several extracurricular activities (e.g. dance class, weight lifting) during the week. S indicated that she used to work with her husband as his office manager, but stopped about five years ago. She described her relationship with her husband as cold and passionless. S did not think that her husband really cared that much for her. She did say that he was a great father to her son and that she should love him, but wondered whether or not she did.

During the *Initial Phase*, S and her therapist began to review her history and the interpersonal events that were associated with the onset of her BN. Although S had a history of dieting, her bingeing and vomiting had begun 10 years ago soon after her marriage to her husband. S has strong religious convictions and did not have sexual intercourse with her husband until their honeymoon. Her husband was fairly forceful with her on their honeymoon night and caused her great physical discomfort. She thought that she would enjoy intercourse but since their honeymoon had not been interested in having intercourse with him. She never raised this issue with her husband, and at the time of treatment had not mentioned to him her dissatisfaction with their sex life. Currently, she let him have intercourse with her about two times per month and resented even this limited sexual relationship. When S's therapist explored with her any other significant interpersonal events connected with the onset of her bingeing and vomiting, S related that soon after their marriage, S and her husband began to have financial problems. Specifically, her husband had lied to her about the amount of debt he had accrued during law school. In addition, they had used her savings to establish a private practice for him. When the practice failed, they went even further into debt. S tried to assist her husband by helping him with billing and collection, but her efforts did not help. At that time S felt angry, resentful and trapped. During that time about five years prior to treatment, her bingeing and vomiting were at their worst. Currently, S found herself bingeing and vomiting more frequently when bills came to the house, and when she knew that her husband was going to want to be with her sexually.

Toward the end of the initial phase, S's therapist asked her if she was interested in working on and improving her relationship with her husband. S confessed that she did still have loving feelings toward her husband, and would be willing to work on the relationship. She indicated however, that she did not understand how talking about her relationship with her husband would help her eating disorder. At this point, S's therapist acknowledged her skepticism and then began to conceptualize her bingeing and vomiting in terms of a role dispute with her husband. The therapist speculated that S was binge eating and vomiting as a means to manage her anger and frustration at her husband over their financial woes and his insensitivity to her sexual needs. To punctuate this point, the therapist reminded her of the several examples she had given in which her bingeing and vomiting occurred either before or after these two events occurred. The therapist then suggested that a focus on helping S resolve her resentment and anger toward her husband would help to improve the quality of her relationship with him and to eliminate her BN. Although still somewhat skeptical, S acknowledged the connection and agreed to work on the role dispute with her husband.[2] At this point, S and her therapist developed a set of goals to guide their work through the remainder of treatment.

In the *Intermediate Phase* of treatment, S and her therapist began working on her goals. The therapist concluded that S's relationship with her husband was at an impasse, because they had not discussed the frustration that S was feeling, nor had they talked about their passionless relationship. S's therapist first encouraged her to be honest with her husband about her current bulimic symptoms (she had told him it stopped five years earlier) and her feelings about their sex life—including the experience she had during their honeymoon. This task took place over several sessions in which the therapist worked closely with S on her communication style and delivery. Although S's husband was initially overwhelmed and angry about her feedback (specifically that she had never told him), he soon acknowledged her feelings and apologized for his behavior on their honeymoon and asked her what, if anything, he could do to make things better. During a joint meeting with S and her husband, the therapist was able to help S's husband verbalize his feelings of love and passion for her feelings that he had locked away because he thought she did not care for him. As a result of this meeting, S began to take more control of their sexual encounters and found herself enjoying intercourse with him for the first time. Her therapist also encouraged her to talk more with her husband about her concerns over their finances, since this was another goal that she had set for herself. As a result, S and her

---

[2] In our clinical experience, we have found that approximately one-fifth of patients are initially skeptical of the interpersonal approach. Nonetheless, most of these patients do agree to work on the identified problem area and typically end up profiting from treatment.

husband began to seek financial advice and developed a concrete plan to decrease their debt. As S and her husband began to engage with one another more actively, S's bingeing began to dissipate.

By the beginning of the *Termination Phase* of treatment, S's bingeing had ceased. During the final sessions with her therapist, S noted the improvements she had made. Specifically, she cited the importance of being able to make the connection between her eating disorder and her relationship difficulties with her husband. She also shared how talking with her husband about her feelings and sharing the distress she felt during their honeymoon was an important breakthrough for her. S realized that as she took more control over her feelings and her relationship with her husband, their marriage improved and her eating disorder resolved. In the final sessions, S and her therapist developed a plan for her to identify and manage periods when she might have an urge to binge. Specifically, her therapist encouraged her to keep sharing with her husband, and to maintain open communication about their relationship.

Interpersonal Deficits: The Case of C

C is a 45-year-old woman who presented for treatment for binge eating. C is a hairdresser and was currently in a live-in relationship with a boyfriend of three years. She was bingeing on average 5-6 times per week. Her pattern was to binge on fast food which she purchased and ate during her drive home, after spending 12 to 14 hour days at work. During her work days, she would often work through lunch and stay late to accommodate her clients' busy schedules. When she arrived home, she would also eat dinner with her boyfriend. She described her relationship with him as okay, but stressful as he keeps telling me that I spend too much time at work and not enough time with him. She indicated that she wanted this relationship to be a perfect one. Therefore, she tried to keep the peace and did her best to please him so he would not be mad at her.

During the *Initial Phase*, C and her therapist began to review her history and the interpersonal events associated with the onset of her binge eating. C had a history of conflict avoidance and a fear of criticism. At the age of 15, she began a series of failed relationships that she hid in order to appear as the perfect daughter and to not disappoint her parents. Accordingly, she binged when she was alone to numb out as a way of managing the feelings that she kept private. Her attempts at secrecy and use of food to disconnect from her feelings continued throughout C's marriage at age 20. Although her husband was cruel and verbally abusive, C worked hard to fool everyone for 15 years into believing that she had a perfect, fulfilling relationship because she did not want anyone to think that she had failed in her marriage. Prior to her divorce at age 35, C's bingeing and weight gain were at their worst. In discussing her current relationship, C indicated that she really liked her boyfriend, but she was always worried that he was angry with her about her work. Consequently, she went out of her way to please him so he would not be upset with her. Similarly, she put in 14-hour days because she felt uncomfortable saying no to her customers' requests to see her before and after their business hours.

Toward the end of the initial phase, C and her therapist began to examine the link between her binge eating and her use of food as a way to avoid the conflicted feelings of wanting to please her boyfriend and clients, but at the same time resenting them for the demands they made on her. Given her history of unfulfilling relationships and an inability to manage her current interpersonal relationships effectively, the therapist identified interpersonal deficits as C's primary problem area. C found it very difficult to see how her eating was related to her difficulties in managing relationships. She shared with the therapist that she did not have problems with relationships. 'I have millions of friends.' Given her history, C's therapist chose not to challenge that perception, but instead talked with her about how she seemed to have a difficult time managing the stress of her work life and her current relationship. The therapist speculated to C that her binge eating might be a way to manage this distress. To highlight this, C's therapist shared some examples that C had discussed in previous sessions. C was able to see this link and, along with her therapist, developed specific goals to guide her work during the remainder of treatment.

In the *Intermediate Phase* of treatment, C and her therapist began working on C's goals. C's therapist used the context of the therapeutic relationship to encourage C to notice that specific behaviors—maintaining a perfect façade, glossing over problems, and avoiding conflict—might be preventing her from having more satisfying relationships. Moreover, they were connected to her episodes of binge eating. In session, the therapist used the IPT techniques of clarification, communication analysis, and encouragement of affect to assist C in finding ways of negotiating the conflicts at work and with her boyfriend. After several attempts, C was finally able to resolve conflicts effectively. In addition, C began to share more with her boyfriend and her sisters, communicate more effectively with coworkers, and set limits with customers by refusing some of their requests. As a result, she reported that her relationships were more satisfying, her binge eating had ceased, and that she and her boyfriend had become much closer.

During the *Termination Phase* of treatment, C was able to reflect on the progress that she had made during treatment. Specifically, C shared that when she began treatment, she did not have good relationships. She noted that glossing over problems and trying to maintain a perfect image had actually hindered her relationships with others, and perpetuated her binge eating. She talked about and reviewed with her therapist ways that she had learned to attend to conflict without feeling as if the world was coming to an end. During the final sessions, C and her therapist outlined a plan for C to stay binge free. That is, she would try to share more with others during times of increased work stress, take steps to decrease her work load, and continue sharing her fears and concerns about conflict with her boyfriend.

Grief: The Case of G

G is an overweight 39-year old man who presented for treatment for binge eating. He is married and has two young children. For the last 10 years, he had worked as a physician in an intensive care unit (ICU). Growing anxiety about the family finances and his children's welfare had pushed G to begin working the 11 p.m. to 7 a.m. shift approximately five years prior to beginning treatment. When he came for treatment, G was bingeing on average 10 times per week. His pattern was to come home in the morning after work and eat a large breakfast with his children. After taking his children to school and his wife to work, he would binge eat by himself when he got back home. He was also binge eating prior to returning to work after his wife and children had gone to bed. G was an excellent doctor, but, he found the ICU stressful. It was quite upsetting for him to lose any of his patients. G also indicated that his relationship with his wife and children had become more distant in the past several years, although he still loved them.

During the *Initial Phase*, G and his therapist reviewed his history and the interpersonal events associated with the onset of his binge eating. At age 16 following the death of his father, G began to over-eat and struggle with weight gain. Because his mother was incapacitated by grief, G began, on his own, to assume the primary care of his younger sister, who suffered with a degenerative muscle disease. At age 29, G finished his residency, was married, and began working in the ICU. Shortly after he assumed these new responsibilities, his younger sister passed away. It was during this time that he began to binge eat and experienced his largest weight gain.

Toward the end of the initial phase, G and his therapist examined the link between his binge eating and weight gain with two very significant life events: the death of his father and the death of his younger sister. The therapist explored with G that he may not have had the opportunity to grieve his father's death because of his mother's grief and his decision to assume responsibility for his sister's care. Instead, he began to use food as a way to comfort himself. Similarly, when his younger sister died, G had the responsibility of a new wife and job and was unable to appropriately grieve the loss of his sister. Consequently, G began to binge eat as a way to regulate his feelings. At the time he initiated treatment, G's work was compounding his distress because he was taking care of critically ill patients, a number of whom would die. G's therapist speculated that this might be one of the reasons why he was bingeing prior to and after work. Prior to receiving IPT, G had never made the link between his grief and his binge eating. As a result of this insight, G and his therapist developed goals to guide G's work during the remainder of treatment.

In the *Intermediate Phase* of treatment, G and his therapist began working on G's goals. Specifically, G's therapist helped to facilitate G's delayed mourning for his father and sister. During the first session of this phase, G needed a lot of reassurance from the therapist that he would not lose it if he began to feel strong emotions or cry. With his therapist's help, G reconstructed his relationship with both his father and sister. When he began to do this, G really noticed the connection between his unresolved grief and his binge eating. As treatment progressed, G brought in pictures of his father, letters his sister had written to him when G was away at college, and a book of poetry that was written by his sister. In reliving the memories these documents evoked, G expressed the grief and pain of the deaths and began to work through his guilt about not being a better caretaker for his sister. He expressed some unresolved anger at his mother for abandoning him and leaving him to care for his sister. During this process, G began to see how his unresolved grief, as manifested in his binge eating, hindered his relationship with his wife and children. As a result of this work, G began to share more with his wife (including the feelings about his father and sister) and worked to develop a stronger relationship with her and with his children. This improvement in his family relationships was a secondary benefit of the work on his grief-related goal. Toward the end of the intermediate phase, G had dramatically reduced his binge eating, and had substantially improved his relationship with his wife and children. In addition, he began to explore the possibility of transferring to a less stressful area in the hospital.

During the *Termination Phase* of treatment, G reviewed the changes he had made in his eating, especially as it related to the improvement in his grief. He shared with his therapist how helpful it had been to talk about and express his feelings of loss. He became aware that his work environment had intensified his feelings of grief, leading him to engage in more out-of-control eating. G acknowledged how helpful it had been to share with his wife the grief and loss that he had experienced. He realized that keeping those feelings to himself created more stress and a rift between him and his wife. To prevent a recurrence of binge episodes, G made a plan to decrease his work stress and to continue sharing his thoughts and feelings about his losses with his wife.

EFFECTIVENESS OF IPT FOR EATING DISORDERS

In comparative research studies, IPT has demonstrated successful long-term outcomes that compare favorably with those of CBT for BN and BED. Indeed, IPT is the only psychological treatment for BN that has demonstrated long-term outcomes comparable to CBT. All controlled studies of IPT have been comparison studies with CBT. Early findings with BN indicated similar short- and long-term outcomes for binge eating between CBT and IPT (Fairburn et al., 1993, 1995). A more recent multi-site study (Agras et al., 2000) that also compared CBT and IPT as treatments for BN found that patients receiving CBT evidenced higher rates of abstinence from binge eating, and lower rates of purging behaviors, at post-treatment. However, these rates were equivalent by long-term follow-up (8 months and 1 year following treatment). Moreover, IPT patients rated their treatment as more suitable, and expected greater success, than did CBT patients. This finding suggests that bulimic patients perceive the interpersonal focus of IPT as more relevant to their disorder and treatment needs than the CBT focus on cognitive distortions concerning weight and shape.

For BED, group IPT has been shown to be significantly more effective than waitlist control at reducing binge eating (Wilfley et al., 1993). In two randomized-controlled trials that examined the efficacy of group IPT as compared to group CBT, IPT showed similar results as CBT, proving to be an effective treatment achieving marked short-term and long-term reductions in binge eating (Wilfley et al., 1993, 2002), with 62% of the patients evidencing abstinence from binge eating at 1-year follow-up (Wilfley et al., 2002). Moreover, the time-course of almost all outcomes with IPT was identical to that of CBT. In addition, IPT (similar to CBT) had significant short- and long-term impact on wide-ranging areas of psychosocial functioning, including improvements in eating disorder and general psychopathology, self-esteem, social adjustment, and interpersonal problems. For BED patients, IPT was rated as credible as CBT, and 53% of the patients actually rated, prior to randomization, a preference for being assigned to IPT over CBT.

Although no studies have yet demonstrated the efficacy of IPT for the treatment of AN, McIntosh and colleagues (2000) are currently conducting a randomized clinical trial comparing IPT, CBT, and routine clinical management for a large sample of young women with AN. This research may support the efficacy of IPT for the treatment of AN, similar to its demonstrated efficacy for BN and BED. Because IPT does not focus directly on disturbed attitudes regarding eating, weight, and shape, it may be a more efficacious treatment than CBT, since CBT and other symptom-focused treatments sometimes encounter resistance from AN patients. However, given the severity of the illness, it is likely that IPT for AN will not be a sufficient stand-alone treatment and instead will need to be delivered in the context of other adjunctive treatments (e.g. pharmacological, nutritional). Moreover, it will be important to determine whether IPT is most well-suited to *bring about* remission of AN or to *prevent relapse or recurrence* of the illness.

FUTURE DIRECTIONS

Several key areas are in need of further investigation. First, data from ongoing clinical trials will be critical to determine whether IPT can be effective for AN, and if so, to document the clinical considerations necessary when delivering IPT for AN. Second, although outcome studies have clearly documented the efficacy of IPT for BN and BED, little is known about the mechanisms by which IPT exerts its effects. A greater understanding of these mechanisms would assist in making further refinements of the treatment and yield insights about the nature of those factors that maintain eating disorder symptoms. Third, increased efforts to improve the effectiveness of IPT are warranted. Because IPT for eating disorders has been exclusively tested as an alternative to CBT, the manualized versions examined in research studies have had no symptom focus during the second and third phases of treatment, which is in stark contrast to IPT as tested for depression. Now that studies of BN and BED have demonstrated that IPT and CBT have equivalent long-term effects, it may be productive to test more symptom-focused versions of IPT to see if its effectiveness could be strengthened. Fourth, there exists a need to translate IPT efficacy data to effectiveness studies and routine clinical practice. Fifth, IPT has been used with specific subgroups of eating-disordered individuals, including adolescents with BN (Robin et al., 1998) and individuals with BN and diabetes mellitus (Peveler & Fairburn, 1992). Given IPT's demonstrated effectiveness with BN and BED, empirical tests of IPT with subpopulations of these disorders is an exciting potential direction for future research. Because BN patients often seek treatment in late adolescence, a time when interpersonal factors play an important role, IPT may prove to be particularly useful for eating-disordered adolescents. Finally, data to date have not identified predictors of response to IPT for eating disorders; this is a high-priority area for continuing research.

SUMMARY

IPT is a focused, goal-driven treatment which targets interpersonal problem(s) associated with the onset and/or maintenance of the eating disorder. There is a strong empirical basis for the use of an interpersonal approach to understand and treat eating disorders. IPT has resulted in significant and well-maintained improvements for the treatment of BN and BED, and it is currently under investigation for the treatment of AN. IPT has also been successfully delivered for eating disorders in both individual and group formats (see Wilfley et al., 1998 and 2000 for considerations and techniques in adapting IPT for group). Further research is needed regarding the mechanisms by which IPT achieves its effects, predictors of treatment outcome, and dissemination of IPT for eating disorders in clinical settings outside of controlled trials. In addition, IPT may be successfully adapted in the future for additional subgroups of BN and BED patients. A viable alternative to CBT, IPT's brief, time-limited nature is consistent with the aims of health care delivery systems to limit costs and maximize delivery, while its interpersonal focus is appealing to therapist and patient alike.

REFERENCES

Agras, W.S., Walsh, T., Fairburn, C.G., Wilson, G.T. & Kraemer, H.C. (2000) A multicenter comparison of cognitive-behavioral therapy and interpersonal psychotherapy for bulimia nervosa. *Archives of General Psychiatry*, **57**, 459–466.

Calam, R. & Waller, G. (1998) Are eating and psychosocial characteristics in early teenage years useful predictors of eating characteristics in early adulthood? A 7-year longitudinal study. *International Journal of Eating Disorders*, **24**, 351–362.

Cattanach, L., Phil, M., Malley, R. & Rodin, J. (1988) Psychologic and physiologic reactivity to stressors in eating disordered individuals. *Psychosomatic Medicine*, **50**, 591–599.

Fairburn, C.G., Jones, R., Peveler, R.C., Carr, S.J., Solomon, R.A. O'Connor, M.E., Burton, J. & Hope, R.A. (1991) Three psychological treatments for bulimia nervosa: A comparative trial. *Archives of General Psychiatry*, **48**, 463–469.

Fairburn, C.G., Peveler, R.C., Jones, R., Hope, R.A. & O'Connor, M.E. (1993) Predictors of 12-month outcome in bulimia nervosa and the influence of attitudes to shape and weight. *Journal of Consulting and Clinical Psychology*, **61**, 696–698.

Fairburn, C.G., Norman, P.A., Welch, S.L., O'Connor, M.E., Doll, H.A. & Peveler, R.C. (1995) A prospective study of outcome in bulimia nervosa and the long-term effects of three psychological treatments. *Archives of General Psychiatry*, **52**, 304–312.

Fairburn, C.G. (1997) Interpersonal psychotherapy for bulimia nervosa. In D.M. Garner & P.E. Garfinkel (Eds), *Handbook for Treatment of Eating Disorders*. New York: Guilford Press.

Fairburn, C.G., Welch, S.A., Doll, H.A., Davies, B.A. & O'Connor, M.E. (1997) Risk factors for bulimia nervosa. *Archives of General Psychiatry*, **54**, 509–517.

Fairburn, C.G., Doll, H.A., Welch, S.L., Hay, P.J., Davies, B.A. & O'Connor, M.E. (1998) Risk factors for binge eating disorder: A community-based, case-control study. *Archives of General Psychiatry*, **55**, 425–432.

Frank, E., Kupfer, D.J., Wagner, E.F., McEachran, A.B. & Cornes, C. (1991) Efficacy of interpersonal psychotherapy as a maintenance treatment of recurrent depression: Contributing factors. *Archives of General Psychiatry*, **48**, 1053–1059.

Garner, D.M., Vitousek, K.M. & Pike, K.M. (1997) Cognitive-behavioral therapy for anorexia nervosa. *Handbook for Treatment of Eating Disorders* (2nd edition; pp. 94–144). New York: Guilford Press.

Ghaderi, A. & Scott, B. (1999) Prevalence and psychological correlates of eating disorders among females aged 18–30 years in the general population. *Acta Psychiatrica Scandinavica*, **99**, 261–266.

Greeno, C.G., Wing, R.R. & Shiffman, S. (2000) Binge antecedents in obese women with and without binge eating disorder. *Journal of Consulting and Clinical Psychology*, **68**, 95–102.

Grissett, N.L. & Norvell, N.K. (1992) Perceived social support, social skills, and quality of relationships in bulimic women. *Journal of Consulting and Clinical Psychology*, **60**, 293–299.

Heatherton, T.F. & Baumeister, R.F. (1991) Binge eating as escape from self-awareness. *Psychological Bulletin*, **110**, 86–108.

Herzog, D.B., Keller, M.B., Lavori, P.W. & Ott, I.L. (1987) Social impairment in bulimia. *International Journal of Eating Disorders*, **6**, 741–747.

Horesh, N., Apter, A., Ishai, J., Danziger, Y., Miculincer, M., Stein, D., Lepkifker, E. & Minouni, M. (1996) Abnormal psychosocial situations and eating disorders in adolescence. *Journal of the American Academy of Child and Adolescent Psychiatry*, **35**, 921–927.

Kenardy, J., Wilfley, D.E., Wiseman, C.V., Stein, R.I., Dounchis, J.Z. & Arnow, B. (2001) *The phenomenology of binge eating precursors and consequences in a prospective examination.* Unpublished manuscript.

Klerman, G.L., Weissman, M.M., Rounsaville, B.J. & Chevron, E.S. (1984) *Interpersonal Psychotherapy of Depression.* New York: Basic Books.

McFall, R.M., Eason, B.J., Edmondson, C.B. & Treat, T.A. (1999) Social competence and eating disorders: Development and validation of the Anorexia and Bulimia Problem Inventory. *Journal of Psychopathology and Behavioral Assessment*, **21**, 365–394.

McIntosh, V.V., Bulik, C.M., McKenzie, J.M., Luty, S.E. & Jordan, J. (2000) Interpersonal psychotherapy for anorexia nervosa. *International Journal of Eating Disorders*, **27**, 125–139.

McManus, F. & Waller, G. (1995) A functional analysis of binge eating. *Clinical Psychology Review*, **15**, 845–863.

O'Mahony, J.F. & Hollwey, S. (1995) The correlates of binge eating in two nonpatient samples. *Addictive Behaviors*, **20**, 471–480.

Peveler, R.C. & Fairburn, C.G. (1992) The treatment of bulimia nervosa in patients with diabetes mellitus. *International Journal of Eating Disorders*, **11**, 45–53.

Powell, A.L. & Thelen, M.H. (1996) Emotions and cognitions associated with bingeing and weight control behavior in bulimia. *Journal of Psychosomatic Research*, **40**, 317–328.

Robin, A.L., Gilroy, M. & Dennis, A.B. (1998) Treatment of eating disorders in children and adolescents. *Clinical Psychology Review*, **18**, 421–446.

Rorty, M., Yager, J., Buckwalter, J.G. & Rossotto, E. (1999) Social support, social adjustment, and recovery status in bulimia nervosa. *International Journal of Eating Disorders*, **26**, 1–12.

Schmidt, U., Tiller, J., Blanchard, M., Andrews, B. & Treasure, J. (1997) Is there a specific trauma precipitating anorexia nervosa? *Psychological Medicine*, **27**, 523–530.

Schupak-Neuberg, E. & Nemeroff, C.J. (1993) Disturbances in identity and self-regulation in bulimia nervosa: Implications for a metaphorical perspective of 'body as self'. *International Journal of Eating Disorders*, **13**, 335–347.

Segrin, Chris. (2001) *Interpersonal Processes in Psychological Problems.* New York: Guilford Press.

Spurrell, E.B., Wilfley, D.E., Tanofsky, M.B. & Brownell, K.D. (1997) Age of onset for binge eating: Are there different pathways to binge eating? *International Journal of Eating Disorders*, **21**, 55–65.

Steiger, H., Gauvin, L., Jabalpurwala, S., Seguin, J.R. & Stotland, S. (1999) Hypersensitivity to social interactions in bulimic syndromes: Relationship to binge eating. *Journal of Consulting and Clinical Psychology*, **67**, 765–775.

Stice, E., Akutagawa, D., Gaggar, A. & Agras, W.S. (2000) Negative affect moderates the relation between dieting and binge eating. *International Journal of Eating Disorders*, **27**, 218–229.

Striegel-Moore, R.H., Dohm, F., Pike, K.M., Wilfley, D.E. & Fairburn, C.G. (2001) Childhood sexual abuse: A risk factor for binge eating disorder? Manuscript submitted for publication.

Tanofsky-Kraff, M., Wilfley, D.E. & Spurell, E. (2000) Impact of interpersonal and ego-related stress on restrained eaters. *International Journal of Eating Disorders*, **27**, 411–418.

Telch, C.F. & Agras, W.S. (1994) Obesity, binge eating and psychopathology: Are they related? *International Journal of Eating Disorders*, **15**, 53–61.

Telch, C.F. & Agras, W.S. (1996) Do emotional states influence binge eating in the obese? *International Journal of Eating Disorders*, **20**, 271–279.

Thelen, M.H., Farmer, J., McLaughlin Mann, L. & Prutit, J. (1990) Bulimia and interpersonal relationships: A longitudinal study. *Journal of Counseling Psychology*, **37**, 85–90.

Thelen, M.H., Kanakis, D.M. & Farmer, J. (1993) Bulimia and interpersonal relationships: An extension of a longitudinal study. *Addictive Behaviors*, **18**, 145–150.

Tiller, J.M., Sloane, G., Schmidt, U., Troop, N., Power, M. & Treasure, J.L. (1997) Social support in patients with anorexia nervosa and bulimia nervosa. *International Journal of Eating Disorders*, **21**, 31–38.

Troop, N.A., Holbrey, A., Trowler, R. & Treasure, J.L. (1994) Ways of coping in women with eating disorders. *Journal of Nervous and Mental Disease*, **182**, 535–540.

Tuschen-Caffier, B. & Vogele, C. (1999) Psychological and physiological reactivity to stress: An experimental study on bulimic patients, restrained eaters and controls. *Psychotherapy and Psychosomatics*, **68**, 333–340.

Van Buren, D.J. & Williamson, D.A. (1988) Marital relationships and conflict resolution skills of bulimics. *International Journal of Eating Disorders*, **7**, 735–741.

Weissman, M.M., Markowitz, J.C. & Klerman, G.L. (2000) *Comprehensive Guide to interpersonal Psychotherapy*. New York: Basic Books.

Welch, S.L. & Fairburn, C.G. (1994) Sexual abuse and bulimia nervosa. *American Journal of Psychiatry*, **151**, 402–407.

Wilfley, D.E., Agras, W.S., Telch, C.F., Rossiter, E.M., Schneider, J.A., Cole, A.G., Sifford, L. & Raeburn, S.D. (1993) Group cognitive-behavioral therapy and group interpersonal psychotherapy for the nonpurging bulimic individual: A controlled comparison. *Journal of Consulting and Clinical Psychology*, **61**, 296–305.

Wilfley, D.E., Pike, K.M. & Striegel-Moore, R.H. (1997) Toward an integrated model of risk for binge eating disorder. *Journal of Gender, Culture, and Health*, **2**, 1–32.

Wilfley, D.E., Frank, M.A., Welch, R., Spurrell, E.B. & Rounsaville, B.J. (1998) Adapting interpersonal psychotherapy to a group format (IPT-G) for binge eating disorder: Toward a model for adapting empirically supported treatments. *Psychotherapy Research*, **8**, 379–391.

Wilfley, D.E., Welch, R.R., Stein, R.I., Spurrell, E.B., Cohen, L.R., Saelens, B.E., Dounchis, J.Z., Frank, M.A., Wiseman, C.V. & Matt, G.E. (2002). A randomized comparison of group cognitive-behavioral therapy and group interpersonal psychotherapy for the treatment of binge eating disorder. *Archives of General Psychiatry*, **59**, 713–721.

Wilfley, D.E., MacKenzie, K.R., Welch, R.R., Ayres, V.E. & Weissman, M.M. (2000) *Interpersonal Psychotherapy for Group*. New York: Basic Book.

Wonderlich, S.A. (1995) Personality and eating disorders. In K.D. Brownell & C.G. Fairburn (Eds), *Eating Disorders and Obesity: A Comprehensive Handbook* (pp. 171–176). New York: Guilford Press.

Woodside, D.B., Shekter-Wolfson, L.F., Brandes, J.S. & Lackstrom, J.B. (1993) *Eating Disorders and Marriage: The Couple in Focus*. New York: Brunner/Mazzel Inc.

CHAPTER 16

Dialectical Behaviour Therapy

Bob Palmer

Brandon Mental Health Unit, Leicester General Hospital, Leicester, UK

and

Helen Birchall

Brandon Mental Health Unit, Leicester General Hospital, Leicester, UK

The treatment of people with eating disorders complicated by comorbid personality disorder is often unsatisfactory (Dennis & Samsone, 1997). The usual treatments, such as manual-based cognitive-behavioural therapy (CBT) for bulimia nervosa, are worth a try but are commonly insufficient. In particular, patients with borderline personality disorder (BPD) may do poorly. The therapeutic relationship often breaks down or becomes so complex as to render such therapies difficult or impossible. Most clinicians are aware of a minority of such patients who consume substantial therapeutic resource with little apparent benefit. Typically they will have other problem behaviours such as repeated self-harm and substance abuse together with affective instability and may be called 'multi-impulsive'. Such patients lead unhappy and chaotic lives with much suffering and substantial risk. Too often those who would help them come to feel that their efforts are overwhelmed by this chaos and distress.

Dialectical behaviour therapy (DBT) is a treatment that has some claim to proven efficacy in the management of women with BPD and recurrent self-harm and/or substance abuse (Linehan et al., 1991, 1999), and may be useful as an approach for people with eating disorders and comorbid BPD.

DIALECTICAL BEHAVIOUR THERAPY

DBT is a complex treatment. It was devised by Marsha Linehan of Seattle and is set out in her book and in the accompanying skills training manual (Linehan, 1993a, 1993b). It is based upon a provisional 'Biosocial Theory' that sees BPD as arising from a probable biological tendency towards emotionality that is shaped by an invalidating environment.

Handbook of Eating Disorders. Edited by J. Treasure, U. Schmidt and E. van Furth.
© 2003 John Wiley & Sons, Ltd.

DBT is usually an outpatient treatment although it has been adapted for inpatient or day patient use (Bohus et al., 2000). Typically it runs for one year although the programme may be repeated. It has four main elements. Three of these are therapeutic activities which involve the patient, namely weekly sessions with an individual therapist, weekly skills training in a group and telephone contact for skills coaching between sessions. DBT is a team treatment and the fourth element is a weekly consultation group in which the team meets together to discuss the patients and the programme. Arguably, one of the strengths of DBT is the clear supportive framework that it supplies for patients and clinicians alike. However, the conceptual underpinnings of DBT are varied. It is a strange hybrid.

Much of the basic thinking of DBT comes from the cognitive-behavioural tradition. DBT espouses the scientific ethos. There is an emphasis on the need for open and explicit collaboration between clinician and patient and there is substantial use of such techniques as self-monitoring. Furthermore, the language of DBT is often very commonsensical or even folksy. It is full of aphorisms. Thus, patients are thought of as 'always doing their best'. The therapist is urged to seek the 'kernel of truth' in the assumptions of the patients. It is said that the patients 'may not have caused all of their own problems but they have to solve them anyway'. Trying to gain something out of a setback or a disaster is described as 'making lemonade out of lemons'.

In contrast, the 'dialectical' in DBT refers to a broad way of thinking that substitutes 'both/and' for 'either/or' and sees truth as an evolving product of the opposition of different views. Its relevance arises from clinical observation of the shifting and non-linear character of human emotion and experience in general and that of the borderline patient in particular. Such thinking pervades the overall style of the therapeutic interaction in DBT. This is sometimes compared to that of a dance to rapidly changing music in which the clinician and patient react to each other. What the 'right' step should be can be judged only in the context of the overall dance. It is important to keep on the move. Humour and irreverence are invoked to this end.

Dialectical thinking emphasises the wholeness and interconnectedness of the world and the potential for the reconciliation of opposites. A further novel element of DBT is the inclusion of ideas and techniques drawn from Zen Buddhism. The key concept is that of mindfulness. The person with BPD is seen as having difficulty in being at all detached from her experience and as being frequently overwhelmed by it. Developing the capacity for mindfulness and living in the moment increases the potential for feeling appropriately in charge of the self. Paradoxically, greater mastery is achieved through an increased ability to be detached. A related idea is that of the balance between acceptance and change. Zen is full of paradox and again there is something paradoxical in the idea that acceptance—for instance, of unchangeable traumatic events in the past—may be necessary for change to be possible.

The overall stance of the therapist in DBT is that of being a 'consultant to the patient'. Although the posture is not rigid, the DBT therapist tends to work with and advise the patient but does not take over except in extreme circumstances. If other professionals become involved then the therapist will tend to help the patient to deal appropriately with them rather than the other way around. The relationship between the patient and the therapist should be quite explicitly a working partnership. The need to cherish and often to repair the therapeutic relationship is seen as central. Time is spent getting explicit commitment and when necessary recommitment from the patient. And, of course, the therapist has reciprocal commitments.

INDIVIDUAL THERAPY

Typically the patient and therapist meet once each week for about an hour. The patient fills in a diary card for the preceding week and this may be used as an initial focus of discussion. Attention is paid to topics according to a hierarchy in which life-threatening behaviours come top, followed by therapy interfering behaviours. Quality of life-impairing behaviours and other issues are dealt with only if these other two topics are satisfactory. In practice, the style of the sessions may vary between therapists. However, there is an overall aim of validating the experience of the patient and encouraging her to become more skilful in the management of her feelings, behaviours and her relationships with others. Detailed chain analysis may be used to explore the antecedents and consequences of troublesome feelings or actions.

Skills Training

The patient is taught skills in a weekly group which typically lasts for two hours or so. The style of the group is didactic. The room may be set out as a classroom with the skills trainers—usually two—facing the patients. Process issues or evident emotion are dealt with only if they threaten the running of the group. Sometimes a skills trainer may also be the therapist of one or more of the patients but this dual relationship is not dealt with in the group. The training is organised around a manual that contains handouts that may be copied freely for this purpose (Linehan, 1993b). There are four modules, *emotional regulation, distress tolerance, interpersonal effectiveness* and *mindfulness*. Each module takes several weeks to teach. Often, the mindfulness module is repeated in brief form between each of the other modules. Typically, each meeting of the group begins and ends with a mindfulness exercise.

Telephone Contact

Patients receiving full DBT may contact their individual therapist between sessions by telephone. Such contact may be planned but is usually in response to crises. The calls are typically quite brief and used to coach the patients in the use of skills to survive and weather their emotional storms. The hours during which such contact is available are agreed between the therapist and the patient. What the therapist can manage is an explicit determinant of the arrangement and is usually the limiting factor. The aim is to provide an alternative to self-harm and the patient is banned from telephoning for 24 hours after such an act.

DBT AND EATING DISORDERS

DBT has been tried out by a number of centres working with eating-disordered patients. However, full DBT has yet to be adequately evaluated. The main work has been conducted by the group at Stanford and has involved the assessment of brief outpatient therapies that have been informed by DBT but which are much abridged compared to the full treatment as described by Linehan (1993a, 1993b). Thus, the group have reported the use of skills training as a treatment for binge eating disorder (Welch & Telch 1999; Telch, Agras & Linehan, 2000). The same team have conducted a trial of an individual outpatient treatment described as DBT for women with bulimia nervosa (Safer, Telch & Agras, 2001a, 2001b). The treatment was found to be superior to a waiting list comparison condition in respect of reduction of binge eating and purging behaviour. The treatment was individual and brief, lasting only 20 weeks. The patients were not selected for comorbid personality disorder. The results of this trial suggest that short treatment based upon affect regulation may be useful in the outpatient treatment of bulimia nervosa. However, it has less relevance to the question of the utility of full DBT in helping people with eating disorders complicated by borderline personality disorder.

Other reported work has been purely descriptive and uncontrolled. Marcus, McCabe and Levine (1999) from Pittsburgh have described a DBT treatment programme for eating-disordered patients. In Leicester, we ran a full DBT programme for 18 months. The seven patients on the programme all had eating disorder and comorbid BPD. Most of them had displayed life-threatening self-harming behaviour and two also had comorbid diabetes mellitus. All of the patients stayed in therapy, all survived and all were improved at 18 months follow-up (Palmer et al., 2003). However, although the improvement of the patients was impressive, formal pre-post measures were not available because of lack of cooperation of several of the patients at the outset. Furthermore, there was no comparison group and improvements may have reflected the settling down of a group of patients initially recruited at the peak of their disturbance. Thus the efficacy and effectiveness of full DBT in the treatment of eating-disordered people has yet to be properly evaluated.

A feature of our programme was the development of an additional skills training module called 'Eatingness' (Gatward, McGrain & Palmer, 2003). This contains psycho-educational material presented in the style of DBT. It was acceptable to the patients and has been used in a number of centres. However, it, too, remains to be formally evaluated.

Case Example

The following case history is fictional. It is included as illustration and not as evidence. However, the story accords broadly to those of women who might be predicted to be suitable for full DBT. Issues set in *italics* are mentioned in the story as illustrations of ideas or techniques characteristic of DBT.

The Story of Jane

Jane is a 28-year-old woman with borderline personality disorder, who had been in touch with psychiatric services since the age of 15. She was born in Scotland, and her parents separated when she was 5 years old. Jane stayed with her mother, who was alcohol dependent and often neglected the physical and emotional care of the children. The mother remarried when Jane was 8, and Jane suffered sexual abuse from her step-father from this time until she left home at 16. Subsequently, Jane had a relationship with a physically abusive man from the age of 17, but left him when she was 22 and moved to England.

Jane began to restrain her eating at the age of 12, and probably fulfilled criteria for anorexia nervosa at this time. When she was 14, Jane began to binge eat, vomit and take amphetamines, in addition to self-harming, which included cutting, burning and pulling her hair out. Soon she was drinking heavily and was truanting from school. This prompted a referral to the local child and adolescent psychiatric services. She had several admissions to the local inpatient unit to try to deal with the eating and self-harm. At 17, she graduated to the Adult services, but continued her chaotic life with multiple admissions.

In her mid-twenties, Jane moved to England. After a year or so, she again came into contact with psychiatric services after a serious overdose that had involved resuscitation and treatment in the Intensive Care Unit. At this time, her body mass index was 18, and she was found to be hypokalaemic. She was found to be actively eating disordered, and was referred to the Specialist Eating Disorders Team, where she was offered psychodynamically informed psychotherapy. However, the therapy did not go smoothly. Jane became abusive and critical of her therapist's efforts to help. After a year or so, the therapeutic relationship broke down, repeating the pattern of other relationships. She continued to self-harm, necessitating recurrent medical admissions sometimes followed by lengthy admissions to the psychiatric unit for containment. Despite attracting many offers of help from concerned professional and lay people, Jane had little sustained support in the community. Typically any relationships were soon damaged beyond repair by her demanding and aggressive behaviour. Her hospital admissions followed a similar pattern, with ward staff feeling angry and frustrated at Jane's behaviour and lack of progress.

Jane said that 'no one can handle me'. This sounded like defiance and a challenge, but superficially covered a desperate fear. Jane was scared, angry, miserable, unable to trust and felt life to be not worth living. The clinical team, too, had problems. There was splitting and disagreement, with some staff members wanting to rescue the patient, and others feeling that she was indeed impossible to manage and was wasting resources that might otherwise have been used for 'people who wanted help'. There was no progress with either the eating or the self-harm and there was the familiar despair and demoralisation.

The Eating Disorders Team decided to offer Jane treatment on their DBT programme, which was a new venture. Jane's problems were seen as her eating disorder, which flipped between partial syndrome AN and BN, and her interpersonal difficulties and self-harm. She was introduced to a new therapist who, although an experienced clinician like the other members of the team, had just finished his DBT training. Jane was his first DBT patient. He met with Jane, and took a history and the *invalidating environment* of Jane's childhood was quickly apparent. The diagnosis of borderline personality disorder was formally reviewed and confirmed. The therapist explained the diagnosis to Jane together with *the biosocial theory*. To his surprise, this made sense to Jane, and she seemed quite relieved that there was some explanation for the way life was for her. Over several weeks, the therapist and patient worked on *committing* to therapy. The therapist said that he would be available from 9am to 9pm seven days a week for *telephone contact*. Jane initially refused the group skills training, but was told this was an integral part of the treatment although she was reminded that she was, of course, under no obligation to accept the *treatment package*.

Jane acknowledged how awful life was for her, and that she did want to improve things, but had no faith that anything could be any better. She finally decided to start DBT.

For the first five months, each session was spent going through the self-harm of the week in great detail. Jane filled in *diary cards* and these were used in *chain analyses* of the antecedents, behaviour and consequences (ABC). She was attending *skills training*, but found this difficult and often missed group. This was discussed within the group as *therapy interfering behaviour* but Jane felt attacked and complained bitterly to her therapist during *individual sessions*, saying she would never return. The therapist was able to say what a pity this was, as he felt she was beginning to make some headway. He said that he would really feel sorry if she were to leave the programme and he was not able to see her any more. Jane was quick to say that she did not want to quit individual therapy, so the therapist coached her on how to address her problems with the group leaders. Here the therapist was being a *'consultant to the patient'*.

Throughout the DBT programme, the professionals involved met weekly in the *consultation group*. Six months into therapy, other members of the team expressed concern that Jane's therapist was overburdened by telephone contact. Jane was ringing him two to three times most days, and although these calls were in general appropriate—dealing with crises by skills coaching—they were interfering with the therapist's working and personal life. The team helped the therapist to look at ways he could manage this, by constructing a *behavioural programme* of reducing phone contact in a planned manner over the coming months. The therapist was able to put this to Jane, saying that in order for him to carry on working with her effectively, this would have to happen. She agreed to this, but on the next phone call, the therapist was unable to respond immediately. He called as soon as practicable, and found the patient to be slurred in speech, having taken an overdose in the interim. He made sure that Jane was not alone, and that she was going to accident and emergency department, before ending the call. The next session was spent dealing with this *therapy interfering behaviour*, and Jane could see that it would be impossible for the therapist to work under the pressure of having to be immediately available, while he validated her distress, which often felt unbearable.

After eight months, Jane began to reduce her self-harming behaviour. She said that she was fed up with doing nothing in sessions but talk about self-harm, and the only way she could get to talk about other things that distressed her was to stop cutting and overdosing. The therapist said he was relieved she had realised this, because it did seem a shame to waste so much session time on 'the same old stuff' (*irreverence*). Group was going better, and Jane was beginning to be able to use the skills to communicate in a more useful way, and was contributing ideas to other group members.

After ten months of treatment, Jane was mugged while in town. The experience frightened her, and brought back memories of past violence she had suffered. She took a large overdose, and was readmitted to hospital, where the long-suffering staff clearly remembered her previous admissions. Jane continued with therapy while in hospital, and the therapist coached Jane on how to manage her interactions with ward staff. Jane began to be able to talk to various members of the ward team, who commented on how she had changed over the last few months. Jane and her primary nurse decided to try to do some work on her eating while she was on the ward, and Jane brought her homework sheets from the 'Eatingness' module to work on with this nurse.

Jane continued in full DBT for 18 months, but finished the skills training group after she had been through each module twice. She remained in weekly therapy for a further nine months and negotiated with her therapist to cut down telephone contact gradually. In sessions they began to explore issues from her past now that the present produced fewer demanding crises. In her life, she began tentatively to build up more social links and Jane used her therapy sessions to discuss problems in doing this. Jane continued to binge and vomit occasionally, but managed to give up her self-harming. She reduced her alcohol intake, and stopped taking illicit drugs.

Towards the end of the third year after entering DBT, Jane moved away to start a degree course and was discharged. However, she would sometimes write to her therapist to say how things were going. She commented upon some of the things that she felt had helped her. She described how contained the therapy had made her feel. She also said that she had valued her therapist's belief in her. She mentioned his comments that she was *trying her hardest* and how this—together with his straight talking when she had behaved unacceptably—had helped her to keep going in the bad times.

CONCLUSION

Full DBT is a complex and expensive treatment. It requires that a team be especially trained. Furthermore, the treatment is personally demanding of the clinicians involved. Nevertheless, it may well have a place in the management of that small group of eating-disordered patients who suffer from comorbid BPD and, furthermore, show a range of highly problematic behaviours. Such patients are familiar to most clinicians working within the field. Helping such unfortunate people within a DBT programme is likely to be more satisfactory and satisfying than trying to do so in an unplanned and reactive manner. It may even be more effective although efficacy has yet to be formally demonstrated for eating-disordered patients. Furthermore, it is unclear how DBT would compare with other special treatments for this patient group (Lacey 1995; Dennis & Samsone, 1997). However, such evaluation and comparison would seem to be warranted by the limited experience currently available.

REFERENCES

Bohus, M., Haaf, B., Stiglmayr, C., Pohl, U., Bohme, R. & Linehan, M. (2000) Evaluation of inpatient dialectical-behavioral therapy for borderline personality disorder—a prospective study. *Behaviour Research and Therapy*, **38**, 875–887.

Dennis, A.B. & Samsone, R.A. (1997) Treatment of patients with personality disorders. In D.M. Garner & P.E. Garfinkel (Eds), *Handbook of Treatment for Eating Disorders*. New York: Guilford Press.

Gatward, N., McGrain, L. & Palmer, R.L. (2003) Eatingness—a new DBT skills training module for use with people with eating disorders (submitted for publication).

Lacey, J.H. (1995) Inpatient treatment of multi-impulsive bulimia nervosa. In K.D. Brownell & C.G. Fairburn (Eds), *Eating Disorders and Obesity: A Comprehensive Handbook*. New York: Guilford Press.

Linehan, M.M. (1993a) *Cognitive-Behavioral Treatment of Borderline Personality Disorder*. New York: Guilford Press.

Linehan, M.M. (1993b) *Skills Training Manual for Treating Borderline Personality Disorder*. New York: Guilford Press.

Linehan, M.M., Armstrong, H.E., Suarez, A., Allman, D. & Heard, H.L. (1991) Cognitive-behavioral treatment of chronically parasuicidal borderline patients. *Archives of General Psychiatry*, **48**, 1060–1064.

Linehan M.M., Schmidt H., Craft J.C., Kanter J. & Comtois K.A. (1999) Dialectical behavior therapy for patients with borderline personality disorder and drug-dependence. *American Journal on Addictions*, **8**, 279–292.

Marcus, M.D., McCabe, E.B. & Levine, M.D. (1999) Dialectical behavior therapy (DBT) in the treatment of eating disorders. Paper presented at the 4th London International Conference on Eating Disorders, London, April 1999.

Palmer, R.L., Birchall, H., Damani, S., Gatward, N., McGrain, L. & Parker, A. (2003) Dialectical behaviour therapy (DBT) programme for people with eating disorder and borderline personality disorder—description and outcome. *International Journal of Eating Disorders* (in press).

Safer, D.L., Telch, C.F. & Agras, W.S. (2001a) Dialectical behavior therapy for bulimia: A case report. *International Journal of Eating Disorders*, **30**, 101–106.

Safer, D.L., Telch, C.F. & Agras, W.S. (2001b) Dialectical behavior therapy for bulimia nervosa. *American Journal of Psychiatry*, **158**, 632–634.

Telch, C.F., Agras, W.S. & Linehan, M.M. (2000) Group dialectical behavior therapy for binge eating disorder: A preliminary, uncontrolled trial. *Behaviour Therapy*, **31**, 569–582.

Welch, S. & Telch, C.F. (1999) Dialectical behavior therapy for binge-eating disorder. *Journal of Clinical Psychology*, **55**, 755–768.

CHAPTER 17

Cognitive Analytic Therapy

Claire Tanner

26 Vancouver Road, Forest Hill, London, UK

and

Frances Connan

Vincent Square Eating Disorders Clinic, London, UK

INTRODUCTION

Cognitive analytic therapy (CAT) was developed by Dr Anthony Ryle at Guy's Hospital, London, during the 1980s. The drive to develop a new therapy came from Ryle's experience of the limited availability and suitability of psychoanalytic therapy for National Health Service patients. His aim was to convey the analytic model in a brief, time-limited, focused therapy that could be delivered by all members of the multidisciplinary team. Importantly, the model was designed to have broad applicability, specifically including patients with severe borderline or narcissistic personality disorders.

The first section of this chapter provides a description of the theoretical basis of CAT, with reference to the specific cognitive and analytic concepts that were influential in the evolution of this model. The second section describes the aims, structure and process of CAT, with reference to the treatment of eating disorders. The evidence base and rationale for the application of CAT to eating disorder is then examined and the chapter concludes with a brief case illustration.

THE THEORETICAL BASIS OF CAT

Anthony Ryle drew from theoretical models of both the analytic and cognitive traditions to produce an integrative and structured therapy model. A detailed rationale of CAT is given in Ryle (1990). The following is a brief overview of some of the theoretical models from which CAT was developed.

Cognitive components of CAT were influenced particularly by the work of Lazarus, Bandura and Kelly. Lazarus made an important contribution to the emotion/cognition debate by conceptualising motivation as an integral component of these processes. He argues that the temporal sequence is not important, rather cognition, emotion and motivation are interdependent and that harmonious integration is essential for psychological well-being.

Handbook of Eating Disorders. Edited by J. Treasure, U. Schmidt and E. van Furth.
© 2003 John Wiley & Sons, Ltd.

Coping is conceptualised as an integral part of emotion, dependent upon both cognition and motivation, and thus several pathways for improved emotional coping are inferred. These include modification of goals, cognitive restructuring and modification of the behavioural response (Lazarus, 1999). Bandura hypothesised that self-efficacy, or perceived control, is a primary determinant of coping behaviour (Bandura, 1977), and thus outcome of efforts to change (Bandura, 1986). Subsequent research has lent support to this contention, particularly in the treatment of anxiety disorders (Mineka & Thomas, 1999). Enhancement of self-efficacy and agency is an important focus of CAT. Kelly's construct theory (Kelly, 1963) was a significant forerunner of both schema theory and CAT. By placing self and others along bipolar constructs, such as good/bad, or caring/uncaring, a tool is constructed through which the patient can visualise and begin to understand his or her interpersonal world. Predictions about the patient's experience of self and others can then be made, facilitating change and a sense of control over the inner and outer world. Bipolar interpersonal constructs lie at the core of interpersonal understanding in CAT, but have been enriched with the incorporation of object relations theory.

Early psychoanalytic theorists, such as Freud, saw conflict as arising from inner drives and destructive forces that needed mastery. Thus issues of power and control are central to traditional psychoanalytic thinking. Object relations theory shifted the emphasis to the importance of relatedness, and thus issues of nuturance and care inherent in the child's earliest experiences of the primary carer, usually the mother, became the focus. While early objects relations theorists such as Klein conceptualised infantile splitting of good and bad as arising from the innate destructive urges and fantasies of the infant, Fairbairn attested that this split in the inner world arises from the infant's experience of a real mother as depriving, rejecting and tantalising. By necessity, the new-born infant is dependent upon the mother figure, but is unable to control her. To split off difficult aspects of experience in relation to the mother is seen as an understandable and necessary strategy for the infant to maintain the relationship and thus to receive care (see also Chapter 6). The cost of such a strategy is a fragmented and inconsistent sense of self. Transition into mature interdependence requires integration of good and bad aspects of self and others. Fairbairn viewed failure to negotiate this transition, and thus failure to develop a consistent and stable sense of self, as the root of psychopathology. Later object relations theorists such as Ogden further developed these ideas, describing bipolar intrapsychic representations that are coloured by affect and form templates for future relationships (see Sheldon & Cashdan, 1988, for review).

These cognitive and object relations theories are drawn together to form the reciprocal role relationship pattern and procedural diagram that is the building block for CAT formulation (see Figure 17.1). Relationship patterns are described as two poles of a dynamic, in which self and other take reciprocal roles. For example, abusive/abused, or controlling/crushed. These reciprocal role patterns are perceived to arise from early experiences of relatedness and maladaptive patterns are therefore conceptualised as understandable responses to unsatisfactory experience. This component of CAT can be seen to reflect the influence of object relations theorists, particularly Fairbairn, Winnicott and Ogden. The reciprocity of the relationship role patterns is important and reflects the capacity of the individual to recruit others, or aspects of themselves, to the reciprocal pole of an active role. Thus, reciprocal roles can be manifest in a relationship, or in patients' relatedness to themselves. Furthermore, an individual will usually move dynamically between the two roles of a relationship pattern. For example, abused children will often abuse themselves or others, while parental

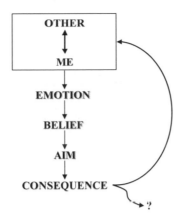

Figure 17.1   Reciprocal role relationship and procedural diagram

over-control nurtures a child that may be controlling of others and over-controlled in themselves. In therapy, these reciprocal role patterns are plotted in a sequential diagram, or map, providing an overview of the patient's self states and interpersonal relationships, much as Kelly attempted to do with his repertory grids.

Drawing from objects relations theorists, an affect arises from reciprocal role patterns. For example, abusive/abused is associated with terror and rage, while the controlling/crushed pattern is associated with rebellious anger. Thus a link is made into cognitive theory. Emotion is interrelated with motivation and cognition, which are represented by aim and belief respectively in the procedural diagram. The term procedure, rather than pattern, is used in CAT to illustrate that problematic relationships and behaviours are a closed system which are part of a sequential loop and thus lead to the same outcome, or consequence (see Figure 17.1). The consequence may be a behavioural response, or a further procedural sequence. Difficulties arise when the consequences are negative, or maintain the individual in the same stuck pattern of maladaptive relationships. Frequently, false assumptions, problems with emotional processing or coping, and maladaptive reciprocal role patterns serve to trap the individual in a vicious negative cycle, create a forced choice dilemma, or prohibit more adaptive choices of response. It is the restriction and lack of flexibility inherent in these features that make them maladaptive. We all have reciprocal role patterns and cognitive procedures arising from our early life experience that serve as templates for relationships with ourselves and others, and it is the maladaptive roles and procedures that are focused upon in therapy.

For example, a common reciprocal role relationship pattern encountered in patients with eating disorders is controlling/crushed (see Figure 17.2). This pattern may arise from an early experience where emotions and needs are felt by the infant to be controlled by the early caretaker. Thus the infant experiences his or her feelings and needs as crushed and disallowed. This early experience gives rise to the belief that feelings and needs are bad and must be controlled. Later in life this experience is replicated both in relationships with others and in relation to oneself. Anorexia nervosa (AN) can be conceptualised as one of the consequences of this type of early experience. That is, anorexia provides a behavioural expression for the need to control the self and others arising from this relationship pattern. The controlling/crushed reciprocal role relationship pattern has obvious parallels with

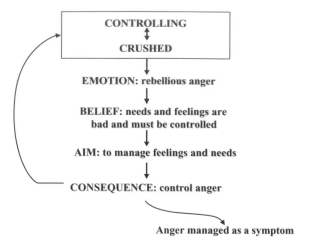

Figure 17.2 The controlling/crushed reciprocal role relationship and procedural diagram. [The experience that feelings and needs are crushed and disallowed by controlling others gives rise to rebellious anger and the belief that feelings and needs are bad and must be controlled. The aim is therefore to manage feelings and needs, including the anger arising from this experience of relationships. Anger may either be controlled, thus maintaining the vicious circle of the controlling/crushed reciprocal role pattern, or the anger is managed as a symptom, such as food restriction or vomiting.]

Fairburn's cognitive theory for anorexia nervosa (Fairburn et al., 1999) in placing the need for control as a central theme. However, CAT extends the cognitive theory into the domain of interpersonal relationships and in doing so offers an understanding of how this need has arisen and how it can be modified.

THE AIMS, STRUCTURE AND PROCESS OF CAT

The aim of CAT, as perhaps any therapy, is to enhance self-efficacy and self-reflection and to generate change. The duration of CAT is fixed at the outset to 16–24 sessions, depending on the underlying level of disturbance in personality structure. The three main processes that promote change in CAT are *reformulation* of the problematic interpersonal and behavioural patterns, *recognition* of these patterns and then through recognition in the here and now and in life outside therapy, *revision* of the patterns. These three processes roughly map onto the three stages of therapy: reformulation is the focus of the first four sessions; the middle sessions focus upon recognition and preparation for revision; and the final four sessions focus upon ending, which if managed successfully facilitates further revision and change.

Reformulation is a process in which both patient and therapist collaborate in developing an understanding of current problems and their evolution from past experience. The therapist takes a thorough history of the patient's early life and evolution of the current difficulties. The patient is asked to complete the Psychotherapy File, a tool developed by Ryle listing commonly occurring problematic procedures. The patient is invited to consider the current situation and, from this, to identify and list patterns of thinking, feeling and behaving that may be contributing to things going wrong and feeling stuck. As part of the reformulation process, two or three target problems will be identified as a focus for the therapy. It is helpful if behavioural, emotional and interpersonal problems are each represented in the list of target problems. Patients with eating disorders are usually ambivalent about change and often do not identify weight and eating behaviour as a problem. By devoting time to negotiate the problems on which to focus, and enhancement of motivation, this issue can be addressed and low weight will usually be accepted as an appropriate focus in AN. Alternatively, a formulation can be offered focusing on why the patient does not see the eating disorder as a difficulty.

Once the target problems have been agreed upon, the procedures that maintain the problem are described. This description not only includes the present, but also links the past to the present. Examples from the patient's childhood situation are used to illustrate experiences that would understandably have led to the development of procedures that were effective coping strategies originally, but now leave the patient with difficulties in current relationships and circumstances. The original relationships underlying current reciprocal roles are also described, particularly those with the patient's attachment figures. Relationship patterns that have an emphasis on over-control, conditionality, admiration, emotional deprivation and abandonment are commonly present in the background of patients with eating disorders. Common procedures focus on issues of avoidance, placation, perfection, splitting and sabotage.

The aim of reformulation is to facilitate understanding, not to apportion blame. Parental roles can be understood by hypothesising about parental experiences. For example, prior to the birth of the child who goes on to develop AN, the frequency of serious birth complications and obstetric loss is elevated (Cnattingius et al., 1999; Shoebridge & Gowers, 2000). High parental concern, over-protection and over-control may be understandable in this context.

Once the therapist has ascertained the procedures that the patient is enacting and the reciprocal role patterns that lead to these procedures, then a letter is constructed by the therapist as a hypothesis with which to understand the difficulties. The letter is written empathically and aims as much as possible to employ the words and metaphors used by the patient to express her difficulties, in order to ensure an emphasis upon collaboration and empathic understanding. The reformulation letter describes the target problems, the problem procedures, and the reciprocal role relationships in such a way as to make clear the understandable links between the patient's past, and possible origin of their procedures, and the way in which the procedures are occurring in the patient's life currently. Predictions are also made in the letter as to how the procedures and reciprocal roles will be re-enacted in the therapy. Goals for change are set out in the letter in terms of recognising and revising the procedures. Rather than challenging the patient to give up her disorder outright, an indication of how change might be achieved is offered. The letter is concluded with a succinct list of target problems and associated procedures.

The patient is offered a draft copy of the reformulation letter at sessions 4–6, when it is read aloud to the patient. The patient takes away the copy and is encouraged to re-read and change or agree to the reformulation. A diagram of the reciprocal roles and procedures is also developed with the patient in the following sessions as a shorthand and more visually accessible version of the reformulation letter. This is used in subsequent sessions to name re-enactments of the procedures as they occur. If the patient disagrees with the reformulation, then further work is done on descriptions of problems and procedures so that the patient and therapist agree on the focus of therapy. Flexibility is important and is encouraged, while avoiding collusion with minimisation of the seriousness of the problems. Flexibility is also useful in the timing of reformulation. For those with very disturbed personality structure and unstable reciprocal role patterns, early reformulation in the form of the map facilitates the process of engagement. Firstly, it helps the patient to feel empathically understood and, secondly, it serves to contain both patient and therapist anxiety.

Constructing reformulations in CAT is a complex set of skills and thus regular supervision is offered to therapists. Once reformulation has been constructed, then supervision is used to enable therapists to recognise when re-enactments are occurring in therapy.

The following 12–20 sessions of CAT are used to enable patients to recognise when they are enacting their procedures. This is accomplished by homework, such as diary keeping, monitoring of mood states, written work such as letter writing etc. Observing the enactment of procedures during a session in the here and now is a particularly effective way of enabling patients to understand the way their procedures operate. By focusing on the procedures, conflict is contained, an understanding of resistance is offered, and thus avoided, and patients are offered the opportunity to reflect upon themselves and understand their motives, behaviours and emotional reactions. The therapist encourages patients to use the map to be able to reflect on the way that both their mind and that of significant others work. Thus the development of a theory of mind and self-reflective function is facilitated by use of the map, which serves as an external example of a theory of mind.

The process of reformulation and recognition helps the patient to feel empathically understood and offers a new experience of relating, in which feelings and needs can be acknowledged and expressed. For patients with eating disorders, the model of CAT can provide meaning for their anorexia or bulimia that was previously beyond their grasp. The offering of an understanding that can be internalised by the patient is one of the key factors for change in CAT. It is through this experience that a therapeutic alliance can be fostered. The structure, focus and tools of CAT help to make this possible with even the most difficult-to-engage patients. A therapeutic alliance is crucial to the process of revision and change (Safran, 1993). Once established, patient and therapist are able to collaborate in developing strategies for revision of maladaptive relationship patterns and procedures. CAT is eclectic in this respect and draws upon a range of therapeutic techniques depending upon the symptom profile of the patient. Thus, guided by clinical assessment and the evidence base, CBT techniques, such as goal modification and cognitive restructuring; intention implementation; expressive therapies and psychodynamic techniques may each be employed as appropriate. Expression of emotions that have perhaps been prohibited is encouraged and tolerated. New behaviours are attempted as experiments, with the support of the therapist.

As CAT is a brief, time-limited therapy, endings are paid particular attention. Endings are often frightening, distressing and can be experienced as rejecting or abandoning. Discussion of the ending begins at least four sessions before the end. Many patients feel subjectively worse towards the end of treatment because they are struggling with painful emotions that have previously been avoided with procedures and symptoms. Many will also have great difficulty expressing their ambivalence and distress and this becomes a focus for the final sessions. The aim is for the patient to be able to acknowledge both the good and bad aspects of the therapy and the therapist, and to accept the experience as having been 'good enough'. For these reasons, endings are a particular challenge for patients with perfectionistic, placating, depriving or abandoning relationship patterns, all of which are common in those with eating disorders. Goodbye letters are exchanged between the therapist and the patient during the penultimate or final session. These letters review changes made, predict potential difficulties and further work to be done, and acknowledge the relationship between the therapist and the patient. Follow-up is offered at regular intervals to monitor change and the revision of procedures. In addition, these sessions, and the letters and maps the patient has received, serve to maintain the attachment after weekly sessions have ended and provide further opportunity for expression and resolution of ambivalent feelings associated with ending.

Many patients are able to achieve considerable change during the follow-up period. For those that continue to experience significant illness at the end of follow-up, further therapy may be offered. In this context, the patient is helped to view the completed therapy not as a failure on the part of either therapist or patient, but as important and helpful preparation for further work.

EVIDENCE AND RATIONALE FOR THE APPLICATION OF CAT TO THE TREATMENT OF EATING DISORDERS

There is little empirical evidence to support the use of CAT in the treatment of eating disorders. There are only two treatment studies reported in the literature. The first was a pilot study in which 30 outpatients with AN, many of whom had poor prognostic features, were randomly allocated to either CAT or educational behaviour therapy (EBT). Those in the CAT group reported significantly greater subjective improvement at 1 year follow-up than the EBT group. The CAT group also showed consistently better outcome on each of the subscales of a standard eating disorders outcome scale (the Morgan and Russell scale), although these differences were not statistically significant in this small sample (Treasure et al., 1995). In a larger scale study comparing CAT with family therapy, psychodynamic psychotherapy and supportive therapy, the specific therapies performed better than supportive therapy, and there were no significant differences between CAT, family therapy and psychodynamic therapy (Dare et al., 2001).

If there is no clear efficacy advantage for CAT over other specific therapies, why chose CAT? A theoretical rationale for CAT in the treatment of AN has been given by Treasure and Ward (1997). Target problems maintain the focus on weight, which can be important for work with placating patients, but also allows focus on other issues which may underly the problem with eating. The open and collaborative style of CAT helps to diffuse the power struggles that are commonly encountered with patients enacting a controlling reciprocal role, and faciliates engagement of ambivalent patients. Patients with AN frequently experience significant interpersonal (Schmidt et al., 1997) and emotional difficulties (Troop et al., 1995) and the dual emphasis upon maladaptive relationship patterns and emotional processing is therefore valuable. Patients with AN perform poorly on theory of mind tasks (Tchanturia et al., 2001), and the disorder has been conceptualized as an empathy disorder (Gillberg et al., 1994). The use of the CAT map to facilitate development of theory of mind may therefore be particularly relevant to this group of patients. CAT provides an excellent set of tools for engaging and working with difficult patients and for managing therapist frustration and collusion. The integrationist style of CAT allows for the use of other techniques, such as motivational enhancement (Ward et al., 1996) to address ambivalence, and CBT techniques to facilitate behaviour change. The time-limited nature of the therapy and the focus upon a well-managed ending is helpful when separation and individuation are issues, as they frequently are in AN. Because the treatment of severe AN often requires prolonged therapeutic input, the brevity of therapy may also be seen as a disadvantage. However, follow-up sessions can be used to extend the therapeutic relationship and, if appropriate, further therapy can be considered after a period of reflection during follow-up. There may also be a cost-effectiveness advantage to CAT: it can be delivered in half the number of sessions of a standard 40-week psychodynamic therapy, but may be as effective. CAT training is also relatively short and is equally applicable to all members of the multidisciplinary team, helping to facilitate a shared model of understanding within the team. Finally, the flexibility of CAT means that it can be generalized to a variety of settings, including inpatient treatment and family work.

Much of the rationale for CAT in the treatment of AN is also applicable to BN. Borderline personality features and comorbid psychiatric symptoms such as substance misuse and self-harm are prevalent among patients with BN, and the CAT model may have particular advantages for this patient group. Firstly, the broad focus of CAT allows for comorbid problems to be addressed alongside the eating disorder. More narrowly focused treatments may require that patients with complex presentations are sent to different centres for different aspects of their care. This fragmentation may reinforce the internal splits and the sense of self as too overwhelming, and renact experiences of rejection and abandonment. Secondly, the map provides a particularly useful tool for understanding and recognising dissociative states and impulsive behaviours.

CASE STUDY

Susie

Susie was a 23-year-old patient who was referred by her GP. Her BMI was 16.8 at the time of referral. The onset of her AN was two years previously, following the death of her father from cancer. As the father's death was so rapid and unexpected, the family (Susie, her mother and her younger sister) did not mourn him, nor were they able to function as a family. Susie's mother knew her daughter had a problem, but was unable to comment upon her daughter's weight, or help her to eat. Susie was very unhappy, terrified of being anorexic and having therapy, but willing to try. This is the reformulation letter read to her at session 4:

Dear Susie,

As promised, here is my reformulation letter to you. In it I will be attempting to describe your present problems and their origins in your past. Some of the difficulties you are having now, you have had before and it would be helpful if we linked the past with the present. To start, however, I would like to describe your present problems.

You have an eating disorder that started at the unexpected death of your father two years ago. Your eating disorder has helped you to feel in control and your life has been both physically and emotionally affected by this eating disorder. It is making you feel depressed and ashamed. Perhaps we can look at the other times in your life when you have needed to be in control when you felt depressed and ashamed.

You described to me a pleasant childhood, and also that you were told that you were a very demanding baby who your mother found difficult to cope with. When you started school you felt all your demanding behaviour stopped and you needed to control yourself, but often felt bad. You felt that you were a good girl, but underneath you felt ashamed because you knew you really were bad. When you were seven years old you were in a very bad car accident and had to be hospitalised for some months. You remember desperately wanting your parents with you but they couldn't be and again you felt bad and ashamed for wanting too much and not getting it. You struggled again to be a good girl, having to learn to walk again, and feeling that you must be in control of yourself, not causing a fuss, and not being demanding towards your parents. This you managed to do.

As an adolescent you felt you couldn't rebel as you caused your father particular distress because you were so bad at maths. He used to tutor you and shout at you because you were so bad at it. You again tried to control yourself emotionally and learn to do maths. But perhaps you were unable to express your fear, anger and shame at his treatment and at your inability to be good at maths. When your father died, perhaps such distressing emotions as fear, loss, anger and grief made you feel ashamed again, as they did not seem able to be expressed by your family. So again you went out of control, this time using control of your eating and body as a way of managing your distress.

The conditional rules of your childhood, be in control, don't be demanding and don't be emotional, are applying to you now. You seem to need to control both your emotions and your needs and this is what the anorexia does. You want to be the good girl again and being in control is the best way to do this, as you perhaps discovered as a child. The problem is that it is the anorexia that is in control and stopping you from having a social life, a boyfriend and causing the shame and distress.

So our task in therapy, Susie, is to find ways for you to express neediness and emotions and not to be in perfect control. Perhaps by changing the definition of being a good girl, we can change your behaviours so that you don't feel ashamed of what you need and feel. Perhaps we can find ways that you can experience your relationships as something other than controlling and conditional both of yourself and of others. You can be demanding, emotional and, angry and still get love, attention and care.

To do this, I suggest that we focus on the following procedures.

I am fearful of making demands because I will upset others, so I try to please and be the good girl. I feel distressed, angry and ashamed so I try even harder to please and be the good girl.

I either keep myself in perfect control but am depressed and ashamed, or I express myself and fear rejection for being too demanding

I am bad and greedy inside so I cannot allow myself to want too much. I must starve and be in control to punish myself for being too demanding.

Susie accepted the letter and worked together with her therapist in developing a map (see Figure 17.3) and on recognising the above procedures. As she started to recognise

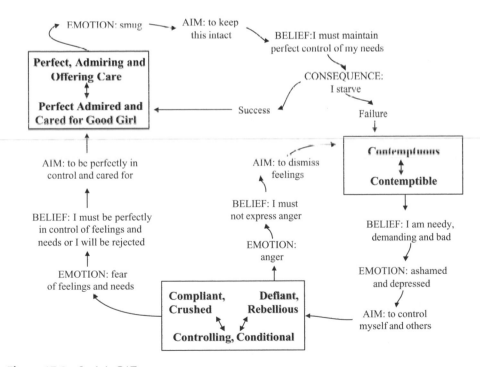

Figure 17.3 Susie's CAT map

> how much she needed to be in control to be the good girl, she was able to start challenging this and express herself emotionally to her family, her friends and her therapist. She found writing to be useful and wrote a letter to her father telling him how she felt about his death. She was able to express the distress of changing and not getting it right, both wanting to get better and fearful of getting better.
>
> The ending of therapy was very difficult as Susie was worried about not having the support of the therapist. She wrote a very moving goodbye letter where she was able to express her disappointment in her not gaining any weight during the therapy, how she would miss the therapist and her fears about the future. However, at her three-month follow-up, Susie had gained 4 kilos and felt she was well on the road to recovery. She had recruited her mother to help her to eat and this was working successfully.

The use of CAT in the above therapy helped both the patient and the therapist to understand the nature of Susie's anorexia, and to find ways for Susie to deal with her difficulties other than anorexia. The control issues were managed between the therapist and the patient by working with the re-enactment of the procedures rather than simply focusing on weight gain or loss. The reformulation letter helped to establish a good therapeutic alliance where control was the main issue rather than anorexia.

REFERENCES

Bandura, A. (1977) Self-efficacy: towards a unifying theory of behavioral change. *Psychol. Rev.*, **84**, 191–215.

Bandura, A. (1986) *Social Foundations of Thought and Action: A Social Cognitive Theory.* Englewood Cliffs, NJ: Prentice Hall.

Cnattingius, S., Hultman, C.M., Dahl, M. & Sparen, P. (1999) Very preterm birth, birth trauma, and the risk of anorexia nervosa among girls. *Arch. Gen. Psychiat.*, **56** (7), 634–638.

Dare, C., Eisler, I., Russell, G., Treasure, J. & Dodge, L. (2001) Psychological therapies for adults with anorexia nervosa: randomised controlled trial of out-patient treatments. *Br. J. Psychiat.*, **178**, 216–221.

Fairburn, C.G., Shafran, R. & Cooper, Z. (1999) A cognitive behavioural theory of anorexia nervosa. *Behav. Res. Ther.*, **37** (1), 1–13.

Gillberg, I.C., Rastam, M., & Gillberg, C. (1994) Anorexia nervosa outcome: six-year controlled longitudinal study of 51 cases including a population cohort. *J. Am. Acad. Child Adolesc. Psychiat.*, **33** (5), 729–739.

Kelly, G. (1963) *Theory of Personality: The Psychology of Personal Constructs.* New York: Norton.

Lazarus, R. (1999) The cognition-emotion debate: a bit of history. In T. Dalgleish & M. Power (Eds) *Handbook of Cognition and Emotion* (pp. 3–19). Chichester: John Wiley & Sons.

Mineka, S. & Thomas, C. (1999) Mechanisms of change in exposure therapy for anxiety disorders. In T. Dalgleish & M. Power (Eds) *Handbook of Cognition and Emotion* (pp. 747–764). Chichester: John Wiley & Sons.

Ryle, A. (1990) *Cognitive Analytical Therapy: Active Participation in Change. A New Integration in Brief Psychotherapy.* Chichester: John Wiley & Sons.

Safran, J. (1993) Breaches of the therapeutic alliance: an arena for negotiating authentic relatedness. *Psychotherapy*, **30** (1), 11–23.

Schmidt, U., Tiller, J., Blanchard, M., Andrews, B. & Treasure, J. (1997) Is there a specific trauma precipitating anorexia nervosa? *Psychol. Med.*, **27** (3), 523–530.

Sheldon & Cashdan (1988) Object relations theory: An overview. In *Object Relations Therapy: Using the Relationship.* New York: W.W. Norton & Co.

Shoebridge, P. & Gowers, S.G. (2000) Parental high concern and adolescent-onset anorexia nervosa. A case-control study to investigate direction of causality. *Br. J. Psychiat.*, **176**, 132–137.

Tchanturia, K., Hape, F., Godley, J., Treasure, J., Bara-Carril, N. & Schmidt, U. (2001) Theory of mind in anorexia nervosa. *Am. J. Psychiat.*

Treasure, J. & Ward, A. (1997) Cognitive analytical therapy in the treatment of anorexia nervosa. *Clin. Psychol. Psychother.*, **4** (1), 62–71.

Treasure, J., Todd, G., Brolly, M., Tiller, J., Nehmed, A. & Denman, F. (1995) A pilot study of a randomised trial of cognitive analytical therapy vs educational behavioral therapy for adult anorexia nervosa. *Behav. Res. Ther.*, **33** (4), 363–367.

Troop, N.A., Schmidt, U.H. & Treasure, J.L. (1995) Feelings and fantasy in eating disorders: a factor analysis of the Toronto Alexithymia Scale. *Int. J. Eat. Disord.*, **18** (2), 151–157.

Ward, A., Troop, N. & Treasure, J. (1996) To change or not to change. *Br. J. Med. Psychol.*, **69**, 139–146.

CHAPTER 18

Family Interventions

Ivan Eisler
*Adolescent Eating Disorder Service, Maudsley Hospital and
Psychotherapy Section, Institute of Psychiatry, London, UK*
Daniel le Grange
Eating Disorders Program, The University of Chicago, USA
and
Eia Asen
Marlborough Family Service, London, UK

SUMMARY

- Family therapy is an effective treatment for anorexia nervosa.
- The majority of adolescents suffering from anorexia nervosa, even when severely ill, can be managed on an outpatient basis providing the family has an active role in treatment.
- Family interventions are best viewed as treatments that mobilize family resources rather than treat family dysfunction (for which there is little empirical evidence).
- Brief, intensive multiple family interventions provide an important alternative to engaging families in treatment and are viewed very positively by families.

FAMILY THERAPY: TREATING DYSFUNCTIONAL FAMILIES OR HELPING FAMILIES TO FIND SOLUTIONS?

Over the past 25 years family therapy has gradually established itself as an important treatment approach in eating disorders, particularly with adolescent anorexia nervosa. The growing empirical evidence for the effectiveness of family-based treatments (reviewed later in the chapter) has added weight to the earlier clinical and theoretical accounts of some of the pioneer figures of the family therapy field, such as Salvador Minuchin (Minuchin et al., 1975) and Mara Selvini Palazzoli (1974) and has undoubtedly been one of the important factors in the major changes in the treatment of eating disorders that the field has witnessed in the past 10 to 15 years.

Paradoxically, alongside of the data for the effectiveness of family therapy, there has also been growing evidence that the theoretical models, from which the family treatment of eating

Handbook of Eating Disorders. Edited by J. Treasure, U. Schmidt and E. van Furth.

disorder was derived, are flawed. Minuchin et al.'s (1978) model of the 'psychosomatic family' which has probably been the most influential, hypothesized that there was a specific family context within which the eating disorder developed. The authors argued that a particular family process (characterized by rigidity, enmeshment, overinvolvement and conflict avoidance or conflict non-resolution) evolved around the symptomatic behaviour in interaction with a vulnerability in the child and the child's role as mediator in cross-generational alliances (Minuchin et al., 1975). Although they were clear that this was not simply an account of a 'family aetiology' of eating disorder and emphasized the evolving, interactive nature of the process, they saw the resulting 'psychosomatic family' as a necessary condition for the development of an eating disorder. The aim of family therapy then was clearly to alter the way the family functioned. This is well illustrated by the following quote: 'The syndrome of anorexia nervosa is associated with characteristic dysfunctional patterns of family interaction. The family therapist conceptualizes anorexia nervosa in relation to the organization and functioning of the entire family [. . .] and plans the therapeutic interventions to induce change in the family' (Sargent et al., 1985, p. 278).

In spite of a considerable amount of research endeavour, the evidence for the existence of the so-called psychosomatic family is unconvincing, as there is growing indication that families in which there is an eating disorder are a heterogeneous group not only with respect to sociodemographic characteristics but also in terms of the nature of the relationships within the family, the emotional climate and the patterns of family interactions (see Eisler, 1995, for a detailed review). While there is some evidence that effective family therapy is, in some families, accompanied by changes in family functioning (Eisler et al., 2000; Robin et al., 1995) the observed changes are not readily explained by the psychosomatic family model. The fact that families in which there is an eating disorder are heterogeneous and do not necessarily change in predictable ways, inevitably raises the question about the targets of effective family interventions and the nature of the underlying process of change.

Whether or not the family environment has a causal role in the aetiology of eating disorders, it is undoubtedly the case that the presence of an eating disorder has a major impact on family life (see Chapter 11 by Nielsen and Bará-Carril in this volume). As time goes on, food, eating behaviours and the concerns that they give rise to begin to permeate the entire family fabric, every relationship in the family, influencing daily family routines, coping and problem-solving behaviours. Steinglass and colleagues have described a similar process in families with an alcoholic member (Steinglass et al., 1987) and in families coping with a wide range of chronic illnesses (Steinglass, 1998). They developed a conceptual model that describes the process of family reorganization around alcohol-related (or illness-related) behaviours. They propose that families go through a step-wise reorganization in response to the challenges of the illness in which illness issues increasingly take centre stage, altering the family's daily routines, their decision-making processes and regulatory behaviours, until the illness becomes *the central organizing principle* of the family's life. They argue that families, in trying to minimize the impact of the illness on the sufferer, as well as on other family members, increasingly focus their attention on the here-and-now, making it difficult for them to meet the changing developmental needs of the family.

The model proposed by Steinglass and colleagues is readily applicable to eating disorders. Families trying to cope with an eating disorder in their midst will often say that they feel as if time had come to a standstill and that all of the family's life seems to revolve around the eating disorder. The way families respond to this invasion into their family life will vary depending on the nature of the family organization, the family style of each individual family and the particular lifecycle stage they are at when the illness occurs. However, like with other illnesses, what may be more predictable is the way in which the centrality of the eating disorder magnifies certain aspects of the family's dynamics and narrows the range of their adaptive behaviours. The following case example illustrates this process:

Jenny, a 16-year-old adolescent, was referred to our service with a 14-month history of anorexia nervosa. From the referral letter we knew that Jenny's parents had divorced when she was 9 and that she was living with her mother, Ann, and mother's new husband, Tom. There was also a 3-year-old sister from the second marriage. Although Tom had been living in the family home for over four years, Jenny did not get on with him and did not consider him as a father figure. As is our customary practice we invited the whole family to attend the first meeting, but only Jenny and her mother attended. Throughout the first interview we were struck by the close, at times even clingy, relationship between Jenny and her mother. Jenny tended to let her mother speak for her, but from time-to-time would angrily contradict any inaccuracy in Ann's description of her problem. Ann would invariably back away from the potential conflict. When the therapist inquired about Tom, Jenny quickly answered that he did not understand and in any case would probably not come. The therapist asked if that was because he did not care or because he did not believe that he might be of any help. Jenny and Ann agreed that Tom did care and that if he thought that he could be of help that he would want to help but Ann hinted that there were difficulties between her and her husband (particularly in how they dealt with Jenny's problem) that might make things more difficult if he was involved. The therapist responded by acknowledging that it might be difficult if Tom was there but that Jenny's problem was far too serious for them not to make use of every resource they had. The fact that he was less involved and had a different perspective on things could be useful, although he probably needed the opportunity to learn more about the problem as well.

It would be relatively easy to construct a hypothesis which would 'explain' Jenny's anorexia as arising out of and/or being maintained by a dysfunctional family system. The very close, intense relationship between Jenny and her mother, Jenny's awkward relationship with Tom and the role that she seemed to play in mediating the marital relationship, the avoidance of overt conflict could all be seen as representing the features of the 'psychosomatic family' described above. However, it would ignore the fact that much of what we observed was also clearly connected with the transitional lifecycle stage that the family was going through (i.e. reconstituting itself as a new family)—or more accurately, because of the presence of anorexia was finding it hard to negotiate. The usual difficulties of a step-father becoming part of the new family were magnified by anorexia and at the same time any uncertainty that Tom had in trying to make sense of Jenny's illness, simply confirmed that he did not understand her and did not belong. Ann's occasional doubts whether she had done the right thing in leaving her first husband, and the effect this might have had on Jenny, turned into feelings of guilt that she might somehow be responsible for the illness.

Trying to work out which of these processes were cause and which effect and which were just incidental is, of course, difficult to disentangle and from a clinical point of view perhaps not very useful in any case. It is more important to explore with the family where things have got stuck and to help them to rediscover some of the resources that they have as a family so that they can become 'unstuck' and start looking for new solutions for the problem at hand. The most important step in engaging the family in treatment, therefore, is to be clear that the family is not seen as the problem but as a resource. In coming together to tackle their daughter's problem, families may sometimes find that there are aspects of the way they function as a family that they want to change. That is, however, not the primary aim of the treatment, which has to be the overcoming of their daughter's eating disorder.

EVIDENCE FOR THE EFFECTIVENESS OF FAMILY THERAPY FOR EATING DISORDERS

Uncontrolled Follow-up Studies of Family Therapy for Adolescent Anorexia Nervosa

The first family therapy study of patients with anorexia nervosa was conducted by Minuchin and his colleagues at the Philadelphia Child Guidance Clinic (Minuchin et al., 1975, 1978). In a follow-up of 53 anorexic patients, for whom family therapy had been the main intervention, Minuchin et al. (1978) reported a very high rate of successful outcomes. The treatments were mixed in that just over half of the patients started out receiving inpatient treatment in conjunction with family therapy, and some of the adolescents were also seen individually while engaged in family therapy. The Philadelphia team reported a remarkably high recovery rate of 86% with their treatment approach, which was in stark contrast to most previous accounts of treatment outcome with children and adolescents suffering from anorexia nervosa (Lesser et al., 1960; Blitzer et al., 1961; Warren, 1968; Goetz et al., 1977). The patient population was mainly adolescent with only three patients being over the age of 18, and the mean duration of illness was just over eight months (range = one month – three years). The very positive results reported by Minuchin et al. (1978), together with the clear and persuasive theoretical model that underpinned their treatment approach, has made the work of the Philadelphia team highly influential even though the study has been criticized for methodological weaknesses (the evaluations were conducted by members of the clinical team, the length of follow-up varied from 18 months to 7 years, there was no comparison treatment).

There have been two other very similar studies, one in Toronto (Martin, 1985) and one in Buenos Aires (Herscovici & Bay, 1996). Both studies were of adolescent anorexia nervosa, with family therapy being the main treatment, but used in combination with a mixture of individual and inpatient treatment. The study reported by Martin (1985) was of a five-year follow-up of 25 adolescent anorexia nervosa patients (mean age 14.9 years) with a short duration of illness (mean 8.1 months). At treatment termination there had been significant improvements although only 23% of patients would have met the Morgan/Russell criteria for good outcome, 45% intermediate outcome and 32% poor outcome. The outcome at follow-up was comparable to Minuchin's results with 80% of patients having a good outcome, 4% intermediate outcome, with the remaining either still in treatment (12%) or relapsed (4%). Herscovici and Bay (1996) report the outcome in a series of 30 patients treated by a pediatrician and family therapist, and followed-up 4–8.6 years after their first presentation. The mean age of these patients at the start of treatment was 14.7 years with a mean duration of illness of 10.3 months. More than 40% of patients were admitted to hospital during the study. They report that 60% of patients had a 'good' outcome, 30% an intermediate outcome, and 10% a poor outcome.

Three other studies have been reported in which family therapy was the only treatment used. The first two (Dare, 1983; Mayer, 1994) were small studies of 12 and 11 adolescent patients respectively, who were seen in outpatient family therapy at the Maudsley Hospital in London and at a General Practice based family therapy clinic in North London. In both studies the treatment was brief (usually less than six months) and 90% were reported to have made significant improvements or were recovered at follow-up.

The third is a larger study from Heidelberg (Stierlin & Weber, 1987, 1989). The sample consisted of families seen at the Heidelberg Centre over a period of 10 years. After excluding male patients, bulimics and those whose treatment had ended less than two years before the follow-up study took place, 42 families were included in the follow-up. The study differs from the other studies in several ways. In the first place the patients were older (mean age when first seen, 18.2 years) and had been ill for an average of just over three years. Approximately two-thirds were still at school, the rest were either at university or were working. All but two of the patients had had previous treatment (56% of whom as inpatients). The therapy lasted on average just under nine months but used relatively few sessions (mean = 6). At follow-up (the average duration of which was $4^1/_2$ years) just under two-thirds were within a normal weight range and were menstruating. The study makes no distinction in the reporting of the findings between adolescents and adults and is not therefore directly comparable to the other studies described. Nevertheless, it adds to the evidence that adolescents, and probably also young adults, do well in family therapy.

Randomized Clinical Trials of Family Therapy in Adolescent Anorexia Nervosa

There have been few randomized trials in anorexia nervosa and all have been relatively small. The first study by Russell and colleagues (1987) compared family therapy with individual supportive therapy following inpatient treatment. This study included patients of all ages and covered 80 consecutive admissions to the inpatient unit at the Maudsley Hospital in London. Twenty-six of these patients were adolescents with anorexia nervosa, 21 with an age of onset on or before 18 years and a duration of illness of less than three years. All patients were initially admitted to hospital for an average of 10 weeks for weight restoration before being randomized to outpatient follow-up treatment. Adolescent patients with a short duration faired significantly better with family therapy than the control treatment (individual therapy), although the findings were inconclusive for those with a duration of illness of more than three years who mostly had a poor outcome. A five-year follow-up of this study (Eisler et al., 1997) showed that in the adolescent subgroup with a short history of illness those who received family therapy continued to do well with 90% having a good outcome. Although the patients who had received individual therapy had also continued to improve, nearly half still had significant eating disorder symptoms, showing that even five years after the end of treatment it was still possible to detect benefits of the family interventions.

Four studies have compared different forms of family intervention. Le Grange et al. (1992) and Eisler et al. (2000) compared conjoint family therapy (CFT) and separated family therapy (SFT) in which the adolescent was seen on her own and the parents were seen in a separate session by the same therapist. Both treatments were provided on an outpatient basis although 4 out of 40 in Eisler et al. (2000) required admission during the course of treatment. The overall results were similar in the two studies, showing significant improvements in both treatments (at the end of treatment two-thirds were classified as having a good or intermediate outcome), but relatively small differences between treatments in terms of symptom improvement. Both studies also showed that families in which there was raised maternal criticism tended to do worse in CFT. On the other hand, the Eisler et al. (2000) study showed that on individual psychological measures and measures of family functioning there was significantly more change in the CFT group. Similar to other studies the patients continued to improve after the treatment ended. Preliminary results from the five-year follow-up show that 75% have a good outcome, 15% an intermediate outcome and 10% have a poor outcome.

Robin et al. (1999) in Detroit also compared two forms of family intervention in a study with a similar design to that of the Maudsley group. They compared a conjoint family therapy (described as behavioural family systems therapy—BFST) with ego-oriented individual therapy (EOIT) in which weekly individual sessions for the adolescent were combined with fortnightly meetings with the parents. Robin et al. (1998, 1999) in describing the features of BFST, point out the similarities with the Maudsley CFT. Both treatments emphasize the role of the parents in managing the eating disorder symptoms in the early stages of treatment with a broadening of focus to individual or family issues at a later stage. Robin et al. have also argued that while EOIT is superficially similar to SFT, the aim is quite different. While in SFT there is again an emphasis on helping the parents to take a strong role in the management of the symptoms, the work with the parents in EOIT aims to help them to relinquish control over their daughter's eating and to prepare them to accept a more assertive adolescent. The parents are 'instructed not to be controlling about eating but rather take a proactive, supportive role, for example, planning menus, shopping for food, arranging meals that are eaten together as a family, supervising lunch preparation, providing snacks during activities and quietly monitoring the progress of the anorectic's food intake in a supportive, nonjudgmental manner' (Robin et al., 1998, p. 434). However, while there may well have been significant differences between the Detroit EOIT and the Maudsley SFT, the similarities between the treatments are equally important. In both treatments the adolescent received regular individual therapy in which she had the opportunity to address her own personal and relationship issues as well as matters directly connected with her eating problems. The parallel sessions with the parents may have had a somewhat different focus in the two studies but in both treatments the parents were encouraged to have an active role in providing support for their daughter in the process of recovery and to reflect on some of the family dynamics that might have got caught up with the eating disorder.

There are some important differences between the Maudsley and Detroit studies which could have had a bearing on outcome. One difference was that Robin et al. hospitalized patients whose weight was below 75% of ideal weight (43% of their sample) at the start of the treatment programme until their weight rose above 80% of ideal, whereas in the le Grange et al. (1992)/Eisler et al. (2000) studies, the protocol allowed for admission only if outpatient therapy failed to arrest weight loss (none of the 18 patients in le Grange et al. and 4 out of 40 in Eisler et al. were admitted during the study). A further difference concerns the length of treatment which was 6 months in le Grange et al. study, 12 months in Eisler et al. study and 12–18 months (with an average of 16 months) in the Robin et al. study. There were also apparent differences between the patient groups in that the patients in the Maudsley studies tended to have a longer duration of illness, the majority had had previous treatment and a higher percentage were suffering from depression.

The end of treatment findings (Robin et al., 1999) showed significant improvements in both treatments with 67% reaching target weight by the end of treatment and 80% regaining menstruation. By the 1-year follow-up, approximately 75% had reached their target weight and 85% were menstruating. BFST led to significantly greater weight gain than EOIT both at the end of treatment and at follow-up and there was also a significantly higher percentage of girls menstruating at the end of treatment in the BFST group. Both treatments produced comparably large improvements in eating attitudes, depression, and self-reported eating-related family conflict although, interestingly, neither group reported much general conflict before or after treatment. Robin et al. (1995) have also reported the results of observational ratings of family interaction in a subsample of their study which showed a significant decease in maternal negative communication (and a corresponding increase in positive communication) in the BFST group which was not found in the EOIT group.

A further study by Geist et al. (2000) compared family therapy with family group psychoeducation (FGP). The effects of the family interventions are difficult to evaluate as nearly half of the family treatments occurred during inpatient treatment and 76% of the weight gain took place before discharge from hospital. There were no differences between the two family interventions. Two other controlled treatment studies in anorexia nervosa included adolescent patients and used family intervention as part of the treatment (Hall & Crisp, 1987; Crisp et al., 1991). In both studies, however, the family interventions were part of a larger treatment package and it is unclear how central the family was in the treatment. Moreover, both studies also included adult patients, and the results are not reported separately for the adolescent subgroup. This makes it difficult to evaluate the effects of family treatment on outcome in adolescent patients in these two studies.

Summary of Family Therapy Studies in Adolescent Anorexia Nervosa

Table 18.1 summarizes the results from the various family intervention studies in anorexia nervosa. The overall findings from these studies are remarkably consistent, showing that adolescents with anorexia nervosa respond well to family therapy, often without the need for inpatient treatment. By the end of treatment between half and two-thirds will have reached a healthy weight, although most will not yet have started menstruating again. By the time of follow-up between 60–90% will have fully recovered and no more than 10–15% will still be seriously ill.

Conclusions about the comparisons between different kinds of family interventions have to be more cautious, given the small size and small number of comparative studies. Treatments that encourage the parents to take an active role in tackling their daughter's anorexia seem the most effective and may have some advantages over involving the parents in a way that is supportive and understanding of their daughter but encourages them to step back from the eating problem. One study (Russell et al., 1987; Eisler et al., 1997) has shown that not involving the parents in the treatment at all leads to the worst outcome and may considerably delay recovery. Seeing whole families together appears to have some advantages in addressing both family and individual psychological issues but may have disadvantages for families in which there are high levels of hostility or criticism. Such families can be difficult to engage in family treatment (Szmukler et al., 1985) and this may be particularly true when the whole family is seen together. There is some evidence that this is associated with feelings of guilt and blame being increased as a consequence of criticisms or confrontations occurring during family sessions (Squire-Dehouck, 1993) and our clinical experience suggests that with such families conjoint family sessions may be more useful at a later stage in treatment when the concerns about eating disorder symptoms are no longer central. It is important to stress, however, that while there may be advantages and disadvantages between different types of family interventions, these differences are relatively small in comparison with the overall improvements in response to any of the family interventions studied.

Table 18.1 Studies of family therapy for adolescents with anorexia nervosa

	Sample	Treatments	End of treatment results	Follow-up results
Open follow-up studies				
Minuchin et al. (1978)	N = 53 Age = 14.8 yrs Duration = 8.6 mths	Average of 6.8 mths FT (2–16) 57% admitted for mean of 2.4 wks	Not reported	FU 2.7 yrs (1.5–7) Recovered 86%; fair 4%; Unimproved or relapsed 10%
Dare (1983)	N = 12 Age = 14.7 Duration = 11.6 mths	Outpatient treatment only FT for mean of 6 mths (1–6)	Not reported	FU 10 mths 33% recovered; 58% fair; 8% unchanged
Martin (1985)	N = 25 Age = 14.9 yrs Duration = 8.1 mths	Average of 11 mths FT (2–39) 72% admitted for mean of 8 wks	23% good; 45% inter; 32% poor	FU 5.1 yrs (2.5–7) 80% good; 4% inter; 16% poor
Stierlin & Weber (1987) Stierlin & Weber (1989)	N = 42 Age = 18.2 Duration = 3.3 yrs	Outpatient treatment only Average of 8.7 mths FT (1–40)	21% > 85% abw; 17% menst	FU 4.4 yrs (2.2–8.8) 57% above 85% abw; 60% menst
Mayer (1994)	N = 11 Age = 17 yrs Duration = 9 mths	Outpatient treatment only FT for 1–9 mths. Mean no. of sessions 6.3 (1–18)	Not reported	Mean FU 1.7 yrs 57% good 29% inter; 14% poor
Herscovici & Bay (1996)	N = 30 Age = 14.7 yrs Duration = 10.3 mths	FT for 24 mths 43% admitted for mean of 4 wks	Not reported	FU 6.1 yrs (4–8.6) 60% good; 30% inter; 10% poor
Randomized treatment trials				
Russell et al. (1987) Eisler et al. (1997)	N = 21 Age = 15.3 yrs Duration = 14.4 mths	10.3 wks inpatient + 1 yr FU of: (a) family therapy (b) individual supportive therapy	(a) 60% good; 30% inter; 10% poor (b) 9% good; 9% inter; 10% poor	FU 6.3 yrs (3.1–9.8) (a) 90% good; 10% poor (b) 36% good; 18% inter; 46% poor
Le Grange et al. (1992) Squire-Dehouck (1993)	N = 18 Age = 15.3 yrs Duration = 13.7 mths	6 mths outpatient FT: (a) conjoint family therapy (b) separated family therapy	(a) 20% good; 50% inter; 30% poor (b) 50% good; 40% inter; 10% poor	FU 2 yrs (a) 33% good; 33% inter; 33% poor (b) 87% good; 13% inter
Robin et al. (1999)	N = 37 Age = 14.2 yrs Duration < 12 mths	1–1.5 yrs FT/IT (43% admitted): (a) behavioural family systems therapy (b) ego-oriented individual therapy	(a) 59% good; 6% inter; 35% poor (b) 38% good; 31% inter; 31% poor	FU 1 yr (a) 73% good; 7% inter; 20% poor (b) 64% good; 29% inter; 7% poor
Eisler et al. (2000)	N = 40 Age = 15.5 yrs Duration = 12.9 yrs	1 yr FT (10% admitted): (a) conjoint family therapy (b) separated family therapy	(a) 26% good; 21% inter; 53% poor (b) 48% good; 28% inter; 24% poor	FU 5 yrs[a] (a) 61% good; 17% inter; 22% poor (b) 76% good; 19% inter; 5% poor

[a]Preliminary unpublished data.

The evidence for the effectiveness of family therapy for adolescent anorexia nervosa is clearly compelling as several reviewers have recently concluded (e.g. Wilson & Fairburn, 1998; Carr, 2000) and on current evidence is probably the treatment of choice. It is important to recognize, however, that this may be, at least in part, due to the lack of research on other treatments. Cognitive or psychodynamic treatments are described in the literature (Bowers et al., 1996; Jeammet & Chabert, 1998) but have not been systematically evaluated with adolescent anorexia nervosa and their relative merits in comparison with family therapy are not known. Similarly, the multiple-family day treatment, described in some detail later in this chapter, is a promising new treatment development but as yet there is no systematic evidence for its effectiveness.

ADULT ANOREXIA NERVOSA

Randomised Treatment Trials

The Russell et al. (1987) controlled trial, described earlier, included 31 adult patients with anorexia nervosa (19 years of age or older) who were randomly assigned to either family therapy or the individual control treatment, following discharge from hospital. There were no differences in outcome between treatments for the group as a whole. However, in the subgroup of patients with an adult onset of the illness ($n = 14$) the results favoured individual therapy in which there was significantly greater weight gain (20%) than family therapy (6%). At five-year follow-up, there were no differences in eating disorder symptoms in this subgroup although there was some evidence that the patients in individual therapy had made a somewhat better psychological adjustment, particularly in the area of psychosexual attitudes and behaviours (Eisler et al., 1997).

Dare et al. (2001) conducted an outpatient study to assess the effectiveness of specific psychotherapies, including family therapy, in the outpatient management of adult patients with chronic anorexia nervosa. Eighty-four patients were randomized to four treatments: (1) focal psychoanalytic psychotherapy, (2) cognitive analytic therapy, (3) family therapy and (4) routine treatment that served as a control. At the end of one-year follow-up, the group of patients as a whole showed modest symptomatic improvements with the specialist treatments proving to be significantly more effective than routine treatment. Of the patients allocated to family therapy or focal psychotherapy, 35% were categorized as recovered or significantly improved at the end of treatment compared to 5% of those in the control treatment. There were no significant differences between the three specialist treatments.

Summary of Studies of Family Therapy in Adult Anorexia Nervosa

The data on the use of family therapy (or indeed other psychotherapies) with adults suffering from anorexia nervosa is still quite limited. Moreover, the existing data comes from studies of mainly chronically ill patients with whom positive treatment results are difficult to achieve in general, which makes it more difficult to demonstrate specific effects of particular treatments. The finding by Dare et al. (2001), that specialized psychotherapies were more effective than routine treatment but did not differ from one another, is worthy of further investigation. The similarity of outcome between the different psychotherapies may be simply another example of the so-called 'Dodo' effect (different psychotherapies leading to similar results) (Luborsky et al., 1975) but it may also be that different subgroups respond differently to particular treatments. Larger studies with greater power than the Dare et al. (2001) study are needed to address these questions.

BULIMIA NERVOSA

Although there have been many accounts in the literature of the use of family therapy in the treatment of bulimia nervosa (e.g. Dare, 1997; Johnson et al., 1998; Fishman, 1996; Garner, 1994), there is very little research data to support the clinical accounts. Schwartz et al. (1985) reported on a follow-up of 30 cases of bulimia nervosa who were treated in family therapy. At the end of treatment 66% were rated as being nearly always in control, with at most one bulimic episode per month. These results were maintained at follow-up (the average length of which was 18 months). In the only study of family therapy with adolescents with bulimia nervosa, Dodge et al. (1995) reported on a small series of eight bulimic patients receiving family therapy on an outpatient basis. Significant improvements in bulimic behaviours were reported at the end of treatment. In terms of the Morgan–Russell outcome scores, one patient achieved a good outcome, five achieved an intermediate outcome, and two a poor outcome. Although these results are encouraging, the results must be viewed with caution given the uncontrolled nature of the study and the very small number of cases. Two centres are currently exploring the efficacy of family therapy for adolescent bulimia nervosa. At the University of Chicago, a controlled treatment study is underway in which bulimics aged 19 or younger are randomized into one of two manualized treatments, family therapy or individual supportive therapy. A multicentre RCT study is also being conducted by the Maudsley team of family therapy and guided self-help CBT.

The only randomized trial of family therapy in bulimia nervosa is the Russell et al. (1987) study described earlier. This trial included a subgroup of 23 adult bulimia nervosa patients. As was the case with the three other subgroups in this trial, bulimic patients were randomly allocated to either family therapy or to individual supportive therapy. In terms of general outcome at the end of the one-year outpatient treatment, patients in neither groups faired well and the distribution for the two treatment groups between the outcome categories did not differ significantly. Five-year follow-up data were obtained for 19 patients in this subgroup (Eisler et al., 1997). On the whole, these patients showed a disappointing outcome with only 16% being asymptomatic and a further 32% bingeing and/or vomiting less than once a week. There were no differences between the two follow-up treatments. The results from this study do not easily compare with other studies of bulimia nervosa in that nearly two-thirds of the patients were significantly underweight and by today's diagnostic criteria would be more appropriately classified as bulimic type anorexia nervosa.

The other, albeit indirect, evidence for the possible value of family interventions in bulimia nervosa comes from studies of interpersonal therapy (Fairburn et al., 1991; Agras et al., 2000). Interpersonal therapy is an individual therapy but, like family or systemic therapies, focuses on the way that symptomatic behaviours become entangled in interpersonal relationships. Interpersonal therapy is comparable in effectiveness in the medium to long term with cognitive-behaviour therapy (although less effective in the short term) which suggests that further study of the possible role of family therapy in bulimia nervosa are warranted.

MULTIPLE-FAMILY THERAPY IN THE TREATMENT OF ADOLESCENT EATING DISORDERS

The effectiveness of family interventions with adolescent eating-disordered patients and the need to develop more intensive forms of family based treatments for those who do not respond to outpatient family therapy alone has recently led to the development of multiple-family therapy day programmes in Dresden (Scholz & Asen, 2001) and at the Maudsley Hospital in London (Dare & Eisler, 2000). Preliminary results from these programmes are very promising and offer an additional approach for helping adolescents with eating disorders and their families. The experience from these programmes also offers new perspectives on the processes underlying family interventions.

The idea of treating a number of families together was first pioneered in the early 1960s by Laqueur (Laqueur et al., 1964). He saw this as a way of providing a context where the resources of all family members could be used more successfully when several families were treated together in one group in order to improve inter- and intra-family communication (Laqueur, 1972). In addition, by identifying with members of other families and learning by analogy (Laqueur, 1973) patients and key relatives could expand their social repertoires. The multiple-family therapy model has been further elaborated over the past three decades (Strelnick, 1977; Steinglass, 1998; Asen, 2002) and applied to various psychiatric populations including drug and alcohol abuse (Kaufman & Kaufman, 1979), chronic medical illness (Gonsalez et al., 1989; Steinglass, 1998), Huntingdon's disease (Murburg et al., 1988), child abuse (Asen et al., 1989), as well as eating disorders (Slagerman & Yager, 1989; Wooley & Lewis, 1987).

In England, Cooklin and his team at the Marlborough Family Service in London (Cooklin et al., 1983, Asen et al., 1982) pioneered a unique multiple-family approach in the late 1970s, creating a day hospital where up to 10 families would attend together for five days a week for 8 hours a day. Bringing a whole number of families together for intensive days or weeks creates a hothouse effect. Interactions are necessarily more intense in a group setting where children and parents are participating in different tasks and where they are required to examine not only their own but also other families' communications and behaviours. This increased intensity can lead to rapid growth—change is more likely to take place as familiar coping and defence mechanisms cannot be employed. Being part of a multiple-family setting requires families constantly to change context, requiring each family member continuously having to adapt to new demands. Such intensity cannot easily be created in individual family sessions.

The therapeutic factors that are described as important in multiple-family work, such as reducing social isolation, de-stigmatization, enhancing opportunities to create new and multiple perspectives, neutralizing chronic staff–patient relationships, etc. (see Asen, 2002), are strongly enhanced by the intensity of the day programme setting.

The Dresden and London projects are very similar (unsurprisingly, since both units have shared their experiences and inspired one another) even though the starting point for each programme was quite different. The Dresden service is based around a large inpatient unit which over the years admitted about 60 anorectic and bulimic teenagers per year, often in rather severe physical states. In addition to other treatments, fortnightly family therapy sessions had been used routinely during admission, and following discharge from hospital (after an average of 12 weeks) the young person would usually continue to attend as a daypatient or outpatient, receiving individual and family therapy and, occassionally, medication. The impetus for developing the experimental multiple-family day treatment (MFDT) was the repeated experience of patients who tended to lose weight rapidly after discharge from hospital, particularly if the parents had not been involved in learning to manage the eating routines of their children.

It seemed obvious that, in order to address this, the parents had to be involved much more centrally in the treatment programme, possibly right from the outset. However, parents are not always welcome visitors on adolescent inpatient wards, particularly when staff believe, consciously or unconsciously, that they are to blame for the eating disorder of their child. There are doctors and nurses who think that the eating-disordered young person needs to be separated from her parents and that an inpatient spell would be extremely useful to help her to cut the umbilical cord and individuate. Moreover, parents might also be experienced as interfering with the well-worked-out ward routines. Rivalries between staff and parents are not uncommon, particularly when it comes to who is the 'best' carer, with the young person inevitably getting caught up in such dynamics. The frequently observed rapid weight loss following discharge from the inpatient unit only serves as confirmation that the hospital staff are 'better' than the parents and seem to confirm the failure of the latter. Parents increasingly feel demoralized and sanction their child's readmission to hospital, more keen to have her discharged later rather than sooner, with an ever-increasing risk of the young person becoming a chronic patient. In this situation the MFDT paradigm seemed highly relevant, since it addresses directly the parents' sense of struggling away in isolation and having to rely heavily on the input of nurses, doctors and therapists. Connecting these parents with other parents seemed a logical step to overcome this isolation. Moreover, involving parents directly in the eating issues of their child seemed another step for them to become expert themselves rather than leave that expertise remaining with the nursing and medical staff.

The starting point of the London group was quite different. The team has for a number of years provided both a local and a national specialist outpatient family therapy service for children and adolescents with an eating disorder. The specialist nature of the service is reflected in the nature of the referrals which are often complex and follow previous attempts at treatment elsewhere. Because of the previous failures and the severity of the illness many of the referrals are requests for inpatient treatment. In spite of this, relatively few cases are admitted to the inpatient eating disorder unit (5–10%) even though more than 70% of the referrals meet recommended criteria for inpatient treatment (APA, 2000). However serious the illness, an attempt is nearly always made to engage the family actively in the treatment, to try to avoid hospitalization. Sometimes the referral is at a point when the child has already been admitted to a general paediatric ward. Providing the physical condition can be stabilized and the medical staff agree that it is safe for the child to be away from hospital at least for a few days, it is often possible to use the crisis to engage the family in effective outpatient work without the need for further admission. The idea of developing a MFDT programme was attractive because it offered a more intensive form of treatment than the standard outpatient family therapy, while at the same time was in keeping with the general principle underlying the outpatient treatment that the most effective help in the long term is to help the family to find its own solutions. While it was initially envisaged that the MFDT programme would be needed mainly for the complex referrals that might otherwise require inpatient treatment, the positive experiences (of both the families and the staff) of taking part in the group suggested that it might be beneficial for all the families referred to the service.

In common with the outpatient family therapy model (Dare & Eisler, 1997), MFDT aims to help families rediscover their own resources by exploring ways in which parents can take an active role in their daughter's recovery. At the same time the families are encouraged to explore how the eating disorder and the interactional patterns in the family have become entangled, making it difficult for the family to follow the normal developmental course of the family lifecycle. The sharing of experiences among families and the intensity of the treatment programme makes this a very different experience for the families than outpatient family therapy. The emphasis on helping families to find their own solutions is much more readily apparent in this context and is an aspect of the treatment that the families themselves frequently comment on.

Although each group develops its own unique dynamic, nearly all the groups very quickly establish a sense of identity which generally evolves around discussions of the shared experience of living with anorexia or bulimia and the effect it has on family life. Given that most parents with an anorectic child have a complex set of feelings—including failure, guilt, anger, fear and embarrassment—having the opportunity to meet with other families who experience similar feelings allows for these to be shared. This has strong destigmatizing effects and creates a sense of solidarity. In a multiple-family setting professional staff are in a minority and this contributes to a 'family' rather than 'medical' atmosphere. Being in the presence of other families also has the effect of making the adolescents and their parents feel less central—they are part of a large group and the feeling of being constantly watched and observed by staff is less intense. This process often quite quickly allows the families to 'externalize' the eating disorder as the enemy or intruder in their family life which they have to join forces to overcome.

The presence of other families also highlights the very real differences between them, which illustrates for the families better than any number of statements by staff, that there is no specific family constellation which leads to the development of an eating disorder. This makes it easier for families to start making comparisons, for example, how other parents handle the food refusal of their teenager—as much as young persons cannot help comparing their own parents' responses to those of other eating-disordered teenagers. The effect of all this is that new and different perspectives are introduced, so important since eating-disordered families tend to have distorted self-perceptions while being often very precise and intuitive about other families. Many people find it easier to use feedback from fellow-sufferers than from staff—it seems more 'credible' because these families all have painful direct experiences around food, hospitalization and dieting. Such feedback gets generated during a whole range of different activities throughout the day, both formal and informal. The role of the therapists is that of a catalyst, enabling families to connect with one another and encouraging mutual curiosity and feedback.

The structure of the Dresden and London programmes is quite similar with a mixture of whole family group discussions, parallel meetings of parents and adolescents and occasional meetings with individual families (see Appendix 18.1 for examples of the day structure). Group discussions are interspersed with a variety of activity techniques including role-plays, family sculpting, body image work, symbolic food preparation, creative art work such as clay modelling, etc (Appendix 18.2 gives examples of a variety of activities used in the programme). At other times individual families will work with a member of staff, e.g. preparing a genogram which they then bring to the whole group for discussion. The ensuing discussions are usually stimulating all round, providing ample opportunity for cross-family discussion. Information giving—sometimes in the form of psychoeducational talks explaining the facts about eating disorders, their physical risks and psychological side-effects, etc., but more often informally, as part of general group discussions—is an important component of the programme.

Lunch is in many respects the central event of the day—at least in the initial stages of MFDT. In London families go shopping to the local supermarket and here major confrontations may ensue between the teenager and her parents as to what is nutritious food. Once the food has been bought, families are in charge of preparing and serving it. The situation is different in Dresden where food is provided by the hospital, with a fixed menu within which there are a few choices. Each family decides what and how much their daughter or son should eat. Needless to say, soon familiar battles will flare up, with the anorectic making out the best possible arguments for not eating anything, and with the parents determined to impose their will. The staff's role is to comment on and, if appropriate, challenge these interactions around food 'in vivo' and to question the parents' tolerance and their willingness to compromise. Sometimes this is videotaped so that parent–child interactions can be viewed and analysed in subsequent video-feedback sessions. Group discussions of the lunch time sessions is a useful time for families to reflect on the 'possibles' and 'impossibles' of managing eating.

Other sessions are also videotaped with the families' permission so that there is opportunity to record interactions which can then be reviewed jointly by families and staff later that day or at some other suitable time. One-way screens can also be used creatively, for instance to facilitate an uninterrupted discussion between the adolescents that the parents can observe (or vice versa).

Since its inception in 1998, the staff of the Dresden Eating Disorder Unit have experimented with a whole range of different lengths and frequencies of the programme (Scholz & Asen, 2001)—from two block days per month, to whole weeks in two-monthly intervals. The team is multidisciplinary, consisting of nurses, occupational therapists, teachers, social workers, psychotherapists, psychologists and psychiatrists. The minimum staff for each multiple-family group is four, with the various different professionals having different functions and tasks, be that direct therapeutic work, observation or supervision. The structure of each day is discussed and decided by the staff, although families also have an opportunity to discuss the programme for the day and their ideas are often used to create a new daily structure.

The London team at the Maudsley has used a less variable time structure, starting generally with a four-day block running from 09.00 to 17.00 hours which is followed by 4–6 one-day follow-ups (the first being within one or two weeks and the rest at longer intervals) and some individual family attendances in between as necessary. The London team makes regular use of family therapy or clinical psychology trainees who are 'assigned' to different families and will, when needed, do specific pieces of work with them such as helping them to complete a genogram, accompanying them on the daily supermarket shopping trip, etc.

Preliminary Findings

To date over 85 eating-disordered teenagers and their families have been seen in MFDT in Dresden and some 40 in London. In Germany both the more traditionally oriented psychiatric practices as well as the more generous funding structure have resulted in there being many more inpatient beds available than in the UK. Clinicians are under pressure to fill these beds as they are otherwise at risk of having these, as well as staff, cut. This means that in effect quite a few adolescents get admitted who would not be considered for admission in the UK. This makes comparisons difficult. Preliminary observations show that the drop-out rate from the MFDT is very low in both centres (2–3%). In Dresden there has been a 30% reduction in admission rates, a 25% shortening of the duration of inpatient treatment for those who have been admitted and a 50% reduction in readmissions (Scholz et al., in preparation). In London, one patient who dropped out of the programme was shortly afterwards admitted to hospital; one patient completed the programme but continued to lose weight and was admitted; and a third patient had been admitted a few weeks before the start of the MFDT programme and was discharged back to the care of her family soon after completing the day programme. We do not as yet have systematic follow-up data to demonstrate the effectiveness of the treatment in bringing about symptomatic improvement. While in many of the adolescents there has been considerable change in weight, stabilization of eating, reduction of bingeing and vomiting, decreased laxative abuse, etc., probably the most immediate and most striking change has been in the way that families have rediscovered a sense of hope and a belief in their own ability to help the patient. This is accompanied by significant reductions in family tension and disputes, and a cooperative and supportive atmosphere and working environment has been created for the young persons and their families.

A user satisfaction survey revealed that, in Dresden, some 93% of parents, 84% of patients and 100% of staff were in favour of a combination of inpatient and multiple day-patient treatment. All parents and 80% of the adolescents regarded working together with other families jointly in a day hospital setting as helpful and desirable (Scholz & Asen, 2001). In London, Lim (2000) found that the MFDT was experienced generally as helpful, with parents in particular commenting on the collaborative nature of the treatment and the value of being able to exchange ideas with other families on how to cope with their common predicament.

CONCLUSIONS

Proponents of different models of psychotherapy are often prone to make exaggerated claims for their own particular therapeutic approach, both in terms of its ability to explain particular disorders and to provide effective treatment. This leads to a polarization between treatment models, that is hardly justified by empirical evidence, which suggests that differences between treatments is generally much less than we would like to believe. For instance, Asay and Lambert (1999), in summarizing many years of psychotherapy research in a variety of disorders, have estimated that, when different psychotherapies are compared, as little as 15% of the outcome variance is accounted for by factors that are unique to a specific mode of psychotherapy, with the rest being divided between individual therapist factors (30%), patient and environmental factors (40%) and a general placebo or expectancy effect (15%). This should not be taken to mean that it does not matter what therapeutic approach we adopt. There are many studies that have shown that while more than one treatment may be effective, there are also treatments that are ineffective. For instance, the study by Fairburn et al. (1991, 1993), which showed a similarity in outcome between cognitive-behaviour therapy (CBT) and interpersonal therapy (IPT), also showed that behaviour therapy was ineffective in the long term, despite initial positive responses to the treatment. Similarly, our own study of outpatients psychotherapies in adult anorexia nervosa (Dare et al., 2001) showed little difference between family therapy, focal psychodynamic therapy and cognitive analytic therapy, but highlighted the greater effectiveness of these specialized treatments in comparison with routine treatment.

The relative similarity in outcome between different treatments has a more important implication, however. Every model of treatment assumes that there is a particular mechanism of change (e.g. cognitive restructuring, changes in interpersonal relationships, etc.) that is specifically targeted by the treatment. The fact that apparently very different treatments can lead to quite similar outcomes suggests that our understanding of the mechanisms which bring about change is limited. When one takes a look at the history of family therapy for eating disorders much of the above is readily applicable. The pioneering work of Selvini Palazzoli (1974), Minuchin (Minuchin et al., 1975, 1978) and others made very strong claims for the approach. While the empirical evidence for the effectiveness of family therapy, particularly for adolescent anorexia nervosa, is strong, the theoretical models from which it derives are almost certainly flawed and our understanding of the way in which family interventions bring about change has required (and will require further) major revision. Our close involvement with the families in the intensive atmosphere of the MFDT programme has highlighted to us the limitations of our understanding of the process of change during effective family interventions. Just as families vary in the way they respond to having a member with an eating disorder so they vary in the way they make use of family treatment interventions. For some families this is an opportunity for the parents to re-stake their claim to parenting and parental authority in a very literal way, by taking very firm charge of the patient's eating until she is out of physical danger. Other families seem to do the same but only very briefly, or in a fairly symbolic way. In yet other families group meetings serve as an opportunity for the adolescent and the parents to start renegotiating the role the parents are going to have not just in relation to eating but in other areas of life as well. What all these solutions seem to have in common is that the family is able to step back and begin to disentangle itself from the way they have been caught up with the symptomatic behaviour and, perhaps even more importantly, that they have regained their belief that they can find a way of overcoming the problem, even though it may take some time.

APPENDIX 18.1

An Example of a Day Programme

9.00–10.15	Each family (separately): 'Plan the year ahead.' Month by month: critical events and threats; planned achievements, goals, and weight of patient. (At a later session the charts are pinned up and each family presents the chart to the whole group.)
10.15–10.45	Morning snack.
10.45–12.15	Dietetic psycho-education.
12.15–1.15	Parents and offspring buy food at supermarket (each family accompanied by a trainee).
1.15–2.30	Family meals: observed and videoed by trainees and family supported by staff.
2.30–3.00	Offspring: spend time with paper plates and food magazines to cut out food to be put on their parents plate: 'What your parents should eat this evening.' Parents: exchanging experiences of 'tricks of the anorexic trade'.

3.00–3.45   Each patient has to feed the meal designed for their parents to one of the parents, who has at all costs to resist being fed.
3.45–4.15   Afternoon snack.
4.15–5.00   Public planning of supper and breakfast.

APPENDIX 18.2

Examples of Exercises used in the Programme

Sculpting the family with and without the eating disorder.

Drawing a family tree.

'Externalising' the problem with a 'speaking' anorexia.

Sculpting the family and the future patterns of family life.

Drawing a 'life line' for the next year. (On the one hand, month by month critical events and threats on the other achievements goals, and weight of patient month by month.)

Offspring spend time with paper plates and food magazines to cut out food to be put on their parents plate: 'What your parents should eat this evening.' Followed by role reversal exercise with the person with the eating disorder 'feeding' one of the parents.

'Opposition' activities, e.g. 'fending off', 'tug of war'.

'Control' activities, e.g. 'following hands', 'leading the blind'.

Role-playing specific problems (using alternate voices, changing roles and other psychodrama techniques).

Clay/Plasticine modelling (the family as I see it and as I would like it to be).

Drawing the family.

Drawing the shape of the person with the eating disorder.

Observing VTR of previous lunchtime.

Body image work (me as I would like to be, as I see me, as you see me; in clay, drawing).

Parents discus what they had learned of the nature of their daughter's problems; what they have bee able to change and the ways that they had been unable to change; what could be different.

Offspring discuss what's the use of being anorexic and are there better things to do with life.

Discussion (parents and offspring separately and then together): What would there be to deal with if there were to be no anorexia?

Siblings Group: Discussion of what are the advantages and disadvantages of their sister being/not being anorexic followed by patient group commenting on what they had heard.

REFERENCES

Agras, W.S., Walsh, B.T., Fairburn, C.G. & Kraemer, H. (2000) A multicenter comparison of cognitive-behavioral therapy and interpersonal psychotherapy for bulimia nervosa. *Archives of General Psychiatry*, **57**, 459–466.

APA (2000) Practice Guideline for the Treatment of Patients with Eating Disorders (revision). *American Journal of Psychiatry*, **157** (Supplement), 1–39.

Asay, T.P. & Lambert, M.J. (1999) The empirical case for the common factors in therapy: Quantitative findings. In M.A. Hubble, B.L. Duncan & D.M. Scott (Eds), *The Heart and Soul of Change. What Works in Therapy*. Washington, D.C., American Psychiatric Association.

Asen, K.E., Stein, R., Stevens, A., McHugh, B., Greenwood, J. & Cooklin, A. (1982) A day unit for families. *Journal of Family Therapy*, **4**, 345–358.

Asen, K.E., George, E., Piper, R. & Stevens, A. (1989) A systems approach to child abuse: Management and treatment issues. *Child Abuse and Neglect*, **13**, 45–57.

Asen, K.E. (2002) Developments in multiple family therapy. *Journal of Family Therapy* (in press).

Blitzer, J.R., Rollins, N. & Blackwell, A. (1961) Children who starve themselves: Anorexia nervosa. *Psychosomatic Medicine*, **23**, 369–383.

Bowers, W.A., Evans, K. & Van Cleve, L. (1996) Treatment of adolescent eating disorders. In M.A. Reinecke, F. M. Dattilio, et al. (Eds), *Cognitive Therapy with Children and Adolescents: A Casebook for Clinical Practice*. New York: Guilford Press.

Carr, A. (2000) Evidence-based practice in family therapy and systemic consultation. I: Child-focused problems. *Journal of Family Therapy*, **22**, 29–60.

Cooklin, A., Miller, A. & McHugh, B. (1983) An institution for change: Developing a family day unit. *Family Process*, **22**, 453–468.

Crisp, A.H., Norton, K., Gowers, S., Halek, C., Bowyer, C., Yeldham, D., Levett, G. & Bhat, A. (1991) A controlled study of the effect of therapies aimed at adolescent and family psychopathology in anorexia nervosa. *British Journal of Psychiatry*, **159**, 325–333.

Dare, C. (1983) Family therapy for families containing an anorectic youngster. In *Understanding Anorexia Nervosa and Bulimia*. Report of the IVth Ross Conference on Medical Research. Ohio, Columbus: Ross Laboratories.

Dare, C., Eisler, I., Russell, G.F.M., Treasure, J. & Dodge, E. (2001) Psychological therapies for adult patients with anorexia nervosa: A randomised controlled trial of out-patient treatments. *British Journal of Psychiatry*, **178**, 216–221.

Dare, C. (1997) Chronic eating disorders in therapy: Clinical stories using family systems and psychoanalytic approaches. *Journal of Family Therapy*, **19**, 319–351.

Dare, C. & Eisler, I. (1997) Family therapy for anorexia nervosa. In D.M. Garner & P.E. Garfinkel (Eds), *Handbook of Psychotherapy for Anorexia Nervosa and Bulimia* (2nd edition). New York: Guilford Press.

Dare, C. & Eisler, I. (2000) A multi-family group day treatment programme for adolescent eating disorder. *European Eating Disorders Review*, **8**, 4–18.

Dodge, E., Hodes, M., Eisler, I. & Dare, C. (1995) Family therapy for bulimia nervosa in adolescents: An exploratory study. *Journal of Family Therapy*, **17**, 59–78.

Eisler, I. (1995) Family models of eating disorders. In G.I. Szmukler, C. Dare & J. Treasure (Eds), *Handbook of Eating Disorders: Theory, Treatment and Research*. London: John Wiley & Sons.

Eisler, I., Dare, C., Russell, G.F.M., Szmukler, G.I., le Grange, D. & Dodge, E. (1997) Family and individual therapy in anorexia nervosa. A 5-year follow-up. *Archives of General Psychiatry*, **54**, 1025–1030.

Eisler, I., Dare, C., Hodes, M., Russell, G.F.M., Dodge, E. & le Grange, D. (2000) Family therapy for adolescent anorexia nervosa: The results of a controlled comparison of two family interventions. *Journal of Child Psychology and Psychiatry*, **41**, 727–736.

Fairburn, C.G., Jones, R., Peveler, R.C., Carr, S.J., Solomon, R.A., O'Conner, M.E., Burton, J. & Hope, R.A. (1991) Three psychological treatments for bulimia nervosa. *Archives of General Psychiatry*, **48**, 463–469.

Fairburn, C.G., Jones, R., Peveler, R.C., Hope, R.A. & O'Conner, M.E. (1993) Psychotherapy and bulimia nervosa: The longer-term effects of interpersonal psychotherapy, behavior therapy and cognitive behavior therapy. *Archives of General Psychiatry*, **50**, 419–428.

Fishman, H.C. (1996) Structural family therapy. In J. Werne (Ed.), *Treating Eating Disorders*. San Francisco: Jossey-Bass Inc.

Garner, D.M. (1994) Bulimia nervosa. In C.G. Last & M. Hersen (Eds), *Adult Behavior Therapy Casebook*. New York: Plenum Press.

Geist, R., Heineman, M., Stephens, D., Davis, R. & Katzman, D.K. (2000) Comparison of family therapy and family group psychoeducation in adolescents with anorexia nervosa. *Canadian Journal of Psychiatry*, **45**, 173–178.

Goetz, P.L., Succop, R.A., Reinhart, J.B. & Miller, A. (1977) Anorexia in children: A follow-up study. *American Journal of Orthopsychiatry*, **47**, 597–603.

Gonsalez, S., Steinglass, P. & Reiss, D. (1989) Putting the illness in its place: Discussion groups for families with chronic medical illnesses. *Family Process*, **28**, 69–87.

Hall, A. & Crisp, A.H. (1987) Brief psychotherapy in the treatment of anorexia nervosa. Outcome at one year. *British Journal of Psychiatry*, **151**, 185–191.

Herscovici, C.R. & Bay, L. (1996) Favourable outcome for anorexia nervosa patients treated in Argentina with a family approach. *Eating Disorders: the Journal of Treatment and Prevention*, **4**, 59–66.

Jeammet, P. and Chabert, C. (1998) A psychoanalytic approach to eating disorders: The role of dependency. In A.H. Esman (Ed.), *Adolescent Psychiatry: Developmental and Clinical Studies*, Vol. 22. *Annals of the American Society for Adolescent Psychiatry*. Hillsdale: The Analytic Press, Inc.

Johnson, S.M., Maddeaux, C. & Blouin, J. (1998) Emotionally focused family therapy for bulimia: Changing attachment patterns. *Psychotherapy*, **35**, 238–247.

Kaufman, E. & Kaufman, P. (1979) Multiple family therapy with drug abusers. In E. Kaufman & P. Kaufman (Eds), *Family Therapy of Drug and Alcohol Abuse*. New York: Gardner.

Laqueur, H.P. (1972) Mechanisms of change in multiple family therapy. In C.J. Sager & H.S. Kaplan (Eds), *Progress in Group and Family Therapy*. New York: Bruner/Mazel.

Laqueur, H.P. (1973) Multiple family therapy: Questions and answers. In D. Bloch (Ed.), *Techniques of Family Psychotherapy*. New York: Grune & Stratton.

Laqueur, H.P., La Burt, H.A. & Morong, E. (1964) Multiple family therapy: Further developments. *International Journal of Social Psychiatry*, **10**, 69–80.

Le Grange, D., Eisler, I., Dare, C. & Russell, G.F.M. (1992) Evaluation of family therapy in anorexia nervosa: A pilot study. *International Journal of Eating Disorder*, **12**, 347–357.

Lesser, L.I., Ashenden, B.J., Debuskey, M. & Eisenberg, L. (1960) Anorexia nervosa in children. *American Journal of Orthopsychiatry*, **30**, 572–580.

Lim, C. (2000) *A pilot study of families' experiences of a multi-family group day treatment programme*. MSc Dissertation. Institute of Psychiatry, Kings College, University of London.

Luborsky, L., Singer, B. & Luborsky, L. (1975) Comparative studies of psychotherapies: Is it true that 'Everybody has one and all must have prizes?' *Archives of General Psychiatry*, **32**, 995–1008.

Martin, F.E. (1985) The treatment and outcome of anorexia nervosa in adolescents: A prospective study and five year follow-up. *Journal of Psychiatric Research*, **19**, 509–514.

Mayer, R.D. (1994) *Family therapy in the treatment of eating disorders in general practice*. MSc Dissertation, Birkbeck College, University of London.

Minuchin, S., Baker, L., Rosman, B.L., Liebman, R., Millman, L. & Todd, T.C. (1975) A conceptual model of psychosomatic illness in childhood. *Archives of General Psychiatry*, **32**, 1031–1038.

Minuchin, S., Rosman, B.L. & Baker, L. (1978) *Psychosomatic Families: Anorexia Nervosa in Context*. Cambridge, MA: Harvard University Press.

Murburg, M., Price, L. & Jalali, B. (1988) Huntington's disease: therapy strategies. *Family Systems Medicine*, **6**, 290–303.

Robin, A.L., Siegel, P.T. & Moye, A. (1995) Family versus individual therapy for anorexia: Impact on family conflict. *International Journal of Eating Disorders*, **4**, 313–322.

Robin, A.L., Gilroy, M. & Dennis, A.B. (1998) Treatment of eating disorders in children and adolescents. *Clinical Psychology Review*, **18**, 421–466.

Robin, A.L., Siegel, P.T., Moye, A.W. Gilroy, M., Dennis, A.B. & Sikand A. (1999) A controlled comparison of family versus individual therapy for adolescents with anorexia nervosa. *Journal of the American Academy of Child and Adolescent Psychiatry*, **38**, 1482–1489.

Russell, G.F.M., Szmukler, G.I., Dare, C. & Eisler, I. (1987) An evaluation of family therapy in anorexia nervosa and bulimia nervosa. *Archives of General Psychiatry*, **44**, 1047–1056.

Sargent, J., Liebman, R. & Silver, M. (1985) Family therapy for anorexia nervosa. In Garner. D.M. & Garfinkel, P.E. (Eds), *Handbook of Psychotherapy for Anorexia Nervosa and Bulimia*. New York: Guilford Press.

Scholz, M. & Asen, K.E. (2001) Multiple family therapy with eating disordered adolescents. *European Eating Disorders Review*, **9**, 33–42.

Schwartz, R.C., Barrett, M.J. & Saba, G. (1985) Family therapy for bulimia. In D.M. Garner and P.E. Garfinkel (Eds), *Handbook of Psychotherapy for Anorexia Nervosa and Bulimia*. New York: Guilford Press.

Selvini Palazzoli, M. (1974) *Self Starvation: From the Intrapsychic to the Transpersonal Approach to Anorexia Nervosa*. London: Chaucer Publishing.

Slagerman, M. & Yager, J. (1989) Multiple family group treatment for eating disorders: a short term program. *Psychiatric Medicine*, **7**, 269–283.

Squire-Dehouck, B. (1993) *Evaluation of conjoint family therapy versus family counselling in adolescent anorexia nervosa patients: A two year follow-up study*. Unpublished MSc Dissertation, Institute of Psychiatry, University of London.

Steinglass, P. (1998) Multiple family discussion groups for patients with chronic medical illness. *Families, Systems and Health*, **16**, 55–70.

Steinglass, P., Bennett, L.A., Wolin, S.J. & Reiss, D. (1987) *The Alcoholic Family*. New York: Basic Books.

Stierlin, H. & Weber, G. (1987) Anorexia nervosa: Lessons from a follow-up study. *Family Systems Medicine*, **7**, 120–157.

Stierlin, H. & Weber, G. (1989) *Unlocking the Family Door*. New York: Brunner/Mazel.

Strelnick, A.H.J. (1977) Multiple family group therapy: A review of the literature. *Family Process*, **16**, 307–325.

Szmukler, G.I., Eisler, I., Russell, G.F.M. & Dare, C. (1985) Parental 'Expressed Emotion', anorexia nervosa and dropping out of treatment. *British Journal of Psychiatry*, **147**, 265–271.

Warren, W. (1968) A study of anorexia nervosa in young girls. *Journal of Child Psychology and Psychiatry*, **9**, 27–40.

Wilson, G.T. & Fairburn, C.G. (1998) Treatments for eating disorders. In P.E. Nathan & J.M. Gorman (Eds), *A Guide to Treatments that Work*. New York: Oxford University Press.

Wooley, S. & Lewis, K. (1987) Multi-family therapy within an intensive treatment program for bulimia. In J. Harkaway (Ed.), *Eating Disorders: The Family Therapy Collections*, **20**. Rockville: Aspen Publ.

CHAPTER 19

Drug Treatments

Tijs Bruna

*National Centre for Eating Disorders, Robert-Fleury Stichting, Leidschendam,
The Netherlands*

and

Jaap Fogteloo

*Department of General Internal Medicine, Leiden University Medical Centre,
Leiden, The Netherlands*

INTRODUCTION

Pharmacotherapy is not the first choice of treatment in eating disorders. The first focus of attention is the physical health of the patient, whether she is suffering from anorexia nervosa, bulimia nervosa, binge eating disorder or other eating disorders. Improvement of the physical condition alone is never sufficient for complete recovery. The dysfunctional attitudes and cognitions towards food, body weight and body size also need to be addressed in treatment. Attention should also be focused on factors contributing to or maintaining the eating disorder.

Psychotherapy is commonly recognised as the treatment of first choice. Individual and family therapy have proved to be effective in the treatment of anorexia nervosa (for a review see van Furth, 1998). Cognitive-behavioural therapy and interpersonal psychotherapy are effective treatment methods in bulimia nervosa and binge eating disorder (for a review see Schmidt, 1998; Agras, 1997; see also Chapters 14 and 15 in this volume). In the treatment of obesity the results of psychotherapy are inconclusive and short lived.

For anorexia nervosa it is striking that, although the treatment results are moderate, relatively few controlled trials with medication have been conducted. New developments within the field of pharmacotherapy make it likely that the number of trials will increase in the coming years. The treatment of bulimia nervosa, with psychotherapy and/or medication, has been studied quite extensively. The results are encouraging but, as with anorexia nervosa, pharmacotherapy is not the first option in treatment. Much is still unknown about the way in which specific drugs contribute to the cessation of bingeing. The quest for new medication which is both more specific and more effective is ongoing and promising. Although binge eating disorder is formally not yet acknowledged as a discrete disorder and questions have been raised about the severity of the disorder (Fairburn et al., 2000), medication has proved

Handbook of Eating Disorders. Edited by J. Treasure, U. Schmidt and E. van Furth.

to contribute to attaining abstinence of bingeing. In the treatment of obesity the long-term results of pharmacotherapy have been disappointing. However, new developments suggest a more promising role for medication in the treatment of obesity.

This chapter will provide an update of the research (RCTs) and clinical implications in the field of pharmacotherapy of eating disorders. Results of clinical trials and clinical recommendations will be described per DSM-IV disorder and separately for obesity. As obesity is considered a somatic (as opposed to mental) disorder, a short introduction will be dedicated to its therapy in general. In every section attention will be paid to new and promising developments.

ANOREXIA NERVOSA

Research

In the only systematic review of the treatment of anorexia nervosa (Treasure & Schmidt, 2001) authors found no evidence for the improvement of outcome by pharmacotherapy. Medication (neuroleptics, tricyclic antidepressants, cyproheptadine, cisapride) may even be harmful by increasing the sometimes already prolonged QT interval. This does not mean that there is completely no role for pharmacotherapy in the treatment of anorexia nervosa. Although anorexia nervosa has been acknowledged as a discrete disorder for a long time, the number of medication trials has been quite limited. The prevalence of the disease is low, the number of patients that seek help is small, and ethical dilemmas may emerge when doing scientific research with a population with a poor physical health (Mayer & Walsh, 1998; van Furth, 1998).

Although the disturbance in the perception of body shape and the disturbance in thinking about food and weight are akin to psychotic phenomenology, only two double-blind placebo controlled trials with antipsychotic medication have been carried out (Vandereycken & Pierloot, 1982; Vandereycken, 1984). These were two cross-over trials with a modest number of inpatients (18 in both trials) and a short-term perspective (3-week periods) with pimozide and sulpiride respectively. The results not only showed an initial beneficial effect on daily weight gain especially in the first treatment period, but also that the changes in eating behaviour and in attitude towards the body were limited. The authors concluded that their general inpatient treatment method appeared to be effective enough to restore body weight in patients with anorexia nervosa and there was no additional value in adding this type of medication. No controlled trials with antipsychotic medication have been published since.

In the 1980s there was interest in the efficacy of antidepressants, but research came to a halt because of the disappointing results. The selective serotonin reuptake inhibitors (SSRIs) are more tolerated and are relatively safe, and open trials were encouraging. Many patients with anorexia nervosa show features of affective disorders and/or of anxiety disorders and a proportion fulfil the full diagnostic criteria for affective disorder (Halmi, 1995). It is often difficult to determine if these symptoms precede or follow the onset.

Serotonin has a role in the regulation of hunger and satiety. There are signs that serotonin activity is altered in eating disorders, not only during the active phase of the disease, but also after weight restoration and symptom remission. Elevated concentrations of 5-hydroxyindoleacetic acid (5-HIAA), the metabolite of serotonin have been found in the cerebrospinal fluid, suggesting that altered serotonin activity is a trait-related characteristic of anorexia nervosa (Kaye et al., 1991, 2001). Abnormal 5HT function is also consistent with traits as behavioural inhibition, high harm avoidance and perfectionism often seen in patients after recovery from anorexia nervosa.

Some of the older antidepressant drugs have been studied in RCTs. Clomipramine (50 mg daily) did not lead to a faster body weight gain than placebo in a double-blind RCT with 16 inpatients (Lacey & Crisp, 1980). Amitriptyline (Biederman et al., 1985) prescribed up to a maximal daily dose of 175 mg in a small mixed in- and outpatient sample did not show significantly better results in comparison to placebo on any of the outcome measures. In a short-term study (Halmi et al., 1986), inpatients were treated with amitriptyline up to 160 mg daily. The patients who achieved target weight and who received amitriptyline gained weight faster than the patients who received placebo (32 days in comparison to 45 days to target weight). There was no significant effect on treatment efficiency. In the only controlled trial with lithium carbonate (Gross et al., 1981), a significant positive result in weight gain was achieved in the last two weeks of the 4-week trial ($N = 16$). This finding was never replicated, probably because of the increased risk of intoxication with lithium in this population.

In a 7-week study of fluoxetine at a target daily dose of 60 mg in 31 women with anorexia nervosa no significant added benefit to the inpatient treatment was found (Attia et al., 1998). Nevertheless, interesting research has been done by Kaye et al. who demonstrated that there may be a role for fluoxetine in the prevention of relapse in patients who regained weight. Following inpatient weight restoration, 10 of 16 (63%) subjects on fluoxetine remained well over a one-year outpatient follow-up period, whereas only 3 of 19 (16%) remained well on placebo (Kaye et al., 2001). Fluoxetine was associated with maintaining a healthy body weight and with a significant reduction in obsessions and ritualistic preoccupations. These contradictory results may be explained because of the differing nutritional status of the two patient groups. In the starved state there may be reduced synaptic 5-HT, due to reduced availability of tryptophan, the essential amino-acid precursor of serotonin.

Cyproheptadine, a serotonin antagonist, prescribed as an anti-allergic medicine with weight gain as a side-effect, showed some positive results in double-blind RCTs (Vigerski & Loriaux, 1977; Goldberg et al., 1979), although the effect on decreasing the number of days to achieve a normal body weight was marginal (Halmi et al., 1986). No significant differences in weight gain were found. Cisapride, a drug that is prescribed for stomach complaints, did not perform better than placebo in one small RCT (Szmukler et al., 1995). In many countries this drug has now been withdrawn because of the potential to cause arrythmias.

Treatment

At present, a review of the results of RCTs does not justify the prescription of drugs in uncomplicated anorexia nervosa. The benefits do not outweight the harms. An intervention with medication in the starting phase of the disorder, may further be conflicting with therapeutic strategies. The use of medication in this phase may undermine the motivational process. Pharmacotherapy should be reserved for cases in which comorbidity interferes with the development of the therapeutic process, in cases of treatment resistance and perhaps in cases in which relapse is likely.

There is some evidence to suggest that the depressive disorder seen in patients with a very low weight is not easily affected by antidepressants (Ferguson et al., 1999). The mild depressive disorder that develops in the process of weight gain can often be addressed best in psychotherapy. If the low mood is not lifted or the depression becomes more severe, the prescription of antidepressant medication should be considered. It seems reasonable to choose a SSRI given the suggested role of serotonin in the pathophysiology of eating disorders. Furthermore, the clinical picture often shows features of anxiety disorders, on which SSRIs often have a favourable effect. The same arguments for prescribing a SSRI are valid in cases of anxiety disorders that interfere with the process of recovery. If an obsessive-compulsive disorder emerges or persists after weight restoration, antidepressants should also be considered. Because of its side-effect profile and the experience in the treatment of eating disorders (although limited in anorexia nervosa) Mayer and Walsh (1998) recommend fluoxetine.

The clinical assessment of a patient sometimes warrants the prescription of antipsy-chotic medication. The patient who, in a phase of weight restoration, increasingly reports chaotic thinking, cannot keep her thoughts ordered and increasingly needs rituals and/or compulsions to prevent her from becoming psychotic, can react positively to (low dose) an-tipsychotics. The relatively new atypical antipsychotics may be of value. Promising results in treatment-resistant patients were described in case studies (La Via et al., 2000) and open label trials are being conducted. It is not yet clear whether there really is a substantial group of patients with anorexia nervosa that can profit from treatment with the atypical antipsychotics, nor is it clear what subgroup this would be. The case studies suggest that there may be a role for these drugs in treatment-resistant patients. A hypothesis about the mode of action of these drugs in patients with anorexia nervosa has not yet been proposed. Do they effect the patient's cognitions, do they reduce the anxiety surrounding weight gain or is the side-effect (weight gain) the main effect? Neither the duration nor the dosage of this new medication have been established in patients with anorexia nervosa, and double-blind placebo controlled trials are needed to provide answers to these unresolved questions. For the time being atypical antipsychotics should be prescribed with reserve, and only in treatment-resistant patients and/or if a psychosis is developing.

BULIMIA NERVOSA

Research

In a recent systematic review (Hay & Bacaltchuk, 2001) the authors found that antidepres-sants reduce bulimic symptoms in the short term. They found insufficient evidence about the persistence of these effects or about the effects of different classes of antidepressants.

Although bulimia nervosa was only recognised as a discrete disorder in the late 1970s, many controlled psychotherapeutic and pharmacotherapeutic studies have been carried out. Bulimia nervosa is far more prevalent than anorexia nervosa (for a review see van Hoeken et al., 1998) and in general causes less metabolic disturbances (Mayer & Walsh, 1998).

The fact that endogenous opiates play a role in the hypothalamic regulation of hunger and satiety led to a limited number of trials with opiate antagonists. The results were inconsistent (de Zwaan & Mitchell, 1992; Marrazzi et al., 1995) and the risk/benefit ratio is considered unprofitable.

Far more controlled trials tested the efficacy of different types of antidepressant medication. Indeed, many patients with bulimia nervosa show features of a depression or even meet the criteria for a major depression (Halmi, 1995). Furthermore, it has been demonstrated that serotonin function has been disordered in bulimia nervosa, although it is not yet clear whether these psychobiological alterations are trait-related and contribute to the pathogenesis or reflect a state-related abnormality (Kaye et al., 1998; Smith et al., 1999; Wolfe et al., 2000).

All sorts of antidepressant medication (tricyclics, selective serotonin reuptake inhibitors (SSRIs), a monoamineoxidase inhibitor, mianserin and trazodon) have been tried out in double-blind placebo-controlled trials. All of these studies consistently showed a positive effect of the antidepressant medication in comparison to placebo in decreasing the frequency of the binges and the frequency of vomiting. A retrospective analysis of two large multi-centre studies with fluoxetine indicated that the reduction of bulimia-symptoms occurred independently of the presence of depressive symptoms (Goldstein et al., 1999). In earlier (smaller) studies, results in this respect were conflicting (Pope et al., 1983; Walsh et al., 1988). In some studies no significant reduction in depression scores could be found, possibly as a result of low baseline scores (Barlow et al., 1988; Walsh et al., 1991).

However, the results of these trials with antidepressant medication in bulimia nervosa should be put in perspective. Although between 30% and 91% of the patients experience a reduction in the frequency of the binges in the different studies, only 4% to 35%, with one exception of 68%, experience complete remission (Crow & Mitchell, 1994). Moreover, most studies lack a long-term follow-up (most studies last only 6-8 weeks, sometimes 16 weeks). A substantial proportion of the patients relapse despite continuation of the medication (Walsh et al., 1991; Agras et al., 1997). More controlled research is needed to make firm conclusions on the subject of relapse and medication.

Fluoxetine is the most researched drug in the treatment of bulimia nervosa (Fluoxetine Bulimia Nervosa Collaborative Study Group, 1992; Goldstein et al., 1995). It also proved to be effective in a (small) group of patients that didn't respond to cognitive-behavioural or interpersonal psychotherapy (Walsh et al., 2000).

In patients with bulimia nervosa, fluoxetine is effective in a daily dose of 60 mg, which is three times the advised dose in depressive disorders. The high dose and the fact that it is effective regardless of the occurrence of a comorbid depression raises questions about the mode of action, which probably differs from that in depression. Another interesting finding which supports the idea that fluoxetine acts differently to its role in depression is the possible effect of ondansetron on bulimic symptoms. A placebo-controlled randomised, double-blind trial with ondansetron—a peripherally active antagonist of the serotonin receptor 5-HT3 marketed for prevention of vagally mediated emesis caused by chemotherapy—led to a 50% decrease in binge/purge episodes after 4 weeks in patients with severe bulimia nervosa (Faris et al., 2000). Also, there was an increase in the number of normal meals. These results suggest a normalisation of the physiological mechanisms controlling meal termination and satiety, mainly vagally mediated functions. They point also to the possibility of affecting bulimia nervosa through a peripheral point of action.

As for the use in clinical practice, certainly more trials of ondansetron are needed, and certainly more knowledge about the pathophysiological mechanisms in bulimia nervosa before it should be prescribed routinely. Apart from that, cost-effectiveness should be looked at, considering the present price.

Treatment

Most experts and users in the field of eating disorders prefer psychotherapy (CBT or IPT) as their treatment of first choice in bulimia nervosa (Walsh et al., 1997, 2000), because of the superior short- and long-term results, the minimal potential to cause harm, and the better acceptability.

There are some indications that adding psychiatric drugs to a psychotherapeutic treatment leads to a small improvement in the results of treatment (Agras, 1997). On the other hand, adding cognitive-behavioural therapy to treatment with antidepressants also seems to be of value (Agras, 1997). However, it is not yet clear what patient-factors are important in the decision to apply one or the other treatment, or a combination of both.

In everyday clinical practice, such factors as the availability of expertise in psychotherapy with eating disorders and the motivation and preference of the patient will play a role in making a choice. Medication should be considered in patients who do not respond to psychotherapy and in patients with psychiatric comorbidity that prevents improvement in bulimia nervosa. Antidepressant medication should be prescribed in these cases, and it is reasonable to start with fluoxetine at 60 mg daily, given the two large trials that had a beneficial outcome. Moreover, it is generally well tolerated with limited side-effects. Only one controlled trial with another SSRI has been conducted and the negative outcome to fluvoxamine was merely alluded to in a review (Freeman, 1998).

In case of non-response to medication a switch to another drug can be helpful. This was suggested in one study in which desipramine was followed by fluoxetine (Walsh et al., 1997). Compared to a previous study in the same centre, the average binge frequency reduced from 69% to 47%.

In the near future there may be a role for peripherally active agents like ondansetron. For the time being prescribing ondansetron is not warranted in view of the limited evidence and the overall expense.

BINGE EATING DISORDER

Research

In 1994 research criteria for Binge Eating Disorder (BED) were described in Appendix B of DSM-IV (APA, 1994). These criteria made it possible to carry out treatment studies (de Zwaan, 2001).

No systematic reviews of treatment studies have been published. Four double-blind placebo-controlled trials involving medication were done. In three, SSRIs were prescribed; in one, dexfenfluramine, a serotonin agonist.

Fenfluramine was taken off the market in many countries because of the serious side effects. In the controlled trial dexfenfluramine performed better than placebo in reducing the frequency of binge episodes in overweight women with binge eating disorder, but no effect was left after follow-up and it did not lead to weight loss (Stunkard et al., 1996).

Fluoxetine (60 mg daily) improved dietary intake in overweight women with and without BED, but it did not affect their binge frequency or mood (Greeno & Wing, 1996).

Fluvoxamine, to a maximum of 300 mg daily, reduced body weight and the frequency of binges significantly better than placebo in a multicentre trial (Hudson et al., 1998).

The intent-to-treat-analysis did not reveal a significant difference in the level of response. There were significantly more drop-outs because of adverse medical events in the group with the active medication. These events included nausea, sedation and lightheadedness. Compared with the placebo group, a significantly greater percentage of fluvoxamine-treated patients experienced insomnia, nausea and abnormal dreams. No serious medical events were observed.

Sertraline, to a maximum of 200 mg/day, was significantly more effective than placebo in decreasing the frequency of binges, clinical global severity and the body mass index in a 6-week trial with 34 BED subjects (McElroy et al., 2000). Eight patients withdrew for several reasons. No patients withdrew because of an adverse medical event. More sertraline-treated patients ($N = 7$) than patients given placebo ($N = 1$) experienced insomnia. Among the patients who completed the study sertraline was associated with a higher response level than placebo, but the difference did not reach statistical significance.

Treatment

There are clear indications that SSRIs decrease binge-eating symptoms in patients with BED, at least in the short term. Given the remarkably high response on placebo in the first week(s) of the three studies, the lack of a long-term follow-up, the possible mild course of the disorder (Fairburn et al., 2000) and the positive results of other kind of treatments, there only seems to be a modest role for drugs in the therapy of binge eating disorder. Cognitive-behavioural therapy, also in self-help format, and interpersonal therapy have proved to be effective, even at follow-up (Carter & Fairburn, 1998; de Zwaan, 2001).

Medication should be considered in patients with resistance to these treatments or in patients with serious comorbidity. Outcome measures used in the studies with SSRIs were different and none of the studies was replicated. It is not even clear what the primary outcome should be. A lot of patients with BED suffer mainly because of their overweight, but the long-term effects of medication on weight are not known. At present it is not possible to give a clear guideline on what medication should be prescribed for patients with BED.

OBESITY

Introduction

The main therapeutic intervention for patients with obesity is to make sure that their daily energy intake is less than their total energy expenditure. This always implies an energy-restricted diet and, if possible, an increase in the energy expenditure. However, an energy-restricted diet is difficult to maintain and induces a decrease in resting energy expenditure, thus diminishing the efficacy of the diet. As a consequence, there is often a demand from patients for the supplementation of their dietary therapy with medication. More generally, at the local health food store, a large and increasing selection of herbs is available for the treatment of obesity.

Unfortunately, the choice of regular medication is limited, and the efficacy is low. In combination with an energy-restricted diet, all available medication when compared to placebo, results in an additional weight loss of 4 kg after six months or one year of treatment. Also, when medication is discontinued, most patients return to their original weight (NIH Conference, 1993; Pi-Sunyer, 1993). However, an additional weight loss of 4 kg would mean a significant risk reduction in the complications of obesity, such as cardiovascular disease or type II diabetes. For example, a weight loss of 10% significantly improves the glycemic control in type II diabetes (Wing et al., 1987), and for every kilogram lost, blood pressure decreases by 1 mmHg and LDL cholesterol by 1% (Schotte, 1990; Wolf & Grundy, 1983). Cosmetically this additional weight loss is not significant, so the additional weight loss is only advantageous for those patients who are at risk of the complications of obesity and for whom every kilogram of weight loss is significant: i.e. patients with a body mass index >27 kg/m^2 and additional risk factors or patient with a body mass index > 30 kg/m^2.

There are several ways in which medication, whether or not in combination with an energy-restricted diet, could reduce body weight. Medication could (1) reduce energy intake, (2) reduce the absorption of nutrients in the gastrointestinal tract or (3) increase the (total) energy expenditure. Theoretically, stimulation of the local fat mobilisation or decreasing the synthesis of triglycerides could also lead to weight loss. The first three possibilities were tested in research, the fourth possibility is only a hypothesis. Perhaps new developments will arise from the research with leptin, the hormone produced by fat cells.

Research

The drugs in the group that reduces energy intake also decrease appetite. Although there are differences in the mechanisms in which they reduce appetite, these differences are not clinically relevant. Because of their side-effects most of these medications are no longer legally available. Amphetamines are effective; in studies they show an additional weight loss when compared to placebo. The main side-effect is their stimulating effect, but they also have addictive properties (Bray, 1993), and for this reason amphetamines are not legally prescribed. Related to amphetamines are the phenylethylamines, which are not available in every country in Europe. Mazindol is comparable to the amphetamines with regards to effects and side-effects, but their efficacy is limited and no recent clinical studies are available.

Another important and, until 1997 (especially in the USA), frequently prescribed group are the serotonin releasers and reuptake inhibitors. The increase in the level of serotonin stimulates receptors in the paraventricular nucleus of the hypothalamus, and so reduces appetite. Well-known compounds are the fenfluramines and sibutramine. Fluoxetine in higher dosages also reduces appetite. The fenfluramines (fenfluramine and dexfenfluramine) were withdrawn from the market in 1997 because of serious side-effects. The first side-effect that became apparent was pulmonary hypertension (Abenhaim et al., 1996) but it was the second side-effect, the increase in the incidence of cardiac valve abnormalities, that finally led to the withdrawal of fenfluramines. Although the absolute risk was low, their limited efficacy was sufficient reason to withdraw them from the market (Devereux, 1998; Jick et al., 1998).

Sibutramine decreases appetite by inhibition of the reuptake of serotonin but it also slightly decreases the reuptake of noradrenalin (norepinephrin). The latter mechanism slightly increases the resting energy expenditure, and in combination with an energy-restricted diet, sibutramine can result in an additional weight loss of 4.8–6.1 kg (depending on the dosage used). The side-effects of pulmonary hypertension or cardiac valve abnormalities were not seen in the clinical studies. An important side-effect is hypertension, probably caused by the slight adrenergic effect of sibutramine (Lean, 1997). With a dosage of 15 mg. daily the diastolic blood pressure rises with an average of 2 mmHg.

In a higher dosage (60 mg daily) fluoxetine can reduce appetite. In at least one study fluoxetine was shown, as compared to placebo, to give an additional weight loss of 3.6 kg, but other studies have failed to demonstrate the effect of fluoxetine on body weight (Wise, 1992). Fluoxetine is not registered for the treatment of obesity.

Another approach to achieving weight loss is to influence the absorption of nutrients in the gastrointestinal tract and so to reduce the daily energy intake. Paraffin, for example, has been tried for a long time; a more recent development is the non-absorbent fat-substitute Olean®. Olean® is available in the USA but not in Europe. Olean® may only be used in snacks.

Orlistat is a relatively new drug that specifically inhibits the enzyme pancreatic lipase. Orlistat reduces the total dietary fat absorption by 30%. In studies orlistat proved to give an additional weight loss of 3.1% (Hill et al., 1999). The side-effects, especially if the dietary compliance to fat restriction is poor, are steatorrhoea and a decrease in the absorption of fat-soluble vitamins. In the case of longer usage or frequent diarrhoea it is advised to substitute the fat-soluble vitamins. In the first clinical studies with orlistat a higher incidence of mamma carcinoma was seen; this could not be confirmed by additional studies and was caused by a statistical artefact. Orlistat is registered in Europe but not all health insurance companies reimburse the use of this drug.

Another possibility for the reduction of body weight is by medically inducing an increase in total energy expenditure. Many well-known compounds (thyroxin, caffeine or ephedrine) do in fact increase the total energy expenditure but are not acceptable as prescription drugs because of their (mainly cardiac) side-effects or addictive properties. The promising results with β_3 agonists in animal studies, showed a poor efficacy and serious side-effects in studies with humans (Carruba et al., 1998).

A recent development is the research into leptin as a possible therapy for obesity. Leptin is produced by white fat cells and passes the blood brain barrier by active transport. The ventro median nucleus of the hypothalamus has leptin receptors. Stimulation of these receptors leads to inhibition of neuro peptide Y and so decreases appetite and increases resting energy expenditure. In all genetic normal mammals, including humans, there is a strong correlation between the body mass index (or total body fat) and serum leptin levels. But with an increase in total body fat the intracerebral leptin levels rise relatively less and the ratio between intracerebral and serum leptin levels decreases (Zhang et al., 1994; Considine et al., 1996). Possibly the transport of leptin over the blood brain barrier is saturable and this might be the explanation for the resistance for higher leptin levels in obese subjects. Exogenous leptin substitution leads to a dramatic increase in serum leptin levels and possibly to an increase in intracerebral levels. This increase might overcome the leptin resistance and subsequently lead to weight loss. However, there is another physiological mechanism which could explain the way in which leptin substitution can lead to weight loss. As a response to fasting or energy restriction, leptin levels drop sharply. This decrease might be the cause of the well-known neuro-endocrine response on fasting. This response results in the stimulation of the appetite and a decrease in resting energy expenditure. In this setting exogenous leptin substitution could prevent the neuro-endocrine response. The appetite will not be stimulated and the resting energy expenditure will remain stable. This could improve dietary compliance and also the efficacy of an energy-restricted diet. The activity of leptin substitution seems to be dose dependent. Leptin needs to be administered by subcutaneous injection; the main side-effect is erythema of the injection site. Leptin is as yet only available for research purposes. Randomised double-blind placebo-controlled trials (Heymsfield et al., 1999; Huckshorn et al., 2000) have not (yet) given positive answers to the questions on the usefulness of leptin in the treatment of obesity.

Treatment

Because of the limited efficacy and the side-effects of the current medication, the pharma-cotherapy of obesity is problematic. On the other hand, many patients ask for medication as they have often had poor results with energy-restricted diets. Also they are often frustrated by the quick return to their original body weight after the period of dieting is finished. Because of this, but also because of the reports on television and internet (there are over 800 websites on orlistat), patients often have great expectations of medication. The current medication has proved to give no more than an additional weight loss of 4 kg. This will not result in the often desired cosmetic effect, so patients wanting to lose weight purely for cosmetic reasons will have little success through medication. However, this additional 4 kg can be significant for the reduction of health risks associated with obesity.

If a reduction of the total alimentary fat intake is indicated (e.g. if the daily intake is high) treatment with orlistat can be considered, but to prevent steatorrhoea, good compliance to the fat restriction is essential.

Sibutramine is effective, but the side-effect of hypertension is a potential problem. At this moment it is not yet clear if there will be a role for leptin in the treatment of obesity.

The perfect drug for obesity does not yet exist. Ideally it should combine a good thera-peutic effect (preferably more weight loss than the average additional 4 kg) with minimal side-effects. Treatment of obesity primarily means a reduction of the (obesity associated) risks of cardiovascular disease or type II diabetes. From this perspective, hypertension as a side-effect of drug treatment is a potential problem.

Like type II diabetes, obesity is a chronic metabolic disease. Without additional therapy, weight loss is often followed by a subsequent weight gain. This implies that the ideal drug for obesity has to be suitable for chronic (possible lifelong) treatment.

REFERENCES

Abenhaim, L., Moride, Y.,Brenot, F., Rich, S., Benichou, J., Kurz, X., Higenbottam, T., Oakley, C., Wouters, E., Aubier, M., Simonneau, G. & Begaud, B. (1996) Appetite-suppressant drugs and the risk of primary pulmonary hypertension. *New England Journal of Medicine*, **335**, 609–616.

APA (1994) *Diagnostic and statistic manual of mental disorders*. (4th edition) Washington, D.C.: American Psychiatric Association.

Agras, W.S. (1997) Pharmacotherapy of bulimia nervosa and binge eating disorder: Longer-term outcomes. *Psychopharmacology Bulletin*, **33** (3), 433–436.

Attia, E., Haiman, C., Walsh, B.T. & Flatter, S.R. (1998) Does fluoxetine augment the inpatient treatment of anorexia nervosa? *American Journal of Psychiatry*, **155**, 548–551.

Barlow, J., Blouin, J., Blouin, A. & Perez, E. (1988) Treatment of bulimia with desipramine: A double blind crossover study. *Canadian Journal of Psychiatry*, **33**, 129–133.

Biederman, J., Herzog, D.B., Rivinus, T.M., Harper, G.P., Ferber, R.A., Rosenbaum, J.F., Harmatz, J.S., Tondorf, R., Orsulak, P.J. & Schildkraut, J.J. (1985) Amitriptyline in the treatment of anorexia nervosa: A double-blind, placebo-controlled study. *Journal of Clinical Psychopharmacology*, **5**, 10–16.

Bray, G.A. (1993) Use and abuse of appetite suppressant drugs in the treatment of obesity. *Annals of Internal Medicine*, **119**, 707–713.

Carruba, M., Tomello, C., Briscini, L. & Nisoli, E. (1998) Advances in pharmacotherapy for obesity. *International Journal of Obesity*, **22**, S13–S16.

Carter, J.C. & Fairburn, C.G. (1998) Cognitive-behavioral self-help for binge eating disorder: A controlled effectiveness study. *Journal of Consulting and Clinical Psychology*, **66**, 616–623.

Considine, R.V., Sinha, M.K., Heiman, M.L., Kriauciunas, A., Stephens, T.W., Nyce, M.R., Ohannesian, J.P., Marco, C.C., McKee, L.J., Bauer, T.L. et al. (1996) Serum immunoreactive-leptin concentrations in normal-weight and obese humans. *New England Journal of Medicine*, **334** (5), 324–325.

Crow, S.J. & Mitchell, J.E. (1994) Rational therapy of eating disorders. *Drugs*, **48**, 372–379.

Devereux, R.B. (1998) Appetite suppressants and valvular heart disease. *New England Journal of Medicine*, **339**, 765–766.

McElroy, S.L., Casuto, L.S., Nelson, E.B., Lake, K.A., Soutullo, C.A., Keck, P.E. & Hudson, J.I. (2000) Placebo-controlled trial of sertraline in the treatment of binge eating disorder. *American Journal of Psychiatry*, **157**, 1004–1006.

Fairburn, C.G., Cooper, Z., Doll, H.A., Norman, P.A. & O'Connor, M.E. (2000) The natural course of bulimia nervosa and binge eating disorder in young women. *Archives of General Psychiatry*, **57**, 659–665.

Faris, P.L. Kim, S.W., Meller, W.H., Goodale, R.L., Oakman, S.A., Hofbauer, R.D.,Marshall, A.M., Daughters, R.S., Banerjee-Stevens, D., Eckert, E.D. & Hartman, B.K. (2000) Effects of decreasing afferent vagal activity with ondansetron on symptoms of bulimia nervosa: A randomised, double-blind trial. *Lancet*, **355**, 792–797.

Ferguson, C.P., La Via, M.C., Crossan, P.J. & Kaye, W.H. (1999) Are serotonin selective reuptake inhibitors effective in underweight anorexia nervosa? *International Journal of Eating Disorders*, **25**, 11–17.

Fluoxetine Bulimia Nervosa Collaborative Study Group (1992) Fluoxetine in the treatment of bulimia nervosa. *Archives of General Psychiatry*, **49**, 139–147.

Freeman, C. (1998) Drug treatment for bulimia nervosa. *Neuropsychobiology*, **37**, 72–79.

Goldberg, S.C., Halmi, K.A., Eckert, E.D., Casper, R.C. & Davis, J.M. (1979) Cyproheptadine in anorexia nervosa. *British Journal of Psychiatry*, **134**, 67–70.

Goldstein, D.J., Wilson, M.G., Thomson, V.L., Potvin, J.H., Rampey Jr, A.H. and the Fluoxetine Bulimia Nervosa Research Group (1995) Long-term fluoxetine treatment of bulimia nervosa. *British Journal of Psychiatry*, **166** (5), 660–666.

Goldstein, D.J., Wilson, M.G., Ascroft, R.C. & Al-Banna, M. (1999) Effectiveness of fluoxetine therapy in bulimia nervosa regardless of comorbid depression. *International Journal of Eating Disorders*, **25**, 19–27.

Greeno, C.G. & Wing, R. (1996) A double-blind, placebo-controlled trial of the effect of fluoxetine on dietary intake in overweight women with and without binge eating disorder. *American Journal of Clinical Nutrition*, **64**, 267–273.

Gross, M.A., Ebert, M.M., Faden, U.B., Goldberg, S.C., Lee, L.E. & Kaye, W.H. (1981) A double-blind controlled trial of lithium carbonate in primary anorexia nervosa. *Journal of Clinical Psychopharmacology*, **1**, 376–381.

Halmi, K.A., Eckert, E.D., La Du, T.J. & Cohen, J. (1986) Anorexia nervosa: Treatment efficacy of cyproheptadine and amitriptyline. *Archives of General Psychiatry*, **43**, 177–181.

Halmi, K.A. (1995) Current concepts and definitions. In G. Szmukler, C. Dare & J. Treasure (Eds), *Handbook of Eating Disorders. Theory, Treatment and Research*, (pp. 29–42). Chichester: John Wiley & Sons.

Hay, P.J. & Bacaltchuk, J. (2001) Extracts from 'clinical evidence': Bulimia nervosa. *British Medical Journal*, **323**, 33–37.

Heymsfield, S.B., Greenberg, A.S., Fujioka, K., Dixon, R.M., Kushner, R., Hunt, T., Lubina, J.A., Patane, J., Self, B. & McCamish, M. (1999) Recombinant leptin for weight loss in obese and lean adults: A randomized, controlled, dose-escalation trial. *JAMA*, **282** (16), 1568–1575.

Hill, J.O., Hauptman, J., Anderson, J.W., Fujioka, K., O'Neil, P.M., Smith, D.K., Zavoral, J.H. & Aronne, L.J. (1999) Orlistat, a lipase inhibitor, for weight maintenance after conventional dieting: A 1-y study. *American Journal of Clinical Nutrition*, **69**, 1108–1116.

Huckshorn, C.J., Saris, W.H., Westerterp-Plantenga, M.S., Farid, A.R., Smith, F.J. & Campfield, L.A. (2000) Weekly subcutaneous pegylated recombinant native human leptin (PEG OB) administration in obese men. *Journal of Clinical Endocrinology and Metabolism*, **85** (11), 4003–4009.

Hudson, J.I., McElroy, S.L., Raymond, N.C., Crow, S., Keck, P.E. Jr, Carter, W.P., Mitchell, J.E., Strakowski, S.M., Pope, H.G. Jr, Coleman, B.S. & Jonas, J.M. (1998) Fluvoxamine in the treatment of binge-eating disorder: A multicenter placebo-controlled, double-blind trial. *American Journal of Psychiatry*, **155**, 1756–1762.

Jick, H., Vasilakis, C., Weinrauch, L.A., Meier, C.R., Jick, S.S. & Derby, L.E. (1998) A population-based study of appetite suppressant drugs and the risk of cardiac-valve regurgitation. *New England Journal of Medicine*, **339**, 719–724.

Kaye, W.H., Gwirtsman, H.E., George, D.T. & Ebert M.H. (1991) Altered serotonin activity in anorexia nervosa after long-term weight restoration: Does elevated cerebrospinal fluid 5-hydroxyindoleacetic acid level correlate with rigid and obsessive behavior? *Archives of General Psychiatry*, **48**, 556–562.

Kaye, W.H., Greeno, C.G., Moss, H., Fernstrom, J., Fernstrom, M., Lilenfeld, L.R., Weltzin, T.E. & Mann, J.J. (1998) Alterations in serotonin activity and psychiatric symptoms after recovery from bulimia nervosa. *Archives of General Psychiatry*, **55**, 927–935.

Kaye, W.H., Nagata, T., Weltzin, T.E., Hsu, L.K.G., Sokol, M.S., McConaha, C., Plotnicov, K.H., Weise, J. & Deep, D. (2001) Double-blind placebo-controlled administration of fluoxetine in restricting- and restricting-purging-type anorexia nervosa. *Biological Psychiatry*, **49**, 644–652.

Lacey, J.H. & Crisp, A.H. (1980) Hunger, food intake and weight: The impact of clomipramine on a refeeding anorexia nervosa population. *Postgraduate Medical Journal*, **56** (1), 79–85.

La Via, M.C., Gray, N. & Kaye, W.H. (2000) Case reports of Olanzapine treatment of anorexia nervosa. *International Journal of Eating Disorders*, **27**, 363–366.

Lean, M.E.J. (1997) Sibutramine: A review of clinical efficacy. *International Journal of Obesity*, **21**, S30–S36.

Marrazzi, M.A., Bacon, J.P., Kinzie, J. & Luby, E.D. (1995) Naltrexone use in the treatment of anorexia nervosa and bulimia nervosa. *International Journal of Clinical Psychopharmacology*, **10**, 163–172.

Mayer, L.E.S. & Walsh, B.T. (1998) The use of selective serotonin reuptake inhibitors in eating disorders. *Journal of Clinical Psychiatry*, **59** (15), 28–34.

NIH Technology Assessment Conference Panel (1993) Methods for voluntary weight loss and control. Consensus Development Conference, 30 March to 1 April 1992. *Annals of Internal Medicine*, **119** (7, Pt 2), 764–770.

Pi-Sunyer, F.X. (1993) Medical hazards of obesity. *Annals of Internal Medicine*, **119** (7, Pt 2), 655–660.

Pope, H.G., Hudson, J.I., Jonas, J.M. & Yurgelun-Todd, D. (1983) Bulimia treated with imipramine: A placebo-controlled, double-blind study. *American Journal of Psychiatry*, **140**, 554–558.

Schmidt, U. (1998) The treatment of bulimia nervosa. In H.W. Hoek, J. Treasure & M.A. Katzman (Eds), *Neurobiology in the Treatment of Eating Disorders*. (pp. 331–361). Chichester: John Wiley & Sons.

Schotte, D.E. (1990) The effects of weight reduction on blood pressure in 301 obese subjects. *Archives of Internal Medicine*, **150**, 1701–1704.

Smith, K.A., Fairburn, C.G. & Cowen, P.J. (1999) Symptomatic relapse in bulimia nervosa following acute tryptophan depletion. *Archives of General Psychiatry*, **56**, 171–176.

Stunkard, A., Berkowitz, R., Tanrikut, C., Reiss, E. & Young, L. (1996) D-Fenfluramine treatment of binge eating disorder. *American Journal of Psychiatry*, **153**, 1455–1459.

Szmukler, G.I., Young, G.P., Miller, G., Lichtenstein, M. & Binns, D.S. (1995) A controlled trial of cisapride in anorexia nervosa. *International Journal of Eating Disorders*, **17**, 347–357.

Treasure, J. & Schmidt, U. (2001) Anorexia nervosa. *Clinical Evidence*, 5, 0–12.

Van Furth, E.F. (1998) The treatment of anorexia nervosa. In H. Hoek, J. Treasure & M. Katzman (Eds), *Neurobiology in the Treatment of Eating Disorders* (pp. 315–330). Chichester: John Wiley & Sons.

Van Hoeken, D., Lucas, A.R. & Hoek, H.W. (1998) Epidemiology. In H. Hoek, J. Treasure & M. Katzman (Eds), *Neurobiology in the Treatment of Eating Disorders*, (pp. 97–126). Chichester: John Wiley & Sons.

Vandereycken, W. & Pierloot, R. (1982) Pimozide combined with behavior therapy in the short-term treatment of anorexia nervosa: A double-blind placebo controlled cross-over study. *Acta Psychiatrica Scandinavica*, **66** (6), 445–450.

Vandereycken, W. (1984) Neuroleptics in the short-term treatment of anorexia nervosa: A double-blind placebo-controlled study with sulpiride. *British Journal of Psychiatry*, **144**, 288–292.

Vigerski, R.A. & Loriaux, D.L. (1977) The effect of cyproheptadine in anorexia nervosa: A double-blind trial. In R.A. Vigerski (Ed.), *Anorexia Nervosa*. New York: Raven Press.

Walsh, B.T., Gladis, M., Roose, S.P., Stewart, J.W., Stetner, F. & Glassman, A.H. (1988) Phenelzine vs placebo in 50 patients with bulimia. *Archives of General Psychiatry*, **45**, 471–475.

Walsh, B.T., Hadigan, C.M., Devlin, M.J., Gladis, M. & Roose, S.P. (1991) Long term outcome of antidepressant treatment for bulimia nervosa. *American Journal of Psychiatry*, **148**, 1206–1212.

Walsh, B.T., Wilson, G.T., Loeb, K.L., Devlin, M.J., Pike, K.M., Roose, S.P., Fleiss, J. & Waternaux, C. (1997) Medication and psychotherapy in the treatment of bulimia nervosa. *American Journal of Psychiatry*, **154**, 523–531.

Walsh, B.T., Agras, W.S., Devlin, M.J., Fairburn, C.G., Wilson, G.T., Kahn, C. & Chally, M.K. (2000) Fluoxetine for bulimia nervosa following poor response to psychotherapy. *American Journal of Psychiatry*, **157**, 1332–1334.

Wing, R.R., Koeske, R., Epstein, L.H., Nowalk, M.P., Gooding, W. & Becker, D. (1987) Long-term effects of modest weight loss in type II diabetic subjects. *Archives of Internal Medicine*, **147**, 1749–1753.

Wise, S.D. (1992) Clinical studies with fluoxetine in obesity. *American Journal of Clinical Nutrition*, **55**, 181S–184S.

Wolf, R.N. & Grundy, S.M. (1983) Influence of weight reduction on plasma lipoproteins in obese subjects. *Arteriosclerosis*, **3**, 160–169.

Wolfe, B.E., Metzger, E.D., Levine, J.M., Finkelstein, D.M., Cooper, T.B. & Jimerson, D.C. (2000) Serotonin function following remission from bulimia nervosa. *Neuropsychopharmacology*, **22**, 257–263.

Zhang, Y., Proenca, R., Maffei, M., Barone, M., Leopold, L. & Friedman, J.M. (1994) Positional cloning of the mouse obese gene and its human homologue. *Nature*, **372**, 425–432.

De Zwaan, M. & Mitchell, J.E. (1992) Opiate antagonists and eating behavior in humans: A review. *Journal of Clinical Pharmacology*, **32**, 1060–1072.

De Zwaan, M. (2001) Binge eating disorder and obesity. *International Journal of Obesity and Related Metabolic Disorders*, 25, S51–S55.

CHAPTER 20

Eating Disorder Services

Lorna Richards

Eating Disorders Unit, Bethlem Royal Hospital, Kent, UK

INTRODUCTION

Mental health services planning is a topic which is high on the agenda in many fora. In Britain there is a progressive move towards clinical practice being guided by national policy. Responsibility for the commissioning of services has shifted during the lifetime of the National Health Service (NHS) with the current desire for a more collaborative, coordinated approach that seeks to maximise quality and health improvement (Thornicroft & Tansella, 1999). It is widely agreed that the basis for the rationing of resources should be the needs of the population. Historically, information on needs has not been accurate but there have been recent innovations in the area of needs assessment including the formulation of specific instruments such as the Camberwell Assessment of Needs (Slade et al., 1999) and the MRC Needs for Care Assessment (Brewin et al., 1987) as well as the use of indirect indicators of need (Lewis, 1999). This may enable the collection of more systematic data on the needs of a population but a more taxing challenge is the translation of these needs into resource allocation. This is the domain of service planners and policy makers.

If we turn to the eating disorders, these conditions have attracted mounting international public concern in recent years. Although the history of these disorders is substantial, the development and planning of comprehensive services in this area is in its infancy. Services across Europe have evolved in a largely unsystematic fashion over the last century. A common feature in all nations is the substantial unmet need in the provision of care for those suffering with eating disorders. The last decade has seen existing services scrutinised and the planning of more rational and evidence-based practice is coming to the fore.

Service development is influenced by current understanding of the disorders and their management, societal pressure and political climates to name but a few. The influence that government policy casts on the development of services can be evidenced in many countries. A powerful example can be seen in the political history of Romania where there is very little documentation of eating disorders during the communist era. Ceausescu had banned psychology in 1977 and there were no psychology departments at Romanian universities during the period 1977 to 1990. The psychological approach to eating disorders was therefore greatly disrupted with psychological investigation and treatments being almost forbidden until the last few years when the concept of eating disorders has acquired a new status.

Handbook of Eating Disorders. Edited by J. Treasure, U. Schmidt and E. van Furth.
© 2003 John Wiley & Sons, Ltd.

In all nations, negotiating the inevitable process of change is set to be exciting and challenging for users, carers, professionals and service planners alike. However the benefits for those suffering with eating disorders will be considerable. In this chapter I aim to discuss the development of eating disorders services, the rationale behind this progress and guidelines for the future expansion of resources. Some of the problems faced in providing a comprehensive service for this patient group will also be covered along with current practical recommendations for what specialist services should comprise and how to deliver appropriate care optimally. I will end with some thoughts on the growing trend of increased user and carer involvement in the evaluation and development of services. I will be concentrating on the picture in the UK, using this as an example, but will make reference to services across Europe where possible.

SERVICE DEVELOPMENT

Historical Perspective

Current services have a strong historical and socio-political legacy. Understanding the development of services requires an appreciation of these factors. Medieval historians debate the first documentation of women suffering with illnesses which appear to fit modern day criteria for anorexia nervosa and discuss early aetiological theories. It was in 1873 that the physician Sir William Gull finally named the disorder while working at Guy's Hospital, London (Gull, 1873). Although psychosocial factors were recognised in the aetiology of the condition it was general physicians who took the lead in the management of anorexia nervosa during the nineteenth century and the first half of the twentieth (see Figure 20.1).

During the latter part of the twentieth century we saw a gradual shift in the management of anorexia nervosa from physicians to psychiatrists in most European countries,

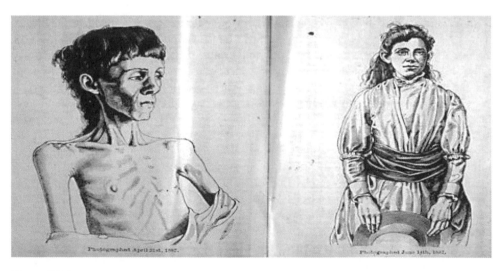

Figure 20.1

with the exception of Germany where there are special psychosomatic clinics. There was also a paradigm shift in research interest from a biological position to the evaluation of psychological treatments.

A significant event in the development of services for eating disorders came with the recognition of a novel form of eating disorder, bulimia nervosa, by Russell in 1979. This actual increase in patient numbers together with growing public awareness of the eating disorders resulted in an increased demand for eating disorders services.

GUIDELINES AND STANDARDS FOR SPECIALIST EATING DISORDERS SERVICES

In response to the call for a more systematic and standardised approach, guidelines for clinical practice and its delivery are being developed internationally. The American Psychiatric Association was the first to publish guidelines for the treatment of eating disorders (APA, 1992) and published a revised edition in 1993 and 2000. Guidelines currently in circulation in the UK are those published from a collaboration between the Royal College of Psychiatrists (2001) and the Eating Disorders Association (1995) and also the British Psychological Society (Bell et al., 2001). The National Institute of Clinical Excellence (NICE) is also planning the development of eating disorder clinical guidelines (www.nice.org.uk). Australian guidelines will shortly appear and the National Commission in Italy are also developing guidelines emphasising evidence-based practice (Ruggiero et al., 2001). Regarding a broader classification of eating disorders, obesity is also a public health concern frequently revisited by the World Health Organisation. In the UK the most comprehensive guidelines for the management of obesity are found in the SIGN report (Scottish Intercollegiate Guidelines Network, 1996) and these are due to be updated.

WHAT SHOULD A SERVICE LOOK LIKE?

The hub and spoke model of service delivery is recognised to be a rational framework throughout mental health in the UK (Audit Commission, 1997). Services for obesity, which affects up to 15% of the population in European countries, are not well coordinated and this model may not fit. For anorexia nervosa and bulimia nervosa the hub and spoke model provides a centralised element offering very specialised treatment such as inpatient beds or other intensive care on a supra-regional level with several 'feeder' clinics based more locally. These components need to allow for the transition of an individual between them through the stages of illness and recovery. The relationship between the specialist centre and local services can be enhanced by shared professional posts and good liaison between clinics.

Localities will vary but, as a rule of thumb, guidelines suggest that a population of 30 000 needs an outpatient eating disorders service, without inpatient or day-care facilities ('a spoke'), to provide an appropriate level of specialist treatment in less severe cases. In addition there should also be a comprehensive service ('hub') for every million people in the population. This service should comprise six dedicated inpatient beds and two or three local outpatient clinics at a cost of approximately 1.4 euros per head of population. The lead health professional (e.g. psychiatrist) should preferably spend at least a third of his or her time treating patients with eating disorders. The multidisciplinary team should include staff with experience of eating disorders such as a clinical psychologist, dietician and psychiatric nurses (Royal College of Psychiatrists, 2001).

PROBLEMS IN PROVIDING A SERVICE

Some inherent problems exist in the provision of effective and comprehensive services for this particular patient group, and these require consideration when planning resources. Eating disorders encompass conditions with a wide range of severity, both physical and psychological.

Many high-profile personalities have spoken candidly about their eating disorders in recent years, and although this has certainly raised public awareness, it has served little in reducing the stigmatisation of such conditions. Many still perceive them as self-inflicted or restricted to vain women aspiring to a supermodel physique. Mild or short-lived cases do occur but the morbidity and mortality attached to many cases rates among the highest of any mental disorder (see Chapter 11 in this volume). At least a third of cases of anorexia nervosa run a chronic course requiring long-term and flexible care packages. There has even been debate about the place of palliative care in the management of exceptionally chronic cases, although this remains controversial and is generally viewed as an extreme solution.

Another difficulty is that sufferers commonly delay in presenting for help and remain ambivalent, if not resistant to attempts at change (see Chapter 13 in this volume). These cases are often complex and a commitment to treatment in both patient and therapist is vital if any consistent improvement is to be made. This may compromise individual's care as well as having an impact on the accuracy of prevalence figures for the population. These hidden needs hamper the planning of suitable and effective services.

Providing for both the physical and psychological aspects of illness has implications on the expertise of staff available in addition to the environment in which care is most safely delivered. Although currently the majority of patients are managed in mental health settings it is often necessary to treat patients on a general medical ward during the course of the illness when severe physical complications take priority. Providing seamless care even within the mental health arena alone has its complications. Most eating disorders will develop in teenage years and early twenties. Conventionally, mental health services are divided into child/adolescent and adult services, and patients therefore, typically, graduate from one to the other during the course of treatment for an eating disorder. This has repercussions on the continuity of care and patient satisfaction. There is also an issue of resources and training with the current split reliant on expertise developing in two separate teams with less direct sharing of experience.

With funding increasingly being awarded preferentially to services that can demonstrate a robust evidence base for treatments, psychiatry as a whole can miss out. The planning process is hindered by the fact that there is no simple way of determining, still less proving, that there is a clear causal link between levels of health care expenditure and states of mental health. Historically, professionals working in mental health have been poor advocates for the development of their services because they have not been able to articulate specific, measurable service objectives. Evaluation of the benefits and efficiency of services has therefore been deficient. In eating disorders there is a lack of systematic data, particularly to support the effectiveness of current treatments. Inpatient management of anorexia nervosa is well known to carry a high cost and has low efficacy in the long term.

Delivery of care

Providing a comprehensive service to those suffering with eating disorders therefore demands manpower and expertise in a range of clinical settings. Treatment of severely ill people with anorexia nervosa and bulimia nervosa ideally requires an integrated treatment team, coordinating medical, mental health, nursing, nutrition and other health professionals. These resources will necessarily be accessed through primary care, secondary care and tertiary/specialist centres. The Audit Commission in the UK states that services should be adjusted to the needs of the population and be acceptable, accessible, equitable, cost-effective and of high quality (Audit Commission, 1997).

Acceptability

The acceptability of services relies on many factors. In recent years there has been an increasing emphasis on patient and public participation in the evaluation of health care. There has been some research on the views of service users although this has introduced some methodological problems. Development of a standardised method of appraising perceptions among interested groups would enable this information to be utilised in clinical decision making and service development (Newton, 2001).

Accessibility and Equity

Regarding the accessibility of care we need to study traditional service models. In most circumstances, individuals with eating disorders initially contact their GP, private counsellor or therapist, or local voluntary organisation. In younger patients this first contact may be through the pastoral care system in schools. Patients who are not successfully treated at this level would usually be referred to secondary care by their GP, with tertiary care reserved for those who are severely ill or whose problems have been difficult to manage at previous levels. This traditional progression of care may not be optimal in all cases and this has been studied with regard to cognitive-behavioural therapy (CBT) services (Lovell, 2000). This is highly relevant to eating disorders, as CBT is the treatment of choice for bulimia nervosa. This chapter argues that for service protocols to promote equity, accessibility and choice, CBT services should be organised around multiple levels of entry and service delivery and should range from self-help to simple single-stranded through to multiple-stranded complex interventions rather than the more usual secondary care referral systems.

Cost-effectiveness

In the USA cost-effectiveness has been addressed with the development of 'managed care systems' to facilitate flexible and complex care packages. The guiding principle which can be generalised to publicly funded health systems is an aim for care that is medically necessary, provided in an appropriate manner, and at the least restrictive level. This indicates that the best treatment setting for a patient is that which provides adequate and effective treatment but is not unnecessarily restrictive, complex or expensive. A patient is thought to have achieved 'maximal benefit' at a certain level of care if improvement has plateaued and the patient can continue to make progress at a lower level of care (Walter et al., 1996).

This method of service delivery acknowledges the need for correspondence between problem severity and the intensity of the intervention offered. Matching patient need to the appropriate level of treatment, however, demands a clear understanding of the individual's characteristics as well as a sound evidence base for treatments available. Accurate determination of both factors may present problems, particularly in the absence of clear prognostic indicators for different forms of treatments when applied to an individual patient. Stepped care is a model in keeping with managed care where treatment is arranged in a series of steps of graded intensity. Those who respond to a minimal intervention are then filtered out, which has advantageous economic implications. Low-intensity models of care are more developed in bulimia nervosa compared to anorexia nervosa. Psycho-education, self-help manuals incorporating education, cognitive-behavioural and motivational elements and group attendance are examples of such.

Thornicroft and Tansella (1999) describe nine leading principles that affect mental health services organisation. In addition to the above requirements of acceptability, accessibility and equity and cost-effectiveness, they suggest that *autonomy, continuity, coordination, comprehensiveness* and *accountability* of services demand consideration. These factors will all influence the capability of a service to meet the needs of a population satisfactorily.

WHAT SERVICES SHOULD BE OFFERED?

A comprehensive eating disorders service should therefore fulfil a number of roles. A specialist service should offer a range of specialised treatments including individual and family psychotherapy. Inpatient and/or day-care places should be available with medical support. The tertiary centre should also take responsibility for coordination of resources and ongoing planning of services in addition to a commitment to research, specialist training and education. This concentration of skills enables the development of and maintenance of a skilled workforce with the advantage of equality of care through implementation of agreed pathways of care and application of evidence-based practice.

However, some argue that this results in the de-skilling of staff in generic services who already report finding treating those with an eating disorder difficult (Kaplan & Garfinkel, 1999). Comorbidity is a common problem in those with eating disorders and patients should therefore not be distanced from generic services who may need to share care with the specialist team. The geographical centralisation may also isolate some patients. Certainly, in Norway many clinicians and decision makers have voiced these concerns, driving public policy towards the improvement of clinical competence and knowledge about eating disorders at all levels of health care rather than building up specialised centres and clinics. Official policy of making primary health care services a cornerstone, has paved the way for the initial priority of prevention (Skarderud & Rosenvinge, 2001).

USERS AND CARERS

In modern health care provision users and carers are gaining a higher profile in both the evaluation and planning of services. In the UK we are beginning to see users present on appointment committees, organisational boards, ethics committees and government advisory bodies. User groups for people with eating disorders have evolved internationally alongside developments in services in the health system. As well as their increasingly influential role in policy making they also provide information and support to individual sufferers and their carers. Attempts have been made to evaluate self-help groups both in terms of service users' views and outcome, but due to the heterogeneity of groups and the interventions offered this has been difficult. As many sufferers use these resources there is a need for further research (Newton, 2000).

Carers feature increasingly in literature across mental health. It is well documented that carers of people with severe adult anorexia nervosa are distressed and experience difficulties in their role (Treasure, 1995; Treasure et al., 2001), and this may have an effect on service uptake and acceptability as well as outcome. Traditional approaches use psycho-education, books and workbooks for the family and incorporate them into family meetings or in groups for carers. More recently multi-family group interventions are being used (Colahan & Robinson, 2001; Dare & Eisler, 2000). Compared to research into the needs of users, there is relatively little on the measurement of needs of carers.

CONCLUSIONS

I think it would be fair to say that population needs will always outstrip health service provision. It is difficult to imagine a situation where this would not be the case. This is not necessarily a negative view, as the need for ever-improving services should drive the development of novel practices and encourage the provision of more comprehensive services. An ideal service for eating disorders is a somewhat intangible concept. With the publication of guidelines it is hoped that services will develop in a more rational manner than previously. However, services need to maintain flexibility and responsiveness. Health care planning is often carried out on the assumption that the planning systems will remain stable and that the characteristics of the population to be served will remain steady. As we have seen in the history of services for eating disorders, influential factors are subject to change. Political and financial climates influence progress and we can predict that these trends will continue. The composition of populations is in a constant state of flux alongside changes in the nature of disorders.

REFERENCES

APA (1992) Practice guidelines for the treatment of patients with eating disorders. *American Journal of Psychiatry*, **150**, 208–228.

Audit Commission (1997) *Higher Purchasing*. London: HMSO.

Bell, L., Clare, L. & Thorn, E. (2001) *Service Guidelines for People with Eating Disorders*. The British Psychological Society Division of Clinical Psychology Occasional Paper No. 3.

Brewin, C.R., Wing, J.K., Mangen, S.P. et al. (1987) *Principles and Practice of Measuring Needs in the Long Term Mentally Ill: The MRC Needs for Care Assessment. Psychological Medicine*, **17**, 971–981.

Colahan, M. & Robinson, P. (2001) Multi-family groups in the treatment of young eating disorder adults. *Journal of Family Therapy* (in press).

Dare, C. & Eisler, I. (2000) A multi-family group day treatment for adolescent eating disorders. *European Eating Disorders Review*, **8**, 4–18.

Eating Disorders Association (1995) *Guide for Purchasers of Services for Eating Disorders.* Norwich: Eating Disorders Association.

Joja, O. (2001) Eating disorders across Europe: History and current state of treatment for eating disorders in Romania. *European Eating Disorders Review*, **9**, 374–380.

Kaplan, A. & Garfinkel, P.E. (1999) Difficulties in treating patients with eating disorders: A review of patient and clinician variables. *Canadian Journal of Psychiatry*, **44**, 665–670.

Lewis, G. (1999) Population-based needs assessment. *Current Opinions in Psychiatry*, **12**, 191–194.

Lovell, K. & Richards, D. (2000) Multiple Access Points and Levels of Entry (MAPLE): Ensuring choice, accessibility and equity for CBT services. *Behavioural and Cognitive Psychotherapy*, **28**, 379–391.

Newton, J.T. (2000) Evaluating non-professional self-help groups for people with eating disorders. *European Eating Disorders Review*, **8**, 1–3.

Newton, T. (2001) Consumer Involvement in the appraisal of treatments for people with eating disorders: A neglected area of research? *European Eating Disorders Review*, **9**, 301–308.

Royal College of Psychiatrists (2001) *Eating Disorders.* Council Report CR87. London: Royal College of Psychiatrists.

Ruggiero, G.M., Prandin, M. & Mantero, M. (2001) Eating disorders across Europe. Eating disorders in Italy: A historical review. *European Eating Disorders Review*, **9**, 292–300.

Skarderud, F. & Rosenvinge, J.H. (2001) Eating disorders across Europe. The history of eating disorders in Norway. *European Eating Disorders Review*, **9**, 217–228.

Slade, M., Thornicroft, G., Loftus, L. et al. (1999) *CAN: Camberwell Assessment of Need.* London: Gaskell.

Thornicroft, G. & Tansella, M. (1999) *The Mental Health Matrix. A Manual to Improve Services.* Cambridge: Cambridge University Press.

Treasure, J.L. (1995) European co-operation in the fields of scientific and technical research, COST B6. Psychotherapeutic treatment of eating disorders. *European Eating Disorders Review*, 3, 119–120.

Treasure, J.L., Murphy, T. & Todd, G. (2001) The experience of care giving for severe mental illness: A comparison between anorexia nervosa and psychosis. *Social Psychiatry and Psychiatric Epidemiology* (in press).

Walter, H., Kaye, M.D., Kaplan, A.S. (1996) Treating eating disorder patients in a managed care environment: Contemporary American issues and a Canadian response. *The Psychiatric Clinics of North America*, **19**, 793–810.

CHAPTER 21

Day Treatments

Paul Robinson

Department of Psychiatry, Royal Free Hospital, London, UK

SUMMARY

- Anorexia nervosa has a high mortality and safety must not be compromised.
- High-quality outpatient and day care may make expensive inpatient care unnecessary.
- A team costing £1m (€ 1.63m) with a whole time consultant psychiatrist can treat eating disorders over 16 years of age arising in a population of around 1m.
- Key quality issues for an effective multidisciplinary team for eating disorders are a broad range of skills including family interventions, effective physical monitoring, good support and supervision for staff and access to a wide range of services including inpatient beds.

INTRODUCTION

Anorexia nervosa is a significant cause of morbidity and mortality with a Standardised Mortality Ratio among the highest of all psychiatric conditions (Harris & Barraclough, 1998). It can therefore result in very high levels of anxiety in families and health care professionals. This anxiety often leads to the demand for inpatient care, and, in some life-threatening situations, admission cannot be avoided. However, inpatient treatment may not be necessary or even desirable for most patients.

There is some inconclusive evidence that hospital inpatient care may adversely affect outcome in young patients (Gowers et al., 2000) while evidence for the advantage of inpatient over outpatient care is lacking, or suggests no significant advantage (Crisp et al., 1991, Gowers et al., 1994). In this chapter, the relative advantages and disadvantages of inpatient versus community care will be described, and a new active model of community care in use at the Royal Free Hospital described.

HOSPITAL VERSUS COMMUNITY

Anorexia Nervosa and the Illusion of Control

The causes of anorexia nervosa remain obscure, while the effects of the illness are profound. The young person, struggling with this serious illness, often gives up social contacts,

Handbook of Eating Disorders. Edited by J. Treasure, U. Schmidt and E. van Furth.
© 2003 John Wiley & Sons, Ltd.

becomes depressed and at risk for physical complications which can prove fatal. It has been suggested that weight control reflects the individual's need for control more generally (Fairburn et al., 1999). Such control is, in fact illusory. The patient becomes surrounded by people who take a great interest in her eating, including family members, doctors, nurses and therapists. Her health may deteriorate to a point at which control over her life is completely removed and she is admitted to hospital involuntarily. In other words, the more successful she is at exerting control over her food intake, the less control she actually has. By asserting her absolute independence (of food) she brings about complete dependence. Her behaviour parodies the adolescent's quest for independence. It is possible that people with anorexia nervosa (like many adolescents) are seeking to be contained by authority figures, while protesting independence and a rejection of such containment.

The Anorexic Pseudo-Conflict

By asserting her independence of food, she often brings herself into conflict with her family. This conflict, like the illusion of control, parodies the healthy conflict that occurs when adolescents challenge their parents, for example, concerning smoking or staying out late. The anorexic's conflict is, however, a fight to the death and is a lethal challenge to the ability of the mother and father to nurture and provide. When this conflict is addressed early in its course, using family approaches to treatment, parental coherence can be reinstated and the patient may recover (Eisler et al., 1997, and Chapter 18 in this volume). However, if the process becomes chronic, or if the patient is removed from home for a prolonged period, the opportunity for the family to organise in a way that finds alternatives to the anorexic lifestyle may be lost.

'Parentectomy': Family Surgery for Anorexia Nervosa

Prolonged admission for anorexia nervosa speaks to both the illusion of control and the anorexic pseudo-conflict. Admission to an inpatient anorexic unit removes control from the patient or the family and places it in the hands of the clinic; but this would appear counter-intuitive, if our aim as therapists is to increase the autonomy and responsibility of the patient and family. Admission can be an enormous relief to all parties, because it appears to provide a solution to the struggle, and to the family conflict. The latter, however, is merely displaced. The struggle between the patient and the parents becomes the struggle between the patient and a set of strangers whose job it is to impose nutrition upon the patient. The family dilemma, which is 'How do we live with a person on a hunger strike?' is hardly solved by moving the 'hunger striker' to another 'family' and persisting with encouragement, until she eats. The family dilemma still remains, and needs to be solved when the patient, now heavier, leaves the clinic. Little wonder that the weight so often falls off in the few months after discharge (Russell et al., 1987). Admission to hospital, while it may be necessary because of physical deterioration, or exhaustion on the part of family, patient and therapist, decreases the patient's control and autonomy and transforms the anorexic's conflict with her family into a pseudo-conflict with hospital staff that can never be resolved.

USE OF COERCIVE METHODS OF TREATMENT

The inpatient unit for anorexia nervosa could have a sign above its doors 'We will make you put on weight'. Many patients respond to this implicit aim with an implicit 'Let me see you try!' of their own. The investment of the unit in weight gain is so great that it will occasionally go to extreme lengths to achieve it. Such measures include 'assisted feeding', in which the patient is held and food pushed into her mouth by a nurse, and 'peer pressure' in which the person refusing to eat may be forced to eat by other patients. Coercive methods are, in the view of the writer, usually counterproductive, and can only be ethically justified when the patient's life (and not just her welfare or her bone density) would be at risk if she were not forced to accept nutrition. The case for coercive treatment would be better if backed by solid evidence of benefit in controlled studies. No satisfactory study has, however, been reported.

Inpatient Units: Systemic Considerations

In some ways, the structure of the inpatient unit (and, to a lesser extent, the day unit) mirrors a family, albeit a dysfunctional one. The nurses, mostly female, have the task of encouraging the person to eat. The consultant, usually but now less often male, may see the team once a week during the archaically named ward round. The father/consultant hears from the mother/nurse how their child/patient has performed. If she has not gained weight, the nurse feels she has failed and a dynamic is set up echoing that of the parents. The mother feels responsible for the child's weight, spends much of her time with her and may become as obsessed with food as her daughter, while the father lives more and more in the world of work, becomes distant from the problem, and cannot understand why his wife is unable to get their daughter to eat properly. On the ward, the nurses, like mothers, spend, collectively, all the time with the patient and a conflict can be set up between medical and nursing staff which is curiously reminiscent of the commonly observed family conflict.

Inpatient psychiatric units often become rigidly hierarchical. This is necessary because of the role such units have in the enforcement of compulsory treatment under legal sanctions, particularly in relation to the care of patients with psychoses who have a history of violence either to themselves or to others. In the UK, The Mental Health Act (1983) enshrines the authority of the Responsible Medical Officer (RMO) who has to sign a paper to allow a detained patient even to leave the ward for a walk. When a patient with anorexia nervosa (or any other problem) is admitted to a psychiatric ward, she already gives up some rights because, even if she enters the ward freely, she can be detained, if she tries to leave, by the signature of only one doctor or one nurse.

Inpatient care is therefore overshadowed by the immense authority of the psychiatrist and the covert threat of detention, and a staff group that wishes to engender a cooperative atmosphere has to overcome these two very significant influences. It is difficult to overestimate the significance of legal sanctions as an influence on the treatment of a person with a mental illness. They organise not only the patient, but also the ward staff and the patient's family. The result is a rigidly hierarchical system, which, it seems to the author, is most unlikely to be able to help the patient to become more autonomous.

Case Examples

A patient was admitted to an inpatient unit with severe anorexia and bulimia nervosa. The consultant demanded of her that she put on 0.5 kg weekly and she was strongly encouraged to finish meals by the nurses. Her weight gradually rose but her appearance and muscle power suggested decline. A spot weighing on one occasion demonstrated a loss of over 3 kg in one morning, and she admitted to water loading prior to weighing. A second patient in the unit began to have suspicious changes in weight suggestive of water loading.

This patient responded to increased supervision by an equivalent increase in her own dysfunctional behaviour, and passed her skills on to another, less experienced, patient.

A patient placed a waste-bin upside down by her door, stood on it and put her head in a noose attached to the door frame, at a time that she knew a particular nurse would open the door to check on her, thereby pushing over the bin. She survived but the nurse was traumatised.

This case demonstrates the way patients who are willing to risk death can engage destructively with nurses deputed to protect them.

FINANCIAL INVESTMENT IN CUSTODIAL TREATMENT

In many European countries, specialist care for eating disorders can be arranged either through the country's national health service or through health insurance. This provides a mechanism whereby specialist care can be provided for patients with eating disorders who would, otherwise, not have been able to obtain such care from the local psychiatric service. However, the funds generated from inpatient admissions are far in excess of those charged for outpatient care and some clinicians have been aware of pressure from hospital authorities to admit patients in order to fill beds, and generate income. An illustrative example will be provided:

A 15-year-old patient was admitted to a private residential eating disorders service for anorexia nervosa. Funding was from the local health authority. She regained a healthy weight, but refused to eat on her return home. She was immediately rehospitalised and spent the following 12 months as an inpatient, with attempts at returning her home thwarted by her refusal to eat. She was transferred to another residential unit, and spent nearly two more years as an inpatient. The cost to her health authority was around £¼m (€ 0.4m). At no time following her initial admission did her weight fall much below the normal range. After her eighteenth birthday she was transferred to the adult service and has required no further admissions.

This case raises questions about prolonged admissions for adolescents with eating disorders. It is not clear that hospitalisation for nearly three years, irrespective of the cost, was the most appropriate treatment for her. At least, it can be argued that those responsible for funding such health care would be well advised to commission their own experts in eating disorders to determine whether treatment they are funding is being appropriately provided.

AVOIDING HOSPITALISATION IN SEVERE ANOREXIA NERVOSA

The problems that occur among patients and staff of an inpatient unit appear proportional to the degree of restraint and coercion applied. This is unsurprising, as the more a patient's will is directly challenged, the more she will retaliate in order to defend her position. The clinician faced with a severe eating disorder has a very difficult dilemma. It is probable that useful change is only likely to occur when the patient concludes that improvement in health brings advantages, which outweigh the sacrifices she would have to make. Weight loss, itself, however, may produce cognitive changes, which may militate against rational thought, and the doctor may be forced to admit a patient whose physical deterioration threatens her survival.

Alternatives to hospitalisation have been developed in a number of centres in diverse parts of the world. The best described are the Day Hospital Program at the Toronto General Hospital (Piran et al., 1989), the Therapy Centre for Eating Disorders in Munich (Gerlinghoff et al., 1998), Our Lady of the Lake Eating Disorders Program in Baton Rouge, Louisiana (Williamson et al., 1998) and the Cullen Centre in Edinburgh (Freeman, 1992). Outcome data from each of these programmes suggest clinical efficacy, although no satisfactory controlled study has been reported from the centres. A comparison of day and inpatient treatment at the Cullen Centre found no significant difference in outcome between the two treatments, but unfortunately the study was curtailed prematurely due to the overwhelming preference of referrers for the Day Programme (Freeman et al., 1992).

Given that hospital admission, under compulsion if necessary, is mandatory for patients who would otherwise die, what can be done for the remainder? Experience at the Royal Free Eating Disorders Service demonstrates that a service which offers intensive outpatient, day hospital and domiciliary management can avoid most admissions. In five years the service has utilised approximately 1 hospital bed per million residents served.

ESSENTIAL ELEMENTS OF THE SERVICE

Referral

Referrals are welcomed from primary and secondary care and referrers are asked to provide the patient's height and weight, in addition to the provisional diagnosis and any other relevant information. If a referral is marked 'Urgent' the referrer is contacted and the case discussed. Assessment can be immediate or within a few days, although in most cases the wait of 6–8 weeks is acceptable. The assessment interview is done by a staff member who may be a doctor, nurse, psychologist or occupational therapist, or a medical student, using a checklist which indicates the areas to cover. The staff members who have seen patients that morning then meet with the consultant and each person recounts the history of the patient he or she has assessed. In the third hour, each patient is then interviewed by the consultant in the presence of the interviewer and other relevant team members, necessary physical examination and tests are arranged and treatment options are explored. In this way, up to five new patients are seen in a three-hour session, and all are seen by the consultant. Moreover, staff learn how to interview and present patients and hear about a number of patients in each session.

Outpatient Treatment

Following the psychiatric and medical assessment, most patients are seen within a few weeks by a psychologist, and then allocated to one or more of the following:

1. *Individual supportive therapy.* This is provided to patients with a variety of eating disorder diagnoses. Nurses, after joining the team, are trained by more experienced nurses, and begin to attend supervision sessions, before taking on patients. Treatment is eclectic and includes physical monitoring, cognitive-behavioural techniques and supportive and educational approaches. The focus of these sessions is on weight gain and reduction of self-destructive symptoms. Other issues including family and relationship difficulties may also be discussed. We have found that nurses with basic mental health training, when properly supervised, can provide extremely helpful therapy to this group of patients.

2. *Individual psychotherapy.* A limited number of patients, with more serious disorders (e.g. eating disorders complicated by self-harm or substance misuse) are taken on for individual psychodynamic or cognitive-behavioural psychotherapy by clinical psychologists.

3. *Cognitive-behavioural therapy (individual (nurse) or group (nurse + psychologist).* CBT, either individually or in a group, is the first line therapy for patients with normal weight bulimia nervosa.

4. *Family therapy.* Patients with anorexia nervosa, and patients with eating disorders who also have children, are offered family therapy using an eclectic mix of structural, Milan-systemic and other systemic approaches. Supervision of family therapists in training is facilitated by a video link. The approach to families is as supportive and collaborative as possible, as long as the patient aggrees for her family to be involved. Initial sessions may be conducted in the home, or in the family doctor's surgery.

5. *Multiple family groups.* This recent development utilises four workshops per day, on three and a half days over three months, for four or five families with a child suffering from anorexia nervosa. Various styles of work, including 'Goldfish Bowl' discussions (in which one group, such as all the children, discuss a topic while their parents look on), task planning discussions, family sculpts, and art and movement therapy, are used. The techniques are promising and have been reported in detail elsewhere (Colahan & Robinson, 2002).

Day Programme

The Eating Disorders Day Programme takes place within the Royal Free Hospital and consists of the following elements:

1. Supported meals on four days per week, which can be increased to seven days, if necessary. These meals are intended to be educational and therapeutic. Patients generally have only a proportion of their meals at the Unit, and if a patient is eating inappropriately, the intervention by the nurse or other team member present is confined to advice, and a post-meal discussion with other patients. This approach is quite stressful for staff, because they have to be able to handle a group of patients, all eating in differently dysfunctional ways. The aim is to foster a culture of recovery, rather than one in which patients compete to be the most eating-disordered person at the table.

2. A variety of groups led by occupational therapy, creative therapy and nursing staff. (Pre- and post-meal, psychodynamic, nutrition, art therapy, drama and dance-movement therapy and current affairs groups.) Individual massage and dance-movement therapy is also provided.

3. Individual key nurse monitoring and therapy.
4. Participation in team meeting.
5. All therapies which are available to outpatients.

Outreach Care

A small team of a senior nurse, family therapist, doctor and other professionals provide an outreach service. Patients who continue to deteriorate in spite of a full day programme can be supported at home with visits from EDS staff at weekends. Staff can also be employed to spend nights at the patient's home to help the family to cope with a severely ill family member.

Less dramatically, family assessments are often conducted at home, by the key nurse, together with a family therapist, in order to engage new families in outpatient or day patient care.

Patients admitted to other hospitals are visited regularly in order help the staff in the other unit and to engage the patient with the aim of attendance at treatment sessions at the Royal Free. The outreach team also supports staff at other hospitals that treat patients with eating disorders.

Persuading Patients to Gain Weight

This is the main aim of most treatment services, and it is self-evident that without weight recovery the anorexia nervosa remains. The nurse providing individual therapy to the patient has a supportive and accepting role, and, most importantly, eliciting the trust of the patient. At the same time, the nurse will be firm and persistent about the need for improvements in diet and weight, and often asks the dietician to provide a session to emphasise the importance of weight recovery. The family sessions are also intended to be supportive, particularly the family support group sessions, but family therapists will also aim to address dysfunctional patterns, for example withdrawal of the father from family life or a parent defending the *status quo* and preventing therapeutic change. Families are invited to team meetings to discuss treatment with the consultant and the rest of the team, and this can prevent unhelpful splits in the team, for example when one team member is seen by patient or family as good and another bad.

In general, patients are encouraged to find their own route to weight gain, and some may gain weight while clearly under-eating within the unit. This would be commented on and discussed in the post-meal group. The patient is finding her own way to a healthy body weight, but has to do so in private.

Management of the Severely Ill Patient with Anorexia Nervosa

Patients who lose weight to a dangerously low level are monitored closely for signs of physical collapse. It is important to measure several variables, as only one or two of them may change in any one patient whose physical state is deteriorating.

- *Body mass index.* If BMI is changing, physical collapse may be imminent. This is particularly the case at levels below 13, although rapid weight loss at higher BMIs can also be dangerous. BMI, if falling, should be measured once or twice weekly. Patients who sense that they may be liable to compulsory hospitalisation may falsify their BMI in a number of ways, particularly by water loading, as in the case described above.
- *Muscle power.* Muscle weakness is a common sign of physical deterioration.

A patient who brought breakfast to her mother each morning was losing weight and began placing the breakfast tray on each step, sitting on the stair and dragging herself up to the next step, once she was unable to climb the stairs.

The SUSS Test of Muscle Power in Anorexia Nervosa

We have chosen two measures of muscle power, the stand-up and the sit-up (SUSS: Sit-Up, Stand Straight). For the stand-up, the patient is asked to squat and to rise without using her hands, if possible. The scale used is as follows:

0: completely unable to rise
1: able to rise only with use of hands
2: able to rise with noticeable difficulty
3: able to rise without difficulty.

For the sit-up, the patient lies flat on a firm surface such as the floor and has to sit up without, if possible, using her hands. The scoring is just as for the stand-up (see Figure 21.1).

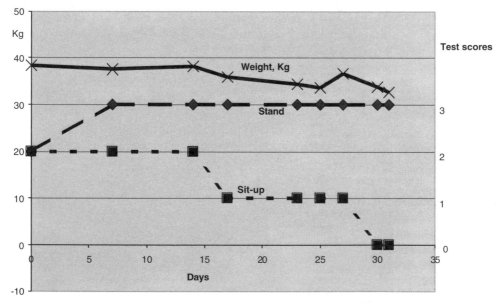

Figure 21.1   Use of the SUSS test in a patient with falling weight. The stand-up test is satisfactory, but the sit-up declines with reduced weight. The transient increase in weight on day 27 was due to water loading. The patient was admitted to hospital on day 31 (BMI 11.4)

Postural Dizziness

This is usually due to fall in blood pressure caused by dehydration and cardiac dysfunction. It is an important sign because it suggests that cardiovascular collapse may occur if further weight or fluid are lost. The scale used for this symptom, tested by asking the patient to stand up after lying down, is:

0: no postural dizziness
1: transient dizziness
2: sustained dizziness
3: unable to stand due to dizziness.

A patient who scores 1 or above should have standing and lying blood pressure monitored.

Blood Tests

These are of limited value, but at times precede other clinical signs of impending collapse. Serum Creatine Kinase may be raised in a patient with anorexic myopathy (Alloway et al., 1988), especially, in our experience, if the patient continues to exercise while losing weight. White blood count and platelets may decline with weight loss, and electrolytes, especially potassium, may fall in a patient with self-induced vomiting or laxative abuse. Thinner patients (i.e. those with anorexia nervosa) are more at risk for hypokalaemia, because of poorer body stores. Liver function tests are also worth monitoring, with rises in transaminase levels indicating liver dysfunction due to malnutrition. A chart suitable for monitoring physical state in this way is provided (Appendix 21.1).

APPENDIX 21.1

The form shown as Figure 21.2 is used to monitor medical state in a patient with anorexia nervosa judged to be at high physical risk. The decision about admission must be taken by the

Name			DOB		Address	Phone	Number
GP (Phone/fax/email)					EDS Contact (Phone/ fax/ email)		
Date	BMI	Stand up[a]	Sit-up[b]		Postural dizziness[c]	Other symptoms/ signs (e.g. oedema)	Tests (K, Na, etc)

[a] Ability to rise from squatting (0, unable to rise even with help from hands; 1, can only rise with help from hands; 2, some difficulty; 3, no difficulty).
[b] Ability to sit up from lying flat (no pillow, firm surface). Scale as for stand-up.
[c] Dizziness on standing up from a lying posture (0, no symptoms; 1, transient; 2, persistent; 3, unable to stand because of dizziness).

Figure 21.2 Medical monitoring of high-risk AN patient

individual clinician and team, and information derived from monitoring several parameters allows a more informed decision than one taken purely on weight. The direction and rate of change are also important. If a patient has a BMI of 12, and is known to have collapsed at a BMI of 10, then it is inappropriate and dangerous to wait until weight goes down, until she is *in extremis*. These decisions are best made in a team context, with contributions from the nurse and therapist who know the patient well, medical staff, family and, if the Mental Health Act might be involved, the social worker.

Where to Admit, and What to do Then

In a service such as that at the Royal Free, with no dedicated beds, a flexible budget is essential. A patient who requires admission because of physical deterioration has the following options:

1. A Medical Bed

In areas in which there are shortages of medical beds, a medical admission may only be only possible for a patient who is very severely ill. Contact between the senior psychiatrist and the consultant physician is essential, and a certain amount of persuasion and diplomacy may be needed in order to secure a medical bed. Once the patient has negotiated Accident and Emergency (ER), and been placed in a bed, a meeting is rapidly arranged between the medical ward staff and the eating disorders team. The patient's key nurse spends time on the ward negotiating between the patient, the nurses and doctors, the catering department and the eating disorders team in what is an exhausting and at times thankless task. The nurse's other duties should be reviewed and shared with other team members in such a crisis. A medical member of the eating disorders staff attends whatever medical meetings are arranged (often in the early morning) and hopes to be involved in treatment planning, particularly around discharge.

A patient with anorexia nervosa lost weight and was admitted to a medical bed, unable to walk due to myopathy. After three days she was deemed no longer to need an intravenous infusion and was discharged by a senior registrar (senior resident) as no longer needing medical services. She was still unable to raise her legs to walk, although she was able to move by sliding her feet along the floor. After two days she collapsed and was readmitted, following a formal complaint by her parents.

In this case, a 'sweep' by the senior registrar (senior resident) in order to clear beds the day before the ward was on take for emergency admissions led to the patient being discharged prematurely without reference to psychiatric medical staff. Her next admission was dealt with much more collaboratively.

2. A Psychiatric Bed

Acute psychiatric wards are often inappropriate for someone with severe anorexia nervosa. However, as long as the ward is reasonably calm, and the patient not too medically unwell, such a bed remains a possibility to be explored. Again, it is very important that eating disorder staff provide support to the general psychiatry staff so that various issues such as lack of information about eating disorders, fears about physical frailty and adverse attitudes to eating disorder patients among staff can be addressed. At the Royal Free Hospital, a women's unit has recently been established, and has provided excellent care to patients with anorexia nervosa requiring admission.

3. A 'Traditional' Inpatient Eating Disorders Bed

Once a patient has been through outpatient, day-patient, medical inpatient and, perhaps, psychiatric inpatient care, the patient should be admitted to an inpatient eating disorders service.

A 19-year-old patient with anorexia nervosa had been treated, initially, with psychoanalytic psychotherapy, then family therapy, day care and two inpatient medical admissions for severe malnutrition. She had developed symptoms of anorexia and bulimia nervosa, and latterly, frankly psychotic symptoms in relation to food. She was admitted to an inpatient eating disorders service for several months, where she made some progress, although her weight fell again rapidly on discharge.

This patient suffers from severe anorexia and bulimia nervosa, together with a paranoid psychosis of uncertain aetiology. Her treatment has proved to be a major challenge to all services with which she has had contact.

Team Structure Support and Supervision

In the last 50 years, psychiatric beds all over the world have given way to community approaches to treatment. In many places, this has proved very successful (Trieman et al., 1999) with hitherto incarcerated patients living freer and more independent lives. However, many patients remain vulnerable, both to self-neglect and self-harm, and to urges to harm others. These patients naturally raise concerns, and society has looked around for systems to replace the asylum walls and contain anxiety. The response has been to charge community staff with responsibility for care and to back that demand with paperwork that can prove oppressive and can, at times, militate against provision of care by engendering a 'tick box' approach to the provision of care. In the eating disorders field, patients are mostly at risk for self-neglect, and the resulting anxiety raised in a service without dedicated beds is absorbed by the staff. It is necessary, therefore, to have a team with sufficient breadth of skill, depth of experience and density of support to cope with the demands. These three essential elements will be addressed individually:

(1) *Breadth of skill.* The skills required are for the administration and management of the service, medical diagnosis and monitoring of patients and the provision of therapy to individuals, groups and families. Specific skills required cover the areas of administration, management, medicine, nursing, psychotherapy, group therapy, family therapy, dietetics and creative therapies.
(2) *Depth of skill.* It is also essential to have a range of depth of skill (usually signifying seniority). Thus, recently qualified staff in any field may be able to take on the care of patients, as long as they are backed by senior medical, nursing and therapeutically

trained staff. In the Royal Free team, 9–11 nurses are employed at five different levels of seniority, providing significant within-profession support while doctors are at all levels from junior psychiatric trainee to consultant. Other professions, including psychology, dietetics, and art, movement and family therapy, do not have multiple levels of seniority, although they do have professional and management structures both within and outside the team.

(3) *Density of support and supervision.* This indicates the amount, variety and frequency of types of communication among team members that occur in relation to patient care and to service development.

    (a) Management structures provide three levels at which information is shared:

> (i) Service manager meets consultant weekly and both liaise with psychiatric service manager monthly.
> (ii) Service manager and consultant with senior administrative and clinical staff (monthly management meeting).
> (iii) All staff on unit (monthly business meeting).

In addition, twice yearly 'away days' provide opportunities for staff to contribute to service planning, informal team outings provide opportunities for interaction outside the work setting, Each professional head meets with his or her staff regularly for appraisal and the consultant meets with all staff members twice yearly for an informal career discussion.

    (b) Clinical supervision takes the form of weekly team meetings, peer support meetings, group and case discussions, and supervision from a consultant psychiatrist in psychotherapy and an eating disorders specialist psychiatrist. There are weekly training sessions provided by team members and outside speakers.

Financial and Managerial Considerations

The service provides assessment and treatment of patients with eating disorders to an area containing 1 100 000 people. Out of area patients are not seen. The lower age limit is 18, although 16–17 year olds will be seen following a referral by a child and adolescent psychiatrist.

Within the budget, which is managed within adult mental health and is designated for eating disorders, is a flexible element, which can be used at the discretion of clinical and managerial staff. Examples of the use of this budget have included:

1. Inpatient care in a private hospital for a patient unresponsive to community approaches.
2. Provision of private analytic psychotherapy when this is unavailable within a reasonable time, and when the Royal Free Clinicians believe that such treatment would be likely to be beneficial.
3. Provision of nurses to work in the home at the weekends, and, if necessary, at night, to help families with the care of their eating disordered family members.
4. Provision of taxis to allow patients to attend the day and outpatient programme.

All treatment for eating disorders under the National Health Service in the designated area is provided through the Royal Free. Any requests for public funding of care outside the

Royal Free service are scrutinised, and appropriate treatment provided by the Royal Free if possible.

This style of service requires a substantial team (Appendix 21.2). The staff budget at 2001 costs, amounts to £800 000 (€ 1.3m). The author suggests that a budget of £1 (€ 1.63) per adult in the community should purchase a satisfactory service for a local population, which should probably not exceed one million. This accords with recent guidelines from the Royal College of Psychiatrists (2001).

APPENDIX 21.2 STAFF RESOURCES AVAILABLE TO THE ROYAL FREE EATING DISORDERS SERVICE

Results in the First Three Years

Of the first 500 patients seen in the service, between 1997 and 1999, the vast majority were treated as outpatients: 25 (5%) were treated as day patients and 5 (1%) were admitted—3 to medical wards, 2 to psychiatric beds (women only unit) and 1 to an inpatient unit for eating disorders. On average, 0.6 beds were used at any one time, and this figure translates to a requirement of 1 bed per million population. (The catchment area population up to 1999 was 650 000.) Over the five years since the service was established, patients with severe, relapsing illness have, however, tended to accumulate, and the eventual need for beds might be a little higher. The service is audited using weight, BMI, and a range of standardised measures of eating disorder and depressive symptoms. Preliminary audit results in the first 81 patients with anorexia nervosa (restrictive or bulimic subtype) followed up at one year showed significant improvements in BMI, eating disorder symptoms and depression. Of these 81 patients, 50 (62%) had gained weight to a BMI over 17.5, the criterion level for anorexia nervosa. Comprehensive audit will extend findings to all diagnostic groups, and a comparison with other services will give some information on relative efficacy of different approaches.

Table 21.1 Staff resources available to the Royal Free EDS

Staff	Grade/Profession	Whole-time equivalent
Medical	Consultant	2
	Psychiatric Trainee	0.5
Nursing	Team leaders	2
	Staff nurses	11
Management	Clinical service manager	1
Therapy	Psychologists	1.5
	Family therapists	1.5
	Occupational therapist	1
	Dietician	1
	Creative therapists	0.4
Administration	Secretaries	2
Total		23.90

Dangers of Avoiding Admission

The approach to service provision is not without drawbacks. When patients are very unwell, managing them in the community, even with high levels of support, can be exhausting and frightening for staff. We have learned, in crisis situations, to try to protect the key worker, as far as possible, from the strain of looking after a very ill patient while managing less acutely needy patients. Liaising with medical and psychiatric units, especially if they are unused to dealing with eating-disordered patients, can be difficult, and requires ready access to senior staff, both clinical and managerial, on both eating disorder and medical or psychiatric teams. Staff in our unit do not get training on how to manage an inpatient eating disorders unit, although they do have contact with patients, generally one at a time, who have been admitted. This problem can be addressed by seconding staff for a period of training to an inpatient unit. There is no evidence that mortality has been increased by the service model. In five years no patient seen and treated by the service has died, although in 2000 one patient who presented to the service in terminal renal failure died in hospital shortly after beginning treatment.

A National Service

If our approach were to be replicated around the UK, a team with responsibility for outpatients, day patients, and for organising brief medical or psychiatric inpatient when appropriate would be provided for every million people. In urban areas, this could be provided from one or two centres, while in rural areas, three or four clinics may need to be set up, according to local needs. The total budget for such a service would amount to 0.5–1% of the general adult psychiatry budget, a reasonable outlay considering that eating disorders are common (1–2% of young women), serious (Ratnasuriya et al., 1991) and treatable, especially if identified early.

REFERENCES

Alloway, R., Shur, E., Obrecht, R. & Russell, G.F. (1988) Physical complications in anorexia nervosa. Haematological and neuromuscular changes in 12 patients. *British Journal of Psychiatry*, **153**, 72–75.

Colahan, M. & Robinson, P.H. (2002) Multi-family Groups in the treatment of young adults with eating disorders. *Journal of Family Therapy* (in press).

Crisp, A.H., Norton, K., Gowers, S., Halek, C., Bowyer, C., Yeldham, D., Levett, G. & Bhat A. (1991) A controlled study of the effect of therapies aimed at adolescent and family psychopathology in anorexia nervosa. *British Journal of Psychiatry*, **159**, 325–333.

Eisler, I., Dare, C., Russell, G.F., Szmuckler, G., le Grange, D. & Dodge, E. (1997) Family and indvidual therapy in anorexia nervosa. A 5 year follow-up. *Archives of General Psychiatry*, **54**, 1025–1030.

Fairburn, C.G., Shafran, R. & Cooper, Z. (1999) A cognitive behavioural theory of anorexia nervosa. *Behaviour Research and Therapy*, **37**, 1–13.

Freeman, C. (1992) Day patient treatment for anorexia nervosa. *British Review of Bulimia and Anorexia Nervosa*, **6**, 3–8.

Freeman, C.P., Shapiro, C., Morgan, S. & Engliman, M. (1992) Anorexia nervosa: A random allocation controlled trial of two forms of treatment. Paper Presented at Fourth International Conference on Eating Disorders, New York.

Gerlinghoff, M., Backmund, H. & Franzen, U. (1998) Evaluation of a day treatment program for eating disorders. *European Eating Disorders Review*, **6**, 96–106.

Gowers, S., Norton, K., Halek, C. & Crisp, A.H. (1994) Outcome of outpatient psychotherapy in a random allocation treatment study of anorexia nervosa. *International Journal of Eating Disorders*, **15**, 165–177.

Gowers, S.G., Weetman, J., Shore, A., Hossain, F. & Elvins, R. (2000) Impact of hospitalisation on the outcome of adolescent anorexia nervosa. *British Journal of Psychiatry*, **176**, 138–141.

Harris, E.C. & Barraclough, B. (1998) Excess mortality of mental disorder. *British Journal of Psychiatry*, **173**, 11–53.

Piran, N., Kaplan, A., Kerr, A., Shekter-Wolfson, L., Winocur, J., Gold, E. & Garfinkel, P.E. (1989) A day hospital program for anorexia nervosa and bulimia. *International Journal of Eating Disorders*, **8**, 511–521.

Ratnasuriya, R.H., Eisler, I., Szmukler, G.I. & Russell, G.F. (1991) Anorexia nervosa: Outcome and prognostic factors after 20 years. *British Journal of Psychiatry*, **158**, 495–502.

Royal College of Psychiatrists (2001) Council Report 87: Eating disorders in the UK. Policies for service development and training. See www.rcpsych.ac.uk

Russell, G.F.M., Szmukler, G.I., Dare, C. & Eisler, I. (1987) An evaluation of family therapy in anorexia nervosa and bulimia nervosa. *Archives of General Psychiatry*, **44**, 1047–1057.

Trieman, N., Leff, J. & Glover, G. (1999) Outcome of long stay psychiatric patients resettled in the community: Prospective cohort study. *British Medical Journal*, **319**, 13–16.

Williamson, D.A., Duchmann, E.G., Barker, S.E. & Bruno, R.M. (1998) Anorexia nervosa. In Van Hasselt and Hersen (Eds), *Handbook of Psychological Treatment Protocols for Children and Adolescents* (pp. 423–465). London: Lawrence Erlbaum Associates.

CHAPTER 22

Inpatient Treatment

Anthony Winston

Eating Disorders Unit, Warwick Hospital, Warwick, UK

and

Peter Webster

Eating Disorders Unit, Institute of Psychiatry, London, UK

HISTORICAL PERSPECTIVE

The inpatient treatment of anorexia nervosa has undergone major changes since the illness was first identified and treated in the 1860s (Lasègue 1873; Gull, 1874). Although prolonged admission was originally the sole recommended treatment (Marce, 1860), early management was pragmatic and both Lasègue and Gull were appropriately reticent about aetiology. They recommended the withdrawal of the patient from the family environment, together with refeeding ' ... at regular intervals and surrounded by persons who would have moral control over them' (Gull, 1874). By the end of the nineteenth century, this had extended to total isolation during treatment (Charcot, 1889), and this approach continued in some centres up to the 1970s. Another early treatment was the use of medication to correct secondary hormonal deficits and promote weight gain; drugs used included thyroid hormone (Berkman, 1930), ovarian and anterior pituitary extracts (Reifenstein, 1946) and insulin with chlorpromazine (Dally & Sargant, 1960; Bhanji and Mattingly, 1988).

In the 1970s, particularly through the influence of Gerald Russell, the approach to treatment started to change. This coincided with a growth in behavioural psychology and an increasing understanding of the role of individual psychological, family and social factors in the cause and maintenance of anorexia nervosa. Initially, there was disagreement between those who advocated psychological treatment prior to weight gain (Bruch, 1970) and those who aimed for weight gain before psychological treatment (Russell, 1970). The latter often employed operant conditioning techniques to increase weight gain (Garfinkel et al., 1973). Over time a multifaceted approach has evolved, which starts with weight gain in an emotionally supportive setting and is then followed by more specific psychotherapy when the patient has reached a weight at which she is able to make use of it (Russell, 1981). Furthermore, the patient's family and environment have come to be seen as supportive tools to be used in therapy, rather than necessarily as maintainers of the illness.

Handbook of Eating Disorders. Edited by J. Treasure, U. Schmidt and E. van Furth.

In the UK, for example, the increased emphasis on community psychiatric care over the last two decades has led to a move away from inpatient care for anorexia nervosa. Concerns have arisen about the harmful effect of removing the patient from her usual environment and the risks of institutionalisation. Furthermore, previous motivational treatment may be compromised by the greater emphasis on controlled refeeding during inpatient treatment. It has been suggested that admission may actually be harmful, perhaps because it disrupts long-term treatment (Morgan et al., 1983; Gowers et al., 2000). However, this may not be the case if inpatient treatment forms part of a comprehensive and integrated treatment programme, delivered by a consistent clinical team. Alternative models of management which have been developed include outpatient, daypatient and home treatment (Piran & Kaplan,1990).

THE CURRENT PLACE OF INPATIENT TREATMENT

The present role of inpatient care in the treatment of anorexia nervosa varies enormously across the world. In Germany and the USA most patients are still treated as inpatients, whereas the trend at present in the UK is towards a 'stepped care' approach employing outpatient, day patient and inpatient care in sequence. Unfortunately, this model is significantly compromised by a lack of specialist units and the variation in services nationally. This often leads to admissions to distant units which are delayed and expensive and are not coordinated with a local treatment programme extending over a longer period. A more rational approach may be the 'hub and spoke' model of service organisation (Audit Commission, 1997), in which a central, specialist unit (the 'hub') provides inpatient care, research and training and local units (the 'spokes') provide outpatient care in collaboration with the 'hub'.

INDICATIONS FOR ADMISSION

Despite its potential disadvantages, it is generally agreed that admission is sometimes necessary as a life-saving treatment. In some cases it may also be a positive therapeutic intervention, particularly if it forms part of a longer term management strategy. The American Psychiatric Association (2000) has summarised in detail the specific indications for admission. These reflect both the life-threatening nature of the illness and the need to provide an alternative approach to treatment when motivation is inadequate or facilities are not available for treatment at home. The indications for admission are summarised in Table 22.1. Severely ill patients, such as those with profound electrolyte disturbance or cardiac dysfunction, may need a period of stabilisation on a medical ward before being transferred to the eating disorders unit.

STRUCTURE OF THE INPATIENT PROGRAMME
FOR ANOREXIA NERVOSA

While the structure of admissions varies somewhat between units, there is a general consensus on several basic aspects of management. Clinical experience strongly suggests that

Table 22.1 Indications for inpatient admission

Life threatening
Medical
Body Mass index <13.5 kg/m^2 or rapid fall > 20% in 6 months
Cardiovascular compromise
• Bradycardia ≤ 40 bpm
• Hypotension ≤ 90/60 mmHg (<16 years ≤ 80/50 mmHg)
• Orthostatic drop ≥10–20 mmHg
• Severe dehydration
Proximal myopathy
Hyoglycaemia
Poor diabetic control
Severe electrolyte disturbance (e.g. K + < 2.5 mmol/L; Na + < 130 mmol/L)
Petechial rash and significant platelet suppression.
Organ compromise   hepatic, renal, bone marrow

Psychiatric
High risk of suicide
Severe comorbidity, e.g. severe depression or OCD
Very low motivation/insight

Compromised community treatment
Intolerable family situation (e.g. high expressed emotion; abuse; collusion)
Social situation (e.g. extreme isolation; lack of support)
Failure to gain weight as outpatient

patients with anorexia nervosa should be treated in specialist units whenever possible and that those treated on general psychiatric or medical wards tend to have a poorer outcome. There are a number of possible reasons for this. Firstly, effective treatment depends on an integrated team which shares a common philosophy and understanding of the disorder. Secondly, anorexia nervosa is a rare disorder and it is difficult for non-specialists to develop sufficient expertise in its management. Thirdly, it is unlikely that a non-specialist team will be able to offer the range of skills needed for effective treatment.

The Multidisciplinary Team

Successful inpatient treatment requires contributions from a number of professional disciplines, who need to work closely together as an integrated team. Nursing patients with anorexia nervosa requires a high level of skill and is most likely to be effective when carried out by a nursing team with experience and training in this area. It is important that nursing staff have an understanding of the complex and ambivalent feelings which patients have about gaining weight and the way in which these reflect fears of psychological change (George, 1997). Nurses need to strike a difficult balance between firmness and sensitivity; this requires an ability to understand the patient's dilemmas and must be based on a firm therapeutic alliance. Developing this alliance is one of the crucial tasks in nursing eating disordered patients. Patients are likely to respond badly to staff whom they perceive as rigid and authoritarian, but at the same time are unlikely to feel safe unless those caring for them are able to set clear and appropriate boundaries. The patient's perception of staff is likely to reflect a disturbed attachment history (Ward et al., 2000) and staff may come to function as good attachment objects. Although this experience of 'reparenting' potentially has many positive aspects, the development of an excessively dependent relationship may hinder the development of a sense of autonomy in the patient.

In most teams, a consultant psychiatrist provides clinical leadership, supported by one or more junior doctors. The psychiatrist's specific contributions include the diagnosis of eating disorders and secondary psychiatric illnesses, the management of medical complications and the prescription of medication. In many units, psychologists play a major role in the assessment and treatment of the primary illness. They may also take the lead in the assessment and treatment of comorbid disorders such as depression, obsessive-compulsive disorder (OCD), social phobia and self-harm. However, it may be necessary to wait until a sufficient degree of weight gain has been achieved before instituting specific psychological treatments for these disorders.

Psychotherapy is essential to the treatment of patients with anorexia nervosa and may be provided by professionals from a variety of disciplines. In some units, a family therapist is included in the team. The dietitian has a central role in supervising the patient's nutritional rehabilitation and may also play a part in nutritional education. The occupational therapist may contribute to the patient's dietary rehabilitation, for example supervising her in buying, preparing and cooking meals. She may also have a role in running groups on the ward. Many inpatients have long histories of anorexia nervosa and the disorder may be complicated by social isolation and delayed psychosocial development. These problems need to be included in the treatment programme and the patient may benefit from 'rehabilitation' in terms of social function, education or employment, sexual relationships and other areas.

It is essential that the multidisciplinary team meets regularly to review the patient's progress. Patients with anorexia nervosa are likely to provoke strong feelings in those who care for them. These may include powerful feelings of frustration and anger on the one hand and a wish to protect and rescue the patient on the other. These feelings should be understood as counter-transference responses to the patient's difficulties and staff need to be able to resist the temptation to 'act out' their feelings. Such 'acting out' can result in ostensibly 'therapeutic' responses which are in fact punitive or humiliating and are ultimately counterproductive. Not uncommonly, the patient will 'split' the therapeutic team, viewing one member as sympathetic and helpful and another as authoritarian and cruel. This can lead to conflict within the team and undermine the therapeutic process. Team members need to develop the ability to reflect on their own emotional responses to the patient and this can be facilitated by the provision of regular supervision.

Length of Admission

The primary aim of admission is to achieve significant weight gain while at the same time providing appropriate psychotherapy and support. Although restoration of a normal weight can be achieved relatively quickly, the pace of psychological change is likely to be much slower. There is little empirical evidence on which to base recommendations about the optimum rate of weight gain or length of admission, and units vary in these respects. Moreover, due to the complexity of the illness, patients have to be treated individually.

This results in considerable variation in the length of admission, both between and within units.

One observational study found that people with a longer duration of illness had a higher likelihood of a good outcome with a longer duration of inpatient treatment, while those with a shorter duration of illness had a higher likelihood of a good outcome with briefer inpatient treatment (Kächele, 1999).

Preparation for Admission

Admission to an eating disorders unit represents a major commitment for both the patient and the hospital. Good preparation can be very helpful in facilitating admission and may increase the chances that the patient will remain in treatment. Every admission must involve a full psychiatric, physical and social assessment, as well as an assessment of the patient's capacity. This should include the patient's understanding of and insight into her illness, its current risks, and the treatment involved and her attitude to hospitalisation. The nature and likely duration of the treatment programme should be explained in detail and, if possible, the patient should have the opportunity to visit the unit before admission. Issues such as meals may need to be discussed in some detail at this point.

Treatment Philosophy

There is always a tension during inpatient treatment between enhancement of the patient's sense of responsibility for herself and the necessity of weight gain. This creates a paradox in the treatment: a behavioural approach to feeding goes hand in hand with psychological work aimed at increasing motivation and autonomy. In many units, the former takes precedence early in treatment and the latter becomes more important as weight and insight increase. This can be a source of confusion for both patients and staff, particularly if these issues are not addressed openly. Over the last century the management of anorexia nervosa has transferred from medical to psychiatric settings, which is an implicit marker of the recognition that psychosocial processes are important in the process of recovery.

Historically, inpatient treatment was based on strict behavioural principles in which privileges were removed and returned as a reward for weight gain. However, such an approach is likely to be experienced by the patient as degrading and thus damaging to the therapeutic alliance (Anonymous, 1995). There is no evidence that such programmes are more effective in promoting weight gain than those which are based on more collaborative principles (Eckert et al., 1979; Touyz et al., 1984). It is our view that programmes based on strict operant conditioning can no longer be recommended. However, the issue of control is central to the psychopathology of anorexia nervosa and this needs to be reflected in the structure of the inpatient programme. Admission to hospital entails giving up the rigid dietary control of anorexia nervosa, which many patients experience as equivalent to emotional control. In order for the patient to feel safe enough to relinquish this control, the treatment programme needs to provide a degree of external control, and a clear treatment structure is therefore essential. However, as the patient develops a greater capacity to tolerate and integrate emotion, this external control can be relaxed and the patient can take progressively more responsibility for her own eating.

Meals and Weighing

In one model meals are taken as a group as this encourages socialisation and can provide additional support, as well as making supervision easier. All meals are supervised by a nurse and are treated as a form of group therapy as well as refeeding; difficulties can be discussed and abnormal eating behaviour challenged by the nurse. Nursing staff can also model normal eating by sharing the meal with patients. Strict boundaries are maintained around finishing meals on time and eating everything provided. These boundaries may be maintained in a variety of ways—for example, by substituting calorific drinks if food is not consumed and only allowing patients to leave the dining room when all have completed the meal. In many units, patients are also supervised for a defined period after meals in order to prevent them concealing food or vomiting. At a later stage in treatment, they may eat their meals without supervision.

Patients should be weighed at least twice weekly; staff need to be aware that some patients will attempt to increase their weight artificially by drinking large quantities of water or concealing heavy objects in their clothes. The regular weighing session is likely to be a difficult time for the patient and one at which staff should be able to offer support. Exercise also needs to be regarded as part of the nutritional equation and should therefore be 'prescribed', particularly during the early stages of treatment. During inpatient treatment, exercise should ideally be under the supervision of a physiotherapist.

Target Weight

It is a common practice in many units to set a 'target weight' at the beginning of treatment. This gives definition to the treatment programme and may help to allay the patient's anxieties that she will be allowed to become overweight. There is no clear consensus as to how the target weight should be determined; it may be set at a specific point within the normal range (BMI of 20–25 kg/m^2) or negotiated with the patient. A reasonably common practice is to base it on a low normal body weight, such as a BMI of 19 or 20 kg/m^2. This is, of necessity, an arbitrary figure and may have to be modified in the light of individual circumstances, for example if the patients' premorbid stable weight was significantly higher or lower than this. It may sometimes be appropriate to agree a lower target weight, for example as part of a specialised treatment plan or in intractable cases where the patient has repeatedly failed to attain a normal weight.

Although setting the target at a normal weight results in lengthy admissions, clinical experience suggests that discharge before this point may allow the patient to avoid the difficult psychological transition to a normal weight. There is limited research evidence that discharge at a low weight is associated with a poorer outcome and a higher readmission rate (Baran et al., 1995; Howard et al., 1999). It should be emphasised that the target represents a minimum healthy weight rather than an ideal. In some units a target weight range is used in preference to a single weight. The return of menstruation may be used as a physiological marker of adequate weight restoration, although patients should be informed that this may be delayed for several months after attaining a normal weight.

Maintenance Treatment

There are advantages, if circumstances allow, in providing a further period of inpatient or day patient treatment after the patient attains a normal weight. It is at this point that the patient is forced to relinquish the psychological safety of the anorexic position and face the prospect of life at a normal weight. In many ways, the most difficult psychological work begins at this point. A period of stabilisation—both psychological and dietary—may help to reduce the chances of relapse after discharge. At this point in treatment, it may be appropriate for the patient to eat meals without supervision and to take responsibility for maintaining her own weight within an agreed range. During the maintenance phase, staff can help the patient to learn how to shop, cook and eat meals in a social situation, while supporting her in working through the feelings that these activities generate.

Other Forms of Inpatient Treatment

Although most inpatient admissions will be directed towards full weight restoration, admission may occasionally be required in other circumstances. These include shorter admissions for those whose physical health is in immediate danger but are not able to commit themselves to full weight restoration, and crisis admissions precipitated by comorbid psychiatric disorders.

SPECIAL GROUPS

Younger Patients

This section describes the treatment of adults—that is, those aged 18 or over. Those below the age of 18 are usually best treated in a specialised adolescent eating disorder unit, although this may not always be possible. Patients between the ages of 16 and 18 are frequently admitted to adult eating disorder units in the UK. In those below the age of 16, the effect of malnutrition on growth needs to be taken into account and developmental psychological issues assume even greater importance. Family therapy is likely to play a larger role in the treatment of this age group than in adults, and various models of integrating the family into treatment have been used, e.g. the use of family flats or partial hospitalisation. Another important aspect is the adolescent's educational needs.

Concern has been expressed about the disruption to a young person's life by admission, and indeed Gowers et al. (2000), in a naturalistic study, showed a poorer outcome in patients who had been admitted. However, as with adult patients, admission is necessary if there are life-threatening risks or if the family situation is profoundly detrimental. Medically, this is particularly so, as younger patients can dehydrate extremely rapidly and prepubescent cases have very low fat stores. In this age group, deterioration can therefore be sudden and severe.

Male Patients

The needs of male patients, who represent a significant minority of those with anorexia nervosa, require special consideration. Issues of self-care and body image may be significantly different in men, as may those related to sexual relationships.

Parents

In the relatively infrequent case of a patient who has children, the parental role needs to be acknowledged and the treatment programme may need to be modified accordingly. Depending on the circumstances, it may be appropriate to involve child and adolescent mental health services or social services in the treatment plan.

COMPULSORY TREATMENT

Provision for compulsory treatment of psychiatric disorders, including anorexia nervosa, varies from country to country. Due to the nature of anorexia nervosa, many patients have impaired insight despite an apparent understanding of the nature and consequences of the illness. This compromises their capacity to make an informed choice about treatment. Until relatively recently, there was uncertainty about the legality of compulsory treatment for anorexia nervosa in the UK but the position has recently been clarified by guidance from the Mental Health Act Commission:

> In certain situations, patients with severe anorexia nervosa whose health is seriously threatened by food refusal may be subject to detention in hospital and ... there are occasions when it is necessary to treat the self-imposed starvation to ensure the proper care of the patient . . . naso-gastric feeding can be a medical process, forming an integral part of the treatment for anorexia nervosa. (Mental Health Act Commission, 1997)

The European Court of Human Rights has ruled that compulsory feeding does not constitute inhuman or degrading treatment; it therefore appears to be consistent with the European Convention on Human Rights, which has been substantially incorporated into British law as the Human Rights Act (Radcliffes Mental Health Law Briefing, No. 34, 2000).

Although it is always preferable to engage ambivalent patients through the gradual development of a therapeutic alliance (Goldner et al., 1997), compulsory treatment may be appropriate for the small minority of patients who refuse treatment despite life-threatening risk. The case for compulsory treatment is strengthened by the evidence that apparently intractable cases can recover fully even after 10 years (Theander, 1992). However, involuntary patients appear to take longer to achieve weight gain than voluntary patients and have a mortality rate about five times higher (Ramsey et al., 1999).

THE INPATIENT TREATMENT OF BULIMIA NERVOSA

This is a complex area and differs from that of anorexia nervosa. As with anorexia nervosa, there are national variations: for example, inpatient treatment appears to be used more

Table 22.2 Recommended investigations on admission

Essential	Additional
Full blood count	Vitamin B12, folate levels
Urea and electrolytes	Erythrocyte transketolase (thiamin)
Glucose	Serum zinc
Serum calcium, magnesium, phosphate	DEXA scan
Serum proteins	Creatine kinase
Liver function tests	
ECG	

commonly in some other European countries than in the UK. Unlike anorexia nervosa, specific indications for admission have not been clearly defined but it is useful to follow the same pattern, i.e. admitting when there is a severe medical, psychiatric or social risk or a failure of outpatient treatment. The main aim of admission is usually to stabilise the patient's eating pattern and support her in giving up vomiting or laxative abuse. Treatment is likely to be of shorter duration than in anorexia nervosa and may be based more clearly on cognitive-behavioural principles (Tuschen & Bents, 1995).

However, the proportion of patients with bulimia nervosa who require admission is relatively small and is likely to consist mostly of those with the 'multi-impulsive' form of the disorder (Lacey & Evans, 1986; Lacey, 1995). These patients are difficult to treat and can be extremely disruptive to the ward routine. Admission to hospital can precipitate a deterioration, in which the patient's behaviour becomes more disturbed and problematic behaviours such as self-harm more frequent. Clinical experience suggests that such patients tend to respond poorly unless treated in specialised programmes, but there are few outcome data available.

PHYSICAL ASSESSMENT AND MONITORING

Patients require a detailed physical assessment on admission to hospital. This should include a full medical history and a thorough physical examination. A range of screening investigations should be carried out, including blood tests and an electrocardiogram (ECG) (American Psychiatric Association, 1993; Sharp & Freeman, 1993; Carney & Andersen, 1996; Winston, 2000). Detailed recommendations for routine investigations are given in Table 22.2; further investigations may be required, depending on the patient's condition. If significant abnormalities are detected, expert advice may be needed from an appropriate specialist.

NUTRITIONAL MANAGEMENT

Weight restoration in hospital is generally considered to be best carried out under the supervision of a dietician, due to the medical risks involved in refeeding at very low weights. Due to the fact that patients with anorexia nervosa have delayed gastric emptying (Robinson et al., 1995), small and frequent meals are preferable to infrequent but larger meals. Patients should have three meals a day and this may be supplemented with snacks in between. Vegetarianism and other special diets may be allowed, but dietary restrictions based on anorexic thinking should be challenged. An average rate of weight gain of 0.5–1.0 kg per week is generally considered appropriate; most patients require a daily calorie intake of around 2500 kcal per day to achieve this but a higher intake may occasionally be required, particularly in men. Recent preliminary research suggests that a minimum weight gain of 0.5 kg per week results in greater weight gain by the time of discharge from hospital than adoption of a higher minimum (Herzog et al., in press).

Weight gain may be relatively rapid during the first week or two of treatment as a result of rehydration and glycogen deposition; this can be minimised by starting refeeding gradually. A progressive increase in calorie intake in the early stages of treatment will also allow the patient time to adjust to the idea of weight gain; a rapid increase in weight early in treatment is likely to alarm her and jeopardise the therapeutic alliance. Conversely, calorie intake may need to be increased in the later stages of treatment as the basal metabolic rate increases (Salisbury et al., 1995) and the patient becomes more active.

Nasogastric Feeding

Artificial means of feeding such as nasogastric tubes should be used only as a last resort. In most cases, a combination of sensitive exploration of the patient's fears and skilled nursing is sufficient to enable the patient to begin to take food normally. The enforced use of enteral feeding may be very damaging to the therapeutic alliance and may reactivate previous experiences of physical or sexual abuse. However, there is a small number of patients who do require nasogastric feeding. These include those who are being treated against their will and those who have life-threatening medical complications. Enteral feeding should always be carried out under the supervision of a dietician. Parenteral feeding should be avoided if at all possible as the risk of medical complications is high and in most cases it is unlikely to have significant advantages over the enteral route.

Nutritional Supplements

The use of nutritional supplements in place of food is generally avoided as re-feeding patients with a normal diet usually provides adequate renutrition; it also encourages normalisation of eating patterns and a return of normal gastrointestinal function. However, a number of micronutrient deficiencies have been identified in anorexia nervosa (Hadigan et al., 2000; Casper et al., 1980; Philipp et al., 1988; Thibault & Roberge, 1987; Beaumont et al., 1981; Rock & Vasantharajan, 1995). Although the clinical significance of many of these deficiencies is at present unclear, it is probably wise to prescribe a multi-vitamin/multi-mineral supplement in oral form.

Deficiencies of zinc and thiamin (vitamin B1) may be of clinical significance (Lask et al., 1993; McClain et al., 1992; Humphries et al., 1989; Katz et al., 1987). It has been suggested that the use of zinc supplements increases the rate of weight gain (Birmingham et al., 1994), but this finding has yet to be confirmed and the routine use of zinc supplements cannot currently be recommended. A significant proportion of patients with anorexia nervosa are deficient in thiamin (Winston et al., 2000) and the increase in carbohydrate metabolism which occurs during refeeding may exhaust inadequate thiamin reserves. The use of prophylactic thiamin supplements may therefore be appropriate.

COMPLICATIONS OF REFEEDING

A number of complications may occur during the course of refeeding, some of them serious. Clinical experience suggests that many of the untoward consequences of refeeding can be minimised or avoided by starting the patient on relatively small amounts of food and increasing progressively.

Electrolyte Disturbances

A range of electrolyte disturbances can occur during refeeding and these are sometimes referred to collectively as the 'refeeding syndrome' (Solomon & Kirby, 1990). It should be borne in mind that serum measurements of electrolytes may be misleading as they may mask a significant total body deficit (Powers et al., 1995). The metabolic demands of refeeding can unmask hidden deficiencies and complex shifts of electrolytes between intracellular and extracellular compartments may further complicate the biochemical picture (Warren & Steinberg, 1979). The use of intravenous fluids may compound the problem.

Hypokalaemia, hypocalcaemia and hypomagnesaemia occur and hypokalaemia appears to be particularly common in those who purge (Palla & Litt, 1988; Koh et al., 1989; Greenfield et al., 1995; Connan et al., 2000). One of the most serious biochemical complications in the short term is hypophosphataemia. Malnourished patients are likely to be phosphate deficient and ingestion of large quantities of carbohydrate, such as occurs during refeeding, may result in a precipitate drop in serum phosphate levels (Fisher et al., 2000; Winston & Wells, 2002). It is essential to monitor the serum potassium, calcium, magnesium and phosphate closely, particularly during the first week or two of treatment. If significant biochemical deficiencies are identified, the patient may require supplementation, either orally or intravenously.

Gastrointestinal Dysfunction

Gastrointestinal symptoms are common. Delayed gastric emptying results in early satiety and sensations of abdominal fullness or bloating in a significant number of patients. Promotility agents such as metoclopramide and cisapride have been used to increase gastric emptying but cisapride has recently been withdrawn from use in the UK due to concerns about cardiac arrythmias. Metoclopramide may be used in a reduced dose of 5 mg t.d.s. but is often only of limited effectiveness.

Many patients complain of colicky abdominal pain. This rarely responds, in our experience, to antispasmodic drugs such as mebeverine and is generally best managed with explanation and reassurance. A shift of fluid into the gut after eating may cause symptoms such as nausea, diarrhoea and faintness, particularly if the patient is given large quantities of carbohydrate; limiting the amount of sodium in the diet may help. Constipation may be a problem in some patients, particularly those who have abused laxatives. Constipation can usually be managed adequately with a combination of sufficient fluid and dietary fibre together, if necessary, with stool softening agents or bulk laxatives. The use of stimulant laxatives is best avoided.

Refeeding Oedema

Some patients develop peripheral oedema in the early stages of refeeding; this appears to be particularly common in those who have abused laxatives or induced vomiting prior to admission. In severe cases, it can lead to rapid weight gain of several kilograms, which is alarming to the patient. Refeeding oedema should be distinguished from cardiac failure, of which other signs are absent. The aetiology of this problem is at present obscure. It may be related to dysregulation of the renin–angiotensin–aldosterone system but this hypothesis has yet to be substantiated (Jonas & Mickely, 1990; Mitchell et al., 1988; Fujita et al., 1991; Mizuno et al., 1992). There is some preliminary evidence that abnormal sensitivity to vasopressin may also be implicated (Kaye et al., 1983; Nishita et al., 1989). Hypoproteinaemia does not appear to be a major factor in most cases.

Some clinicians believe that the use of a low sodium diet during the early stages of treatment is helpful in preventing refeeding oedema; although rational, there is no research evidence to support this practice. The use of diuretics to treat refeeding oedema is probably best avoided, as the short-term benefits are likely to be offset by intravascular dehydration, which may perpetuate the problem. The most appropriate management in most cases is to reassure the patient that the oedema and weight gain are transient and that they will resolve as the body's homeostatic mechanisms return to normal. In cases where the use of diuretics is unavoidable, the most logical choice would appear to be the aldosterone antagonist spironolactone.

Cardiac Complications

Cardiac failure does occasionally occur and is most likely when patients are fed artificially, particularly parenterally. Patients with severe anorexia nervosa have evidence of impaired cardiac function and loss of left ventricular muscle (Gottdiener et al., 1978; Moodie & Salcedo, 1985; St John Sutton et al., 1985). In this situation, a large salt, water and protein load (such as occurs in parenteral feeding) can overload the circulation and result in cardiac failure. Other factors which may predispose to cardiac failure include hypophosphataemia and thiamin deficiency . Specific care should be taken when using antidepressants and antipsychotics, due to the already heightened risk of arrythmias and the need for lower therapeutic doses at low weight. As QT interval prolongation can occur at very low weights, drugs which prolong this interval should be avoided due to the risk of arrythmias.

PSYCHOTHERAPY

As discussed in other chapters, psychotherapy plays a central role in inpatient and day-patient treatment. Despite the fact that there is a more intense focus on refeeding in inpatient treatment, and the patients are generally of lower weight, psychotherapy should still form an integral part of the inpatient treatment programme. Effective treatment depends on weight gain and psychological change going hand in hand (Agras, 1987). Appropriate psychological interventions enable the patient to gain weight and, conversely, weight gain generates further psychological issues which need to be addressed in therapy. However, patients who are severely underweight have evidence of cognitive impairment (Szmukler et al., 1992; Kingston et al., 1996; Lauer et al., 1999) which may reduce their ability to make use of psychotherapy. Individual psychotherapy during the early stages of treatment may therefore need to be focused primarily on the development of a therapeutic alliance and exploration of the patient's anxieties about change. It should be emphasised to the patient that inpatient treatment is only the beginning of the therapeutic process and that therapy and psychological change are likely to continue for some considerable time after discharge from hospital.

There is at present little evidence on which to base recommendations about the type of therapy for adults with anorexia nervosa, although both psychoanalytic psychotherapy and family therapy appear to be beneficial in out-patients (Dare et al., 2001). Some units adopt a cognitive-behavioural approach (Andersen et al., 1997) whereas others use a predominantly psychodynamic model (Crisp et al., 1985). Therapy may consist of any combination of individual, group and systemic therapy. Family therapy appears to be particularly beneficial for younger patients (Russell et al., 1987; Dare et al., 1990; le Grange et al., 1992; Eisler et al., 1997, 2000).

Whatever approach is adopted, it is important that there is a coherent theoretical model underpinning all aspects of patient care. Ideally, inpatient psychotherapy should form part of a continuum with both pre-admission and post-discharge therapy. There are significant advantages in having the same therapist working with the patient throughout all three phases of treatment. Although the primary focus of treatment is on issues related to food, psychotherapy will need to focus on more complex underlying issues. In this sense, attaining a normal weight should not be seen as an endpoint but rather as the beginning of a new phase in the patient's life, which will bring new challenges and opportunities. It may be helpful to frame this transition as leaving the safety of anorexia nervosa and facing the psychological difficulties from which the illness had previously offered protection.

A group culture is likely to develop among the patients on the unit, which can be supportive or destructive depending on the group dynamics. Relationships within the patient group and between patients and staff may come to recapitulate aspects of family dynamics and transference issues are often prominent. Recovery from anorexia nervosa entails change for both the patient and those around her. The family or partner may require help to adapt to these changes and family or couple therapy should be available if required.

DRUG TREATMENT

Although a number of drugs have been used in the treatment of anorexia nervosa, the place of medication remains unclear at present. Cyproheptadine (Halmi et al., 1986) and pimozide (Vandereycken & Pierloot, 1982) have been shown to increase weight gain when compared to placebo. However, weight gain seems to be restricted to the short term and these drugs are not generally considered cost-effective methods of treatment. Some research suggests that fluoxetine might be effective in reducing the risk of relapse following inpatient treatment (Kaye et al., 1991); however, a more recent study indicates no benefit (Strober et al., 1997). There have also been case reports of olanzepine causing resolution of anorexic cognitions (Hansen, 1999; Jensen et al., 2000). These findings, however, are confounded by weight gain and the concurrent use of other therapies and thus only present a case for further clinical trials.

Symptomatically, medication may be used to reduce the patient's level of arousal and agitation; this can be achieved with standard anxiolytics. Moderate to severe depression occurs in a significant number of patients (Corcos et al., 2000) but often does not respond to antidepressants until weight is significantly restored. This is also generally true of OCD; as both disorders are often present together it is often useful to prescribe an antidepressant which is effective for both, such as a selective serotonin reuptake inhibitor. In general, if depressed mood persists after weight gain it should be managed in the conventional way. Patients with anorexia nervosa may be very sensitive to the effects of drugs and a reduced dose may be necessary; calculating the dose on the basis of body weight is generally best. Prescribers should also be aware of potential contra-indications arising from physical complications such as compromised bone marrow or liver function or an abnormal ECG.

DISCHARGE AND FOLLOW-UP

Preparation for discharge and subsequent follow-up treatment are essential if improvement is to be maintained and admission is to serve a purpose beyond weight gain alone (Crisp et al., 1991). Before discharge the patient should be helped to optimise her skills in managing her own illness; this may be addressed particularly during the maintenance phase of treatment. Concurrently, it is important to educate carers, such as the patient's family, in providing the appropriate level of support. This often needs to be negotiated between the therapist, patient and family in order to achieve an appropriate balance between patient responsibility and external support.

Once discharged, the patient should be offered appropriate help in managing her own eating, while continuing to work on underlying psychological issues. In practice, the type and intensity of care provided after discharge will depend on a number of factors including: the patient's level of insight and motivation, the extent of comorbidity and the availability of services in the area. Eating disorder day units and psychotherapeutic supported accommodation can offer a useful 'half-way house' between inpatient care and independent living. Another important area is planning for any possible relapses or 'crises' and the use of a 'crisis card' may be helpful (see Appendix 22.2).

OUTCOME OF INPATIENT TREATMENT

Although it is well established in clinical practice, data on the effectiveness of inpatient treatment are sparse. Published studies have yielded confusing results. Crisp et al. (1991) found no difference in one-, two- and five-year outcome in a randomised trial comparing four treatment modalities: inpatient treatment; a combination of individual and family therapy; group therapy; and assessment only. However, methodological difficulties reduce the impact of this study and leave the question still open (Gowers et al., 1988). A later study indicated significant differences in mortality between areas with and without specialised eating disorder services (Crisp et al., 1992).

As mentioned a naturalistic study found that adolescents treated as inpatients had a considerably worse outcome at 2–7 years than those who received outpatient treatment alone. The authors of this study argue that inpatient treatment may actually be damaging to treatment in the long term (Gowers et al., 2000). However, it should be noted that no adjustment was made for case mix and that these conclusions may not be applicable to adults. Furthermore, the results of Kächele's study in adults do not support the conclusions of Gowers et al. (Kächele, 1999). A recent review concluded that at present there is no clear evidence of any significant outcome difference between in- and outpatient treatment. (Meads et al., 2001).

Drop-out rates of patients with anorexia nervosa from inpatient treatment are high and concerning. Kahn and Pike (2001) found that one-third of inpatients dropped out early, the only predictors being length of illness and bulimic subtype. Early drop-out is a risk factor for relapse in the first year post-hospitalisation (Baran et al., 1995), as well as a predictor of the illness progessing to a severe, chronic course (Strober et al., 1997). Thus, more research is needed to identify predictors of drop-out and reduce the chance of relapse post-discharge.

CONCLUSION

Despite limited and sometimes conflicting research evidence, inpatient treatment has a well-established place in the treatment of severe anorexia nervosa and a less clearly defined place in that of bulimia nervosa. It is increasingly recognised that it must form part of a package of care that extends well beyond discharge from hospital. Further research is needed to determine the essential components of effective treatment, to clarify who is most likely to benefit from it and to establish whether some aspects may actually impede recovery.

Keypoints

- Inpatient treatment has progressively played a smaller role in the management of eating disorders.
- Admission should generally be limited to life-threatening situations, intolerable social situations, and failure of extensive community management.
- Management involves refeeding and psychotherapy and should be multidisciplinary.
- Clear evidence is still lacking for outcome measures compared to community treatment.
- Engagement in treatment and relapse prevention is essential in improving prognosis.

REFERENCES

Agras, W.S. (1987) *Eating Disorders; Management of Obesity, Bulimia and Anorexia Nervosa.* Elmsford, NY: Pergamon Press.
American Psychiatric Association (1993) Practice guideline for eating disorders. *Am. J. Psychiat.*, **150** (2), 207–228.
American Psychiatric Association (2000) Practice guideline for eating disorders. *Am. J. Psychiat.*, **157** (1 Supplement).
Andersen, A.E., Bowers, W. & Evans, K. (1997) In-patient treatment of anorexia nervosa. In D.M. Garner & P.E. Garfinkel (Eds), *Handbook of Treatment for Eating Disorders* (pp. 327–348). New York: Guilford Press.
Anonymous (1995) *Br. Med. J.*, **3111**, 635–636.

Audit Commission (1997) *Higher Purchase; Commissioning Specialised Services in the NHS*. London: Audit Commission.

Baran, S.A., Weltzin, T.E. & Kaye, W.H. (1995) Low discharge weight and outcome in anorexia nervosa. *Am. J. Psychiat.*, **152**, 1070–1072.

Berkman, J.M. (1930) Anorexia nervosa, anorexia, inanition and low metabolic rate. *Am. J. Med. Sci.*, **180**, 411.

Bhanji, S. & Mattingly, D. (1988) *Medical Aspects of Anorexia Nervosa*. London: Wright.

Birmingham, C.L., Goldner, E.M. & Bakan, R (1994) Controlled trial of zinc supplementation in anorexia nervosa. *Int. J. Eat. Disord.*, **15**, 251–255.

Bruch, H. (1970) Instinct and interpersonal experience. *Compr. Psychiat.*, **11**, 495–506.

Carney, C.P. & Andersen, A.E. (1996) Eating disorders: Guide to medical evaluation and complications. *Psychiat. Clin. N. Am.*, **19**, 657–679.

Casper, R.C., Kirschner, B., Sandstead, H.H., Jacob, R.A. & Davis, J.M. (1980) An evaluation of trace metals, vitamins and taste function in anorexia nervosa. *Am. J. Clin. Nutrit.*, **33**, 1801–1808.

Charcot, J.M. (1889) *Diseases of the Nervous System*. London: New Sydenham Society.

Corcos, M., Guilbaud, O., Speranza, M., Paterniti, S., Loas, G., Stephan, P. & Jeammet, P. (2000) Alexithymia and depression in eating disorders. *Psychiat. Res.*, **10** (93), 263–266.

Crisp, A.H., Callender, J.S., Halek, C. & Hsu, L.K.G. (1992) Long-term mortality in anorexia nervosa: A twenty-year follow-up of the St. George's and Aberdeen cohorts. *Br. J. Psychiat.*, **161**, 104–107.

Crisp, A.H., Norton, K.R.W., Gower, S., Halek, C., Bowyer, C., Yeldham, D., Levett, G. & Bhat, A. (1991) A controlled study of the effect of therapies aimed at adolescent and family psychopathology in anorexia nervosa. *Br. J. Psychiat.*, **159**, 325–333.

Crisp, A.H., Norton, K.R.W., Jurczak, S., Bowyer, C. & Duncan, S. (1985) A treatment approach to anorexia nervosa—25 years on. *J. Psychiat. Res.*, **19**, 399–404.

Dally, P.J. & Sargant, W. (1960) Treatment and outcome of anorexia nervosa. *Br. Med. J.*, **2**, 793.

Dare, C., Eisler, I., Russell, G.F.M. & Szmukler, G.I. (1990) Family therapy for anorexia nervosa: Implications from the results of a controlled trial of family and individual therapy. *J. Marital Family Ther.*, **16**, 39–57.

Dare, C., Eisler, I., Russell, G., Treasure, J. & Dodge, L. (2001) Psychological therapies for adults with anorexia nervosa: Randomised controlled trial of out-patient treatments. *Br. J. Psychiat.*, **178**, 216–221.

Eckert, E.D., Goldberg, S.C., Halmi, K.A., Casper, R.C. & Davis, J.M. (1979) Behaviour therapy in anorexia nervosa. *Br. J. Psychiat.*, **134**, 55–59.

Eisler, I., Dare, C., Russell, G.F.M., Szmukler, G.I., le Grange, D. & Dodge, E. (1997) Family and individual therapy in anorexia nervosa: A 5 year follow-up. *Arch. Gen. Psychiat.*, **54**, 1025–1030.

Eisler, I., Dare, C., Hodes, M., Russell, G., Dodge, E. & le Grange, D. (2000) Family therapy for adolescent anorexia nervosa: The resuts of a controlled comparison of two family interventions. *J. Child Psychol. Psychiat.*, **41**, 727–736.

Ferguson, C.P., La Via, M.C., Crossan, P.J. & Kaye, W.H. (1999) Are serotonin reuptake inhibitors effective in underweight anorexia nervosa? *Int. J. Eat. Disord.*, **25**, 11–17.

Fisher, M., Simpser, E. & Schneider, M. (2000) Hypophosphatemia secondary to oral refeeding in anorexia nervosa. *Int. J. Eat. Disord.*, **28**, 181–187.

Garfinkel, P.E., Kline, S.A. & Stancer, H.C. (1973) Treatment of anorexia nervosa using operant conditioning techniques. *J. Nervous Mental Disord.*, **157**, 428–433.

George, L. (1997) The psychological characteristics of patients suffering from anorexia nervosa and the nurse's role in creating a therapeutic relationship. *J. Adv. Nursing*, **26**, 899–908.

Goldner, E.M., Birmingham, C.L. & Smye, V. (1997) Addressing treatment refusal in anorexia nervosa: Clinical, ethical, and legal considerations. In D. Garner & P. Garfinkel (Eds), *Handbook of Treatment for Eating Disorders* (2nd edn; pp. 450–461). New York: Guilford Press.

Gottdiener, J.S., Gross, H.A., Henry, W.L., Borer, J.S. & Ebert, M.H. (1978) Effects of self-induced starvation on cardiac size and function in anorexia nervosa. *Circulation*, **58**, 425–433.

Gowers, S.G., Weetman, J., Shore, A. et al. (2000) Impact of hospitalisation on the outcome of adolescent anorexia nervosa. *Br. J. Psychiat.*, **176**, 138–141.

Gowers, S., Norton, K., Yeldham, K., Bowger, C., Levett, G., Heavey, A., Bhat, A. & Crisp, A. (1988) The St. George's prospective treatment study of anorexia nervosa: A discussion of methodological problems. *Int. J. Eat. Disord.*, **8**, 445–454.

Greenfield, D., Mickley, D., Quinlan, D.M. & Roloff, P. (1995) Hypokalemia in outpatients with eating disorders. *Am. J. Psychiat.*, **152**, 60–63.

Gull, W.W. (1874) Anorexia nervosa (apepsia hysterica, anorexia hysterica). *Trans. Clin. Soc. Lond.*, **7**, 22.

Hadigan, C.M., Anderson, E.J., Miller, K.K., Hubbard, J.L., Herzog, D.B., Halmi, K.A., Eckert, E., LaDu, T.J. et al. (1986) Anorexia nervosa. Treatment efficacy of cyproheptadine and amitriptyline. *Arch. Gen. Psychiat.*, **43**, 177–181.

Hansen, L. (1999) Olanzepine in the treatment of anorexia nervosa (letter). *Br. J. Psychiat.*, **175**, 592.

Herzog, T., Zeeck, A., Hartmann, A. & Nickel, T. (in press) Lower targets for weekly weight gain lead to better results in inpatient treatment of anorexia nervosa. *Eur. Eat. Disord. Rev.*

Howard, W.T., Evans, K.K., Quintero-Howard, C.V., Bowers, W.A. & Andersen, A.E. (1999) Predictors of success or failure of transition to day hospital treatment for in-patients with anorexia nervosa. *Am. J. Psychiat.*, **156**, 1697–702.

Humphries, L., Vivian, B., Stuart, M. & McClain, C.J. (1989) Zinc deficiency and eating disorders. *J. Clin. Psychiat.*, **50** (12), 456–459.

Jensen, V.S., Mejlhede et al. (2000) Anorexia nervosa: Treatment with olanzepine (letter). *Br. J. Psychiat.*, **177**, 87.

Kächele, H. for the study group MZ-ESS. (1999) Eine multizentrische Studie zu Aufwand und Erfolg bei psychodynamischer Therapie von Eßstörungen. *Psychother. Med. Psychol.*, 49, 100–108.

Kaplan, A.S. & Olmstead, M.P. (1997) Partial hospitalisation. In D.M. Garner & P.E. Garfinkel (Eds), *Handbook of Treatment of Eating Disorders* (2nd edn; pp. 354–360). New York: Guilford, Press.

Kahn, C. & Pike, K.M. (2001) In search of predictors of dropout from inpatient treatment for anorexia nervosa. *Int. J. Eat. Disord.*, **30**, 237–244.

Katz, R.L, Keen, C.L., Litt, I.F., Hurley, L.S., Kellams-Harrison, K.M. & Glader, L.J. (1987) Zinc deficiency in anorexia nervosa. *J. Adolesc. Health Care*, **8** (5), 400–406.

Kaye, W.H., Gendall, K. & Kye, C. (1998) The role of the central nervous system in the psychoneuroendocrine disturbances of anorexia and bulimia nervosa. *Psychiat. Clin. N. Am.*, **21**, 381–396.

Kaye, W., Weltzin, T.E., Hsu, L.G. & Bulik, C.M. (1991) An open trial of fluoxetine in patients with anorexia nervosa. *J. Clin. Psychiat.*, **52** (11), 464–471.

Kingston, K., Szmukler, G., Andrewes, D., Tress, B. & Desmond, P. (1996) Neuropsychological and structural brain changes in anorexia nervosa before and after refeeding. *Psychol. Med.*, **26**, 15–28.

Klibanski, A. & Grinspoon, S.K. (2000) Assessment of macronutrient and micronutrient intake in women with anorexia nervosa. *Int. J. Eat. Disord.*, **28**, 284–292.

Koh, E., Onishi, T., Morimoto, S, Imanaka, S., Nakagawa, H. & Ogihara, T. (1989) Clinical evaluation of hypokalemia in anorexia nervosa. *Japan. J. Med.*, **28** (6), 692–696.

Lacey, J.H. & Evans, C.D.H. (1986) The impulsivist: A multi-impulsive personality disorder. *Br. J. Addict.*, **81**, 641–649.

Lacey, J.H. (1995) In-patient treatment of multi-impulsive bulimia nervosa. In K.D. Brownell & C.G. Fairburn (Eds), *Eating Disorders and Obesity*. New York: Guilford Press.

Lasègue, C. (1873) De l'anorixie hysterique. *Arch. Gen. de Med.*, **21** (April), 385–403.

Lask, B., Fosson, A., Rolfe, U. & Thomas, S. (1993) Zinc deficiency and childhood-onset anorexia nervosa. *J. Clin. Psychiat.*, **54** (2), 63–66.

Lauer, C.J., Gorzewskie, B., Gerlinghoff, M., Backmund, H. & Zihl, J. (1999) Neuropsychological assessments before and after treatment in patients with anorexia nervosa and bulimia nervosa. *J. Psychiat. Res.*, **33** (2), 129–138.

Le Grange, D., Eisler, I., Dare, C. & Russell, G.F.M. (1992) Evaluation of family therapy in anorexia nervosa: A pilot study. *Int. J. Eat. Disord.*, **12**, 347–357.

Meads, C., Gold, L. & Burls, A. (2001) How effective is outpatient care compared to inpatient care for thetreatment of anorexia nervosa? A systematic review. [Journal Article] *Eur. Eat. Disord. Rev.*, **9**, 229–241.

Marcé, L.V. (1860) Note sur une forme de délire hypochondriaque consécutive aux dyspepsies et caractérisée principalement par le refus d'aliments. *Annales Médico-Psychologiques*, **6**, 15–28.

McClain, C.J., Stuart, M.A, Vivian, B., McClain, M., Talwalker, R., Snelling, L. & Humphries, L. (1992) Zinc status before and after zinc supplementation of eating disorder patients. *J. Am. Coll. Nutrit.*, **11** (6), 694–700.

Moodie, D.S. & Salcedo, E. (1985) Cardiac function in adolescents and young adults with anorexia nervosa. *J. Adolesc. Health Care*, **4**, 9–14.

Morgan, H.G., Purgold, J. & Welbourne, J. (1983) Management and outcome in anorexia nervosa: A standardised prognostic study. *Br. J. Psychiat.*, **143**, 282–287.

Nishita, J.K., Ellinwood, E.H., Rockwell, W.J.K. et al. (1989) Abnormalities in the response of arginine vasopressin during hypertonic saline infusion in patients with eating disorders. *Biol. Psychiat.*, **26**, 73–86.

Palla, B. & Litt, I.F. (1988) Medical complications of eating disorders in adolescents. *Pediatrics*, **81** (5), 613–623.

Philipp, E., Pirke, K.-M., Seidl, M., Tuschl, R.J., Fichter, M.M., Eckert, M. & Wolfram, G. (1988) Vitamin status in patients with anorexia nervosa and bulimia nervosa. *Int. J. Eat. Disord.*, **8**, 209–218.

Piran, N. & Kaplan, A.S. (Eds) (1990) *A Day Hospital Treatment Programme for Anorexia Nervosa and Bulimia Nervosa*. New York: Brunner/ Mazel.

Radcliffes Mental Health Law, Briefing No. 34 (2000) London: Radcliffes Solicitors.

Ramsey, R., Ward, A., Treasure, J. & Russell, G.F.M. (1999) Compulsory treatment in anorexia nervosa. *Br. J. Psychiat.*, **175**, 147–153.

Reifenstein, E.C. (1946) Psychogenic or 'hypothalamic' amenorrhea. *Med. Clin. N. Am.*, **30**, 1103.

Rock, C.L. & Vasantharajan, S. (1995) Vitamin status of eating disorder patients: relationship to clinical indices and effect of treatment. *Int. J. Eat. Disord.*, **18**, 257–262.

Russell, G.F.M. (1981) Comment: The current treatment of anorexia nervosa. *Br. J. Psychiat.*, **138**, 164–166.

Russell, G.F.M., Szmukler, G.I., Dare, C. & Eisler, I. (1987) An evaluation of family therapy in anorexia nervosa and bulimia nervosa. *Arch. Gen. Psychiat.*, **44**, 1047–1056.

Salisbury, J.J., Levine, A.S., Crow, S.J. & Mitchell, J.E. (1995) Refeeding, metabolic rate and weight gain in anorexia nervosa: A review. *Int. J. Eat. Disord.*, **17** (4), 337–345.

St John Sutton, M.G., Plappert, T, Crosby, L., Douglas, P., Mullen, J. & Reichek, N. (1985) Effects of reduced left ventricular mass on chamber architecture, load and function: A study of anorexia nervosa. *Circulation*, **72**, 991–1000.

Sharp, C.W. & Freeman, C.P.L. (1993) The medical complications of anorexia nervosa. *Br. J. Psychiat.*, **163**, 452–462.

Strober, M., Freeman, R., DeAntonio, M. et al. (1997) Does adjunctive fluoxetine influence the post-hospital course of restrictor-type anorexia nervosa? A 24-month prospective, longitudinal followup and comparison with historical controls. *Psychopharmacol. Bull.*, **33**, 425–431.

Strober, M., Freeman, R. & Morrell. (1997) The long-term course of severe anorexia nervosa in adolescents: Survival analysis of recovery, relapse and outcome predictors over 10–15 years in a prospective study. *Int. J. Eat. Disord.*, **22**, 339–360.

Szmukler, G.I., Andrewes, D., Kingston, K., Chen, L., Stargatt, R. & Stanley, R. (1992) Neuropsychological impairment in anorexia nervosa before and after refeeding. *J. Clin. Exp. Neuropsychol.*, **14**, 347–352.

Theander, S. (1992) Chronicity in anorexia nervosa: Results from the Swedish long-term study. In W. Herzog, H.-C. Deter & W. Vandereycken (Eds), *The Course of Eating Disorders*, (pp. 214–227). Berlin: Springer Verlag.

Touyz, S.W., Beumont, P.J.V., Glaun, D., Phillips, T. & Cowie, I. (1984) A comparison of lenient and strict operant conditioning programmes in refeeding patients with anorexia nervosa. *Br. J. Psychiat.*, **144**, 517–520.

Tuschen, B. & Bents, H. (1995) Intensive brief in-patient treatment of bulimia nervosa. In K.D. Brownell & C.G. Fairburn (Eds), *Eating Disorders and Obesity*. New York: Guilford Press.

Vandereycken, W. & Pierloot, R. (1982) Pimozide combined with behaviour therapy in the short-term treatment of anorexia nervosa. A double-blind placebo-controlled cross-over study. *Acta Psychiat. Scand.*, **66**, 445–50.

Ward, A., Ramsay, R. & Treasure, J. (2000) Attachment research in eating disorders. *Br. J. Med. Psychol.*, **73** (1), 35–51.

Warren, S.E. & Steinberg, S.M. (1979) Acid-base and electrolyte disturbances in anorexia nervosa. *Am. J. Psychiat.*, **136** (4A), 415–418.

Winston, A.P. (2000) Physical assessment of the eating disordered patient. *Eur. Eat. Disord. Rev.*, **8**, 188–191.

Winston, A.P. & Wells, F.E. (2002) Hypophosphataemia following self-treatment for anorexia nervosa. *Int. J. Eat. Disord.*, **32** (2), 245–8.

Winston, A.P., Jamieson, C.P., Madira, W., Gatward, N.M., Palmer, R.L. (2000) Prevalence of thiamin deficiency in anorexia nervosa. *Int. J. Eat. Dis*, **28** (4), 451–454.

CHAPTER 23

Eating Disorders in Males

Manfred Fichter

*Department of Psychiatry, University of Munich and Klinik Roseneck,
Prien, Germany*

and

Heidelinde Krenn

Department of Psychiatry, University of Munich, Germany

SUMMARY

This chapter considers differences in certain aspects of eating disorders in males and females:

- There is a much lower prevalence of eating disorders in males than in females.
- Eating disorder symptomatology has been found to be quite similar in males and females.
- There are differences in age at onset, premorbid weight, body image and dieting, athletic pursuits and substance abuse/dependence.
- Males and females have both shown concern with sex role identity.
- Psychopathology is on average less severe in male as compared to female cases with an eating disorder.

INTRODUCTION

- Historical accounts.
- Prevalence of eating disorders in males.
- Methodological issues.

Anorexia and bulimia nervosa are rare diseases in males, so why is the analysis of male cases of importance to theories of eating disorders? The study of male cases opens intriguing opportunities to enhance our knowledge on aetiology and pathophysiology of eating disorders in general. Very few disorders in psychiatry or in general medicine show such a skewed gender distribution as anorexic and bulimic eating disorders. This raises a number of questions: Why are there not more males with eating disorders? How frequently are men with an eating disorder seen in other cultures? What is unusual about those males who, against all odds, develop an eating disorder? How do these males compare to females in

Handbook of Eating Disorders. Edited by J. Treasure, U. Schmidt and E. van Furth.

psychopathology, comorbidity, treatment and course? Studying eating-disordered males may shed light on our understanding of eating disorders from a different angle. An important point is that eating disorders *do occur* in males, although not frequently. Males differ biologically from females and puberty in males generally occurs later than in females. Thus, genetic or biological gender differences may potentially account for an unusual gender distribution in eating disorders. On the other hand, there are a number of differences between boys and girls in their socialization process as well as in values and ideals, which expose them to different kinds of social expectations and pressures.

Looking at the *history* of publications about eating disorders, the first English publication by Richard Morton was published in 1694, five years after his book had appeared in Latin. He referred to a condition for which he gave case examples as 'a nervous consumption' caused by 'sadness and anxious cares'. His first case describes a girl, the second a boy with anorexia nervosa (AN). In the eighteenth century there were two accounts of male cases, one by Robert Whytt in 1764, who described a 14-year-old anorexic boy, and one by Robert Willan (1790), who described the death of a young man who had fasted for 78 days. These three old accounts of anorexia nervosa in males were all observed in Great Britain. Later William Gull (1874) presented an important paper, in which he renamed the former 'apepsia hysterica' into 'anorexia nervosa' to make clear that the disorder does not exclusively occur in females. Then, for many decades the topic of eating disorders in males was largely neglected, partially because it did not fit into certain psychoanalytic theories such as the hypotheses of the 'origin of anorexia nervosa through oral impregnation'. Following the 1970s some case reports (Gwirtsman et al., 1984; Robinson & Holden, 1986) or studies with small samples were published. Then Burns and Crisp (1984, 1985) and Fichter and Daser (1987) published on somewhat larger groups of anorexic males. In 1990 a book edited by Andersen on 'males with eating disorders' was published and in 1997 Carlat et al. published a report on 135 eating-disordered male patients. Thus, while first reports on the subject were published centuries ago our wider and more detailed knowledge about eating disorders in males is quite recent.

There are actually very limited epidemiological data from community samples as to the prevalence of *anorexia nervosa* (AN) in male subjects. The large epidemiological study by Garfinkel et al. (1995) focused on bulimic individuals; limited data were reported on bulimic males and no data on anorexic individuals. Götestam and Agras (1995) also excluded males from their general population-based epidemiological study of eating disorders in Norway. Even today, most psychotherapy or psychopharmacology treatment studies exclude males for reasons of sample homogeneity. Males typically accounted for only 5–10% of anorexia nervosa cases (Burns & Crisp, 1985). One reason for neglecting anorexia nervosa in males, especially in the 1960s and 1970s, was that amenorrhoea was a necessary condition for the diagnosis of this disorder.

Carlat and Camargo (1991) have examined 24 epidemiological studies on the prevalence of *bulimia nervosa* (BN) in males and conclude that bulimia affects approximately 0.2% of adolescent boys and young adult men and that males account for 10–15% of all bulimic subjects identified in community-based studies. However, the majority of the studies they cite used questionnaires only for case identification and the samples frequently consisted of high school or college students. In the studies based on interview data on bulimia (nervosa) the prevalence rates were as follows: Schotte and Stunkard (1987) reported a prevalence for male BN of 0.1% (ratio 1 : 7.0) in college students; Drewnowski et al. (1988) reported a prevalence of 0.2% (ratio 1 : 5.0) in college students; King (1989) reported a prevalence of

0.5% (ratio 1 : 2.2) in general practice-patients aged 16–35. In a large Canadian community sample of 8116 males and females aged <65 years, Garfinkel et al. (1995) used the CIDI-interview for case identification and reported a prevalence rate for BN according to DSM-III-R of 1.1% for female and 0.1% for male subjects; of those who fulfilled criteria for BN, 8.3% were men (ratio 1 : 11). Kinzl et al. (1999) assessed a community sample of 1000 Austrian men and reported a prevalence of 0.8% for *binge eating disorder* (BED) and 4.2% for partial BED syndrom (fewer and smaller binges); they concluded that males may carry a risk of developing subthreshold eating disorders and that high body weight may be an indicator of increased bingeing pathology. Using self-report questionnaires, Taraldsen et al. (1996) examined lifetime and point prevalence of AN, BN, BED and eating disorders not otherwise specified (EDNOS) in male psychiatric outpatients in Norway. The lifetime prevalence in males was 0% for AN, 10.7% for BN, 6.7% for BED and 4% for EDNOS. The authors found a considerable discrepancy between staff-reported and self-reported prevalences of eating disorders. This means that either patients under-reported symptoms of disordered eating towards their therapist, or staff members were not able to identify certain symptoms as being related to an eating disorder. Hence, there might be a considerable number of unrecorded cases, which never present for treatment and, even if they do, are not identified as eating disordered. The prevalence rates for BN, BED and EDNOS in this study are probably overestimated as a result of the self-report questionnaire procedure. There are some indications that the percentage of *treated* eating-disordered men has increased over the past decades. Braun et al. (1999) reported that the percentage of all first inpatient admissions of eating-disordered male patients at the New York Presbyterian Hospital at Westchester County increased from about 2% to 9% between 1984 and 1997. According to the authors there appears to be a high threshold for men to seek treatment 'for a typical women's disease' but this threshold may have come down over time because of hightened awareness in the public, media publications and higher levels of awareness by health care professionals.

In conclusion, the percentage of male cases in eating disorders appears to be smallest in AN (8%), somewhat higher in BN (roughly 15%) and possibly around 20% for BED.

Many studies on eating disorders in males suffer from *methodological shortcomings*. As Striegel-Moore et al. (1999b, p. 410) point out, 'this area of research is characterized by an almost complete lack of methodological consistency across research studies'. Male samples are often too small to be representative due to low prevalence rates and a higher threshold to report disordered eating. Prospective designs are difficult to realize. Moreover, studies often use mixed samples of AN, BN, BED, EDNOS patients or mixed samples of in- and outpatients. Data on distinct DSM-IV subgroups like 'AN-restricting type' vs 'AN-binge eating/purging-type' and 'BN-purging type' vs 'BN-non-purging type' are scarce. Binge eating disorder, as subtyped in the DSM-IV appendix, is rarely ever mentioned with regards to males. Methods of case detection vary considerably across studies. When psychiatric inpatients are screened for eating disorders, male cases are not uncommon. However, these data cannot be generalized to community samples (Carlat et al., 1997). In addition, most studies use self-report questionnaires only for case identification, and this approach is less reliable than using structured interviews. In studies using a two-stage-design for case identification, results depend largely on the positive predictive power (PPP) of the screening instrument (Fairburn & Beglin, 1990). In addition, most instruments were designed for and evaluated on female samples; therefore core psychological issues of eating-disordered men may not be addressed by these instruments.

CLINICAL PRESENTATION

- Eating disorder symptomatology in males
- Psychiatric comorbidity in eating-disordered males
- Endocrinological findings.

Several authors concur on the central finding that *eating disorder symptomatology* in the clinical presentation of AN and BN is quite similar for males and females (Beumont et al., 1972; Burns & Crisp, 1985; Crisp et al., 1986; Margo, 1987; Sharp et al., 1994; Olivardia et al., 1995; Carlat et al., 1997; Braun et al., 1999; Woodside et al., 2001). There are, however, some areas of symptomatology where eating-disordered males seem to differ from their female counterparts. Several groups reported an increased tendency in *anorexic* males to exercise excessively (Fichter & Daser, 1987; Oyebode et al., 1988; Sharp et al., 1994). Physical hyperactivity was found more commonly among male as compared to female anorexics (Burns & Crisp, 1985). A less frequent laxative and diet pill use in males has been reported by Fichter and Daser (1987), Sharp et al. (1994) and Braun et al. (1999). In bulimic males Mitchell and Goff (1984) found a similar tendency and most males had marked weight fluctuations. Garfinkel et al. (1995) found the following compensatory behaviours to a lesser extent in bulimic males: strict dieting, use of diuretics, laxatives or enemas, self-induced vomiting, fasting and taking diet pills. Carlat and Camargo (1991) in their review conclude that "male bulimic subjects are less troubled by their binge eating and are less concerned with strict weight control than are their female counterparts" (p. 838). This was also confirmed by Woodside and Kaplan (1994), who found lower scores on the Eating Disorders Inventory (EDI) and on the Eating Attitudes Test (EAT) for the subscales 'dieting' and 'oral control' in anorexic and bulimic males ($n = 15$). There are very few studies comparing eating disorder symptoms in male and female BED patients. Tanofsky et al. (1997) reported that there are very few differences between BED in males and females concerning the eating disorder symptomatology.

High *comorbidity rates* in eating disorders have been found across genders, especially for mood disorders, personality disorders and substance use disorders. Striegel-Moore et al. (1999a) used an administrative data set combining data bases of 155 Veterans Affairs medical centers in the USA. On the basis of routine clinical diagnoses, 0.30% of the female veterans and 0.02% of the male veterans were diagnosed with a current ICD-9-CM eating disorder. Ninety-two percent of the male veterans and 95% of the female veterans carried a comorbid psychiatric diagnosis. In males the eating disorder diagnosis was frequently given not as a primary, but as a secondary diagnosis. Men with eating disorders were found to have high rates of comorbid organic mental, schizophrenic/psychotic, substance use and mood disorders. Although the sample was very large, data are not representative for the community. The ICD-9 diagnostic criteria were vague and there were limitations in the method of case identification.

In a large study on 135 males suffering from AN, BN or EDNOS, Carlat et al. (1997) found equally high rates of major depression, anxiety disorders, personality disorders and especially elevated rates of substance abuse among bulimic males. High rates of mood disorder and substance abuse among first-degree family members of males suffering from eating disorders are also common (Carlat et al., 1997). Thirty-six percent of eating disordered college men in Olivardia et al.'s (1995) study reported to have at least one first-degree relative with major depression. Nevertheless, this figure was significantly lower than that reported by females (67%). The few existing results on comorbidity in males with BED suggest higher rates of axis-I psychopathology and substance dependence in males compared to females (Tanofsky et al., 1997).

Endocrinological changes or dysfunctions of the pituitary gonadal axis in female AN patients are manifested clinically through the cessation of menstruation. Several attempts have been made to find an analogous disturbance in males afflicted by the condition. Beumont et al. (1972) reported testosterone levels far below normal in emaciated males with AN; this finding indicates a diminution of testicular function and total gonadotropic activity. After refeeding, these hormonal abnormalities did not disappear entirely, which led the authors to the conclusion that these endocrinological disturbances may only partly be due to malnutrition. Pirke et al. (1979) and Fichter (1985, pp. 118ff) reported on 'the 24-hour secretion pattern of the pituitary luteinizing hormon (LH) in 18 anorexia nervosa patients'. One of these patients was an 18-year-old male. At 73% of ideal body weight (IBW) his secretion pattern was pubertal; after some weight gain (90% of IBW) his LH secretion pattern was infantile and after further weight increase to 94% IBW the LH secretion pattern became pubertal. These data do not contradict, but also do not confirm the overwhelmingly clear findings for the 17 remaining female patients whose endocrine secretion was studied during refeeding. They showed an infantile pattern upon admission with low body weight; with weight gain their patterns progressed to pubertal and, in some cases to adult LH secretion levels. Generally the literature leads to the conclusion that LH and FSH secretion, as well as gonadal hormone secretion, are suppressed during starvation and restored with adequate weight gain. This restitution, however, occurs at a slower rate than that of the hypothalamo–pituitary–adrenal axis. Other data (Fichter et al., 1990) suggest that bingeing and purgeing at normal body weight may also affect hormonal secretion, including gonadotropins and gonadal hormons. Gwirtsman et al. (1984) reported on three cases of men with BN and found at least one neuroendocrine abnormality in each case. According to Andersen (1995) testosterone levels rise during weight restoration in about 80–90% of male patients, with the remaining 10–20% still showing signs of testicular abnormalities after weight restoration. The question whether these abnormalities have aetiological relevance or whether they are merely a consequence of dieting and/or purgeing has to be examined further. Excessive motor activity has also been shown to reduce testosterone levels (Beumont, 1972), resulting in decreased libido and sexual drive. Many anorexic men do not complain about this, but rather feel relieved (Crisp & Burns, 1983; Fichter & Daser, 1987). The constant pattern of hormonal secretion in males, in contrast to the cyclic pattern in women, has been discussed as a possible protective factor for males in respect to eating disorders; however, research results are contradictory (Carlat & Camargo, 1991).

In the course of DSM and ICD revisions, there has been quite a debate concerning the diagnostic relevance of endocrine disturbances. Comparison of amenorrhoeal and nonamenorrhoeal women indicated that amenorrhoea may not be a useful criterion for diagnosing AN (Cachelin & Maher, 1998).

RISK FACTORS

- Age at onset
- Premorbid weight

- Body image and dieting
- Occupations and athletic pursuit
- Psychosexual development and sex-role-identity
- Personality traits
- Substance- and alcohol abuse

Several risk factors for young men to develop an eating disorder have been discussed in the literature.

Age at Onset

Carlat and Camargo (1991) in their review on BN in males found that the average age at onset of the disorder was higher in males (18–26 years) than in females (15–18 years). Anorexic males in Sharp et al.'s (1994) study on 24 subjects also had a higher mean age at onset (18.6 years) than their female counterparts. The 51 males in Braun et al.'s study (1999) had a significantly higher age at onset of their eating disorder (20.56 years) compared to females in the study (17.15 years). Striegel-Moore et al.'s (1999a,b) results also reached statistical significance and point in the same direction. Different results were, however, reported by Olivardia et al. (1995); their 25 men with an eating disorder had a mean age of 14.7 years at onset of the disorder.

One biological difference between boys and girls concerns the onset of puberty. Girls reach puberty about two years earlier than boys. The resulting discrepancy between biological and psychological maturity, together with increasing body dissatisfaction, may put girls (but also to a lesser extent boys) at higher risk for developing an eating disorder during these years (Eller, 1993). Along with the changes of puberty girls have a higher percentage of body fat in their mid-teens (Andersen, 1992) and a lower resting metabolic rate in comparison to boys (Striegel-Moore et al., 1986). Taken together these factors may predispose girls for dieting and purging. Age at onset as a predictor of outcome has yielded contradictory results in studies with female samples and is often confounded with other variables like duration of illness (Fichter & Quadflieg, 1995).

Premorbid Weight

Studies repeatedly found overweight or obesity to be a precursor of eating disorders in males. Bulimic men in Carlat et al.'s (1997) sample were significantly more likely to report premorbid obesity and showed a higher weight at study onset compared to men with AN or EDNOS. Fifty-three percent of subjects in this study also reported a parental history of overweight, but again only in bulimic males did this finding reach statistical significance. More than 60% of males examined by Andersen (1992) had experienced obesity in childhood or adolescence. Along with obesity in childhood and adolescence, eating-disordered males quite frequently report teasing by peers. Sixty-four percent of bulimic males in the study of Herzog et al. (1984) had a history of being overweight compared to 37% of females, a difference that did not reach statistical significance. Crisp et al. (1986) reported that their anorexic males were significantly more overweight at onset of the disorder. Sharp et al.

(1994) also noted a tendency towards obesity prior to the onset of AN in 24 anorexic males, with a premorbid mean weight of 114.7% of matched population mean weight.

Body Image, Body Dissatisfaction and Dieting

Dieting is closely related to premorbid obesity and body dissatisfaction and seems to be a logical consequence of the two. According to Andersen (1995, p. 178) 'most females who diet *feel* fat, while slightly more than half of the males who diet *are* medically obese to some degree'. In contrast to their female counterparts young men do not regard low body weight as the primary goal of their dieting efforts: they rather want to build up lean muscle mass and attain a muscular body (Andersen, 1995). Eating disorders in both genders manifest in cultural settings that value slimness. However, the sociocultural pressures to be thin in industrialized countries appear to be higher for women than for men (Garner et al., 1980). Thus, Andersen and DiDomenico (1992) hypothesized that the number of dieting-concerned advertisements should be higher in magazines for young women (age 18–24) than for men of the same age group. They found a ratio of 10:1 advertisements addressed to women and men respectively, matching almost exactly the ratio of male to female cases of anorexia and bulimia nervosa.

Pope et al. (1999) examined the hypothesis that cultural expectations of body ideal in males might be mirrored in toys used in the USA over the last 30 years. They found that male action toys like 'GI Joe' or 'Star Wars' figures have grown more muscular and increased in sharp muscle definition over these years. Using methods of classical allometry the authors found body shapes that would far exceed the physique of any bodybuilder in the real world. It is not clear whether these results reflect changing ideals of male body shape in society or if toys and newly emerging beauty and health magazines for men simply set trends.

In order to examine weight-losing and weight-gaining ambitions among adolescent girls and boys Rosen and Gross (1987) examined 1.373 high school students. Whereas girls were four times more likely than boys to be involved in weight reduction activities like dieting and exercise, boys were three times more likely than girls to be involved in efforts at gaining weight. All these results show that there exists a close link in western societies between thinness or ectomorphic body shape and femininity, whereas masculinity on the other hand is associated with mesomorphic, muscular body shapes (Striegel-Moore et al., 1986; Mickalide, 1990). Methods of weight control, like dieting, are therefore a means for women to reach their ideal, whereas for some men in fact the contrary holds true (Carlat & Camargo, 1991).

Research into transcultural differences in body dissatisfaction in males to date is scarce. Findings by Mangweth et al. (1997) strongly suggest that such differences exist. They found that dissatisfaction with body image was consistently stronger in American compared to Austrian men. Although the mean BMI was slightly higher in Austrian subjects, more Americans reported that they felt 'fat' and this held true not only for eating-disordered males but also for controls.

Regarding outcome, Burns and Crisp (1985) did not find specific dietary habits to be strongly predictive of outcome in 27 anorexic males at a minimum of two years after initial assessment. Contrary to the females, there was a weak trend for the absence of bulimic symptoms to be related to poor outcome in the male sample. The authors interpreted this somewhat paradoxical finding as an effect of a subgroup of severely ill abstainers in their male sample.

Occupations and Athletic Pursuit

To examine the question whether eating-disordered men are over-represented in certain 'high-risk' jobs, Carlat and Camargo (1997) categorized 109 males in their sample according to the jobs they held. They found that 16% these of males worked in appearance-based or food-related jobs or jobs traditionally held by females. Some patients reported that their job (e.g. acting, modelling) was clearly associated with the onset of their eating disorder. In addition to occupational reasons, athletic pursuit in males is considered an important risk factor for disordered eating. Yates et al. (1983) hypothesized that increased motor activity and obsessive running in male anorexics could be an equivalent to the dieting efforts of their female counterparts. In a comparison of 20 male and 20 female habitual runners and anorexia nervosa patients, Powers et al. (1998) did not find significant similarities in regard to psychopathology and physiological measures between runners and AN patients. AN patients scored higher on depression (BDI), several MMPI subscales and on body image distortion measures.

Certain sports, such as boxing and wrestling, put great emphasis on different weight categories, and for some sports a low body weight is advantageous. For individuals practicing such a sport there are pressures to monitor eating behaviours and to diet. Significantly more males than females in Braun et al.'s study (1999) reported 'being involved in an occupation or athletic team in which control of weight is important for good performance' (p. 419). In 3 of 12 bulimic males in Mitchell and Goff's study, bulimic behaviour started in association with school athletic training and the need to meet certain weight-class standards. In order to assess the prevalence of what they call 'subclinical eating disorders' (an analogue to EDNOS) in male rowers and wrestlers of low-weight categories Thiel et al. (1993) examined 59 rowers and 25 wrestlers using the Eating Disorder Inventory (EDI). Eleven percent of athletes were identified as having a subclinical eating disorder and 52% reported bingeing; both figures clearly exceed those for the normal male population. Another motivation for men to control their weight and closely related to excessive motor activity is the wish to avoid medical illnesses common in western society, e.g. diabetes, coronary diseases or cancer (Andersen, 1992). It is not by accident that one of the most popular magazines for men promoting values of fitness and an ideal male body shape today is called *Men's Health*.

Sex Role Identity, Homosexuality and Sexual Inhibition

The prevalence of homosexuality among males in the community ranges from 1 to 6% (Seidman & Rieder, 1994). Compared to this, several studies found increased rates of homosexuality in males with an eating disorder: in the sample of the Boston group (Herzog et al., 1984 and Carlat et al., 1997) 26–42% of the eating-disordered males depicted themselves as being homo- or bisexual. Only very few of the eating-disordered females did so. In Fichter and Daser's sample of 42 anorexic males 25% reported homosexual experiences. In contrast to these findings Pope et al. (1986), as well as Burns and Crisp (1984), did not find elevated rates of male homosexuality in their samples. Possible reasons for these discrepant findings are (1) differences in sample selection and (2) differences in the strictness of the definition for homosexuality. Both, Pope et al. (1986; homosexual experience to orgasm within the preceding five years) and Burns and Crisp (1984; established homosexual relationship) used rather strict criteria.

Not only homosexuality but also asexuality or sexual anxieties and inhibition have been documented in males, especially in those suffering from AN. In their comparison of 29 male and 23 female subjects with 'primary' AN, Fichter and Daser found males to be significantly more anxious regarding sexuality (expert-rating), with 95% having tried to suppress their sexual drive and feeling relieved by loss of libido secondary to weight loss. Seventy-five percent of males even reported feelings of disgust regarding sexual relationships, and sexual anxieties were present in regard to hetero- as well as homosexual behaviour although 72% of patients were age 18 or older. As males in this study also had high 'femininity'-scores on personality measures, the authors concluded that males with atypical gender role behaviour have an increased risk of developing an eating disorder. Burns and Crisp (1985) followed 27 male subjects with AN for a minimum of two years after assessment. Outcome categories were defined in terms of body weight and sexual activity in the six months prior to assessment. Interestingly the authors found that 'active sexual fantasy, masturbation and general sexual activity were strong predictors of good outcome and their absence of poor outcome' (p. 326).

Heffernan (1994) reviewed the literature on sexual orientation as a possible risk factor for disordered eating; she hypothesized that—in focusing on physical appearance and attractiveness—gay men resemble heterosexual women. They want to be physically attractive to men, who themselves place great value on attractiveness. Silberstein et al. (1989) found that for gay men physical appearance was very central for their sense of self-worth. Gay men also exercised more than heterosexual men to improve attractiveness. These pressures in their specific culture may make gay men more vulnerable to eating disorders.

Personality Traits

According to Andersen (1990) males with eating disorders have more extreme personality traits, especially obsessive-compulsive and antisocial traits. Carlat et al. (1997) reported from their sample of 135 males with AN, BN and ED-NOS that 71% of bulimic men with axis-II comorbidity suffered from a cluster B personality disorder (borderline, antisocial, narcissistic). Anorexic men with personality disorders were evenly divided across clusters A, B and C. Each of the three male bulimic cases reported by Gwirtsman et al. (1984) had borderline personality, one had additional features of antisocial personality disorder. In studies on female samples with high rates of personality disorders, the borderline diagnoses was most prevalent one (Rossiter et al., 1993; Carroll et al., 1996). Keel and Mitchell's (1997) review on 88 studies of BN in females reports that impulsivity as a personality trait is predictive of poor outcome. To examine a potential overlap of eating disorders and obsessive-compulsive disorder Pigott et al. (1991) compared 27 males with obesessive-compulsive disorder to normal controls on measures of disordered eating. Male patients with obsessive-compulsive disorder scored significantly higher than controls on seven of the eight EDI-subscales and they had more symptoms of disordered eating as measured by the EDI than females. More than half of the 24 anorexic males examined by Sharp et al. (1994) also showed obsessional features. However, further studies are needed to substantiate the preliminary findings of high rates of obsessive-compulsive, antisocial and borderline personality disorder in eating-disordered males.

Substance and Alcohol Abuse

Besides frequently cited comorbidity of alcohol abuse in males with eating disorders, Carlat and Camargo (1991) pointed out that cocaine-abusing males are likely to show bulimic features. The authors commonly observed BN in association with alcohol and cocaine abuse. Males suffering from BED in Tanofsky et al.'s (1997) sample also were significantly more likely than the females to have a lifetime diagnosis of cocaine abuse. Concerning alcohol abuse, Carlat et al. (1991) conclude that 'being a child of an alcoholic parent particularly increases a male's risk of having an eating disorder' (p. 837). Similarly, Sharp et al. (1994) found a family history of alcohol abuse in over one-third of their 24 male anorexics. In a study on BN and alcohol abuse among adolescents in the community Suzuki et al. (1995) found that male and female binge eaters who fulfilled four of five DSM-III-R criteria for BN showed significantly more alcohol abuse than non-bulimic controls. Similarly, Ross and Ivis (1999) found that, among adolescent boys from a school-based sample, those who were classified as non-compensating bingers were the most likely to use tobacco or alcohol. On the other hand, males classified as compensating bingers were the most likely to use cannabis or other drugs. All in all, binge eating was shown to be related to more problematic and heavier substance abuse.

TREATMENT AND OUTCOME

- Course of male eating disorders
- Mixed male/female therapy.

Data on the *course of eating disorders* and treatment outcome in males are scarce. Andersen (1997, p. 395) concluded that 'male gender is not an adverse factor in short-term or long-term treatment outcome'. As is the case with many disorders, early diagnosis and treatment result in a better prognosis and outcome (Andersen, 1990). Woodside and Kaplan (1994) compared 15 males to 15 females with AN or BN who had been treated for 8–14 weeks in their programme. Global clinical outcome was similar in both, though slightly worse for the men: 28.6% of men had a good outcome, 71% had a poor outcome. Intermediate outcome in terms of symptom reduction over time was not scored in order to foster attitudinal shifts in the subjects. In Oyebode et al.'s (1988) study of 13 male and 13 female anorexics, males had a marginally worse outcome on the Morgan–Russell scale than females. Seventy percent of men, compared to only 30% of women, were still preoccupied with dieting or body shape after a mean follow-up period of 9.22 years. Burns and Crisp (1984) measured outcome in 27 anorexic males (20 inpatients, 2 outpatients) within a follow-up period of 2–20 years using the Morgan–Russell Outcome Scale and measures of sexual activity six months prior to assessment. Forty-four percent of subjects showed a good outcome, 26% intermediate and 30% poor according to these categories. Predictors of poor outcome were a longer duration of illness, a greater number of previous treatments, more weight loss in the acute phase of the illness, reduced or absent sexual activity and also a disturbed relationship with parents during childhood. Because of the latter finding the authors concluded that elements of family therapy should be included in the treatment of eating-disordered men to ameliorate prognosis. Andersen (1992) found a 'rule of thirds' to hold true in the largest male follow-up studies, i.e. one-third with good, intermediate and poor outcome, respectively. Findings in females to date concur largely with this rule. However, it has to be mentioned that this 'rule' is an oversimplification and does not hold on methodological grounds. Between studies different definitions of poor, intermediate and good outcome have been used, and frequently outcome has not been assessed reliably in outcome studies.

Mixing male and female eating-disordered patients in a therapy group sometimes may be difficult, as men normally are under-represented in these groups and therefore may feel that their typical male problems are not being addressed adequately. In addition, some eating-disordered women may feel threatened by or prejudiced towards eating disordered men (Andersen, 1995). Contrary to this view, Woodside and Kaplan (1994) experienced no difficulties integrating male subjects in their group therapy day treatment programme.

There are indications that case identification and referral to specialist services differ between patients with AN and BN. In Carlat et al.'s (1997) sample of 135 men with eating disorders, bulimic men were significantly older at first treatment and were mostly self-referred. On the other hand, anorexic patients (whose disorder is more visible to lay persons and doctors) due to low body weight were referred to specialist services earlier; referral in the case of AN is frequently initiated by relatives. Usually bulimic patients have more or less normal body weight and handle their symptoms rather secretively. Most likely this is a major reason for the longer delay between onset of illness and referral to treatment. Apparently, over the past decade public as well as professional awareness of eating disorders has increased (Braun et al., 1999). Waller and Katzman (1998) recently have examined opinions of therapists concerning the role of the therapist's gender for treatment. However, at this point of time we do not know if the gender of the therapist has effects on treatment outcome. Gender-specific problems in eating disorders, e.g. anxieties or inhibition regarding sexuality in male anorexics, have only recently been addressed by research (Balakrishna & Crisp, 1998).

Regarding prognosis of eating-disordered men, Andersen (1990) concluded that 'no evidence has emerged that a pessimistic outlook is warranted for males on the basis of gender' (p. 157). In a follow-up of eating-disordered inpatients six month to six years after treatment, the average male patient had maintained a thin-normal weight (92% Ideal Body Weight) and adequate overall improvement in functioning. Others, however, have reported more pessimistic data about treatment outcome and course of illness in eating disordered males.

CONCLUSIONS AND OUTLOOK

- Future needs of research in the area
- Current studies.

Eating disorders are best represented by a continuum of behaviours ranging from normal eating behaviour to partial symptoms and full syndrome manifestation (Carlat & Camargo, 1991). For a better understanding of the extremes of this continuum *future research* should also focus on those atypical and subsyndromal cases, which DSM-IV summarizes under EDNOS. This relatively heterogeneous category has to be studied and subtyped further, as research into BED or atypical cases of AN and BN can yield important information about core features of disordered eating. Striegel-Moore et al. (1999b) suggest that EDNOS cases might even be those with the highest prevalence rates. Findings of Kinzl et al. (1999) point into the same direction. Striegel-Moore et al.'s (1999a) sample of eating disordered male veterans had a mean age of 51.7 years (SD = 14.2) and EDNOS subjects were the subgroup with the highest mean age. Although the authors did not give information about age at onset of the disorder, this relatively high mean age draws attention to more atypical, but still at-risk cases of eating disorders.

For future research there exists also a clear need for multi-centre studies to compensate for the effects of small sample sizes on the one hand (Oyebode et al., 1988) and to facilitate cross-cultural research on the other. As has been mentioned above, only few studies have adequately adressed intercultural issues in eating disorders in males (e.g. Mangweth et al., 1997). Questions about possible sociocultural factors in the aetiology of disordered eating in males therefore remain largely unanswered.

At this time we do see a need for a thorough comparison of larger samples of matched male and female pairs of patients with AN, BN, BED and EDNOS. In our current follow-up-study (Fichter et al., 2002) we have assessed a sample of men with AN (N = 62), BN (N = 55) and BED (N = 29) according to DSM-IV criteria. Subjects have been followed-up for up to 20 years after their first presentation as inpatients in cooperating German hospitals specializing in the treatment of eating disorders. All the subjects treated in these hospitals received CBT. This sample of male inpatients will be compared to a (diagnosis, age, and follow-up interval) matched inpatient female sample. Results on the six-year-course of a large sample of women with AN, BN and BED have already been presented by Fichter and Quadflieg (1997, 1999) and Fichter et al. (1998a). In our present study eating disorder symptomatology as well as comorbid disorders (axis-I and axis-II) in men and women have been recorded using self-report questionnaires as well as standardized expert interviews (SCID, SIAB; Fichter et al., 1998b). The interviews are conducted by trained psychologists either personally or by telephone. Special emphasis will be put on the evaluation of personality disorders (axis-II) and impulsive behaviour, as results concerning axis-II comorbidity in males with eating disorders are still scarce. Questions concerning bodily appearance, fitness or muscularity may also play an important part in the aetiology of eating disorders in males (Pope et al., 2000) and will also be examined in our study. Preliminary results of our current study indicate that eating disorder specific and general psychopathology tend to be more pathological in female as compared to male patients with a major eating disorder.

According to Andersen (1992), in the overall course of eating disorders males and females show substantial similarities in the acute illness phase, where eating disorder and comorbid symptomatology manifest in similar ways. Anderson hypothesizes that men and women with eating disorders differ mainly *before* and *after* their acute phase of the eating disorder. Before and after the acute phase of illness, differences between genders in respect to biological and social learning processes and gender role identity come to bear. Future research has to focus on these phases, as similarities in symptom manifestation in males and females have repeatedly been proved. There is still very little data on possible biological vulnerability factors (genetic, neurochemical, neuroendocrine, etc.) in males suffering from eating disorders. Finally, future research should also focus on sociocultural aspects. e.g. values of slimness and fitness in both genders, and their manifestation in different cultural settings.

REFERENCES

Andersen, A.E. (Ed.) (1990) *Males with Eating Disorders*. New York: Brunner/Mazel.

Andersen, A.E. (1992) Follow-up of males with eating disorders. In W. Herzog, H.C. Deter & W. Vandereycken (Eds), *The Course of Eating Disorders*. Berlin: Springer.

Andersen, A.E. (1995) Eating disorders in males. In K.D. Brownell & C.G. Fairburn (Eds), *Eating Disorders and Obesity*. New York, London: Guilford Press.

Andersen, A.E. & DiDomenico, L. (1992) Diet vs. shape content of popular male and female magazines: a dose-response relationship to the incidence of eating disorders. *International Journal of Eating Disorders*, **10** (4), 389–394.

Andersen, A.E. & Holman, J.E. (1997) Males with eating disorders: Challenges for treatment and research. *Psychopharmacology Bulletin*, **33** (3), 391–397.

Balakrishna, J. & Crisp, A.H. (1998) A pilot programme of sex education for inpatients with anorexia nervosa. *European Eating Disorders Review*, **6**, 136–142.

Beumont, P.J.V., Beardwood, C.J. & Russell, G.F.M. (1972) The occurrence of the syndrome of anorexia nervosa in male subjects. *Psychological Medicine*, **2**, 216–231.

Braun, D.L., Sunday, S.R., Huang, A. & Halmi, K.A. (1999) More males seek treatment for eating disorders. *International Journal of Eating Disorders*, **25**, 415–424.

Burns, T. & Crisp, A.H. (1984) Outcome of anorexia nervosa in males. *British Journal of Psychiatry*, **145**, 319–325.

Burns, T. & Crisp, A.H. (1985) Factors affecting prognosis in male anorexics. *Journal of Psychiatric Research*, **19** (2/3), 323–328.

Cachelin, F.M. & Maher, B.A. (1998) Is amenorrhoea a critical criterion for anorexia nervosa? *Journal of Psychosomatic Research*, **44**, (3/4) 435–440.

Carlat, D.J. & Camargo, C.A. (1991) Review of bulimia nervosa in males. *American Journal of Psychiatry*, **148**, 831–843.

Carlat, D.J., Camargo, C.A. & Herzog, D.B. (1997) Eating disorders in males: A report on 135 patients. *American Journal of Psychiatry*, **154**, 1127–1132.

Carroll, J.M., Touyz, S.W. & Beumont, P.J.V. (1996) Specific comorbidity between bulimia nervosa and personality disorders. *International Journal of Eating Disorders*, **19**, 159–170.

Crisp, A.H. & Burns, T. (1983) The clinical presentation of anorexia nervosa in males. *International Journal of Eating Disorders*, **2**, 5–10.

Crisp, A.H., Burns, T. & Bhat, A.V. (1986) Primary anorexia nervosa in the male and female: A comparison of clinical features and prognosis. *British Journal of Medical Psychology*, **59**, 123–132.

Drewnowski, A., Hopkins, S.A., & Kessler, R.C. (1988) The prevalence of bulimia nervosa in the US college student population. *American Journal of Public Health*, **78**, 1322–1325.

Eller, B. (1993). Males with eating disorders. In A.J. Giannini & A.E. Slaby (Eds), *The Eating Disorders*. New York: Springer.

Fairburn, C.G. & Beglin, S.J. (1990) Studies of the epidemiology of bulimia nervosa. *American Journal of Psychiatry*, **147**, 401–408.

Fichter, M.M. (1985) *Magersucht und Bulimia*. Berlin, Heidelberg, New York: Springer Verlag.

Fichter, M.M. & Daser, C. (1987) Symptomatology, psychosexual development and gender identity in 42 anorexic males. *Psychological Medicine*, **17**, 409–418.

Fichter, M.M., Pirke, K.M., Pöllinger, J., Wolfram, G. & Brunner, E. (1990) Disturbances in the hypothalamo-pituitary-adrenal and other neuroendocrine axes in bulimia. *Biological Psychiatry*, **27**, 1201–1037.

Fichter, M.M. & Quadflieg, N. (1995) Comparative studies on the course of eating disorders in adolescents and adults: Is age at onset a predictor of outcome? In H.C. Steinhausen (Ed.), *Eating Disorders in Adolescence*, Berlin: de Gruyter.

Fichter, M.M. & Quadflieg, N. (1997) Six-year-course of bulimia nervosa. *International Journal of Eating Disorders*, **22**, 361–384.

Fichter, M.M., Quadflieg, N. & Gnutzmann, A. (1998a) Binge eating disorder: Treatment outcome over a 6-year course. *Journal of Psychosomatic Research*, **44**, 385–405.

Fichter, M.M., Herpertz, S., Quadflieg, N. & Herpertz-Dahlmann, B. (1998b) Structured interview for anorexic and bulimic disorders for DSM-IV and ICD-10: Updated (third) revision. *International Journal of Eating Disorders*, **24**, 227–249.

Fichter, M.M. & Quadflieg, N. (1999) Six-year course and outcome of anorexia nervosa. *International Journal of Eating Disorders*, **26**, 359–385.

Fichter, M.M., Krenn, H., Quadflieg, N., Nutzinger, D. & Küchenhoff, H. (2002) A comparative study of men and women with an eating disorder. Paper presented at the 8th annual meeting of the Eating Disorders Research Society (EDRS), Charleston, S.C., USA, Nov. 21–23.

Garfinkel, P.E., Lin, E., Goering, P., Spegg, C., Goldbloom, D.S., Kennedy, S., Kaplan, A.S. & Woodside, D.B. (1995) Bulimia nervosa in a Canadian community sample: Prevalence and comparison of subgroups. *American Journal of Psychiatry*, **152**, 1052–1058.

Garner, D.M., Garfinkel, P.E., Schwartz, D. & Thompson, M. (1980) Cultural expectations of thinness in women. *Psychological Reports*, **47**, 483–491.

Götestam, K.G. & Agras, W.S. (1995) General population-based epidemiological study of eating disorders in Norway. *International Journal of Eating Disorders*, **18** (2), 119–126.

Gull, W.W. (1874) Anorexia nervosa. *Transactions of the Clinical Society of London*, **7**, 22–28.

Gwirtsman, H.E., Roy-Byrne, P., Lerner, L. & Yager, J. (1984) Bulimia in men: Report of three cases with neuroendocrine findings. *Journal of Clinical Psychiatry*, **45** (2), 78–81.

Heffernan, K. (1994) Sexual orientation as a factor in risk for binge eating and bulimia nervosa: A review. *International Journal of Eating Disorders*, **16**, 335–347.

Herzog, D.B., Norman, D.K., Gordon, C. & Pepose, M. (1984) Sexual conflict and eating disorders in 27 males. *American Journal of Psychiatry*, **141**, 989–990.

Keel, P.K. & Mitchell, J.E. (1997) Outcome in Bulimia Nervosa. *American Journal of Psychiatry*, **154**, 313–321.

King, M.B. (1989) Eating disorders in a general practice population: Prevalence, characteristics and follow-up at 12 to 18 months. *Psychological Medicine Monograph Supplement*, **14**, 1–34.

Kinzl, J.F., Traweger, C., Trefalt, E., Mangweth, B. & Biebl, W. (1999) Binge eating disorder in males: A population-based investigation. *Eating Weight Disorders*, **4**, 169–174.

Mangweth, B., Pope, H.G., Hudson, J.I., Olivardia, R., Kinzl, J. & Biebl, W. (1997) Eating disorders in Austrian men: An intracultural and crosscultural comparison study. *Psychotherapy Psychosomatics*, **66**, 214–221.

Margo, J.L. (1987) Anorexia nervosa in males: a comparison with female patients. *British Journal of Psychiatry*, **151**, 80–83.

Mickalide, A.D. (1990). Sociocultural factors influencing weight among males. In A.E. Andersen (Ed.), *Males with Eating Disorders*. New York: Brunner/Mazel.

Mitchell, J.E. & Goff, G.G. (1984) Bulimia in male patients. *Psychosomatics*, **25** (12), 909–913.

Morton, R. (1694) *Phthisiologia: Or a Treatise of Consumptions*. London: S. Smith & B. Walford.

Olivardia, R., Pope, H.G., Mangweth, B. & Hudson, J.I. (1995) Eating disorders in college men. *American Journal of Psychiatry*, **152**, 1279–1285.

Oyebode, F., Boodhoo, J.A. & Schapira, K. (1988) Anorexia nervosa in males: Clinical features and outcome. *International Journal of Eating Disorders*, **7**, 121–124.

Pigott, T.A., Altemus, M., Rubenstein, C.S., Hill, J.L., Bihari, K., L'Heureux, F., Bernstein, S. & Murphy, D.L. (1991) Symptoms of eating disorders in patients with obsessive-compulsive disorders. *American Journal of Psychiatry*, **148**, 1552–1557.

Pirke, K.M, Fichter, M.M., Lund, R. & Doerr, P. (1979) Twenty-four hour sleep-wake pattern of plasma LH in patients with anorexia nervosa. *Acta Endocrinologica*, **92**, 193–204.

Pope, H.G., Hudson, J.I. & Jonas, J.M. (1986) Bulimia in men: A series of fifteen cases. *Journal of Nervous and Mental Disease*, **174** (2) 117–119.

Pope, H.G., Olivardia, R, Gruber, A. & Borowiecki, J. (1999) Evolving ideals of male body image as seen through action toys. *International Journal of Eating Disorders*, **26**, 65–72.

Pope, H.G., Phillips, K.A. & Olivardia, R. (2000) *The Adonis Complex. The Secret Crisis of Male Body Obsession*. New York: The Free Press.

Powers, P.S., Schocken, D.D. & Boyd, F.R. (1998) Comparison of habitual runners and anorexia nervosa patients. *International Journal of Eating Disorders*, **23**, 133–143.

Robinson, P.H. & Holden, N.L. (1986) Bulimia nervosa in the male: A report of nine cases. *Psychological Medicine*, **16**, 795–803.

Rosen, J.C. & Gross, J. (1987) Prevalence of weight reducing and weight gaining in adolescent girls and boys. *Health Psychology*, **6**, 131–147.

Ross, H.E. & Ivis, F. (1999) Binge eating and substance use among male and female adolescents. *International Journal of Eating Disorders*, **26**, 245–260.

Rossiter, E.M., Agras, W.S., Telch, C.F. & Schneider, J.A. (1993) Cluster B personality disorder characteristics predict outcome in the treatment of bulimia nervosa. *International Journal of Eating Disorders*, **13**, 349–357.

Schotte, D.E. & Stunkard, A.J. (1987) Bulimia vs bulimic behaviors on a college campus. *Journal of American Medical Association*, **258**, 1213–1215.

Seidman, S.N. & Rieder, R.O. (1994) A review of sexual behavior in the United States. *American Journal of Psychiatry*, **151**, 330–341.

Sharp, C.W., Clark, S.A., Dunan, J.R., Blackwood, D.H.R. & Shapiro, C.M. (1994) Clinical presentation of anorexia nervosa in males: 24 new cases. *International Journal of Eating Disorders*, **15**, 125–134.

Silberstein, L.R., Mishkind, M.E., Striegel-Moore, R.H., Timko, C. & Rodin, J. (1989) Men and their bodies: A comparison of homosexual and heterosexual men. *Psychosomatic Medicine*, **51**, 337–346.

Striegel-Moore, R.H., Garvin, V., Dohm, F.-A. & Rosenheck, R.A. (1999a) Psychiatric comorbidity of eating disorders in men: A national study of hospitalized veterans. *International Journal of Eating Disorders*, **25**, 399–404.

Striegel-Moore, R.H., Garvin, V., Dohm, F.-A. & Rosenheck, R.A. (1999b) Eating disorders in a national sample of hospitalized female and male veterans: Detection rates and psychiatric comorbidity. *International Journal of Eating Disorders*, **25**, 405–414.

Striegel-Moore, R.H., Silberstein, L.R. & Rodin, J. (1986) Toward an understanding of risk factors for bulimia. *American Psychologist*, **41** (3), 246–263.

Suzuki, K., Takeda, A. & Matsushita, S. (1995) Coprevalence of bulimia with alcohol abuse and smoking among Japanese male and female high school students. *Addiction*, **90**, 971–975.

Tanofsky, M.B., Wilfley, D.E., Borman Spurrell, E., Welch, R. & Brownell, K.D. (1997) Comparison of men and women with binge eating disorder. *International Journal of Eating Disorders*, **21**, 49–54.

Taraldsen, K.W., Eriksen, L. & Götestam, K.G. (1996) Prevalence of eating disorders among Norwegian women and men in a psychiatric outpatient unit. *International Journal of Eating Disorders*, **20**, 185–190.

Thiel, A., Gottfried, H. & Hesse, F. W. (1993) Subclinical eating disorders in male athletes: A study of the low-weight category in rowers and wrestlers. *Acta Psychiatrica Scandinavica*, **88**, 259–265.

Waller, G. & Katzman, M.A. (1998) Female or male therapists for women with eating disorders? A pilot study of experts' opinions. *International Journal of Eating Disorders*, **23**, 117–123.

Whytt, R. (1764) *Observations on the Nature, Causes, and Cure of those Disorders which have been Commonly Called Nervous, Hyochondriac or Hysteric to which are Prefixed some Remarks on the Sympathy of the Nerves*. Edinburgh: Becket, DeHondt, & Balfour

Willan, R. (1790) A remarkable case of abstinence. *Medical Communications*, **2**, 113–122

Woodside, D.B. & Kaplan, A.S. (1994) Day hospital treatment in males with eating disorders—response and comparison to females. *Journal of Psychosomatic Research*, **38** (5), 471–475.

Woodside, D.B., Garfinkel, P.E., Lin, E., Goering, P., Kaplan, A.S., Goldbloom, D.S. & Kennedy, S.H. (2001) Comparison of men with full or partial eating disorders; men without eating disorders, and women with eating disorders in the community. *American Journal of Psychiatry*, **158**, 570–574.

Yates, A., Leehey, K. & Shisslak, C. (1983) Running: an analogue of anorexia? *New England Journal of Medicine*, **308**, 251–255.

CHAPTER 24

Athletes and Dancers

Jorunn Sundgot-Borgen

The Norwegian University of Sport and Physical Education and The Norwegian Olympic Training Centre, Oslo, Norway

Finn Skårderud

University of Oslo and The Norwegian Olympic Training Centre, Oslo, Norway

and

Sheelagh Rodgers

Adult Psychological Therapies, Pontefract General Infirmary, W. Yorkshire, UK

SUMMARY

There is an increased prevalence of eating disorders among athletes and dancers compared with the general population. This is not a surprise, as within sport and dance there is a greater focus on body, food and performance. A key concept is control through bodily techniques, and in both cultures boundaries are pushed. With regard to dieting behaviour, there are a lack of 'norms for normalcy'. Ideally, the health professional treating athletes and dancers with eating disorders should be familiar with, and have an appreciation for, the athlete's sport or knowledge of the demands placed upon a dancer. Educational programmes are needed to help those involved with sport and dance to both recognise eating disorders, and to begin to change the attitudes towards eating disorders that exist in both athletes and dancers.

INTRODUCTION

Eating disorders are more prevalent among athletes and dancers than in the general population. While there has been considerable interest shown and research carried out into eating disorders in the general population, it is only relatively recently that researchers have turned their investigations to the special populations within the sport and dance worlds.

The high prevalence of eating disorders in sport and dance is not a surprise. If we consider the two cultures, that of sport and dance on the one hand, and that of eating disorders on the other, there are many similarities. This is particularly true when we study sport and dance at elite and professional levels. In both areas there is a great focus on body and food. Nutrition generally plays a big part in the training programmes. In both areas we find the pressure

Handbook of Eating Disorders. Edited by J. Treasure, U. Schmidt and E. van Furth.
© 2003 John Wiley & Sons, Ltd.

to perform. It is generally accepted that professional dance or elite sport places extreme demands on the participants. Both for the athlete and the anorectic, the body serves as a tool to achieve something, which may be extreme performance and/or self-esteem. A key concept is *control* through bodily techniques. It has been claimed that female athletes are at increased risk for developing eating disorders due to the focus upon low body weight as a performance enhancer, comments from coaches or important others, and the pressure to perform (Otis et al., 1997; Sundgot-Borgen, 1994; Wilmore, 1991).

This phenomenological likeness may partly explain an additional problem: signs and symptoms of eating disorders are often ignored by athletes and dancers. To some extent disordered eating seems to be regarded as a natural part of being an athlete (Sundgot-Borgen, 1996) or dancer. One may meet subcultures of normalisation of symptomatic behaviour. Some athletes and dancers do not consider training or exercise as sufficient to accomplish their idealised body weight or percent body fat. Therefore, to meet their goals, a significant number of them diet and use harmful, though often ineffective weight-loss practices such as restrictive eating, vomiting, laxatives and diuretics to meet their goals (Sundgot-Borgen, 1993).

In this chapter we review the definitions, diagnostic criteria, prevalence and risk factors for the development of eating disorders in sport and dance. Practical implications for the identification and treatment of eating disorders in athletes and dancers are also discussed.

DEFINITIONS

Athletes and dancers constitute a unique population, and special diagnostic considerations should be made when working with these groups (Sundgot-Borgen, 1993; Szmukler et al., 1985; Thompson & Trattner Sherman, 1993). Despite similar symptoms subclinical cases may be easier to identify than in non-athletes (Sundgot-Borgen, 1994) and non-dancers. Since athletes and dancers, at least at the elite level, are evaluated by their coach more or less daily, changes in behaviour and physical symptoms may be observed. However, symptoms of eating disorders in competitive athletes and professional dancers are too often ignored or not detected by coaches. Reasons for this may be lack of knowledge of symptoms, lack of developed strategies for approaching the eating-disordered athlete, and the coaches' own feeling of guilt (Sundgot-Borgen, 1993).

The DSM-IV (APA, 1994) diagnostic criteria distinguish two subtypes for anorexia nervosa, the restrictive type and the binge-eating/purging type. Eating-disordered athletes often move between these two subtypes. However, it is the authors' experience that chronicity leads to an accumulation of eating-disordered athletes in the binge-eating/purging subgroup.

The Eating Disorder Not Otherwise Specified (EDNOS) category (APA, 1994) acknowledges the existence and importance of a variety of eating disturbances. In the early phase of research on athletes and eating disorder the term 'anorexia athletica' was introduced (Sundgot-Borgen, 1993). Most athletes meeting the criteria listed for 'anorexia athletica' will also meet the criteria described in EDNOS.

PREVALENCE OF EATING DISORDERS

Different sports such as aesthetic, power, endurance, weight-class and ball sports place different demands on the athlete. There is also different emphasis on body shape and size, depending on the type of dancing that is performed. Extreme leanness seems to be more important among classic dancers as compared to modern dancers. Classical ballet is one area of dance where there appears to be a higher prevalence of eating disorders.

The populations studied in both dance and sports have been very different. Within dance a range of ages and different styles of dance have been studied, as have professional dancers who perform with both the national and smaller regional dance companies. Sports research has looked at populations ranging from elite athletes, to recreational sports people, and in the USA many studies have concentrated on athletes from the American Collegiate system. There are gender differences too, with female athletes and dancers being studied more than their male counterparts.

A further consideration in the work on prevalence in athletes is that some of the research tools used have not been validated for use with athletes. Neither the Eating Disorders Inventory (EDI; Garner & Olmstead, 1984) nor the Eating Attitudes Test (EAT; Garner & Garfinkel, 1979) was designed for use with a specific sporting population, and may not consider the special problems shown by athletes and performers. It is also difficult to get accurate figures for the prevalence as athletes and dancers may have a different perception of what eating disorders are, and many athletes and dancers deny or want to conceal that they have a problem.

EATING DISORDERS AMONG ATHLETES

Estimates of the prevalence of the symptoms of eating disorders and clinical eating disorders among female athletes range from less than 1% to as high as 75% (Gadpalle et al., 1987; Sundgot-Borgen, 1994; Warren et al., 1990). In a recent Norwegian study the prevalence of anorexia nervosa is 2.2%, bulimia nervosa 7.2% and subclinical eating disorders is 10%. These figures show a higher prevalence than among non-athletes. Furthermore, this study showed that eating disorders are more frequent among female elite athletes competing in aesthetic and weight-class sports than among other sport groups where leanness is considered less important (Figure 24.1).

Only two previous studies on male athletes (wrestlers) (Lalim, 1990; Oppliger et al., 1993) have based their results on DSM diagnostic criteria (DSM-III-R). They reported 1.7% and 1.4%, respectively, of male wrestlers with bulimia. A recent Norwegian study reported the prevalence of eating disorders to be as high as 8% among male elite athletes and 0.6% in age-matched controls. As many as 4.0%, 3.5% and 0.4% met the criteria for EDNOS, bulimia nervosa and anorexia nervosa, respectively (Torstveit et al., 1998). The prevalence of clinical eating disorders in male elite athletes is highest among those competing in weight-class sports (i.e. wrestling, rowing) and gravitation sports (ski jumping, high jump) (Figure 24.1).

EATING DISORDERS AMONG DANCERS

Eating disorders are common among dancers (le Grange et al., 1994). Abraham (1996) examined the eating patterns of 60 young (mean age 17 years) female ballet dancers and concluded that 1.7% had anorexia nervosa, and a further 1.7% had bulimia nervosa, while overall 12% had some form of eating disorder. Moreover, 34% had a body mass index below 17 kg/m^2, 13% abused laxatives, 11.7% regularly vomited, 28% reported cycles of binge eating and starvation, 30% worried about becoming obese, and menstruation was absent

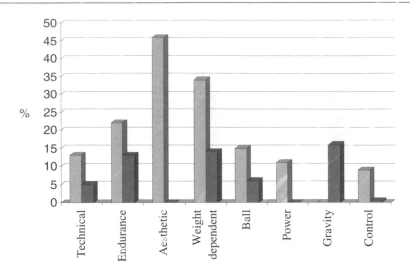

Figure 24.1 Prevalence of eating disorders in female ($N = 572$) and male ($n = 687$) elite athletes. None of the female athletes in the power and gravitation sports and none of the male athletes in the aesthetic or power sports met the DSM-IV criteria

in 58% of the sample. Seventy-three percent of the dancers had problems controlling their eating, while 52% claimed to experience ongoing problems of controlling their weight. While eating disorders do seem to be a major problem within the world of ballet, it appears to be less common in other dancers where different emphasis is placed on body definition.

To reduce the methodological problems associated with dancers' perceptions of anorexia nervosa and bulimia nervosa, some studies have used a two-stage design method to identify cases of eating disorders in dancers. The initial stage involved a screening questionnaire. In the second stage a clinician interviewed the subject using a set of operational criteria for the diagnosis of eating disorders. Using these techniques Garner and Garfinkel (1980) reported that 6.5% of dancers (mean age 18.5 years) had anorexia nervosa. This is a slightly higher figure than that reported by le Grange et al. (1994) who found that 4% of their dancers had anorexia nervosa. Studies by Szmukler et al. (1985) and Garner et al. (1987) suggested that between 7 and 25% of 15-year-old dancers were affected.

Studies of professional adult dancers by Hamilton et al. (1985, 1988) have shown that up to 23% of dancers currently have or had previously had problems with eating disorders.

A study by Doyle et al. (1997) that looked at young dancers attending specialist dance schools, showed that 4% aged between 11 and 13 years had anorexia nervosa, and 3% aged between 14 and 16 years had anorexia nervosa. Comparison groups for age and at boarding schools showed no such problems.

RISK FACTORS FOR THE DEVELOPMENT OF EATING DISORDERS

The aetiology of eating disorders is multifactorial (Garfinkel et al., 1987; Katz, 1985). More than to sum up possible factors, the challenge is to develop *risk models* that can organise our understanding of how different risk factors interact. The essence of such models is how the individual with his or her biological, relational and social history meets different contexts.

A simple model will describe how *predisposing factors* contribute to a 'vulnerability'. These may be genetic, temperamental predispositions, personality traits, traumas or the emotional climate in the family. Whether such a disposition is realised as an eating disorder or other psychopathology, will depend on *precipitating factors*. These may be specific for different contexts, like the pressure to diet within some sports and ballet. In addition we have the *maintaining factors*, which perpetuate the disorder. These are psychological symptoms secondary to the physiology of hunger and chaotic eating, 'war' in the family, social isolation, or that the person strongly identifies with risk behaviour and the risk milieu.

In working with eating disorders among athletes and dancers we must remember that many of the risk factors may lie outside sport or dance.

Life events (Schmidt et al., 1997) and risk factors such as childhood sexual abuse, parenting practices and psychiatric problems (Fairburn & Welch, 1998; Fairburn et al., 1997) can affect athletes as well as their non-sporting peers, and it is important in assessing an athlete and formulating a treatment plan that a wide range of possible risk factors are taken into account.

Davis (1992) and Davis et al. (1995) have looked at the personality characteristics of athletes and how these factors might interact with the sports environment. Predisposing personality traits include low self-esteem, perfectionism and obsessiveness. These are traits often found in eating-disordered populations, but combined with characteristics that are shown by many athletes of self-control, self-drive, self-sacrifice and goal orientation, these traits can help to maintain an eating disorder for some considerable time, seemingly without ill effects.

Dancers in general often exhibit some of the characteristics thought to be associated with anorexia nervosa, such as an elevated need to achieve, perfectionism, fear of fatness, concerns with their body, compliance, dieting and high levels of activity (Bruch, 1978; Vincent, 1981). This profile of dancers may put them at higher risk of developing an eating disorder but the psychological profile is only part of the problem.

Some authors argue that specific sports attract individuals who are anorectic before commencing their participation in sports, at least in attitude if not in behaviour or weight (Sacks, 1990; Thompson & Trattner Sherman, 1993). It is the authors' opinion that the attraction to sport hypothesis might be true for the general population, but athletes and dancers do not achieve the elite level if the only motivation is weight loss.

In our clinical work (The Norwegian Olympic Training Centre) we have asked elite athletes in treatment for eating disorders about how they consider the relationships between their careers as athletes and an eating disorder. From the interviews three main narratives were extracted:

Elite Sport is a High-Risk Culture

Under this headline there were many different examples, but many stressed the general overemphasis or 'hyperfocus' on body and nutrition, both aesthetically (i.e. gymnastics) and in terms of performance (i.e. the myth about higher achievement through lower weight in some endurance sports). Some of the athletes gave concrete examples of coaches stimulating and/or pressing the athletes to lose weight (i.e. in gymnastics). Some of these examples need to be categorised as mobbing. One sailor who mentioned the pressure to increase weight, was more or less pushed into binge-like eating sessions by her coaches. The rationale for this was 'fat is speed'. She increased in weight, started to diet, and her eating disorder began.

In this narrative other important elements were the descriptions of what we can call the 'lack of norms for normalcy'. In these subcultures where the aim is to move boundaries in achievement, both athletes and coaches may lose the contact with what is normal, i.e. the normalisation of purging techniques. This situation is not improved by the fact that some of the coaches and leaders also have abnormal eating patterns.

- *'I might have got it anyhow.'* In this narrative there were different descriptions of what above is called predisposing factors; dysfunctional families, psychiatric disorders in the family, trauma, etc. Some described entering the elite sport milieu as the trigger factor. As one athlete said: 'When I with my history came into sport, it was like one added to one became three.'
  Others, however, described sports as a protecting milieu. There athletes meet other people who care for them and are genuinely interested in them. They have a peer group, and some stated that they were convinced that the ability to use physical activity on a very intense level helped them to regulate and control psychological tension as well as difficult thoughts and feelings.
- *Eating disorder as a way of getting out of sports.* This narrative is relatively rare, but useful to be aware of. Two athletes connected their symptoms of eating disorders partly because of how stressful it was to be at an elite level: 'This is not a life for a teenager!' Both these athletes had great problems telling their parents, coaches, leaders and sponsors about their doubts whether to continue. Their symptoms were real and severe enough, but they also served the function of legitimising the withdrawal from competing. Both recovered apparently quickly when they terminated performing at an elite level.

What can be Said about Sport- and Dance-Specific Factors?

Pressure to reduce weight has been the common explanation for the increased prevalence of eating-related problems among athletes and dancers. One of the reasons that ballet dancers may be at risk for developing eating disorders is that they may have to diet in order to maintain the sylph-like bodies that are required for the discipline of ballet. Lowenkopf and Vincent (1982) have suggested that female adolescent dancers run eight times the risk of developing eating disorders compared to their non-dieting peers. Ballet is also an activity that is low in energy expenditure, and Cohen et al. (1982) reported that while age-matched swimmers or skaters might expend 500 calories in a similar length session, a dancer would only expend 200 calories.

However, the important factor may not be dieting per se, but rather the situation in which the performer is told to lose weight, the words used and whether the athlete receives guidance. It is very worrying to experience how unprofessionally some professional teachers and trainers may behave. There is anecdotal evidence of how they set their own standards for body shape and weight, and pass on abnormal eating and dieting myths to the new generations of performers.

In addition to the pressure to reduce weight, athletes are often pressed for time, and they have to lose weight rapidly to make or stay on the team. As a result they often experience frequent periods of restrictive dieting or weight cycling (Sundgot-Borgen, 1994). Weight cycling has been suggested as an important risk or trigger factor for the development of eating disorders in athletes (Brownell et al., 1987; Sundgot-Borgen, 1994). Wrestlers have been characterised as high-risk athletes for developing eating disorders. A study on wrestlers (Dale & Landers, 1999) concluded that although in-season wrestlers are more weight-conscious than non-wrestlers, these feelings and attitudes are transient. It is the authors' impression that whether male athletes competing in weight-class sports have a transient condition or true clinical eating disorder seems to depend on the competitive level and years of practising weight-loss techniques with weight fluctuation.

From subjective experience athletes report that they developed eating disorders as a result of traumatic events, such as the loss or change of a coach, injury, illness, or overtraining (Katz, 1985; Sundgot-Borgen, 1994; Sundgot-Borgen & Klungland, 1998). An injury can curtail the athlete's and dancer's exercise and training habits. As a result, they may gain weight owing to less energy expenditure, which in some cases may develop into an irrational fear of further weight gain. Then the athlete may begin to diet to compensate for the lack of exercise (Thompson & Trattner Sherman, 1993). Poor nutritional intake may hinder recovery, injuries can become chronic, and a vicious cycle of dieting is continued.

Another sport- and dance-specific risk factor may be the level of competitiveness. National ballet companies showed a higher incidence of eating disorders than did the regional companies (Homak, 1984). The study found that ballet dancers who danced for the big national companies thought that the ethos of these companies actually promoted eating disorders. In the same study, Homek also reported that the national companies required dancers to exercise more and set more rigorous standards for thinness and expected their dancers to diet more frequently.

One retrospective study indicates that a sudden increase in training load may induce a caloric deprivation in endurance athletes, which in turn may elicit biological and social reinforcements leading to the development of eating disorders (Sundgot-Borgen, 1994). Female athletes with eating disorders have been shown to start sport-specific training at an earlier age than healthy athletes (Sundgot-Borgen, 1994). Another factor to consider is that if female athletes start sport-specific training at prepubertal age, they might not choose the sport that will be most suitable for their adult body type. Longitudinal studies with close monitoring of a number of sport-specific factors (volume, type, and intensity of the training) in athletes are needed to answer questions about the role played by different sports in the development of eating disorders.

Figure 24.2 describes the ways in which eating disorders might develop in both dancers and athletes. Connors (1996) presents a model of eating disorders that explores the vulnerabilities that predispose some people to develop an eating disorder, while some others will be discontent with their bodies and just diet, and yet another group may develop other psychopathologies that do not include eating disorders. Connors suggests that the risk factors involved are sociocultural (young, white, middle-upper class) particular body types, teasing about childhood weight and maternal influences on dieting practices and weight. The psychological variables may be having a negative body image, low self-esteem, mood problems and personality characteristics such as perfectionism, as well as parental problems and poor family interactions. Both the sociocultural and psychological factors may interact with other triggers such as life events and other traumas. Connors proposes that dissatisfaction with one's body and affective dysregulation are necessary and sufficient conditions for the development of eating disorders. For athletes or dancers, failure to achieve 'the right weight' or body shape for their activity may be a trigger for dieting. If dieting fails to achieve the right body and there is still pressure from teachers or coaches, the dancer or athlete may feel pressured to diet still further, and an eating disorder may develop. The context of the

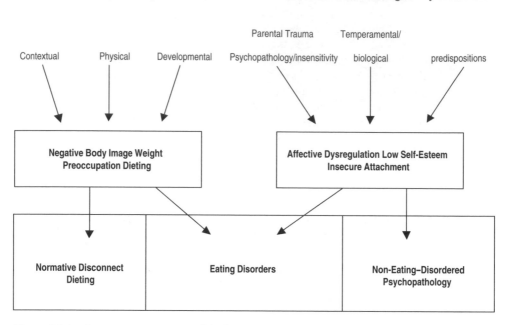

Figure 24.2 A two-component model of eating disorder (Connors 1996)

dance or athletic world, coupled with personal characteristics, traumas, parental or other influences may all interact with the end result of an eating disorder.

MEDICAL ISSUES

Eating disorders cause serious medical problems and can even be fatal. Whereas most complications of anorexia nervosa occur as a direct or indirect result of starvation, complications of bulimia nervosa occur as a result of binge eating and purging (Thompson & Trattner Sherman, 1993). Hsu (1990), Johnson and Connor (1987) and Mitchell (1990) provide information on the medical problems encountered in eating-disordered patients.

Mortality rates of eating disorders among athletes are not known. However, a number of deaths of top level female athletes in the sports gymnastics, running, alpine-skiing and cycling have been reported in the media. Five (5.4%) of the female elite athletes diagnosed in the Norwegian study (Sundgot-Borgen, 1994) reported suicide attempts.

The long-term effects of body weight cycling and eating disorders in athletes are unclear. Biological maturation and growth have been studied in girl gymnasts before and during puberty, suggesting that young female gymnasts are smaller and mature later than females from sports that do not require extreme leanness, such as swimming (Mansfield & Emans, 1993; Theintz et al., 1993). However, it is difficult to separate the contributions of physical strain, energy restriction, and genetic predisposition to delayed puberty.

Besides increasing the likelihood of amenorrhea and stress fractures, early bone loss may inhibit achievement of normal peak bone mass. Thus, athletes with frequent or longer periods of amenorrhea may be at high risk of sustaining fractures. Longitudinal data on fast and gradual body weight reduction and cycling in relation to health and performance parameters in different groups of athletes are clearly needed.

The nature and the magnitude of the effect of eating disorders on health and athletic performance are influenced by the severity and chronicity of the eating disorder and the physical and psychological demands of the sport. In addition to the negative health consequences, repeated or severe weight loss attempts will result in poor recovery and impaired sports performance (Fogelholm & Hilloskopri, 1999; Hsu, 1990; Sundgot-Borgen, 1994). Norwegian female elite athletes reported increased fatigue, anger, or anxiety when attempting to lose body weight rapidly (Sundgot-Borgen & Klungland, 1998).

IDENTIFYING ATHLETES WITH EATING DISORDERS

We know that many individuals with eating disorders do not realise that they have a problem and therefore do not seek treatment on their own. Athletes might consider seeking help only if they experience that their performance level is leveling off.

In contrast to the athletes with anorectic symptoms, most athletes suffering from bulimia nervosa are at or near normal weight, and therefore their disorder is difficult to detect. Hence the team staff must be able to recognise the physical symptoms and psychological characteristics listed in Table 24.1. It should be noted that the presence of some of these characteristics does not necessarily indicate the presence of the disorder. However, the

Table 24.1 Physical symptoms, psychological and behavioural characteristics of athletes with eating disorders

Physical	Psychological and behavioural
Significant weight loss beyond that necessary for adequate sport performance[a]	Anxiety, both related and unrelated to sport performance
Frequent and often extreme weight fluctuations[b]	Avoidance of eating and eating situations
	Claims of 'feeling fat' despite being thin
Low weight despite eating large volumes[b]	Resistance to weight gain or maintenance
Amenorrhea or menstrual irregularity	Dieting that is unnecessary for appearance,
Reduced bone mineral density	health, or sport performance
Stress fractures	Binge eating[b]
Dehydration	Agitation when bingeing is interrupted[b]
Hyperactivity	Unusual weighing behaviour (i.e. excessive
Electrolyte abnormalities	weighing, refusal to weigh, negative
Bradycardia	reaction to being weighed)
Fatigue beyond that normally expected in training or competition	Compulsiveness and rigidity, especially regarding eating and exercise[a]
Gastrointestinal problems (i.e. constipation, diarrhoea, bloating, postprandial distress)	Excessive or obligatory exercise beyond that required for a particular sport
Hypothermia[a]	Exercising while injured despite prohibitions
Lanugo[a]	for medical reasons
Muscle cramps, weakness or both	Restlessness
Swollen parotid glands	Social withdrawal
	Depression and insomnia
	Excessive use of the restroom[b]
	Self-critical, especially concerning body, weight, and performance
	Substance abuse
	Use of laxatives, diuretics (or both)

[a] Anorexia nervosa.
[b] Bulimia nervosa.

likelihood of the disorder being present increases as the number of presenting characteristics increases (Thompson & Trattner Sherman, 1993).

TREATMENT

Here we present some general experiences and recommendations for treatment, and some more specific experiences from our national contexts, respectively Norway and England.

At the Norwegian Olympic Training Centre we have developed a special team for eating disorders among elite athletes. This team is involved in preventive work through seminars and courses for athletes, coaches and leaders (judges, administrators), contributions in media, and through booklets, etc. We also offer treatment including individual psychotherapy, a modified cognitive group therapy programme and nutrition counselling. The team consists of a psychiatrist, a dietician and a consultant educated in sports medicine with eating disorders as a special area of interest. The team is an integrated part of the treatment services offered by The Norwegian Olympic Committee. This gives possibilities for close cooperation with other specialists within medicine—nurses, laboratory services, physiotherapists—and the training centre.

Through our work we have experienced the usefulness of developing such a special team, not least in the context of creating an alliance for treatment. The first consultation with an athlete with suspected or manifest eating disorder is extremely important. Eating-disordered athletes are more likely to accept the idea of going for a single consultation than the idea of committing themselves to prolonged treatment. Putting it very simply: the aim in the first session is to engage the patient enough to have a second session. We have heard many sad stories about eating-disordered athletes who have been in contact with the general health service. They were given the advice that they should stop competing or reduce their training drastically. Typically, the consequence of this is that they continue the training, but drop out from treatment.

It is our experience that it is easier to establish a trusting relationship when the eating-disordered athlete realises that the therapist knows the athlete's sport in addition to being trained in treating eating disorders. Therapists who have good knowledge about eating disorders and know the various sports will be better able to understand the athlete's training setting, daily demands, and relationships that are specific to the sport/type of events, and competitive level.

Building a sound therapeutic relationship will often include respecting the athlete's desire to be lean for athletic performance and expressing a willingness to work together to help the eating-disordered athlete to become lean and healthy, of course within the frames of a healthy body, like regular menstruation. The treatment team needs to accept the athlete's fears and irrational thoughts about food and weight, and then present a rational approach for achieving self-management of a healthy diet, weight, and training programme (Clark, 1993).

Themes and questions that should be included in the first consultations with athletes suspected to suffer from an eating disorder are listed in Table 24.2, which also shows what should be included in the system review, examination, lab tests and treatment.

At the Norwegian Olympic Training Centre, athletes with eating problems have their first consultation without any physical examination, blood tests or nutritional evaluation. The very first consultations are focused on the athlete's presentation of her/his 'problem'. After

Table 24.2   History and medical examination of female elite athletes with disordered eating

History related to eating disorders	Review of systems, evaluation, lab tests and treatment
Exercise Athlete's sport participation (is it fun, does she want to continue competing?) Hours spent training per week and intensity: aerobic and anaerobic training Time spent exercising outside of normal training regimen, continue training in spite of injury	*Symptoms of starvation and purging* Cold intolerance Amenorrhea, delayed menarch Light-headedness/lack of concentration Abdominal bloating Fatigue Constipation/diarrhoea Sore throat and chest pain Face and extremity oedema
Nutrition Eating pattern 24-hour food recall/3-day weighing Number of meals/snacks per day List of foods avoided (e.g. meat, sweets) How does she feel about her present weight/percent body fat? What does she consider her ideal weight/percent body fat? Has she ever tried to control her weight using vomiting, laxatives, diuretics, other drugs, fasting or excessive exercise?	*Physical exam* Dry skin, brittle hair and nails Decreased subcutaneous fat Hypothermia Bradycardia Lanugo Cold and discoloured hands and feet Orthostatic blood pressure changes Parotid gland enlargement Erosion of dental enamel
Menstrual history Age of menarche Frequency and duration of periods Date of last menstrual period Degree of regularity since menarche Use of hormonal therapy How does she feel about menstruating/not menstruating?	*Laboratory evaluation* Urine analysis Complete blood count and sedimentation rate Chemistry panel including electrolytes, calcium, magnesium and renal, thyroid and liver function tests Indication for an electrocardiogram Pulse is less than 50 bpm[a] (dependent on sport participation) Electrolyte abnormality Frequent purging behaviour

Family, medical and psychological history
Family:
  including weight history
  eating disorders or any other psychiatric disorders
Medical:
  chronic disease
  infections
  previous surgery
  medications
  injuries (including stress fractures)
Psychological:
  present stress factors in her life
  general mood, self-esteem and body image
	Treatment
	Multidisciplinary team approach:
	  Physician
	  Nutritionist
	  Psychologist/mental health professional
	  Coach (?)[b]
	  Trainer (?)[b]
	Criteria for hospitalisation:
	  Weight 30% below normal
	  Hypotension/dehydration
	  Electrolyte abnormalities

[a] Take into consideration that low pulse could be training induced.
[b] Dependent on the coach or trainer and athlete relationship. A good relationship is assumed to have a positive effect on treatment.

an assessment, which includes standardised questionnaires, the athletes are presented with the possible treatment options. This may be nutrition counselling only, such counselling in combination with short-term psychotherapy (10–20 sessions) and to a limited extent there is a possibility for long-term psychotherapy. Time limited group therapy may also be an alternative. Different types of treatment strategies have been described in detail elsewhere (Thompson & Trattner Sherman, 1993).

For a number of athletes with eating disorders we have to redefine their ambitions and clarify the therapist's involvement in training and competition programmes. The coaches play an important role in such dialogues and negotiations. But it is important to stress that the treatment of athletes with eating disorders should be undertaken by health care professionals. The role of the coaches is not to diagnose or treat eating disorders, but they must be educated about the signs and symptoms, to be specific about any suspicions they may have and strategies for supporting the eating-disordered athlete. Furthermore, coaches should encourage medical evaluation, and support the athlete during treatment.

A total suspension of training during treatment is not, or is seldom, a good solution. Therefore unless severe medical complications are present, training at a lower volume and at a decreased intensity should be allowed. For athletes with an eating disorder, it is important to acknowledge that some aspects of their dysregulated eating patterns may be the result of self-discipline and long-term goals. Moreover, it may be necessary for the athletes to continue with a dietary regimen or intensive training programme that would automatically be targeted for elimination in a non-athlete. In general, to avoid a message of sport performance as more important than health, it is recommended that athletes do not compete during treatment. Nevertheless, competitions during treatment might be considered for individuals with less severe eating disorders who are engaged in low-risk sports.

It is important to emphasise that the basic ethos for treatment is the psychological and physiological well-being of the patient, and not the gold medals. Some of the patients get well and achieve better in their sport. Others are supported in their wish, or are advised to stop competing.

While the Norwegian Olympic Training Centre offers a treatment package for athletes with eating disorders the situation in the UK remains bleak. Problems begin before an athlete can even seek help in that many coaches are unaware of the symptoms of eating disorders. Even if the athlete admits to having a problem and wants to get treatment there are further problems with obtaining a referral to a qualified and interested professional, who is aware of the particular demands of sport or dance.

The normal referral route in the UK is via a doctor who is a general practitioner, to a psychologist or psychiatrist or other health professional who specialises in eating-disorder treatments. One difficulty is that few therapists have any awareness of the special problems faced by athletes and dancers. Long waiting lists within the National Health Service or a patchy delivery of eating disorder services means than many people will look to the private sector for treatment.

Recent concern about treatment for athletes has led the Eating Disorders Association (EDA) and UK Athletics to set up a working party to educate athletes, coaches, family and friends. The group has organised workshops for coaches and medical and other sports scientists, and has produced leaflets about eating disorders. It is hoped to extend these workshops to other sports beyond athletics, but progress remains very slow.

Brinson and Dick (1996) carried out a national inquiry into dancers' health and injury. The report called for support structures to be set up for dancers to help them to deal with injuries and rehabilitation. The report called for support structures to be put into place that complemented those that existed for sports people, which would prevent dancers having to seek help from the private sector. It is ironic that the report called for the same provision as given to sports people. Whereas good facilities and practice does exist for physical injuries the problem of eating disorders is still under provided for.

Dance UK has published a booklet for dancers called *Your body, your risk* which provides information on the problems of eating disorders in dance and where to seek help. Preventive work with dance teachers is also planned. There is still resistance in the dance world in that it is not thought that science has anything to offer that could improve artistic performance.

PROGNOSIS

For most athletes, the reason for the development of an eating disorder seems to be related to extreme dieting, over-training, injury, or other more sport-specific factors. Data from the Norwegian team indicate that it may be easier to treat athletes, and that their prognoses should be better. However, this has not been fully investigated. When it comes to treatment, athletes may have some advantages compared to non-athletes. They are used to complying with rules and programmes and few have personality disorders or clinical depression. However, there are some possible negative factors that may delay the treatment progression in some athletes: low psychological mindedness, limited social experiences connected to spending so much of their time within a narrow subculture, and 'brainwashed' parents.

PREVENTION OF EATING DISORDERS

In contrast to prevention programmes from the general adolescent population (Gresko & Rosenvinge, 1998; Rosenvinge & Gresko, 1997), talking to athletes and coaches about eating disorders and related issues such as reproduction, bone health, nutrition, body composition, and performance prevents eating disorders in that population (Sundgot-Borgen & Klungland, 1998). Therefore, coaches, trainers, administrators and parents should receive information about eating disorders and related issues such as growth and development and the relationship between body composition, health, nutrition and performance. In addition, coaches should realise that they can strongly influence their athletes. Coaches or others involved with young athletes should not comment on an individual's body size, or require weight loss in young and still growing athletes. Without further guidance, dieting may result in unhealthy eating behaviour or eating disorders in highly motivated and uninformed athletes (Eisenman et al., 1990).

Because of the importance that athletes ascribe to their coaches, the success of a prevention programme tends to be related to the commitment and support of the coaches and 'important others' involved.

Early intervention is also important since eating disorders are more difficult to treat the longer they progress. Therefore professionals working with athletes should be informed about the possible risk factors for the development of eating disorders, early signs and symptoms, the medical, psychological and social consequences of these disorders, how to approach the problem if it occurs, and what treatment options are available.

CONCLUSION

Many studies have shown an increased prevalence of eating disorders among athletes and dancers compared with the general population. Eating disorders in both athletes and dancers can easily be missed unless they are specifically searched for. If untreated, eating disorders can have long-lasting physiological and psychological effects and may even be fatal. Treating athletes and dancers with eating disorders should be undertaken by qualified health care professionals. Ideally, these individuals should also be familiar with, and have an appreciation for, the athlete's sport or knowledge of the demands placed upon a dancer.

REFERENCES

Abraham, S. (1996) Characteristcs of eating disorders amongst young ballet dancers. *Psychopathology*, **29**, 223–229.

APA (1994) *Diagnostic and Statistical Manual of Mental Disorders* (4th edn.). Washington, D.C.: American Psychiatric Association.

Brinson, P. & Dick, F. (Eds) (1996) *Fit to Dance?* London: Calouste Gulbenkian Foundation.

Brownell, K.D., Steen, S.N. & Wilmore, J.H. (1987) Weight regulation practices in athletes: Analysis of metabolic and health effects. *Medicine and Science in Sports and Exercise*, **6**, 546–560.

Bruch, H. (1978) *The Golden Cage*. Cambridge: Harvard Press.

Clark, N. (1993) How to help the athlete with bulimia: Practical tips and case study. *International Journal of Sport Nutrition*, **3**, 450–460.

Cohen, J., Chung, S., May, P. & Ertel, N. (1982) Exercise, body weight and amenorrhea in professional ballet dancers. *Physician and Sports Medicine*, **10**, 92–101.

Connors, M.E. (1996) Developmental vulnerability for eating disorders. In L. Smolak, M. Levine & R. Striegal Moore (Eds), *The Developmental Psychopathology of Eating Disorders*. Hillsdale, NJ: Lawrence Erlbaum Associates.

Dale, K.S. & Landers, D.M. (1999) Weight control in wrestling: Eating disorders or disordered eating? *Medicine and Science in Sports and Exercise*, **31**(10), 1382–1389.

Davis, C. (1992) Body image, dieting behaviours and personality factors: A study of high performance female athletes. *International Journal of Sports Psychology*, **23**, 179–192.

Davis, C., Kennedy, S.H., Ralevski, E., Dionne, M., Brewer, H., Neiert, C. & Ratunsey, D. (1995) Obsessive compulsiveness and physical activity in anorexia nervosa and highlevel exercising. *Journal of Psychosomatic Research*, **39**(8), 967–976.

Doyle, J., Bryant Waugh, R., Plotkin, H. & Lask, B. (1997) *Emotional well being in children and adolescents attending specialist schools for the performing arts*. Unpublished PhD Thesis, University of London. [Quoted in Lask, B. & Bryant-Waugh, R. (1999) *Anorexia Nervosa and Related Eating Disorders in Childhood and Adolescents* (2nd edition). Psychology Press.]

Dyke, S. (Ed.) (2000) *Your Body Your Risk. The Facts: Can you Ignore Them?* Dance UK.

Eisenman, P.A., Johnson, S.C. & Benson, J.E. (1990) *Coaches Guide to Nutrition and Weight Control* (2nd edn). Champaign, Illinois: Leisure Press.

Fairburn, C., Welch, S., Doll, H., Davies, B. & O'Conner, M. (1997) Risk factors for bulimia nervosa. *Archives of General Psychiatry*, **54**, 509–517.

Fairburn, C. & Welch, S. (1998) *Risk Factors for Eating Disorders*. Oxford: University Department of Psychiatry.

Fogelholm, M. & Hilloskopri, H. (1999) Weight and diet concerns in Finnish female and male athletes. *Medicine and Science in Sports and Exercise*, **31**(2), 229–235.

Gadpalle, W.J., Sandborn, C.F. & Wagner, W.W. (1987) Athletic amenorrhea, major affective disorders and eating disorders. *American Journal of Psychiatry*, **144**, 9339–9343.

Garner, D. & Garfinkel, P. (1979) The eating attitudes test. *Psychological Medicine*, **9**, 273–279.

Garner, D. & Garfinkel, P. (1980) Sociocultural factors in the development of anorexia nervosa. *Psychological Medicine*, **10**, 647–656.

Garner, D., Garfinkel, P., Rockert, W. & Olmstead, M. (1987) A prospective study of eating disturbances in ballet. *Psychotherapy and Psychosomatics*, **48**, 170–175.

Garner, D. & Olmstead, M. (1984) *Manual for Eating Disorders Inventory (EDI)*. Odessa Psychological Assessment Resources.

Garfinkel, P., Garner, D. & Goldbloom, D.S. (1987) Eating disorders implications for the 1990s. *Canadian Journal of Psychiatry*, **32**, 624–631.

Gresko, R.B. & Rosenvinge, J.H. (1998) The Norwegian School-based prevention model: Development and validation. In W. Vandereycken & G. Noordenbos (Eds), *The Prevention of Eating Disorders*. London: Athlone Press/New York: New York University Press.

Hamilton, L., Brooks Gunn, J. & Warren, M. (1985) Sociocultural influences on eating disorders in female professional dancers. *International Journal of Eating Disorders*, **4**, 465–477.

Hamilton, L., Brooks Gunn, J., Warren, M. & Hamilton, W. (1988) The role of selectivity in the pathogenesis of eating problems in ballet dancers. *Medicine and Science in Sports and Exercise*, **20**, 560–565.

Homak, L.H. (1984) *The Effect of Competition on Eating Behaviour in Professional Ballet Dancers*. New York: Fordam University.

Hsu, L.K.G. (1990) *Eating Disorders*. New York: Guilford Press.

Johnson, C. & Connor, S.M. (1987) *The Etiology and Treatment of Bulimia Nervosa*. New York: Basic Books.

Katz, J.L. (1985) Some reflections on the nature of the eating disorders. *International Journal of Eating Disorders*, **4**, 617–626.

Le Grange, D., Tibbs, J. & Noakes, T. (1994) Implications of a diagnosis of anorexia nervosa in a ballet school. *International Journal of Eating Disorders*, **15**, 369–376.

Lowenkopf, E. & Vincent, L. (1982) The student ballet dancer and anorexia. *Hillside Journal of Clinical Psychology*, **4**, 53–64.

Mansfield, M.J. & Emans, S.J. (1993) Growth in female gymnasts: Should training decrease during puberty? *Pediatrics*, **122**, 237–240.

Mitchell, J.E. (1990) *Bulimia Nervosa*. Minneapolis: University of Minnesota Press.

Otis, C.L., Drinkwater, B., Johnson, M., Loucks, A. & Wilmore, J. (1997) The female athlete triad. *Medicine and Science in Sports and Exercise*, **29**, i–ix.

Oppliger, R.A., Landry, G., Foster, S.W. & Lambrecht, A.C. (1993) Bulimic behavior among interscholastic wrestlers: A statewide survey. *Pediatrics*, **91**, 826–831.

Rosenvinge, J.H. & Gresko, R.B. (1997) Do we need a prevention model for eating disorders? *Eating Disorders: The Journal of Treatment and Prevention*, **5**, 110–118.

Sacks, M.H. (1990) Psychiatry and sports. *Annals of Sports Medicine*, **5**, 47–52.

Schmidt, U., Tiller, J., Blanchard, M., Andrews, B. & Treasure, J.L. (1997) Is there a specific trauma precipitating anorexia nervosa? *Psychological Medicine*, **27**, 523–530.

Skårderud, F. (1998) Portrett av atleten i nød. In S. Loland (Ed.), *Toppidrettens pris*. Oslo: Universitetsforlaget. (In Norwegian.)

Sundgot-Borgen, J. (1993) Prevalence of eating disorders in female elite athletes. *International Journal of Sports Nutrition*, **3**, 29–40.

Sundgot-Borgen, J. (1994) Risk and trigger factors for the development of eating disorders in female elite athletes. *Medicine and Science in Sports and Exercise*, **4**, 414–419.

Sundgot-Borgen, J. (1996) Eating disorders, energy intake, training volume, and menstrual function in high-level modern rhythmic gymnasts. *International Journal of Sport Nutrition*, **6**, 100–109.

Sundgot-Borgen, J. & Klungland, M. (1998) The female athlete triad and the effect of preventive work. *Medicine and Science in Sports and Exercise*, Suppl. **5**, 181.

Szmukler, G.I., Eisler, I. & Gillies, C. & Hayward, M.E. (1985) The implications of anorexia nervosa in a ballet school. *Journal of Psychiatric Research*, **19**, 177–181.

Thompson, R.A. & Trattner Sherman, R. (1993) *Helping Athletes with Eating Disorders*. Champaign, Illinois: Human Kinetic.

Theintz, M.J., Howald, H. & Weiss, U. (1993) Evidence of a reduction of growth potential in adolescent female gymnasts. *Journal of Pediatrics*, **122**, 306–313.

Torstveit, G., Rolland, C.G. & Sundgot-Borgen, J. (1998) Pathogenic weight control methods and self-reported eating disorders among male elite athletes. *Medicine and Science in Sports and Exercise*, Suppl. **5**, 181.

Vincent, L. (1981) *Competing with the Sylph. Dancers and the Pursuit for the Ideal Body*. Kansas City, Kansas: Andrews & McMeel.

Warren, B.J., Stanton, A.L. & Blessing, D.L. (1990) Disordered eating patterns in competitive female athletes. *International Journal of Eating Disorders*, **5**, 565–569.

Wilmore, J.H. (1991) Eating and weight disorders in female athletes. *International Journal of Sports Nutrition*, **1**, 104–117.

CHAPTER 25

Comorbidity of Diabetes Mellitus and Eating Disorders

Stephen Herpertz

Clinic of Psychosomatic Medicine and Psychotherapy, University of Essen, Essen, Germany

and

Søren Nielsen

Psychiatric Youth Centre, Storstrøm County Psychiatric Services, Næstved, Denmark

INTRODUCTION

Diabetes mellitus is the most common of the serious metabolic diseases of humans. The disease is characterized by a series of hormone-induced metabolic abnormalities, by long-term complications involving the eyes, kidneys, nerves, and blood vessels. The basic categories are type 1 or insulin-dependent diabetes (IDDM) and type 2 or non-insulin-dependent diabetes (NIDDM). Insulin dependence in this classification is not equivalent to insulin therapy. Rather, the term means that the patient is at risk for ketoacidosis in the absence of insulin. The overall prevalence in western societies is thought to be about 2.4% to 4.0% (Waldhäusl & Gries 1996). The most prevalent form of diabetes is type 2-diabetes, which accounts for 80% of the diabetic population. Type 1-diabetes is characterized by absolute lack of insulin production due to autoimmune destruction of the pancreatic cell. This type of diabetes usually begins before the age of 40, often in childhood or adolescence. Insulin resistance plays a major role in subjects within type 2-diabetes. The onset is usually during mid-life. In 60% to 90% of the patients, type 2-diabetes is accompanied by obesity. Individuals affected by diabetes must learn self-management skills and make lifestyle changes to effectively manage diabetes and avoid or delay the complications associated with this disorder.

Contrary to type 2-diabetes, insulin therapy is required in type 1-diabetes once symptoms have developed. Intensification of insulin therapy combined with comprehensive diabetes education lead to a significant and lasting improvement of metabolic control. In type 2-diabetes symptoms begin more gradually and the diagnosis is frequently made when an asymptomatic person is found to have an elevated plasma glucose on routine laboratory examination. Weight reduction is considered the treatment of choice for obese patients with type 2-diabetes. The positive short-term effects of weight loss on metabolic control have been well documented (Wing et al., 1987), long-term effects, however, are uncertain (Goodrick & Foreyt, 1991; Wing, 1993).

ETIOLOGY

Type 1-Diabetes and Eating Disorders

The earliest reference to concurrent diabetes mellitus and eating disorder date back to 1974 when Bruch described a 19-year-old anorectic girl, who also suffered from diabetes. There have been a succession of reports, special studies and surveys describing comorbidity of diabetes mellitus and eating disorders. As the age at onset of anorexia peaks from 14 to 18 years, and the mean age of onset of bulimia nervosa is 18 years, the prevalence of eating disorders and diabetes mellitus has been predominantly studied in adolescent type 1-diabetes patients.

There is some theoretical rationale to predict that eating disorders may be more prevalent in adolescent and young adult women with type 1-diabetes than in their nondiabetic peers. Thus the order of onset is of interest when evaluating the influence of one disorder on another. As Nielsen and Mølbak (1998) demonstrated in their recent review, most studies indicate that type 1-diabetes precedes the eating disorder (Fairburn & Steel, 1980; Hillard et al., 1983; Powers et al., 1983; Hudson et al., 1985; Rodin et al., 1986–1987; Nielsen et al., 1987; Steel et al., 1987; Pollock et al., 1995; Ward et al., 1995; Herpertz et al., 1998a, 1998b) implicating that type 1-diabetes may be a significant risk factor.

Several aspects of type 1-diabetes and its management might lower the threshold for the expression of an eating disturbance in vulnerable young women. Because of insulin deficiency and glycosuria a period of significant weight loss usually precedes the diagnosis of type 1-diabetes.

- The institution of insulin and intensive insulin therapy are both associated with weight gain (Copeland & Anderson, 1995) and may augment the cognitive and emotional preoccupation with questions concerning body shape and form as well as eating habits which are prevalent in this developmental stage (Engström et al., 1999). A weight gain, associated with diabetes mellitus, may therefore make this stage of development even more crucial and represent an important etiological factor in the development of eating disorders (Steel et al., 1990).

Although new diabetes treatment strategies liberalized food consumption, adherence to a prescribed dietary regimen and corresponding daily doses of exogenous insulin remains to be a key component of type 1-diabetes care:

- Constant dieting might cause bingeing by promoting the adoption of a cognitively regulated eating style, which is necessary if the physiological defense of body weight is to be overcome. By substituting physiological regulatory controls with cognitive controls, dieting makes the dieter vulnerable to disinhibition and subsequent over-eating (Polivy & Herman, 1985). According to this theory, dieting and binge eating, for example, are closely related and may explain a possible higher prevalence of bulimia or binge eating disorder in both type 1 and type 2-diabetes patients.

- Hypoglycemia as a result of insufficient adherence to dietary regimen and insulin-dosage may trigger a binge.
- Of the self-care behavior, omission or intentional underdosing of recommended levels of self-administered insulin is one of the most serious adherence problems. Omission of insulin in type 1-diabetes leads to hyperglycemia, excessive urination, volume depletion, and ketoacidosis. Some young diabetic patients omit or underdose insulin in order to reduce their weight, thus inducing glucosuria. This highly risky attempt to lose weight called 'insulin-purging' is considered to be a diabetes-specific method of preventing weight gain. When insulin is reinstituted after having been omitted for some time, the patient typically has temporary weight gain as a result of rehydration. This phenomenon makes it extremely difficult for a woman who is already terrified of becoming fat, and believing that insulin makes her fat, to continue taking insulin.

Type 2-Diabetes and Eating Disorders

There has been considerably less research on the comorbidity of type 2-diabetes and eating disorders. Not only young women but also older, especially overweight, women have likewise been found to be concerned about eating, body weight, and physical appearance (Pliner et al., 1990) and to exhibit significant body dissatisfaction across the life span (Tiggerman, 1992; Stevens & Tiggerman, 1998). Being overweight is a major correlate of type 2-diabetes and weight reduction is considered one effective approach to manage the disease not only in the early stage but for some time (Wing et al., 1995). Furthermore, it has been suggested that dieting, and its almost inevitable failure and link with bingeing (Polivy & Herman, 1985), might mediate or moderate the relationship between perceived overweight and self-esteem.

Wing et al. (1989) observed binge eating to be a common problem in obese type 2-diabetic patients and Herpertz et al. (1998a, 1998b) demonstrated the distribution of the eating disorders to be different in the diabetes subtypes, with a predominance of bulimia nervosa in type 1-diabetes and binge eating disorder in type 2-diabetes. Contrary to type 1-diabetes, nearly 90% of type 2-diabetic patients developed an eating disorder before the metabolic illness was diagnosed. The majority of type 2-diabetic patients indicated the age of onset of the eating disorder between 15 and 35 years, suggesting that the eating disorder preceded type 2 diabetes even in the state of asymptomatic hyperglycemia. In several studies, there is evidence that the onset of binge eating disorder more commonly precedes the onset of significant dieting (Spitzer et al., 1992, 1993; Wilson et al., 1993). Thus, binge eating disorder does not seem to be primarily the consequence of weight reduction connected with restraint eating, as a supreme therapy goal for overweight type 2-diabetic patients enhancing their susceptibility to dietary disinhibition and bingeing. Because of the lack of compensatory measures, however, a steady rise in body weight usually is the consequence of the binge eating disorder. By being overweight and obese, binge eating may lead to type 2-diabetes in some patients.

EPIDEMIOLOGY

In spite of the discussed predisposing aspects, reported prevalence of eating disorders within type 1-diabetes patients has varied considerably with prevalence rates ranging from 0.0%

(Striegel-Moore et al., 1992) to 35.0% (Hudson et al., 1985). The different findings depend upon the population, the response rate in the sample studied, and the measures, methods, and diagnostic criteria used. Early exclusively observational studies suggested high rates of eating disorders in young women with type 1-diabetes (Hudson et al., 1985). Recent controlled studies (Rosmark et al., 1986; Robertson & Rosenvinge, 1990; Fairburn et al., 1991; Striegel-Moore et al., 1992; Peveler et al., 1992; Vila et al., 1995; Engström et al., 1999; Jones et al., 2000)—some of them using a two-stage epidemiological strategy, with screening tests and validated semistructured interviews as more rigorous methods—have found lower rates of clinical eating disorders.

At least 26 studies have examined the frequency of eating disorder behaviors or diagnoseable eating disorders in type 1 and type 2 diabetes. Studies which used criterion-based diagnoses demonstrated lower estimates of rates of eating disorders.

- Controlled trials did not show evidence of greater prevalence of eating disorders in type 2-diabetes. The overall findings for type 1-diabetes can be summarized as follows—there is no support for a hypothesis on an increased occurrence of AN, but there seems to be a significant three-fold increase in the odds ratio for bulimia nervosa, as well as a significant two-fold increase in odds ratio for both EDNOS and subthreshold eating disorders (Nielsen, 2002). Crow et al. (1998) cautions that important dimensional information about pathological eating behavior might be missed by structured interviews, as it might not fit any of the specific diagnostic categories. Fairburn et al. (1991) demonstrated that disturbed eating is common in patients with diabetes mellitus.
- Binge eating disorder seems to be the most prevalent eating disorder in type 2-diabetes.

INTENTIONAL OMISSION OF INSULIN: 'INSULIN-PURGING'

A number of studies have examined the prevalence rate of intentional insulin omission in order to counteract food eaten or to lose weight. According to these data, the frequency of insulin omission reported by subjects varies rather widely. The wide variability in rates of insulin omission across studies may reflect a number of methodologic issues, including the survey of different age groups, different clinical populations, and different assessment methods.

The data of most studies suggest that 'insulin-purging' is a fairly frequent phenomenon within the broad population of diabetic persons and tends to be higher than the rate of diagnosable eating disorders in type 1-diabetes.

Rodin et al. (1991) pointed out that omission of insulin is far more common in those persons with a diagnosable eating disorder (52% vs 12%) and that insulin manipulation is a more common method of weight control than self-induced vomiting and laxative or diuretic abuse. Other controlled studies have similar findings (see Nielsen, 2002). These findings support the notion that 'insulin purging' is often eating disorder-related rather than a reflection of general problems with compliance and may serve as a useful marker of elevated risk for an eating disorder.

- According to population-based type 1-samples, young women—but not men—frequently omit insulin.

Table 25.1 Studies on the comorbidity of diabetes mellitus and eating disorders

Author	Year	No.	Type of diabetes	Sex	Mean age (years)	AN (%)	BN (%)	BED & EDNOS (%)	Methods
Hudson et al.	1985	80	type 1	female	18.4	0	35.0	n.i.	not standardized
Rodin et al.	1986	58	type 1	female	17.6	6.9	6.9	20.7	questionnaire
Rosmark et al.	1986	102	type 1	male/female	28.4	2.9	0.9	n.i.	questionnaire*
Lloyd et al.	1987	208	type 1	female	n.i.	5.0	1.0	1.5	not standardized
Steel et al.	1987	208	type 1	female	20.5	4.3	1.4	n.i.	not standardized
Stancin et al.	1989	59	type 1	female	21.5	0.0	12.0	36.0	questionnaire
Popkin et al.	1989	75	type 1	male/female	31.0	0.0	1.3	n.i.	interview*
Birk & Spencer	1989	385	type 1	female	28.2	1.0	16.2	n.i.	not standardized
Wing et al.	1989	98	type 2	male/female	52.5	0.0	0.0	15.0	questionnaire
Powers et al.	1990	97	type 1	male/female	15.6	0.0	1.0	n.i.	questionnaire
Robertson & Rosenvinge	1990	56	type 1	female	26.2	0.0	1.8	15.0	quest & interv.*
Fairburn et al.	1991	100	type 1	male/female	21.5	1.0	3.0	3.0	interview*
Rodin et al.	1991	103	type 1	female	15.1	0.0	12.0	n.i.	questionnaire
Striegel-Moore et al.	1992	46	type 1	female	13.0	0.0	0.0	n.i.	interview*
Peveler et al.	1992	76	type 1	male/female	15.3	0.0	0.0	n.i.	quest. & interv.*
Vila et al.	1993	52	type 1	female	15.9	0.0	6.0	35.0	quest. & interview*
Lorini et al.	1993	74	type 1	male/female	9.2	4.1	0.0	6.8	not standardized
Kenardy et al.	1994	50	type 2	male/female	63.0	0.0	0.0	6.0	quest & interv.*
Friedman et al.	1995	40	type 1	female	23.0	0.0	2.0	39.0	quest. & interv.*
Pollock et al.	1995	79	type 1	male/female	10.5	0.0	3.4	2.1	interview
Cantwell & Steel	1996	147	type 1	female	23.0	0.0	3.4	2.1	quest. & interv.
Affenito et al.	1997	90	type 1	female	28.2	4.4	11.1	14.4	quest. & interv.
Bryden et al.	1999	76	type 1	male/female	15.2	0.0	0.0	4.6	stand. interv.
Engström et al.	1999	89	type 1	female	16.3	0.0	0.0	6.0	quest. & interv.*
Pinhas-Hamiel et al.	1999	42	type 2	male/female	14.5	0.0	0.0	7.1	interview
Carroll et al.	1999	125	type 2	female	58.1	n.i.	n.i.	5.8Φ	questionnaire*
Herpertz et al.	1999	341	type 1	male/female	36.3	0.3	1.5-2.1	3.5-4.7	quest. & interv.
		322	type 2	male/female	54.2	0.0	0.3	6.2-8.7	
Jones et al.	2000	356	type 1	female	14.9	0.0	1.0	9.0	quest. & interv.*

AN = Anorexia Nervosa; BN = Bulimia Nervosa; BED = Binge Eating Disorder; EDNOS = Eating Disorder Not Otherwise Specified;
n.i. = not investigated; Φ binge eating; *controlled study

Table 25.2 Intentional insulin omission ('insulin purging') in patients with type 1-diabetes, lifetime prevalence

Authors	Year	No.	Type of diabetes	Gender	Average age	Insulin purging lifetime %	Method
Hudson et al.	1985	80	type 1	female	18.4	14.0	questionnaire
Birk & Spencer	1987	385	type 1	female	28.2	4.9	questionnaire
Stancin et al.	1989	59	type 1	female	21.5	39.0	questionnaire
Powers et al.	1990	97	type 1	male/female	15.6	14.1	questionnaire
Fairburn et al.	1991	100	type 1	male/female	21.5	54.7	interview
Rodin et al.	1991	103	type 1	female	15.1	12.0	questionnaire
Striegel-Moore et al.	1992	46	type 1	female	13.0	6.5	quest. & interv.
Peveler et al.	1992	76	type 1	male/female	15.3	15	interview
Biggs et al.	1994	42	type 1	female	28.0	35.7	quest. & interv.
Dunning et al.	1995	59	type 1	male/female	23.0	38.0	questionnaire
Polonsky et al.	1995	341	type 1	female	33.1	30.5	questionnaire
Cantwell et al.	1995	147	type 1	female	24.4	6.8	questionnaire
Affenito et al.	1997	90	type 1	female	28.8	13.3	quest. & interv.
Rydall et al.	1997	91	type 1	female	15.0	14.0	questionnaire
Bryden et al.	1999	76	type 1	male/female	15.2	13.2	interview
Herpertz et al.	1999	341	type 1	male/female	36.3	5.9	quest. & interv.
Herpertz et al.	1999	322	type 2	male/female	54.2	2.2	quest. & interv.
Jones et al.	2000	356	type 1	female	149	11	quest. & interv.

COURSE OF EATING DISORDERS IN DIABETES

Little is known about the long-term course of eating disorders and eating pathology in diabetes mellitus. Rydall et al. (1997) performed a sophisticated study of 91 type 1-diabetes young women over a period of four years. Disordered eating behavior was common and persistent in these women. A variety of pathological behavior was more frequent, including insulin omission, dieting, and self-induced vomiting. Disordered eating was associated with impaired glycemic control and a higher risk of diabetic retinopathy. In a longitudinal study, Bryden et al. (1999) interviewed 65 of originally 76 male and female adolescents after eight years. An increase in body weight from adolescence to adulthood could be observed and was associated with higher levels of concern over shape and weight and more intense dietary restraint, especialy among females. This study failed to show evidence of increase in the prevalence of clinical and subclinical eating disorders. There was no relationship between those subjects with an eating disorder and glycemic control, nor was there a significant difference between the glycemic control of those subjects who admitted intentional insulin misuse and glycemic control of the rest of the females at both baseline and follow-up. A register study by Nielsen, Emborg and Mølbak (2002) indicate increased mortality in this group of patients.

RISK FACTORS

Numerous studies have examined the relationship between eating disorder rating-scale scores, eating disorders, and glycemic control in diabetics. Rodin et al. (1986) and Wing et al. (1986) reported a positive correlation between the frequency of binge eating and HbA1c concentration. The findings of Cantwell and Steel (1996) could not corroborate this. Eight of the 14 studies listed in Table 25.3 show diabetic patients with an eating disorder to have significantly higher glycosylated hemoglobin levels compared to diabetic patients without an eating disorder. However, five studies, two of them with control groups could not find significant differences in glycemic control between diabetics with and without an eating disorder. One reason for these divergent findings might be different therapy strategies. The more intensive diabetes treatment is, the more flexible food consumption and even a binge can be handled and counterregulated by a flexible amount of short and very short effective insulin.

Several groups have examined the relationship between insulin omission and glycemic control (Biggs et al., 1994; Herpertz et al., 1998b; Jones et al., 2000; La Greca et al., 1987; Polonsky et al., 1994; Takii et al., 1999). In three of the studies (Biggs et al., 1994; Jones et al., 2000; La Greca et al., 1987; Polonsky et al., 1994; Takii et al., 1999), glycosylated hemoglobin levels were significantly higher in the insulin-omitting subjects.

- Eating disorders and especially the intentional omission of insulin to influence body weight is often associated with poor control of glycemia in diabetic individuals.

DIABETIC COMPLICATIONS

There is a strong relationship between glycemic control and the development of complications in diabetes mellitus (DCCT Research Group, 1995). Numerous studies, which have

Table 25.3 Glycemic control of diabetic patients with and without an eating disorder

Authors	Sample (n)	Type of diabetes	Glycemic control (HbA1(c)) (%)	Eating disorder +	Eating disorder −	Type of eating disorder
Rodin et al., 1986	58	type 1	HbA1	12.1	11.5	AN, BN, EDNOS
Birk & Spencer, 1989	154	type 1	HbA1c	8.44+	7.0	AN, BN
Rodin et al., 1991	103	type 1	HbA1	10.0+	8.9	AN, BN
Fairburn et al., 1991	100	type 1	HbA1	13.3+	11.1	BN, EDNOS*
Colas et al., 1991	58	type 1	HbA1c	10.8+	8.1	AN, BN*
Friedman et al., 1995	69	type 1	HbA1c	8.8	8.2	EDNOS*
Cantwell & Steel, 1996	48	type 1	HbA1	11.3+	10.2	EAT-scores
Affenito et al., 1997	90	type 1	HbA1c	10.4+/10.0+	8.3	clinical/subclinical EDs*
Rydall et al., 1997	91	type 1	HbA1c	11.1+/8.9	8.7	highly/moderately disordered eating
Engström et al., 1999	89	type 1	HbA1c	8.7	8.3	EDNOS*
Bryden et al., 1999	76	type 1	HbA1c	10.3	9.5	EDNOS, insulin omission
Takii et al., 1999	33	type 1	HbA1c	12.3+/9.7+	6.2	BN, EDNOS*
Herpertz et al., 1999	341	type 1	rel. HbA1(c)	1.6	1.5	AN, BN, EDNOS, BED
	322	type 2	rel. HbA1(c)	1.7	1.7	BN, EDNOS, BED
Jones et al., 2000	356	type 1	HbA1c	9.4+	8.6	BN, EDNOS*

+ significant; *controlled study.

Table 25.4 Frequency of clinically significant retinopathy in cases with concurrent eating disorder and type 1-diabetes

	Retinopathy		
Authors	+	−	%
Steel et al., 1987	11	4	73
Nielsen et al., 1987	2	3	40
Colas et al., 1991	18	11	62
Ward et al., 1995	7	10	41
Affenito et al., 1997	5	9	36
Rydall et al., 1997	12	9	57

exclusively been performed on type 1-diabetes patients, have demonstrated a relationship between the co-occurrence of an eating disorder and diabetes mellitus and elevated risk for medical complications of either the eating disorder or diabetes.

Two longitudinal studies examined the relationship between eating disturbances and insulin-omission and diabetic lesions. Rydall et al. (1997), but not Bryden et al. (1999), could demonstrate a strong relationship between disordered eating, impaired glycemic control and higher risk of diabetic retinopathy after a four- and eight-year follow-up respectively. However, Bryden et al. (1999) showed that 50% of diabetics who had developed microvascular complications had deliberately misused their insulin in the past.

PREVENTION AND MANAGEMENT OF EATING DISORDERS IN PATIENTS WITH DIABETES MELLITUS

Type 1-Diabetes

Given the potential health risks resulting from the combination of type 1-diabetes and an eating disorder, routine assessment of eating attitudes and behavior in adolescent and young adult women is discussed (Daneman & Rodin, 1999). With regard to epidemiologic data this procedure seems to be justified in high-risk groups of eating disorders like young adolescent girls. Furthermore, a sophisticated investigation of an eating disorder must be taken into consideration in all cases of poor glycemic control without any medical explanation.

Type 1-diabetes has long been thought to complicate the treatment and outcome of persons with eating disorders; however, treatment outcome data of these comorbid diabetics are rare and are commonly based on case reports of type 1-diabetic patients (Nielsen et al., 1987; Peveler & Fairburn 1989, 1992; Spurdle & Giles, 1990; Mannuai et al., 1997; Pitel et al., 1998). Recently, Carney et al. (1996) compared 27 female patients with an eating disorder with and without type 1-diabetes over a period of four years to evaluate the influence of diabetes on the presentation, course, and outcome of the eating disorder pathology. With the exception of bone density, they found only few differences between these two samples and outcomes were similar.

On the condition that type 1-diabetic patients with an eating disorder usually had an intensive diabetic education in the past, the common assumption that there is a knowledge deficit about the risk of diabetic complications is often inaccurate. On the contrary, their knowledge about therapy regimen is usually excellent often exceeding the knowledge of ordinary nurses or even medical doctors not working in the field of diabetes. Educational efforts may be more effective when directed toward themes typically addressed in eating disorder treatment. These include information on attitudes about shape and weight in Western societies, the role of dietary restriction as a precipitant of binge eating, and the biological determinants of body weight.

A careful assessment for psychiatric comorbidity is an important aspect of the initial evaluation. In a longitudinal study of diabetic adolescents Pollock et al. (1995) showed that eating disorders occured almost exclusively in the context of a DSM-III psychiatric diagnosis other than eating disorder and that in each case the psychiatric illness temporally preceded the period of disordered eating and was comorbid with it. The association of eating disorders with psychiatric illness suggests that a subgroup of type 1-diabetes patients have various difficulties in coping with their diabetes. The impact of combining various psychiatric disorders has yet to be determined but might contribute to a higher risk of poor glycemic control and diabetic lesions. Divergent findings in glycemic control in comorbid diabetic samples may result from different psychiatric comorbidities other than eating disorders with different coping styles, and adherence to diabetes care.

- Future research on the comorbidity of eating disorders and diabetes mellitus should include the precise evaluation of psychiatric disorders other than eating disorders with regard to adherence to diabetes care, glycemic control, and diabetic lesions.

Multidimensional structured therapy approaches consisting of various treatment interventions are common in the treatment of eating disorders and appear to yield somewhat better results (Herzog et al., 1996). There is little evidence that a special treatment approach is necessary for comorbid type 1-diabetic patients; however, in order to establish a confident therapeutic relationship, psychiatrists or psychologists should be familiar with diabetes and its treatment regimen. For example, keeping a protocol of the blood sugar levels is, at least for type 1-diabetes patients, mandatory; this could then be implemented along with an eating disorder protocol as an important factor in the treatment of patients with an eating disorder.

Type 2-Diabetes

Patients with type 2-diabetes are usually obese and suffer from other obesity-related medical problems such as hypertension and hyperlipidemia. In the sense of weight cycling, the majority of these patients have engaged in numerous weight loss programs but eventually end up with a weight gain instead of a weight loss. Therefore therapy strategies need to be aimed at eating disorders, particularly binge eating, and weight reduction with regard to decreasing the metabolic risks of these patients. As yet, we know little about the treatment of the binge eating disorder in relation to obesity. Several studies on treatment outcome of the binge eating disorder has not shown that an improvement of the binge eating symptomatology was necessarily connected with weight loss (Castonguay et al., 1995; Fichter et al., 1998). The treatment of obese patients with an eating disorder is regarded to be less successful compared to obese patients without an eating disorder (Marcus & Wing, 1987). However, Yanovsky and Sebring (1994) showed no difference in outcome of behavioral weight loss programs of obese subjects with and without binge eating. Diabetic and diet counseling, joint shopping, and preparation of meals as well as the motivation for physical exercise are further elements of an integrated treatment approach. Long-term follow-up studies of obese patients with and without diabetes undergoing behavior therapy (Brown et al., 1996; NHLBI Obesity Education Initiative Expert Panel, 1998; Wing et al., 1997) show a return to baseline weight in the vast majority of subjects in the absence of continued behavioral intervention. Therefore, the emphasis is placed on the great importance of continuing a maintenance program on a long-term basis.

CLINICAL IMPLICATIONS

For diabetic patients there is no such thing as 'subclinical' or 'subthreshold' eating disorders. It is necessary to screen the diabetic population, especially young and adolescent females for eating pathology. If possible, the high risk population should be subjected to a psychiatric interview. A useful first step might be intensified contact with a dietician, followed by psychotherapeutic contact if necessary. Close liaison between psychotherapist and diabetes team is essential, as well as a basic understanding of management of diabetes on the therapist's part.

RESEARCH IMPLICATIONS

Multicenter cooperative efforts are needed—as demonstrated by the Toronto group (Rodin et al., 1991; Rydall et al., 1997; Jones et al., 2000) and the German group (Herpertz et al., 1998a, 1998b)—to give sufficient power to the data. The model with three controls per proband (Jones et al., 2000) seems very efficient. Population-based studies of the epidemiology of eating disorders in type 2-diabetes are needed. Initial screening for (diabetic) complications at entry and control for weight would be very helpful as well as careful assessment of specific eating patterns and transgressions of the optimal treatment plans for diabetes. Well-planned and executed controlled outcome studies of preventive and treatment efforts are much needed.

REFERENCES

Biggs, M.M., Ramirez, M., Patterson, G. & Raskin, P. (1994) Insulin withholding for weight control in women with diabetes. *Diabetes Care*, **17**, 1186–1189.

Bruch, H. (1973) *Eating Disorders: Obesity, Anorexia and the Person Within.* (pp 356–357), New York, Basic Books.

Bryden, K.S., Neil, A., Mayou, R.A., Peveler, R.C., Fairburn, C.G. & Dunger, D.B. (1999) Eating habits, body weight, and insulin misuse. *Diabetes Care*, **22**, 1956–1960.

Cantwell, R. & Steel, J.M. (1996) Screening for eating disorders in diabetes mellitus. *Journal of Psychosomatic Research*, **40**, 15–20.

Carney, C., Andersen, A., Barsness, J. & Holman, J. (1996) The influence of type 1 diabetes mellitus on the course and outcome of the eating disorders. A comparative analysis. Seventh New York International Conference on Eating Disorders, April 26–28.

Castonguay, L.G., Eldredge, K.L. & Agras, W.S. (1995) Binge eating disorder: Current state and future directions. *Clinical Psychology Review*, **15**, 865–890.

Colas, C.L., Mathieu, P. & Tchobroutsky, G. (1991) Eating disorders and retinal lesions in type 1 (insulin-dependent) diabetic women. *Diabetologia*, **34**, 288.

Copeland, P.M. & Anderson, B. (1995) Diabetes mellitus and eating disorders. *Harvard Review of Psychiatry*, **3**, 46–50.

Crow, S.J., Keel, P.K. & Kendall, D. (1998) Eating disorders and insulin-dependent diabetes mellitus. *Psychosomatics*, **39**, 233–243.

Daneman, P. & Rodin, G. (1999) Eating disorders in young women with type 1 diabetes: A cause for concern? *Acta Paediatr.*, **88**, 175–180.

DCCT Reseach Group (1995) The effect of intensive treatment of diabetes on the development and progression of long-term complications in insulin-dependent diabetes mellitus. *New England Journal of Medicine*, **329**, 977–986.

Engström, I., Kroon, M., Arvidsson, C.-G., Segnestam, K., Snellman, K. & Aman, J. (1999) Eating disorders in adolescent girls with insulin-dependent diabetes mellitus: A population-based case-control study. *Acta Paediatrica*, **88**, 175–180.

Fairburn, C.G. & Steel, J.M. (1980) Anorexia nervosa in diabetes mellitus. *British Medical Journal*, **280**, 1167–1168.

Fairburn, C.G., Peveler, R.C., Davies, B., Mann, J.I. & Mayou, R.A. (1991) Eating disorders in young adults with insulin-dependent diabetes mellitus: A controlled study. *British Medical Journal*, **303**, 17–20.

Fichter, M.M., Quadflieg, N. & Gnutsmann, A. (1998) Binge eating disorder: Treatment outcome over a 6 year course. *Journal of Psychosomatic Research*, **44**, 385–404.

Goodrick, G.K. & Foreyt, J.P. (1991) Why treatments for obesity don't last. *Journal of the American Dietitian's Association*, **91**, 1243–1247.

Herpertz, S., Albus, C., Wagener, R., Kocnar, M., Wagner, R., Henning, A., Best, F., Foerster, H., Schulze Schleppinghoff, B., Thomas, W., Köhle, K., Mann, K. & Senf, W. (1998a) Comorbidity of diabetes mellitus and eating disorders: Does diabetes control reflect disturbed eating behavior? *Diabetes Care*, **21**, 1110–1116.

Herpertz, S., Wagener, R., Albus, C., Kocnar, M., Wagner, R., Best, F., Schulze Schleppinghoff, B., Filz, H.-P., Förster, H., Mann, K., Köhle, K. & Senf, W. (1998b) Diabetes mellitus and eating disorders: A multicenter study on the comorbidity of the two diseases. *Journal of Psychosomatic Research*, **44**, 503–515.

Herzog, T., Hartmann, A. & Falk, C. (1996) Symptomorientierung und psychodynamisches Gesamtkonzept bei der stationären Behandlung der Anorexia Nervosa. *Psychotherapy and Psychosomatics in Medical Psychology*, **46**, 11–22.

Hillard, J.R., Lobo, M.C. & Keeling, R.P. (1983) Bulimia and diabetes: A potentially life-threatening combination. *Psychosomatics*, **24**, 292–295.

Hudson, J.I., Wentworth, S.M., Hudson, M.S., Harrison, G. & Pope, J. (1985) Prevalence of anorexia nervosa and bulimia among young diabetic women. *Journal of Clinical Psychiatry*, **46**, 88–89.

Jones, J.M., Lawson, M.I., Daneman, D., Olmsted, M.P. & Rodin, G. (2000) Eating disorders in adolescent females with and without type 1 diabetes: Cross sectional study. *British Medical Journal*, **320**, 1563–1566.

La Greca, A.M., Schwarz, L.T. & Satin, W. (1987) Eating patterns in young women with IDDM: Another look. *Diabetes Care*, **10**, 659–660.

Mannuai, E., Ricca, V. & Rotella, C.M. (1997) Clinical features of binge eating disorder in type 1 diabetes: A case report. *International Journal of Eating Disorders*, **21**, 99–102.

Marcus, M.D. & Wing, R.R. (1987) Binge eating among the obese. *Annals of Behavioral Medicine*, **9**, 23–27.

NHLBI Obesity Education Initiative Expert Panel (1998) Clinical guidelines on the identification, evaluation, and treatment of overweight and obesity in adults—the evidence report. *Obesity Research*, **6**, 51–210.

Nielsen, S. (2002) Eating Disorders in Females with Type 1 Diabetes: An Update of a Meta-analysis. *European Eating Disorders Review*, **10**, 241–254.

Nielsen, S., Børner, H. & Kabel, M. (1987) Anorexia nervosa/bulimia in diabetes mellitus. *Acta Psychiatrica Scandinavica*, **75**, 464–473.

Nielsen, S., Emborg, C. & Mølbak, A.G. (2002) Mortality in Concurrent Type 1 Diabetes and Anorexia Nervosa. *Diabetes Care*, **25**, 309–312.

Nielsen, S. & Mølbak, A.G. (1998) Eating disorder and type 1-diabetes: Overview and summing-up. *European Eating Disorders Review*, **6**, 1–24.

Peveler, R.C. & Fairburn, C.G. (1989) Anorexia nervosa in association with diabetes mellitus—a cognitive-behavioural approach to treatment. *Behaviour Research and Therapy*, **27**, 95–99.

Peveler, R.C. & Fairburn, C.G. (1992) The treatment of bulimia nervosa in patients with diabetes mellitus. *International Journal of Eating Disorders*, **11**, 45–53.

Peveler, R.C., Fairburn, C.G., Boller, I. & Dunger, D. (1992) Eating disorders in adolescents with IDDM. *Diabetes Care*, **15**, 1356–1360.

Pliner, P., Chaiken, S. & Flett, G.L. (1990) Gender differences in concern with weight and physical appearance over the life span. *Person Soc Psychol Bull*, **16**, 263–273.

Polivy, J. & Herman, C.P. (1985) Dieting and bingeing: A causal anaysis. *American Psychology*, **40**, 193–201.

Pollock, M., Kovacs, M. & Charron-Prockownik, D. (1995) Eating disorders and maldaptive dietary/insulin management among youths with childhood-onset insulin-dependent diabetes mellitus. *Journal of the American Academy of Child and Adolescent Psychiatry*, **34**, 291–296.

Polonsky, W.H., Anderson, B.J., Lohrer, P.A., Aponte, J.E., Jacobson, A.M. & Cole, C.F. (1994) Insulin omission in women with IDDM. *Diabetes Care*, **17**, 1178–1181.

Powers, P.S., Malone, J.I. & Duncan, J.A. (1983) Anorexia nervosa and diabetes mellitus. *Journal of Clinical Psychiatry*, **44**, 133–135.

Robertson, P. & Rosenvinge, J. (1990) Insulin-dependent diabetes mellitus. A risk factor in anorexia nervosa or bulimia nervosa? An empirical study of 116 women. *Journal of Psychsosomatic Research*, **34**, 535–541.

Rodin, G., Craven, J., Littlefield, C., Murray, M. & Daneman, D. (1991) Eating disorders and intentional insulin undertreatment in adolescent females with diabetes. *Psychosomatics*, **132**, 171–176.

Rodin, G.M., Johnson, L.E., Garfinkel, P.E., Daneman, D. & Kenshole, A.B. (1986–1987) Eating disorders in female adolescents with insulin-dependent diabetes mellitus. *International Journal of Psychiatry in Medicine*, **16**, 49–57.

Rosmark, B., Berne, C., Holmgren, S., Lago, C., Renholm, G. & Sohlberg, S. (1986) Eating disorders in patients with insulin-dependent diabetes mellitus. *Journal of Clinical Psychiatry*, **47**, 547–550.

Rydall, A.C., Rodin, G.M., Olmstead, M.P., Devenyi, R.G. & Daneman, D. (1997) Disordered eating behavior and microvascular complications in young women with insulin-dependent diabetes mellitus. *New England Journal of Medicine*, **336**, 1849–1854.

Spitzer, R.L., Devlin, M., Walsh, B.T., Hasin, D., Wing, R., Marcus, M., Stunkard, A., Wadden, T., Yanovski, S., Agras, S., Mitchell, J. & Nonas, C. (1992) Binge eating disorder: A multisite field trial of the diagnostic criteria. *International Journal of Eating Disorders*, **1**, 191–203.

Spitzer, R.L., Yanovski, S., Wadden, T., Wing, R., Marcus, M.D., Stunkard, A., Devlin, M., Mitchell, J., Hasin, D. & Horne, R.L. (1993) Binge eating disorder: Its further validation in a multisite study. *International Journal of Eating Disorders*, **2**, 137–153.

Spurdle, E.P. & Giles, T.R. (1990) Bulimia complicated with diabetes mellitus: A clinical trial using exposure with reponse prevention. *Psychology and Health*, **4**, 167–174.

Steel, J.M., Young, R.J., Lloyd, G.G. & Clarke, B.F. (1987) Clinically apparent eating disorders in young diabetic women: Associations with painful neuropathy and other complications. *British Medical Journal*, **294**, 859–862.

Steel, J.M., Young, G., Lloyd, G.G. & Macintyre, C.C.A. (1989) Abnormal eating attitudes in young insulin-dependent diabetics. *British Journal of Psychiatry*, **155**, 515–521.

Steel, J.M., Lloyd, G.G., Young, R.J. & Macintyre, C.C.A. (1990) Changes in eating attitudes during the first year of treatment for diabetes. *Journal of Psychosomatic Research*, **34**, 313–318.

Stevens, C. & Tiggerman, M. (1998) Women's body figure preferences across the life span. *Journal of Genetic Psychology*, **159**, 94–102.

Striegel-Moore, R.H., Nicholson, T.J. & Tamborlane, W.V. (1992) Prevalence of eating disorder symptoms in preadolescent and adolescent girls with IDDM. *Diabetes Care*, **15**, 1361–1368.

Takii, M., Komaki, G., Uchigata, Y., Maeda, M., Omori, Y. & Kubo, C. (1999) Differences between bulimia nervosa and binge-eating disorder in females with type 1 diabetes: The important role of insulin omission. *Journal of Psychosomatic Research*, **47**, 221–231.

Tiggerman, M. (1992) Body-size dissatisfaction: Individual differences in age and gender, and relationship with self-esteem. *Person Insiv Diff*, **13**, 39–43.

Vila, G., Robert, J.-J., Nollet-Clemencon, C., Vera, L., Crosnier, H., Rault, G., Jos, J. & Mouren-Simeoni, M.-C. (1995) Eating and emotional disorders in adolescent obese girls with insulin-dependent diabetes mellitus. *European Child and Adolescent Psychiatry*, **4**, 270–279.

Waldhäusl, W. & Gries, F.A. (1996) *Diabetes in der Praxis* (pp. 3–4). Berlin, Heidelberg, New York: Springer.

Ward, A., Troop, N., Cachia, M., Watkins, P. & Treasure, J. (1995) Doubly disabled: Diabetes in combination with an eating disorder. *Postgraduate Medical Journal*, **71**, 546–550.

Wilson, G.T., Nonas, C.A. & Rosenblum, G.D. (1993) Assessment of binge eating in obese patients. *International Journal of Eating Disorders*, **13**, 25–33.

Wing, R.R., Nowalk, M.P., Marcus, M.D., Koeske, R. & Finegold, D. (1986) Subclinical eating disorders and glycemic control in adolescents with type 1 diabetes. *Diabetes Care*, **9**, 162–167.

Wing, R.R., Marcus, M.D., Epstein, L.H., Blair, E.H. & Burton, L.R. (1989) Binge eating in obese patients with type II diabetes. *International Journal of Eating Disorders*, **8**, 671–679.

Wing, R.R., Koeske, R., Epstein, L.H., Nowalk, M.P., Gooding, W. & Becker, D. (1997) Long-term effect of modest weight loss in type II diabetic patients. *Archives of Internal Medicine*, **147**, 1749–1753.

Yanovsky, S.Z. & Sebring, N.G. (1994) Recorded food intake of obese women with bing eating disorder before and after weight loss. *International Journal of Eating Disorders*, **2**, 135–150.

Further Reading

Affenito, S.A., Backstrand, J.R., Welch, G.W., Lammi-Keefe, C.J., Rodriguez, N.R. & Adams, C.H. (1997) Subclinical and clinical eating disorders in IDDM negatively affect metabolic control. *Diabetes Care*, **20**, 182–184.

Birk, R. & Spencer, M. (1989) The prevalence of anorexia nervosa, bulimia, and induced glycosuria in IDDM females. *Diabetes Educator*, **15**, 336–341.

Brown, S.A., Upchurch, S., Anding, R., Winter, M., Ramírez, G. (1996) Promoting weight loss in type II diabetes. *Diabetes Care*, **19**, 613–624.

Carroll, P., Tiggerman, M. & Wade, T. (1999) The role of body dissatisfaction and bingeing in the self-esteem of women with type II diabetes. *Journal of Behavioural Medicine*, **22**, 59–74.

Friedman, S., Vila, G., Timsit, J., Boitard, C. & Mouren-Simeoni, M.-C. (1994) Troubles des conduites alimentaires et équilibre métabolique dans une population de jeunes adultes diabétiques insulino-dépendants. *Annales Médico-Psychologiques*, **153**, 282–285.

Kenardy, J., Mensch, M., Bowen, K. & Pearson, S.-A. (1994) A comparison of eating behaviors in newly diagnosed NIDDM patients and case-matched control subjects. *Diabetes Care*, **17**, 1197–1199.

Lloyd, G.G., Steel, J.M. & Young, R.J. (1987) Eating disorders and psychiatric morbidity in patients with diabetes mellitus. *Psychotherapy and Psychosomatics*, **48**, 189–195.

Lorini, R., d Ànnunzio, G. & Cortona, L. (1993) Eating disorders in adolescents and young women with insulin-dependent diabetes mellitus (IDDM). *Advances in the Biosciences*, **90**, 507–510.

Pitel, A.U., Monaco, L., Geffken, G.R. & Siverstein, J.H. (1998) Diagnosis and treatment of an adolescent with comorbid type 1 diabetes mellitus and anorexia nervosa. *Clinical Pediatrics*, **8**, 491–496.

Pinhas-Hamiel, O., Standiford, D., Hamiel, D., Dolan, L.M., Cohen, R. & Zeitler, P.S. (1999) The type 2 family. A setting for development and treatment of adolescent type 2 diabetes mellitus. *Archives of Pediatric and Adolescent Medicine*, **153**, 1063–1067.

Popkin, M.K., Callies, A.L., Lentz, R.D., Colon, E.A. & Sutherland, D.E. (1988) Prevalence of major depression, simple phobia, and other psychiatric disorders in patients with long-standing type-I diabetes mellitus. *Archives of General Psychiatry*, **45**, 64–68.

Powers, P.S., Malone, J.I., Coovert, D.L. & Schulman, R. (1990) Insulin-dependent diabetes mellitus and eating disorders: A prevalence study. *Comprehensive Psychiatry*, **31**, 205–210.

Stancin, L., Link, D.S. & Reuter, J.M. (1989) Binge eating and purging in young women with IDDM. *Diabetes Care*, **12**, 601–603.

Wing, R.R. (1993) Behavioral treatment of obesity. *Diabetes Care*, **16**, 193–199.

Wing, R.R., Jeffery, R.W., Wendy, L. & Hellerstedt, L. (1995) A prospective study of effects of weight cycling on cardiovascular risk factors. *Archives of Internal Medicine*, **155**, 1416–1422.

It is important to differentiate this form of active food avoidance from the loss of appetite that occurs commonly in association with depression. Depression may be present, but often the food avoidance exists as an isolated symptom. We have come to use the term FAED when food avoidance is marked and merits treatment intervention in its own right. When comorbid disorders exist, either physical or psychological, they need to be addressed in addition to the eating difficulty.

Psychogenic Vomiting

Psychogenic vomiting is a diagnostic category in ICD-10, although little clinical elaboration is provided other than to make the clear distinction between 'vomiting associated with other psychological disturbances' and vomiting as seen in bulimia nervosa. The diagnosis includes vomiting in association with dissociative disorders and in hypochondriacal disorder. The symptom may be anxiety related, in which case it might simply be seen as a symptom of food phobia or other anxiety disorder. Overt anxiety is not always present however, and it may be that the child has developed an extreme sensitivity to emetic triggers. A child who has a past history of gastro-oesophageal reflux or of vomiting associated with other illness may be more at risk. Occasionally the vomiting may be of sufficient severity to inhibit all food intake. In these cases anxiety management techniques in combination with family work can be effective once nutritional intake has been re-established. As with any anxiety disorders, the key is in an understanding and non-confrontational approach, and provision of appropriate support.

Anxiety Disorders

Phobias Associated with Food Avoidance

Phobias involving food may occur in isolation (i.e. as simple phobias), or as part of a more generalised anxiety disorder. The overlap with other eating problems is evident, since food avoidance is a feature of most of the problems we describe. There are children who develop specific circumscribed fears in relation to food, however, which are associated with specific cognitions (unlike in FAED) and are not associated with obsessional rumination and checking/compulsive behaviours (see below). The nature of the specific fear will vary with, among other things, the child's developmental stage, but it is probably the case that other severe food phobias are more common than phobic fear of fatness in the 8 to 10-year-old age group. The fears that are common are a fear of vomiting and a fear of contamination or poisoning. This may mean that only certain family members can be entrusted to prepare foods. One paper of interest in this area describes three boys, aged 6 to 8, consuming between 41 and 75% of their estimated daily needs for normal growth and development (Singer et al., 1992). The authors describe an approach to treatment, based on family involvement and anxiety management.

Obsessive-Compulsive Disorder

The coexistence of AN and obsessive-compulsive disorder (OCD) is well recognised, as is the difficulty in separating some aspects of the disorders. AN is associated with OC symptoms, particularly in boys who may alternate between episodes of AN and OCD (Shafran et al., 1995). In addition, OCD without AN can present as food-related obsessions, where the primary behavioural symptom is unusual food-related behaviours. For example, a child may develop obsessional fear about the cholesterol content of food, as one boy did following the death of his father from myocardial infarction; or about the freshness of food, such that food intake is limited to those sources which are of 'known' safety in terms of cleanliness. In children, factors determining the extent of elaboration of OCD rituals include contextual factors as well as responses to the symptoms. Presentation features may include rigid eating patterns and associated conflict (usually intrafamilial), restricted range of foods and, in more extreme cases, restricted quantity of food leading to weight loss.

Developmental Disorders

Selective Eating

'Selective eating' describes a highly selective pattern of food intake in terms of the range of foods eaten (Bryant-Waugh, 2000). This phenomenon is also known as 'few foods', or 'faddy eating', both of which have the potential problem of confusion between limited quantity (calorie intake) and limited range (numbers of different foods). 'Faddy' implies that the eating pattern is temporary, a criterion specifically excluded from this group. We have chosen 'selective eating' as a term that conveys the extreme selectivity in preferred foods.

A number of features differentiate selective eating from the other eating difficulties described so far. The first is the highly limited range of foods that is long-standing, often stemming from the time of weaning, but may also be secondary to some traumatic event. A range of less than 10 foods in total is usual in those presenting for help (Nicholls et al., 2001). The foods will typically be predominantly carbohydrate based, and may be brand specific, e.g. only McDonald's chips. The second feature is an extreme unwillingness to try new foods. In order to exclude other eating difficulties, the child should be in the normal range for weight and height, and not losing or gaining significant amounts of relative weight. In addition, in order to be considered outside the normal developmental range, selective eating should have persisted well into middle childhood and/or adolescence. In the majority of cases selective eating problems tend to resolve with age. Some will, however, persist in accepting only a very narrow range of foods, becoming adult selective eaters (Bryant-Waugh, 2000).

The issue of treatment is unclear. Highly motivated children can change selective eating behaviour using child-centred cognitive-behavioural techniques (Christie, 2000; Nicholls et al., 2001). Parents are facilitated to support but not become involved in trying to influence this process of change. Where parents are motivated to change the child but the child is not, attempts at intervention can be counter-productive and result in food refusal. Given the lack of known physical risk of selective eating, the best policy is to offer a review or 'come back when you're ready'. Is there a rationale for offering treatment at all? Selective eating may render a child vulnerable to later weight loss problems, as shut down on eating is a common response to emotional distress. Selective eaters may not have the reserve to maintain an adequate diet if this occurs.

Chronic Illness

Eating difficulties in the context of chronic illness is mentioned here in order to emphasise the need for comprehensive assessment of eating difficulties and their differential diagnoses. Food refusal associated with illness has recently been comprehensively reviewed (Harris et al., 2001). The review highlights the interactional nature of physical and psychological problems, and the role of temperament in the nature of the eating problem, both issues that are true of eating disorders.

Over-eating Associated with Childhood Obesity

Children may present because of concerns about excessive weight gain. In the majority of cases this will be associated with over-eating—i.e. that energy intake exceeds energy expenditure for that particular individual. It is important to take a number of factors into account when talking about 'over-eating' as many overweight children may actually eat less than their leaner peers. Differences in genetic make-up, metabolism, and energy expenditure through exercise may all contribute to a tendency to gain weight. Once the child is overweight there is often a tendency to decrease activity (because it becomes harder, but also because the child may become more self-conscious and less likely to become involved in peer sports), hence also energy expenditure which in turn can contribute to continuing weight gain.

In our experience, obese children often have a very poor sense of hunger and satiety, and have developed habitual patterns of over-eating. It is important to understand the psychological mechanisms underlying eating behaviour, and where possible to attempt to differentiate between eating in response to emotional arousal and eating in response to environmental cues. These different underlying mechanisms suggest a number of possible strategies to work with to help the child manage their eating.

Although many obese children suffer from low self-esteem this is by no means always the case. In particular, prepubertal children tend in our experience to have a reasonably positive self-concept.

MEDICAL ISSUES

In some countries paediatricians (usually in Adolescent Medicine) manage young people with anorexia nervosa, and this can mean a highly medicalised approach to care (see, for example, Lock, 1999). When children and adolescent eating disorder patients are cared for primarily by mental health specialists (and often by adult specialists) the limitations of little or no paediatric involvement become apparent. This is particularly so for the early onset population, where the medical risks may differ in type and severity from those of older patients. In addition to aiding diagnosis and management decisions, information obtained from physical assessments can be a powerful psycho-educational tool for both sufferers and parents/carers, improving motivation to change. Medical assessment and ongoing evaluation are crucial aspects of a biopsychosocial approach to early onset eating disorders.

Those complications that are unique to younger patients are growth retardation, pubertal delay or arrest, and reduction of peak bone mass (Kreipe et al., 1995). Certain age-related differences in eating disorder pathology also influence the likely medical complications. For example, while many high-risk behaviours in children are comparable to those of adults (reduced energy intake, purging, increased exercise), others are more closely related to increasing age, independence and culture (e.g. laxative and diuretic abuse, substance misuse). In addition there are a higher number of boys in the early onset population (Fosson et al., 1987), particularly among those with atypical eating problems.

Because growth is dynamic, severe nutritional difficulties can occur during the growth period without weight loss. There is a literature on medical complications in the younger patient (see Fisher et al., 1995; Katzman & Zipursky, 1997; Nicholls et al., 1999, for reviews). Significant gaps in knowledge remain, however. There is no internationally agreed cut-off for health versus malnutrition in children, no weight and height adjusted for pubertal maturation, and no standards for expected catch up after a period of growth failure. The concept of 'target weight' in early onset populations remains one of controversy, with the need for clinical precision at odds with the complexity and heterogeneity of adolescence. As such there is no 'evidence base' on which recommendations can be based, and wide variation in clinical practice exists. Discussions about the need for adult patients to achieve adequate weight gain during the nutritional rehabilitation stage of treatment (Russell & Gross, 2000) are even more pertinent in the early onset population. It seems likely that failure to attain sufficient weight restoration is contributing to the trend in increased severity of illness and complications.

Overall the mortality rate in early onset and adolescent eating disorders is low (Steinhausen, 1997). This may in part be due to a lower threshold for intervention and/or hospitalisation in children (up to 80% of adolescents receive some inpatient care (Kreipe et al., 1989; Nussbaum et al., 1985; Steiner et al., 1990). More likely it is because the majority of complications are compounded by chronicity of illness.

Assessing Malnutrition

Assessment of the degree of protein calorie malnutrition is important both as a guide to management and as a predictor of outcome. Children dehydrate more quickly than adults (Irwin, 1984) and often fluid restrict as part of the illness. Clinical judgement, together with vital signs (pulse, blood pressure, temperature and circulation), may be the best indicator of the need for rehydration. Measures such as % Body Mass Index (BMI) (Cole et al., 1995) can be valuable pointers and screening instruments, but may be a poor reflection of a child's fat reserves, which in turn will vary with stage of development. Amenorrhoea is less helpful than in adults, as adolescents often miss three or more cycles in the first 1–2 years, or may have primary amenorrhoea. Skinfold thickness and other measure of body composition adds a further level of refinement when %BMI and clinical findings do not tally. For example, a child may be exercising sufficiently to maintain body mass, while having so little fat reserve that endocrine function (and hence growth and puberty) are disturbed. As with all measurements in growing children, skinfold thickness should be compared to age and sex-matched norms using charts or standard deviation scores (SDS) scores.

Complications in growing young people can result from underestimating target weight due to failure to adjust for growth. Weight and height charts are of more value for monitoring change than for assessing the significance of a single measurement. A weight measurement in the normal range may represent significant weight loss, or be of concern when adjusted for the child's height. More importantly, growth charts emphasise the rate of expected weight gain for a child. Over the past few years many countries have published BMI centiles for children (e.g. Cole et al., 1995; Luciano et al., 1997; Williams, 2000), which should help to bring the language for children and adolescents closer to that used for adult patients and ensure that nutritional status can be more conveniently and routinely assessed.

Impact on Growth

The impact of an episode of altered nutrition on a growing body is likely to have different implications from that on a body that has already reached its adult potential, although the question of adolescence as a 'critical period' for nutritional programming (Lucas, 1991) has not been adequately addressed. The key paper raising this dilemma was Russell's (1985) description of 20 women in whom anorexia nervosa had onset prior to menarche. As a group they had shorter stature and incomplete pubertal development. The question remains as to what severity, intensity, duration or timing of illness is necessary to permanently alter the course of development in such a way that long-term outcome is altered, even if the patient subsequently recovers from the disorder. Inherent in this, and equally unevaluated in the early onset population, is the capacity of the body for self healing, or 'catch-up'. One case report has documented a male patient who completed growth and developed secondary sexual characteristics at 27 years old following psychogenic food refusal (Magner et al., 1984). One entry in Russell's case series reached menarche at the age of 25.

Puberty and Menstruation

On the restoration of weight, endocrine function is restored, heralding continuing pubertal development and ultimately the onset or resumption of menses. The impact of endocrine activity can be seen on serial pelvic ultrasound scans (Lai et al., 1994; Nicholls et al., 1999), which are of particular value when no premorbid menstrual weight is available as a guide or when target weight is in dispute. The %BMI at which menses occurs is normally distributed within ±2 BMI SDS, and there is no evidence that this is any different for eating-disordered patients than for normal adolescents (Nicholls et al., 1999). There is no equivalent technique to pelvic ultrasound for assessing progress in boys, other than observing pubertal development by Tanner staging (Tanner & Whitehouse, 1966).

Impact on Bone Density

The problem of bone loss in anorexia nervosa is compounded in adolescents by failure of bone accretion. Sixty percent of bone accretion occurs during puberty (Golden, 1992) and the aim is to achieve as high a 'peak bone mass' as possible, as a store that will be slowly depleted during adulthood. Measurement of bone density is usually performed by dual x-ray absorptiometry (DXA). However, there are major problems with the interpretation of bone density results in younger patients with anorexia nervosa, the most important of which is the need to adjust bone density measurements for bone size. Failure to do so results in falsely low readings. Other methods of evaluating bone density in childhood are being evaluated (Mather et al., 1999), most notably calcaneal (heel) ultrasound. Whatever technique, the terms osteoporosis and osteopenia have little value in younger patients, since these are defined in relation to peak bone mass (t-score) and not to developing bone mass (z-score). Nevertheless, in such a high-risk population for osteoporosis, DXA scans are a useful way of evaluating progress and assessing risk. The best reference for a child is her/himself.

The potential for catch-up in bone density is not yet clear (Bachrach et al., 1991; Ward et al., 1997), but it is likely that in children who have not completed growth and puberty, bone loss can be at least partially compensated for.

ASSESSMENT

Assessment forms one of the most important aspects of any approach to management. It can in itself be a powerful intervention. Its components should ideally be based on the use of a theoretical or conceptual model for the development of eating difficulties in children. Bearing in mind that children with eating problems encompass a wide range of types of diagnoses and clinical features, any assessment protocol will need to be comprehensive enough to gather relevant information. The main components of our assessment protocol, based on a developmental/systemic understanding of eating difficulties, are set out below. Suggested routine and optional physical assessments and investigations are presented in Table 26.1.

Table 26.1 Suggested routine and optional physical assessment and investigations for children and young adolescents with eating disorders

	Routine	Optional
Examination	Height[a] Weight[a] Parents' height and weight %BMI or BMI[a] Pubertal stage[a] Peripheral circulation Pulse/Blood pressure/Temperature *Ask about*: Previous growth records Menarche/LMP Medication/other illnesse	Skinfold thickness[a]/body fat measure Mid arm circumference[a] Fundi/Eye movements Reflexes/Power/Gait If male or atypical Cranial nerves Peripheral nerves Coordination
Investigation	Bone age x-ray ECG Urea and electrolytes/Full blood count Liver function test Urine specific gravity Baseline bone density scan Pelvic ultrasound	LH & FSH Thyroid function Prolactin Immunoglobulins Food allergies Structural brain scan (e.g. MRI)

[a]Plot on gender appropriate centile chart.

Assessment of Clinical Presentation

Medical assessment, which forms an important part of any first visit, has been fully discussed above. Besides this we would recommend a discussion with the child and parents about the history and development of the eating difficulty, starting from the time when someone first became aware that there might be a problem. This might have been a parent, the child, a relative, or another person—for instance, someone at the child's school. We have found it quite helpful to draw a time line that includes changes in eating, weight, and related concerns. At presentation it is also necessary to conduct a mental state examination (to contribute to a risk assessment), which would include assessment of comorbid disorders. Specific eating disorder psychopathology is useful to assess (e.g. using the child version of the EDE, Bryant-Waugh et al., 1996; Fairburn & Cooper, 1993). Finally the child's current general functioning should also be assessed (including school and social functioning).

Assessment of Developmental Issues

We have found it useful to take a personal history including important events in the child's life. This can be drawn on a time line that can then be placed next to the one with weight and eating history, enabling potential links to be explored more easily. The personal history should also include a developmental history, including early feeding, milestones, etc., the child's medical history, plus any past history of emotional and/or behavioural problems.

Assessment of Systemic Context

Assessment of systemic context involves gathering information about the family, its wider context and the family's past contact with health professionals. We recommend starting with drawing a family tree. This can be done with the child with the eating problem (plus any siblings), using the parents to prompt when the children get stuck. It is helpful to include three generations. While drawing, useful information can be gathered about family history of weight and shape issues as well as family medical and psychiatric history.

A family history including family life events and stresses that have not yet been discussed is helpful, and again can be drawn on a time line to place against those already generated. Using visual means of recording information can help children to participate in the process and can help to facilitate an understanding of problems arising within a systemic context. Further questioning about present family circumstances and social or support networks can help the treatment team to better understand other stresses on parents as well as potential resources. It is important to gain some impression of the family's social context, their ethnic background and any relevant associated beliefs and practices.

With regard to the eating difficulty, we would routinely ask each member of the family how they understand it and how it affects them. Finally, we would ask parents what they have tried in terms of managing the problem.

It is important also to try to get a picture of the child's and the family's wider context, in particular relationships with the child's school and other health professionals. As part of this it can be helpful to review the route by which the family have reached your clinic and what their expectations are both of the assessment process and of you or your team.

Assessment of Perceived Mechanisms and Possibilities for Change

A final important part of the assessment process is to ascertain where the child and the parents are up to in terms of their wish to change, to assess their perception of their own ability to achieve change, and to assess their understanding of the process by which change can be achieved.

Such an assessment procedure (which in our case requires the family to attend for one two-and-a-half-hour session, plus the child and parents to make a second visit lasting approximately four hours) allows the team to do a number of important things. Specifically, it enables a diagnosis to be made as well as a statement about level of risk (usually subdivided in terms of physical risk; risk of suicide/self-harm; vulnerability to abuse/neglect; and risk of aggression/violence to others). It also enables the team to assess the impact of the eating difficulty on the child's development and general functioning. The child's and the parents' expectations of treatment will be clear, and some information about their level of motivation and readiness to change will have been gathered. Potential obstacles to successful intervention may now be apparent, and material has been elicited that enables a formulation to be made within a developmental/systemic framework.

Such an approach to assessment facilitates engagement and sets the scene for a collaborative approach to management. It enables problems and difficulties to be owned in a non-blaming way, which consequently makes them more amenable to change.

MANAGEMENT

Specific treatments for adolescents with eating disorders are discussed elsewhere in this handbook. Many aspects of the work described, in particular aspects of family work, may be applicable to the management of children. At this time there is no separate body of evidence-based treatments for children with eating disorders, including anorexia nervosa. The following ideas are based on developmental and systemic theory and have been developed through clinical practice.

The type of treatment offered, or even appropriate, will depend on the context of the country and its service. This reflects the fact that children with eating difficulties are seen by a variety of professionals in a variety of settings, including generic and specialist services, outpatient, inpatient and daypatient services, paediatric or psychiatric settings and across a wide range in terms of age and type of eating problems seen. Whatever the context, treatment of children with eating difficulties differs in certain important respects to the situation with adult patients.

Firstly, the patient/client is not a single individual. Issues about engagement in treatment and help seeking, and expectations regarding motivation and wish to change need to take into account the fact that children are brought for treatment. Secondly, physical considerations may be more urgent and necessitate prompt action. Related to this is the need for awareness of statutory responsibilities regarding child protection and consideration of legal and ethical frameworks for all aspects of capacity, consent, and responsibility.

An individual management plan depends on findings from the assessment, which will provide answers to questions in the following areas.

- What is the problem?
- Are there any immediate risks?
- How can we understand the problem?
- What is maintaining it?
- Is everyone at an agreed starting point?
- What might facilitate or stand in the way of change?
- Is everybody ready for change?

As the answers to these questions will differ across the types of disorder, with the age of the child, across cultures, and within individual families, prescriptive plans for intervention are inappropriate. Some important principles apply however. The first is that successful intervention involves understanding, not just identifying or recognising a problem. As described above, the process of assessment will have revealed a complexity of contextual issues around an individual diagnosis. In this age group in particular, understanding the eating problem includes a consideration of developmental and systemic issues.

A second principle of intervention in the younger population is that change is best achieved through enhancing and supporting the child and parents' problem solving and communication skills. In this model, the role of the therapist is to elicit, enhance, encourage, and even suggest.

Finally, treatment of choice is to treat the eating disorder not the complication. This does not mean addressing 'underlying issues' at the expense of eating behaviour. The aim of treatment from this perspective is two-fold—to enable the child to eat and drink sufficiently for normal growth and development to occur, and to facilitate emotional communication through a medium other than food. The aim is to restore the child to the right developmental track in terms of physical, social and psychological well-being.

Agreeing a Management Plan

With these principles in mind, the process of intervention begins with feedback from the assessment process, concluding with construction of a mutually acceptable formulation. It can be helpful to use time lines, diagrams and drawings to illustrate the shared understanding of how the eating problem developed. Accepting the family's account of the problem, the 'personal logic' that has resulted in this solution in this situation, can facilitate ownership of the problem. During this stage of the process, it is important to clarify expectations of treatment, talk about readiness to change and explore anxieties around change. Looking at the implications of change may include an analysis of the gains and losses involved in changing the problem. Learning to engage all those who have come for treatment is a core skill in the management of younger patients and their families and one that requires particular time and attention.

Early in the treatment, process lines of communication require clarification, in particular about how information will be shared and what the procedures and possibilities are for doing so. This may be highlighted in individual work with young people, where issues of confidentiality and autonomy on the part of the young person may conflict with parental involvement in treatment. The purpose and practice of therapy should be overt and understandable to everyone, whatever its nature. This includes agreeing a format, identifying shared and (non-shared) aims and expectations, and identifying how progress in treatment can be reviewed.

The management plan needs to build in physical monitoring, and responsibility for this clarified, together with how the information will be fed back to parents, young person and all others involved in treatment? Agreeing boundaries and responsibilities includes agreeing responsibility for care with parents, including responsibility for food provision, reporting concerns, ensuring attendance, etc.

Informed decision making requires information. Since we ask children and parents to be involved in the decision-making process, we provide information at every stage— information about onset, course, prognosis, and outcome; information about physical aspects, behavioural aspects and emotional aspects; contact addresses, and a reading list; and encourage questions. This process of information sharing has a number of functions: it demystifies the diagnosis, and can provide a framework for understanding the development and the maintenance of the eating disorder. But perhaps, more importantly, it allows parents and young people to make informed decisions regarding treatment in a way that attempts to minimise the escalation of issues around power and control.

Once a formulation, a framework for management, goals and expectations, boundaries and responsibilities, have been clarified and agreed, therapeutic work can continue in a number of formats. In the younger age group it is our expectation that intervention will involve those with parental responsibility.

Family Work

The nature of family work has changed considerably over the years, as have assumptions about the role of the family in aetiology of eating difficulties. Family work is the first line treatment for anorexia nervosa (with or without binge–purges) in younger patients. Controlled studies have demonstrated maximum utility in those with relatively short duration of illness (less than three years' duration), living within a family context (Russell et al., 1987). In this framework, the young person has some identity within the family other than her illness. The treatment developed for the treatment trials has recently been published in manual form (Lock et al., 2000) and will enable specific questions regarding the efficacy of this treatment approach in different patient subpopulations to be addressed. For example, the approach may be useful for some patients with bulimia nervosa and other eating problems, but may not be sufficient alone. The manual has the obvious benefit of making an effective treatment more widely accessible. Based on an outpatient model of treatment, the therapy adopts a systemic approach that emphasises parental responsibility and authority in response to their child's crisis. These structural family therapy principles rest squarely on the work of Minuchin and colleagues (1978), who pioneered much of the work in this area. The other key concept in this form of therapy is the 'externalisation' of the illness (White, 1989)—a technique which enables detachment from the problem, and allows relationships to the problem (anorexia) to be the subject of scrutiny rather than the more intrusive exploration of relationships between people.

'Conjoint family therapy', when all family members are present, is not always ideal, and alternatives should be considered if parents are highly critical of their child, or intrafamilial abuse is suspected. Parental counselling uses the same principles as family work, but without the young person present, and has been shown to be just as effective as conjoint family therapy (Eisler et al., 2000). Some parents find this easier if they have their own difficulties, and worry that they may be impinging on treatment, or are severely burdened with guilt.

An alternative form of therapeutic work is in a family group context, otherwise known as multi-family therapy (Scholz & Asen, 2001). Involving the whole family allows family strengths and resources to be utilised, while connecting parents to other parents helps to overcome the feeling of isolation.

Individual Work

Individual therapy can have many formats, e.g. CBT, psychodynamic, play therapy, but younger patients can find individual therapy extremely difficult, particularly those with more concrete cognitive styles. Therapist style needs to be flexible and developmentally appropriate and parental support for the therapy is crucial. The nutritional state of the child, as well as cognitive and emotional development stages, are important in assessing suitability. The focus of work may be to encourage the child to address issues more directly with her parents by rehearsing with the therapist. Other specific indications for individual work include treatment for concurrent depression, obsessive-compulsive disorder or specific anxieties such as fear of swallowing or choking. Here, age appropriate cognitive-behaviour therapy (CBT) would be the treatment of choice (Christie, 2000).

Group Work

Group work with young people and with parents can be task focused or not. Group therapy is an established part of most treatment programmes for adolescents with eating disorders, the focus usually being on the development of self-esteem. Groups for younger children are less well established. The provision of unstructured time for children to explore peer relationships and to develop freedom of expression can be infinitely more accessible and acceptable to the child than individual therapy, in which a child can feel persecuted.

A parents' group can address issues such as coping with rejection, and provides an opportunity for parents to share their knowledge and their skills, and to learn from and support each other (Nicholls & Magagna, 1997). As one parent in our group commented '(anorexia nervosa) as an illness makes you feel as if your parenting is not good enough, but also that your common sense isn't common sense. It challenges you to understand something completely different and your normal responses are no longer valid.'

Physical Intervention

The paucity of work in the area of physical interventions in young patients makes it hard to give clear evidence-based guidelines for intervention. There are no randomised trials of nutritional supplementation, nor for psychopharmacology in this age group. The use of hormonal treatments has not been systematically evaluated, but may be worth considering in severe chronic anorexia nervosa in consultation with appropriate specialists, the young person and her family. Thresholds for hospitalisation may be somewhat lower in younger patients, although the Society of Adolescent Medicine guidelines for admission to hospital may be somewhat over-inclusive (Fisher et al., 1995). For example, arrested growth and development would be expected in pubertal children with anorexia nervosa, and whether inpatient admission improves or worsens the prognosis is an issue much in debate. Arrested growth would, however, suggest the need for specialised care from both a physical and therapeutic point of view.

Thresholds for nasogastric feeding vary in the younger patient. On occasions when this is necessary, appropriate dietetic advice and a feeding rate suited to the age and nutritional status of the child is sought. The most important aspect of treatment interventions of this kind is the careful consideration of issues relating to consent for both the child and parents. Manley et al. (2001) offer a framework for considering ethical decision making in the care of young people with eating disorders, intended as guidance when difficult decisions regarding care, such as those outlined above, need to be addressed.

The task for the clinician is to return the child to her appropriate developmental track, physically and psychologically. In this context, provision of information about normal physical development, feedback about progress and growth potential and ongoing monitoring of physical health and pubertal development, whether through growth assessment, pelvic ultrasound scanning or other forms of physical assessment, are in themselves interventions and can be powerful therapeutic tools.

Working with the Wider System

Points for consideration in working with a complex network of professionals, as is often the case for specialist services, include agreement about communication, both written and verbal, within the network and within the family, and about sharing information. The potential for disagreement and misunderstanding is high and views can easily become polarised if communication breaks down. For similar reasons, consideration of how the team will respond to crises, expectations regarding availability, clarifying and documenting policies and procedures, identifying statutory roles and responsibilities, staff support, teaching and training all merit specific attention. It can be helpful to identify a central point of contact as well as a system for feedback and review of treatment, which may be independent of, but include, the therapist and wider system or referrer and is documented.

Consent for the young person and his or her parents is complex and the precise legal issues will differ from country to country. Some issues merit highlighting. The first is the difference between giving and withholding consent. A young person may not have the capacity, either on the basis of age or mental state, to give consent, while being within his or her rights to withhold consent (refuse). A second and related issue is that consent and competence are specific. A young person is not 'competent or not', but rather 'competent to make decision x'. This means that each specific decision for which consent is required needs to be considered from the young person's point of view, and his or her opinion sought. This concept is incorporated in the working principles we have described thus far. For those occasions where agreement cannot be achieved, local policies regarding child protection and legal responsibilities are important to clarify.

We started this section saying that management was context dependent, provided consideration was given to the issues outlined. A number of elements are, in our view, essential. Treatment of young people with eating disorders works best when it is collaborative, and based on a comprehensive, multidisciplinary assessment. Treatment should be appropriate to level of complexity. As the study by Ben-Tovim et al. (2001) has demonstrated, not all patients need intensive psychotherapy. Treatment should be responsive to the developmental need and degree of autonomy of the child within the family—family therapy may be appropriate for a 20 year old, and not be viable in a 13 year old. Treatments need to be flexible enough to be responsive to the child's immediate and wider context, i.e. treatment should fit the patient. The treating team needs clear policies and guidelines, enabling them to respond to medical and psychiatric urgency when needed. And finally, approaches need to be reviewed, developed and evaluated. Our treatments are evolving, and we must be ready and prepared to adapt to changing situations.

REFERENCES

Arnow, B., Sanders, M.J. & Steiner, H. (1999) Premenarcheal versus postmenarcheal anorexia nervosa: A comparative study. *Clin. Child Psychol. Psychiat.*, **4**, 403–414.

Bachrach, L.K., Katzman, D.K., Litt, I.F., Guido, D. & Marcus, R. (1991) Recovery from osteopenia in adolescent girls with anorexia nervosa. *J. Clin. Endocrin. Metab*, **72**, 602–606.

Ben-Tovim, D., Walker, K., Gilchrist, P., Freeman, R., Kalucy, R.S. & Esterman, A. (2001) Outcome in patients with eating disorders: A 5 year study. *Lancet*, **357**, 1254–1257.

Bryant-Waugh, R. (2000) Overview of the Eating Disorders. In B. Lask & R. Bryant-Waugh (Eds), *Anorexia Nervosa and Related Eating Disorders in Childhood and Adolescence* (2nd edn; pp. 27–40). Hove, East Sussex: Psychology Press.

Bryant-Waugh, R., Cooper, P., Taylor, C. & Lask, B. (1996) The use of the Eating Disorder Examination with children: A pilot study. *Int. J. Eat. Disord.*, **19**, 391–397.

Bryant-Waugh, R., Knibbs, J., Fosson, A., Kaminski, Z. & Lask, B. (1988) Long term follow-up of patients with early onset anorexia nervosa. *Arch. Dis. Child.*, **63**, 5–9.

Bryant-Waugh, R., Lask, B., Shafran, R. & Fosson, A. (1992) Do doctors recognise eating disorders in children? *Arch. Dis. Child.*, **67**, 103–105.

Christie, D. (2000) Cognitive-behavioural techniques for children with eating disorders. In B. Lask & R. Bryant-Waugh (Eds), *Anorexia Nervosa and Related Eating Disorders in Childhood and Adolescence2* (2nd edn; pp. 205–226). Hove, East Sussex: Psychology Press.

Cole, T.J., Freeman, J.V. & Preece, M.A. (1995) Body mass index reference curves for the UK, 1990. *Arch. Dis. Child.*, **73**, 25–29.

De Vile, C.J., Sufraz, R., Lask, B. & Stanhope, R. (1995) Occult intracranial tumours masquerading as early onset anorexia nervosa. *Br. Med. J.*, **311**, 1359–1360.

Eisler, I., Dare, C., Hodes, M., Russell, G., Dodge, E. & le Grange, D. (2000) Family therapy for adolescent anorexia nervosa: The results of a controlled comparison of two family interventions. *J. Child Psychol. Psychiat.*, **41**, 727–736.

Fairburn, C.G. & Cooper, Z. (1993) The Eating Disorders Examination (12th Edition). In C.G. Fairburn & G.T. Wilson (Eds), *Binge Eating: Nature, Assessment and Treatment* (pp. 317–332) New York: Guilford Press.

Fisher, M., Golden, N.H., Katzman, D.K., Kreipe, R.E., Rees, J., Schebendach, J., Sigman, G., Ammerman, S. and Hoberman, H. (1995) Eating disorders in adolescents: A background paper. *J. Adolesc. Health*, **16**, 420–437.

Fosson, A., Knibbs, J., Bryant-Waugh, R. & Lask, B. (1987) Early onset anorexia nervosa. *Arch. Dis. Child.*, **62**, 114–118.

Golden, N.H. (1992) Osteopenia in adolescents with anorexia nervosa. *Children's Hospital Qtly.*, **4**, 143–148.

Gowers, S.G., Crisp, A.H., Joughin, N. & Bhat, A. (1991) Premenarcheal anorexia nervosa. *J. Child Psychol. Psychiat.*, **32**, 515–524.

Halmi, K.A. (1985) Classification of the eating disorders. *J. Psychiat. Res.*, **19**, 113–119.

Harris, G., Blissett, J. & Johnson, R. (2001) Food refusal associated with illness. *Child Psychol. Psychiat. Rev.*, **5**, 148–156.

Higgs, J.F., Goodyer, I.M. & Birch, J. (1989) Anorexia nervosa and food avoidance emotional disorder. *Arch. Dis. Child.*, **64**, 346–351.

Irwin, M. (1984) Early onset anorexia nervosa. *South Med. J.*, **77**, 611–614.

Jacobs, B.W. & Isaacs, S. (1986) Pre-pubertal anorexia nervosa: A retrospective controlled study. *J. Child Psychol. Psychiat.*, **27**, 237–250.

Katzman, D.K. & Zipursky, R.B. (1997) Adolescents with anorexia nervosa: The impact of the disorder on bones and brains. *Ann. NY Acad. Sci.*, **817**, 127–137.

Kent, A., Lacey, J.H. & McCluskey, S.E. (1992) Pre-menarchal bulimia nervosa. *J. Psychosomat. Res.*, **36**, 205–210.

Kreipe, R.E., Churchill, B.H. & Strauss, J. (1989) Long term outcome of adolescents with anorexia nervosa. *Am. J. Dis. Child.*, **43**, 1322–1327.

Kreipe, R.E., Golden, N.H., Katzman, D.K., Fisher, M., Rees, J., Tonkin, R.S., Silber, T.J., Sigman, G., Schebendach, J., Ammerman, S.D. et al. (1995) Eating disorders in adolescents. A position paper of the Society for Adolescent Medicine [see comments]. *J. Adolesc. Health*, **16**, 476–479.

Lai, K.Y., de Bruyn, R., Lask, B., Bryant-Waugh, R. & Hankins, M. (1994) Use of pelvic ultrasound to monitor ovarian and uterine maturity in childhood onset anorexia nervosa. *Arch. Dis. Child.* **71**, 228–231.

Lask, B. & Bryant-Waugh, R. (2000) *Anorexia Nervosa and Related Eating Disorders in Childhood and Adolescence.* (2nd edn). Hove, East Sussex: Psychology Press.

Lock, J. (1999) How clinical pathways can be useful: An example of a clinical pathway for the treatment of anorexia nervosa. *Clin. Child Psychol. Psychiat.*, **4**, 331–340.

Lock, J., le Grange, D., Agras, S. & Dare, C. (2000) *Treatment Manual for Anorexia Nervosa.* New York: Guilford Press.

Lucas, A. (1991) Programming by early nutrition in man. *Ciba Found Symp.*, **156**, 38–50.

Luciano, A., Bressan, F. & Zoppi, G. (1997) Body mass index reference curves for children aged 3–19 years from Verona, Italy. *Eur. J. Clin. Nutrit.*, **51**, 6–10.

Magner, J.A., Rogol, A.D. & Gorden, P. (1984) Reversible growth hormone deficiency and delayed puberty triggered by a stressful experience in a young adult. *Am. J. Med.*, **76**, 737–742.

Manley, R., Smye, V. & Srikameswaran, S. (2001) Adressing complex ethical issues in the treatment of children and adolescents with eating disorders: Application of a framework for ethical decision making. *Eur. Eat. Disord. Rev.*, **9**, 144–166.

Mather, S.J., de Bruyn, R., Pokropek, T. & Lask, B. (1999) Ultrasound bone analysis in 53 children and adolescents with eating disorders and 100 healthy children and adolescents. 1st International Conference on Children's Bone Health Maastricht (Abstract).

McCabe, R.J.R., Rothery, D.J., Wrate, R.M., Aspin, J. et al. (1996) Diagnosis in adolescent inpatients: Diagnostic confidence and comparison of diagnoses using ICD-9 and DSM-III. *Eur. Child Adolesc. Psychiat.*, **5**, 147–154.

Minuchin, S., Rosman, B. & Baker, L. (1978) *Psychosomatic Families: Anorexia Nervosa in Context.* Cambridge, Mass.: Harvard University Press.

Nicholls, D., Chater, R. & Lask, B. (2000) Children into DSM IV don't go: A comparison of classification systems for eating disorders in childhood and early adolescence. *Int. J. Eat. Disord.*, **28**, 317–324.

Nicholls, D., Christie, D., Randall, L. & Lask, B. (2001) Selective eating: Symptom, disorder or normal variant? *Clin. Child Psychol. Psychiat.* **6**, 257–270.

Nicholls, D., de Bruyn, R. & Gordon, I. (1999) Physical assessment and complications. In B. Lask & R. Bryant-Waugh (Eds), *Childhood Onset Eating Disorders* (2nd edn). Hove, East Sussex: Earlbaum.

Nicholls, D. & Magagna, J. (1997) A group for the parents of children with eating disorders. *Clin. Child Psychol. Psychiat.*, **2**, 565–578.

Nussbaum, M., Shenker, I.R., Baird, D. & Saravay, S. (1985) Follow-up investigation in patients with anorexia nervosa. *J. Pediat.*, **106**, 835–840.

Russell, G.F., Szmukler, G.I., Dare, C. & Eisler, I. (1987) An evaluation of family therapy in anorexia nervosa and bulimia nervosa. *Arch. Gen. Psychiat.*, **44**, 1047–1056.

Russell, G.F.M. (1985) Pre-menarchal anorexia nervosa and its sequelae. *J. Psychiat. Res.*, **19**, 363–369.

Russell, J. & Gross, G. (2000) Anorexia nervosa and body mass index. *Am. J. Psychiat.*, **157**, 2060.

Scholz, M. & Asen, E. (2001) Multiple family therapy with eating disordered adolescents: Concepts and preliminary results. *Eur. Eat. Disord. Rev.*, **9**, 33–42.

Shafran, R., Bryant-Waugh, R., Lask, B. & Arscott, K. (1995) Obsessive-compulsive symptoms in children with eating disorders: A preliminary investigation. *Eat. Disord. J. Treat. Prevent.*, **3**, 304–310.

Singer, L.T., Ambuel, B., Wade, S. & Jaffe, A.C. (1992) Cognitive-behavioral treatment of health-impairing food phobias in children. *J. Am. Acad. Child Adolesc. Psychiat.*, **31**, 847–852.

Steiner, H., Mazer, C. & Litt, I.F. (1990) Compliance and outcome in anorexia nervosa. *West J. Med.*, **153**, 133–139.

Steinhausen, H.C. (1997) Outcome of anorexia nervosa in the younger patient. *J. Child Psychol. Psychiat.*, **38**, 271–276.

Strober, M., Freeman, R. & Morrell, W. (1997) The long-term course of severe anorexia nervosa in adolescents: Survival analysis of recovery, relapse, and outcome predictors over 10–15 years in a prospective study. *Int. J. Eat. Disord.*, **22**, 339–360.

Tanner, J.M. & Whitehouse, R.H. (1966) Standards from birth to maturity for height, weight, height velocity and weight velocity: British Children 1965. Part 2. *Arch. Dis. Child.*, **41**, 613–635.

Treasure, J. & Thompson, P. (1988) Anorexia nervosa in childhood. *Br. Med. J.*, **40**, 362–369.

Walford, G. & McCune, N. (1991) Long-term outcome in early onset anorexia nervosa. *Br. J. Psychol.*, **159**, 383–389.

Ward, A., Brown, N. and Treasure, J. (1997) Persistent osteopenia after recovery from anorexia nervosa. *Int. J. Eat. Disord.*, **22**, 71–75.

Watkins, E., Bryant Waugh, R., Cooper, P. & Lask, B. (2000) The nosology of childhood onset eating disorders. Anonymous.

White, M. (1989) The externalising of the problem and the re-authoring of lives and relationships. Dulwich Centre Newsletter 3–20.

Williams, S. (2000) Body Mass Index reference curves derived from a New Zealand birth cohort. *N.Z. Med. J.*, **113**, 308–311.

CHAPTER 27

From Prevention to Health Promotion

Runi Børresen

Organization for Health and Social Affairs, Buskerud County, Norway

and

Jan H. Rosenvinge

Department of Psychology, University of Tromsø, Tromsø, Norway

SUMMARY

- Paradoxically eating disorders are not the issue in the primary prevention of eating disorders
- Disease prevention should be integrated in a health promotion perspective
- Health promotion includes both schools, and a supportive environment to enable teachers, parents and other adults to be good role models
- Empowerment in health promotion means learning personal skills to cope with stress in order to be able to take charge over one's own life
- Preventive programmes should take on a longitudinal and multicomponent approach
- The Internet may become an important arena for doing preventive work
- Prevention programmes should be evaluated using a variety of research methods
- Health promotion may highlight difficult, conflicting political priorities in the development of society.

INTRODUCTION: WHY IS PRIMARY PREVENTION IMPORTANT?

Is primary prevention in general, and of eating disorders in particular, a nice, but unrealistic wish? The drive to diminish human suffering and prevent a fatal outcome of eating disorders is laudable. However, over time, professional opinions have oscillated between unrealistic optimism and fatalism. In this chapter we review what can be learned from the past, and describe a new model of prevention work in eating disorders. This is a middle way in a spirit of realistic optimism.

Handbook of Eating Disorders. Edited by J. Treasure, U. Schmidt and E. van Furth.
© 2003 John Wiley & Sons, Ltd.

THE DIETING CULTURE

Many children, and girls in particular, believe that thinness is important to attractiveness, academic and social success, and a happy life in general. Even small children believe that fat is undesirable (Richardsen et al., 1961; Smolak & Levine, 1996). For instance, girls prefer thin rather than fat dolls (Dyrenforth et al., 1980), and 50% of girls aged 7–13 years want to lose weight despite the fact that only 4% actually are overweight (Davis & Furnham, 1986). Moreover, among girls aged 11–16, years, 15–20% may display weight and shape preoccupation as well as strict dieting (e.g. Cooper & Goodyer, 1997; Gresko & Rosenvinge, 1998). Thinness is an important component of how attractive and desirable a woman is perceived to be (Smith et al., 1990; Tiggerman & Rothblum, 1988) and physical attractiveness is more strongly associated with opposite-sex popularity for women than for men (Feingold, 1990, 1991). Excessive dieting disturbs school performance and interpersonal relations, affects general mental and physical health (Rosenvinge & Gresko, 1997; Smolak & Levine, 1996), and may increase the risk for developing eating disorders (Patton, 1999). Moreover, body dissatisfaction and dieting as well as diagnosable eating disorders seem to occur among still younger age groups (Bryant-Waugh & Lask, 1995).

THE RECEPTOR: INDIVIDUAL VULNERABILITY

Numerous studies report on factors that may explain the inclination to diet. Some of these studies focus on the impact of mass media, family and friends. For instance, media convey salient or hidden messages to girls about what they should look like (Andersen & DiDomenico, 1992; Waller & Shaw, 1994). This points to the negative impact of an increasingly aggressive media culture, viewing children as consumers. Moreover, the strong correspondence between dietary restraint of 10-year-old girls and their mothers' dieting behaviour (Hill et al., 1990) becomes important because 60–80% of mothers may be on a diet (Edlund, 1997; Maloney et al., 1989). Also, almost 60% of girls aged 14 years reported that they had a friend who used to diet, and four times more girls than boys may have a friend who would like them more if they were thinner (Edlund, 1997). The question then, is how primary prevention can address and counteract negative external influences from poor human role models as well as from dysfunctional advertising. On the other hand, social influence, whether it comes from significant others or from mass media, needs a 'receptor'. Hence, other studies explaining the inclination to diet focus on psychological factors like body dissatisfaction, interoceptive awareness, concurrent psychological stress, poor self-esteem, and the vicious circle between dieting, poor self-esteem, and general distress (Hsu, 1990; Polivy & Herman, 1993; Rosenvinge, 1994; Rosenvinge et al., 1999; Striegel-Moore et al., 1986). The question then, is how to conduct primary prevention in a manner that diminishes these kind of psychological factors.

Models of understanding using 'external–internal' or 'continuous–discontinuous' dichotomies may represent oversimplifications. For instance, the inclination to diet may not stem from sociocultural pressures per se, and commercials with a slimness message may affect only those individuals who for some reason are vulnerable to this kind of message. A social-cognitive model (Fairburn & Wilson, 1993) may offer a framework bridging the dichotomies. Hence, sociocultural messages of thinness as the key to success, popularity and the resolving of psychological problems may be introjected and incorporated in the cognitive-affective schemata of individuals who are vulnerable because they are looking for solutions to personal problems. Such a model also predicts that watching other people dieting becomes a model learning effect only if the behaviour is viewed as attractive and performed by significant others. Thus, cognitive schemata and negative model learning may be important targets for primary prevention.

Normal developmental transitions are a risk period for developing eating problems and eating disorders. For boys, physical maturation brings them closer to the masculine ideal, but it takes the girls further away. Thus, boys gain weight due to an increase of muscle-and-skeleton mass, while girls gain weight due to an increase in body fat. For girls, particularly among those who mature earlier or later than their peers (Killen et al., 1992, 1994), physical changes may elicit body dissatisfaction and an inclination to lose weight. Furthermore, normal development may imply psychological changes in roles and responsibilities, and those who cope with such challenges in a more dysfunctional way may come to believe that to resolve problems is to improve on their appearance by reducing the size of the body by losing weight (Smolak & Levine, 1996; Striegel-Moore, 1993). Hence, information about normal physical changes in order to prepare adolescents for developmental challenges may be another important arena for primary prevention.

An unknown number of children and adolescents on a diet actually develop diagnosable eating disorders. This low predictive value of risk factor studies to date inhibits creative thinking about prevention. To some extent, there has been too narrow a focus on preventing anorexia nervosa, bulimia and binge eating. To widen the perspective, one should focus on individual suffering regardless of whether one develops an eating disorder or not. Eating problems which never reach the criteria for anorexia nervosa, bulimia nervosa or binge eating disorder are associated with a lot of suffering and problems which reduce the quality of life. A further widening of perspectives may include a shift of paradigm of prevention, i.e. from disease prevention to health promotion (Rosenvinge & Børresen, 1999).

PRIMARY PREVENTION: PAST EXPERIENCES AND FUTURE CHALLENGES

History is the best teacher. Primary prevention and health promotion do work. The history of preventive medicine is a history of resourcefulness—of how new insights are translated into new standards of practice which have radically improved the standard of living. This, however, requires efficient models and the continuous revision of models according to theoretical innovations, practical experience and empirical research. Traditionally, preventive work has been guided by the disease prevention paradigm and with the KAP model (knowledge–attitude–practice) as the guiding principle for practical work. According to this model, if you provide people with knowledge about the hazards of a given illness or disease this will lead them to change their attitude, values or self image and will stop unhealthy behaviours. For instance, there is a tacit assumption that information about eating disorders and the unveiling of 'false' cultural ideals may bring about 'insight', and hence, attitudinal change and a reduction in dieting. This theoretical model of attitude and behaviour change does not take into account the complex relationship between attitudes and behaviours, and how to influence people's choices. Moreover, this KAP model has not been supported by emprical research (see Rosenvinge & Børresen, 1999, for a review). The KAP model has generally been abandoned within other domains, such as the prevention of suicide, and substance abuse. It is therefore surprising that this model is still widespread within the field of eating disorders. It is possible that people working on prevention in eating disorders rather than being driven by empirical research, have been too focused on the hazards of eating disorders, and driven by good will and by the wish to act. The pitfalls of this way of working is individual burnout and disappointment when no visible results emerge.

Research in social psychology research has highlighted the complex interaction which exists between communicators, the characteristics of the target population and the nature of the information. Fact-oriented information may be preferred in situations were the recipients already agree with the delivered message. For example, athletes may strongly benefit from fact-oriented information about eating disorders because they are used to this sort of information about training—and nutritional advice to increase their competitive level—and because they view the coach who gives this information as an authority with high credibility. Fear-inducing information may lead to change if the recipients actually understand that the risk is personal and does not concern others, and if they are instructed about how to lower their risk. It is difficult to make a credible argument about personal risk in the case of eating disorders, given the low prevalence and the low predictive validity of empirically derived risk factors. High-risk individuals can remain well, and clinical cases can occur among people not at conspicuous risk (Rose, 1993). Thus, the message may be experienced as irrelevant. This activates the peripheral route of cognitive processing (Petty & Cacioppo, 1986) in which irrelevant features of the communicator may make a difference, rather than the message itself. It is impossible to produce educational materials or large-scale oral presentations that will fit the various combinations of communicator and recipient variables that will be encountered in the widespread distribution of educational material. If the recipients are hostile or indifferent, a balanced material would be optimal. A more one-sided message would create most impact among those who are initially positive to the message in the first place. Even in small group discussions it may be difficult to convey messages which match the individual needs in a manner which can change thinking and behaviours. This need to match the intervention to the indiduals' readiness to hear the message is similar to what we recognise in the clinical domain (see Chapter 13 by Treasure & Bauer, this volume).

Another difficulty, particularly with the widespread distribution of fact-oriented educational materials, relates to the risk of unwittingly teaching someone about eating disorder symptoms. This effect may be augmented if the information appears to increase the interest in eating disorders as a 'hot' and 'exciting' topic, which is politically correct for the media, teachers, health care professionals, and others to engage in. Young people in more or less difficult life situations may view eating disorder symptoms as a gateway to get help and, hence, resort to symptom imitation (Bruch, 1985; Habermas, 1992). Such symptom imitations may be likely to appear if adolescents, through the engagement in eating disorders by health professionals or school teachers, come to believe that such symptoms are the most 'efficient' way to get their attention in order to talk about a difficult life situation. Also, 'expert advice' on 'healthy' nutrition often has a hidden moralistic touch. This may increase food preoccupation and, hence, undermine self-control and confidence about eating. Therefore, we believe that while information about natural pubertal growth and development most certainly deserves a place in primary prevention, giving information about eating disorders does not. Still, this does not imply that one should avoid talking to young people about eating disorders at all costs. It might deserve a place when such talking is explicitly wanted by the adolescents, and where it serves a particular purpose, for instance, to reduce personal fear. In secondary prevention, however, information about eating disorders to school and health care personnel is a basic requirement (see Chapter 28, on Early Identification, in this volume).

A basic, though ignored requirement is to measure attitudes and behavioural correlates at the same level of specificity. Hence, attitudes may predict behaviour change if attitudes and behaviour are specified relative to a given context and if the attitudes are related to a given class of behaviours (Azjen & Fishbein, 1980). To overlook this point can either cause errors of measurement, which mask positive effects of prevention, or increase the risk of the intervention failing. From cognitive dissonance theory (Festinger, 1957), one would predict that a voluntary behaviour change that is inconsistent with a given attitude might be followed by an attitudinal change to reduce arousal or resolve 'cognitive dissonance'. Here, behaviour change is a procedural variable, while attitudinal change is the effect variable. In terms of prevention, such a change may be accomplished by mild positive incentives or pressures (persuasion). Another line of strategy is to rely on modelling or observational learning (Bandura, 1977). Social learning theory is often cited as the predominant model used to design programmes, because social learning theory addresses both the psychosocial dynamics underlying health behaviour and the methods of promoting behaviour change. To some extent, this has been used in our prevention programme with respect to teachers. However, behaviour change will not occur if those people who act as models are not perceived as models. This important point is frequently overlooked. A third perspective focuses on attitudes as effect variables. According to the elaboration-likelihood model (Petty & Cacioppo, 1986), it is important to find the optimal point of exposure to the prevention message. Repeated exposure facilitates cognitive elaboration of the message, which, in turn, leads to more lasting attitudes and attitudinal change. Obviously, this is a strong argument against short-lived prevention campaigns.

Thus, social psychology theories of persuasion, as well as communication theory, may give guidance about *how to communicate*. However, within a disease prevention model, the negative effect of *content of information* and the pitfalls of a high risk strategy are the main arguments for incorporating disease prevention within the paradigm of health promotion in primary prevention. Thus there is a paradox in the sense that the prevention of eating disorders is best served if there is no intention to prevent eating disorders (Rosenvinge & Gresko, 1997). In the following, we will outline some methods and strategies emerging from such a paradigm.

INTEGRATING DISEASE PREVENTION AND HEALTH PROMOTION

We argue that a model for the primary prevention of eating disorders alone is not warranted. Rather the focus should be to enable people to increase control of their own health (WHO, 1986). This salutogenic perspective implies a focus on factors which increase the likelihood that people manage to stay healthy, rather than on disputable risk factors for a particular illness. Educational policy and the school system form the basis and the premise for health promotion and primary prevention. For instance, the most recent version of the Norwegian prevention material (Børresen, 1999) follows this more general, health promotion approach. It includes issues like self-esteem, self-assertion, positive and negative coping strategies, stress management, puberty and what it means to grow up, and the developmental stressors of adolescents. The cultural obsession with slenderness is, of course, also emphasised, because it is important to address not only behavioural change at the individual level but also change within the environment to support behavioural change.

The salutogenic thinking of health promotion does not exclude disease prevention. Rather, disease prevention should be integrated in the health promotion paradigm. Knowledge is a necessary, though not a sufficient requirement to change behaviour at the individual or population level. Motivation to change arises from many factors. Health promotion incorporates many interventions (Green & Kreuter, 1991). The key concepts are the relevance of the knowledge, and motivation among recipients to integrate what is communicated. Obviously, messages about how, for instance, to cope with stress and increase self-esteem may stand a better chance in population health education than information about a given disease perceived as being only a remotely personal risk. Moreover, there is a great deal of knowledge to be communicated about more general risk factors. Within a developmental perspective there is evidence that specific diseases have many risk factors in common. 'Multifaceted vulnerability' is a useful concept. This is the flip side of poor predictive validity of disease-specific risk factors. Several studies have focused on more general risk factors predicting poor mental health. For children and adolescents, such risk factors relate to the quality of child–parent relations (Londerville & Main, 1981), child abuse (Gauthier et al., 1996), parental conflicts (Dadds & Powell, 1991) or substance abuse and parent depression (Cummings & Davies, 1994; Steinhausen, 1995). Other studies (Werner et al., 1971; Werner & Smith, 1982; Rutter et al., 1976) also focus on the impact of family disharmony, parent criminality, poverty, parent psychopathology and a low social status as predictive of poor mental health. Also, negative affectivity, poor self-esteem and lack of dispositional optimism have a cumulative negative impact on mental as well as physical health (Watson & Clark, 1989). Several studies (Rutter et al., 1976; Rutter, 1981) show a cumulative negative impact of general risk factors. Thus the presence of 2–3 general risk factors gives a four-fold increase in the risk for a mental disorder, whereas the presence of four or more factors further increases the risk to about 20%. This evidence not only helps in planning how to prevent mental health problems but also can pinpoint high-risk groups. Thus, a health promotion paradigm of primary prevention may be defined either as universal, and population based, or as part of a selective strategy to target subgroups where general risk factors may be present (Mrazek & Haggerty, 1994). There may also be general resiliency factors.

THE SCHOOL AS AN ARENA FOR PRIMARY PREVENTION AND HEALTH PROMOTION

The WHO's definition of health promotion may require a united effort from many actors and agencies in society. Public schools are an important arena for health promotion. Schools are everywhere, and everyone is obliged to attend school. Hence, school-based programmes give the opportunity to reach the entire child and adolescent population. Moreover, the school educates people and education follows detailed governmental plans. Also, the teachers are not only instructors and counsellors for children; they also have to work with parents, other professionals, and the authorities, which together form essential elements of the school's broad educational environment. In total, the school is a powerful arena for socialisation of children and adolescents into cultural standards and ideals as well as helping them to take a critical look at standards, ideals and norms. Hence, the school's role is not only to promote an intellectual understanding of culture, but also actually to focus on peer interactions, and how teachers can act as good role models. Thus, the social relations among the pupils and the values embedded in the youth culture are integrated parts of the learning environment. A Swedish study showed that 75% of the pupils wanted to be remembered as a popular student, and only 10% for their technical skills (Haugen, 1994). This highlights that schools are an important arena for social, not just intellectual, learning (Weare, 1992). This arena for social and relational learning may become increasingly important given the change in living conditions. For instance, the widespread access to Internet, computer games and the decrease in practical work may promote an anomic and introverted adolescent culture (Kraut et al., 1998; Stein, 1997). For some, this may result in poor socialisation and poor social skills, which may create feelings of helplessness and despair. In addition, their increasing exposure to the mass media places them easily in the passive role of the spectators and exposes them to conflicting views and values. To counteract these negative influences is a general aspect of promoting health, but the school may have a special responsibility and a unique possibility to teach young people how to cope with and fight negative cultural messages.

THE TEACHER AS A ROLE MODEL

Parents have the primary responsibility for educating and bringing up their children, and they are the most obvious and significant health role models. However, as a result of modern family life, teachers may become one of the adults with whom children and youth interact, perhaps not most closely with, but at least most frequently.

Hence, the schoolteacher may become a significant role model, not just an individual who provides information. In this respect, teachers must venture to project themselves clearly, alert and assured in relation to knowledge, skills and values to be transmitted. This aspect of a teacher's role is, in our opinion, highly undervalued. Teachers must acknowledge their own personality and character, and to stand forth as robust and mature adults in relation to young people who are in the process of emotional and social development, and exposed to many confusing and conflicting messages and values from the society at large. Teachers with a trustworthy self-image increase the likelihood that adolescents actually perceive them as such a role model.

FROM SCHOOLS TO COMMUNITIES: CREATING SUPPORTIVE ENVIRONMENTS

For the majority, childhood and adolescence are vulnerable periods, if not a time of turbulence or turmoil (Alsaker & Olweus, 1992; Verhulst & van der Ende, 1992). A supportive environment imbued with assurance and warmth is a prerequisite for learning, development and self-confidence, and may protect against many of today's leading health threats. This highlights the concept of *population-attributable risk*. When a risk is widely distributed in the population like, for instance, a risk for mental disorders in general, small changes in the entire population are likely to yield greater improvements in the population-attributable risk than larger changes among a smaller number of high-risk individuals, if ever such high-risk individuals could be identified. Hence, a large number of people exposed to a small risk may generate more cases than a small number exposed to a high risk (Rose, 1992), and the total cost–benefit of population strategies to create supportive environments may then be higher.

A supportive environment is highlighted in the Ottawa Charter of Health Promotion (WHO, 1986) as well as by Green and Kreuter (1991). Here, health promotion is defined as the combination of educational and environmental supports for actions and conditions of living conducive to health. This supports the idea that the educational challenge in schools goes much further than providing knowledge (Weare, 1992). In planning health education, the environment in which learning occurs has to be taken into account. The whole institutional context can, if organised effectively, become a health-promoting environment. It is important not to see this exclusively in the context of health education, but that this in fact has to be taken seriously in planning education in general.

Creating supportive environments for girls might be a particular challenge. For instance, if conflict and disruption are allowed to dominate the classroom atmosphere in schools, as so often happen, girls especially are the losers. It is a common experience among teachers that boys often dominate in the classroom and set the tone for the atmosphere. Therefore, they usually get most attention from the teacher. Also, among girls, there is a conflict between academic achievement and the wish to be popular among boys, a conflict that many girls resolve by becoming underachievers (Striegel-Moore, 1993). Young women may feel forced to choose between success at school or work, or success in relationships. This poses a dilemma, because each choice means denying many of their physical and interpersonal needs (Shisslak & Crago, 1994). The consequences may be to produce or enlarge a basic feeling of being helpless, and unable to cope with life. Such feelings may easily become a starting point for developing signs of poor mental health as a way to 'regain' control or autonomy or to display emotional stress. From an educational point of view this is perhaps one of the greatest challenges—to enable people to find a balance between autonomy and dependence (Weare, 1992). However, a paradox of health promotion is that autonomy also means to be free to choose, even if the choice is unhealthy (Weare, 1992). Some people in the field of health promotion dislike the idea that people should be completely free to choose, and want people to adopt their ideas about what is healthy or unhealthy. This highlights the conflict between accepting the huge statistical variation in the population with respect to coping styles, 'symptoms' and behaviours, and some more or less narrow, normative standards of living in the mind of the professional health-care worker.

Health promotion might be important in reducing risks for morbidity and mortality, but the ultimate value lies in the contribution to the quality of life of those for whom it is intended. The Ottawa Charter (WHO, 1986) puts it this way: 'Health is seen as a resource for everyday life, and not the objective for living.'

In the 1980s, the World Health Organisation (WHO), the European Commission (EC) and European Union (EU) developed the concept 'Health Promoting Schools'. The idea of 'Health Promoting Schools' is based on the principles and strategies of the Ottawa Charter (WHO, 1986) The main goal of this network is to develop good models for health promotion through collaboration between many schools. The main objective for most schools is the well-being of students, but the schools are free to choose their own targets and objectives and to design their intervention. However, being accepted as a member of the network is perhaps the main organisational benefit. In this way, every teacher may get support from the leadership of the school. Furthermore, the leadership is obliged to ensure that someone at their school is responsible for integrating health promotion into the school's daily life as well as the curricular plans.

In order to change the school into a health promoting school, five factors are crucial:

1. A holistic approach, including the social, emotional, spiritual and physical dimensions of health and well-being, should be emphasised.
2. Students should be active in a classroom democracy, with teaching that uses experimental, active learning to help them to develop interpersonal relationships and increase their self-esteem and confidence.
3. Teachers should collaborate to promote cross-curricular teaching.
4. Parental support and co-operation should be enhanced as an addition to the school health services and other relevant outside partners.
5. There should be a continuous focus on a healthy and safe social environment at school, both for students and staff (Colquhoun et al., 1997; Conference report, 1997; WHO, 1993; Williams, 1994). Such approaches are effective when schools and the entire community are involved (see Sorensen et al., 1998, for a review), and when many sectors—for instance, politicians, mass media, education and business—take responsibility. In particular, this way of thinking has been recognised within the field of preventing adolescent obesity (Neumark-Sztainer et al., 2000; Pronk & Boucher, 1999; Zwiauer, 2000).

Hence, the theoretical scope of primary prevention may be expanded from social psychology and communication theory (making persuasive health messages more effective) to social ecology theory (Bronfenbrenner, 1979; Stokols, 1996, 2000). Within such a framework, the aetiology as well as the interventions relative to mental health problems are placed in a wider context highlighting the interplay between mental health, social class, living and economic conditions, life span development, personal dispositions and family factors. Creating a supporting school environment may then become an important part of a supportive community in general.

PARENTS AS ROLE MODELS

A developmental prerequisite for optimal identity formation is the development of a stable sense of self (Kohut, 1971). By and large, early development of a child's sense of self arises from a history of parental empathy and parental frustrating of the child's immature grandiose 'self'. This is the starting point for parents as role models, i.e. the extent to which the child develops inner representations of attachment figures. Attachment disturbances may lead to deficits in these inner representations as well as a lack of a secure base for exploration and experimentation necessary for future identity achievement (Erikson, 1963, Grotevant & Cooper, 1985; Kroger & Haslett, 1988). In some cases, this may result in identity diffusion. These problems may increase or become evident in adolescence, where the individual is subject to conflicting values and interests. In some cases, a state of identity diffusion could indicate a fragmented self, feelings of emptiness, gender dysphoria, and a susceptibility to external influences. This may create a vulnerability to dysfunctional impulse regulation typical of, for instance, bulimic symptoms, suicide attempts and substance abuse, as well as indices of personality disorders and, in particular, borderline personality disorder (Akhtar & Samuel, 1996; Kroger & Rosenvinge, 2003).

Thus child-rearing practices are a primary target for health promotion. Parents may need to reflect on, and receive counselling about, the following: (1) the child's need for basic trust and parent confirmation; (2) the balance between stimulating and frustrating the child; (3) recognising and appreciating the child's own feelings; (4) distinguishing between the parent's needs and the child's needs; (5) the child's need for predictability, stability and control, and (6) the parents' awareness of themselves as basic role models with respect to coping style, attitudes and behaviours (Rosenvinge & Børresen, 1999). Previous universal, health promotion studies (Singletary, 1993) show that programmes which teach parents about such issues have a positive effect on the children's social and cognitive development. Thus, the fatalism of early child experiences may be exchanged with a realistic optimism with respect to the potentials for later health education and counselling.

DEVELOPING PERSONAL SKILLS

Empowerment is a key term in education as well as in health promotion. Empowerment does not only help pupils to take command of their own life and set their own boundaries, it also helps them to realise their potentials, appreciate their uniqueness and worth and encourage the acknowledgement and expressions of their feelings.

Such high demands are not the sole responsibility of the school. Moreover, even if such goals are met, it does not protect from stress, conflicts or other negative experiences. They are necessarily a part of life. Then, coping strategies should be equally focused to enable pupils to handle the different tasks and challenges they meet in life. According to Antonovsky's salutogenic model centred on the concept of 'sense of coherence' (Antonovsky, 1987) this includes 'manageability', 'comprehensibility' and 'meaningfulness'. Manageability refers to the feeling of having sufficient personal resources to meet internal and external stimuli, comprehensibility to the feeling that the world makes sense and that information about the environment is structured, ordered and consistent. Finally, meaningfulness refers to the feeling that different areas of life are worthy of emotional investment. The foundation of functional coping strategies lies in the interaction with primary caretakers. On the other hand, universal, health promotion programmes (Shure, 1997; Shure & Spivack, 1982) may significantly impact on problem solving and coping with frustrations. Similar to parental skills, this shows the significance of training and education and the potentials for primary prevention.

PRACTICAL CONSEQUENCES

Throughout the years health professionals and teachers have been visiting schools and youth organisations to target children and adolescents with programmes in order to prevent eating disorders. The most usual approach has been that the school arrange a day where the focus is eating disorders. In other words, the pupils listen to various topics related to eating disorders, and maybe watch a video of the development of eating disorders or a patient presenting the story of her life. Usually, the school staff and the pupils are very satisfied after such a day. Recent research (Westjordet & Rosenvinge, 2002) also indicates that pupils by and large experience this as providing facts about eating disorders. However, students view this as informative and not harmful, and they do not think that it will increase the likelihood that someone will develop an eating disorder. However, the crucial question is: 'Does it actually reduce the incidence of eating disorders or the frequency of eating disorder symptoms?' Consumer satisfaction aside, experiences as well as research indicate that this is not the way to target the problems of eating disorders. The traditional 'away day' with eating disorders might just be a fascinating break for the students, as well as satisfying the need 'do something' and the wishful belief that it just might help.

As previously mentioned, knowledge or health education has a place also in health promotion, but behaviour change usually comes from sources other than factual knowledge. In addition, we must be aware of how and in which context facts are communicated. Teachers and health care workers proclaim that pupils of today are disenchanted and bored by facts. We believe, however, that students are not turned off by facts, but rather, they are turned off by moralisation, superficial coverage of subject matter, scare tactics, and tedious methods of presentation.

A more fruitful approach is longitudinal and community-based programmes. Recent evidence (Rosenvinge, 2003) indicates that even within a health promotion paradigm, short-lived programmes do not affect coping skills, self-esteem, and the number of health complaints or dieting. This means that effective health promotion programmes should target the entire school environment on a long-term basis in order to change the adolescent subculture. Hence, by targeting the teachers, the school health personnel, and the parents as well as the pupils it is possible to start a process of awareness, and a lasting synergistic effect, that may increase individual resilience and create a supportive environment that may protect against developing eating problems and other mental problems. Previous studies (see Durlak & Wells, 1997; Weissberg et al., 1991 for a review) show lasting effects of longitudinal ecological and multicomponent programmes in promoting prosocial behaviours and reducing drug addictions. Such a longitudinal approach goes well with the elaboration-likelihood model (Petty & Cacioppo, 1986), where repeated exposure facilitates cognitive elaboration and a more lasting attitudinal change. Also, this fits with the social ecology theory as a framework for health research and practice (Stokols, 2000).

Behaviour may not change immediately in response to new awareness. Rather, change may be the result of cumulative effects of heightened awareness, increased understanding, and greater command (recognition and recall) of facts which seep into the system of beliefs, values, attitudes, intentions and self-efficacy, and then finally into behaviour (Green & Kreuter, 1999).

This is the strategy that can be outlined as a result of our best knowledge at present. However, the crucial point is not general models only, but also concrete guidelines on how to do the practical work. We believe that the following goals should guide practical health promotion strategies (Rosenvinge & Børresen, 1999):

1. To develop a broader emotional register and improve contact with own feelings.
2. To promote healthy stress management, coping and assertiveness.
3. To increase self-esteem, confidence and self-respect.
4. To create a balance between autonomy and dependency in relation to family members, and peers.
5. To increase confidence in expressing own needs and emotions.
6. To reduce ambitions and perfectionism.
7. To enhance a more positive body experience.
8. To connect self-esteem to other factors than weight and physical appearance.
9. To enforce a critical approach to superficial sociocultural ideals.
10. To enforce healthier eating habits.

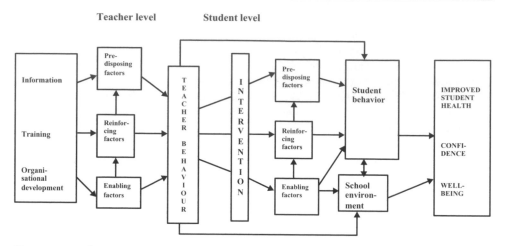

Figure 27.1   The PRECEDE–PROCEED model (Green & Kreuter, 1991, 1999)

Hence, general health promotion goals seems to be the best way to protect against eating disorders, rather than a focus on eating disorders in particular. This may be supported from findings that patients with a previous eating disorder actually focus things like a supportive environment and social network as well as coping and an internal locus of control as helpful in their recovery (Pettersen & Rosenvinge, 2002).

However, many prevention programmes or health-promoting interventions have become stuck, not because of a lack of goals and objectives, but of a lack of a theoretical framework as well as adequate strategies and comprehensive planning. One notable exception in this respect is the 'PRECEDE–PROCEED' model (Figure 27.1) (Green & Kreuter, 1991, 1999). This theoretical framework of planning is founded on the disciplines of epidemiology, the social, behavioural and educational sciences as well as health administration.

The PRECEDE framework takes into account the multiple factors which shape health status, and helps the planner to arrive at a highly focused subset of those factors as targets for intervention. However, it is important to have in mind that in the PRECEDE framework, the focus is on the outcome. This forces and encourages us to ask *why* and *how*, instead of merely stepping in to design and implement an intervention when a problem occurs. What is important is the final outcome one wants to accomplish. The PROCEED framework provides additional steps for developing policy and initiating the implementation and evaluation process.

Predisposing factors include a person's or a populations' knowledge, attitudes, beliefs and values and the perceptions which facilitate or block motivation change. *Reinforcing factors* are the rewards and feedback the learner receives from performing a certain class of health behaviours. According to learning theory, the nature of these reinforcers determines the probability of the behaviours occurring in the future. *Enabling factors* are the skills, resources, or barriers that can help or block the desired behavioural changes as well as environmental changes.

The basic steps in the use of this process are to identify and sort factors into predisposing, reinforcing and enabling categories, and to set priorities among and within those categories. The factors selected will then determine the learning objectives and community organisation objectives. This determination will then lead to the selection of materials and methods for programme implementation.

The three categories of predisposing, reinforcing and enabling are not mutually exclusive, and thus, a factor can appropriately be placed in more than one category (Green & Kreuter, 1991). For example, a family may be predisposed to dieting, and may reinforce (negatively or positively) that behaviour once it has been undertaken. Thus, Green and Kreuter (1991) underline that the content definition of categories should be viewed as practical, and not mirror a theoretically rigid model. Rather, the purpose of the categories is to sort causal factors into three classes of targets for subsequent intervention according to the three broad classes of intervention strategy: *direct* communication to change the predisposing factors, *indirect* communication (through, for instance, family, peers, and teachers) to change the reinforcing factors, and *organisational* or *training* strategies to change the enabling factors.

Furthermore, Green and Kreuter (1991) point to the fact that motivation is something that happens *within* the person and is not something that is done *to* the person by others.

HEALTH PROMOTION AND THE INTERNET

The Internet and the fact that it has quickly become an everyday tool for a growing part of the population may open new challenges and opportunities in health promotion. As for the latter, the Internet offers an opportunity for effective dissemination of information to large segments of the population, and could be an efficient tool in building healthier communities (Fawcett et al., 2000). Moreover, the Internet facilitates interactive communication, such as online supportive groups. On the other hand, negative aspects include Internet addiction, which may result in a breakdown of *in vivo* social relations (Kraut et al., 1997; Stein, 1997), and in the quality of Internet information which varies. Another concern might be that access to computers and the Internet services may be less frequent among low-income groups who may be in most need. Thus, the Internet may enhance social inequality (Eng et al., 1998). Some studies (Finfgeld, 2000; Johnsen et al., 2002; Kummervold et al., 2002) indicate that, compared to support groups for cancer, general psychiatric problems or sexually abused individuals, active participation from professionals may be necessary to prevent eating-disordered groups becoming destructive. Yet other studies (e.g. DiSogra & Glanz, 2000) show the benefit of the Internet in promoting sound nutrition among schoolchildren. Obviously, the role of the Internet in health promotion is just beginning, and it is important for health care workers and the health and education authorities to take an active role in this new development.

EVALUATION

To go back to the beginning we have made several critical points to the non-empirical approach to practical prevention work. The future challenge is not to remain in the hope that a longitudinal, multicomponent health promotion approach just might work, but to conduct scientifically valid studies to entangle the outcome of such an approach with a focus on outcome variables relevant for the field of eating disorders as well as other mental disorders.

Whether universal or indicative school-based or population-based programmes, the intervention phase needs to be expanded far beyond what has been customary in previous studies. Given the difficulties to change complex behaviours like eating patterns, and the time it takes to mobilise a community, at least five years intervention time has been recommended (Mittlemark et al., 1993). Given the concept of population-attributable risk, the outcome measure should be changed from clinical significance to public health significance. Public health significance comprises the efficacy in producing individual change as well as the reach, defined as the penetration of the intervention within the population. Furthermore, several authors (Pearce, 1996; Susser, 1995) have argued against the randomised-controlled design as appropriate for the research questions within community intervention trials. While the randomised-controlled design is suitable for the restricted hypotheses, the complexity of communities may involve a huge number of dependent and independent variables, which may become impossible to keep track of, and the loss of statistical power in the randomisation may be substantial. This is a reminder that methods are subordinate to the research questions, and that the complex nature of health promotion may require the implementation of a variety of methods.

CONCLUSIONS AND PROSPECTS FOR THE FUTURE

The primary prevention of eating disorders within a health promotion perspective is paradoxical as it is best not to have eating disorders at the focus. This is because the disease prevention paradigm can have negative effects such as giving information about eating disorders to healthy people who do not want it, and the risk of planting unhealthy ideas into vulnerable people. Also, any model must take into account the irrationality of the mind and our decision making, the complexity of the information forces in the multimedia society, as well as the complexity of eating disorders per se.

Rather, a health promotion perspective on primary prevention puts eating disorders in a wider context by including the complex mix of risk and resilience factors. This opens a large box of methods, including information and counselling to parents about good parenting, to teachers about how to become good role models, as well as to adolescents directly. Such multifaceted and longitudinal intervention programmes aim to impact on their self-esteem, sense of coherence and identity formation and, finally, systems rewarding and promoting healthy behaviours.

For the individual health care worker, school nurse, teacher or others who work with adolescents, the future challenge is to counteract the tendency to seek easy solutions. Resist the temptation to make a stab on eating disorders prevention by acting only in the 'here and now'. Do not fall into the trap of merely mirroring the present cultural fascination with eating disorders which are currently used to express distress or general maladjustment. Rather critically appraise your professional role in the wider context.

For scientists, politicians and the community planner, the focus on eating disorders in primary prevention may be politically correct and elicit funds for research or campaigns. It is tempting to seek quick results in a field highlighted in the mass media. However, this must not be to the detriment of hard work on a broader, health promotion level. A health promotion perspective may highlight difficult, conflicting political priorities (Albee, 1996). Much is known about health promotion goals, strategies, and methods for implementation but the challenge is to facilitate multicomponent, longitudinal studies using appropriate designs and methods to document the impact on individuals, groups and communities.

Two hundred years ago the German doctor, Franck, proclaimed that 'poverty is the mother of sickness'. Time and again in the centuries that followed, living conditions have been shown to play an important role in the development of public health. We also know that cultural changes have a strong influence on the health of individuals—though perhaps in slightly subtler ways. Images of the ideal body become translated into pathological eating habits. The words of Dr Franck are still valid, but there is another kind of poverty in today's society—the poverty of the heart and the soul. Today, it is important that children are seen, heard and loved by parents, peers, teachers and health care personnel. To see, to notice and to love is our greatest challenge and the pathway to a realistic optimism with respect to mental health promotion.

REFERENCES

Akhtar, S. & Samuel, S. (1996) The concept of identity. *Harvard Review of Psychiatry*, **3**, 254–267.

Albee, G.W. (1996) Revolutions and counterrevolutions in prevention. *American Psychologist*, **51**, 1130–1133.

Alsaker, F.D. & Olweus, D. (1992) Stability of global self-evaluation in early adolescence. A cohort longitudinal study. *Journal of Research on Adolescence*, **2**, 123–145.

Antonovsky, A. (1987) *Unraveling the Mystery of Health*. San Francisco: Jossey-Bass.

Azjen, I. & Fishbein, M. (1980) *Understanding Attitudes and Predicting Social Behaviour*. Englewood-Cliffs., NJ: Prentice Hall; New York: New York University Press, 1998.

Andersen, A.E. & DiDomenico, L. (1992) Diet vs. shape content of popular male and female magazines: A dose-response relationship to the incidence of eating disorders? *International Journal of Eating Disorders*, **11**, 283–287.

Bandura, A. (1977) *Social Learning Theory*. Englewood-Cliffs, NJ: Prentice Hall.

Bronfenbrenner, U. (1979) *The Ecology of Human Development. Experiments by Nature and Design*. Cambridge, MA.: Harvard University Press.

Bryant-Waugh, R. & Lask, B. (1995) Eating disorders in children. *Journal of Child Psychology and Psychiatry*, **36**, 191–202.

Børresen, R. (1999) *Om kultur, kropp og kommunikasjon. Undervisningsmateriell for ungdomsskolen og videregående opplæring. (About culture, body and communication. Teaching materials for teachers and school health personnel.* In Norwegian.) Sosial og helsedepartementet, Oslo:

Bruch, H. (1985) Four decades of eating disorders. In D.M. Garner & P.E. Garfinkel (Eds), *Handbook of Psychotherapy for Anorexia Nervosa and Bulimia*. New York: Guilford Press.

Davis, E. & Furnham, A. (1986) The dieting and body shape concerns of adolescent female. *Journal of Child Psychology and Psychiatry*, **27**, 417–428.

DiSogra, L. & Glanz, K. (2000) The 5 a day virtual classroom: An on-line strategy to promote healthful eating. *Journal of the Americal Dietician Association*, **100**, 349–352.

Dyrenforth, S.R., Wooley, O.W. & Wooley, S.C. (1980) A women's body in a man's world: A review of findings on body image and weight control. In J.R. Kaplan (Ed.), *A Woman's Conflict: The Special Relationship between Women and Food*. New Jersey: Prentice Hall, Inc.

Durlak, J.A. & Wells, A.M. (1997) Primary prevention mental health programs for children and adolescents: A meta-analytic review. *American Journal of Community Psychology*, **25**, 115–152.

Colquhoun, D., Goltz, K. & Sheehan, M. (1997) *The Health Promoting School. Policy, Programmes and Practice in Australia*. Harcourt Brace & Company.

Cooper, P.J. & Goodyer, I. (1997) Prevalence and significance of weight and shape concerns in girls aged 11–16 years. *British Journal of Psychiatry*, **171**, 542–544.

Conference Report (1997) 'The Health Promoting School—an investment in education, health and democracy'. First conference in the European Network of Health Promoting Schools. Thessaloniki–Halkidiki, Greece.

Cummings, E.M. & Davies, P.T. (1994) Maternal depression and child development. *Journal of Child Psychology and Psychiatry*, **35**, 73–112.

Dadds, M.R. & Powell, M.B. (1991) The relationship of transparental conflict and global marietal adjustment to aggression, anxiety, and immaturity in aggressive and nonclinic children. *Journal of Abnormal Child Psychology*, **19**, 553–567.

Edlund, B. (1997) *Dieting in Swedish children and adolescents*. Doctoral dissertation. Centre for Caring Sciences, University of Uppsala.

Eng, T.R., Maxfield, A., Patrick, K., Deering, M.J., Ratzan, S.C. & Gustafson, D.H. (1998) Access to health information and support: A public highway or a private road? *Journal of the America Medical Association*, **280**, 1371–1375.

Erikson, E.H. (1963) *Childhood and Society*. New York: Norton.

Fairburn, C.G. & Wilson, G.T. (1993) *Binge Eating. Nature, Assessment and Treatment*. New York: Guilford Press.

Fawcett, S.B., Francisco, V.T., Schultz, J.A., Berkowitz, B., Wolff, T.J. & Nagy, G. (2000) The Community Tool Box: A web-based resource for building healthier communities. *Public Health Report*, **115**, 274–278.

Feingold, A. (1990) Gender differences in effects of physical attractiveness on romantic attraction: A comparison across five research paradigms. *Journal of Personality and Social Psychology*, **59**, 981–993.

Feingold, A. (1991) Sex differences in the effects of similarity and physical attractiveness on opposite-sex attraction. *Basic and Applied Social Psychology*, **12**, 981–993.

Festinger, L. (1957) *A Theory of Cognitive Dissonance*. Evanston, IL: Row Peterson.

Finfgeld, D.L. (2000) Therapeutic groups online: The good, the bad, and the unknown. *Issues in Mental Health Nursing*, **21**, 241–255.

Gauthier, L., Stollak, G., Messe, L. & Aronoff, J. (1996) Recall of childhood neglect and physical abuse as different predictors of current psychological functioning. *Child Abuse and Neglect*, **20**, 549–559.

Green, L.W. & Kreuter, M.W. (1991) *Health Promotion Planning: An Educational and Environmental Approach* (2nd edition). Mountain View, CA: Mayfield Pulishing Company.

Green, L.W. & Kreuter, M.W. (1999) *Health Promotion Planning: An Educational and Environmental Approach* (3rd edition). Mountain View, CA: Mayfield Pulishing Company.

Gresko, R.B. & Karlsen, A. (1994) The Norwegian program for the primary, secondary and tertiary prevention of eating disorders. *Journal of Treatment and Prevention*, **2**, 57–63.

Gresko, R.B. & Rosenvinge, J.H. (1998) The Norwegian school-based prevention model: Development and evaluation. In W. Vandereycken & G. Noordenbos (Eds), *Prevention of Eating Disorders* (pp. 75–98). London: Athlone.

Grotevant, H.D. & Cooper, R.C. (1985) Patterns of interaction in family relations and the development of identity exploration in adolescence. *Child Development*, **56**, 415–428.

Habermas, T. (1992) Possible effects of the popular and medical recognition of bulimia. *British Journal of Medical Psychology*, **65**, 59–66.

Haugen, R. (1994) Trivsel, selvoppfatning og sosialt miljø i klassen. En analyse av sammenhenger. (Well-being, self-concept and social climate in the school class: an analysis of relations. In Norwegian). *Norsk Pedagogisk Tidsskrift*, **3**, 163–174.

Hill, J.A., Weaver, C. & Blundell, J.E. (1990) Dieting concerns of 10-year old girls and their mothers. *British Journal of Clinical Psychology*, **29**, 346–348.

Hsu, L.K.G. (1990) *Eating Disorders*. New York: Guilford Press.

Johnsen, J.A., Rosenvinge, J.H. & Gammon, D. (2002) Online group interaction and mental health. *Scandinavian Journal of Psychology*, **43**, 445–449.

Killen, J.D., Haywars, C., Litt., I., Hammer, L.D., Wilson, D.M., Miner, B., Taylor, C.B., Varady, A. & Shisslak, C.M. (1992) Is puberty a risk factor for eating disorders? *American Journal of Diseases in Childhood*, **146**, 323–325.

Killen, J.D., Hayward, C. & Wilson, D.M. (1994) Factors associated with eating disorder symptoms in a community sample of 6th and 7th grade girls. *International Journal of Eating Disorders*, **15**, 357–367.

Kohut, H. (1971) *The Analysis of the Self*. New York: International Universities Press.

Kummervold, P.E, Gammon, D., Bergvik, S., Johnsen, J.A.K, Hasvold, T. & Rosenvinge, J.H. (2002) Social support in a wired world—use of mental health discussion forums in Norway. *Nordic Journal of Psychiatry*, **56**, 59–65.

Kraut R., Lundmark V., Patterson, M., Kiesler, S., Mukopadhyay, T. & Scherlis, W. (1998). Internet paradox: A social technology that reduces social involvement and psychological well-being? *American Psychologist*, **53**, 1017–1031.

Kroger, J. & Haslett, S.J. (1988) Separation-individuation and ego identity status in late adolescence: A two-year longitudinal study. *Journal of Youth and Adolescence*, **17**, 59–79.

Kroger, J. & Rosenvinge, J.H. (2003) Identity disorders. In R. Fernandez Ballesteros (Ed.), *Encyclopedia of Psychological Assessment*. London: Sage (in press).

Londerville, S. & Main, S. (1981) Security of attachment, compliance and maternal training methods in the second year of life. *Developmental Psychology*, **17**, 289–299.

Maloney, M.J., McGuire, J., Daniels, S.R. & Specker, B. (1989) Dieting behaviour and eating attitudes in children. *Pediatrics*, **84**, 482–489.

Mittlemark, M., Hunt, M., Heath, G. & Schmid, T. (1993) Realistic outcomes: lessons from community-based research and demonstration programs for the prevention of cardiovascular diseases. *Journal of Public Health Policy*, **14**, 437–462.

Mrazek, P.J. & Haggerty, R.J. (1994) *Reducing Risks for Mental Disorders: Frontiers for Preventive Intervention Research*. Washington, D.C.: National Academy Press.

Neumark-Sztainer, D., Martin, S.L. & Story, M. (2000) School-based programs for obesity prevention: What do adolescents recommend? *American Journal of Health Promotion*, **14**, 232–235.

Patton, G.C. (1999) Onset of adolescent eating disorders: Population base cohort study over 3 years. *British Medical Journal*, **318**, 765–788.

Pearce, N. (1996) Traditional epidemiology, modern epidemiology, and public health. *American Journal of Public Health*, **86**, 678–683.

Pettersen, G. & Rosenvinge, J.H. (2002) Recovery from eating disorders: A patient perspective. *Journal of Treatment and Prevention*, **10**, 61–71.

Petty, R.E. & Cacioppo, J.T. (1986) *Communication and Persuasion: Central and Peripheral Routes to Attitude Change*. New York: Springer.

Polivy, J. & Herman, C.P. (1993) Etiology of binge eating: Psychological mechanisms. In C.G. Fairburn & G.T. Wilson (Eds), *Binge Eating. Nature, Assessment and Treatment* (pp. 173–205). New York: Guilford Press.

Pronk, N.P. & Boucher, J. (1999) Systems approach to childhood and adolescent obesity prevention and treatment in a managed care organization. *International Journal of Obesity and Related Metabolic Disorders*, **23**, 238–232.

Richardson, S.A., Hastorf, A.H., Goodman, N. & Dornbusch, S.M. (1961) Cultural uniformity in reaction to physical disabilities. *American Sociological Review*, **26**, 241–247.

Rose G. (1992) *The Strategy of Preventive Medicine*. New York: Oxford University Press.

Rose, G. (1993) Mental disorder and the strategies of prevention. *Psychological Medicine*, **23**, 553–555.

Rosenvinge, J.H. (1994) *Eating disorders in clinical and non-clinical samples*. Doctoral dissertation, Institute of Psychology, University of Oslo.

Rosenvinge, J.H. (2003) Adolescent health promotion: Effects of time or programme? A controlled intervention study. (Submitted for publication).

Rosenvinge, J.H., Sundgot-Borgen, J. & Gresko, R.B. (1999) The prevalence and psychological correlates of anorexia nervosa, bulimia nervosa and binge eating among 15-year-old students: A controlled epidemiological study. *European Eating Disorders Review*, **7**, 382–391.

Rosenvinge, J.H. & Børresen, R. (1999) Prevention of eating disorders: Time to change programmes or paradigms? Current update and future recommendations. *European Eating Disorders Review*, **7**, 6–16.

Rosenvinge, J.H. & Gresko, R.B. (1997) Do we need a prevention model for eating disorders? Recent developments in the Norwegian school-based prevention model. *Journal of Treatment and Prevention*, **5**, 110–118.

Rutter, M. (1981) *Maternal Deprivation Reassessed*. London: Penguin.

Rutter, M., Tizard, J., Yule, W., Graham, P. & Witmore, K. (1976) Research report: Isle of Wright studies, 1964–1974. *Psychological Medicine*, **6**, 313–332.

Shisslak, C.M. & Crago, M. (1994) Toward a new model for the prevention of eating disorders. In P. Fallon, M.A.Katzman & S.C.Wooley (Eds), *Feminist Perspective on Eating Disorders.* (pp. 419–438). New York/London: Guilford Press,

Shure, M.B. (1997). Interpersonal problem solving: Primary prevention of early high-risk behaviors in pre-school and primary years. In G.W. Albee & T.P. Gullotta (Eds), *Primary Prevention Works* (pp. 167–190). London: Sage.

Shure, M.B. & Spivack, G. (1982) Interpersonal problem solving in young children: A cognitive approach to prevention. *American Journal of Community Psychology*, **10**, 341–356.

Singletary, W.M. (1993) Education for parenting. In H. Parens & S. Kramer (Eds), *Prevention in Mental health* (pp. 149–166). Northvale: Jason Aronson.

Smith, J.E., Waldorf V.A. & Trembath, D.L. (1990) 'Single white male looking for thin, attractive . . . ' *Sex Roles*, **23**, 675–685.

Smolak, L. & Levine, M.P. (1996) Adolescent transition and the development of eating problems. In L. Smolak, M.P. Levine & R. Striegel-Moore (Eds), *The Developmental Psychopathology of Eating Disorders. Implications for Research, Prevention, and Treatment* (pp. 207–235). New Jersey: Lawrence Erlbaum Associates.

Stein, D.J. (1997) Internet addiction, Internet psychotherapy. *American Journal of Psychiatry*, **153**, 890.

Steinhausen, H.C. (1995) Children of alchoholic parents: A review. *European Child and Adolescent Psychiatry*, **4**, 143–152.

Striegel-Moore, R.H., Silberstein, L.H. & Rodin, J. (1986) Toward an understanding of risk factors for bulimia. *American Psychologist*, **41**, 246–263.

Striegel-Moore, R.H. (1993) Etiology of binge eating: A developmental perspective. In C.G. Fairburn & G.T. Wilson (Eds) *Binge Eating. Nature, Assessment and Treatment* (pp. 144–172). New York: Guilford Press.

Stokols, D. (1996) Translating social ecological theory into guidelines for community health promotion. *American Journal of Health Promotion*, **10**, 828–898.

Stokols, D. (2000) Social ecology and behavioral medicine: Implications for training, practice, and policy. *Behavioral Medicine*, **26**, 129–138.

Sorensen, G., Emmons, K., Hunt, M.K. & Johnston, D. (1998) Implications of the results of community intervention trials. *Annual Reviews of Public Health*, **19**, 379–416.

Susser M. (1995) Editorial: The tribulations of trials: Intervention in communities. *American Journal of Public Health*, **85**, 156–160.

Tiggerman, M. & Rothblum, E.D. (1988) Gender differences in social consequences of perceived overweight in the United States and Australia. *Sex Roles*, **18**, 75–86.

Verhulst, F. & van der Ende, J. (1992) Six year stability of parent-reported problem behaviour in an epidemiological sample. *Journal of Abnormal Child Psychology*, **20**, 595–610.

Waller, G. & Shaw, J. (1994) The media influence on eating problems. In B. Dolan & I. Gitzinger (Eds), *Why Women. Gender Issues and Eating Disorders* (pp. 44–54). London: Athlone Press.

Watson, D. & Clark, L.A. (1989) *Vulnerable but Invincible. A Longitudinal Study of Resilient Children and Youth.* New York: McGraw-Hill.

Weare, K. (1992) The contribution of education to health promotion. In R. Bunton & G. MacDonald (Eds), *Health promotion Disciplines and diversity* (pp. 66–85). London: Routledge.

Weissberg, R.P., Caplan, M. & Harwood, R.L. (1991) Promoting competent young people in competence-enhancing environments: A systems-based perspective on primary prevention. *Journal of Consulting and Clinical Psychology*, **59**, 830–841.

Werner, E.E., Bierman, J.M. & French, F.E. (1971) *The Children of Kwai. A Longitudinal Study from the Prenatal Period to Age 10.* Honolulu: University of Hawai Press.

Werner, E.E. & Smith, R.S. (1982) *Vulnerable but Invincible: A Longitudinal Study of Resilient Children and Youth.* New York: McGraw-Hill.

Westjordet, M.Ø. & Rosenvinge, J.H. (2002) Is information about eating disorders experienced as harmful? A consumer perspective on primary prevention (submitted for publication).

WHO (1984) *Health Promotion: A Discussion Document on the Concept and Principles.* Copenhagen: WHO Regional Office of Europe.

WHO (1986) *The Ottawa Charter for Health Promotion*. Geneva: World Health Organisation.

WHO (1993) *ENHPS Resource Manual*. Copenhagen: WHO.

Williams, M.I (Ed.) (1994) *Promoting the Health of Young People in Europe. Health Education in Schools*. A training manual for teachers and others working with young people. Health Education Board of Scotland, WHO, CE, CEC.

Zwiauer, K.F. (2000) Prevention and treatment of overweight and obesity in children and adolescents. *European Journal of Pediatrics*, **159**, 156–168.

CHAPTER 28

Early Identification

Greta Noordenbos

Department of Clinical Psychology, Leiden University, Leiden, The Netherlands

SUMMARY

1. In order to implement secondary prevention both patient and doctor delays have to be shortened.
2. General practitioners who are more familiar with the (early) and subclinical signs of anorexia and bulimia nervosa, are better able to identify eating disorders.
3. General practitioners need to adopt a sympathetic and non-judgemental manner when enquiring about patients' eating disorder symptoms and psychopathology.
4. An important task for general practitioners is to help the patients to recognize the seriousness of their disorder and to prepare and motivate them for specialist trreatment.
5. Early referal to specialized care for eating disorders is important. However, in bulimia nervosa specialist treatment can be adapted for primary care by delivering brief formats of CVBT or manual-based self-help guides.

INTRODUCTION

Given the severe physical, psychological, social and financial consequences of eating disorders for patients and their families—and the considerable potential for chronicity—secondary prevention of these disorders by early identification and intervention is an important topic. Parents, teachers and general practitioners play a pivotal role in identifying individuals with eating disorders before serious morbidity has developed. Having said that, there is little information available in the scientific literature about early identification of eating disorders by parents and teachers. However, there are a growing number of websites on eating disorders which can provide information to faciliate early detection by patients and their families and work assessing their quality is currently underway (Schmidt, personal communication). Most scientific articles about the possibilities of secondary prevention are about what can be done in primary care. A computer search showed that little research has been done on the experiences of general practitioners themselves. Rather the focus is on informing general practitioners about the characteristics of eating disorders and how to arrive at a diagnosis. These articles typically also give suggestions on how to treat these

Handbook of Eating Disorders. Edited by J. Treasure, U. Schmidt and E. van Furth.

patients in primary care and how to decide when more specialized treatment might be necessary.

In this chapter I will first describe the results of research on the possibilities of, and some of the barriers to, early identification and intervention with eating disorders. The most common difficulties in the interaction between patients with anorexia nervosa and general practitioners will also be described. In the second part suggestions will be made on how to improve the primary care physician's ability to identify eating disorders at an earlier stage; their attitudes towards and their communication with these patients, and their interventions and referrals to more specialized treatment.

RESEARCH ON SECONDARY PREVENTION IN PRIMARY CARE

Research on secondary prevention in primary care reveals that there is substantial under-diagnosis of eating disorders in primary care. A network of Dutch general practitioners, who together see nearly 150 000 patients a year (i.e. about 1% of the Dutch population), have maintained a register of morbidity since 1970 (Bartelds et al., 1989). These general practitioners are experienced in registering illnesses and every year they record the data on a few selected disorders. Using this registration system Hoek et al. (1995) studied the registration of anorexia and bulimia nervosa by 58 general practitioners from 1985 to 1989. Annually these doctors received detailed information on eating disorders by means of a circular with information about anorexia and bulimia nervosa and through special meetings convened for this purpose, in which they received oral instructions about the detection of eating disorders. In the period concerned, these general practitioners were asked to consider in every patient they saw whether this might be a case of anorexia or bulimia nervosa (according to the DSM-III-R criteria). In doubtful cases the researchers asked the physicians for more detailed information or made the decision for them.

With the aforementioned registration system, before 1985 only 28 patients with anorexia nervosa and 31 patients with bulimia nervosa had been detected (Hoek et al., 1995). After the intervention 60 patients received a first diagnosis of anorexia nervosa (an incidence of 8.1 per 100 000 persons/year) and 85 patients a first diagnosis of bulimia nervosa (an incidence of 11.5 per 100 000 persons/year) during the period of 1985 to1989. These figures were higher than those found in earlier research. These findings show that special and ongoing training of general practitioners can improve their ability to diagnose eating disorders. However, the study also illustrates the difficulties in detecting eating disorders. Although the general practitioners in this study were better informed than the average GP, they invariably missed some cases, because eating disorders are characterized by taboo and denial. In general, it was difficult to detect patients with normal-weight bulimia nervosa, even though this is the most common condition in clinical samples (Hoek et al., 1995). Based on their epidemiological research in the Netherlands, Hoek (1993) concluded that less than half of the patients with anorexia nervosa are correctly diagnosed by their general practitioner and only about 10% of the patients with bulimia nervosa (see Table 28.1).

In Britain, King (1989) studied four group practices of general practitioners in south London: a screening of 748 patients between the ages of 16 and 35 years revealed 1.1% of females (6 women) and 0.5% of males (1 case) diagnosed with bulimia nervosa; no case of anorexia nervosa was found. When partial syndromes were included, the prevalence

Table 28.1   One year prevalence rates per 100 000 young females at different levels of care (Hoek, 1993)

Level of morbidity	AN N (%) Filter	BN N (%)
1. Estimated in the community	370	1500
	Illness behavior	
2. Total in primary care	260 (70)	1050 (70)
	Detection behavior	
3. Conspicuous in primary care	160 (43)	170 (11)
	Referral to psychiatrist	
4. Total of psychiatric patients	127 (34)	87 (6)
	Admission to psychiatric unit	
5. Psychiatric inpatients	30 (8)	? (?)

in females rose to 3.9%. A similar study in Cambridge by Whitehouse and colleagues (1992) found a prevalence of anorexia nervosa of 0.2% (1 case), full bulimia nervosa 1.5% (8 cases) and partial bulimia nervosa 5.4% (29 cases). Half of the people with bulimia nervosa, however, had not been identified by the general practitioner and two of these patients had been refered to medical specialists for treatment of secondary complications of their eating disorder. According to Whitehouse et al. (1992), hidden cases of bulimia, or partial syndromes, are relatively common in primary care, but many of these patients remain undetected, even when the help of specialists is sought for what are likely to be secondary complications of the eating disorder. In Austria, only 12% of the patients with bulimia nervosa, and only 45% of the patients with anorexia nervosa, are diagnosed by general practitioners (de Zwaan, 1999).

BARRIERS TO EARLY IDENTIFICATION OF EATING DISORDERS BY GENERAL PRACTITIONERS

Thus epidemiological research from different European countries points to the fact that eating disorders are being under-diagnosed in primary care. What are the reasons for this? A number of different reasons seem to be potent barriers to early diagnosis and intervention. These include:

- patient delay in presenting their eating problems;
- doctor delay in diagnosing eating disorders at an early stage;
- communication difficulties between doctors and eating-disordered patients;
- attitudinal biases of general practitioners towards these patients;
- gender differences between general practitioners and eating-disordered patients;
- inadequate interventions by general practitioners including referrals to other specialists.

Each of these problems will be described below.

Patient Delay

Patient delay severely hampers early identification of eating disorders by general practitioners. Research in the Netherlands by de Bloois (1987) and Noordenbos (1998) showed that nearly 90% of the patients with anorexia or bulimia nervosa went to their general practitioner with complaints related to their eating disorder. The mean period between the start of their eating disorder and the first visit to the doctor was nearly four years (Daaleman, 1991). The reason for this 'patient delay' is often that at the onset of an eating disorder the patients do not realize they have a problem. On the contrary, they often feel well because their slimming behaviour is 'successful' and seems to be the 'solution' for other problems. Thus, in the early phase of their eating disorder these patients are seldom willing to see a doctor because they do not see themselves as being ill (Yanovski, 1991). Some of these patients may even ask their physician to help them with their weight loss. Indeed, in a study of case ascertainment from primary care in the UK, 27/100 cases of bulimia nervosa had previously been prescribed laxatives (Turnbull et al., 1996).

In a Dutch sample of 108 individuals with anorexia and bulimia nervosa, who were recruited by advertisements in newspapers and the journal of the Dutch Foundation of Anorexia Nervosa and Bulimia Nervosa, only 45% took the initiative to see their general practitioner; 23% mentioned that others advised them to go, while 32% were sent by others who insisted they should visit their general practitioner (Noordenbos, 1992). The younger patients with eating disorders are often brought to the general practitioner by their family who become concerned about her eating habits and weight. For these patients, denial and non-compliance are hallmarks of their eating problems (Deters, 1998).

Most patients with anorexia and bulimia nervosa find it very difficult to tell their doctor directly about their eating behaviour, because they feel too ashamed to do so. They often fear that they have to give up their weight loss behaviour, and hence will become fat. Some are worried that they will be sent to a hospital or be labelled as mentally ill and admitted to a psychiatric unit. Exhausted and desperate families may reinforce these fears by using threats of compulsory admission as a way of coercing their anorexic daughter into eating. When the sufferer finally agrees to visit the doctor, it is often for secondary complications of her eating and slimming behaviour, such as menstrual irregularities, loss of hair, fatigue, weakness and dizziness, dental problems, persistent sore throat, abdominal pain and constipation (Noordenbos, 1992; Ogg et al., 1997; Yanovski, 1991). The patient's main complaint is often constipation, for which she requests a special diet or laxatives. Some patients are quite successful in this strategy. They hide their 'real' problems by only mentioning secondary complaints. However, others hope that their doctor will ask more questions about their eating problems (Noordenbos, 1992).

Doctor Delay

General practitioners have many different and often conflicting pressures and priorities, and as each general practitioner will only see a few eating-disordered cases per year it is difficult for them to bear eating disorders in mind as a diagnostic possibility. This problem may be compounded further by lack of knowledge about (early) signals of anorexia and bulimia nervosa. Moreover, general practitioners often are confronted with 'subclinical forms' of anorexia and bulimia nervosa, which lack the characteristics of the full-blown clinical picture (King, 1989; Meadows et al., 1986; Szmukler, 1983) and are therefore more difficult to identify (Button & Whitehouse, 1981; Dhondt et al., 1989; Bryant-Waugh et al., 1992; Hoek, 1991; Whitehouse et al., 1992). Even when the patients meet the full diagnostic criteria (APA, 1994) for eating disorders, early diagnosis can be difficult. The doctor may need to be very observant to pick up the emaciation of someone with anorexia nervosa, who covers her body in multiple layers of baggy clothes. Bulimia nervosa is even more difficult to diagnose, because these patients usually have a normal weight and appear healthy, although marked weight fluctuations can sometimes provide a clue over time (Yanovski, 1991).

Attitudinal Biases and Communication Difficulties

General practitioners, like the wider public, may have stereotyped ideas about anorexia and bulimia nervosa as 'female' disorders, which affect only white, middle-class women. This makes it very likely that they will overlook eating disorders in male sufferers, irrespective of whether they suffer from anorexia nervosa or bulimia nervosa (Andersen & Mickalide, 1983; Bryant-Waugh et al., 1992; Mitchell & Goff, 1984). Additionally, male patients may be reluctant to tell their doctors about their eating disorder, because many of them feel ashamed that they have a 'girl's disease'.

Physician bias may also explain why eating disorders are overlooked in non-whites or in lower socio-economic classes (King, 1989; Striegel-Moore & Smolak, 1996). Research shows that women from non-western cultures tend to adopt the cultural ideal of slenderness when they live in western societies, and hence are equally at risk for developing an eating disorder (Nasser, 1986).

Moreover, eating disorders are often trivialized/stigmatized as they are widely seen as self-inflicted conditions (Gowers & Shore, 1999). Health professionals in general, and GPs are unlikely to be an exception to this (Fleming & Szmukler, 1992; Vandereycken, 1993), typically have negative attitudes to these patients and see them in a similarly negative light to those who take recurrent overdoses—another group of patients whose needs are widely neglected. These attitudinal biases are likely to contribute to poor detection rates and poor communication between the general practitioner and their eating-disordered patients (Noordenbos, 1998; Vandereycken, 1993). Unsurprisingly, therefore in a survey of members of the Eating Disorders Association 43% of 1638 respondents said that their initial consultation with a GP was unhelpful (Newton et al., 1993).

Vandereycken (1993) pointed out that people with anorexia nervosa challenge the medical knowledge and the authority of doctors. They evoke mistrust and even hostility because many clinicians believe that the patient's reluctance to eat could be controlled with adequate exercise of will power on her part. Physicians have great difficulty in dealing with their patients' denial of illness and their reluctance to be treated. 'Anorexics often evoke frustration and outrage in doctors who regard them as imposters because they do not have a "genuine illness", deliberately harm themselves, and refuse to co-operate in treatment, just like self-poisoners and addicts do' (Vandereycken, 1993, p. 13). Hence, physicians tend to see anorectic patients as untrustworthy, obstinate, demanding, bothersome, manipulative, and likely to polarize people, not only their family, but also therapists. Feelings of helplessness in the middle of a power struggle—the battle of control, wherein the doctor tries to restore his authority—may lead to counter-aggressive reactions disguised as therapeutic measures, ranging from hospitalization to tube feeding (Vandereycken, 1993). (See also Bauer & Treasure in this volume for a further discussion on this topic.)

Gender Differences between Doctors and Patients

Communication problems between patients and doctors can also be caused by gender differences. The vast majority of patients with eating disorders are female, whereas most GPs are male. Gender differences make it more difficult for patients to trust their doctors, and for physicians to understand these patients (Dolan & Gitzinger, 1994). For female patients it is more difficult to reveal their eating behaviour because they assume that male doctors do not understand why women are so concerned about growing fat (Noordenbos, 1998).

Treatment in Primary Care and Referrals

When the general practitioner has passed the difficult stage of diagnosing anorexia or bulimia nervosa, the question is how to treat the patient at this early stage and when to refer her for more specialized treatment in the case of more severe problems. A Dutch survey of 108 patients with eating disorders showed that 38% of the patients received medication from their general practitioners. These included vitamins, laxatives (for constipation), hormones (to induce menses) and drugs to stimulate or suppress the appetite; however, in many cases the patients did not take the prescribed medication (Noordenbos, 1992). Forty-five percent of people with bulimia nervosa were prescribed an antidepressant by their general practitioner in the UK (Turnbull et al., 1996). Although some form of psychological therapy in patients with a subclinical or partial eating disorder can be helpful, most doctors do not take this on themselves due to lack of time, and many practices do not have access to practice-based counsellors. King (1989), in his UK-based study, showed that intervention by general practitioners in eating-disordered patients was minimal and in no case did the GP attempt to manage the problem on a one-to-one basis. In the UK 80% of cases of anorexia nervosa, and 60% of cases of bulimia nervosa, are referred on for specialized help (Turnbull et al., 1996). More recently, in the UK, the National Service Framework for Mental Health has specified that each health authority has to implement guidelines for the treatment and referral pathways of common mental disorders in primary care, including eating disorders. This could lead to an improvement of primary care-based interventions if it is posssible to overcome the barriers of lack of time and skills .

Referrals to other specialists is not always successful. The Dutch survey of 108 patients with an eating disorder revealed that of the 93 patients who visited their general practitioner with an eating disorder, 53% were referred to a medical specialist, 19% to a psychiatrist and 10% to a psychologist. The remainder were 'treated' by the general practitioner who prescribed either a diet (16%) or medication (38%) (Noordenbos, 1992). The retrospective information from this survey applied to the patients' management in the 1980s. A study of 30 general practitioners several years later showed a changing picture in the way in which GPs handle eating disorders: the prescription of medication was reduced to 23% and the patients were more often referred to a community mental health centre (31%), to a psychologist (23%) or a psychiatrist (23%), while only 8% were sent to a medical specialist (Aerts, 1992; Dresscher, 1993). However, referrals to more specialized treatment were not often successful because 27% of the patients completely denied their eating disorder, 46% minimized their problems and were reluctant to be treated and 19% dropped out after some weeks or months. Only 8% had a positive attitude towards treatment. Thus an important task for the general practitioner is to help the patients to recognize the seriousness of their disorder and to prepare and motivate them for specialist treatment (Silber & DeAngelo, 1991; Spaans & Bloks, 1997).

IMPROVEMENT OF SECONDARY PREVENTION BY GENERAL PRACTITIONERS

Improvement of Early Identification

General practitioners have to be better informed about the (early) signals of anorexia and bulimia nervosa and the so-called subclinical eating disorders (Button & Whitehouse, 1981) or partial syndromes (King, 1989). Important signals of (partial) anorexia nervosa are weight loss, amenorrhoea, pubertal delay, cold hands and low body temperature, and a persistent overconcern with body weight and shape. Other signals can be anaemia, constipation, fatigue, dehydration, dry skin, brittle hair and nails and dental problems. Important signals for bulimia nervosa are abrasions and scars on the dorsum of the hands (caused by scraping the hands against the teeth during self-induced vomiting), dental erosions and swelling of the salivary glands, weight fluctuations, fatique and sleep disturbances (Yanovski, 1991). When a general practioner sees these characteristics, he or she can ask further questions to verify the diagnosis. However, GPs have to realize that patients with eating disorders often start to tell only a part of their real story and expect that the doctor will ask more questions about their eating behaviour. General practitioners should realize that for these patients it is often threatening to discuss their eating and slimming behaviour. When an eating disorder is presumed, one can start with the following questions (Yanovski, 1991): 'Many young women have concerns about food and weight. Do you have such concerns?' or 'Many young people have trouble with eating too much. Has this been a problem for you?'. If the patient says 'yes', the physician can ask in a sympathetic and non-judgemental manner about the following topics:

- eating behaviour
- (self-induced) vomiting
- use of laxatives and diuretics
- general physical condition
- attitudes towards body shape and weight
- history of highest and lowest weight
- physical exercises and sports
- self-criticism and lack of self-esteem
- mood disturbances, stress and depression
- perfectionistic behaviour and fear of failure
- social contacts with peers
- relationship with parents (boyfriend, spouse)
- menstruation pattern
- possible negative sexual experiences.

Although the patient often is too ashamed to answer these questions, merely asking them gives the patient the feeling that the physician is informed about the features and background of anorexia and bulimia nervosa (Noordenbos, 1998). The conversation should take place in a non-judgemental atmosphere and without showing distrust, even when the physician senses that the patient is not (yet) willing to reveal 'the whole truth'. In younger patients it is important to include the parents in the assessment, because their information might lead more quickly to the diagnosis, especially in denying patients (Vandereycken et al., 1989).

The diagnosis should be based mainly on behavioural characteristics of the disorder instead of being the result of an exclusion process. More specialized physical examinations should only be carried out in case of doubt about the diagnosis. All too often patients are subjected to inappropriate or intrusive physical examinations which can delay the start of an appropriate treatment (Vandereycken & Meermann, 1984; Whitehouse et al., 1992). When physical examination is necessary the following tests should be included, according to Gilchrist et al. (1998) and Crisp and McClelland (1996):

- Full blood count
- Serum biochemistry, including electrolytes and urea, glucose, calcium, phosphate, liver function studies
- Thyroid function
- Electrocardiogram.

Improving Communication with Eating-Disordered Patients

Patients with eating disorders often hesitate about disclosing their behaviours, thoughts and feelings, and general practitioners should view this as part of the problem of having an eating disorder. Eating disorders often have the function of avoiding or resolving underlying problems (Gilchrist et al., 1998). It is important to acknowledge and compliment the patient on her courage in deciding to come and discuss her eating disorder, even when she only reveals a small part of it. The first contacts are the most difficult, because these patients often 'test' whether the clinician can be trusted. One should avoid a battle over 'who is in control here', which implies that the physician may temporarily have to accept feeling helpless or manipulated. 'It is precisely when the patient can attribute these feelings to a therapist who can accept and endure these feelings himself, that the patient is first able to achieve personality changes and to experience a greater sense of intrapsychic integration' (Cohler, 1977, p. 386).

The patients' denial of being ill, secretiveness of eating habits and pseudo-cheerfulness are only a camouflage for their own helplessness and lack of basic trust. General practitioners have to understand that their patient's resistance to eating is not a deliberate decision. Moreover, starvation by itself leads to narrowed awareness and cognitive dysfunction. Only over the course of therapy will the clinician be able to witness the patient's growing awareness and recognition of her real emotional state (Vandereycken, 1993). Also, gender aspects should be taken into account, because specific gender-related issues such as body experience and sexuality and ambivalence about gender identity are more easily discussed with a female doctor than a male (Zunino et al., 1991).

Improving the Motivation of Eating-Disordered Patients

Once the diagnosis has been ascertained, patients will need treatment for their eating dis-order, but most patients are not motivated to change their behaviour. They are often very afraid of the prospect of treatment, because their disorder serves too often as a strategy to cope with their psychological problems and often functions as a coping strategy (Deters, 1998). Motivation techniques are very important for these patients (Spaans & Bloks, 1997; See also Treasure & Bauer in this volume). Patients have to know clearly what the goals and activities of the treatment are, and the time it will take to reach these goals. Also, the gender of the therapist should be taken into account. Feminist therapists claim that women should be treated by a female doctor or therapist (Stockwell & Dolan, 1994). It may be best to leave this choice to the patients themselves.

In order to inform patients and their families about the consequences of their eating disorder and the possibilities of treatment short brochures in the waiting room of general practitioners can be very useful. The Dutch Association of Anorexia and Bulimia Nervosa has distributed such a brochure among general practitioners, entitled *When the Scales are your Enemy*. This brochure informs them of the characteristics of anorexia and bulimia nervosa, the physical, psychological and social consequences, and the possibilities of treatment. Patients can find this brochure in the waiting room of their doctor. The Dutch Center for Women and Health Care has published similar brochures, one for physicians with the title *To Eat or Not to Eat, That is the Question*, and one for lay-people entitled *Do I Eat or Not?* Both brochures are widely distributed among general practitioners. There are a number of excellent books which address most of the common questions that family members ask and may assist the general practitioner in their task, e.g. Crisp et al. (1996), Bryant-Waugh and Lask (1999), Palmer (1996), and Treasure (1998). Parents might also be encouraged to join self-help organizations, such as the UK-based Eating Disorders Association, which runs a number of carer support groups.

Brief Interventions Suitable for Use in Primary Care

Because of lack of time and knowledge, general practitioners often find it difficult to take on the treatment of their eating disordered patients. However, recently a number of studies have addressed the issue of how specialist treatments for eating disorders, in particular for bulimic type disorders, can be adapted for primary care, e.g. by delivering brief formats of CBT (Waller et al., 1996) or use of psycho-educational groups, which focus on symptom management (Davies et al., 1990). A number of manual-based self-help treatments for bulimia nervosa and binge eating disorder have also become available, which can be used by the patient on her own or with minimal clinician support (Cooper, 1993; Schmidt & Treasure, 1993; Fairburn, 1995). The findings from this research can be summarized as follows (Treasure et al., 1994, 1996; Thiels et al., 1998; Banasiak et al., 2000; Carter & Fairburn, 1998): Pure self-help with a book leads to recovery rates in bulimia nervosa of 20%, i.e. is roughly as effective as treatment with an antidepressant like fluoxetine. If a patient is given a self-help book in addition to some sessions (up to 8) with a therapist either concurrently or after having worked through the book on her own, the outcome can be as good as that with full cognitive behavioural treatment, even if the therapist is not a trained cognitive behavioural therapist (Cooper et al., 1996; de Zwaan et al., 2000). Thus GPs and practice-based counsellors may be able to deliver these interventions.

CONCLUSION

General practitioners play an important role in secondary prevention (early identification and intervention) of eating disorders, but they are hampered by many problems, such as patient delay in presentation, doctor delay in diagnosis, inadequate communication between doctors and eating-disordered patients, negative attitudes of general practitioners towards these patients, gender differences between general practitioners and eating-disordered patients, ineffective interventions and inadequate referrals to other specialists. To make secondary prevention effective both patient and doctor delay have to be shortened and the treatment of anorectic and bulimic patients has to be improved.

A major problem for developing a special prevention programme in primary care is that for physicians eating disorders constitute only a marginal problem; on average they have relatively few (new) patients with anorexia or bulimia nervosa (King, 1989; Hoek, 1991, 1993; Whitehouse et al., 1992). Articles have been written for general practitioners, aiming to improve the early identification and diagnosis of eating disorders and to improve their knowledge, attitude and communication with eating-disordered patients and knowledge about treatment. However, we lack scientific data about the effects of these 'secondary prevention' activities on the diagnostic and therapeutic abilities of general practitioners. Nevertheless, research in the Netherlands shows that general practitioners who became more familiar with eating disorders were better able to diagnose them (Hoek et al., 1995) prescribed less medication, and made more referrals to dieticians, psychologists, psychiatrists, or outpatient clinics for eating disorders (Noordenbos, 1998). These results are promising for the future, as better information may lead to earlier diagnosis and more adequate treatment in an earlier stage.

REFERENCES

Aerts, J.J.M. (1992) *Early identification and diagnosis of anorexia and bulimia nervosa by general practitioners* (in Dutch). Dissertation, University of Maastricht.

APA (1994) *Diagnostic and Statistical Manual of Mental Disorders* (4th edition; DSM-IV). Washington, D.C.: American Psychiatric Association.

Andersen, A.E. & Mickalide A.D. (1983) Anorexia nervosa in the male: An underdiagnosed disorder. *Psychosomatics*, **24**, 1066–1075.

Banasiak, S.J., Paxton, S.J. & Hay, P.J. (2000) Cognitive-behavioural guided self-help for bulimia nervosa in primary care. Paper presented at the Academy of Eating Disorders' 9th International Conference on Eating Disorders, New York, 4–7 May.

Bartelds, A.I.M., Fracheboud, J. & Van der Zee, J. (1989) *The Dutch Sentinel Practice Network: Relevance for Public Health Policy*. Utrecht: Netherlands Institute of Primary Health Care (NIVEL).

Bloois, M. de (1987) *Anorexia nervosa from within. How do patients with anorexia nervosa evaluate their treatment?* (in Dutch). Dissertation, University of Leiden.

Bryant-Waugh, R.J., Lask, B.D., Shafran, R.L. & Fosson, A.R. (1992) Do doctors recognise eating disorders in children? *Archives of Diseases in Childhood*, **67**, 103–105.

Bryant-Waugh, R. & Lask, B. (1999) *Eating Disorders—A Parents Guide*. Harmondsworth. Penguin Books.

Button, E.J. & Whitehouse, A. (1981) Subclinical anorexia nervosa. *Psychological Medicine*, **11**, 509–516.

Carter, J.C. & Fairburn, C.G. (1998) Cognitive behavioural self help for binge eating disorder: A controlled effectiveness study. *Journal of Consulting and Clinical Psychology*, **66**, 616–623.

Cohler, B.J. (1977) The significance of therapists' feelings in the treatment of anorexia nervosa. In F.A. Feinstein & P.L. Giovacchini (Eds), *Adolescent Psychiatry: Volume 5* (pp. 352–386). New York: Jason Aronson.

Cooper, P. (1993) *Bulimia Nervosa*. Robinson: London.

Cooper, P.J., Coker, S. & Fleming, C. (1996) An evaluation of the efficacy of supervised cognitive behavioural self-help for bulimia nervosa. *Journal of Psychosomatic Research*, **40**, 281–287.

Crisp, A.H., Joughin, N., Halek, C. & Bowyer, C. (1996) *Anorexia Nervosa. The Wish to Change*. Hove, East Sussex: Psychology Press.

Crisp, A.H. & McClelland, L. (1996) *Anorexia Nervosa: Guidelines for Asessment and Treatment in Primary and Secondary Care* (2nd edition) Redwood Books, Trowbridge: Psychology Press.

Daaleman, C.J. (1991) *More or less: Research on the Prevalence of Anorexia Nervosa, Bulimia Nervosa, and Obesity* (in Dutch). Warnsveld: RIGG Oost Gelderland.

Davies, R., Olmsted, M.P. & Rockert, W. (1990) Brief group psychocducation for bulimia nervosa: Assessing the clinical significance of change. *Journal of Consulting and Clinical Psychology*, **58**, 882–885.

Deters, S.H. (1998) What patients want physicians to know. *North Caroline Medical Journal, Health Watch*, **59** n(1), 31–34.

Dhondt, A.D.F., Volman, H.G., Westerman, R.F., Weeda-Mannak, W.L. & Van der Horst, H.E. (1989) Bulimia nervosa: Do general practitioners signal this disorder? (in Dutch). *Medisch Contact*, **44**, 231–233.

Dolan, B. & Gitzinger, I. (Eds) (1994) *Why Women? Gender Issues and Eating Disorders*. London: Athlone Press.

Dresscher, C.J.M. (1993) *Early recognition and diagnosis of eating disorders by general practitioners* (in Dutch). Dissertation, University of Leiden.

Fairburn, C. G. (1995) *Overcoming Binge Eating*. New York: Guilford Press.

Fleming, J. & Szmukler, G.I. (1992) Attitudes of mental health professionals towards patients with eating disorders. *Australian and New Zealand Journal of Psychiatry*, **26**, 436–434.

Gilchrist, P.N., Ben-Tovim, D.I., Hay, P.J., Kalucy, R.S. & Walker, M.K. (1998) Clinical practice. Eating disorders rivisited I: Anorexia nervosa, *MJA*, **169**.

Gowers, S.G. & Shore, A. (1999) The stigma of eating disorders. *International Journal of Clinical Practice*, **53**, 386–388.

Hoek, H.W. (1991) The incidence and prevalence of anorexia nervosa and bulimia nevosa in primary care. *Psychological Medicine*, **21**, 455–460.

Hoek, H.W. (1993) Review of the epidemiological studies of eating disorders. *International Review of Psychiatry*, **5**, 61–74.

Hoek, H.W., Bartelds, A.I.M., Bosveld, J.J.F., van der Graaf, J., Limpens, V. Maiwald, M. & Spaaij, C.J.K. (1995) Impact of urbanization on detection rates of eating disorders. *American Journal of Psychiatry*, **152**, 1272–1278.

King, M.B. (1989) Eating disorders in a general practice population. Prevalence, characteristics and follow-up at 12–18 months. *Psychological Medicine*, (Supplement).

Meadows, G.N., Palmer, R.L., Newball, E.U.M. & Kenrick, J.M.T. (1986) Eating attitudes and disorders in young women: A general practice based survey. *Psychological Medicine*, **16**, 351–357.

Mitchell, J.E. & Goff, G. (1984) Bulimia in male patients. *Psychosomatics*, **25**, 909–913.

Nasser, M. (1986) Comparative study of the prevalence of abnormal eating attitudes among Arab females students of both London and Cairo universities. *Psychological Medicine*, **16**, 621–625.

Newton, T., Robinson, P. & Hartley, P. (1993) Treatment for eating disorders in the UK. Part 2. Experiences of treatment: A survey of members of the EDA. *Eating Disorders Review*, **1**, 10–21.

Noordenbos, G. (1992) Important factors in the process of recovery according to patients with anorexia nervosa. In W. Herzog, H.C. Deter & W. Vandereycken (Eds), *The Course of Eating Disorders. Long-Term Follow-up Studies of Anorexia and Bulimia Nervosa* (pp. 304–323). Berlin, Heidelberg: Springer Verlag.

Noordenbos, G. (1998) Eating disorders in primary care: Early identification and intervention by general practitioners. In W. Vandereycken & G. Noordenbos (Eds), *The Prevention of Eating Disorders* (pp. 214–229). London: Athlone Press; New York: New York University Press.

Ogg, E.C., Millar, H.R., Pusztai E.E. & Thom, A.S. (1997) General practice consultation patterns preceding diagnosis of eating disorders. *International Journal of Eating Disorders*, **22**, 89–93.

Palmer, R.L. (1996) *Understanding Eating Disorders*. London. Family Doctor Publication.

Silber, T.J. & DeAngelo, L.J. (1991) The role of the primary care physician in the diagnosis and management of anorexia nervosa. *Psychosomatics*, **32**, 221–225.

Schmidt, U. & Treasure, J. (1993) *Getting Better Bit(e) by Bit(e). A Survival Kit for Sufferers of Bulimia Nervosa and Binge Eating Disorder.* Hove, Sussex: Lawrence Erlbaum Associates.

Spaans, J.A. & Bloks, J.A. (1997) 'Motivation'. In J.A. Bloks, E.E. van Furth & H.W. Hoek (Eds), *Strategies to Treat Anorexia Nervosa. Care and Cure Development* (pp. 30–42). Houten: Bohn Stafleu Van Loghum.

Szmukler, G.I. (1983) Weight and food preoccupation in a population of English schoolgirls. In J.D. Bergman (Ed.), *Understanding Anorexia Nervosa and Bulimia: Fourth Ross Conference on Medical Research* (pp. 21–28). Columbus (Ohio): Ross Laboratories.

Stockwell, R. & Dolan, B. (1994) Women therapists for women clients? In B. Dolan & I. Gitzinger (Eds), *Why Women? Gender Issues and Eating Disorders*. London: Athlone Press.

Striegel-Moore, R. & Smolak, L. (1996) The role of race in the development of eating disorders. In L. Smolak, M.P. Levine & R. Striegel-Moore (Eds), *The Developmental Psychopathology of Eating Disorders* (pp. 259–284). Mahwah, NJ: Lawrence Erlbaum Associates.

Thiels, C., Schmidt, U., Garthe, R., Treasure, J. & Troop, N. (1998) Guided self change for bulimia nervosa. *American Journal of Psychiatry*, **155**, 947–953.

Treasure, J., Schmidt, U., Troop, N. Tiller, J., Todd, G., Keilen, M. & Dodge, E. (1994) First step in managing bulimia nervosa: A controlled trial of a therapeutic manual. *British Medical Journal*, **308**, 686–689.

Treasure, J., Schmidt, U., Troop, N., Tiller, J., Todd, G. & Turnbull, S. (1996) Sequential treatment for bulimia nervosa incorporating a self care manual. *British Journal of Psychiatry*, **168**, 94–98.

Treasure, J. (1998) *Anorexia Nervosa: A Survival Guide for Families, Friends and Sufferers.* Hove, East Sussex: Psychology Press.

Turnbull, S., Ward, A., Treasure, J., Jick, H. & Derby, L. (1996) The demand for eating disorder care: A study using the general practice research data base. *British Journal of Psychiatry*, **169**, 705–712.

Vandereycken, W. (1993) Naughty girls and angry doctors: Eating disorder patients and their therapists. *International Review of Psychiatry*, **5**, 13–18.

Vandereycken, W., Kog, E. & Vanderlinden, J. (1989) *The Family Approach to Eating Disorders: Assessment and Treatment*. London: PMA Publications.

Vandereycken, W. & Meermann, R. (1984) *Anorexia Nervosa: A Clinican's Guide to Treatment.* Berlin, New York: Walter de Gruyter.

Waller, D., Fairburn, C.G., McPherson, A., Kay, R., Lee, A. & Nowell, T. (1996) Treating bulimia nervosa in primary care: A pilot study. *International Journal of Eating Disorders*, **19**, 99–103.

Whitehouse, A.M., Cooper, P.J., Vize, C.V., Hill, C. & Vogel, L. (1992) Prevalence of eating disorders in three Cambridge general practices: Hidden and conspicuous morbidity. *British Journal of General Practice*, **42**, 57–60.

Yanovski, S.Z. (1991) Bulimia nervosa: The role of the family physician. *American Academy of Family Physicians*, **44**, 1231–1238.

Zunino, N., Agoos, E. & Davis, W.N. (1991) The impact of therapist gender on the treatment of bulimic women. *International Journal of Eating Disorders*, **10**, 253–263.

Zwaan, M. de (1999) Anorexie und Bulimie-Grenzen und Möglichkeiten in der ärztlichen Praxis. *Themenheft: Psychotherapeutische Medizin*, **11**, 326–330.

Zwaan, M. de, Bailer, U., El-Giamal, N., Leenkh, C. & Strand, A. (2000) Guided self-help versus cognitive behavioural, group therapy in the treatment of bulimia nervosa. Paper presented at the World Psychiatric Congress, Paris France, 26–30 June.

Index

Index compiled by Indexing Specialists (UK) Ltd